The New Chess Player

Le Nouveau Joueur d'Échecs

Der neue Schachspieler

De Nieuwe Schaakspeler

Den nye Schackspelaren

Il Nuovo Giocatore di Scacchi

El Nuevo Ajedrecista

Новый Шахматист

5

1979

A

PITMAN

PITMAN PUBLISHING LIMITED
39 Parker Street, London WC2B 5PB

Associated Companies
Copp Clark Limited, Toronto
Fearon-Pitman Publishers Inc., Belmont, California
Pitman Publishing New Zealand Ltd., Wellington
Pitman Publishing Pty Ltd., Melbourne

Distributed in Italy by
Edizioni Scolastiche APE SpA
Via Tanaro 14, 20128 Milano

© The Chess Player Ltd 1979

First published in Great Britain 1979

Printed and bound in England by
Billing & Son Ltd., Guildford

ISBN 0 273 01404 8

Contents

+ = white stands slightly better les blancs ont jeu un peu meilleur Weiss steht etwas besser wit staat er iets beter voor vit står nagot bättre il bianco sta un po' meglio el blanco está algo mejor белые стоят немного лучше

= + black stands slightly better les noirs ont jeu un peu meilleur Schwarz steht etwas besser zwart staat er iets beter voor svart står nagot bättre il nero sta un po' meglio el negro está algo mejor черные стоят немного лучше

± white has the upper hand les blancs ont le meilleur jeu Weiss steht besser wit staat beter vit står bättre il bianco sta meglio el blanco está mejor белые стоят лучше

∓ black has the upper hand les noirs ont le meilleur jeu Schwarz steht besser zwart staat beter svart står bättre il nero sta meglio el negro está mejor черные стоят лучше

+ − white has a decisive advantage les blancs ont un avantage décisif Weiss hat entscheidenden vorteil wit heeft een beslissend voordeel vit har avgörande fördel il bianco è in vantaggio decisivo el blanco tiene una ventaja decisiva белые имеют решающее преимущество

− + black has a decisive advantage les noirs ont un avantage décisif Schwarz hat entscheidenden vorteil zwart heeft een beslissend voordeel svart har avgörande fördel il nero è in vantaggio decisivo el negro tiene una ventaja decisiva черные имеют решающее преимущество

= the game is even le jeu est égal das Spiel ist ausgeglichen de stellingen zÿn gelÿkwaardig spelet är jamnt giuoco pari el juego está equilibrado игра равна

≈ approximately equal plus où moins égal ungefähr gleich ongeveer gelÿkwaardig narmelsevis jämnt piu o meno eguale más o menos igual приблизительно равно

∝ the position is unclear le jeu est incertain das Spiel ist unklar de posities zÿn onduidelÿk ställningen är oklar il giuoco è poco chiaro la posición no es clara неясная позиция

! a very good move un tres bon coup ein sehr guter Zug een zeer goede zet ett bra drag una buona mossa una jugada muy buena очень хороший ход

!! an excellent move un excellent coup ein ausgezeichneter Zug een uitstekende zet ett utmärkt drag una mossa ottima una jugada excelente отличный ход

? a mistake un coup faible ein schwacher Zug een fout ett dåligt drag una mossa debole una mala jugada плохой ход

?? a blunder une grave erreur ein grober Fehler een ernstige fout ett grovt fel un grave errore un gran error грубая ошибка

!? a move deserving attention un coup qui mérite l'attention ein beachtenswerter Zug een zet die de aandacht verdient ett drag som fortjäner uppmärksamhet una mossa degna di considerazione una jugada que merece atención ход, заслуживающий внимания

?! a dubious move un coup d'une valeur douteuse ein Zug von zweifelhaftem wert een dubieuze zet ett tvivelaktigt drag una mossa dubbia una jugada de dudoso valor ход, имеющий сомнительную ценность

Δ with the idea . . . avec l'idée . . . mit der Idee . . . met het idee om . . . med idén . . . con l'idea . . . con idea . . . с идеей...

N a novelty une innovation eine Neuerung een nieuwtje en nyhet un'innovazione una novedad новинка

Contributors

A. Adorjan	GM		R. Maric	IM
B. Balogh			R. Marszalek	
R. Bellin	IM		S. Mechkarov	
J. Bielczyk			A. Miles	GM
G. Botterill	IM		K. Pytel	IM
W. Browne	GM		I. Rogers	
M. Ciamarra			S. Samarian	
V. Ciocaltea	IM		L. Santos	
W. J. Donaldson			W. Schmidt	GM
F. Gheorghiu	GM		? Shakarov	
T. Ghitescu	IM		G. Sigurjonsson	GM
A. Gipslis	GM		A. Smith	
P. Hardicsay			R. Snyder	
R. Hubner	GM		A. Soltis	IM
A. Kapengut			J. Speelman	IM
H. Kasparov			M. Stean	GM
R. Keene	GM		M. Suba	GM
? Kindermann			A. Suetin	GM
R. Knaak	GM		S. Taulbut	IM
L. Kovacs	IM		J. Tompa	
J.-C. Letzelter			Mik. Tseitlin	IM
B. Malich	GM		L. Vogt	GM
			M. Vukic	GM

Journals

Ajedrez, British Chess Magazine, Butlleti D'Escacs, Ceskoslovensky Sach, Chess, Chess Bulletin (Canada), Chess in Australia, Chess Life and Review, Deutsche Schachblatter, Deutsche Schachzeitung, Europe Echecs, Fernschach, Jaque, Jaque Mate, Le Courrier Des Echecs, L'Italia Scacchistica, Magyar Sakkelet, Modern Chess Theory, Revista Romana de Sah, Rochade, Sahovski Glasnik, Scacco, Schaakbulletin, Schach, Schach-Echo, Schack nytt, Schakend Nederland, Shahmat, Shakhmatna Mis'l, Skakbladet, South African Chessplayer, Suomen Shakki, Szachy, Tidskrift for Schack, 64 Шахматы Шахматный Бюллетень Шахматы в СССР

Bulletins

1977-8: Montpellier

1978: Albufieri Zonal, Amsterdam Zonal, Argentina Final, Baguio City, Bucharest, Buenos Aires, Buenos Aires Olympiad, Bucharest, Canada Final, CSSR Final, Eksjo, Erbeek, Graz, Halle, Hungary Final, II Ciocco, Kirovakan, London (Lloyds Bank), Malgrat de Mar, Maribor, Mexico Olympiad, Nijmegen, Novi Sad, Pazardjik, Penang, Pernik, Piotrkon Trybunalsk, Sombor, Tehran, Tiruchirapalli, Virovitica.

1978-9: Groningen, Hastings, Stockholm.

1979: Burevestnik-Partizan, Malta, Warsaw, Wijk aan Zee.

Combinations

8	Gheorghiu	– Panno		161	Knaak	– J.Fernandez
20	Gheorghiu	– Lein		162	Gheorghiu	– F.Portisch
25	Seirawan	– Browne		171	Suba	– Botterill
35	Suba	– Roos		173	Djindjihashvili	– Torre
36	Rivas-Pastor	– Letzelter		174	Ghitescu	– Sikora
74	Gheorghiu	– Radulov		176	Nemet	– Smejkal
76	Ribli	– Prandstetter		188	Gaprindashvili	– Miles
77	Tal	– Geller		191	Makropoulos	– Gheorghiu
86	Haik	– Gheorghiu		192	Rickford	– Browne
88	Segal	– Riemsdyk		194	Kindermann	– Fleck
102	Korchnoi	– Miles		195	Kavalek	– Hubner
106	Gutman	– Vitolins		197	Veingold	– Levchenkov
112	L.Popov	– Kuligowski		260	Szmetan	– Gheorghiu
116	Gheorghiu	– Sunye		279	Gaprindashvili	– Nikolac
127	Barczay	– Tompa		282	Timman	– Bellon
134	Alburt	– Lengyel		296	Kupreichik	– Kakageldiev
				332	Hort	– Seirawan
				342	Skrobek	– Bielczyk
				349	Portisch	– Radulov

Novelties

2	Ree	– Miles		94	Petran	– Nicevski
13	Ivanov	– Kapengut		96	Alburt	– Tukmakov
20	Gheorghiu	– Lein		107	Hartston	– Suba
24	Schmidt	– Haik		118	Petrosian	– Browne
25	Seirawan	– Browne		122	Miles	– Hubner
26	Filguth	– Byrne		124	Miles	– Rivas
32	Ghitescu	– Calvo		131	Korchnoi	– Gheorghiu
35	Suba	– Roos		136	Polugaevsky	– Miles
37	Gipslis	– Vitolins		140	Ghitescu	– Smejkal
44	Bagirov	– Romanishin		144	Kaunas	– Levchenkov
46	Langeweg	– Miles		152	Gheorghiu	– Jansa
50	Hubner	– Miles		155	Speelman	– Biyiasas
51	Kuligowski	– Ghitescu		159	Sapi	– Ozsvath
52	Eperjesi	– Marszalek		160	Kuligowski	– Liberson
63	Tseitlin	– Volchichin		163	Gheorghiu	– Sznapik
66	Deze	– Kovacs		205	A.Smith	– Petersen
70	Kovacs	– Radulov		206	Browne	– Whitehead
79	Sosonko	– Morrison		223	Auzins	– Ausmanis
82	Miles	– Meulders		275	Soltis	– Shamkovich
91	Smirnov	– Kapengut		280	Kapengut	– Roizman
				289	Snyder	– Shmeteff
				337	Dobsa	– Bullocks
				340	Sveshnikov	– Romanishin

Name	Title	ELO
Adamski	IM	2415
Adorjan	GM	2525
Aingorn		2410
Alburt	GM	2515
Andersson	GM	2560
Angantysson		2400
Anikaev	IM	2455
Antoshin	GM	2440
Antunac	IM	2455
Arapovic		2420
Armas		2405
J.Arnason		2410
Asmundsson		2400
Augustin	IM	2430
Averbach	GM	2515
Averkin	IM	2455
Bagirov	GM	2545
Baikov		2400
Balashov	GM	2600
Balshan		2430
Barcza	GM	2420
Barczay	GM	2470
Barle	IM	2420
Basman		2405
Beljavsky	GM	2595
Bellin	IM	2425
Benko	GM	2495
M.Bernat	IM	2410
Y.Bernstein		2425
Bielczyk		2410
Bilek	GM	2460
Bilunov		2420
Birnboim	IM	2460
Bisguier	GM	2445
Biyiasis	GM	2485
Bjelalac	IM	2410
Bleiman	IM	2465
Blocker		2435
Bobotsov	GM	2405
Boey	IM	2415
Bogdanovic	IM	2420
H.Bohm	IM	2410
Bohosian	IM	2410
Bojkovic		2410
Bonsch	IM	2460
Borisenko		2430
Bouaziz	IM	2420
Brandts		2400
Bronstein	GM	2555
L.Bronstein	IM	2420
Browne	GM	2540
Buchman		2430
Bukal	IM	2405
Bukic	GM	2495
Buljovcic	IM	2430
Butnoris		2400
Byrne	GM	2535
Calvo	IM	2425
Campora		2400
Capelan	IM	2425
R.Cappello		2405
Castro	IM	2430
Cebalo	IM	2450
Chebanenko		2410
Chekhov	IM	2470
Cherepkov		2425
Chernikov		2465
Chi		2415
Christiansen	GM	2475
Ciocaltea	GM	2430
Ciric	GM	2440
Cleghorn		2405
Commons	IM	2465
Cosulich		2425
Cserna		2400
Csom	GM	2510
Cuartas	IM	2425
Cuasnicu		2400
Damjanovic	GM	2420
Darga	GM	2505
Debarnot	IM	2425
De Firmian		2415
Dely	IM	2445
Dementiev		2485
Deze	IM	2415
Didishko		2415

Diesen	IM	2460	Gazic			2460
Diez del Corral	GM	2485	Geller		GM	2550
Djindjihashvili	GM	2595	Georgadze		GM	2535
Doda	IM	2400	Georgiev		IM	2440
Dolmatov	IM	2495	Gerusel		IM	2425
A.Donchenko		2405	Gheorghiu		GM	2540
O.Donchenko		2400	Ghinda		IM	2455
Donchev		2400	Ghizdavu		IM	2415
Donner	GM	2465	Ghitescu		IM	2400
Donoso		2435	Gipslis		GM	2525
Dorfman	GM	2595	Gligoric		GM	2560
Doroshkevic		2420	Godes			2400
Dricta		2405	Gofstein			2400
Duckstein	IM	2420	Gouveia			2405
Dueball	IM	2455	Govedarica			2410
Duric	IM	2415	Grefe		IM	2400
Dvoretsky	IM	2525	Grigorian			2480
Dzibuan		2440	Grinberg			2400
Eliskases	GM	2430	Y.Grunfeld		IM	2430
Emma	IM	2435	Gufeld		GM	2530
Enklaar	IM	2400	Guimard		GM	2405
Ermenkov	GM	2495	Gulko		GM	2585
Ermolinsky		2450	Gurgenidze		GM	2505
Espig	IM	2450	V.Gusev			2410
Estrin	IM	2430	Gutop			2430
Evans	GM	2520	Haag		IM	2430
Faibisovic		2460	Haik		IM	2435
Farago	GM	2510	Hamann		IM	2475
Fedder		2415	Harandi		IM	2410
Fedorowicz		2405	Hartston		IM	2485
Filip	GM	2475	Hasin		IM	2405
Flesch	IM	2430	Hazai		IM	2420
Forintos	GM	2425	Haritonov			2460
Formanek	IM	2410	Hecht		GM	2490
Frey	IM	2405	Heinicke		IM	2410
Frias		2410	Helmers		IM	2405
Ftacnik	IM	2430	Henley			2405
Gaprindashvili	GM	2460	Hennings		IM	2450
Gild.Garcia		2410	Henry			2400
Guil.Garcia	GM	2490	Hermann			2405
R.Garcia	IM	2430	R.Hernandez		GM	2500
S.Garcia	GM	2465	P.Hesse			2420
Garcia-Padron	IM	2400	Holmov		GM	2550
Garcia-Palermo		2415	Holzl			2425

8

Honfi	IM	2420	Kochner			2400
Hort	GM	2600	Kogan			2400
T.Horvath	IM	2410	Kolarov	IM	2430
Hubner	GM	2595	P.Kondratiev		2450
Hug	IM	2460	Korchnoi	GM	2695
Hulak	GM	2450	Korensky		2435
Ignatiev		2400	V.N.Kozlov		2445
Ilic		2440	Kotov	GM	2470
Ilijevsky		2415	Kovacevic	GM	2500
Inkiov	IM	2460	Kovacs	IM	2430
I.Ivanov		2415	Kraidman	GM	2445
Ivanovic	GM	2460	Krogius	GM	2550
S.Ivarsson		2410	Kuindzki		2435
Ivkov	GM	2525	Kuijpers	IM	2410
Jakobsen	IM	2415	Kuligowski		2495
Jamieson	IM	2425	Kupreichik	IM	2540
Janosevic	GM	2400	Kurajica	GM	2515
Jansa	GM	2495	Kuzmin	GM	2565
Jansson		2410	Kyarner		2415
Jelen		2420	Lengeweg	IM	2440
Johannsson	IM	2440	Lanka		2440
Juferov		2450	Larsen	GM	2620
Jusupov	IM	2490	Lau		2440
Kagan	IM	2445	Lechtynsky	IM	2415
Kaiszauri	IM	2405	Lederman	IM	2415
Kakageldiev		2415	Lein	GM	2535
Kaldor	IM	2420	Lekovic		2405
Kapengut		2465	Lengyel	GM	2455
Kaplan	IM	2460	Lerner	IM	2475
Karaklaic	IM	2460	Liberzon	GM	2515
Karasev	IM	2465	Liebert	IM	2410
Karpov	GM	2705	Ligterink	IM	2440
Katalimov		2415	S.Lim	IM	2440
Kavalek	GM	2590	Liptay		2410
Keene	GM	2465	P.Littlewood		2405
Kelecevic	IM	2410	Liu		2405
Keller	IM	2410	Ljubisaljevic		2415
Kestler	IM	2405	Ljubojevic	GM	2590
Kirov	GM	2420	Lombardy	GM	2520
Kirpichnikov		2405	Luczak		2440
Klovan	IM	2490	Lukacs	IM	2420
Knaak	GM	2565	Lukin		2460
M.Knesevic	GM	2500	Lutikov	GM	2515
Kochiev	GM	2545	O.Magnusson		2400

Magerramov		2435	Nikolic	GM	2440
Makarov		2400	Nogueiras	IM	2435
Makarichev	GM	2500	Novopashin		2435
Makaropoulos		2400	Nun	IM	2400
Malevinsky		2440	Nunn	GM	2500
Malich	GM	2530	Øgaard	IM	2445
Marangunic	IM	2495	O'Kelly	GM	2420
Maric	IM	2420	Olafsson	GM	2555
Mariotti	GM	2485	H.Olafsson	IM	2440
Marjanovic	GM	2505	Ornstein	IM	2445
Marovic	GM	2470	Orso		2455
Martinovic	IM	2410	Osnos	IM	2470
Martz	IM	2405	Ostermeyer		2400
Matanovic	GM	2495	Ostojic	GM	2410
Matera	IM	2415	Pachman	GM	2510
Matulovic	GM	2510	Padevsky	GM	2510
Mazul		2405	Pahtz		2400
Mechkarov		2420	Palatnik	GM	2515
Mecking	GM	2615	Panchenko	IM	2485
Mednis	IM	2510	Panno	GM	2545
Meduna	IM	2405	Parma	GM	2530
Menakov		2450	Partos	IM	2420
Messing	IM	2420	Pavicic		2450
Mestel	IM	2475	Pavlov	IM	2410
Mestrovic	IM	2465	Peev	IM	2435
Mihaljcicin	IM	2420	Peltz		2435
Mihalchishin	GM	2480	Penrose	IM	2420
Mikadze		2425	Peresipkin		2445
Miles	GM	2560	Peters		2475
Mishuchkov		2420	Petkevich		2445
Michjalov		2450	Petran	IM	2410
Mnazakanian	IM	2425	A.Petrosian	IM	2430
Mohring	IM	2400	Petrosian	GM	2610
Mohrlock	IM	2440	Petursson	IM	2420
Moiseev	IM	2425	Pfleger	GM	2545
Moratov		2415	Piasetski	IM	2425
Murei		2430	Pilnik	GM	2435
Musil	IM	2405	J.Pinter	IM	2445
Nagy		2415	Plachetka	GM	2445
Najdorf	GM	2515	Planinc	GM	2445
Navarovsky	IM	2400	Plaskett		2410
Nemet	GM	2470	Platonov		2455
Nei	IM	2500	Podgaets	IM	2450
Nikolac	IM	2450	Polugaevsky	GM	2625

Name			Name		
Pomar	GM	2435	Saidy	IM	2430
L.Popov	IM	2430	Sanguineti	IM	2485
N.Popov	IM	2435	Savon	GM	2550
Popovic	IM	2410	Sax	GM	2590
F.Portisch	IM	2475	Schiffer		2425
Portisch	GM	2640	Schinzel		2400
Pribyl	IM	2420	L.Schmid	GM	2520
Pritchett	IM	2405	B.Schmidt		2420
Psahis		2480	W.Schmidt	GM	2430
Pukshansky		2405	Schneider	IM	2420
Pytel	IM	2425	Schussler	IM	2460
Quinteros	GM	2545	Schweber	IM	2450
Radovici	IM	2410	Segal	IM	2400
Radulov	GM	2485	Seirawan		2485
Rajcevic	GM	2440	Shamkovich	GM	2495
Rajkovic	GM	2460	Sharif	IM	2445
Rakic	IM	2430	Shashkin		2425
Rantanen	IM	2460	Sheliandinov		2425
Rashkovsky	IM	2500	Shereshevsky		2460
Razuvaev	GM	2470	Shmit		2420
Ree	IM	2480	Shpilker		2480
Regan		2420	Sigurjonsson	GM	2490
Reshevsky	GM	2485	Sikora		2430
Reshko		2425	C.Silva		2400
Ribli	GM	2595	Simic	IM	2420
Rind		2410	Sloth		2400
Robatsch	GM	2435	Smejkal	GM	2550
A.Rodriguez	GM	2465	Smyslov	GM	2560
O.Rodriguez	GM	2495	Sofrevski	IM	2440
Rogoff	GM	2515	S.Sokolov		2420
Rogulj	IM	2440	Soltis	IM	2445
Rohde	IM	2405	Soos	IM	2430
Romanishin	GM	2560	Sosonko	GM	2535
Rossetto	GM	2410	Spassky	GM	2640
Rubinetti	IM	2430	Spassov	GM	2470
Rubinstein		2430	Speelman	IM	2470
Ruderfer		2400	Spiridonov	IM	2440
Rukavina	IM	2420	Spraggett	IM	2445
Rusakov		2435	Stean	GM	2540
Ryabchenok		2420	Stoica	IM	2430
Rytov		2400	Stolyar		2435
A.Saharov	IM	2475	Suba	GM	2435
Y.Saharov		2475	Suetin	GM	2535
Sahovic	GM	2520	Suttles	GM	2470

Sveshnikov	GM	2545	Van Riemsdyk	IM	2435
Szabo	GM	2515	Van Wijgerden	IM	2445
Szekely	IM	2430	Varlamov		2460
P.Szilagyi		2405	Varnusz		2410
Szmetan	IM	2400	Vasyukov	GM	2560
Sznapik	IM	2435	Vatnikov	IM	2480
Taimanov	GM	2510	Velikov	IM	2440
Tal	GM	2615	Velimirovic	GM	2515
Tarjan	GM	2525	Veselovsky		2420
Tatai	IM	2475	Vilela	IM	2460
Taylor		2445	Vitolinsh		2430
Terentiev		2415	B.Vladimirov	IM	2465
Teschner	IM	2430	E.Vladimirov		2445
Timman	GM	2625	Vogt	GM	2500
Timoshenko	IM	2530	Vorotnikov		2410
Todorcevic	IM	2455	Vukcevic		2460
Tomaszewski		2435	Vukic	GM	2485
Tompa		2420	Webb	IM	2420
Toncev		2460	Wedberg	IM	2425
Toran	IM	2445	Weinstein	IM	2465
Torre	GM	2520	Westerinen	GM	2465
Toth	IM	2470	Wibe	IM	2425
Tringov	GM	2460	Wirthensohn	IM	2410
Trois	IM	2415	Wolf		2410
I.Tseitlin		2490	Yanofsky	GM	2420
Ma.Tseitlin	IM	2505	Yudovich		2400
Mi.Tseitlin	IM	2505	Zaichev	GM	2505
Tseshkovsky	GM	2560	Zaichik	IM	2465
Tukmakov	GM	2575	Zaltsman	IM	2470
Tuzovsky		2410	Zhuravlev		2490
Ubilava	IM	2430	Zilber		2410
Uddenfeldt		2405	Zilberman		2415
Uhlmann	GM	2530	Zilberstein		2455
Ungureanu	IM	2405	Zivkovic		2425
Unzicker	GM	2530	Zlotnik		2430
Vadasz	GM	2490	Zlotnikov		2435
Vaganian	GM	2570	Zidkov		2520
Vainger		2455	Zuckerman	IM	2480
Valvo		2460	Zuidema	IM	2450
Van der Sterren		2400	Zwaig	IM	2450

Theory

Owen's Defence

1 c4 b6 2 d4 e6
2...♗b7?! 3 d5 e6 4 a3 ♗d6 (4...♘f6 5 ♘c3 ♗d6 6 ♘f3 0-0 7 e4 exd5 8 exd5 ♖e8+ 9 ♗e2 += Torre-Bordonada, Tiruchirapalli 1978) 5 ♘f3 ♕e7 6 ♘c3 ♘f6 7 ♗g5 h6 8 ♗h4 ♘a6 9 e3 c6 10 ♗e2 ♘c7 11 ♘e4± Timman-Speelman, Amsterdam 1978
3 e4
a) 3 a3 ♘f6 4 ♘c3 d5 N (4...♗b7 5 d5 ♗d6 6 ♗g5 N [6 ♘f3 0-0 7 ♗g5 ♗e7!≈ Sosonko-Planinc, Ljubljana 1977] 6...h6 7 ♗h4 ♗e5 8 ♕d2 d6 9 ♘f3 ♗xc3 10 ♕xc3 exd5 11 cxd5 ♗xd5 12 0-0-0∞ Flear-Forintos, London 1978) 5 cxd5 ♘xd5 6 e4 ♘xc3 7 bxc3 ♗b7 8 ♗d3 c5 9 ♘f3 ♗e7 10 0-0 0-0 11 ♖a2 ♘c6 12 d5 exd5 13 exd5 ♘a5 14 c4 b5≈ Stean-Miles, Amsterdam 1978;
b) 3 a3 d5 4 cxd5 exd5 5 ♘c3 ♗b7 6 g3 ♘f6 7 ♗g2 ♗e7 8 ♘f3 0-0 9 0-0 ♘bd7 10 ♗f4 += Gheorghiu-Hartston, Moscow 1977;
c) 3 a3 d5 4 g3 N ♘f6 5 ♗g2 ♗e7 6 ♘c3 ♗b7 7 ♘h3 0-0 8 0-0 ♘bd7 9 ♘f4 c6 10 b3 += Petursson-Plaskett, Groningen 1978/79;
d) 3 a3 d5 4 ♘c3 N ♗b7 5 ♘f3 ♗e7 6 cxd5 exd5 7 ♕a4+ c6 8 ♘e5 ♘f6 9 g3 0-0 10 ♗g2 ♗d6 11 ♗g5 += Zaichik-Ornstein, Kirovakan 1978;
e) 3 ♘c3 ♗b7 4 e4 (4 ♘f3 ♗b4 5 e3 f5 6 ♗d3 ♘f6 7 0-0 0-0 8 ♘e1 ♗xc3 9 bxc3 d6 10 f3 c5 11 ♕e2 ♘c6= Vranesic-Piasetski, Canada Final 1978) 4...♗b4 5 ♗d3 (5 d5 ♕e7 6 ♗e3 exd5 7 exd5 ♘f6 8 ♗d3 c6 9 dxc6 ♗xc3+ 10 bxc3 ♘xc6∞ Haik-Benjamin,

London 1978; 5 f3 ♕h4+ 6 g3 ♕h5 7 ♘h3!? ♗xc3+ 8 bxc3 f5 9 ♘f4 ♕f7 10 exf5 ♕xf5 11 ♗d3 [11 ♗h3! Δ d5] 11...♕f7 12 ♗e4 ♘c6 Donner-Miles, Bristol 1978, 13 d5 ♘a5∞) 5...f5 6 ♕e2 (6 ♕h5+ g6 7 ♕e2 ♘f6 8 ♗g5 fxe4 9 ♗c2 c5 10 d5 exd5 11 0-0-0∞ Shirazi-Bordonada, Tiruchirapalli 1978) 6...♘f6 7 f3? (7 ♗g5 fxe4 8 ♗xe4 ♗xc3+ 9 bxc3 ♗xe4 10 ♗xf6 ♕xf6 11 ♕xe4 ♘c6= Garces-Keene, Lausanne 1977) 7...fxe4 8 ♗c2 ♘c6 9 ♗e3 e5 10 a3 exd4 11 ♗xe4 ♗xc3+ 12 bxc3 dxe3 0-1 Rasmussen-Goldenberg, II Ciocco 1978;
f) 3 d5 ♘f6 4 a3 ♗a6 5 b3 N (5 e3 exd5 6 cxd5 ♗xf1 7 ♔xf1 ♗d6 8 ♘c3 0-0 9 ♘ge2 ♖e8 10 f3 c6 11 e4 cxd5 12 ♘xd5 ♘c6= Hofland-Ree, Netherlands Final 1978) 5...♗c5 6 ♘h3 exd5 7 cxd5 c6 8 b4 ♗d6 9 ♗b2 cxd5 10 g3 0-0 11 ♗g2 ♖e8 12 ♗f3 ♘c6= Cordes-Morrison, Graz 1978;
g) 3 d5 ♗a6 4 e4 exd5 5 exd5 ♗b4+ N (5...♘f6 6 ♘c3 ♗b4 7 ♕e2+ ♗e7 8 ♕c2 c6 Browne-Christiansen, Mentor 1977, 9 ♗f4!±) 6 ♗d2 ♕e7+ 7 ♕e2 ♗xd2+ 8 ♔xd2 ♘f6 9 ♘c3 ♕xe2+ 10 ♗xe2 += Cordes-Sisniega, Graz 1978;
h) 3 d5 ♕h4!? 4 e3 ♘f6 5 a3 ♗b7 6 ♘c3 N (6 ♘f3 ♕h5 7 dxe6 fxe6 8 ♗e2 ♕g6 9 ♘h4 ♕h6 10 ♗f3 ♘c6 11 g3 g5 −+ Ogaard-Miles, Reykjavik 1978) 6...exd5 7 cxd5 ♘e4 8 ♕f3 ♘xc3 9 bxc3 ♘a6 10 c4 ♗d6 11 ♗b2 0-0 12 g3 ♕h6 =+ Anelli-Giardelli, Buenos Aires 1978;
i) 3 ♘f3 ♗b7 4 ♘c3 ♗b4 5 ♕b3 ♕e7 6 a3 ♗xc3+ 7 ♕xc3 a5 8 b3 ♘f6 9 e3 d6 10 ♗e2 += Dementiev-Forintos, Kirovakan 1978
3...♗b7 4 f3
4 ♗d3 ♕h4!? (4...♗b4+ 5 ♗d2 ♗xd2+

6 ♛xd2 f5 7 ♘c3 fxe4 8 ♗xe4 ♗xe4 9 ♘xe4 ♘f6= Robatsch-Supancic, Maribor 1978) 5 ♘f3 ♛g4 6 ♛e2 f5 7 h3 ♛xg2 8 ♖h2 ♛g6 9 exf5 ♛h5 10 ♗e4 ♘c6 11 fxe6 ♘xd4!∓ Riveiro-Giardelli, Buenos Aires 1978

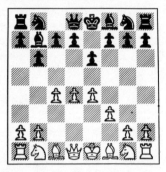

4...f5
a) 4...♗b4+ N 5 ♗d2 ♛h4+ 6 g3 ♛e7 7 ♗xb4 ♛xb4+ 8 ♛d2 ♛e7 9 ♘c3 d6 10 ♗d3 c5 11 ♗c2 ♘c6= Szymczak-Forintos, Kirovakan 1978;
b) 4...e5!? N 5 d5 ♗c5 6 ♘c3 a5 7 ♘ge2 ♘a6 8 g3 ♘e7 9 ♗h3 0-0= Pytel-Piasetski, Buenos Aires 1978
5 exf5 ♞h6!? N
5...exf5 6 ♘h3 ♗b4+ 7 ♘c3 ♛h4+ 8 g3 ♛e7+ 9 ♔f2 ♗xc3 10 bxc3 ♘c6= Sosonko-Keene, Bad Lauterberg 1977
6 fxe6 ♞f5 7 ♞e2 ♗d6 8 h4 0-0 9 ♞bc3 ♛f6 10 c5 ♗e7∞ Ree-Miles, Wijk aan Zee 1979

English

1 c4 c5 2 ♞f3 ♞f6 3 ♞c3 d5
3...♘c6 4 d4 cxd4 5 ♘xd4 e6 6 ♘db5 ♗b4 7 ♗f4 0-0 8 ♗d6 ♗xd6 9 ♘xd6 ♘e8 (Euwe) 10 e3 b6? (10...♛b6! 11 ♖b1! ♛c5 12 ♘de4 ♛e7 13 ♗e2 b6 14 0-0 ♗b7= Prats-Horton, Corr. 1978) 11 ♗e2 ♘xd6 12 ♛xd6 ♗b7

13 0-0 ♛e7 14 ♖ad1± Suba-Monier, Buenos Aires 1978
4 cxd5 ♞xd5 5 e4 ♞b4 6 ♗c4
6 ♗b5+ ♘8c6 7 d4 cxd4 8 a3 dxc3 9 ♛xd8+ ♔xd8 10 axb4 cxb2 (10...g6? 11 bxc3 ♗g7 12 ♖a3± Csom-Stean, Las Palmas 1978; 10...♗d7 11 bxc3 g6 12 0-0 ♗g7 13 ♖a3 ♖c8 14 ♖d1 a6 15 ♗e2± Stean-Browne, Buenos Aires 1978) 11 ♗xb2 e5! N 12 0-0-0+ ♔c7 13 ♗xc6 bxc6 14 ♗xe5+ ♔b7= Miles-Schmidt, Buenos Aires 1978
6...♗e6
6...♛d3+ 7 ♔e2 ♘xc1+ 8 ♖xc1 ♘c6 9 ♗b5 ♗d7 10 d4 cxd4 Suba-Dobrev, Varna 1978, 11 ♗xc6!±
7 ♗xe6 ♞d3+ 8 ♔f1 fxe6

9 ♞g5 ♞c6
9...♛d7 10 ♛f3 ♘e5 11 ♛h3 ♛d3+ 12 ♛xd3 ♘xd3 13 g3! N (13 ♔e2 ♘f4+ 14 ♔f3 h6 15 ♔xf4 hxg5+ 16 ♔g3 += Suba-Alburt, Bucharest 1978) 13...♘c6 14 ♘xe6± Suba-Farago, Boras 1978
10 ♞xe6 ♛d7 11 ♞xc5!? N
11 ♘d5 ♖c8 12 ♛h5+ g6 13 ♛h3 c4 14 b3 ♘d8 15 ♘xd8 ♛xh3 16 gxh3 ♔xd8 17 bxc4 b5 =+ Adorjan-Langeweg, IBM 1978
11...♞xc5 12 ♛h5+ g6 13 ♛xc5 ♛d3+ 14 ♔g1 Timman-Stean,

14

Amsterdam 1978, 14...0-0-0∞

1 c4 e5 2 ♘c3 ♘f6 3 ♘f3

3 g3 ♗b4 4 ♕b3 ♘c6 5 ♘d5 (5 e3 ♗xc3 6 ♕xc3 0-0 7 ♗g2 d5 8 d4? exd4 9 exd4 dxc4 10 ♘e2 ♖e8∓ Sammut-Trabattoni, Malta 1979) 5...♘xd5 (5... ♗d6 6 e3 ♘xd5 7 cxd5 ♘e7 8 ♘e2 c6= Korchnoi-Lein, USSR 1966) 6 cxd5 ♘d4 7 ♕d1 0-0 8 e3 ♖e8!∓ Sammut-Povah, Malta 1979

3...♘c6 4 e3

a) 4 d4 exd4 5 ♘xd4 ♗c5 6 ♘xc6 bxc6 7 g3 ♗b4 N (7...d5 8 ♗g2 ♗e6 9 0-0 0-0 10 cxd5 cxd5 11 ♗g5 c6 12 ♖c1 ♗e7 13 ♘a4 += Pytel-Dussol, Montpellier 1977/78) 8 ♗g2 0-0 9 ♗d2 ♖e8 10 0-0 ♕e7 11 ♖e1 ♗xc3 12 ♗xc3 ♘e4 14 ♖c1 += Pytel-Birnboim, Buenos Aires 1978;

b) 4 g3 ♗c5 5 ♘xe5 ♗xf2+ 6 ♔xf2 ♘xe5 7 e4 c5 8 h3 d6 9 d3 0-0 10 ♗g2 N a6 11 ♖f1 b5 12 ♔g1 h6= Palermo-Djindjihashvili, Buenos Aires 1978;

c) 4 g3 ♗b4 5 ♗g2 0-0 (5...♗xc3 6 bxc3 ♕e7 7 ♕c2 0-0 8 0-0 e4 9 ♘d4 d6 10 ♘xc6 bxc6= Omuku-Baghli, Albufieri 1978) 6 0-0 e4 7 ♘e1 ♗xc3 8 dxc3 h6 9 ♘c2 d6 10 ♘e3 ♖e8 11 ♕c2 ♖e5= Casas-L.Bronstein, Buenos Aires 1978;

d) 4 g3 ♘d4 5 ♗g2 ♘xf3+ 6 ♗xf3 ♗b4 7 0-0 (7 ♕b3 N ♗c5 8 0-0 0-0 9 d3 h6 10 ♕c2 c6 11 ♖b1 d5= Tomaszewski-Botto, Graz 1978) 7... 0-0 8 d3 N c6 9 ♗g2 ♖e8 10 ♕b3 ♗c5 11 ♗d2 ♕b6 12 ♘a4 ♕xb3 13 axb3± Uhlmann-Ungureanu, Bucharest 1978

4...♗b4

4...d5 5 cxd5 ♘xd5 6 ♗b5 ♘xc3 7 bxc3 ♗d6 8 d4 exd4 9 cxd4 0-0 10 0-0 ♗d7 11 ♖b1± Hubner-J. de Metz,

Nijmegen 1978

5 ♕c2 0-0

a) 5...d6 6 ♗e2 0-0 7 0-0 ♗g4 8 d3 ♗xc3 9 bxc3 ♕e7 10 e4 ♘e8 11 h3 ♗d7 12 ♖b1 += Petursson-Muir, Groningen 1978/79;

b) 5...d6 6 ♘d5 a5!? N 7 ♘xb4 ♘xb4 8 ♕b3 e4 9 ♘d4 c5 10 ♘b5 a4 11 ♕c3 0-0 12 a3 ♘c6 13 d3 ♖e8= Marcus-Bouwmeester, Nijmegen 1978;

c) 5...d6 6 a3 ♗xc3 7 ♕xc3 ♗g4 8 ♗e2 (8 b4) 8...e4 9 ♘d4 ♗xe2 10 ♘xc6 bxc6 11 ♔xe2 ♕d7 12 ♖e1 0-0 13 b4 Hubner-Bouwmeester, Nijmegen 1978, 13...♕g4+ 14 ♔f1 ♕h4 15 h3 ♘d7 Δ f5 =+

6 ♘d5

6 d3 ♖e8 7 ♗d2 ♗xc3 8 ♗xc3 d5 9 cxd5 ♘xd5 10 ♗e2 ♕d6= Torre-Smyslov, Buenos Aires 1978

6...♖e8

6...a5 7 a3 ♗c5 8 ♗d3 (8 ♗e2 d6 9 ♘g5 g6 10 ♘xf6+ ♕xf6 11 ♘e4 ♕e7 12 d3 f5= Robatsch-Kavalek, Buenos Aires 1978; 8 ♘g5!?) 8...h6 9 b3 d6 10 ♗b2 ♘xd5 11 cxd5 ♘e7 12 ♗c4 ♗f5 13 ♕c3 b5∞ Hubner-Enklaar, Nijmegen 1978

7 ♕f5 d6 8 ♘xf6+ ♕xf6

8...gxf6 9 ♕h5 d5 10 a3 ♗f8 11 d4 ♗e6 12 ♗d3 e4 13 ♗c2 ♘e7 14 ♘d2 f5 15 cxd5 ♕xd5 16 f3 f4 N

15

(16...♕c6 17 ♘xe4!! +− Goodman-Nunn, London 1978) 17 ♘xe4 ♗g7 18 ♕g5± Akesson-Kaiszauri, Stockholm 1978/79
9 ♕xf6 gxf6 10 a3 ♗a5 11 b3 ♘e7 12 ♗b2 c6 13 ♗e2 += Piasetski-Roos, Buenos Aires 1978

1 c4 ♘f6 2 ♘c3 e6 3 e4 d5

3...c5 4 e5 ♘g8 5 ♘f3 ♘c6 6 d4 cxd4 7 ♘xd4 ♘xe5 8 ♘db5 a6 9 ♘d6+ ♗xd6 10 ♕xd6 f6 11 b3 ♘e7 12 ♗a3 N ♘f5 13 ♕d2 b5! 14 cxb5 ♕a5∝ Piasetski-Nickoloff, Canada Final 1978
4 e5

4 cxd5 exd5 5 e5 ♘fd7 6 d4 c5 7 ♘f3 N ♘c6 8 ♗b5 a6 9 ♗xc6 bxc6 10 0-0 += Popov-Antonov, Pernik 1978
4...d4 5 exf6 dxc3 6 bxc3 ♕xf6 7 ♘f3!?

7 d4 c5 8 ♘f3 cxd4 9 cxd4 ♗b4+ 10 ♗d2 ♗xd2+ 11 ♕xd2 ♘c6 12 ♗e2 0-0 13 ♖d1 += Raicevic-Kluger, Sombor 1978

7...e5 N **8 ♕e2 ♘c6 9 d4 ♗g4 10 dxe5 ♗xf3 11 exf6+ ♗xe2 12 ♗xe2 gxf6 13 ♗e3 0-0-0 14 ♖b1 +=** Timman-Sosonko, Nijmegen 1978

Trompowszky

1 d4 ♘f6 2 ♗g5 c5

a) 2...d5 3 ♗xf6 exf6 4 e3 c6 (4... ♗f5 5 ♗d3 ♕d7 6 ♘e2 ♘c6 7 ♘bc3 0-0-0 8 a3 ♘e7= Laird-Bachtiar, Penang 1978) 5 c4 dxc4 6 ♗xc4 ♗d6 7 ♘c3 0-0 8 ♘f3 f5 9 0-0 ♘d7 10 ♕b1!? g6 11 b4 ♘b6 =+ Pantaleev-Kirov, Bulgaria Final 1978;

b) 2...d5 3 ♗xf6 gxf6 4 ♘c3 c5 5 e3 e5 6 dxc5 ♗xc5 7 ♘d2 ♘c6 8 ♗d3 ♗e6 9 ♕h5 ♕d7 10 ♘e2 0-0-0 11 ♘g3 ♖dg8 12 ♘f3? e4 13 ♗xe4 dxe4 0-1 Kourkounaky-Karolyi, Graz 1978;

c) 2...d5 3 ♗xf6 gxf6 4 ♘c3 c5!? 5 e4 dxe4 6 dxc5 ♕a5 7 ♕h5! ♘c6 8 ♗b5 f5 9 a3 ♗g7 10 ♘e2 e6 11 g4!± Bellin-Lobo, London 1978;

d) 2...♘e4 3 ♗h4 c5 4 f3 g5 5 fxe4 gxh4 6 e3 ♕b6 (6...♗h6! =+) 7 ♘f3 ♕h6 8 ♔f2 ♗g7 9 c3 d6 10 ♘bd2 0-0∝ Joukl-Felix, CSSR 1978

e) 2...♘e4 3 ♗f4 c5 (3...d5 4 f3 ♘f6 5 ♘c3 e6 6 e4 ♗b4 7 ♕d3 c5 8 dxc5 ♘c6 9 0-0-0 ♗xc3 10 ♕xc3 d4 11 ♕d2 e5 ∝/= Tichy-Smejkal, CSSR Final 1978) 4 f3 (4 d5!? e6 5 f3 ♕a5+ 6 c3 ♘f6 7 e4 exd5 8 exd5 d6 9 ♕d2 ♗e7 10 c4 += Bennett-Webb, London 1978) 4...♘f6 (4...♕a5+! 5 c3 ♘f6 6 d5 d6 7 e4 g6∝ Alburt-Dorfman, USSR 1977) 5 dxc5 ♕a5+ 6 ♘c3 ♕xc5 7 e4 ♘c6 8 ♕d2 d6 9 ♗e3 ♕a5= Joukl-Matous, CSSR 1978;

f) 2...g6!? 3 ♗xf6 exf6 4 e3 f5 (4... d5 5 ♘e2 ♗d6 6 g3 c6 7 ♗g2 0-0 8 ♘gf3 a5 9 0-0 ♖e8= Arias-Fischdick, Buenos Aires 1978) 5 ♘f3 ♗g7 6 ♘c3 d6 7 ♗d3 ♘d7 8 h4 ♘f6 9 ♘e2 ♘h5 10 c3 ♗e6= Casas-Anelli, Buenos Aires 1978;

g) 2...e6 3 ♘d2 h6 4 ♗h4 d5 5 e3 b6 6 ♘gf3 ♗e7 7 ♗d3 ♗a6 8 ♗xa6 ♘xa6 9 0-0 0-0= Tichy-Plachetka, CSSR Final 1978;

h) 2...e6 3 Nc3 h6 4 Bxf6 Qxf6 5 e4 d6 6 Nf3 Nd7 7 Bc4 g6 8 0-0 Bg7 9 Re1 0-0= Jansa-Spiridonov, Novi Sad 1978;

i) 2...e6 3 e4 h6 4 Bxf6 Qxf6 5 Nf3 b6 6 Bd3 Bb7 7 Qe2 d6 8 Nc3 Qd8 9 0-0-0 Be7 10 Kb1 a6 11 g4 Nd7 12 h4± Wicker-Ginsberg, London 1978

3 Bxf6

3 d5 Ne4 4 Bf4 (4 Bh4 Qb6 5 Qc1 g5 6 Bg3 Bg7 7 c3 Qh6! 8 Bxb8 Rxb8 9 Nd2 Nxd2 10 Qxd2 b5∓ 11 e4 b4 12 Ne2 bxc3 13 Nxc3 Qb6 14 Rb1 Qa5 15 Bd3? Rxb2! 0-1 Wicker-Nicholson, London 1978) 4...Qb6 5 Qc1 c4! 6 e3 Qa5+ 7 c3 Qxd5∓ Pribyl-Baljon, Erbeek 1978

3...gxf6

3...exf6 4 e3 Qb6 5 Nc3 cxd4 6 Qxd4 Qxb2 7 Rb1 Qa3 8 Bc4 Nc6 9 Qe4+ Be7 10 Nge2 0-0 11 0-0 Qa5 12 Nd5 Qd8 13 Nd4 Bc5 14 Nf5 Ne5 15 Bb3 Ng6∞ Wicker-Gruenfeld, London 1978

4 d5 Qb6

4...f5 5 c4 e5 6 dxe6 dxe6 7 Qxd8+ Kxd8 8 Nc3 Bg7 9 e3 Be7 10 Nge2 Rd8 =+ Kohout-Mokry, CSSR 1978

5 Qc1 f5 6 e3

6 g3 Bg7 7 c3 e5 8 Bh3 Nf6 9 Nf3 0-0 10 Na3 d6 11 Qc2 Na6 12 Nh4± Alexandria-Schikova, Buenos Aires 1978

6...Bg7 7 c3 d6

7...e5!? 8 Na3 d6 9 Qc2 Qd8 10 Bb5+ Kf8 11 Bd3 Qg5 12 f4 exf4 13 Nf3± Barbero-Mateu, Graz 1978

8 Na3 Nd7 9 Qc2 Nf6 10 Rd1 a6 11 Ne2 Qc7 12 Ng3 e6∞ Neunschwander-Grinberg, Groningen 1978/79

Queen's Gambit Accepted

1 d4 d5 2 c4 dxc4 3 Nf3 Nf6 4 e3

4 Nc3 a6 5 e4 b5 6 e5 Nd5 7 a4 Nxc3 (7...Bb7 8 e6 f6?! 9 Be2 Nxc3 10 bxc3 Qd5 11 0-0 Qxe6 12 Re1 Qd7 13 Nh4 g6 14 Bg4 f5 15 Bf3± Peev-Lehmann, Plovdiv 1978; 7...c6 8 axb5 Nxc3 9 bxc3 cxb5 10 Ng5 f6 11 Qf3 Ra7 12 e6 Qb6!? N [12...Bb7 13 Qf4 Qc8 14 Be3 Bd5 15 Qf5 Qb7 16 Nf7∞ Ligterink-van der Sterren, Amsterdam 2 1978] 13 d5 fxg5 14 Qf7+ Kd8 15 Bxg5

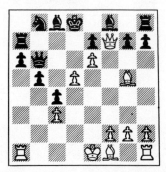

15...Rd7!!∓ Sosonko-Rivas, Amsterdam 3 1978) 8 bxc3 Qd5 9 g3 Bf5 10 Bg2 e6 11 0-0 Qb7 12 Nh4 Be4 13 Qg4! ±/∞ Langeweg-Miles, Amsterdam 3 1978

4...Bg4 5 Bxc4 e6 6 h3 Bh5 7 Nc3 Nbd7

7...a6 8 g4 Bg6 9 Ne5 Nbd7 10 Nxg6 hxg6 11 g5 Nd5! 12 Nxd5 exd5 13 Bxd5 c6 14 Bb3 Qxg5 15 Qf3 Bb4+

2. Lg5 h6 3. Lh4 g5
4 e4? Lg7 5 Lg3 f4 6. Lf4: gf:
7. Dh5+ Kf8 8 Df5+ △ e5

2. Lg5 h6 3. Lh4 g5 4. e3 sf6
5 Le2 d6! (6 Lh5+ Kd7!)

= Petrosian-Djindjihashvili, Buenos Aires 1978
8 0-0 ♗d6 9 ♗e2 0-0 10 e4 e5 11 dxe5 ♘xe5 12 ♘d4 ♗c5
12...♗xe2 13 ♛xe2 ♘c5 N (13...♘g6 14 ♘db5 N [14 ♘f5 ♗e5 15 f4 ♗xc3 16 bxc3 ♖e8 17 e5 ♘d5 18 c4 ♘e7= Quinteros-Ghitescu, Polanica Zdroj 1977] 14...♗c5 15 ♘a4 ♛e7 16 ♘xc5 ♛xc5 17 ♘c3 ♖fe8 18 ♗e3 += Kuligowski-Ghitescu, Warsaw 1979) 14 ♘b3 ♗b6 15 ♖d1 ♛e7 16 ♗g5 c6 17 ♘d4 ♖ad8= Eperjesi-Kovacs, Hungary Final 1978

13 ♘b3 13 ♗xh5 N ♗xd4 14 ♘d5 c5 15 ♗g5 ♘ed7 16 ♖e1 h6 17 ♗h4 ♖e8 18 ♗f3 ♛b8 19 ♔h1 ♘xd5 Hubner-Miles, Wijk aan Zee 1979
13...♛xd1 14 ♗xd1 ♗b6 15 a4
15 ♗g5 N ♗xd1 16 ♖axd1 ♘fd7 17 ♘d5 f6 18 ♗e3 ♖f7= Padevsky-Hase, Buenos Aires 1978
15...♗xd1 16 ♖xd1 a5 N
16...c6 17 a5± Portisch-Miles, Lone Pine 1978
17 ♗g5 c6 18 ♛f1 ♖fd8 19 ♛e2 ♘c4 =/=+ Andersson-Miles, Wijk aan Zee 1979

Dutch

1 d4 f5 2 c4

a) 2 ♗g5 h6 3 ♗h4 g5 4 ♗g3 ♘f6 5 e3 ♗g7 6 ♘d3 d6 7 h4 g4 8 ♘e2 ♘c6 9 ♘bc3 e5= Schussler-Kristiansen, Stockholm 1978/79;
b) 2 ♗g5 g6 3 ♘c3 ♗g7 4 e4 fxe4 5 ♘xe4 ♘f6 6 ♘xf6+ exf6 7 ♗e3 d5!? 8 h4 ♗e6 9 h5 += Langeweg-Meulders, Amsterdam 1978;
c) ♗g5 c5 3 dxc5 ♘a6 4 e4! N (4 c4 ♘xc5 5 ♘c3 d6 6 ♗d2 ♘c6 7 ♘f3 g6 8 ♛c1 ♗g7 9 ♗h6 0-0= Cuderman-Vukcevic, Jugoslavia 1957) 4...fxe4 5 ♘c3 ♘xc5 6 ♗e3 ♘e6 7 ♘xe4 ♘f6 8 ♗d3 g6 9 h4 ♗g7 10 ♘xf6+ exf6 11 ♘f3 += Miles-Meulders, Amsterdam 1978
2...♘f6 3 ♘f3 g6 4 g3 ♗g7 5 ♗g2 0-0 6 0-0 d6 7 ♘c3
a) 7 d5!? ♘a6 8 ♘c3 ♘c5 9 ♘d4! e5 10 dxe6 c6 11 ♗f4 ♘fe4 12 ♘xe4 ♘xe4 13 ♛d3 ♛f6 14 ♖ad1 ♗e6 15 ♘xe6 ♛xe6 16 ♛c2± Gheorghiu-Grunberg, Rumania Final 1976;
b) 7 d5!? c6 8 ♘d4 c5 9 ♘f3 ♘a6 10 ♘c3 ♘c7 11 a4 ♔h8 12 ♖b1± Kochiev-Tal, USSR 1978
7...♘c6
7...c6 8 d5 ♘h5!? N 9 dxc6 bxc6 10 ♘d4 ♗d7 11 e3 ♔h8 12 b4 e5 13 ♘b3 ♗e6 14 ♘a5 ♛c7 15 ♗b2 ♖d8 16 ♖c1± L.Radulov-Carlsson, Corr. 1976-78

4...f4 5 e3 e5 6 ef: ef: 7 Dh5+ Ke7 8 Lf4:
:f6 (g 8...gf 9 De5+) 9 De2+

8 d5 ♘a5 9 ♘d2 c5 10 ♖b1

10 ♕c2 e5 11 dxe6 ♗xe6 12 b3 d5 (Taimanov) 13 cxd5 ♘xd5 14 ♗b2 ♘b4 15 ♕b1 ♖c8 16 ♖d1 ♕e7 17 a3 ♕f7? 18 ♘b5! +− Suba-Bjelajac, Pernik 1978

10...e5?! N

10...♗d7 11 ♕c2 a6 12 b3 b5 13 ♗b2 ♖b8 14 e3 ♕c7 15 ♘e2 ♘b7 16 ♘f4 ♘d8 17 h4! ♕c8 18 ♘f3 ♘f7 19 ♖fd1! ± Ribli-Horvath, Hungary Final 1976

11 dxe6 ♗xe6 12 b3 d5 13 ♗a3 ♖c8 14 ♘a4 b6 15 b4 cxb4 16 ♗xb4 dxc4?! 17 ♗xf8 ♕xf8 18 ♘c3± Pinter-Bjelajac, Pernik 1978

Benko Gambit

1 d4 ♘f6 2 c4 c5 3 d5 b5 4 cxb5

a) 4 ♘f3 bxc4? 5 ♘c3 d6 6 e4 g6 7 ♘d2 N (7 ♗xc4 ♗g7 8 0-0! ♘bd7 9 ♖e1 0-0 10 ♗g5 += Tal-Diaz, Biel 1976) 7...♗g7 8 ♘xc4 0-0 9 ♗e2 ♘bd7 10 0-0 ♘b6 11 ♘e3 += Vacek-Prochazka, CSSR 1978;

b) 4 a4 bxc4 5 ♘c3 d6 6 e4 g6 7 ♗xc4 ♗g7 8 ♘f3 ♗g4 9 h3 ♗xf3 10 ♕xf3 0-0 11 ♕e2 ♘bd7 12 0-0 N (12 a5 ♘e5 13 ♗a6 ♖b8 14 ♘b5 c4 Δ ♘d3∓ Marjanovic-Gaprindashvili, Dortmund 1978) 12...♘e8 13 f4 ♘c7 14 ♗e3 += Tichy-Gross, CSSR Final 1978

4...a6 5 bxa6

a) 5 f3 axb5 N 6 e4 d6 7 ♗xb5+ ♗d7 8 ♗xd7+ ♘bxd7 9 ♘e2 g6 10 ♗d2 ♗g7 11 ♘c3 0-0 12 ♘d2 ♘b6= Goodman-Webb, London 1978;

b) 5 b6 ♕xb6 6 ♘c3 d6 7 e4 g6 8 ♘f3 ♗g7 (8...♗g4 9 ♗e2 ♗g7 10 0-0 0-0 11 ♖b1 ♘bd7= Hadjitoffi-Santos, Albufieri 1978) 9 a4 0-0 10 a5 ♕c7 11 ♗c4 ♗g4= Happel-Eriksson, Stockholm 1978/79;

c) 5 ♘c3 axb5 6 e4 b4 7 ♘b5 d6 8

♘f3 g6 9 e5 dxe5 10 ♘xe5 ♗g7 11 ♘c4 0-0 12 0-0 ♘e4 N (12...♘fd7 13 f4 ♘b6 14 b3 ♗b7= Gligoric-Deze, Novi Sad 1976) 13 ♘d3 ♘d6 14 ♘xd6 exd6 15 ♗f4 ♗a6 16 ♕c2 ♕f6 Δ ♕d4∓ Vaisman-Ungureanu, Bucharest 1978

5...♗xa6 6 ♘c3

6 g3 d6 7 ♗g2 g6 8 b3 ♗g7 9 ♗b2 0-0 10 ♘h3 ♘bd7 11 0-0 ♕b6 12 ♗c3 ♕c7 (12...♕b7 13 ♕c2 ♘b6 14 ♖d1 c4 15 b4 ♗b5 16 ♖d2 ♘a4∞ Giffard-Dussol, Montpellier 1977/78) 13 ♖e1 ♘b6 14 a4 ♖ab8 15 e4 ♘bd7= Gheorghiu-Diez del Corral, Buenos Aires 1978

6...d6 7 ♘f3

7 e4 ♗xf1 8 ♔xf1 g6 9 ♘ge2 ♗g7 10 h3 0-0 11 ♔g1 ♘bd7 12 ♔h2 ♕a5 13 ♕c2 ♖fb8 14 ♗d2 N (14 ♖b1 Kuijpers-Dueball, Hitzacker 1971, 14...♘e8! 15 ♖f1 ♘c7 16 f4 ♘a6=) 14...♘e5 15 ♖hb1 ♕a6 16 b3 ♘d3∓ Bellin-Popov, Pernik 1978

7...g6 8 e4 ♗xf1 9 ♔xf1 ♗g7 10 g3 0-0 11 ♔g2 ♘a6 N

11...♘bd7 Δ ♕b6, ♕a6, ♘b6∞

12 ♕e2 ♕b6 13 ♖d1 ♖fb8 14 ♖b1 ♘d7 15 ♗f4 ♘c7 16 e5± Hort-Gaprindashvili, Wijk aan Zee 1979

Budapest Gambit

19

1 d4 ♘f6 2 c4 e5!? 3 dxe5 ♘g4

3...♘e4? 4 ♘f3 ♗b4+ 5 ♘bd2 ♘c6 6 g3 ♕e7 7 ♗g2 ♘xe5 8 0-0 ♘xd2 9 ♘xd2 0-0 10 ♕c2 ♘c6 11 e3 b6 12 ♘e4 ♗b7 13 a3 ♗d6 14 ♘xd6± Bagirov-Kalashyan, Kirovakan 1978

4 e4

4 ♘f3 ♗c5 5 e3 ♘c6 6 ♗e2 ♘gxe5 (6...0-0 7 0-0 ♖e8 8 ♘c3 ♘gxe5 9 ♘xe5 ♖xe5 10 b3 b6 11 ♗b2 ♖e6 12 ♗f3± Malypetrova-Dobson, Belgrade 1969) 7 ♘xe5 (7 0-0 d6 8 ♘c3 a6 9 b3 0-0 10 ♗b2 ♘xf3+ 11 ♗xf3 ♘e5 12 ♘e4 ♗a7 13 ♕d5!± Sigurjonsson-Segal, Ybbs 1968) 7...♘xe5 8 0-0 0-0 9 ♘c3 d6 10 b3 ♕h4! 11 ♗b2 ♘g4 12 ♗xg4 ♗xg4 13 ♕d2 ♖ae8 =+ Williams-Barbero, Mexico 1978

4...♘xe5 5 f4 ♘ec6

5...♘bc6! 6 fxe5 ♕h4+ 7 ♔d2 ♕f4+ =; 6 ♗e3 ♗b4+ 7 ♘d2 ♘g6= Gibbs-Hardy, Hastings 1968

6 ♘f3

a) 6 a3!;

b) 6 ♗e3 ♗b4+ 7 ♘d2 ♕e7 8 ♗d3 ♘a6 9 ♘f3 ♘c5 10 ♗xc5 ♗xc5∓ Plukker-Drimer, Whitby 1968

6...♗c5 7 ♘c3 d6 8 ♗d3 a5 9 h3 ♘a6 10 ♘d5 ♗e6 11 a3 0-0 12 f5 ♗xd5 13 cxd5 ♘e5 14 ♘xe5 ♕h4+! =+ Vaganian-Weber, Mexico 1978

Queen's Indian Defence

1 d4 ♘f6 2 c4 e6 3 ♘f3 b6 4 g3

4 ♗f4 ♗b7 5 e3

a) 5...♘h5 N 6 ♗g3 ♗e7 7 ♘c3 d6 8 ♗d3 ♘d7 9 ♕c2 g6 10 e4 c5= Ree-Csom, Buenos Aires 1978;

b) 5...♘e4 N 6 ♘fd2 ♗e7 7 ♘xe4 ♗xe4 8 ♘c3 ♗b7 9 ♗d3 0-0 10 d5 f5 11 h3 ♗b4 12 ♕b3 ♘a6 13 ♗e2 d6= Day-Keene, Buenos Aires 1978;

c) 5...♗e7 6 h3 0-0 7 ♘c3 d5 8 cxd5 ♘xd5 9 ♘xd5 ♗xd5 10 ♗d3 ♗b4+ 11 ♔e2 ♗d6 12 ♗xd6 ♗xf3+ N (12...cxd6 13 ♕c2 f5 14 ♗c4 ♗xf3+ 15 gxf3± Miles-Browne, IBM 1978) 13 ♔xf3!? ♕xd6 14 ♕c2 f5 15 ♖ac1 f4 16 ♕xc7!± Miles-Rivas, Amsterdam 1978;

d) 5...♗b4+ 6 ♘fd2! 0-0 7 a3 ♗e7 8 ♘c3 c5 N 9 d5! exd5 10 cxd5 ♗xd5?! 11 ♘xd5 ♘xd5 12 ♕f3 ♘c7 13 ♕b7 d6 14 ♘e4 ♕d7 15 0-0-0 ♘c6 16 ♘xd6 ♕xb7 17 ♘xb7 ♘e6 18 ♗g3± Miles-Timman, Wijk aan Zee 1979

4...♗a6

4...♗b7 5 ♗g2 ♗e7 6 ♘c3 0-0 (6...♘e4 7 ♗d2 f5 8 d5! ♗f6 9 ♖c1 ♘a6 10 0-0 0-0 11 a3 ♘ac5 12 b4 ♘xc3 13 ♗xc3 ♘e4 14 ♗xf6 ♕xf6 15 ♘d4± Browne-Najdorf, Buenos Aires 1978) 7 0-0 ♘e4 8 ♗d2 ♗f6 9 ♖c1 c5 10 d5 exd5 11 cxd5 ♘xc3 12 ♗xc3 d6= Browne-Palermo, Buenos Aires 1978

5 b3

a) 5 ♕c2 c5 6 ♗g2 ♗b7 7 dxc5 bxc5 8 ♘c3 ♗e7 9 0-0 0-0 10 ♗g5 ♕b6= Rukavina-Toth, II Ciocco 1978;

b) 5 ♕a4 c6 6 ♘c3 b5 (6...♗e7 7 ♗g2 0-0 8 0-0 d5 9 ♗f4 ♗xc4 10 ♗xb8 ♕xb8 11 ♘e5 ♗d6 12 ♘xc6 ♕b7 13 ♘e5 ♗a6 =+ Tan-Sharif, Penang 1978) 7 cxb5 cxb5 8 ♘xb5 ♕b6 9 ♘c3 ♗b4 10 ♗g2 0-0 11 0-0 ♗xc3 12

bxc3 ♗xe2 13 ♖e1 ♗b5 14 ♕c2 N
d5= Odendahl-Van der Sterren,
London 1978;
c) 5 ♕a4 c5 (Keres) 6 ♗g2 ♗b7 7 0-0
♗e7 (7...cxd4 8 ♖d1 ♗c5 9 ♘xd4 ♗xg2
10 ♔xg2 ♕c8 11 ♘c3 ♕b7+ 12 f3 0-0=
Radev-Eperjesi, Pazardjik 1978) 8 ♘c3
0-0 9 ♖d1 (9 ♕c2 cxd4 10 ♘xd4
♗xg2 11 ♔xg2 ♕c8 12 ♕d3 ♘c6 13
b3 ♘b4 14 ♕f3 ♗c5 =+ Arafih-
Giardelli, Buenos Aires 1978) 9...cxd4
10 ♘xd4 ♗xg2 11 ♔xg2 ♕c8 12 e4
♕b7 13 f3 a6 14 ♗e3 d6 15 ♕c2
♘bd7= Schmidt-Adorjan, Warsaw
1979
5...♗b4+!
5...d5 6 ♗g2 ♗d6 N 7 0-0 ♘8d7 8
♗b2 ♖c8 9 cxd5 exd5 10 ♘e5 c6 11
♘d2 ♕e7 12 ♖e1 += Polugaevsky-
Guil.Garcia, Wijk aan Zee 1979

6 ♗d2 ♗e7 7 ♗g2
7 ♘c3 N 0-0?! 8 e4 d5 9 cxd5 ♗xf1
10 ♔xf1 exd5 11 e5 ♘e4 12 ♕e2 ♘xc3
13 ♗xc3 += Kuligowski-Keene, Buenos
Aires 1978
7...c6 8 0-0 d5
8...0-0 9 ♗c3 d5 10 ♘e5 ♘fd7 11
♘xd7 ♘xd7 12 ♘d2 ♖c8 13 a4 N ♗f6
14 e4 c5 15 exd5 cxd4 16 ♗b4 ♗e7
17 ♗xe7 ♕xe7 18 dxe6 fxe6∞
Morrison-Miles, Amsterdam 1978
9 ♗c3!? N

9 ♘e5 0-0 10 cxd5 cxd5 11 ♘c3 ♘fd7
12 ♘f3 ♘c6 13 ♕c1 ♖c8 14 ♕b2 ♘f6
=+ Cicovacki-Vilela, Sombor 1978
9...♘e4?! 10 ♗b2 ♘d7 11 ♘fd2!
♘xd2 12 ♘xd2 b5!? 13 c5
13 ♕c2
13...b4 14 ♖e1 f5 15 e4?! dxe4 16
f3 0-0 17 fxe4 e5! ∞/∓ Barczay-
Tompa, Hungary Final 1978

Nimzo Indian

1 d4 ♘f6 2 c4 e6 3 ♘c3 ♗b4 4 e3
a) 4 ♕c2 c5 5 dxc5 ♘a6 6 a3 ♗xc3+
7 ♕xc3 ♘xc5 8 b4 ♘ce4 9 ♕d4 d5
10 c5 h6?! (10...b6 11 f3 bxc5 12
bxc5 ♕a5+ 13 ♕b4 += Lein-Toth,
Rome 1976) 11 f3 ♘g5 12 h4 N ♘gh7
13 g4 ♘f8 14 ♗f4 ♘g6 15 ♗d6± Soos-
Perkins, London 1978;
b) 4 ♕c2 d5 5 a3 ♗xc3+ 6 ♕xc3 ♘e4
7 ♕c2 c5 8 dxc5 ♘c6 9 cxd5 exd5
10 ♘f3 ♗f5 11 b4 0-0 12 ♗b2 d4
13 ♕c4 ♖e8 14 ♖d1 ♕f6 15 b5! N
(15 ♗xd4 ♘xd4 16 ♖xd4 a5∞
Bagirov) 15...♘c3! 16 bxc6 ♘xd1 17
♔xd1 ♕xc6 18 ♘xd4 ♖ad8 19 e3
+=/± Toth-Yilmaz, Albufieri 1978;
c) 4 g3 d5 5 ♗g2 0-0 6 ♘f3 dxc4
7 0-0 ♘c6 8 e3 (8 ♖e1 ♖b8 9 a3 ♗xc3
10 bxc3 ♘a5 11 ♖b1 b6 12 e4 ♗b7
13 ♗g5± Romanishin-Savon, Erevan
1976; 9...♗e7≈ Gulko-Tal, USSR
Final 1977) 8...♖b8 N (8...♘d5 9
♕c2 ♗e7 10 ♖d1 ♖b8 11 e4 ♘cb4
12 ♕b1 ♘xc3 13 bxc3 ♘d3=
Romanishin-Lerner, USSR 1974) 9
♕e2 b5 10 ♖d1 ♘d5! 11 ♗d2! ♕e7
12 a4!± Zaichik-Plachetka, Kirovakan
1978;
d) 4 g3 c5 5 ♘f3 cxd4 6 ♘xd4 ♘e4 7
♕d3 ♕a5 (7...♗xc3+ 8 bxc3 ♘c5 9
♕d2 b6 10 ♘b5 0-0 11 ♘d6 ♗a6 12
♗g2 ♘c6 13 ♗a3 ♖b8 14 0-0 ♘a5 15

♕d4 ♕c7 N .[15...♘ab7 Georgadze-Inkiov, Primorsko 1977, 16 ♘b5! ♗xb5 17 cxb5 ♕c7 18 c4±] 16 ♖fd1 ♘c6 17 ♕e3 ♘a5 18 ♖d4!? ♘ab7 19 ♘b5 ♗xb5 20 cxb5 d5∞ Farago-Tompa, Hungary Final 1978) 8 ♘b3 ♕f5 9 ♕e3 ♘a6 10 ♗g2 ♘xc3 11 bxc3 ♗e7 12 0-0 0-0!? N (12...d6 13 ♗a3 ♘c5 14 ♘d4 Schmidt-Schinzel, 1977, 14...♕f6 △ 0-0 =) 13 c5! d5 14 cxd6 ♗xd6 15 ♖d1± Ribli-Langeweg, Amsterdam 1978
4...c5 5 ♘f3 0-0 6 ♗d3 d5 7 0-0 dxc4 8 ♗xc4

8...♕e7
a) 8...♘c6 9 a3 ♗xc3 10 bxc3 ♕c7 11 ♗a2 ♖d8 12 ♗b2 e5 13 h3 ♗f5 14 ♕e2 ♕e7 N (14...♖d7 15 d5 ♘e7 16 c4 += Luckis-Caro, Mar del Plata 1962) 15 d5 ♘b8 16 c4 e4 17 ♘e5 ♘e8 18 f4 += Lein-Mascarinas, Tehran 1978;
b) 8...cxd4 9 exd4 b6 10 ♗g5 ♗b7 11 ♖c1 ♘bd7 (11...♗e7 12 a3 ♘c6 13 ♗a2 ♖c8 14 ♕d3 ♖c7! 15 ♖fd1 ♖d7 =+ Ogaard-Browne, Reykjavik 1978) 12 a3 ♗xc3? 13 ♖xc3 ♕b8 14 ♖e1 ♗d5 15 ♗xd5 ♘xd5 16 ♖c6± Vranesic-Lipnowski, Canada Final 1978;
c) 8...♘bd7 9 ♕e2 b6 10 d5 ♗xc3 11 dxe6 ♘e5 12 bxc3 ♘xf3+ 13 ♕xf3 ♗xe6 14 ♗xe6 fxe6 15 ♕e2 N (15 e4

♕d7= Gligoric-Unzicker, Moscow 1956) 15...♕d7 16 f3 ♖ad8 17 ♕c4 ♕d5 18 ♕xd5 ♖xd5∓ Woodhams-Parma, Buenos Aires 1978
9 a3 ♗a5 10 ♕c2 ♗d7 11 dxc5 ♕xc5 12 ♘e4 ♗xe4 13 b4 ♕h5 14 bxa5 N
14 ♕xe4 ♗c6 15 ♕f4 ♗b6 16 ♗b2 ♘d7= Gligoric-Smyslov, Jugoslavia 1959
14...♗d6 15 ♗d3 ♖c8 16 ♕d2 ♗c6 17 ♘d4 ♗d5= Gligoric-Smyslov, Burevestnik v Partisan 1979

Grunfeld

1 d4 ♘f6 2 c4 g6 3 ♘c3 d5 4 ♗f4
a) 4 ♗g5 ♘e4 5 ♗h4 c5 6 cxd5 ♘xc3 7 bxc3 ♕xd5 8 e3 cxd4 9 ♕xd4 ♕xd4 10 cxd4 e6! 11 ♖b1 ♗e7=; 11 ♘f3 N ♗b4+ 12 ♘d2 ♘c6 13 ♖b1 ♗e7 14 ♗g3 0-0= Tichy-Jansa, CSSR Final 1978;
a) 4 ♘f3 ♗g7 5 ♕b3 dxc4 6 ♕xc4 0-0 7 e4 ♗g4 8 ♗e3 ♘fd7 9 ♕b3 ♘b6 10 ♖d1 c6 N 11 ♗e2 ♘a6 12 0-0 ♕d6 13 a3 ♘c7 14 h3 ♗e6 15 ♕c2 ♖ad8 16 ♘g5!? ♗c4! ∞/=+ Keene-Smyslov, Buenos Aires 1978;
b) 4 ♘f3 ♗g7 5 ♗f4 0-0 6 e3 (6 ♖c1 c5 7 dxc5 ♗e6 8 ♘d4 ♘c6 9 e3 ♘xd4 10 exd4 dxc4 11 ♗e2 ♕a5 12 0-0 ♖fd8 13 ♕a4 ♕xa4 14 ♘xa4 ♘d5!∓ Villeneuve-Pytel, Montpellier 1977/78) 6...c5 7 dxc5 ♘e4 8 ♖c1! ♘xc3 9 bxc3 ♕a5 10 cxd5 ♗xc3+ 11 ♘d2 ♗f5!? 12 e4! ♗xe4 13 ♕b3! ♗xd2+ N (13...♗d4 Farago-Ftacnik, Kiev 1978 NCP 3/102) 14 ♗xd2 ♕d8 15 ♗h6± Pinter-Kirov, Pernik 1978;
c) 4 ♘f3 ♗g7 5 ♗g5 ♘e4 6 cxd5 ♘xg5 7 ♘xg5 e6 8 ♕d2 (8 ♘f3 exd5 9 e3 0-0 10 b4 ♗e6 11 ♗e2 c6 12 0-0 ♘d7 13 ♖c1 ♕e7 14 ♕b3 f5= Calvo-Sax, Buenos Aires 1978) 8...h6 (8...exd5

9 ♛e3+ ♔f8 10 ♛f4 ♗f6 11 h4 c6 12 e4 h6 13 ♘f3 ♗e6 14 e5 ♗e7≈ Lechtynsky-Ftacnik, CSSR Final 1978) 9 ♘f3 exd5 10 e3 0-0 11 ♗e2 c6 12 0-0 ♗e6 13 b4 ♛d6 =+ Basagic-Radev, Pazardjik 1978

4...♗g7 5 e3 0-0 6 ♛b3

a) 6 cxd5 ♘xd5 7 ♘xd5 ♛xd5 8 ♗xc7 ♘a6 9 ♗xa6 ♛xg2 10 ♛f3 ♛xf3 11 ♘xf3 bxa6 12 ♖c1 ♗b7 N 13 ♔e2 f6 14 ♖c5 e6 15 ♖hc1 ♖f7 16 ♗g3 += Fedder-Vadasz, Buenos Aires 1978;

b) 6 ♖c1 c5 7 dxc5 ♗e6 8 ♘f3 ♘c6 9 ♗e2 ♘e4 10 ♘d4 ♘xd4 11 exd4 ♘xc3 12 bxc3 dxc4 13 0-0 += Vaganian-Plachetka, Kirovakan 1978

6...a5!? N

6...c6 7 ♘f3 ♛a5 8 ♘d2 ♘bd7 9 ♗e2 ♘h5 10 ♗xh5 dxc4 11 ♘xc4 ♛xh5 12 0-0 b5?! (12...b6 Beljavsky-Ftacnik, Kiev 1978 NCP 3/105) 13 ♘a5 e5 14 ♗g3! exd4 15 exd4 c5 16 ♗d6 b4 17 ♗xf8 ♗xf8 18 ♛d5 ♛xd5 19 ♘xd5 cxd4 20 ♖fd1 ♘c5 21 ♖xd4 Inkiov-Witkowski, Lodz 1978

7 ♘f3 c5! 8 cxd5

a) 8 dxc5! a4 9 ♛a3!? ♘c6 10 ♗e2 ♛a5 11 0-0 dxc4 12 ♘d2! Δ ♘xc4±;

b) 8 ♗xb8!? cxd4 9 ♘xd4 a4! 10 ♘xa4 ♖xb8 11 ♘b6 e5 12 ♘f3 d4! 13 ♖d1 ♗g4 14 ♗e2 ♘d7 15 ♘xd7 ♛xd7 16 0-0 ♛e7 17 h3 ♗xf3 18 gxf3 ♗h6∓

8...a4! 9 ♘xa4

9 ♛c4 a3!

9...♘xd5 10 ♗xb8 cxd4! 11 ♘xd4 ♖xb8 12 ♘c3 ♗xd4! 13 exd4 ♘f4! 14 ♖d1 b5 ∞/∓ Beljavsky-Gutman, Ashkabad 1978

King's Indian Defence

1 d4 ♘f6 2 c4 g6 3 ♘c3 ♗g7 4 e4 d6 5 f3

5 f4 0-0 6 ♘f3 c5 7 d5 e6

a) 8 dxe6 ♗xe6!? 9 ♗d3 ♘c6 10 f5! ♗d7 11 ♗g5 (11 0-0 ♘b4 12 ♗b1 ♗c6 13 a3 ♘a6 14 ♗g5!± Lombardy-Westerinen, Lone Pine 1978) 11...♛b6 N (11...♛a5 12 0-0 ♖ae8 13 ♛d2 ♘b4 14 ♗b1 ♗c6 15 a3 ♘a6 16 ♛xd6± Lazarev-Zeliandinov, USSR 1966) 12 ♛d2 ♘d4 13 0-0 ♗c6 14 ♘xd4 cxd4 15 ♘d5 ♗xd5 16 exd5 ♖ae8 =+ Shirazi-Torre, Tiruchirapalli 1978;

b) 8 dxe6 fxe6 9 ♗d3 ♘c6 10 0-0 ♘d4 (10...♛e7 11 ♛e1 N [11 ♛e2 ♘d4 12 ♘xd4 cxd4 13 ♘b5 e5 14 fxe5 dxe5 15 b3 ♗g4 16 ♛d2± Minev-Vukic, Varna 1968] 11...♗d7 12 ♗d2 a6 13 ♔h1 b5 14 e5± Marjanovic-Popovic, Sombor 1978) 11 ♗d2 N (11 ♔h1 N b6 12 ♗e3 ♘xf3 13 ♛xf3 ♗b7 14 ♛h3 ♔h8 15 e5!± Meduna-Hausner, CSSR Final 1978) 11...♘d7 12 ♘g5 ♛e7 13 ♛g4 ♘b8 14 e5! ♘f5 15 ♛h3 h6 16 ♘ge4± Vaganian-Torre, Buenos Aires 1978;

c) 8 ♗e2 exd5 9 cxd5 ♗g4!? 10 0-0 ♗xf3 11 ♗xf3 ♘bd7 12 a4 ♖e8 13 ♛c2 c4∞ Bohm-van der Sterren, Erbeek 1978

5...0-0 6 ♗e3

6 ♗g5 c5 7 d5 e6 (7...♛a5 8 ♛d2 a6 9 0-0-0?! N [9 ♘ge2 b5 10 ♘g3 ♘bd7

11 cxb5 ♖b8 12 a4± Bobotsov-Golz, Leipzig 1968] 9...b5 10 cxb5 axb5 11 ♗xb5 ♗a6 12 ♗a4 ♘xe4! 13 ♘xe4 ♕xa4 14 ♔b1 ♕xa2+!! −+ Jansson-Vangelov, Albena Open 1978) 8 ♕d2 exd5 9 cxd5 ♘bd7?! (9...b6!? Day-Piasetski, Belleville 1971) 10 ♘h3 a6 11 a4 ♕a5 12 ♖a3 ♘e5 13 ♘f2 ♖e8 14 ♗e2 += Day-Biyiasas, Canada Final 1978

6...e5 7 d5 c6 8 ♗d3
8 ♕d2 cxd5 9 cxd5 a6 10 ♗d3 ♘h5 11 g4 ♘f4 12 ♗xf4? exf4 13 ♕xf4 ♕b6∓ Szmukler-Wexler, Buenos Aires 1978
8...cxd5 9 cxd5 ♘e8 10 ♕d2 f5 11 ♘ge2 ♘d7 12 exf5 gxf5 13 0-0 ♘df6
N
13...♔h8 14 ♖ac1 ♘df6 15 ♔h1 ♕e7 16 ♗g5 ♕f7= Polugaevsky-Geller, Petropolis 1973
14 ♖ac1 ♕e7 15 ♗g5 ♕f7 16 ♘g3 f4 17 ♘ge4 += Gheorghiu-Sznapik, Warsaw 1979

1 e4 b6

1 e4 b6 2 d4 ♗b7 3 ♘c3
a) 3 ♗d3 e6 (3...d5 4 exd5 ♕xd5 5 ♘f3 e6 6 ♘c3 ♕d8 7 ♗e4 ♗xe4 8 ♘xe4 ♕d5 9 ♕e2 ♘f6 10 ♘c3 ½-½ Diesen-Sahovic, Sombor 1978) 4 ♘f3

c5 5 0-0 (5 c3 ♗a6!? 6 c4 cxd4 7 ♘xd4 ♕f6 8 ♘b5 ♗xb5 9 cxb5 ♗b4+ 10 ♘d2 ♘e7 11 0-0 ♘g6 12 ♘f3 ♘e5= Chiong-Khan, Penang 1978) 5...cxd4 6 ♘xd4 ♗c5 7 ♘b3 ♗e7 8 ♘c3 ♘c6 9 ♕g4 g6 10 ♕f3 ♘f6 11 ♗h6 ♘h5 12 ♕e3 d6≈ Geller-Sahovic, Novi Sad 1978;
b) 3 ♘d2 e6 4 ♘gf3 ♘f6 (4...c5 5 c3 ♗e7 6 ♗d3 d6 7 0-0 ♘f6 8 a3 0-0 9 ♕e2 ♘c6= Farago-Sahovic, Novi Sad 1978) 5 ♗d3 c5 6 c3 ♕c7 7 0-0 ♗e7 8 ♖e1 0-0 9 ♘f1 d6 10 ♗g5 ♘bd7? (10...h6) 11 e5! +− Silman-Basman, London 1978
3...e6 4 ♗d3
a) 4 ♘f3 ♗b4 5 ♗d3 ♘f6 6 e5?! ♘e4 7 ♗xe4 ♗xe4 8 a3? ♗xc3+ 9 bxc3 0-0 10 ♕e2 ♗b7 11 0-0 f6! 12 ♖e1 ♕e8∓ Popov-Kluger, 1977;
b) 4 a3 g6?! 5 ♘f3 ♗g7 6 d5 ♘e7 7 ♗c4 0-0 8 0-0 exd5 9 exd5 ♗xc3 10 bxc3 ♘f5 11 ♖e1 ♗a6∝ Shamkovich-Basman, London 1978
4...c5 5 ♘f3 a6 6 0-0 cxd4 7 ♘xd4 d6 8 f4 ♘f6 9 ♕e2 ♗e7 10 ♘f3 ♘fd7!?
11 f5 ♗f6 12 fxe6 fxe6 13 ♗c4 ♕e7 Antonov-Govedarica, Pernik 1978, 14 ♗f4 △ ♖ad1

Sicilian

1 e4 c5 2 ♘f3 d6 3 ♗b5+ ♗d7
a) 3...♘c6 4 0-0 ♗d7 5 ♖e1 a6 (5...♘f6 6 c3 a6 7 ♗xc6 [7 ♗f1 ♗g4 8 d3 e5 9 ♘bd2 ♗e7 10 h3 ♗h5 11 ♘c4 0-0 12 ♗g5 h6= Angantysson-Iskov, Stockholm 1978/79] 7...♗xc6 8 d4 ♗xe4 9 ♗g5 ♗d5! [9...d5 10 ♘bd2 ♗g6 11 dxc5 e6 12 ♕a4+ ♕d7 13 ♕d4 ♖c8 14 b4 += Gaprindashvili-Djindjihashvili, Wijk aan Zee 1979] 10 ♘bd2 e6 11 c4 ♗xf3 12 ♕xf3 cxd4

24

13 ♕xb7 ♕c8 14 ♕b6 ♕c5 15 ♕b7
♕c8 16 ♕b6 ♕c5 17 ♕b7 ♕a7?! 18
♕c6+± Timoshenko-Kupreichik,
Ashkabad 1978) 6 ♗f1 ♗g4 7 h3 ♗xf3
(7...♗h5!? 8 c3 e6 9 g4! ♗g6 10 d4
h5 11 g5 ♗e7 12 ♗g2 h4 13 d5! ♘e5
14 dxe6 ♘xf3+ Taulbut-Csom,
Hastings 1978/79, 15 ♗xf3!±) 8 ♕xf3
g6 9 c3 ♗g7 10 ♘a3 ♘f6 11 ♘c2 ♕b6
12 d3 0-0= Balshan-Csom, Hastings
1978/79;
b) 3...♘d7!? 4 d4 (4 0-0 ♘f6 [4...a6
5 ♗xd7+ ♗xd7 6 d4 cxd4 7 ♕xd4
♘c6 8 ♘c3 ♘f6 9 ♗g5 e6 10 ♘d5!
♗xd5 11 exd5 e5 12 ♗xf6 ♕xf6 13
♕a4+± Vasyukov-Mascarinas, Tiruchirapalli 1978] 5 ♖e1 e5 6 b4!? [6 c3
a6 7 ♗f1 ♗e7 8 d4 0-0 9 ♘bd2 b5
10 h3 ♕b6 11 b3 ♖e8 12 ♗b2 +=
Vasyukov-Mestel, Hastings 1978/79]
6...cxb4 7 a3 bxa3 8 d4 a6 9 ♖xa3
♗e7 Zaichik-Eolyan, Kirovakan 1978,
10 dxe5 dxe5 11 ♗xd7+ ♗xd7 12
♘xe5 ♗xa3 13 ♗xa3 ♗e6 14 ♗d6!∝)
4...cxd4 (4...♘f6 5 0-0!? N ♘xe4 6
♕e2 ♘f6 7 ♗g5 cxd4 8 ♗xf6 gxf6 9 ♘x
d4 a6 10 ♗xd7+ ♗xd7 11 ♘c3 ♕a5 12
♕f3 0-0-0 13 ♘d5! e6! 14 ♘xf6 ♗g7∝
Peters-Mestel, Hastings 1978/79) 5
♕xd4 e5 6 ♕d3 h6 (6...a6!?) 7 c4 ♘f6
8 ♘c3 ♗e7 9 0-0 0-0 10 ♗xd7 (10
♗e3 a6 11 ♗xd7 ♗xd7 12 a4 ♗c6 13
a5 ♘xe4 14 ♗b6 Peters-Balshan,
Hastings 1978/79, 14...♕d7 15 ♘xe4
f5∝) 10...♗xd7 11 b3 (11 ♖d1 a6
12 a4 ♗e6 13 b3 ♕b6 14 a5 ♕c7 15
♗e3 += Sharif-Chiong, Penang 1978)
11...a6 12 a4 ♗e6 (12...♕c7 13 ♘h4!?
♖fd8 14 ♗e3 b6 15 f3 ♕b7 16 ♖fd1
♗f8 17 g4 Δ ♘f5± Peters-van Barle,
London 1978) 13 ♖fd1 ♖c8 14 ♗a3
♕a5 15 h3 ♖fd8 16 ♕e3± Duckstein-
Nemet, Virovitica 1978
4 ♗xd7+ ♘xd7

4...♕xd7
a) 5 c4 e5 6 ♘c3 ♘c6 7 d3 ♗e7 8 0-0
♗d8 9 ♘d5 ♘ge7 10 ♕a4 ♘xd5 11
cxd5 ♘b4= Szell-Szekely, Hungary
Final 1978;
b) 5 c4 ♘c6 6 d4 cxd4 7 ♕xd4 g6 8
♘c3 ♗g7 9 ♗e3 ♘f6 10 f3 0-0 11 0-0
♖fc8 12 ♘de2 (12 b3 ♘e8 13 ♕d2
b6 14 ♖ad1 ♖ab8 15 f4 += Mednis-
Byrne, USA Final 1978) 12...b6!?
13 ♕d2 ♕b7 14 ♖ac1 ♖ab8 15 ♘d5 +=
Botterill-Lein, Hastings 1978/79;
c) 5 0-0 e6 6 c3 ♘f6 7 e5?! (7 ♕e2
♘c6 8 d4 cxd4 9 cxd4 d5 10 e5 ♘e4
11 ♗e3 ♗e7 12 ♘e1 h6 13 f3 ♘g5 14
♘c3 += Ambroz-Gross, CSSR Final
1978) 7...dxe5 8 ♘xe5 ♕d5 9 ♕a4+
♘bd7 10 d4 a6! 11 ♗f4 b5 12 ♕d1
cxd4 13 cxd4 ♗b4!∓ Taulbut-
Andersson, Hastings 1978/79;
d) 5 0-0 ♘c6 6 c3 d5 (6...♘f6 7 ♖e1
g6 8 d4 ♖c8 9 ♗g5 ♗g7 10 ♘bd2
0-0= Stanojevic-Notaros, Novi Sad
1978) 7 exd5 ♕xd5 8 d4 e6 9 ♕a4
♘f6 10 ♗g5 cxd4 11 ♘xd4 ♖c8 12
♘xc6 ♕xc6 13 ♕xc6+ ♖xc6= Hebert-
Kavalek, Buenos Aires 1978;
e) 5 0-0 g6 6 ♘c3 ♗g7 7 d3 ♘c6 8
♖b1 e6 9 ♗f4 ♘ge7 10 ♕d2 0-0=
Coutin-Lipiniks, Buenos Aires 1978;
f) 5 0-0 ♘f6 6 e5 dxe5 7 ♘xe5 ♕c8!
8 ♘c3 (8 ♕f3 e6 9 ♘c3 ♗e7 10 d3
0-0 11 ♗f4 ♘a6= Bellin-Ubilava,
Tbilisi 1977) 8...♘c6 9 ♘xc6 ♕xc6
10 ♕e2 e6 11 ♕b5 ♕xb5 12 ♘xb5
♔d7= Kalashin-Zaichik, Kirovakan
1978

Diagram

5 0-0
a) 5 c4 ♘gf6 6 ♘c3 g6 7 0-0 ♗g7 8
♖b1 0-0 9 d3 a6 10 a3 ♘e8 11 ♗e3
♖b8= Sharif-Torre, Tiruchirapalli 1978;

25

b) 5 c4 ♘e5!? 6 0-0 ♘f6 7 d3 ♕d7 8 a3 e6 9 b4 ♗e7 10 bxc5 ♘xf3+ 11 ♕xf3 dxc5 12 e5 ♘g8 13 ♘c3 += Sharif-O'Kelly, Penang 1978
5...♘gf6
5...g6 6 c3 ♘gf6 7 ♖e1 ♗g7 8 d4 e5 9 dxe5 dxe5 10 c4 0-0 11 ♘c3 ♖e8= Szmetan-Kilenc, Buenos Aires 1978
6 ♖e1
a) 6 d3 e6 7 c4 ♗e7 8 ♘c3 0-0 9 b3 a6 10 ♗b2 ♕b8= Lein-Ribli, Buenos Aires 1978;
b) 6 ♕e2 e6 7 ♘c3 ♗e7 8 b3 0-0 9 ♗b2 a6 10 d4 cxd4 11 ♘xd4 ♕c7 12 ♖ad1 += Lawton-Aaron, London 1978
6...e6 7 b3 ♗e7 8 ♗b2 0-0 9 d3
9 c4 a6 10 d4 cxd4 11 ♘xd4 ♕c7 12 ♘c3 ♖fe8 13 ♖c1 += Ghinda-Kuligowski, Warsaw 1979
9...♕c7 10 a4 ♖fd8 11 ♘bd2 ♘e8 12 ♘c4 ♗f6= Stanojevic-Geller, Novi Sad 1978

1 e4 c5 2 ♘f3 ♘f6 3 e5 ♘d5 4 ♘c3 e6 5 ♘xd5 exd5 6 d4 ♘c6 7 dxc5 ♗xc5 8 ♕xd5
a) 8 ♗e2 d4!? 9 0-0 d6 10 ♗g5 ♕c7 11 exd6 ♕xd6 12 ♕d2 0-0 13 ♖fe1 ♗f5= Boleslavsky;
b) 8 ♗d3 N d6 9 exd6 0-0 10 0-0 ♕xd6 11 c3 h6 12 ♗e2 ♗g4 13 ♕d3 ♕g6 14 ♗e3! ♕xd3 15 ♗xd3 +=

Biyiasas-Peters, Hastings 1978/79
8...♕b6 9 ♗c4 ♗xf2+ 10 ♔e2 0-0 11 ♖f1 ♗c5 12 ♘g5 ♘d4+ 13 ♔d1 ♘e6 14 ♘e4 ♗e7!? N 14...d6 **15 c3±** Suetin **15...♕c6 16 ♗e3 b5 17 ♕xc6 dxc6 18 ♗b3 ♘c7 19 ♔c2±** Rivas-Feller, Amsterdam 1978

1 e4 c5 2 b3!?
2 ♘f3 e6 3 b3 ♘c6 (3...d6 4 ♗b5+ ♗d7 5 ♗xd7+ ♘xd7 6 0-0 ♘gf6 7 ♖e1 ♗e7 8 ♗b2 0-0 9 d4 cxd4 10 ♘xd4 += Biriescu-Padevsky, Bucharest 1978) 4 ♗b2 d6 5 ♗b5 ♗d7 6 0-0 ♘f6 7 ♖e1 ♗e7 8 d4 (8 ♗f1 0-0 9 d4 cxd4 10 ♘xd4 ♖c8 11 c4 ♘xd4 12 ♗xd4 e5 13 ♗b2 += Gazik-Yurtseven, Groningen 1978/79) 8...cxd4 9 ♘xd4 0-0 10 ♘xc6 bxc6 11 ♗d3 e5 12 c4 ♗g4 13 ♗e2 ♗e6! 14 ♘c3 ♕b8! =+ Palermo-Najdorf, Buenos Aires 1978
2...d6
a) 2...♘f6 3 e5 ♘d5 4 ♗b2 ♘c6 5 ♘f3 d6 6 ♗c4 ♘c7 7 exd6 exd6 8 0-0 d5 9 ♗e2 d4= Hartston-Guttierrez, Buenos Aires 1978;
b) 2...♘c6 3 ♗b2 e6 4 ♘f3 ♘f6 (4...d5 5 ♗b5 ♘f6 6 e5 ♘d7 7 ♗xc6 bxc6 8 d3 ♗e7 9 0-0 0-0 10 ♖e1 f6 11 exf6 ♗xf6 12 ♘c3 += Spassky-Giardelli, Buenos Aires 1978) 5 e5 ♘d5 6 ♗b5 ♗e7 7 0-0 0-0 8 ♗xc6 bxc6 9 d3 f6 10 ♘bd2 N (10 ♘c3 fxe5 11 ♘xe5 ♕e8?! 12 ♘e4 d6 13 ♘c4 ♕d8 14 a3 e5 15 ♕e1 += Spassky-Hernandez, Buenos Aires 1978) 10...♕c7 11 ♘e4 fxe5 12 ♘xe5 d6 13 ♘c4 e5 14 a3 ♘f4 15 ♘g3 ♗f6 16 b4 += Ornstein-Welin, Stockholm 1978/79
3 ♗b2
3 ♗b5+ ♗d7 4 c4?! ♗xb5 5 cxb5 a6 6 ♘c3 ♘f6 7 ♘f3 g6 8 ♗b2 axb5 9 ♘xb5 ♗g7 10 0-0 0-0 =+ Lein-Polugaevsky, Buenos Aires 1978

26

3...a6!?
3...♘f6 4 ♘c3 e6 5 ♘f3 ♗e7 6 ♗b5+ ♘bd7 7 a4 0-0 8 0-0 b6 9 d4 a6 10 ♗d3 cxd4 11 ♘xd4 += Dolmadjan-Georgiev, Bulgaria Final 1978

4 f4 ♘c6 5 ♘f3 e6 6 g3 ♘f6 7 e5 dxe5 8 fxe5 ♘g4 9 ♗g2 h5 10 ♕e2 ♘b4 11 ♘a3 ♗d7 12 h3 ♘h6 13 c3 ♘d5 14 0-0± Spassky-Hebert, Buenos Aires 1978

1 e4 c5 2 ♘f3 ♘c6 3 ♗b5 g6
3...♕b6 4 ♘c3 e6 5 0-0 ♘ge7 6 ♖e1 ♘d4 7 ♗f1 ♘ec6 8 d3 ♗e7 9 ♘xd4 cxd4 10 ♘e2 0-0 11 ♘g3 N (11 c4?! ♗b4 12 ♗d2 e5 13 f4 d6 14 f5 a5!?∝ Rath-Larsen, Esbjerg 1978) 11...d6 12 c4 a5 13 f4 ♗d7 14 ♖e2 f5= Lein-Franco, Buenos Aires 1978
4 0-0 ♗g7 5 ♖e1 e5
5...♘f6 6 c3 0-0 7 d4 cxd4 8 cxd4 d5 9 e5 ♘e4 10 ♗xc6 bxc6 11 ♘bd2 c5 12 dxc5 ♘xc5 13 ♘b3 ♘xb3 14 ♕xb3 (∝ Gufeld) 14...♗e6 15 ♕a4 ♕d7 16 ♕xd7 ♗xd7 17 ♗g5 e6 18 ♖ac1 ♖fc8 =+ Angantysson-Schneider, Stockholm 1978/79

Diagram

6 c3 ♘ge7 7 d4 cxd4 8 cxd4 exd4
8...♘xd4?! 9 ♘xd4 exd4 10 e5 ♘c6

11 ♗f4 0-0 12 ♘d2 ♕a5 13 a4± Werner-Watson, London 1978
9 ♗f4
9 ♘bd2!? N 0-0 10 ♘b3 d5 11 e5 ♗g4 12 ♗f4 ♕b6 13 ♗e2 ♖ac8 14 ♘fxd4 ♗xe2 15 ♖xe2 ♘xd4 16 ♘xd4 ♘c6= Pelitov-Radev, Pazardjik 1978
9...a6 10 ♗c4 d6 11 ♘bd2 0-0 12 ♖c1 h6 13 h3 d5 14 ♗b3 ♗e6 15 e5 ♕b6 =+/∓ Short-P.Littlewood, London 1978

1 e4 c5 2 ♘f3 ♘c6 3 d4 cxd4 4 ♘xd4 e5 5 ♘b5 a6 6 ♘d6+ ♗xd6 7 ♕xd6 ♕f6 8 ♕a3
8 ♕d1 ♘ge7 9 ♘c3 ♕g6 10 h4 f5?! N (10...h5 11 ♗g5±) 11 h5 ♕e6 12 exf5 ♘xf5 13 ♕d5± Stirling-Frostick, London 1978
8...♘ge7 9 ♘c3 ♖b8! 10 ♗e3 b5 11 ♘d5 ♘xd5 12 exd5 b4 13 ♕d3 ♘e7 14 ♕d2 N
14 d6 ♘f5 15 0-0-0 ♗b7 16 ♗c5 0-0 = Fichtl-Smejkal, CSSR Final 1963
14...0-0 15 0-0-0 ♗b7 16 ♗c4 ♖fc8 17 ♗b3 ♕g6∓ Matous-Sejkora, CSSR 1978

1 e4 c5 2 ♘f3 e6 3 d4 cxd4 4 ♘xd4 a6 5 ♗d3 g6
a) 5...♗c5 6 ♘b3 ♗a7 7 ♕e2! (7 0-0 ♘c6 8 c4 d6 9 ♕e2 ♘f6 10 ♗e3 ♗xe3 11 ♕xe3 0-0 12 ♘c3 b6 13 f4 +=

Holmov-Bohlig, Halle 1978) 7...♘c6 8 ♗e3 ♗xe3 9 ♕xe3 d6 10 ♘c3 ♘f6 11 0-0-0 0-0 12 f4 ♕c7 13 g4 += Georgadze-Bohlig, Halle 1978;
b) 5...♘e7 6 f4 N ♘ec6 7 ♘b3 d6 8 0-0 ♗e7 9 ♗e3 ♘d7 10 a4 b6 11 ♘1d2 ♕c7 12 c3 0-0 13 ♕f3 += Tseshkovsky-Mestres, Malgrat de Mar 1978;
c) 5...♘e7 6 0-0 ♘ec6 7 ♘b3 (7 c3 N d6 8 ♗e3 ♗e7 9 ♘d2 0-0 10 f4 ♘d7 11 ♔h1 ♖e8 12 ♕e1 += Georgiev-Mishuchkov, Primorsko 1978) 7...♗e7 8 ♘c3 0-0 9 f4 d6 10 ♗e3 ♘d7 11 ♕e2 b6 12 ♖ad1 ♘b4 13 e5!? ♘xd3 14 ♖xd3 dxe5 15 fxe5 ♕c7 ∝/=+ Rodriguez-Kochiev, Mexico 1978;
d) 5...♘f6 6 0-0 d6 7 f4 ♘bd7 8 ♕f3 ♘c5 9 ♗e3 ♗e7 10 ♘c3 ♘xd3 11 cxd3 0-0 12 ♖ad1 ♘d7 13 ♕g3 ♗h4 14 ♕h3 ♗f6= Stean-Gheorghiu, Buenos Aires 1978;
e) 5...♘f6 6 f4 N ♗c5!? 7 ♘b3 ♗a7 8 ♕e2 ♘c6 9 ♗e3 ♗xe3 10 ♕xe3 d5 11 e5 d4? 12 ♕g3± Timman-Hubner, Nijmegen 1978

6 0-0
6 ♗e3 ♗g7 7 ♘c3 ♕c7 8 ♕d2 d6 9 0-0-0 ♘c6 10 ♘de2 b5 11 ♔b1 h6 12 f4 ♘f6? 13 ♗xb5 axb5 14 ♘xb5 ♕b8 15 ♘xd6+ +− Ermenkov-Merdinian, Plovdiv 1978
6...♗g7 7 c3 N

7 ♗e3 ♘e7 8 ♘c3 0-0 9 ♕d2 b6 10 ♘de2 ♗d7 11 ♖h6 ♘bc6 12 ♗xg7 ♔xg7 13 ♘g3 ♕b6 14 ♔h1± Garcia-Lombardy, Buenos Aires 1978
7...d6 8 ♘d2 ♗f6 9 ♕e2 0-0 10 ♘c4 e5 11 ♘b3 b5 12 ♘ca5 ♗d7 13 ♗d2 ♘c6 14 c4 ♘d4! =+ Westerinen-Andersson, Buenos Aires 1978

1 e4 c5 2 ♘f3 d6 3 d4 cxd4 4 ♘xd4 ♘f6 5 ♘c3 e6 6 g4 a6
a) 6...h6 7 h4!? ♘c6 8 ♖g1 d5 9 ♗b5 ♗d7 10 exd5 ♘xd5 11 ♘xd5 exd5 12 ♕e2+ ♗e7 13 ♗e3 ♘xd4 14 ♗xd7+ ♕xd7 15 ♗xd4 0-0 16 0-0-0 += Wedberg-Wagman, Eksjo 1978;
b) 6...h6 7 ♗g2 ♘c6 8 h3 ♘xd4 N 9 ♕xd4 ♗d7 10 b3 ♗c6 11 ♗b2 ♕a5 12 0-0-0 += Horvath-Dely, Hungary Final 1978;
c) 6...h6 7 g5 hxg5 8 ♗xg5 ♘c6 9 ♕d2 ♕b6 10 ♘b3 a6 11 0-0-0 ♗d7 12 h4 ♗e7 13 ♗e2 N (13 f4 0-0-0 14 ♗g2∝ Deuball-Ribli, Bath 1973) 13...♕c7 14 f4 0-0-0 15 ♔b1 ♔b8 16 ♗f3 ♗c8∝ Chi-Andersson, Buenos Aires 1978

7 g5 ♘fd7 8 ♗e3 b5 9 a3 ♘b6 9...♗b7 10 f4 N ♘c6 11 ♕g4 b4!? 12 ♘xc6 ♗xc6 13 axb4 ♕b8 14 ♗d3 ♕xb4 15 0-0 g6 16 ♕e2 ♗g7 17 ♘d5!± Sorensen-Hollis, Corres 1977/79

28

10 ♖g1 ♘8d7 11 f4 ♗b7 12 f5 e5
13 ♘e6!? N
13 ♘b3 ♖c8 14 ♗d3 ♘c4? (14...d5!
15 ♘xd5 ♘xd5 16 exd5 ♘b6!
Shamkovich) 15 ♗xc4 ♖xc4 16 ♕d3
♕a8 17 ♘d2 ♖c8 18 0-0-0± Balashov-
Malich, Leipzig 1973
13...fxe6 14 ♕h5+ g6?
14...♔e7 15 fxe6 ♔xe6 16 0-0-0!
♔e7 17 g6 ♘f6 18 ♗g5! Δ ♕xh7 ∝/±
15 fxg6 ♔e7 16 gxh7 ♗g7 17 0-0-0±
Shamkovich-Benko, USA Final 1978

1 e4 c5 2 ♘f3 d6 3 d4 cxd4 4 ♘xd4
♘f6 5 ♘c3 a6 6 ♗g5
6 ♗e3 e5 7 ♘b3 ♗e7 (7...♕c7 8 ♗e2
♗e7 9 0-0 b5 10 f4 ♗b7 11 ♘d5 ♘xd5
12 exd5 ♘bd7 13 a4 += Vrabec-
Sobek, CSSR 1978) 8 ♕d2 ♗e6 9
f3 ♘bd7 10 g4 h6 (10...b5 11 a4 b4
12 ♘d5 ♗xd5 13 exd5 += Hartston)
11 ♘d5 ♗xd5 12 exd5 ♘h7 13 0-0-0
♗g5 14 ♔b1 += Hartston-Csom,
Hastings 1978/79
6...e6 7 f4

7...♕b6
a) 7...♕c7 8 ♕f3 b5 9 ♗xf6 gxf6 10
e5 ♗b7 11 ♕h5 dxe5 12 ♘xe6 ♕b6
13 ♘xf8 ♕e3+ 14 ♕e2 ♕xf4! N
15 g3 ♕f3 16 ♕xf3 ♗xf3 =+ Szmetan-
Quinteros, Buenos Aires 1978;
b) 7...♘bd7 8 ♕e2 ♕c7 9 0-0-0 ♗e7

10 g4 b5 11 ♗g2 ♗b7 12 f5!? N e5
13 ♘b3 ♖c8 14 ♔b1 b4 15 ♗xf6
♘xf6 16 ♘d5 ♘xd5 17 exd5 0-0=
Chiong-Bachtiar, Penang 1978;
c) 7...♘bd7 8 ♕f3 ♕c7 9 0-0-0 b5
10 ♗xb5 (10 ♗d3 ♗b7 11 ♖he1
♕b6 12 ♘b3 ♗e7 N 13 ♕g3 b4 14
♘b1 a5 15 e5 ♘h5 16 ♕h4 ♗xg5 17
♕xg5 g6∝ Webb-Britton, London
1978) 10...axb5 11 e5 ♗b7! N 12
♘dxb5 ♕c8 13 ♕e2 dxe5 14 fxe5
♘d5 15 ♘e4 ♖a6 16 ♘bd6+ ♗xd6 17
♕xa6! ♗xe5! −+ Karadimov-
Georgiev, Primorsko 1978;
d) 7...♗e7 8 ♕f3 ♕c7 (8...h6 9 ♗h4
♕c7 10 0-0-0 ♘bd7 11 ♗d3 g5 12
fxg5 ♘e5 13 ♕e2 ♘fg4 14 ♘f3 ♘xf3
15 gxf3 hxg5 16 ♗g3 ♘e5 17 h4 gxh4
18 f4 ♘xd3+ 19 ♖xd3 ♗d7 20 f5 N
[20 ♕e1 ♗b5 21 ♖d1 h3 21 f5 ♖d8≈
Ljubojevic-Browne, Wijk aan Zee
1975] 20...0-0-0 21 ♗h2 ♗c6∝ Wibe-
Ljubojevic, Buenos Aires 1978) 9
0-0-0 ♘bd7 10 g4 (10 ♗d3 h6 11 ♕h3
♘b6 12 f5 e5 13 ♘b3 ♗d7 14 ♗e3
♘c4 15 ♗xc4 ♕xc4 16 ♘d2 ♕c7! N
[16...♕c6 17 ♗g5 ♖c8 18 ♗xf6 ♗xf6
19 ♕d3 0-0 20 ♔b1± Timman-
Hamann, Amsterdam 1975] 17 ♗g5
♗c6= Gamarra-Byrne, Buenos Aires
1978) 10...b5 11 ♗xf6 ♘xf6 (11...
gxf6 12 f5 ♘c5 13 fxe6 fxe6 14 b4!
N [14 a3 0-0 15 ♗d3 ♖b8 16 h4±
Capelan-Donner, Solingen 1968] 14...
♘a4 15 ♘xa4 bxa4 16 ♖d3 0-0 17
♖c3 ♕b6 18 ♘c6 ±/+− Hubner-
Hort, Wijk aan Zee 1979) 12 g5 ♘d7
13 h4 (13 f5 ♗xg5+ 14 ♔b1 0-0?!
N 15 fxe6 ♘b6 16 ♘d5 ♘xd5 17
exd5 ♗f6 18 ♗d3± Matulovic-
Baghli, Albufieri 1978) 13...b4 14
♘ce2 ♗b7 15 ♘g3 ♘c5 N (15...d5
16 e5 g6 17 ♗d3 ♘c5 18 h5 0-0-0=
Kljenovic-Bukic, Jugoslavia 1972) 16

f5 d5 17 fxe6 fxe6 18 exd5 ♖f8 (18...
♗xd5 19 ♘xe6!) 19 ♕h5+ g6 20
♕xh7 ♕xg3 21 ♕xg6+ +− Ljubojevic-
Bouaziz, Albufieri 1978
8 ♕d2 ♕xb2 9 ♘b3
9 ♖b1 ♕a3 10 f5 ♘c6 11 fxe6 fxe6
12 ♘xc6 bxc6 13 e5 dxe5 (13...♘d7
14 exd6 ♕xd6 15 ♗d3 ♕e5+ 16 ♘e4
♘c5 17 0-0 ♕d4+ 18 ♔h1 ♘xe4 19
♗xe4 ♕xd2 20 ♗xd2 ♗d7 21 ♗c3±
Valkesalmi-Arnold, Groningen 1978/
79) 14 ♗xf6 gxf6 15 ♘e4 ♕xa2!? N
(15...♗e7 16 ♗e2 h5 17 ♖b3 ♕a4 18
♘xf6+ ♗xf6 19 c4 ♗h4+ 20 g3 ♗e7
21 0-0 ♗d7 22 ♕c2 ♕a5 23 ♖fb1
e4! 24 ♕xe4 ♕f5 25 ♖b8+ ♖xb8 26
♖xb8+ ♗d8 27 ♕h4 0-0 0-1 Geszosz-
Tringov, Greece v Bulgaria 1978)
16 ♖d1 ♗e7 17 ♗e2 0-0 18 0-0 f5 19
♕h6 fxe4 20 ♖xf8+ ♗xf8 21 ♕g5+
♔h8 22 ♕f6+ ♔g8= Szmetan-
Quinteros, Buenos Aires 1978
9...♘c6
9...♕a3 10 ♗d3 ♘c6?! N 11 0-0 ♗e7
12 ♖ae1 h6 13 ♗h4 0-0 14 ♖f3±
de Firmian-Patterson, London 1978

**10 ♗xf6 gxf6 11 ♗e2 ♕a3 12 0-0 ♗d7
13 ♔h1**
a) 13 f5 ♘e5 14 fxe6 fxe6 15 ♗h5+
♔d8∞ Tal-Portisch, Varese 1976;
b) 13 f5 h5! N 14 fxe6 fxe6 15
♖f3 0-0-0 16 ♖b1 ♗h6 17 ♕e1 ♖dg8∓

Suradiradja-Palatnik, Plovdiv 1978;
c) 13 ♘b1 ♕b4 14 ♕e3 ♘e7!? N 15
c4 f5 16 a3 ♕a4 17 ♘c3 ♕c6 18 ♖ad1
♗g7∞   Matulovic-Marjanovic,
Jugoslavia 1978
13...♖c8 14 ♗h5 ♗g7 15 ♖f3 0-0≈
Liberzon-Ribli, Buenos Aires 1978

**1 e4 c5 2 ♘f3 ♘c6 3 d4 cxd4 4 ♘xd4
♘f6 5 ♘c3 d6 6 ♗g5 e6 7 ♕d2**
7 ♕d3 a6 8 ♗e2 ♗d7 9 0-0 ♗e7 10
♘b3 ♕c7 (10...b5 11 ♗xf6 gxf6 12
♕g3 ♕b6 13 a4 b4= Biriescu-Stoica,
Bucharest 1978) 11 ♔h1 0-0 12 f4
b5 13 e5?! dxe5 14 fxe5 ♘d5 =+
Biriescu-Banas, Satu Mare 1978
7...a6 8 0-0-0 ♗d7
8...h6 9 ♗e3 ♕c7 N (9...♗d7 10 f3
♕c7 11 g4 ♘e5 12 h4 b5 13 ♕g2 b4
14 ♘ce2 ♘c4= Tringov-Radulov,
Bulgaria 1978) 10 f3 ♖b8 11 g4
♘xd4 12 ♗xd4 b5 13 e5 ♘d7 14
exd6 ♗xd6 15 ♘e4 += Chiburdanidze-
Gaprindashvili (11) 1978
9 f4 ♗e7
9...b5 10 ♗xf6 gxf6 11 f5 (11 ♘xc6
♗xc6 12 f5?! b4 13 ♘e2 ♗xe4 14
fxe6 fxe6 15 ♕e3 f5∓ Roos-Morrison,
Amsterdam 1978; 11 g3 ♕b6 12 ♘ce2
0-0-0 N 13 ♔b1 ♔b8 14 ♗g2 ♗g7
15 ♖hf1 += Sax-Ribli, Warsaw 1979)
11...♘xd4 (11...♕b6 12 ♘xc6 ♕xc6
[12...♗xc6 13 fxe6 fxe6 14 ♕f4 ♗e7
15 ♕g4 ♕e3+ 16 ♔b1 b4= Bordonada-
Torre, Tehran 1978] 13 ♗d3 ♕c5
14 ♔b1 0-0-0 15 ♖hf1 ♔b8 16 fxe6
fxe6 17 ♖xf6± Georgadze-Kuzmin,
USSR Final 1978) 12 ♕xd4 ♗h6+
13 ♔b1 ♗f4 14 ♘e2 ♗e5 15 ♕d3!?
♕b6 16 g3 ♖c8∞ Prandstetter-
Hausner, CSSR Final 1978

Diagram

10 ♘f3 b5 11 ♗xf6

11 e5 b4 12 exf6 bxc3 13 ♕xc3 gxf6 14 ♗h4 d5 15 f5?! N ♘b4 16 ♕b3 ♕a5 17 a3 ♘xc2! −+ Chiong-Torre, Penang 1978

11...gxf6

11...♗xf6 12 ♕xd6 ♖a7 13 e5 ♗e7 14 ♕d2 ♕a5 15 ♔b1 ♗b4 16 ♘g5! N ♗xc3 17 ♕xc3 ♕xc3 18 bxc3 ♘a5 19 ♖d6 ♗c6 20 ♗d3 h6 Inkiov-Spassov, Pernik 1978, 21 ♘e4 +=

12 ♔b1

12 ♗d3 ♕b6 13 ♔b1 0-0-0 14 f5 ♔b8 15 ♘e2 ♕c5= Popovic-Martinovic, Novi Sad 1978

12...♕b6 13 f5 0-0-0 14 fxe6

14 g3 ♔b8 15 fxe6 fxe6 16 ♗h3 ♗c8 17 ♕h6?! ♕c5 18 ♖hf1 a5 =+ Harandi-Torre, Tehran 1978

14...fxe6 15 a4!? ♘a5?!

15...b4 16 ♘a2 a5∞

16 ♘d4 b4 17 ♘a2 d5?! 18 exd5 e5 19 ♕e2 ♔b7 20 ♕e4± Browne-Torre, Buenos Aires 1978

---

1 e4 c5 2 ♘f3 e6 3 d4 cxd4 4 ♘xd4 ♘c6 5 ♘c3 a6 6 g3 ♘ge7 7 ♘b3 d6

7...♘g6 8 h4 d5 9 h5 ♘ge5 10 f4 ♘d7 11 ♗e3 h6 12 ♕e2 ♕c7 13 0-0-0 b5∞ Szmetan-Zapata, Buenos Aires 1978;
b) 7...♘a5 8 ♕h5 ♘ec6 9 ♗g5 ♕c7 10 ♗f4 d6 11 0-0-0 ♘xb3+ 12 axb3 ♗e7 13 ♕c5 dxc5 14 ♗xc7 b5=

Szmetan-Grinberg, Buenos Aires 1978;
c) 7...b6!? N 8 ♗g2 ♗b7 9 0-0 ♘c8 10 ♗f4 d6 11 ♕g4 ♕c7 12 ♖ad1 g6≈ Roos-Speelman, Amsterdam 1978

8 ♗g2 ♗d7 9 ♗g5!? N

a) 9 0-0 ♘c8 10 a4 ♗e7 11 ♕e2 0-0 12 ♗e3 ♕c7 13 f4 ♗f6 14 a5± Szmetan-Langeweg, Buenos Aires 1978;
b) 9 a4 ♘c8 10 a5 ♗e7 11 0-0 0-0 12 ♕e2 ♕c7 13 ♖d1 ♘e5 14 ♗f1 ♗f6 15 ♗e3 += Skrobek-Jansa, Warsaw 1979

9...♕c7 10 0-0 h6!? 11 ♗e3 ♘c8 12 f4 ♗e7 13 f5?!

13 a4 +=

13...♗g5! 14 ♗f2 ♘8e7 =+ Taulbut-Kochiev, Hastings 1978/79

Caro-Kann

1 e4 c6 2 d4

2 ♘c3 d5
a) 3 ♕f3!? dxe4 4 ♘xe4 ♘f6 5 ♘xf6+ exf6 6 ♗c4 ♘d7 7 ♘e2 ♘e5 8 ♕e4 ♕e7 9 ♗b3 a5 10 a3 a4= Feller-Bellon, Amsterdam 1978;
b) 3 ♕f3!? ♘f6 4 e5 ♘fd7 5 d4 e6 6 ♘h3 f6 7 ♗d3 ♕e7 8 exf6 ♕xf6 9 ♕g4 ♘a6 10 ♗g5 ♕f7 11 0-0-0± Baran-Ramik CSSR 1978;

31

c) 3 ♘f3 ♗g4 4 h3 ♗h5 (4...♗xf3 5 ♕xf3 ♘f6 6 d3 e6 7 ♗d2 ♗e7 8 0-0-0 ♘a6 9 g4 d4 10 ♘e2 += Matous-Michalek, CSSR 1978; 7...♗b4 8 e5 ♘fd7 9 ♕g4 ♗f8 10 ♕g3 c5 11 f4 += Matous-Mlynek, CSSR 1978) 5 exd5 cxd5 6 ♗b5+ ♘c6 7 g4 ♗g6 8 d4 e6 9 ♕e2 ♗b4 10 ♘e5 ♘e7 11 h4± Sikora-Meduna, CSSR Final 1978

2...d5 3 exd5

a) 3 e5 ♗f5 4 ♘c3 (4 g4!? ♗e4 5 f3 ♗g6 6 h4 h5 7 e6 ♕c7 8 ♗d3 ♕g3+ 9 ♔f1 hxg4 10 ♗xg6 fxg6 11 ♕d3± Baghli-Yilmaz, Albufieri 1978) 4...e6 5 g4 ♗g6 6 ♘ge2 c5 7 h4 cxd4 8 ♘xd4 h5 9 ♗b5+ ♘d7 10 ♗g5 ♗e7 11 f4 hxg4 12 ♕xg4 a6 13 ♗xd7+ ♕xd7 14 h5 += Kupreichik-Bagirov, Kirovakan 1978;

b) 3 ♘c3 dxe4 4 ♘xe4

1) 4...♗f5 5 ♘c5!? ♕c8 N 6 ♘f3 e6 7 ♘e5 b6 8 ♘cd3 ♘f6 9 g4 ♗e4 10 f3 ♗xd3 11 ♗xd3 ♘bd7 12 ♕e2 ♘xe5 13 dxe5 += Peters-Lein, Hastings 1978/79;

2) 4...♗f5 5 ♘c5!? ♕c8 6 ♘f3 ♘f6 7 ♗d3 ♗g4 8 h3 ♗h5 9 ♗f4 ♘bd7 10 ♘b3 e6 11 c3 ♗e7 12 ♕e2 ♘d5 13 ♗h2 += Ermenkov-Bagirov, Titovo Uzice 1978;

3) 4...♗f5 5 ♘c5!? b6 6 ♘b3 e6 7 ♘f3 ♗d6 8 g3! ♘e7 9 ♗g2 ♘d7 N (9...h6 10 0-0 0-0 11 ♕e2 += Bronstein-Petrosian, USSR 1966) 10 0-0 h6 11 ♖e1 ♕c7 12 ♘bd2 g5!? 13 c4 += Barczay-Vukic, Novi Sad 1978;

4) 4...♗f5 5 ♘g3 ♗g6 6 h4 h6 7 ♘f3 ♘d7 8 h5 ♗h7 9 ♗d3 ♗xd3 10 ♕xd3 e6 11 ♗d2 ♕c7 12 0-0-0 ♘gf6 13 ♘e4 (13 ♕e2 c5 14 ♖h4 ♖c8 N 15 ♘f5 cxd4 16 ♘3xd4 ♕c4 17 ♕xc4 ♖xc4= Gaprindashvili-Chiburdanidze, (14) 1978, 15 ♗f4∞) 13...0-0-0 14 g3 c5!? N (14...♘xe4 15 ♕xe4 ♗e7 16 ♔b1 ♖he8 17 ♕e2! N [17 c4 c5 18 ♗f4 ♗d6 19 ♗xd6 ♕xd6= Geller-Vukic, Novi Sad 1978] 17...♗d6 18 ♖he1 ♘f6 19 ♘e5 += Geller-Kasparov, USSR Final 1978) 15 ♗f4 c4 16 ♕e2 ♕c6 17 ♘xf6 gxf6 18 d5! exd5 19 ♘d4 ♕a6 20 ♔b1 += Tseshkovsky-Kasparov, USSR Final 1978;

5) 4...♘f6 5 ♘xf6+ exf6 6 ♘f3 (6 ♗c4 ♘d7 7 ♘e2 ♗d6 8 ♗f4 ♘b6 9 ♗b3 ♗e6 10 ♗xe6 fxe6 11 0-0 0-0= Martinovic-Sahovic, Novi Sad 1978) 6...♗d6 7 ♗e2 ♘a6!? 8 0-0 ♘c7 9 c4 0-0 10 ♗e3 ♖e8 11 ♕d2 ♗f5 12 ♖ad1 ♗e4 =+ Torre-Korchnoi, Buenos Aires 1978;

6) 4...♘f6 5 ♘xf6+ gxf6 6 c3 ♗f5 7 ♘e2 ♘d7 (7...e6 8 ♘g3 ♗g6 9 h4 h5 10 ♗d3 ♗xd3 11 ♕xd3 ♘d7 12 ♗f4 ♕a5 13 0-0 0-0-0 14 b4 ♕d5!∓ Casas-Campora, Buenos Aires 1978) 8 ♘g3 ♗g6 9 h4 h5 10 ♗e2 ♕a5 11 b4 ♕c7 12 0-0 0-0-0 13 ♕b3 e6= Bhend-Bellon, Buenos Aires 1978;

7) 4...♘f6 5 ♘xf6+ gxf6 6 ♘f3 ♗g4 7 ♗e2 e6 8 c4 ♗b4+ 9 ♔f1 ♗d6 10 h3 ♗h5 11 ♕b3 b6 12 ♗h6 ♘d7 13 ♖d1 ♕c7≈ Zoric-Duckstein, Virovitica 1978;

8) 4...♘f6 5 ♘xf6+ gxf6 6 ♘f3 ♖g8 7 g3 ♕d5 8 ♗g2 ♗g4 9 ♗e3 ♘d7 10 ♕e2 e5 11 h3 ♗e6 12 0-0 e4 13 ♘d2 f5= Tringov-Belton, Buenos Aires 1978;

9) 4...♘f6 5 ♘xf6+ gxf6 6 ♗c4 ♗f5 7 ♘f3 e6 8 c3 ♗d6 9 ♕e2 ♕e7 10 ♘h4 ♗g6 11 f4 f5 12 g3 ♘d7 13 ♗d2 ♘f6 =+ Keogh-Bellon, Amsterdam 1978;

10) 4...♘f6 5 ♘xf6+ gxf6 6 ♗e2 ♖g8 7 ♗f3 e5 8 ♘e2 ♗g4 9 ♗xg4 ♖xg4 10 0-0 ♕d5 11 f3 ♖g6 =+ Timman-

32

Bellon, Amsterdam 1978
3...cxd5 4 ♗d3 ♘c6 5 c3 ♘f6
5...♕c7!? 6 ♘a3 a6 7 ♘c2 ♘f6 8 ♘e3
e5 9 dxe5 ♘xe5 10 ♗c2 ♗e6 =+
Szell-Orso, Hungary Final 1978

6 ♗f4
6 ♗g5 ♗g4 7 f3 ♗h5 8 ♘e2 ♗g6 9 ♘a3
e6 10 ♘c2 ♗d6 11 ♘e3 ♕c7 12 ♗xf6
gxf6 13 g3 b5= Marjanovic-Bagirov,
Kirovakan 1978
6...♗g4
a) 6...g6 7 ♘f3 ♗g7 8 0-0 ♘h5 9 ♗c1
♗g4 10 ♘bd2 ♘f4 11 ♗c2 ♕d6 12
♖e1 ♕f6 =+ Eolian-Bronstein,
Kirovakan 1978;
b) 6...e6 7 ♘f3 ♗e7 8 0-0 0-0 9 ♘bd2
♘h5 10 ♗e3 f5!? 11 ♘b3 ♘f6 12
♖c1 ♘e4= Wagman-Paoli, Eksjo 1978
7 ♕b3 ♕c8
7...♘a5!? 8 ♕a4+ ♗d7 9 ♕c2 g6 10
♘f3 ♗g7 Spraggett-Coudari, Canada
Final 1978, 11 ♘e5! +=
8 ♘d2 e6
8...♗h5 9 ♘gf3 ♗g6 10 ♗xg6 hxg6
11 0-0 e6 12 ♖ae1 ♗e7 13 ♘e5 ♘xe5
14 dxe5 ♘d7 15 ♖e3 += Gazik-dos
Santos, Groningen 1978/79
9 ♘gf3 ♗e7
9...♗h5 10 0-0 ♗e7 11 ♘e5 0-0 12
♗g5 ♕c7 13 f4 ♖fc8 14 ♖ac1 h6=
Lein-Bordonada, Tehran 1978

10 0-0 0-0 11 ♖fe1
11 ♖ae1 ♗h5 12 ♘e5 ♘d7 13 ♘df3
♘cxe5 14 ♘xe5 ♘xe5 15 ♗xe5 ♗g6 16
♕d1 ♖d8 17 ♖e3 ♗d6 18 f4 (18 ♗xg6
hxg6 19 f4 ♗f8 20 ♖h3 ♖d7 21
♕g4 ♕d8≈ Dowden-Taruffi, Graz
1978) 18...♗f8 19 ♗xg6 hxg6 20
♕g4 ♖d7 21 ♖h3 ♗e7? 22 f5 exf5 23
♖xf5 ♖d8 24 f5 exf5 23 ♖xf5 ♖d8
24 ♖fh5 1-0 West-Taruffi, Graz 1978
**11...♗h5 12 ♘e5 ♘xe5 13 ♗xe5 a6
14 c4 ♕d7 15 c5 ♘g4 16 ♘f3 f6 17
♗g3** += Georgadze-Meduna, Halle
1978

Centre Counter

1 e4 d5 2 exd5 ♘f6 2.. ♕xd5 3 ♘c3
♕a5 (3...♕d6 4 d4 c6 N [4...♘f6 5
♗g5 c6 6 ♗c4 ♗g4 7 f3 ♗f5 8 ♘ge2
e6 9 ♕d2 ♗e7 Turichev-Gubnitsky,
USSR 1978 10 0-0-0±] 5 ♘f3 ♘f6
6 h3 ♗f5 7 ♗d3 ♗g6 8 ♗e3 e6= Wiese-
B.Pytel, Piotrkow Trybundalsk 1978)
4 d4 (4 ♗c4 ♘c6! 5 d4? ♘f6 6 ♘f3 ♗g4
7 ♗e3 e5! =+ Bellon-Biriescu,
Bucharest 1978; 4 b4!? ♕xb4 5 ♖b1
♕d6 6 ♘f3 a6 N 7 ♗e2 ♘f6 8 0-0 b5
9 d4 ♘bd7 10 ♗g5 ♗b7∓ Ekstrom-
Persson, Stockholm 1978/79) 4...♘f6
5 ♘f3 ♗g4 6 h3 ♗h5 7 g4 (7 ♗b5+!?
N c6 8 ♗e2 ♗xf3 9 ♗xf3 e6 10 0-0
♗e7 11 ♘e2 0-0 12 c4 += Szmetan-

Scalise, Buenos Aires 1978) 7...♗g6 8 ♘e5 e6 (8...c6 Wedberg-Thornblom, Stockholm 1978/79, 9 h4 ♘bd7 10 ♘c4 ♕c7 11 h5 ♗e4 12 ♘xe4 ♘xe4 13 ♕f3±; 8...♘bd7? Stoica-Bellon, Bucharest 1978, 9 ♘c4 ♕a6 10 ♗d3 ♕e6+ 11 ♘e3 0-0-0 12 d5 ♕b6 13 ♘c4 ♕b4 14 a3 ♕c5 15 ♗e3 1-0 Alekhine-Schroder, New York 1924) 9 ♘c4 ♕a6 10 ♘e5 N (10 h4 ♕c6 11 ♖h3 ♗b4 12 h5 ♗e4 13 ♗d2 ♗xc3 14 ♖xc3 += Zuckerman-Shamkovich, Cleveland 1975) 10...♕b6 11 ♗g2 ♘bd7 12 ♘xg6 hxg6 13 ♕d3 c6 14 ♗d2 ♘d5 15 ♗xd5 cxd5 16 0-0-0 += Bellin-Bohm, Erbeek 1978

3 d4

a) 3 ♗b5+ ♘bd7!? N 4 c4 a6 5 ♗a4 b5 6 cxb5 ♘xd5 7 ♘c3 ♗b7 8 ♘xd5 ♗xd5 9 ♘f3 axb5 10 ♗xb5 c6 11 ♗e2 ♘c5 Δ ♘b3≈ Anguiano-Wieter, Mexico 1978;

b) 3 ♗b5+ ♗d7 4 ♗c4 ♗g4 (4...b5!? 5 ♗b3 N [5 ♗e2 ♘xd5 6 d4 e6 7 ♘f3 c5 8 0-0 ♕b6 9 c4 bxc4 10 ♗xc4 ♗e7 11 ♖e1 ♘c7 12 d5± Voronov-Mikenas, Leningrad 1971] 5...♗g4 6 f3 ♗c8 7 ♗e2 ♗b7 8 ♘bc3 a6 9 d4 ♘bd7 10 ♗g5 h6 11 ♗h4 += Sellos-Bellon, Buenos Aires 1978) 5 f3 ♗c8 6 ♘c3 ♘bd7 7 d4 ♕b6 8 ♗b3 (8 ♗b5+ N ♗d7 9 ♗d3 ♘bxd5 10 ♘xd5 ♘xd5 11 a3 b5 12 ♘e2 e6 13 0-0 ♗d6= Mateu-Valkesalmi, Groningen 1978/79) 8...♘fxd5 9 ♘xd5 ♘xd5 10 c4 ♘f6 11 ♗e3 g6 N (11...c6 12 ♕d2 g6 13 ♘e2 ♗g7 14 0-0 0-0 15 ♖ad1± Alexandria-Gaprindashvili (4) 1975) 12 ♕d2 ♗g7 13 ♘e2 0-0 14 0-0 ♖e8 15 ♖ad1± Alexandria-Burndred, Buenos Aires 1978

3...♘xd5 4 ♘f3

4 c4 ♘b6 5 ♘f3 ♗g4 6 h3 N (6 ♗e2 e6 7 0-0 ♘c6 8 ♘c3! N [8 b3 += Dely-

Karaklaic, Belgrade 1965] 8...♗xf3 9 ♗xf3 ♘xd4 10 ♗xb7 ♖b8 11 ♗a6 ♗e7 12 ♗e3 ♘f5 13 ♗b5+ ♔f8 14 ♕f3 ♘xe3 15 fxe3± Biyiasas-Green-Krolki, Canada Final 1978) 6...♗xf3 7 ♕xf3 ♕xd4 8 ♕xb7 e6 9 ♘c3 ♗c5 10 ♕f3 ♘8d7 11 ♗e3 ♕e5 =+ Gruenfeld-Peters, London 1978

4...♗g4

4...g6 5 ♗e2 ♗g7 6 0-0 0-0 7 h3 ♘c6 8 c4 ♘b6 9 ♗e3 e5 10 d5 += Lind-Harman, London 1978

5 ♗e2 ♘c6 6 0-0 e6 7 h3 ♗h5 8 c4 ♘b6 9 ♗e3

9 ♘c3!

9...♗xf3 10 ♗xf3 ♘xc4 11 ♕b3 N

11 ♗xc6+ bxc6 12 ♕a4 ♘b6 13 ♕xc6+ ♕d7= Garcia-Christiansen, Mexico 1978

11...♘b6 12 d5 exd5 13 ♗xb6 axb6 14 ♗xd5 ♕f6 15 ♘c3∞ Rodriguez-Christiansen, Mexico 1978

Spanish

1 e4 e5 2 ♘f3 ♘c6 3 ♗b5 a6 4 ♗a4 ♘f6 5 d4 exd4

5...♘xd4 6 ♘xd4 exd4 7 e5 ♘e4 8 ♕xd4 ♘c5 9 ♘c3 b5 N (9...♗e7 10 ♕g4 0-0 11 ♗h6 ♘e6 12 ♗b3 ♔h8 13 ♗xe6 gxh6 14 ♗b3 +− Szabo-Pachman, 1948) 10 ♗b3 ♘xb3 11

axb3 ♗b7 12 0-0 c5 13 ʼ♕e3 ♕h4!=
Szmetan-Seidler, Buenos Aires 1978

6 0-0 ♗e7

6...b5 7 ♗b3 ♗e7 8 e5 ♘e4 9 ♗d5
♘c5 10 ♘xd4 ♗b7 11 ♘f5 ♗f8 N 12
♗e3 ♘e6 13 ♘c3± Michalek-Walowy,
CSSR 1978

7 ♖e1

7 e5 ♘e4

a) 8 b4!? 0-0 9 a3 b5 10 ♗b3 d5 11
h3?! N ♗b7 12 ♗b2 a5!∓ Leiw-
Vasyukov, Tiruchirapalli 1978;

b) 8 ♘xd4 ♘c5 9 ♘f5 ♘e6 N 10 ♘xe7
♕xe7 11 ♗xc6 dxc6 12 f4 ♗d7 13
♗e3 0-0-0 14 ♕e2 += Aaron-Liew,
Penang 1978;

c) 8 ♘xd4 0-0 9 ♘f5 d5 10 ♗xc6
bxc6 11 ♘xe7+ ♕xe7 12 ♖e1 ♖e8!
(12...f6 13 f3 ♘g5 14 ♘c3 ♘e6 15
♕e2 += Marjanovic-Kluger, Sombor
1978) 13 f3 ♘d6! 14 b3 f6 15 ♗b2
♘f7 =+ Marjanovic-Honfi, Subotica
1978;

d) 8 ♘xd4 ♘xd4 9 ♕xd4 ♘c5 10
♘c3 0-0 11 ♗g5 ♗xg5 12 ♕xc5 ♗e7
13 ♕e3 d5 14 ♖ad1 c6 15 ♗b3 ♕a5!=
Marjanovic-Petrosian, Kirovakan 1978

7...0-0

7...d6?! N 8 ♘xd4 ♗d7 9 ♗xc6 bxc6
10 e5 dxe5 11 ♘f3 e4 12 ♘e5 0-0
13 ♘xd7 ♘xd7 14 ♖xe4± Povah-
Pettursson, London 1978

8 e5 ♘e8 9 ♗f4

9 c3 dxc3 10 ♘xc3 d6 11 exd6 ♘xd6
12 ♘d5 ♗f6 13 ♗f4 ♗g4 14 ♘xc7!
♕xc7 15 ♗xd6± Mascarinas-Liew,
Tiruchirapalli 1978

9...b5 10 ♗b3 d5 11 c3

a) 11 ♘xd4 ♘xd4 12 ♕xd4 c6 13 ♕d3
♘c7 14 c3 ♘e6 15 ♗c2 g6= Supanic-
Barle, Maribor 1978;

b) 11 a4?! N b4 12 a5 ♗g4 13 ♕d3
♗h5 14 ♗a4 ♗g6= de Boer-Zimmerman,
Groningen 1978/79

**11...♗f5 12 ♘xd4 ♘xd4 13 cxd4
c6 14 ♘c3 +=** Ligterink-Saren, Buenos
Aires 1978

**1 e4 e5 2 ♘f3 ♘c6 3 ♗b5 a6 4 ♗a4
♘f6 5 0-0 ♗e7 6 ♖e1 b5 7 ♗b3 d6 8
c3 0-0 9 d4 ♗g4 10 d5**

a) 10 a3!? N exd4 11 cxd4 d5 12 e5
♘e4 13 ♗a2 ♕d7 14 ♘c3 ♘xc3 15
bxc3 ♘a5= Rantanen-Littlewood,
London 1978;

b) 10 ♗e3 exd4 11 cxd4 ♘a5 (11...
d5?!) 12 ♗c2 ♘c4 13 ♗c1 c5 14 b3
♘b6 15 ♘bd2 ♖c8 16 ♗b2 cxd4 17 h3
♗h5 18 ♗xd4 ♘bd7!?∞ Ligterink-
Klovan, Jurmala 1978

10...♘a5

10...♘b8!? 11 ♘bd2 ♖e8 12 ♘f1
♘bd7 13 h3 ♗h5 14 ♗c2 ♗g6 15 a4
♘c5 16 ♘g3 += L.Bronstein-Casanave,
Buenos Aires 1978

11 &c2 c6 12 h3 &xf3

a) 12...&c8 13 dxc6 ♕c7 14 ♘bd2
♕xc6 15 ♘f1

1) 15...&e6 16 ♘g3 ♖fe8 N (16...g6
17 &h6 ♖fc8 18 ♘g5 &f8 19 &xf8
♖xf8= Ligterink-Timman, Amsterdam
1978) 17 ♕e2 &f8 18 ♘g5 &d7 19 ♘h5
&e7= Tseshkovsky-Savon, Ashkabad
1978;

2) 15...&b7 N 16 ♘g3 g6 17 &h6
♖fe8 18 ♕c1 ♔h8 19 ♘g5± Van der
Sterren-Taylor, Erbeek 1978;

3) 15...♘c4 16 ♘g3 ♖e8 17 a4 &f8
Nunn-Littlewood, London 1978, 18
♘h4! +=;

b) 12...&h5 13 dxc6 ♕c7 (13...♘xc6
N 14 &g5 ♘e8 15 &xe7 ♕xe7 16
♘bd2 ♖c8 17 ♘f1 &xf3 18 ♕xf3 +=
Vogt-Holmov, Halle 1978; 14...♕b6
15 ♘bd2 ♖ad8 16 &b3 ♘d7 17 &e3
♕c7 18 ♘f1 ♘a5 19 ♘g3 &g6 20 a4
+= Beljavsky-Kuzmin, USSR Final
1978) 14 ♘bd2 ♘xc6 (14...♖ad8?!
N 15 ♕e2 ♘xc6 Taulbut-Biyiasas,
Hastings 1978/79 16 a4 +=) 15 ♘f1
♖ad8 16 ♘e3 d5 17 ♘xd5 ♘xd5 18
exd5 f5 19 ♕e2 e4 20 dxc6 &c5 21
&g5 &xf3 22 ♕f1 N (22 &b3+ ♔h8
23 &xd8 ♖xd8∓ Wagner-Perecz,
Dortmund 1978) 22...♖de8 23 a4≈
Kuzmin-Lukacs, Budapest 1978

13 ♕xf3 cxd5 14 exd5 ♘c4 14...♖c8
15 ♘d2 g6 16 b4! N (16 &d3 ♘h5
17 a4 f5 18 axb5?! e4 19 ♘xe4 fxe4
20 ♕xe4 ♘b3! −+ Stein-Geller,
Kislovodsk 1966) 16...♘c4 17 ♘xc4
♖xc4 18 &d2 ♘h5 19 &d3 ♖c7 20 a4
+= Tseshkovsky-Beljavsky, Ashkabad
1978

Diagram

15 ♘d2 ♘b6 16 ♘f1 ♘e8

a) 16...♕c7 N 17 ♘g3 g6 18 &h6 ♖fc8

19 ♖ad1 ♘fd7 20 ♘f5 &f8 21 ♖e4
♕d8= Timman-Hubner, Wijk aan Zee
1979;

b) 16...♘bxd5 17 ♘g3 ♘c7 18 a4
b4!? N 19 ♘f5 ♘e6 20 ♕b7 (20 &b3
Δ ♕g3) 20...♖e8∞ Kurajica-Smejkal,
Titovo Uzice 1978 **17 a4 bxa4 18
&xa4 ♘xa4 19 ♖xa4 f5 20 c4 ♕c8
21 ♕a3** N

21 &d2 ♘f6 22 ♘g3 g6 23 ♖ea1 ♘d7
24 ♕e2 ♘b6 25 ♖b4 += Gufeld-
Tseitlin, USSR 1976

**21...&f6!? 22 ♕a2 ♔h8 23 b4 ♘c7
24 &b2 +=** Sharif-Harandi, Tehran
1978

1 e4 e5 2 ♘f3 ♘c6 3 &b5 f5 4 ♘c3

4 d3 fxe4 5 dxe4 ♘f6 6 0-0 &c5!?
(6...d6 7 ♕d3 &e7 8 ♖e1 &g4 9 h3
&xf3 10 ♕xf3 0-0 11 c3 ♕e8 12
♘d2 ♔h8= Matanovic-Preissmann,
Buenos Aires 1978) 7 ♘c3 d6 8 &g5
0-0 9 ♘d5 ♔h8 10 ♘h4 ♘d4 11 &d3
c6 12 &xf6 gxf6 13 ♘e3 ♘e6=
Grinberg-Parma, Buenos Aires 1978

4...♘d4

4...fxe4 5 ♘xe4 ♘f6!? 6 ♘xf6+ ♕xf6
7 0-0 &e7 8 &xc6 dxc6 9 ♕e2 &g4 10
♕xe5 0-0-0! 11 ♕xf6 &xf6 12 ♖e1
♖he8= Darga-Parma, Buenos Aires
1978 **5 &a4**

5 &c4 d6 6 0-0 c6 7 exf5 ♘f6!? 8
♘xd4 exd4 9 ♖e1+ &e7 10 ♘e4 &xf5

36

11 ♘xf6+ gxf6 12 d3± Plaskett-Gozik, Groningen 1978/79
5...♗f6
5...c6 6 exf5 d6 7 ♘xd4 exd4 8 ♕h5+ ♔d7 9 ♘e2 ♕f6 10 d3 ♔c7 11 ♘g3± Lukov-Atanasov, Bulgaria Final 1978
6 0-0
6 exf5 ♗c5 7 ♘xe5 (7 ♘xd4 exd4 8 ♘e2 0-0 9 0-0 d5 10 b4 ♗b6 11 ♗b2 += Keres) 7...0-0 8 0-0 d5 9 ♘f3 ♗xf5 10 ♘xd4 ♗xd4 11 ♘e2 ♗g4! 12 ♕e1 N c6! 13 c3 ♖e8 14 ♗d1 ♖e6∞ Grinberg-Szmetan, Buenos Aires 1978

6...♗c5 7 ♘xd4 7 exf5 0-0 8 ♘xe5 d5 9 ♘e2 ♕d6 10 ♘xd4 ♗xd4 11 ♘f3 ♘g4 12 c3 ♖xf5! 13 cxd4 ♖xf3= Liberzon-Preissman, Buenos Aires 1978 **7...♗xd4 8 exf5 0-0 9 ♘e2 d5 10 c3 ♗b6 11 ♗c2 ♘e4 12 d3 ♘d6 13 d4±** Tseshkovsky-Rodriguez, Malgrat de Mar 1978

1 e4 e5 2 ♘f3 ♘c6 3 ♗b5 a6 4 ♗a4 ♘f6 5 0-0 ♗e7 6 ♖e1 b5 7 ♗b3 d6 8 c3 0-0 9 h3 ♘b8 10 d4 ♘bd7 11 ♘bd2 11 c4 ♗b7 12 ♘c3 c6 13 a3 N (13 ♗g5 b4! 14 ♘a4 Peters-Lombardy, Lone Pine 1977, 14... c5! 15 d5 a5=) 13...h6 14 ♗e3 exd4 15 ♘xd4 ♘c5 16 ♘f5 ♗xb3 17 ♕xb3 ♗c8= Peters-Kraidman, London 1978

11...♗b7 12 ♗c2 ♖e8
12...c5 13 d5 (13 ♘f1 ♖e8 14 ♘g3 ♗f8 15 d5 g6 16 b3 ♗b6 17 ♗e3 ♗c8 18 a4 += Tal-Gligoric, Leningrad 1973) 13...♖e8 14 ♘f1 ♕c7 15 ♘g3 ♘f8 16 ♘f5 ♘g6 17 ♗g5 += Blackstock-Zaffarese, Malta 1979
13 b3
13 a4 ♗f8 14 b3 g6 15 ♗b2 ♗g7 16 ♗d3 c6 17 ♕c2 ♘h5 18 ♗f1 ♕b6= Matanovic-Ivkov, Belgrade 1978
13...c6 14 a4 ♗f8 15 ♗b2 g6 16 ♘f1 ♘h5 17 ♘e3 ♕c7= Morrison-Timman, Amsterdam 1978

Ponziani

1 e4 e5 2 ♘f3 ♘c6 3 c3 ♘f6 3...f5 4 d4 fxe4 (4...d6 N 5 d5!? ♘ce7 6 c4 ♘f6 7 ♘c3 g6 8 ♗d3 ♗g7 9 ♕c2 0-0= Seidler-Wibe, Buenos Aires 1978) 5 ♘xe5 ♘f6 (5...♕f6 6 ♘g4! ♕g6 7 ♗f4 d6 8 ♘e3 ♘f6 9 ♘a3 += Ljubojevic-Pachman, Manila 1976) 6 ♗b5 N (6 ♗g5 ♗e7 7 ♘d2 0-0 8 ♗e2 += Schneider-Westerinen, Jurmala 1978) 6...♕e7 7 ♗f4 ♘d5? 8 ♕h5+ g6 9 ♘xg6 ♕f7 10 ♗xc6 +– Drvota-Kolar, CSSR 1978
4 d4 exd4
a) 4...♘xe4 5 d5 ♗c5 (5...♘b8 6 ♘xe5 ♕e7 7 ♕d4 N d6 8 ♕xe4 += Miles-Gligoric, Bad Lauterberg 1977; 5...♘e7

6 ♘xe5 ♘g6 7 ♘xg6 hxg6 8 ♕f3 N
[8 ♕e2 ♕e7 9 ♗e3 ♖h5= Liebert-
Minev, Berlin 1962] 8...♕e7 9 ♗e3
♘f6 10 ♗c4 ♕e4= Seidler-Casas,
Buenos Aires 1978) 6 dxc6 ♗xf2+
7 ♔e2 bxc6 8 ♕a4 f5 9 ♘bd2 0-0
10 ♘xe4 fxe4 11 ♔xf2?! (11 ♕xe4±
Maroczy!) 11...exf3 N (11...d5! 12
♔e1 exf3 13 gxf3 c5!∓ Minev-Sax,
Baja 1971) 12 g3! ♕f6 13 ♗e3 d5∞
Krejci-Michalek, CSSR 1978;
b) 4...d6 5 ♗b5 ♗d7 6 ♘bd2 ♗e7 7
dxe5 ♘xe5 8 ♘xe5 dxe5 9 ♕b3 0-0
10 ♗xd7 ♘xd7 11 ♕c2 ♘c5 12 ♘f3!
+= Miles-Smyslov, Hastings 1976/77;
c) 4...d6 5 h3!? N ♗e7 6 d5 ♘b8 7
♗d3 0-0? 8 ♗e3 ♘e8 9 g4! c6 10 c4
g6 11 ♗h6± Macropoulos-Ivkov, Praia
da Rocha 1978
5 e5 ♘e4
5...♘d5?! 6 cxd4 d6 7 ♗c4 dxe5 8
0-0 ♘b6 9 ♗b5 ♗d7 10 ♗xc6 ♗xc6 11
♘xe5± Shirazi-Rodriguez, Bagiuo City
1978

6 ♕e2
6 cxd4 ♗b4+ 7 ♘bd2 d5 8 ♗e2 0-0 9
0-0 ♗xd2 10 ♗xd2 ♗g4= Parreren-
Cazou, Buenos Aires 1978
6...f5 7 exf6 d5 8 ♘bd2 N
8 ♘xd4 ♘xd4 9 cxd4 ♔f7 10 fxg7
♗b4+ = Levy-Boey, Siegen 1970
8...d3 9 ♕e3 ♗f5 10 ♗xd3 ♗c5 11

fxg7 ♖g8 12 ♘d4 ♖xg7 13 ♗xe4 dxe4
14 ♘xc6 ♗xe3 15 ♘xd8 ♗xd2+ 16
♗xd2 ♖xd8 17 g3 += Supancic-Flear,
London 1978

Petroff

1 e4 e5 2 ♘f3 ♘f6 3 ♘xe5
3 d4 exd4 4 e5 ♘e4 5 ♕xd4 d5 6 exd6
♘xd6 7 ♘c3 ♘c6 8 ♕f5 ♗f5 9 ♗b5
♕e7+ 10 ♗e3 ♘xb5 11 ♘xb5 ♕b4+
12 ♕xb4 ♗xb4+ 13 c3 ♗d6 14 ♘xd6+
cxd6 15 0-0-0 ♗e6 16 ♖xd6 ♗xa2
17 ♖e1!? (17 ♗c5 0-0 18 ♖xc6 bxc6
19 ♗xf8 ♔xf8 20 ♘d2 ♗d5 21 f3±
Matulovic-Holmov, Sochi 1968) 17...
0-0= Vechet-Tichy, CSSR 1978
3...d6
3...♘xe4?! 4 ♕e2 ♕e7 5 ♕xe4 d6 6
d4 ♘c6 N (6...♘d7 7 ♘c3 dxe5 8
♘d5 ♘f6 9 ♘xf6+ gxf6 10 ♗b5+ ♗d7
11 ♗xd7+ ♔xd7 12 0-0 +– Sozin)
7 ♗b5 ♗d7 8 0-0 dxe5 9 d5 f5 10
♕e2 ♘b8 11 ♖e1 ♗xb5 12 ♕xb5+
c6 13 ♕b3 cxd5 14 ♗g5 +– Speelman-
Keogh, Amsterdam 1978
4 ♘f3
4 ♘c4 ♘xe4 5 ♕e2 N ♕e7 6 d3 ♘f6 7
♗g5 ♕xe2+ 8 ♗xe2 ♘bd7 9 0-0 h6 10
♗h4 d5 11 ♘e3 g6 12 ♗f3 Ljubojevic-
Toth, Albufieri 1978, 12...c6≈
4...♘xe4 5 d4
5 ♕e2 ♕e7 6 d4 ♘f6 7 ♗g5 ♘bd7 8
♘c3 ♕xe2+ 9 ♗xe2 h6 10 ♗d2 g6 11
♘b5 ♔d8 12 0-0 a6 13 ♘c3 ♗g7=
Bouaziz-Toth, Albufieri 1978

Diagram

5...d5 6 ♗d3 ♗e7 7 0-0 ♗g4 8 h3
8 c4!
8...♗f5 9 c4 dxc4 10 ♗xc4 0-0 11 ♘c3
♘d7 12 ♖e1 ♘d6
12...♘xc3 13 bxc3 ♘b6 14 ♗b3 c5=

38

13 ♗b3 c6 14 ♗f4 += Emma-Campara, Buenos Aires 1978

Latvian Gambit

1 e4 e5 2 ♘f3 f5 3 ♘xe5
3 exf5 e4 4 ♘e5 ♘f6 5 d4 N (5 ♗e2 d6 6 ♗h5+ ♔e7 7 ♘f7 ♕e8 8 ♘c3 ♘xh5 9 ♘d5+ ♔xf7 10 ♕xh5+ g6 11 fxg6+ += Keres) 5...d6 6 ♘c4 ♗xf5 7 ♘e3 ♗g6 8 h4 d5 9 c4 ♘c6 10 ♘c3 dxc4 11 d5 ♘e5 12 ♘xc4 ♘xc4 13 ♗xc4 a6 =+ Crouch-Kindermann, London 1978

3...♕f6 4 d4 d6 5 ♘c4 fxe4 6 ♗e2 ♕f7 N
6...♘c6 7 d5 ♘e5 8 0-0 ♘xc4 9 ♗xc4 ♕g6 10 ♗b5+ += Bronstein-Mikenas, USSR 1941

7 ♘c3 ♘f6 8 ♗g5 ♘bd7 9 ♘b5 ♔d8 10 ♕d2 ♗e7 11 0-0-0 b6 12 ♘e5! +– P.Littlewood-Kindermann, London 1978

King's Gambit

1 e4 e5 2 f4 exf4
a) 2...♕h4+ 3 g3 ♕e7 4 fxe5 ♕xe5? (4...d6!) 5 ♘c3 ♗b4 6 ♘f3 ♕e7 7

♕e2 ♗xc3 8 bxc3 ♘c6 9 ♗g2 d6 10 0-0± Basman-Haik, London 1978;
b) 2...♗c5 3 ♘f3 d6 4 ♘c3 ♘f6 5 ♗c4 ♘c6 6 d3 a6 7 fxe5 ♘xe5 N (7... dxe5 8 ♗g5 ♕d6 9 ♗xf6 ♕xf6 10 ♘d5 ♕d6= Spielmann-Yates, Moscow 1925) 8 ♘xe5 dxe5 9 ♗g5 ♗e6? 10 ♖f1± Basman-Large, London 1978

3 ♘f3
3 ♗c4 ♘f6 4 ♘c3 c6 5 ♗b3 d5 6 exd5 cxd5 7 d4 ♗d6 8 ♘f3 N (8 ♘ge2 0-0 9 0-0 g5 10 ♘xd5 ♘c6 =+ Spielmann-Bogolyubov, Mahrisch-Ostrau 1923) 8...0-0 9 0-0 ♘c6 10 ♘xd5 ♘xd5 11 ♗xd5 ♗g4∝ Pirttimaki-Ekstrom, Stockholm 1978/79

3...d6
a) 3...g5 4 h4 g4 5 ♘e5 h6 6 ♗c4 ♘h6 7 d4 d6 8 ♘d3 f3 9 gxf3 g3 N (9... gxf3 10 ♕xf3 ♗g4 11 ♕f2 ♕d7 12 ♘c3 c6 13 ♗g5± Peev-Atanasov, Bulgaria 1954) 10 ♗g5 ♗e7 11 ♕d2 ♗xg5 12 hxg5 ♘g8 13 ♕f4± Fonseca-Estrada, Mexico 1978;
b) 3...h6 4 d4 g5 5 h4 ♗g7 6 hxg5 hxg5 7 ♖xh8 ♗xh8 8 ♕d3 N g4 9 ♘e5 ♕h4+ 10 ♔d1 d6 11 ♘c4 ♕f2∓ Basman-Rantanen, London 1978;
c) 3...♗e7 4 ♗c4 ♘f6 5 e5 (5 ♕e2 0-0 N 6 0-0 d5 7 ♗xd5 ♘xd5 8 exd5 c6∝ Yeo-Berry, London 1978) 5... ♘g4 6 0-0 d5 7 exd6 ♕xd6 8 d4 0-0 9 ♘c3 ♕h6 N (9...♘e3 10 ♗xe3 fxe3 Bronstein-Koblents, Moscow 1945, 11 ♘b5 ♕d8 12 ♘e5± Boleslavsky) 10 h3 ♘f6 11 ♘e5 g5 12 ♕e1 ♗d6 13 h4!± Cappello-Schlich, II Ciocco 1978

4 ♗c4
4 d3 g5 5 h4 g4 6 ♘g1 ♕f6 7 ♘c3 ♘e7 8 ♗d2 ♖g8 9 ♕c1 f3∝ Zimmermann-Cramling, Groningen 1978/79

4...h6 5 d4 g5 6 0-0
6 g3 fxg3 N (6...♘c6 7 gxf4? g4 8

♘g1 ♕h4+∓ Spassky-Portisch, Budapest 1967) 7 hxg3 ♗g7 8 0-0 ♘f6 9 ♘c3 ♗e6 10 ♗xe6 fxe6 11 ♕e2 0-0∓ Swanson-Beljavsky, Mexico 1978
6...♗g7 7 g3 g4 8 ♘h4 f3 9 c3 ♘e7 10 ♗f4 c6 11 ♘d2 d5 12 ♗d3 ♗e6∓ Osterman-Kaiszauri, Stockholm 1978/79

French

1 e4 e6 2 d4
2 f4!? d5 3 e5 c5 4 ♘f3 ♘c6 5 c3 ♗d7 6 ♗e2 ♘ge7 7 0-0 ♘f5 8 d3 h5 9 ♘a3 ♗e7 10 ♘c2 b5= Kalashin-Ornstein, Kirovakan 1978

2...d5 3 ♘c3
3 e5 c5 4 ♘f3 ♘c6 5 c3 ♕b6 6 ♗d3 cxd4 7 cxd4 ♗d7 8 0-0 a6 9 ♘c3 ♘xd4 10 ♘xd4 ♕xd4 11 ♖e1 ♕b6 12 ♕g4 0-0-0!? (12...f5) Hebert-Jauregui, Canada Final 1978, 13 a3±

3...♗b4
3...dxe4 4 ♘xe4 ♗d7 5 ♘f3 ♘c6 6 ♗d3 ♘d7 7 0-0 ♘gf6 8 ♕e2 (8 ♘xf6+ ♕xf6 9 ♗e2 h6 10 c4 0-0-0 11 ♗e3 b6 12 ♖c1 += Chandler-Tan, Penang 1978) 8...♗e7 9 c4 0-0 10 ♖d1 ♘xe4 11 ♗xe4 ♗xe4 12 ♕xe4 += van der Wiel-Kardyi, Groningen 1978/79

4 e5
a) 4 a3 ♗xc3+ 5 bxc3 dxe4 6 ♕g4 ♘f6 7 ♕xg7 ♖g8 8 ♕h6 c5 9 ♘e2 ♗d7 10 ♗g5 N ♘g4 11 ♗xd8 ♘xh6 12 ♗c7 ♗a4 13 ♘g3 += Nogueira-Augdela, Mexico 1978;
b) 4 ♘e2 dxe4 5 a3 ♗e7 6 ♘xe4
1) 6...♘c6 7 ♗f4 N ♘f6 8 ♕d3 0-0 9 0-0-0 (9 g3 ♘xe4 10 ♕xe4 ♗d7 11 0-0-0 ♗d6 12 ♗g2 ½-½ Ghinda-Uhlmann, Bucharest 1978) 9...b6 10 ♘2c3 ♘d5 11 ♘xd5 exd5 12 ♘c3 += Stoica-Uhlmann, Bucharest 1978;
2) 6...♘c6 7 ♗e3 ♘f6 8 ♘xf6+ ♗xf6

9 ♕d2 L.Bronstein-Bielicki, Buenos Aires 1978, 9...e5!=;
3) 6...♘f6 7 ♘2g3 0-0 8 c3 ♘c6 9 f4 b6 10 ♗d3 ♗b7 11 0-0 ♕d5 12 ♘xf6+ ♗xf6 13 ♗e4 += Filipowicz-Rajna, Poland 1978;
4) 6...♘f6 7 ♘xf6+ ♗xf6 8 ♗e3 c5 9 ♕d2 ♘c6 10 0-0-0 cxd4 11 ♘xd4 ♗xd4 12 ♗xd4 ♕xd4 13 ♕xd4 ♘xd4 14 ♖xd4 ♗d7= Gheorghiu-Vaganian, Buenos Aires 1978;
5) 6...♘f6 7 ♕d3 N 0-0 8 ♗f4 ♘d5 ♗d2 b6 10 c4 ♗a6 11 b4 ♘f6 12 ♘2g3 ♘bd7 13 ♗c3 ♗b7= Biriescu-Uhlmann, Bucharest 1978;
c) 4 ♗d2!? dxe4 5 ♕g4 ♕xd4 6 0-0-0 h5 7 ♕e2!? (Keres) 7...♗d7 (7...♘f6 8 ♗g5 ♕b6 9 ♗xf6 gxf6 10 ♘xe4 ♗e7 11 ♕f3 f5 12 ♕c3 e5∓ Feller-Roos, Amsterdam 1978; 8 ♘h6!?) 8 ♘xe4 ♗xd2+ 9 ♖xd2 ♕a4 10 a3 ♗c6 11 ♘c5 ♕h4? (11...♕f4) 12 ♕e5!± ♘f6? 13 ♘xe6 fxe6 14 ♕xe6+ ♔f8 15 ♗c4 1-0 Sanz-Roos, Amsterdam 1978

4...c5
4...♕d7 5 ♗d2 b6 6 ♘f3 ♗a6 7 ♗xa6 ♘xa6 8 ♕e2 ♕b8 9 ♘d1! N ♗f8 10 ♘e3 ♘e7 11 ♖c1 ♘bc6 12 0-0 h6 13 c4 dxc4 14 ♕xc4± Timman-Panno, Nijmegen 1978

5 a3 5 ♕g4 ♘e7 6 ♘f3 ♘bc6 7 ♗b5 (7 dxc5 d4 8 ♗b5 ♕a5 9 ♗xc6+

bxc6 10 ♕xd4 ♘f5 11 ♕c4 N ♗a6 12
♕b3 ♕b5∞ Banas-Prandstetter, CSSR
Final 1978) 7...cxd4 8 ♘xd4 0-0!
9 ♘xc6 ♗xc3+ 10 bxc3 bxc6 11 ♗d3
Grigorov-Marszalek, Pazardjik 1978,
11...f5=

5...♗xc3+ 6 bxc3 ♘e7

6...♕c7 7 ♕g4 f5 8 ♕g3 cxd4 9 cxd4
♘e7 10 ♗d2 0-0 11 ♗d3 b6 12 ♘e2
♗a6 13 ♗b4 N ♗xd3 14 cxd3 ♘bc6=
Diez del Corral-Portisch, Buenos Aires
1978

7 ♘f3

7 ♕g4 ♕c7 8 ♕xg7 ♖g8 9 ♕xh7 cxd4
10 ♘e2 ♘bc6 11 f4 ♗d7 12 h4 dxc3
13 h5 0-0-0 14 ♕d3 d4 15 h6 ♖g6 16
h7± Carleton-Sowray, London 1978

7...♗d7

a) 7...♕c7 8 a4! b6 9 ♗b5+ ♗d7 10
♗d3 ♘bc6 11 0-0 h6 12 ♖e1 (12 ♕d2
c4 13 ♗e2 0-0-0 14 ♗a3 ♗e8 15 ♗d6
♖xd6!? 16 exd6 ♕xd6∞ Timman-
Garcia, Wijk aan Zee 1979) 0-0 13
♗d2 c4 14 ♗f1 f6 15 g3 ♘g6?! 16
♗h3! += Spassky-Portisch, Buenos
Aires 1978;

b) 7...♕a5 8 ♗d2 ♘bc6 9 ♗e2 ♗d7
10 0-0 ♕c7 11 ♖e1 0-0-0 12 ♗f1 f6
13 g3 += Kurajica-Duckstein,
Virovitica 1978;

c) 7...♘bc6 8 a4 ♕a5 9 ♕d2 (9 ♗d2
♗d7 10 ♘g5 h6 11 ♘h3 ♕c7 12 ♕g4
♘f5 13 ♗d3 cxd4 14 cxd4 ♘xe5 —+
Kukic-Drasko, Sarajevo 1978) 9...♗d7
10 ♗d3 c4 11 ♗e2 f6 12 exf6 gxf6 13
0-0 0-0-0 14 ♗a3 ♘f5 15 ♖fb1 ♕c7=
Yurtseven-Nikolic, Groningen 1978/79

Diagram

8 a4

a) 8 ♗e2!? ♗a4 9 ♖b1 ♕c7 10 ♗b5+
♗xb5 11 ♖xb5 ♘d7 12 ♗e3 ♘f5 13
♗f4 a6= Yurtseven-Karolyi, Groningen

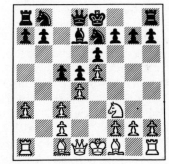

1978/79;

b) 8 dxc5!? ♗a4 9 ♗d3 ♘d7 10 ♗e3
♕c7 11 0-0 ♘xc5 12 ♗xc5 ♕xc5 13
♘g5 h6 14 ♕h5 g6 15 ♕h4 ♗d7=
Planinc-Farago, Novi Sad 1978

8...♘bc6

8...♕a5 9 ♕d2 ♘bc6 10 ♗d3 f6 11
exf6 gxf6 12 dxc5 e5 13 c4 dxc4 14
♗xc4 ♕xc5 15 ♗b3 ♕b4= Arnold-
Boer, Groningen 1978/79

**9 ♗e2 ♕a5 10 ♗d2 c4 11 0-0 f6 12
♖e1 fxe5** Szalanczay-Sinkovits,
Hungary 1978, 13 dxe5 h6 14 ♗f1
0-0 15 g3=

Alekhine

1 e4 ♘f6 2 e5 2 ♘c3 d5 3 exd5 (3 e5
♘e4 4 ♕f3 ♘xc3 5 dxc3 g6 6 ♗f4
♗g7 7 0-0-0 c6 8 h4 h5= Dolmadjan-
Donchev, Bulgaria Final 1978) 3...
♘xd5 4 ♕f3 e6 5 ♗c4 ♗b4 6 ♗b3
♘8c6 7 ♘ge2 ♗e7 N (7...♘a5 8 ♗a4+
♗d7 9 a3 ♘d5 10 ♘xd5 ♗xa4 11
♘e3 += Simagin-Bagirov, Moscow
1968) 8 a3 ♘e5 9 ♕g3 ♘bc6 10 d4
♘g6 11 d5 exd5 12 ♘xd5 ♗d6=
Bellon-Alburt, Bucharest 1978

2...♘d5 3 c4

a) 3 ♘c3 ♘xc3 4 dxc3 d6 5 ♗c4 e6
6 ♘f3 ♘c6?! 7 ♗f4 N (7 ♕e2 ♗e7 8
♗f4 0-0 9 0-0-0 d5 10 h4± Cvetkovic-
Marangunic, Jugoslavia 1970) 7...dxe5

41

8 ♘xe5 ♕xd1+ 9 ♖xd1 ♘xe5 10 ♗xe5 ♗d7 11 0-0 0-0-0= Laird-Khan, Penang 1978;
b) 3 d4 d6 4 ♘f3 ♗g4 (4...g6 5 ♗c4 ♘b6 6 ♗b3 d5 7 h3 a5 8 a4 ♗g7 9 0-0 ♘c6 10 ♘c3 0-0 11 ♖e1 ♗f5 12 ♘e2 ♕d7 13 ♘g3 ♗e6 14 ♘g5± Ghinda-Popov, Warsaw 1979) 5 ♗e2 e6 (5...c6 6 ♘g5 ♗f5 7 ♗d3 [7 e6!] 7... ♗xd3 8 ♕xd3 h6 9 ♘e4 dxe5 10 dxe5 ♘c7 N 11 ♕e2 ♘e6 12 0-0 ♘d4= Subasic-Knezevic, Sarajevo 1978) 6 0-0 ♗e7
1) 7 c4 ♘b6 8 ♘c3 0-0 9 ♗e3 (9 exd6 cxd6 10 b3 ♘c6 11 ♗e3 d5 12 c5 ♘d7 13 b4 ♘xb4 14 ♖b1 ♘c6 15 ♖xb7 ♖b8 16 ♖xb8 ♕xb8 [16...♘bxd7 17 h3 ♗xf3 18 ♗xf3 ♕a5= Tal-Vasjukov, USSR 1967] 17 ♕a4 ♕c7 18 g3 ♖c8 19 ♔g2 ♗f6 20 ♘b5± Wagman-Wademark, Eksjo 1978) 9...♘c6 10 exd6 cx d6 11 d5 exd5 12 cxd5! ♗xf3 13 ♗xf3 ♘e5 14 ♗e2 ♘bc4 15 ♗d4 ♖c8 16 b3± Sahovic-Schmidt, Sombor 1978;
2) 7 h3 ♗h5 8 c4 ♘b6 9 ♘c3 0-0 10 ♗e3 d5 11 c5 (11 cxd5 ♘xd5 12 ♕b3 ♘b6 13 ♖fd1 c6 14 a4 ♕d7 15 ♖ac1 ♘a6 16 a5± Stoica-Alburt, Bucharest 1978) 11...♗xf3 12 gxf3 ♘c8 13 f4 ♘c6 14 b4 (14 f5!?) 14...a6! N (14... ♗h4 15 ♖b1 N ♘8e7 16 ♗d3 g6 17 ♕g4 += Razuvaev-Alburt, Ashkabad 1978) 15 ♖b1 ♗h4 16 ♗d3 f5 17 ♔h2 ♕e8 18 ♖g1 ♘8e7= Kuzmin-Bagirov, USSR Final 1978
3...♘b6 4 c5
a) 4 d4 d6 5 f4 dxe5 6 fxe5 ♘c6 7 ♗e3 ♗f5 8 ♘c3 e6 9 ♘f3 ♗e7 10 d5 exd5 (10...♘b4 11 ♘d4 ♗g6 12 a3 c5 13 axb4 cxd4 14 ♕xd4 ♗xb4 15 dxe6 0-0 16 0-0-0 ♕e8 17 c5 ♗xc3 18 bxc3 ♕xe6∞ Felix-Zvolanek, CSSR 1978) 11 cxd5 ♘b4 12 ♘d4 ♗d7 13 ♕f3 (13 e6 fxe6 14 dxe6 ♗c6 15 ♕g4

♗h4+ 16 g3 ♗xh1 17 0-0-0 ♕f6 18 gxh4 0-0≈ Marjanovic-Cicovacki, Sombor 1978) 13...c5 14 dxc6 bxc6 15 e6 N fxe6 16 0-0-0 ♘6d5 17 a3! ♘xc3 18 ♘xe6! ♕a5 19 ♘xg7+ ♔d8 20 ♖xd7+!! +− Velimirovic-Kovacevic, Jugoslavia 1978;
b) 4 b3!? g6 5 c5 N ♘d5 6 ♗c4 e6 7 d4 d6 8 cxd6 cxd6 9 ♘f3 ♗g7 10 0-0 dxe5 11 ♘xe5 0-0= Camilleri-Oney, Albufieri 1978;
c) 4 b3!? d6 5 exd6 exd6 (5... ♕xd6!?) 6 ♗b2 d5 N (6...♘8d7 7 ♕e2+ ♕e7 8 ♕xe7+ ♔xe7 9 ♘c3 ♘f6 10 ♗e2 ♗f5 11 ♘f3± Gusev-Fedul, USSR 1967) 7 ♘f3 ♘c6 8 ♗e2 d4 9 d3 ♗e7 10 0-0 0-0 11 ♘a3 ♗f6 12 ♕d2± Ljubojevic-Oney, Albufieri 1978
4...♘d5 5 ♘c3
a) 5 ♗c4 c6 6 ♕e2!? ♕a5 7 ♘f3 ♕xc5 N (7...e6 8 0-0 ♗xc5 9 d4 ♗e7 10 ♗g5 ♕d8 11 ♗xe7 ♕xe7 12 ♘bd2∞ Gurgenidze-Breitman, USSR 1968) 8 d4 ♕b4+ 9 ♘bd2 d6 10 0-0 ♗g4 11 h3 ♗xf3 12 ♘xf3 e6 Makarichev-Alburt, Ashkabad 1978, 13 ♗d2! ♕b6 14 ♘g5 dxe5 15 ♘xe6! fxe6 16 ♕xe5±;
b) 5 ♗c4 e6 6 d4 d6 7 cxd6 cxd6 8 ♘f3 ♘c6 (8...♗e7 9 0-0 0-0 10 ♕e2 ♘c6 11 ♘c3 ♘xc3 12 bxc3 d5 13 ♗d3 += Sikora-Neckar, CSSR Final 1978) 9 0-0 ♗e7 10 ♘bd2 ♘b6 11 ♗b3 (11 ♗b5!) 11...d5 12 ♕e2 ♗d7 13 ♖d1 a5 14 ♘f1 += Hon-Torre, Penang 1978

Diagram

5...c6
5...e6 6 ♗c4 ♘xc3 7 dxc3 ♘c6 8 ♗f4 ♕h4 9 g3 ♕e7∓ (Vukic) 10 ♘f3 ♕xc5 11 ♕e2 h6 12 h4 b6!?∞ Berry-Harper, Canada Final 1978; 12...d5 =+

6 ♘f3

6 ♗c4 d6 7 ♕b3 ♘d7 8 ♘xd5! cxd5
9 ♗xd5 e6 10 ♗xe6! N fxe6 11 ♕xe6+
♕e7 12 ♕xe7+ ♔xe7 13 cxd6+ ±/+−
Franzoni-Henttinen, Graz 1978
**6...d6 7 ♘xd5 cxd5 8 cxd6 exd6 9
d4 ♘c6 10 ♗e2 ♗e7 11 0-0 0-0=**
Sikora-Ghinda, Warsaw 1979

Pirc

1 e4 g6 2 d4 ♗g7 3 ♘c3 d6 4 f4
4 ♗c4 ♘f6 5 ♕e2 ♘c6 6 e5
a) 6...♘h5 (Shamkovich) 7 g4 ♘xd4 8
♕d1 ♗xg4 9 ♕xd4 ♕c8∞ Bennett-
Valvo, London 1978; 7 ♗b5!! N
(Δ d5/g4) 7...dxe5 8 d5 a6 9 dxc6
axb5 10 cxb7 +−; 7...0-0 8 ♗xc6 bxc6
9 g4 c5 10 d5 (10 dxc5!) 10...♗b7
11 gxh5 e6 ∞/±;
b) 6...♘xd4!? 7 exf6 ♘xe2 8 fxg7
♖g8 9 ♘gxe2 ♖xg7 10 ♗h6 ♖g8 11
0-0-0± Kindermann-Balinas, London
1978 **4...♘f6**
4...c6 5 ♘f3 ♗g4 (5...♕b6!?) 6 ♗e3
♕b6
a) 7 ♕d2 ♗xf3 8 gxf3 e6!? 9 0-0-0
♕a5 10 ♔b1 ♘d7 11 e5 d5≈ Ambroz-
Ftacnik, CSSR Final 1978;
b) 7 ♕d3 ♗xf3 8 gxf3 ♘f6 9 0-0-0
♕a5 10 ♔b1 a6?! 11 h4 ♘bd7 12 ♗h3
0-0-0 13 f5± Sorm-Vokoun, CSSR
1978;

c) 7 ♕d3 ♘f6 8 0-0-0 d5 9 e5 ♘e4 10
♘e2 ♗f5 11 ♕a3 ♕a6 12 ♕b3 ♕b6=
Marjanovic-Szymczak, Kirovakan 1978
5 ♘f3 0-0
5...c5 6 ♗b5+ ♗d7 7 e5 ♘g4 8 e6
♗xb5 9 exf7+ ♔d7 10 ♘xb5 ♕a5+
11 ♘c3 cxd4 12 ♘xd4 ♗xd4 13 ♕xd4
♘c6 14 ♕c4 ♖ac8 N (14...♕f5!) 15
h3 (15 ♗d2 ♖hf8 16 ♘d5 ♕c5 17
♕xc5 dxc5 18 h3± Borkowski-Pribyl,
Eksjo 1978) 15...♘h6 16 0-0 ♘f5 17
♗d2 ♕b4 18 ♕e2± Szmetan-Torre,
Buenos Aires 1978
6 ♗d3
a) 6 e5 dxe5 7 dxe5 (7 fxe5 ♘d5 8
♗c4 ♗e6 9 ♘xd5 ♗xd5 10 ♗xd5 ♕xd5
11 ♕e2 b5 12 0-0 ♘d7 13 c3 ♘b6=
Unzicker-Chandler, Buenos Aires
1978) 7...♕xd1+ 8 ♔xd1 ♘g4 (8...
♖d8+ 9 ♗d3 ♘d5 10 ♘xd5 ♖xd5 11
♔e2 ♗g4 N 12 ♗e4 ♖b5 13 c3±
Teichmann-Dymond, London 1978) 9
♔e1 ♘c6 10 ♗b5 f6 11 h3 ♘h6 12
exf6 exf6 13 ♔f2 N ♖d8= Szmetan-
H.Garcia, Argentina Final 78; 10
h3 ♘h6 11 g4 ♘b4 12 ♖h2!; 11...f6∞;
b) 6 ♗e3 ♘a6 7 e5 N ♘g4 8 ♗g1 ♘c5
9 h3 cxd4 10 ♕xd4 ♘h6 11 0-0-0
♕a5 12 g4 ♗d7 13 ♘d5± Tseshkovsky-
Vadasz, Malgrat de Mar 1978;
c) 6 ♗e3 b6 7 ♗d3 ♗b7 8 f5! c5 9
fxg6 hxg6 10 d5 ♘bd7 11 0-0
Sigurjonsson-Nielsen, Esbjerg 1978,
11...♘g4∞;
d) 6 ♗e3 b6 7 e5 ♘g4 8 ♗g1 c5 (8...
♗b7 N 9 e6!? ♘h6 10 exf7+ ♘xf7
11 ♕d2 e5 12 fxe5 ♗xf3 13 gxf3
dxe5 14 0-0-0 ♘c6∞ Wedberg-
Schussler, Stockholm 1978/79) 9 h3
♘h6 10 d5 (10 dxc5?! bxc5 11 ♕d2
♘c6 12 ♗b5 ♗b7 13 0-0-0 ♘f5∓
Chiong-Chandler, Penang 1978) 10...
♘d7 (10...♘f5 11 ♗f2 dxe5 12 fxe5
♘d7 13 ♕e2 Balashov-Timman,

43

Tilburg 1977, 13...♕c7∞) 11 ♕e2 b5 N (11...♕c7 12 ♘h2 ♘f5 13 0-0-0 a6 14 g4 ♘d4 15 ♘xd4 cxd4 16 ♖xd4 dxe5∓ Peters-Botterill, Hastings 1978/ 79) 12 0-0-0 b4 13 ♘e4 ♘b6 14 g4 ♗b7 =+ Radulov-Sznapik, Warsaw 1979

6...♘a6

a) 6...♘c6 7 e5 dxe5 8 dxe5 ♘g4!? 9 0-0 ♘b4 10 ♗e4 c6 11 ♕e2 ♘d5= Jezierska-Szmacinska, Piotrkon Trybunalsk 1978;

b) 6...♘c6 7 0-0 ♗g4 8 e5 ♘h5?! N 9 ♗e3 dxe5 10 dxe5 f6 11 exf6 ♗xf6 12 h3 ♗xf3 13 ♕xf3± Mednis-Vadasz, Budapest 1978;

c) 6...♘c6 7 0-0 e5 8 dxe5 dxe5 9 f5 gxf5 (9...♘b4? 10 fxg6 hxg6 11 ♗g5 c6 12 ♔h1 ♘xd3 13 cxd3± Sax-Donner, Buenos Aires 1978) 10 exf5 ♘b4 (10...e4) 11 ♔h1 ♘xd3 12 cxd3 ♗xf5 13 ♘xe5 Parma-Ligterink, Buenos Aires 1978, 13...♗g6 14 ♗g4 ♕d4!∞

7 0-0

7 e5 dxe5 (7...♘d7 8 h4!? ♘b4 9 h5 ♘b6 10 hxg6 ♘xd3+ 11 cxd3 hxg6= Horvath-Hazai, Hungary Final 1978) 8 dxe5 ♘d5 9 ♘xd5 ♕xd5 10 ♕e2 ♗f5 11 ♗xf5 gxf5 12 0-0 ♘c5= Marjanovic-Zaichik, Kirovakan 1978

7...c5 8 d5

8 ♗xa6?! cxd4 9 ♕xd4 bxa6 10 ♗e3 ♘g4 11 ♕d3 ♘xe3 12 ♕xe3 ♖b8∓ Roos-Roth, II Ciocco 1978

8...♘c7

8...♖b8 N 9 ♕e1 ♘b4 10 ♕h4 b5 11 a3 ♘xd3 12 cxd3 ♗a6!? 13 b4 cxb4 14 axb4 ♕b6+ 15 ♔h1 ♘xe4? 16 ♖xa6! ±/+− Lein-Keene, Buenos Aires 1978; 15...♖bc8 Δ ♘g4!?

9 a4

9 ♕e1 ♖b8 10 a4 ♗d7 11 ♔h1 b6 12 ♕h4 a6 13 f5± Savereide-Polihroniade, Buenos Aires 1978

9...b6 10 ♕e1 a6 11 ♕h4 ♗d7 12 f5 b5 13 ♗h6 c4 14 ♗e2 gxf5 15 ♘g5 e6 16 ♖f3 +− Bellin-Pribyl, Erbeek 1978

1 e4 g6 2 d4 ♗g7 3 ♘f3 d6 4 ♘c3 ♘f6 5 ♗e2 0-0 6 0-0 ♘c6 7 ♗e3 7 d5 ♘b8 8 h3 e5 (8...c6 9 ♖e1 a5 10 a4 ♘a6 11 ♗e3 ♘b4 12 ♗c4 ♗d7 13 ♗b3 += Jansa-Popovic, Novi Sad 1978) 9 dxe6 ♗xe6 10 ♗g5 h6 11 ♗f4 ♘c6 12 ♕d2 g5!? 13 ♗h2 ♖e8 14 ♖fe1 += Hutchings-Gulko, Buenos Aires 1978

7...♗g4 8 ♕d3 ♘d7

8...e5 9 d5 ♘b4 10 ♕d2 a5 11 h3 ♗d7 12 ♗g5 ♕e8 13 ♘h2 += Karpov-Korchnoi (18) 1978

9 ♖ae1 N

9 ♘d2 ♘b4! 10 ♕c4 ♗xe2 11 ♘xe2 c5 12 dxc5 dxc5 13 ♖ad1 ♕c7 14 ♘f3 b6= Polugaevsky-Sax, Buenos Aires 1978

9...a5 10 ♔h1 e6 11 ♗g5 f6?! 12 ♗e3 e5 13 dxe5 ♗xf3 14 ♗xf3 fxe5 15 ♗g4 ♔h8 16 ♘d5± Vasyukov-Christiansen, Hastings 1978/79

1 e4 d6 2 d4 ♘f6 3 ♘c3 g6 4 f3 c6

4...♗g7 5 ♗e3 c6 6 ♕d2 h6 7 0-0-0 b5 8 ♔b1 a6 9 ♗d3 ♘bd7 10 ♘ge2 ♗b7 11 ♘c1 ♕c7 12 f4 0-0-0= Ardiansah-Hon, Penang 1978

5 ♗e3 ♘bd7

5...a6 6 a4 ♘bd7 7 ♕d2 ♕c7 8 ♘h3 ♗g7 9 ♘f2 ♖b8 10 a5 b5 11 axb6 ♕xb6 12 b3 c5= Enklaar-de Metz, Nijmegen 1978

6 ♕d2 b5 7 ♘h3 ♗b7 8 ♗e2 a6 9 0-0 ♗g7 10 ♖fd1 0-0 11 ♗h6 e5 12 ♗xg7 ♔xg7 13 a4 b4 14 ♘a2 a5= Aaron-Chandler, Penang 1978

1 e4 d6 2 d4 ♘f6 3 ♘c3 g6 4 ♗g5 c6

a) 4...h6 5 ♗e3 ♗g7 6 f3 c6 7 ♕d2 b5 8 a3 ♘bd7 9 ♘ge2 a6 10 g3 ♗b7

11 ♗g2 e5 12 ♖d1 ♕e7 13 0-0 += Raaste-Kaiszauri, Buenos Aires 1978;

b) 4...♗g7 5 f4 c6 6 ♕d2 0-0 7 0-0-0!? (7 ♘f3 b5 8 a3 h6 9 ♗h4 ♘bd7 10 e5 ♘e8 11 ♘e4 ♘b6 12 ♗d3 ♕c7 13 0-0 a6= Mascarinas-Chandler, Penang 1978) 7...b5 8 e5 b4! 9 exf6 bxc3 10 ♕xc3 exf6 11 ♗h4 ♕b6 12 ♘f3 ♘a6 13 ♗c4 ♘b4 14 ♖he1 ♗f5 15 ♖e2 d5 16 ♗b3 ♕a6 17 ♕d2 ♖ab8 18 a3 ♗xc2! −+ Feller-Timman, Amsterdam 1978

5 ♕d2

5 ♗d3!? ♕b6 6 ♘ge2 ♕xb2 7 ♖b1 ♕a3 8 ♗d2 ♕a5 9 0-0 ♗g7 10 f4∞ Mascarinas-Torre, Baguio City 1978

5...b5

a) 5...♗g7 6 f3 b5 7 a3 ♘bd7 8 ♘h3 0-0 9 ♘f2 a6 10 ♗e2 c5 11 d5 ♘b6 12 0-0 ♗d7 13 ♗h6 += Diez del Corral-Djindjihashvili, Buenos Aires 1978;

b) 5...♘bd7 6 f4 b5 7 ♗d3 h6 8 ♗h4 ♘b6 9 ♘f3 ♗g7 10 0-0 0-0 11 ♖ae1 ♗g4 12 e5 dxe5 13 fxe5 ♘fd5 14 ♘e4± Roth-Rukavina, Il Ciocco 1978

6 ♗d3 ♗g7 7 ♘ge2 0-0 8 ♗h6 e5 9 ♗xg7 ♔xg7 10 0-0 ♖e8 11 dxe5 dxe5 12 ♘g3 ♘bd7 =+ Aaron-Torre, Penang 1978

45

Warsaw i.79   1 2 3 4 5 6 7 8 9 0

				1	2	3	4	5	6	7	8	9	0	
1	Ribli	GM	2595	x	1	½	½	½	½	½	1	1	½	6
2	Prandstetter		2385	0	x	1	½	½	½	½	1	1	1	6
3	Gheorghiu	GM	2540	½	0	x	½	½	½	½	½	1	1	5
4	Sznapik	IM	2435	½	½	½	x	½	1	½	0	1	0	4½
5	Lengyel	GM	2455	½	½	½	½	x	½	½	½	½	½	4½
6	Radulov	GM	2485	½	½	½	0	½	x	1	½	0	1	4½
7	Inkiov	IM	2460	½	½	½	½	½	0	x	½	½	½	4
8	F.Portisch	IM	2475	0	0	½	1	½	½	½	x	½	½	4
9	Skrobek	IM	2370	0	0	0	0	½	1	½	½	x	1	3½
10	Jansa	GM	2495	½	0	0	1	½	0	½	½	0	x	3

Warsaw i.79   1 2 3 4 5 6 7 8 9 0

				1	2	3	4	5	6	7	8	9	0	
1	Smejkal	GM	2550	x	½	1	½	½	½	½	1	½	1	6
2	Sax	GM	2590	½	x	1	½	½	½	½	½	½	1	5½
3	Ghinda	IM	2455	0	0	x	½	1	1	1	½	½	1	5½
4	Adorjan	GM	2525	½	½	½	x	½	½	½	½	½	1	5
5	Ermenkov	GM	2495	½	½	0	½	x	½	½	½	1	1	5
6	L.Popov	IM	2430	½	½	0	½	½	x	½	½	½	1	4½
7	W.Schmidt	GM	2430	½	½	0	½	½	½	x	½	1	0	4
8	Ghitescu	IM	2400	0	½	½	½	½	½	½	x	1	0	4
9	Sikora		2430	½	½	½	½	0	½	0	0	x	½	3
10	Kuligowski		2495	0	0	0	0	0	0	1	1	½	x	2½

Final   1 2 3 4 5 6 7 8

				1	2	3	4	5	6	7	8	
1	Ribli	GM	2595	x	0	½	½	½	1	1	1	4½
2	Sax	GM	2590	1	x	½	½	½	½	½	½	4
3	Gheorghiu	GM	2540	½	½	x	½	½	½	1	½	4
4	Smejkal	GM	2550	½	½	½	x	½	½	1	½	4
5	Adorjan	GM	2525	½	½	½	½	x	½	½	1	4
6	Ghinda	IM	2455	0	½	½	½	½	x	½	½	3
7	Prandstetter		2385	0	½	0	0	½	½	x	1	2½
8	Sznapik	IM	2435	0	½	½	½	0	½	0	x	2

Hastings xii.78-i.79

			1	2	3	4	5	6	7	8	9	0	1	2	3	4	5	
1	Andersson	GM 2545	x	½	½	½	½	½	1	½	1	½	1	½	1	½	1	9½
2	Kochiev	GM 2555	½	x	½	½	½	½	½	1	½	½	1	1	½	½	½	8½
3	Csom	GM 2510	½	½	x	½	½	½	1	0	½	½	1	½	1	½	1	8½
4	Speelman	IM 2410	½	½	½	x	0	½	0	1	½	1	½	½	1	1	1	8½
5	Vasyukov	GM 2555	½	½	½	1	x	½	0	1	0	½	½	1	½	1	1	8½
6	Lein	GM 2505	½	½	½	½	½	x	½	1	0	½	½	½	½	1	1	8
7	Christiansen	GM 2490	0	½	0	1	1	½	x	0	½	½	½	1	1	½	1	8
8	Mestel	IM 2450	½	0	1	0	0	0	1	x	0	½	1	1	1	1	1	8
9	Biyiasas	GM 2450	0	½	½	½	1	1	½	1	x	0	½	½	½	1	0	7½
10	Hartston	IM 2475	½	½	½	0	½	½	½	½	1	x	½	0	½	1	1	7½
11	Taulbut	IM 2405	0	0	0	½	½	½	½	0	½	½	x	½	½	1	½	5½
12	Suba	GM 2430	½	0	½	½	0	½	0	0	½	1	½	x	0	1	0	5
13	Botterill	IM 2400	0	½	0	0	½	½	0	0	½	½	½	1	x	0	1	5
14	Peters	2430	½	½	½	0	0	0	½	0	0	0	0	0	1	x	1	4
15	Balshan	2415	0	½	0	0	0	0	0	0	1	0	½	1	0	0	x	3

GM = 9   IM = 7

Belgrade 18.i-2.ii.79

			1	2	3	4	5	6	7	8	9	0	1	2	3	4	
1	Marjanovic	GM 2505	x	½	1	½	½	½	1	1	1	1	1	1	½	1	10½
2	Szabo	GM 2515	½	x	½	½	1	1	½	½	½	0	1	1	½	1	8½
3	Tringov	GM 2480	0	½	x	½	½	1	½	½	½	½	½	1	1	1	8
4	Matulovic	GM 2510	½	½	½	x	1	½	1	0	½	½	1	½	½	1	8
5	Rajkovic	GM 2460	½	0	½	0	x	1	½	1	½	½	1	1	0	1	7½
6	Pribyl	IM 2420	½	0	0	½	0	x	½	0	1	1	½	1	1	1	7
7	Ciocaltea	GM 2430	0	½	½	0	½	½	x	½	1	1	½	½	½	1	7
8	Raicevic	GM 2440	0	½	½	1	0	1	½	x	1	½	0	0	½	1	6½
9	Adamski	IM 2415	0	½	½	½	½	0	0	0	x	½	1	1	1	1	6½
10	Todorcevic	IM 2455	0	1	½	½	½	0	0	½	½	x	1	½	½	½	6
11	S.Cabarkapa	2280	0	0	½	0	0	½	½	1	0	0	x	½	1	1	5
12	Baretic	2300	0	0	0	½	0	0	½	1	0	½	½	x	1	½	4½
13	Dukanovic	2300	½	½	0	½	1	0	½	½	0	½	0	0	x	½	4½
14	D.Knezevic		0	0	0	0	0	0	0	0	0	½	0	½	½	x	1½

Category 7 (2406)   GM = 10   IM = 7½

Munich ii-iii.79

			1	2	3	4	5	6	7	8	9	0	1	2	3	4	
1	Spassky	GM	2640	x	½	½	1	½	½	½	½	½	1	1	1	0	1	8½
2	Balashov	GM	2600	½	x	1	½	½	½	½	½	½	½	1	½	1	1	8½
3	Andersson	GM	2560	½	0	x	½	½	1	½	1	½	1	1	½	1	½	8½
4	Hubner	GM	2595	0	½	½	x	½	1	½	½	½	½	1	1	1	1	8½
5	Pachman	GM	2510	½	½	½	½	x	½	½	½	½	½	½	1	0	1	7
6	Robatsch	GM	2435	½	½	0	0	½	x	½	½	½	1	½	½	1	1	7
7	Stean	GM	2540	½	½	½	½	½	½	x	½	½	½	½	1	½	½	7
8	Unzicker	GM	2530	½	½	0	½	½	½	½	x	½	½	½	1	1	0	6½
9	Olafsson	GM	2555	½	½	½	½	½	½	½	½	x	½	0	½	½	1	6½
10	Sigurjonsson	GM	2490	0	½	0	½	½	0	½	½	½	x	½	½	1	1	6
11	Pfleger	GM	2545	0	0	0	0	½	½	½	½	1	½	x	1	1	½	6
12	Lau		2440	0	½	½	0	0	½	0	0	½	½	0	x	1	1	4½
13	Lieb			1	0	0	0	1	0	½	0	½	0	0	0	x	1	4
14	Dankert		2360	0	0	½	0	0	0	½	1	0	0	½	0	0	x	2½
15	Karpov			1					½		½		½				1	
16	Adorjan			0			0	½		½							½	

Category 10 (2500)   IM = 6½

Bucharest 6-22.iii.79

				1	2	3	4	5	6	7	8	9	0	1	2	3	4	5	6	
1	Taimanov	GM	2510	x	½	½	½	1	½	½	½	1	½	½	½	1	½	½	1	9½
2	Suba	GM	2430	½	x	½	1	½	½	1	½	½	½	1	½	1	½	0	½	9
3	Ghitescu	IM	2400	½	½	x	½	½	1	½	½	½	1	0	½	1	½	½	1	9
4	Ciocaltea	IM	2430	½	0	½	x	½	½	½	½	½	½	1	1	1	½	1	½	9
5	Bellon	GM	2395	0	½	½	½	x	1	1	½	½	½	½	1	0	1	0	1	8½
6	Biriescu		2390	½	½	0	½	0	x	1	1	0	½	1	½	1	1	½	½	8½
7	Uhlmann	GM	2530	½	0	½	½	0	0	x	1	1	½	1	½	½	½	1	1	8½
8	Stoica	IM	2430	½	½	½	½	½	0	0	x	½	½	1	½	½	1	½	1	8
9	Haik	IM	2435	0	½	½	½	½	1	0	½	x	½	0	0	1	½	1	1	7½
10	Barczay	GM	2475	½	½	0	½	½	½	½	½	½	x	½	½	½	½	0	½	6½
11	Rogulj	IM	2440	½	0	1	0	½	0	0	0	1	½	x	½	0	1	1	½	6½
12	Bielczyk		2410	½	½	½	0	0	½	½	½	1	½	½	x	½	½	½	0	6½
13	Foisor		2310	0	0	0	0	1	0	½	½	0	½	1	½	x	½	1	1	6½
14	Negulescu			½	½	½	½	0	0	½	0	½	½	0	½	½	x	1	½	6
15	Peev	IM	2420	½	1	½	0	1	½	0	½	0	1	0	½	0	0	x	0	5½
16	Lanc	IM	2395	0	½	0	½	0	½	0	0	0	½	½	1	0	½	1	x	5

Category 7 (2413)   GM = 11½   IM = 8½

Wijk aan Zee 18.i-1.ii.79

			1	2	3	4	5	6	7	8	9	0	1	2	
1	Polugaevsky	GM	2625	x	½	½	½	½	½	1	½	½	1	1	1	7½
2	Andersson	GM	2565	½	x	½	½	½	½	½	½	½	½	1	1	6½
3	Miles	GM	2560	½	½	x	½	½	½	1	½	½	½	½	1	6½
4	Sosonko	GM	2535	½	½	½	x	½	½	½	½	1	½	1	½	6½
5	Hort	GM	2600	½	½	½	½	x	0	½	½	½	½	1	1	6
6	Hubner	GM	2595	½	½	½	½	1	x	½	0	½	½	1	½	6
7	Timman	GM	2625	0	½	0	½	½	½	x	1	½	½	1	1	6
8	Djindjihashvili	GM	2595	½	½	½	½	½	1	0	x	0	1	0	½	5
9	Ree	IM	2480	½	½	½	0	½	½	½	1	x	½	½	0	5
10	Guil.Garcia	GM	2490	0	½	½	½	½	½	½	0	½	x	½	0	4
11	Gaprindashvili	GM	2460	0	0	½	0	0	0	0	1	½	½	x	1	3½
12	Nikolac	IM	2450	0	0	0	½	0	½	0	½	1	1	0	x	3½

Category 12 (2547)   GM = 7

Sao Paulo 10-24.ii.79

			1	2	3	4	5	6	7	8	9	0	1	2	3	4	
1	Korchnoi	GM	2695	x	½	½	1	½	½	½	1	1	½	1	1	1	1	10
2	Ljubojevic	GM	2590	½	x	½	½	½	½	1	1	½	1	1	1	1	1	10
3	Gheorghiu	GM	2540	½	½	x	½	1	½	1	½	½	½	1	½	½	½	8
4	Andersson	GM	2560	0	½	½	x	½	1	½	½	1	1	½	1	1	0	8
5	Lein	GM	2535	½	½	0	½	x	1	½	1	0	½	½	1	1	1	8
6	Stean	GM	2540	½	½	½	0	0	x	½	½	1	½	½	1	1	1	7½
7	Panno	GM	2545	½	0	0	½	½	½	x	1	½	½	1	0	1	½	6½
8	Rocha		2365	0	0	½	½	0	½	0	x	1	1	1	1	½	½	6½
9	Segal	IM	2400	0	½	½	0	1	0	½	0	x	½	½	1	1	1	6½
10	Byrne	GM	2535	½	0	½	0	½	½	½	0	½	x	½	1	1	1	6½
11	Sunye		2375	0	0	0	½	½	½	0	0	½	½	x	½	½	1	4½
12	Braga		2390	0	0	½	0	0	0	1	0	0	0	½	x	½	1	3½
13	Filguth		2335	0	0	½	0	0	0	0	½	0	0	½	½	x	1	3
14	H.Riemsdyk	IM	2435	0	0	½	1	0	0	½	½	0	0	0	0	0	x	2½

Category 10   GM = 8½   IM = 6

Belgrade iii.79

			1	2	3	4	5	6	7	8	9	0	
Ljubojevic	GM	2590	1	1	0	½	0	1	½	0	1	½	5½
Gligoric	GM	2560	0	0	1	½	1	0	½	1	0	½	4½

Dubna 1979

				1	2	3	4	5	6	7	8	9	0	1	2	3	4	5	6	
1	Zaitsev	GM	2505	x	½	½	½	½	½	½	½	1	1	½	½	½	1	1	½	9½
2	Razuvaev	GM	2470	½	x	½	1	½	½	½	½	½	0	½	½	1	1	1	1	9½
3	Suetin	GM	2535	½	½	x	½	½	0	½	½	1	0	½	1	1	1	1	1	9½
4	Sahovic	GM	2520	½	0	½	x	½	1	1	1	½	0	½	1	½	1	½	1	9½
5	Sveshnikov	GM	2545	½	½	½	½	x	½	½	0	1	1	1	½	1	½	0	½	8½
6	Forintos	GM	2425	½	½	1	0	½	x	½	½	½	½	½	1	½	0	1	1	8½
7	Rashkovsky	GM	2500	½	½	½	0	½	½	x	1	½	½	½	½	½	½	½	1	8
8	Ungureanu	IM	2405	½	½	½	0	1	½	0	x	0	½	½	½	1	½	1	1	8
9	Plachetka	GM	2445	0	½	0	½	0	½	½	1	x	1	½	½	½	½	½	1	7½
10	Georgiev	IM	2440	0	1	1	1	0	½	½	½	0	x	½	½	0	½	1	½	7½
11	Knezevic	GM	2500	½	½	½	½	0	½	½	½	½	½	x	½	½	½	½	½	7
12	Panchenko	IM	2485	½	½	0	0	½	0	½	½	½	½	½	x	1	1	½	½	7
13	Kaidanov			½	0	0	½	0	½	½	0	½	1	½	0	x	1	½	½	6
14	Lukacs	IM	2420	0	0	0	0	½	1	½	½	½	½	½	0	0	x	½	1	5½
15	Farago	GM	2510	0	0	0	½	1	0	½	0	½	0	½	½	½	½	x	0	4½
16	Gusev		2410	½	0	0	0	½	0	0	0	0	½	½	½	½	0	1	x	4

Category 9 (2457) GM = 10½ IM = 7½

Tallinn iii.79

				1	2	3	4	5	6	7	8	9	0	1	2	3	4	5	6	7	
1	Petrosian	GM	2610	x	½	½	1	1	1	½	½	½	½	½	1	1	½	1	1	1	12
2	Vaganian	GM	2570	½	x	½	½	½	½	½	1	1	1	1	½	1	1	1	0	1	11½
3	Tal	GM	2615	½	½	x	½	½	1	1	1	1	½	1	½	½	1	1	0	1	11½
4	Bronstein	GM	2555	0	½	½	x	1	½	½	0	½	1	½	½	1	1	1	1	½	10
5	Veingold		2370	0	½	½	0	x	½	1	1	1	½	½	½	½	½	½	1	1	9½
6	Sax	GM	2590	0	½	0	½	½	x	½	1	½	0	1	1	1	1	1	0	1	9½
7	Zilberstein		2455	½	½	0	½	0	½	x	½	½	½	½	0	1	½	½	1	1	8
8	Knaak	GM	2565	½	0	0	1	0	0	½	x	½	1	½	½	0	½	1	1	1	8
9	Lechtinsky	IM	2415	½	0	0	½	0	½	½	½	x	1	½	½	0	1	½	1	1	8
10	Hartston	IM	2485	½	0	½	0	½	1	½	0	0	x	½	0	1	½	1	1	1	8
11	Christiansen	GM	2475	½	0	0	½	½	0	½	½	½	½	x	1	½	0	½	1	1	7½
12	Nei	IM	2500	0	½	½	½	½	0	1	½	½	1	0	x	½	½	½	½	½	7½
13	Vilela	IM	2460	0	0	½	0	½	0	0	1	1	0	½	½	x	½	½	0	1	6
14	Voorema		2395	½	0	0	0	½	0	½	½	½	0	½	1	½	x	½	½	½	6
15	Ritov			0	0	0	0	½	0	½	0	½	0	½	½	½	½	x	1	1	5½
16	B.Ivanovic	GM	2460	0	1	1	0	0	1	0	0	0	0	0	½	1	½	0	x	0	5
17	Rantanen	IM	2460	0	0	0	½	0	0	0	0	0	0	0	½	0	½	0	1	x	2½

Category 8 (2431) GM = 12 IM = 8½

Trstenik 8-22.iii.79

				1	2	3	4	5	6	7	8	9	0	1	2	3	
1	S.Marjanovic	GM	2505	x	½	½	½	0	1	1	1	1	1	1	1	0	8½
2	S.Martinovic	GM	2410	½	x	½	½	1	½	1	1	½	½	0	1	1	8
3	Rajkovic	GM	2460	½	½	x	½	½	½	1	½	½	½	1	1	1	8
4	Pytel	IM	2425	½	½	½	x	½	½	½	½	1	½	1	½	1	7½
5	Ciric	GM	2440	1	0	½	½	x	½	1	½	½	1	½	½	1	7½
6	Honfi	IM	2420	0	½	½	½	½	x	0	½	1	½	½	1	1	6½
7	P.Popovic	IM	2420	0	0	0	½	0	1	x	1	1	½	½	1	1	6½
8	Tringov	GM	2460	0	0	½	½	½	½	0	x	½	½	1	1	1	6
9	Inkiov	IM	2460	0	½	½	0	½	0	0	½	x	1	1	1	1	6
10	Sellos		2360	0	½	½	½	0	½	½	½	0	x	½	1	1	5½
11	Schussler	IM	2460	0	1	0	0	½	½	½	0	0	½	x	½	1	4½
12	Bzenic			0	0	0	½	½	0	0	0	0	0	½	x	1	2½
13	Jelesijevic			1	0	0	0	0	0	0	0	0	0	0	0	x	1

Category 7 (2407)

Rome 18-29.iii.79

				1	2	3	4	5	6	7	8	9	0	1	2	
1	Pinter	IM	2445	x	½	½	1	½	½	1	½	½	½	1	1	7½
2	Mariotti	GM	2485	½	x	1	0	½	1	1	½	½	½	1	½	7
3	Csom	GM	2510	½	0	x	1	1	½	½	½	1	½	0	1	6½
4	Toth	IM	2470	0	1	0	x	½	1	0	1	0	1	½	1	6
5	Cappello		2405	½	½	0	½	x	0	½	½	1	½	1	1	6
6	Tatai	IM	2475	½	0	½	0	1	x	½	½	½	½	1	1	6
7	Schmidt	GM	2430	0	0	½	1	½	½	x	½	½	½	1	1	6
8	Hug	IM	2460	½	½	½	0	½	½	½	x	½	½	1	½	5½
9	Keene	GM	2465	½	½	0	1	0	½	½	½	x	½	½	1	5½
10	Marovic	GM	2470	½	½	½	0	½	½	½	½	½	x	½	½	5
11	Passerotti		2340	0	0	1	½	0	0	0	0	½	½	x	½	3
12	Coppini		2285	0	½	0	0	0	0	0	½	0	½	½	x	2

Category 8 (2437)   GM = 8   IM = 6

Tallinn i-ii.79 ?

1	Kuzmin	GM 2565	1 ½	0 ½	½ ½	½ ½	½ 1	5½
2	Tseshkovsky	GM 2560	0	0 1	½ ½	½ ½	1 ½	1	5½
3	Romanishin	GM 2560	½ 1	½ ½	½ ½	½ 0	0 0	4

Kutaisi x 78   Category 8 (2445)
(1-4) Lutikov, Gurgenidze, Dolmatov, Dvoretsky 7½; (5) Azmaiparashvili 7; (6-10) Gedevanishvili, Gufeld, Lerner, Sturua, Holmov 6½; (11-12) Osnos, Podgaets 6; (13) Estrin 5; (14) Zaichik 4½.

Leipzig xii.78
Category 5 (2371)   IM = 7½
(1-2) Hennings IM 2445, Vogt GM 2520 7½; (3) Knaak GM 2520 7; (4) Hausner 2365 6; (5-6) Neckar 2340, Schurade 2350 5½; (7-8) Bohnisch 2365, Sapi 2380 5; (9-10) Baumbach 2375, Tichy 4½; (11-12) Casper 2325, Heinig 2270 4.

Stary Smokovec xii.78
Category 5 (2365)   IM = 8
(1) Ftacnik IM 2380 9; (2) Plachetka GM 2470 8½; (3) Peresipkin 2430 7½; (4) Trejbal 7; (5-6) Djuric IM 2350, Joksic 2405 6½; (7-9) Cvetkovic 2390, Mohring IM 2405, Franzen 2290 5½; (10-11) Sikora 2415, Banas 2385 5; (12) Ujtelky IM 2280 4; (13) Novak 2355 2½.

Groningen 13 Rd SS xii.78-i.79
(1) Van der Wiel 11; (2) Dolmatov 10½; (3) Plaskett 9; (4-5) P.Nikolic, Petursson 8; (6-7) Gazik, Valkesalmi 7½; . . . . (28)

Prague 26.xii.78-7.i.79
Category 4 (2346) IM = 8½
(1) Hausner 2365 8½; (2-4) Pokjowczyk IM 2385, J.Arnason 2470, Mokry 2310 7½; (5-6) Spacek 2285, Liebert IM 2420 7; (7-8) Meduna IM 2425, Dobosz IM 2375 6½; (9) Modr 2310 6; (10) Trapl IM 2390 5; (11) Drovota

3½; (12) Janak 3; (13) Witkowski IM 2365 2½.

Stockholm 1978-9 9 Rd SS
(1) Schussler 7½; (2) Bednarski 7; (3-8) Miralles, Eslon, Angantysson, Schneider, Iskov, Wedberg 6½; (9-15) Karlsson, Plachetka, Kaiszauri; . . . (80)

Reggio Emilia 27.xii.78-6.i.79
Category 4   IM = 7½
(1) Hess 2285 8; (2) Bykhovsky 2440 7½; (3-4) Cappello 2365, S.Nikolic GM 2350 6½; (5-6) Messa, Taruffi 2340 6; (7-9) Zichichi IM 2365, Bertok IM 2415, Goldenberg 2300 5½; (10) Kovacs IM 2400 4; (11-12) Ljungquist 2240, Pederzoli 2255 2½.

Hamar 9 Rd SS 9-16.i.79
(1) Petursson 6; (2-6) Goodman, Karlsson, Schussler, Niklasson, Arnasson 5½; (7-8) Westerinen, Iskov 5; (9-10) Bednarski, Bjork 4½; . . . (18)

Malta 10-22.i.79
(1-2) Povah 2325, Barlov 2340 9; (3-4) Krause 2230, Blackstock 2340 7½; (5-6) Rosino 2290, Camilleri 2230 7; (7) Trabattoni 2330 6½; . . . (12)

Stara Zagora 1979
Category 5   GM = 9   IM = 7½
(1) Lukov IM 2385 8; (2-3) Velikov IM 2440, Ermenkov GM 2495 7; (4-5) Ochoa 2350, Spassov GM 2470 6½; (6-7) Radulov GM 2485, Kirov GM 2420 6; (8) Ekstrom 2385 5½; (9) Danailov 4½; (10) Giffard 2330 4; (11) Witkowski IM 2330 3½; (12) Mikov 1½.

Copenhagen 1 i-ii.79
Category 7 (2408) GM = 8½ IM = 6½
(1) Larsen GM 2620 8; (2-3) Hoi 2355, Westerinen GM 2465 7½; (4) Iskov 2370 7; (5-6) Mikhalchishin GM 2480, J.Kristiansen 2365 6½; (7) Schussler IM 2460 6; (8-10) Wahlbom 2375, Brinck-Claussen 2375, Krnic IM 2390 4; (11) Djuric IM 2415 3½; (12) Auchenberg 2225 1½.

Jugoslavia Final, Bjelovar 11-25.ii.79
13 Rd SS
(1) Nemet 10; (2-4) P.Nikolic, Rogulj, Vukic 8½; (5-10) Kelecevic, Raicevic, Messing, Karaklaic, Nikolac, Todorcevic 8; (11-14) Velimirovic, Z.Nikolic, Janosevic, Popovic 7½; (15-20) Matulovic, Bjelajac, Marjanovic, Maksimovic, Vl.Kovacevic, Antunac 7; (21-22) Planinc, Sprecic 6½; . . . (42)!

Poland Final 12-26.ii.79 13 Rd SS
(1) Przewoznik 9½; (2-3) Pytel, Kruszynski 9; (4-6) Filipowicz, Schinzel, J.Adamski 8½; (7-13) Bernard, Bugajski, Marszalek, Pokojowczyk, Maciejewski, A.Adamski, Barwinski 8 . . . Schmidt 7½ . . . (74).

Copenhagen 2 16-25.iii.79
Category 5 (2364) IM = 6
(1) Schneider IM 2420 6½; (2-3) J.Kristiansen 2365, Hoi 2355 6; (4-5) Arnason 2410, J.Fries Nielsen 2310 5½; (6) Wedberg IM 2425 5; (7-8) Mortensen 2365, Niklasson IM 2385 3½; (9) Fulsang 2½; (10) Kaiszauri IM 2405 1.

Trnava 18-31.iii.79
Category 8 (2435) GM = 9½ IM = 7
(1) Plachetka GM 2445 9½; (2-3) Trapl IM 2395, Tseitlin IM 2505 8; (4-5) Mohring IM 2400, Ftacnik IM 2430 7½; (6) Banas 2395 7; (7-8) Lengyel GM 2455, Espig IM 2450 6½; (9-10) Pavlov IM 2410, Vadasz GM 2490 6; (11) Vilela IM 2460 5½; (12) Pribyl IM 2420 5; (13) Bohosian IM 2410 4½; (14) Kovacs IM 2430 3½.

Helsinki iii.79
Category 7 (2421) IM = 5½
(1-3) Hort GM 2600, Szabo GM 2515, Westerinen GM 2465 6; (4) Rantanen IM 2460 5½; (5-6) Hurme 2320, Sznapik IM 2435 5; (7-8) Ornstein IM 2445, Ristoja 2305 4; (9) Raaste 2330 3½; (10) Kivipelto 2335 0.

Lone Pine 25.iii.-4.iv.79 9 Rd SS
(1-4) Liberzon, Gheorghiu, Gligoric, Hort 6½; (5-10) Lombardy, Sosonko, Ree, Larsen, Gruenfeld, Sahovic 6; (11-22) Seirawan, Kaplan, Reshevsky, Peters, Morris, Korchnoi, Diesen, Lein, Shamkovich, Tarjan, Bisguier, Pachman 5½; (23-33) de Firmian, Biyiasas, H.Olafsson, Odendahl, Miles, Zaltsman, Ligterink, Sigurjonsson, Benko, Browne, Rajkovic 5; (34-44) Ostojic, Quinteros, Janosevic, Christiansen, . . . 4½; . . . (72)

1 Hoffman-Soltis
New York 78

✓ **1 ♘c3 b6!? 2 ♘f3** 2 e4 e6 3 d4 ♗b4
♗b7 3 g3 ♗xf3!? 3...e6 4 ♗g2 ♘f6
5 0-0 d5 6 d3 ♘bd7 **4 exf3 e6 5 ♗g2**
5 f4 ♘f6 6 ♗h3 △ f5 **♘f6 6 0-0 ♗e7 7**
b3! 0-0 8 ♗b2 c6 9 f4 d5 10 ♖e1
♘bd7 11 ♕f3 11 a4! ♗d6 **12 ♘e2**
b5! △ 13 ♘d4 ♕b6 △ ♗c5 **13 ♘c1**
♕a5 14 ♕e2 ♗a3 15 ♖xa3?! 15 ♗c3
b4 16 ♗xf6!? ♘xf6 17 ♘d3 += **♕xa3**
16 ♘d3 a5 17 h4 ♖fe8? 17...a4 18
b4; 17...♖fc8! **18 g4! g6 19 ♗f3?**
c5! 20 ♘e5 20 g5 c4 21 ♘c1 ♕b2;
21 ♘e5 ♘xe5 22 ♕xe5 ♘d7 =+ **c4**
21 h5 ♘xe5 22 fxe5? 22 ♕xe5 ♘d7
23 ♕c7♕c5! 24 ♕xd7 ♖e7; 24 ♕xc5
♘xc5 =+ **♘d7 23 ♕g2 ♖ec8 24 ♖h1**
cxb3 25 axb3 25 cxb3 ♕b2! 26
♖ae1 ♖c2 **♕b2 26 c3 ♕xb3 27 ♕e3**
♕c4 28 hxg6 fxg6 **29 ♕g5** 29 ♖xh7
♕xh7 30 ♖h1+ ♔g8 31 ♕h6 ♘f8 -+
♘f8 30 ♖h6 ♖c7 -+ **31 ♖e1 ♖f7 32**
♗e2 ♕c5! 33 f4 b4 34 ♗d3 ♖g7 35
♖eh1 bxc3 36 dxc3 ♕xc3 37 ♖1h3
♕d2+ 0-1 Soltis

1 c4 b6

✓ ## 2 Ree-Miles
Wijk-aan-Zee 79

1 c4 b6 2 d4 e6 3 e4 ♗b7 4 f3 f5!?
5 exf5 ♘h6!? N **6 fxe6** 6 ♗xh6 ♕h4+
7 g3 ♕xh6∞ **♘f5! 7 ♘e2 ♗d6∞ 8**
h4 0-0 9 ♘bc3 9 ♗g5 ♕e8∞ **♕f6?!**
10 c5! ♗e7 10...bxc5? 11 e7 △ ♕b3+
+-; 10...♗g3+ 11 ♘xg3 ♘xg3 12
♖h3 += **11 exd7** 11 ♗g5 ♕xe6 12
♕b3 ♕xb3 13 axb3 ♗xg5 14 hxg5
♘c6 +=/∞ **♕f7! 12 ♕b3 ♕xb3?** 12...
♘xd7!∞ **13 axb3 ♘xd7 14 b4 ♗xh4+**
15 ♔d1± ♖fd8 15...♘f6 16 ♘f4!±;
15...♖fe8 16 ♘b5!± **16 ♔c2?** 16
♖xh4! ♘xh4 17 ♗g5 ♘f5 18 ♗xd8

♘e3+ 19 ♔d2 ♘xf1+ 20 ♖xf1 ♖xd8
±/+- **♗f6 17 ♘b5 ♗f8! 18 ♘xc7**
♖ac8 **19 ♘b5 a6 20 ♘a7 ♖a8 21**
c6 ♖xa7 22 cxb7 ♖xb7 23 ♖xa6
♘e6!∞ 24 ♔b1 h6 25 g4 ♗fxd4 26
♘xd4 ♖xd4 27 ♖a8+ ♔f7 28 ♖c8
b5 29 ♖h5 ♗g5 30 ♖h2 ♖xc1 31 ♖xc1
♖xb4 32 ♗d3 ♖d4 33 ♗e4 ♖e7 34
♗c2? 34 ♖c6= **♕f6 35 ♗b3 ♖d3 36**
♗xe6 ♖xe6 =+ 37 ♖f2 b4! 38 ♔c2?
Zeitnot **♖ee3 39 f4 b3+?** Zeitnot
39...♖g3 -+ **40 ♔b1 ♖d6∓** 40...
♖g3 **41 ♖ff1!** 41 ♖g1 ♖g3! 42 ♖ff1
♖xg1 43 ♖xg1 ♖d4 44 ♖f1 ♖d3!
∓/-+ **♖g3 42 ♖c3 ♖xc3?** 42...♖dd3
43 ♖c6+ ♔e7! 44 ♖e1+ ♔f7∓ **43**
bxc3 ♖d2 44 c4!= ♖g2 45 g5+ hxg5
46 fxg5+ ♔xg5 47 ♖c1 ♔f6 48 ♖c3
b2 49 ♖e3 g5 50 c5 ♖h2 51 c6 g4
52 ♖c3 ♖h8 53 ♔xb2 ♕e6 54 ♔c2
♖g8 55 c7 ♖c8 ½-½ Miles

3 Vukic-Stanojevic
Novi Sad 78

1 d4 ♘f6 2 c4 b6 3 ♘c3 ♗b7 4 d5
e5?! 4...e6!? 5 a3! += 5 a3 a5 6 ♘f3
d6 7 e4 ♘bd7 8 ♗d3 8 g3!? △ ♗g2
♗e7 9 0-0 0-0 10 ♗e3 ♘h5 11 b4?!
11 ♖e1! ♘f4 12 ♗f1 △ g3 **♘f4 12**
♗c2 g5 13 ♘d2 ♗c8 14 ♘b3 ♘f6 15
bxa5 bxa5 16 a4 ♘h8 17 ♗d2 ♖g8
18 ♕e1?! 18 ♘e2! ♗h3 19 gxh3
♕d7 20 f3 ♕xh3 21 ♖f2 g4 22 ♘xf4
exf4 23 ♔h1 gxf3 24 ♗xf4 ♖g2
25 ♖xf3 +- **♖g6 19 ♘e2 ♗h3**

Diagram

20 gxh3 ♕d7 21 f3 ♕xh3 22 ♖f2
g4 23 ♘xf4 exf4 24 e5! +- gxf3+
24...g3? 25 ♗xg6 gxf2+ 26 ♕xf2 ♖g8
27 exf6 ♖xg6+ 28 ♔h1 ♗xf6 29 ♖g1
+- **25 ♗xg6 ♖g8 26 exf6 ♖xg6+**
27 ♔h1 ♖g2 28 ♗xf4 ♗xf6 29

♖aa2 1-0 Vukic

4 Balogh-Sliva Poland 78
1 d4 e6 2 ♘f3 b6 3 c4 ♗b7 4 e3 4
d5 ♗b4+ 5 ♗d2 ♗xd2+ 6 ♕xd2 ♘f6
7 ♘c3 0-0 8 e4 d6= f5 4...♘f6 **5 ♗d3**
♗b4+ 6 ♗d2 ♕e7 7 0-0 ♗xd2!? 8
♘bxd2 ♘f6 9 ♕c2 9 d5!? 0-0 10
♘d4 g6! =+ **♘a6!? 10 a3 0-0 11 e4**
11 b4 c5 12 bxc5 bxc5 13 ♖ab1
♖ab8 14 d5= **fxe4 12 ♘xe4 c5!?**
12...♘h5!? (△ ♖xf3) 13 ♘fd2 ♘f4
14 ♖ae1 ♖f7 15 ♖e3 ♖af8 16 ♖g3=
13 ♘xf6+ 13 d5 gxf6 **14 d5 ♕g7** 14...
exd5 15 cxd5 d6 (15...♘c7 16 d6)
16 ♗f5± **15 ♘h4 f5 16 f4 ♘c7 17**
♖f3 ♔h8 18 ♖h3 ♖f6 19 ♖f1 ♖h6
20 ♗xf5 ♖xh4 21 ♖xh4 exf5 22
♕xf5 ♖g8 23 ♖xh7+ ½-½ 23...♕xh7
24 ♕f6+ ♖g7 25 ♕d8+ = ♘e8? 26
♕xe8+ ♖g8 27 ♕e5+ ♖g7 28 ♖f3
+= **Balogh**

5 Donner-Miles England 78
1 c4 b6 2 e4 ♗b7 3 ♘c3 e6 4 d4
♗b4 5 f3!? ♕h4+!? 6 g3 ♗xc3+ 6...
♕h5 7 ♗d2∞ Ree-Miles, Amsterdam
78 **7 bxc3 ♕h5 8 ♘h3 f5 9 ♘f4 ♕f7**
10 exf5 ♕xf5 11 ♗d3 ♕f7 12 ♗e4?!
12 0-0∞ **♘c6!** 12...♘xe4? 13 fxe4
♘e7 14 0-0± **13 d5 exd5 14 ♘xd5**
14 cxd5 ♘a5∞ **0-0-0 15 ♗e3?!** 15
c5!? ♘f6 16 ♘xc7? ♔xc7 17 ♕d6+

♔c8 18 ♗f4 ♘e8 −+; 15 ♗f4 d6 =+
♘f6 16 ♘xf6 ♕xf6 17 ♗d4 17 ♕d2
♘e5 −+ **♗xd4 18 ♕xd4 ♗xe4** 18...
♕xd4? 19 ♗xb7+ += **19 ♕xf6** 19
♕xe4 ♖de8 −+ gxf6 20 fxe4 ♖de8
−+ **21 0-0 ♖xe4 22 ♖xf6 ♖xc4 23**
♖f3 h5 24 h4 ♖e8 25 ♖af1 ♔b7 26
♖1f2 ♖e5 27 ♔g2 ♖ec5 28 ♖d2 d6
29 ♖d4 ♖xd4 30 cxd4 ♖d5 31 ♖f4
c5 32 dxc5 bxc5 33 g4 hxg4 34 ♔g3
♖d1 35 h5 ♖h1 36 ♔xg4 d5 37
♖f5 ♔c6 38 ♔g3 c4 39 ♔g2 ♖e1 40
h6 ♖e8 41 h7 c3 42 ♖h5 ♖h8 43
♖h1 c2 44 ♖c1 ♖xh7 45 ♖xc2+ ♔b5
46 ♖c3 ♖f7 47 ♔g3 d4 0-1 Miles

6 Csom-Christiansen Hastings 78/9
1 c4 b6 2 ♘c3 e6 3 ♗b7 4 ♗b4
♗b4 5 ♕b3 a5 5...♗xc3 6 ♕xc3 ♗xe4
7 d3 ♗xf3 8 ♕xg7 ♕f6 9 ♗h6 ♗b7 - allows Qf8++
10 ♕xf6 ♘xf6 11 ♗g7 ♖g8 12 ♗xf6;
7...♗b7? 8 ♕xg7 ♕f6 9 ♗h6!; 5...♘a6;
5...c5 **6 a3 ♗xc3 7 ♕xc3 ♘f6 8 d3**
d6 8...a4!? 9 e5 ♘g8 10 ♗e2 **9 b4**
♘c6 10 ♖b1 10 ♗b2? axb4 11 axb4
♖xa1 12 ♗xa1 **axb4 11 axb4 0-0 12**
♗e2 b5!? 13 cxb5 ♘a7 14 b6 ♘b5!?
14...cxb6 15 0-0± **15 bxc7 ♘xc3**
16 cxd8♕ ♖fxd8 17 ♖b3 ♖dc8 18
♗b2 ♘xe2 19 ♔xe2 d5!? 20 e5 ♖c2
20...d4!? 21 exf6 ♗d5 22 ♖a3 ♖c2+
23 ♘d2 ♖xb2 24 ♖xa8+ ♗xa8 25
♖c1 (25 ♖b1) ♗b7 26 ♖c4; 21 ♘xd4
21 ♘d2 21 ♔d1? ♖xb2! ♘d7 22
♘d4 ♖aa2 23 ♖d1 f6 24 f4 ♔f7
24...fxe5 25 fxe5 ♘f8 △ ♘g6-e7-f5
25 ♖bb1! ♘f8 26 g3 ♘g6 27 ♖a1!
♘e7 28 ♖xa2 ♖xa2 29 ♖a1 ♖xa1
30 ♗xa1 ♗a6 31 exf6! gxf6 32 ♘f3
♘c6 33 ♗c3 △ g4-5 **h5 34 ♔e3 ♔e7**
35 h3 f5!? 36 ♗d4 ♗b5 37 ♗c5+ ♔d7
38 ♘g5 △ ♘h7-f6+ **d4+ 39 ♔d2 e5**
40 ♘f3 exf4 41 gxf4 ♔e6 42 ♘g1 △
♘e2-g3; 42 ♘xd4+? ♘xd4 43 ♗xd4=

Game 6. Instead of 9...B6?, 9...Qxg7 10.Bxg7
10...B45 11.Bxh8 f6 △ Kf7

♗a6 43 ♘e2 ♔f7 44 ♘g3 ♔g6 45
♔e2 ♗b5 46 ♘f1 ♔f7 47 ♘g3 ♔g6 48
h4 ♗a4 49 ♘f1 ♔f7 50 ♘d2 ♔e6

51 ♘c4! ♗b5 52 ♘a3! ♗a4 53 b5
♔d5 54 bxc6 ♔xc5 55 c7 ♗d7 56
♘c2 ♗c8 57 ♔d2 +− ♗a6 58 ♘e1
♗c8 59 ♘f3 ♗d7 60 ♔c2 ♗c8 61 ♘g1
♔d6 62 ♘e2 ♔c5 62...♔xc7 63 ♘xd4
♗d7 64 ♘e2 ♗e8 65 ♔c3; 63...♔d6
64 ♘e2 △ ♘g3 +− 63 ♘g3 ♔d6 64
♘xh5 ♔xc7 65 ♘g3 ♔d6 66 ♘e2
♔d5 67 h5 ♗e6 68 ♘g1 ♗g8 69 ♘f3
△ ♘g5, h6-7 ♔e6 70 ♘xd4+ ♔f6 71
♘e2 ♗f7 72 ♘g3 ♔e6 73 ♔c3 ♔d5
74 h6 ♗g6 75 ♘e2 ♔e6 76 ♘d4+ ♔f6
77 ♘f3 1-0 Speelman/Taulbut

7 Vaganian-Pytel
Buenos Aires 78

1 ♘f3 ♘f6 2 c4 c5 3 ♘c3 b6 4 e4
♗b7!? 4...d6∞ 5 e5 ♘g4 6 h3 ♘h6
7 d4 cxd4 8 ♘xd4 e6 9 ♗f4+ a6 10
♘f3 f5 11 g3 ♘f7 12 ♗g2! ♗e7 12...
g5?? 13 ♗xg5!? ♗xg2 14 ♕h5 ♔e7;
13 ♗xg5! ♘xg5 14 ♘xg5 ♗xg2 15
♕h5+ +− 13 0-0 0-0 14 ♖e1 ♘c6
15 h4 h6 16 h5!± ♘g5 17 ♘h4!
♖f7 18 ♘g6 ♗c5 19 ♗e3 ♕c7 20
♗xc5 bxc5 21 f4! ♘d4 22 fxg5

Diagram

22...♗xg2 23 ♔xg2 ♕b7+ 24 ♔f2
f4 25 gxf4 ♖af8 26 ♖e4 ♕xb2+
27 ♘e2 ♖b8 28 gxh6 ♘c2 29 ♖c1
♘b4 30 ♖c3 ♕xa2 31 hxg7 ♔xg7
32 ♖ee3 ♘c6 33 ♖b3 ♖b4 34 ♖g3
♔h6 35 ♖xb4 ♘xb4 36 ♘f8!! +−
△ ♖g6+ ♖xf4+ 37 ♔g1 ♖xf8 38
♖g6+ ♔xh5 39 ♘f4+ ♔h4 40 ♕h5
mate 1-0 Gheorghiu

8 Gheorghiu-Panno
Sao Paulo 79

1 c4 c5 2 ♘f3 ♘f6 3 ♘c3 b6!? 4 e4!
♗b7 4...d6 5 e5 ♘g4 5...♘g8 6 d4
♗xf3 7 ♕xf3 ♘c6∞; 5...♘e4?? 6 ♘e2!
△ 7 d3 +− 6 h3 ♘h6 7 d4! cxd4 8
♘xd4 g6!? 9 ♗f4! ♘c6 9...♗g7? 10
♕d2 10 ♘f3! ♘f5 11 ♕d2 11 g4?
♘cd4! ♖c8 12 ♗e2 ♗g7 13 ♖d1!±
♘a5 14 b3 ♗xf3 15 ♗xf3 ♘c6 16
♗xc6! dxc6 17 ♕e2! 17 ♕c1 ♕c7 18
e6 ♗e5!∞ ♕c7 18 0-0 0-0?! 18...h5!±
19 g4! ♘h4 20 ♘g3! g5 20...♗xe5?!
21 ♗xe5! ♕xe5 22 ♕xe5 ♘f3+ 23
♔g2 ♘xe5 f4! +−

Diagram

21 e6! ♗e5 22 ♖d7 +− ♗xg3!?
22...♕b8 23 ♘e4! +− 23 ♖xc7
♗xc7 24 exf7+ ♔f7 24...♖xf7 25
♕e6! △ ♘e4 +− 25 ♘e4! h6 25...
♔g6 26 ♘xg5! ♔xg5 27 ♕xe7+
♖f6 28 f4+! +− 26 c5! b5 27 ♘g3!

+− ♗e5 28 ♘f5! ♘xf5 29 ♕xe5 ♘h4
30 f4! +− ♔e8 31 ♕e6! 31 fxg5
♘f3+ 32 ♖xf3 Δ gxh6 +− **1-0**
Gheorghiu

9 Olafsson-Gheorghiu
Buenos Aires 78
**1 ♘f3 c5 2 c4 ♘f6 3 ♘c3 b6 4 e4
d6** 4...♗b7 5 e5 ♘e4? 6 ♘e2 Δ d3
+− **5 d4 cxd4 6 ♘xd4 ♗b7 7 ♗d3 e6
8 0-0 ♗e7 9 b3 0-0 10 ♗b2 ♘c6!=
11 ♘xc6 ♗xc6 12 ♗c2 a6 13 ♕d3!**
g6 13...b5 14 ♘d5!± **14 ♖fe1 ♖e8
15 ♖e2 ♗f8 16 ♖d1 ♕c7** 16...b5?!
17 cxb5 axb5 18 ♘xb5 ♖xa2 19
♗b1 Δ ♘xd6±; 18...♗a6 19 a4± **17
a4! ♗d7!** 18 ♕g3 a5 19 h4 ♘c5 20 h5
e5!= **21 ♗c1 ♖ad8 22 ♘d5 ♗xd5
23 cxd5** 23 ♖xd5∞ ♗g7 23...♗e7!∞
24 ♕h4 ½-½ Gheorghiu

✔10 Andersson-Segal
Sao Paulo 79
**1 ♘f3 ♘f6 2 c4 b6 3 g3 ♗b7 4 ♗g2
c5 5 0-0 e6 6 ♘c3 ♗e7 7 d4 cxd4
8 ♕xd4** 8 ♘xd4 ♗xg2 9 ♔xg2 ♕c8!=
d6 **9 b3 0-0?!** 9...♘bd7! **10 ♗a3**
♘c5= **10 ♖d1 a6** 10...♘a6 11 ♘b5
♕b8!∞ **11 ♗a3!± ♘c6 12 ♕f4 d5
13 cxd5 exd5** 13...♗xa3 14 dxc6 +−
**14 ♗xe7 ♕xe7 15 ♘h4! ♖ad8 16
♘f5 ♕e6 17 ♖ac1 g6 18 ♘d4 ♘xd4
19 ♕xd4 ♖c8 20 ♘a4! ♖xc1 21 ♖xc1**

♘d7 **22 e3!± b5 23 ♘c5 ♘xc5 24
♖xc5 ♖c8 25 ♖xc8+** 25 ♗xd5??
♖xc5! **26** ♗xe6 ♖c1 mate **♕xc8
26 ♗xd5 ♗xd5 27 ♕xd5 ♕c1+** 27...
♕c2!± **28 ♔g2 ♕a3 29 ♕d8+ ♔g7
30 ♕d2! +− a5?** 31 g4 h6 32 ♔f3
♔g8 33 ♔e2 ♔g7 34 f3 ♔g8 35 f4
♔g7 36 ♔f3 ♔g8 37 f5! gxf5 38 gxf5
♔g7 39 ♕d4+! f6 40 ♕d7+ ♔g8
41 ♕e8+! **1-0** 41...♔g7 42 ♕g6+
Gheorghiu

11 Rukavina-Saladen
Monaco 78
**1 ♘f3 ♘f6 2 c4 c5 3 ♘c3 d5 4 cxd5
♘xd5 5 ♕a4+!? ♘c6?!** 5...♗d7 6
♕b3 Δ ♘e5 **6 ♘e5 ♗d7?!** 6...♘b6
7 ♕b5!; 6...♘xc3! 7 bxc3 ♗d7 8
♘xd7 ♕xd7 **7 ♘xf7! ♘d4** 7...♘xc3
8 ♕c4? ♘a5 9 ♕f4 ♘d5 10 ♕f3 ♕b6!
11 ♘xh8 ♘f6∓; 8 ♕f4! ♘d5 (8...e5
9 ♘xe5!±) 9 ♕f3 ♘d4 10 ♘xd5 ♕a5
11 ♘xh8±; 7...♔xf7 8 ♘xd5 ♘d4
9 ♕d1 ♗f5 10 ♘e3 += **8 ♕d1 ♗b4!?
9 ♘xd8 ♘dc2+ 10 ♕xc2 ♘xc2+
11 ♔d1 ♘xa1 12 ♘xb7± e5** Δ a5∓
**13 ♘a5 ♗d6 14 b3 ♗c7 15 ♘c4 a5!?
16 ♘d5!** 16 ♗b2?! a4! 17 ♗xa1 axb3∞
♗d8 **17 ♘db6 ♗xb6 18 ♘xb6 ♖b8
19 ♘xd7 ♔xd7 20 ♗b2 +−** a4 20...
♘xb3 21 axb3 ♖xb3 22 ♔c2 Δ e3
+− **21 ♗xa1 axb3 22 axb3 ♖xb3
23 ♗xe5 ♖a8 24 e3 ♖a2 25 ♗c4!
♖b1+ 26 ♔e2 ♖xd2+ 27 ♔xd2 ♖xh1
28 ♗xg7 ♖xh2 29 ♗d5 ♔d6 30 ♗e4
c4 31 ♔c3 ♔c5 32 f4 ♖h1 33 ♗d4+
♔b5 34 g4 ♖c1+** Zeitnot **35 ♔d2
♖g1 36 ♔c3 ♖xg4 37 ♗xh7 ♖g1 38
♗c2 ♖a1 39 f5 ♖a3+ 40 ♔b2 ♖a8
41 f6 ♖c8 42 f7 ♔b4 43 ♗g7 c3+
44 ♔c1 1-0 Maric**

12 Christiansen-Botterill
Hastings 78-9

1 c4 ♘f6 2 ♘c3 c5 3 ♘f3 d5 4 cxd5 ♘xd5 5 d4 g6!? 5...♘xc3 6 bxc3 g6 **6 ♗d2** 6 dxc5 ♘xc3 7 ♕xd8+ ♔xd8 8 bxc3 += **cxd4 7 ♘xd4 ♗g7** 7... ♘b6 8 ♗g5! **8 e4 ♘b6** 8...♘xc3 9 ♗xc3 ♘c6 10 ♘xc6 ♗xc3+ 11 bxc3 ♕xd1+ 12 ♖xd1 bxc6 13 ♗c4=/+=; 8...♘b4 9 ♕a4+ ♘8c6 10 ♘xc6 ♘xc6 11 ♗e3 += **9 ♗e3 0-0 10 ♗e2 ♘c6 11 ♘xc6 bxc6 12 0-0 ♗e6 13 ♕c2 ♕c8** 13...♘c4 14 ♗xc4 ♗xc4 15 ♖fd1 ♕a5 16 ♘a4± **14 ♖fd1 c5 15 ♖ac1 += ♕b7!? 16 ♗xc5 ♖fc8 17 ♗e3!?** 17 b4 a5!; 17 ♗d4 ♗h6 18 ♖a1 ♘c4 19 ♗xc4 ♖xc4 += **♗xa2 18 b3 ♖xc3 19 ♕xa2 ♖xc1 20 ♖xc1 ♖c8?** 20... ♖d8 += **21 ♖xc8+ ♘xc8 22 ♕a4! ♔f8 23 ♗a6 ♕c7**

24 ♕c4!? 24 ♗xc8 ♕xc8 25 ♕xa7 f5± **♕xc4 25 bxc4 ♘b6 26 c5 ♘a8 27 c6 ♘c7 28 ♗c4 a6 29 f4 ♔e8** Δ 30 ♗b6 ♘a8 31 ♗a5 ♗d4+ **30 ♔f2 e6 31 e5 ♗f8 32 ♔e2 ♗b4 33 ♔d3 ♔d8 34 ♘b6 ♔c8 35 ♔c2 a5** 35...h5= **36 ♔b3 ♗d2 37 g3 ♗b4 38 ♔a4 ♗e1 39 ♗xa5 ♗xa5! 40 ♔xa5 ♘a8 41 ♔b5 ♔c7 42 ♔c5 ♘b6 43 ♗b3 ♘c8 44 ♗c2?!** 44 ♗d2 Δ ♗f3! **♘e7** 44...h5 45 f5 gxf5 46 ♗d1 ♘e7 47 ♗xh5 ♘xc6 48 ♗xf7 ♘xe5 49 ♗xe6 f4!= **45 g4?!**

♔g8? 45...♘xc6 46 ♗a4 ♘e7 47 ♗e8 ♘d5 48 f5 ♘e3 49 ♗xf7 exf5=; 45...♔d5! 46 f5 ♘e3 47 fxe6 fxe6 48 ♗b3 ♘xg4= **46 ♗e4 ♘e7 47 h3 ♘g8 48 h4 ♘e7** 48...♘h6= 49 ♗f3 ♘g8 **49 ♗f3 ♘g8 50 h5** Δ ♗e4, f5 **♘e7?** 50...♘h6= **51 ♗e4 gxh5 52 gxh5 h6 53 ♔b5 ♘c8 54 ♔c5 ♘e7 55 ♗g2 ♘f5 56 ♗f3 ♘e7?** 56...♘g3 57 ♗g4 ♘e4+ 58 ♔d4 ♘g3= **57 ♗e4 +− ♘g8 58 f5 exf5** 58...f6 59 fxe6 fxe6 60 ♔d5 +− **59 ♗xf5 ♘e7** 59...f6!? 60 ♗e6 ♘e7 61 exf6 ♘xc6 62 f7 ♘d8 63 f8♘! +− **60 ♗e4 ♘c8 61 ♗f3 ♘b6 61**...♘e7 62 ♗d5 **62 ♗d1 ♘c8 63 ♗b3 ♘b6 64 ♗xf7 ♘a4+ 65 ♔d4 ♘b6 66 ♗e8 ♘c8 67 ♗d7 ♘b6 68 ♔e4 ♔d8 69 ♔f5 ♔e7 70 ♗e6 1-0 Botterill**

13 Ivanov-Kapengut
Ashkhabad 78

1 ♘f3 ♘f6 2 c4 c5 3 ♘c3 d5 4 cxd5 ♘xd5 5 e3 ♘xc3 6 bxc3 g6 7 d4 ♗g7 8 ♗d3 0-0 9 0-0 ♕c7?! 9...♕a5?= 10 ♗b2 ♘c6 11 ♘d2 ♕c7 12 ♘b3 b6 13 ♕e2 ♖d8 14 ♗e4 ♖b8 15 ♖fd1 cxd4 16 cxd4 ♘b4 17 ♗a3 a5 18 ♗xb4 axb4 19 ♖ac1± Juferov-Tseitlin, Daugavpils 78; 9...♘c6 10 ♗a3 b6 11 dxc5 ♕c7 12 ♗e4 ♗b7 13 ♕c2 ♘a5 14 ♖ab1 ♖fe8 15 c4 ♖ab8 16 ♖fc1 bxc5 17 ♘g5 e6 18 ♗xb7 ♘xb7 19 ♘e4 f5 20 ♘c3 ♘d6= Tal-Miles, Bugojno 78 **10 ♕e2** 10 ♗a3 ♘d7 11 e4 e5 12 ♗b5 a6 13 ♗xd7 ♗xd7 14 ♗xc5 ♖fe8 15 ♘xe5 ♗b5 16 c4 ♗xe5 17 dxe5 ♕xc5 18 cxb5 axb5 ½-½ Spassky-Karpov, Moscow 73; 11 ♕e2 b6 12 e4 ♗b7 13 ♖fd1 ♖fd8 14 ♖ac1 ♖ac8 15 ♕e3 ♘f6 16 ♗b2 e6 17 h3 ♕c6 18 ♘d2 ♕a4 19 a3 ♗a6 Portisch-Tal, Milan 75; 11 ♗b5 b6 12 e4 a6 13 ♗d3 b5 14 ♗b2 ♘b6 15 h3 ♗e6

16 Ng5 Nc4 17 Nxe6 fxe6 18 Qe2 cxd4 19 cxd4 Nxb2 20 Qxb2 **Qd6∓** Osnos-Zilberstein, Tbilisi 73; 10...b6! 11 dxc5 Bb7! 12 cxb6 axb6 13 Bb2 Nd7 14 Nd4 e5 15 Nb3 e4 16 Bb5 Ne5 17 Nd4 Rfd8 18 Qe2 Rd5 19 Rfc1 Nf3+! 20 gxf3 Rg5+ 21 Kf1 Qxh2 22 Ke1 exf3∓ Furman-Timoshenko, Moscow 77 **Nc6 11 Rb1 Rd8 12 Be4 e5 13 d5!?** N 13 dxc5 h6 14 c4 Be6 15 Ba3 Na5 16 Bb4 Nxc4 17 Rfc1 f5 18 Bc2 e4 19 Bb3 exf3 20 gxf3 Ne5 21 Bxe6+ Kh7 22 Bc3 Nd3 23 Rc2 Qc6 24 Rd1 Nxf2 25 Kxf2 Qxe6= Tal-Vaganian, Leningrad 77 **Ne7 14 c4 f5 15 Bc2 e4!? 16 Nd2 Bd7** 16...b5!? 17 Rxb5 Ba6 Δ Nxd5; 17 cxb5 Nxd5 18 Bb3 Kh8 19 Bxd5= **17 f3! exf3 18 Nxf3?!** 18 Qxf3!? b6 19 Qf4 Be5 20 Qh4 Qd6 21 Nf3 Qf6 **Rf8 19 Rd1 Nc8 20 d6!? Qc6 21 e4?** 21 Bb2 Bxb2 22 Rxb2 Nxd6 23 Ne5 Qc7 24 Qd3 Rf6 25 Qd5+ Kh8! **Nxd6! 22 Qd3 fxe4 23 Qxd6 exf3 24 Qxd7 Bd4+ 25 Rxd4 f2+ 26 Kf1 Qxg2+! 27 Kxg2 f1Q+ 28 Kg3 Qg1+?!** 28...Rf3+ 29 Kh4 Qf2+ 30 Kg5 cxd4 31 Qd5+ Rf7 32 Rxb7 Qg2+ 33 Kh4 Qxh2+ 34 Kg4 Qh5+ −+ **29 Kh4 Qxh2+ 30 Kg4!** 30 Kh3 Qf2+ 31 Kg3 Qxc2 −+ **Qg2+ 31 Kh4 Qf2+ 32 Kg4 h5+ 33 Kg5 Qf6+ 34 Kh6 Rf7 35 Rxb7! Qg7+ 36 Kg5 ½-½ Kapengut**

14 Miles-Schmidt
Buenos Aires 78
1 c4 c5 2 Nf3 Nf6 3 Nc3 d5 4 cxd5 Nxd5 5 e4 Nb4 6 Bb5+ 6 Bc4 Be6 7 Bxe6 Nd3+ 8 Kf1 fxe6 9 Ng5∞ Nc6 10 Nxe6 Qd7 11 Nd5 Rc8 12 Qb3 Nce5 13 Qb5 Qxb5 14 Nec7+ Kf7 15 Nxb5 e6 16 Ne3 a6 17 Na3

c4 18 Nac2 g5 19 Ne1 Bg7 20 Rb1 Rhd8∞ Ornstein-Schmidt, Malmo 76 **N8c6 7 d4!?** 7 a3?! Nd3+ 8 Ke2 Nf4+ 9 Kf1 Ne6∓ Poutianen-Tal, Tallinn 77; 7 0-0 a6 8 Ba4 b5 9 a3 Nd3 10 Nxb5 axb5 11 Bxb5 Qd6 12 Qb3 Ba6! 13 Qa4 Bxb5 14 Qxa8+ Nd8 15 b4 Nc6 16 bxc5 Qg6∓ Tukmakov-Tal, Leningrad 77 **cxd4 8 a3!? dxc3 9 Qxd8+ Kxd8 10 axb4 cxb2!?** 10...Bd7 11 bxc3 g6 12 0-0 Bg7 13 Ra3 Rc8 14 Rd1 a6 15 Be2 Ke8 16 b5 axb5 17 Bxb5 f6 18 Be3 e5 19 Nd2 Bf8 20 Raa1± Stean-Browne, Buenos Aires 78 **11 Bxb2 e5! 12 0-0-0+ Kc7 13 Bxc6 bxc6 14 Bxe5+ Kb7 15 Bc3** 15 Nd6 Bg4!? **Be7!= 16 Ne5** 16 Kb2 Re8 17 Rhe1 g6 18 Nd4 c5 19 bxc5 Bxc5 20 f3 Rb8 21 Kc2 Bd7 22 Ra1 Rbc8 ½-½ Lein-Schmidt, Buenos Aires 78 **f6** 16...Be6? 17 Nxf7! **17 Nf7 Re8 18 e5 fxe5 19 Rhe1 Bf8!?** 19...Rf8? 20 Rxe5 Rxf2 21 Nf3± **20 Nd8+** 20 Nxe5 c5 **Kb6 21 Bxe5 Qb5 Bc3 Rxe1 23 Rxe1 Bd7** 23...Bxb4 **24 Ne6 Bxe6 25 Rxe6 c5 26 bxc5 Rc8 27 Qd2 Bxc5 28 f4 ½-½ Schmidt**

Extremely vigorous early attack

15 Riemsdyk-Ljubojevic
Sao Paulo 79
1 c4 Nf6 2 Nc3 c5 3 Nf3 d5 4 cxd5 Nxd5 5 g3 Nc6 6 Bg2 Nc7 7 d3 e5 8 Nd2 8 0-0 Be7 9 Be3∞ **Bd7 9 0-0 h5!?** Δ h4∞ **10 Nc4 h4 11 Ne4 Be6! 12 Be3** 12 Ng5 f6!∓; 12 Ng5 Bd5!∓ **Bd5 13 Qd2 f5!∓ 14 Bg5 Qd7 15 Nc3 Bxg2 16 Kxg2 b5! 17 Ne3 b4 18 Ncd1 hxg3 19 fxg3 f4! 20 gxf4 Qh3+ 21 Kf2 Qxh2+ 22 Ng2 Rh3 23 Nde3 Qg3+ 24 Kg1 Nd4 25 Nc4 Nce6 26 Qd1 Qh2+ 27 Kf2 exf4** Δ Qg3+, Rh2 **0-1 Gheorghiu**

16 Djindjihashvili-Browne
Buenos Aires 2 78

1 c4 Nf6 2 Nc3 c5 3 g3 d5 4 cxd5
Nxd5 5 Bg2 Nxc3 5...e6 6 bxc3 g6
7 Rb1 Qc7 7...Nd7?! 8 Bxb7 Bxb7
9 Rxb7 Nb6 10 Qb3 Qc8 11 Qb5+
Kd8 12 Qa6 += 8 Qa4+!? Nd7 8...
Bd7? 9 Qb3! Na6?! 9 Nf3 Bg7 10
0-0 0-0 11 d4 11 Kh4!? Nb6 12 Qa5
cxd4! 12...Bf5 13 Rb5 cxd4 14
cxd4 Be4 15 Bf4 += 13 cxd4 Be6!
14 Ba3 14 Bf4 Qc2! Qd7 14...Bxa2?
15 Bxe7 Bxb1 16 Bxf8 += 15 Bc5
Nd5! 16 Qd2 16 Qb5? Qxb5 17 Rxb5
Nc3 18 Rb2 Na4 =+ b6 17 Ba3 Rac8
18 Rbc1 18 Rb3 Nc7! 19 Rd3 Bc4!
20 Rc3 Nb5 21 Rxc8 Rxc8 22 Bb4
Nxd4 -+ Qa4! 19 Qb2 19 Bb2 Qxa2
20 Ra1 Qb3 -+ Bh6! 20 Rxc8 20
e3 Nxe3 21 fxe3 Bxe3+ 22 Kh1 Bxc1
23 Rxc1 Rxc1+ 24 Qxc1 Rc8 25
Qb2 Rc2 -+ Rxc8 21 e4! Nc3! 21...
Rc2? 22 Qb3 Qxb3 23 axb3 Nc3
24 d5! 22 d5 Bg4 23 Ne5 23 Bxe7?
Qxe4 -+; 23 h3 Bxf3 24 Bxf4 Nxe4
25 Bxe7 Nd2 -+ Bc1! 23...Ne2+
24 Kh1 Bg7 25 f4

24 Qb3 Qxb3! 25 axb3 Bxa3 26
Nxg4 Ne2+ 27 Kh1 Nd4∓ 28 Ne5
Bxb3! 29 Nc6 a5 30 e5 Rc7 31
Rd1 a4?! 31...Bc5 32 Bf1 e6! -+;
32 f4 b5 33 Bf1 Rb7 34 Nd8 Rb6

-+ 32 Bf1 Bb2 32...Bc5 33 Bb5 a3
34 Bc4 Na5∓ 33 Bb5 a3 34 d6 exd6
35 exd6 Rxc6? 35...Rb7 36 d7??
Rxd7 37 Rxd7 a2 -+; 36 Bc4! Nc5∓
36 Bxc6 a2 37 d7 Bf6 38 d8Q+ Bxd8
39 Rxd8+ Kg7 40 Ra8?? Na5 0-1
40 Rd1 a1Q 41 Rxa1 Na1 42 Ba4=
Browne

17 Filguth-Ljubojevic
Sao Paulo 79

1 c4 Nf6 2 Nc3 c5 3 e4 e6 4 e5
Ng8 5 d4 cxd4 6 Qxd4 Nc6 7 Qe4
b6 8 Nf3 Bb7∞ 9 h4?! 9 Be2 △
0-0 Rc8 10 Nb5 a6 11 Bg5 f6 12
Nd6+ Bxd6 13 exd6 Na5! 13...fxg5
14 Nxg5?! Nf6 14 Qg4 Bxf3 15 gxf3
fxg5 16 hxg5

16...Rc5! -+ 17 Rg1 b5! 18 b3 bxc4
19 bxc4 Qb6 20 Bd3 Qxd6 21 Rd1
Qe5+ 22 Kf1 Ne7 23 f4 Qc7 24 Re1
g6 0-1 Gheorghiu

18 Schmidt-Portisch
Buenos Aires 78

1 Nf3 c5 2 c4 Nf6 3 Nc3 e6 4 g3
Nc6 5 Bg2 d5 6 cxd5 Nxd5 7 0-0
Be7 8 d4 0-0 9 e4 9 Nxd5 exd5 10
dxc5 Bxc5 11 Bg5 f6 12 Rc1 Bb6
Ndb4!? 9...Nxc3 10 bxc3 Bf6 11
Be3 Qa5 ½-½ Torre-Bukic, Vrsac 77
10 d5 10 a3 cxd4 11 axb4 dxc3

12 bxc3 += b6 13 ♕e2 ♗b7 14 ♗f4
♕c8 15 ♘d2 e5 16 ♗e3 ♖d8 17 ♖fc1
h6 18 ♗f1 ♕c7 19 f3 ♘g5 20 ♘c4
♗xe3+ 21 ♕xe3 ½-½ Filip-Pachman,
Moscow 67 **exd5 11 exd5 ♘d4 12
♘xd4 cxd4 13 a3** 13 ♕xd4? ♘c2;
13 ♘b5 **dxc3 14 axb4 ♗xb4** 14...
cxb2 15 ♗xb2 ♗xb4?? 16 ♕d4; 15...
♕b6 16 ♕d4 **15 ♕d4 ♗d6 16 ♕xc3**
16 ♖xa7? ♗e5! a5!∞ **17 ♗e3 ♗d7 18
♗d4 f6 19 ♕d3 b5 20 ♖ac1 ♖c8 21
♖fe1 a4 22 ♗e4 f5 23 ♗f3 ♖xc1 24
♖xc1 ♕b8 25 ♕d2 h6 26 b4!? ♖c8**
26...axb3 27 ♕b2

27 ♖xc8+?! 27 ♗c5!?∞ **♕xc8 28 ♕b2**
♕f8 29 ♗c3 f4!∓ **30 ♗e4 ♘h3! 31 ♕d2
♗f5 32 ♗xf5** 32 ♕d3 ♕xf5 **33 ♕d4
♕g6! 34 ♔g2** 34 ♔f1 f3∓ **h5 35 ♗d2??**
35 ♔f1 f3∓ **f3+ -+ 36 ♔xf3 ♕f6+
37 ♔e4 a3 38 ♕a7 ♕e5+ 39 ♔d3
♕xd5+ 40 ♔e3 ♕b3+ 41 ♔e2 a2 42
♕a8+ ♔f7 0-1 Schmidt**

19 Guil.Garcia-Miles
Wijk aan Zee 79
**1 ♘f3 ♘f6 2 c4 c5 3 d4 cxd4 4 ♘xd4
a6!? 5 ♘c3 e6 6 ♗g5** 6 e4; 6 g3 ♕c7∞
h6 7 ♗h4 ♗b4 8 f3 8 ♖c1 g5 9 ♗g3
♘e4∞; 8 ♕b3!? **♘c6** 8...♗xc3+ 9
bxc3 d6∞ **9 ♖c1** 9 e4 **d5! 10 cxd5
exd5 11 a3** 11 ♕a4!? ♗e7!? 12 ♘xc6
bxc6 13 ♗xf6 ♗xf6 14 ♕xc6+ ♗d7

15 ♕xd5 0-0∞ **♗e7 12 e3 0-0 13 ♗e2
♖e8 14 0-0 ♗c5** 14...♘e5 △ ♘c4 **15
♗xf6?** 15 ♗f2 =+ **♕xf6 16 ♘xd5 ♕d6
17 ♘b3** 17 ♘c7 ♖xe3 18 ♖xc5 ♕xc5
19 ♘xa8 ♘xd4 -+; 17 ♘xc6 bxc6 18
♕c2 ♗a7 19 ♕xc6 ♕xc6 20 ♖xc6
♗b7 21 ♖d6 ♗xd5 22 ♖xd5 ♖xe3 -+
♗a7 18 ♔h1 ♖d8 18...♗e6?? 19
♘f6+ +- **19 e4 ♗e6 20 ♗c4 b5** 20...
♘e5 21 ♘a5∞; 20...♖c8 21 ♘d2∞
21 ♗e2 21 ♗d3!? **♖ac8?** 21...♘e7!∓
22 ♖c3!∞ ♗xd5 23 exd5 23 ♕xd5
♕g6 =+ **♘e7** 23...♕xd5? 24 ♕xd5
♖xd5 25 ♖fc1 +- **24 ♖d3 ♕e5** 24...
♖c4?! (△ ♕xh2+ 26 ♔xh2 ♖h4+ 27
♔g3 ♘f5 mate) 25 g3; 24...♕xd5?
25 f4 △ ♗f3; 24...♕g6!? **25 f4** 25
d6 ♘f5 26 d7?? ♕g3+ 27 hxg3 ♕h5
mate **♕xb2 26 d6 ♘f5 27 ♗g4 ♕f6
28 d7 ♖c4 29 ♗xf5 ♕xf5 30 ♖d5
♕f6∞ ½-½** Zeitnot **Miles**

20 Gheorghiu-Lein
Sao Paulo 79
**1 c4 c5 2 ♘f3 ♘f6 3 d4 cxd4 4 ♘xd4
a6!= 5 ♘c3 e6** 5...d5!∞ **6 e4 d6** 6...
♗b4 7 ♗d3± **7 ♗d3 ♗d7!?** N **8 f4!**
♘c6 9 ♘f3 △ e5± **e5 10 f5! ♗e7 11
0-0 ♖c8 12 ♔h1 0-0 13 ♗e3 ♘b4
14 ♗e2 a5!** 14...b5? 15 a3!± **15
♘d2 ♗c6 16 a3 ♘a6 17 ♗d3 ♘d7 18
♖b1!** △ b4± **b6 19 b4 axb4 20 axb4
♘c7 21 ♘d5! ♖b8** 21...♗xd5 22 cxd5±
22 ♖c1 22 ♖a1 △ ♖a7± **♘e8 23
♘xe7+ ♕xe7 24 ♘b1** △ ♘c3-d5±
**♘c7 25 ♘c3 ♖fc8 26 ♕e2 ♕d8 27
♖fd1 ♖a8 28 ♕f2! ♘e8 29 h3 ♖a3
30 ♕b2! ♖ca8 31 ♖a1 ♖xa1 32
♖xa1 g6 33 fxg6 hxg6 34 ♖f1!±
♕h4?!** Zeitnot **35 ♕d2! ♖a3 36
♗g5 ♕h5** 36...♕g3? 37 ♖f3 ♖a1+
38 ♘d1 +- **37 ♗e2 ♕h7 38 ♔g1
♖xc3?! 39 ♕xc3 ♗xe4 40 c5! +-
bxc5 41 ♗b5! f6**

42 bxc5!?± 42 Qb3+! Kh8 43 Qa4!
+− fxg5 43 cxd6 Nxd6 44 Qb3+!
Kh8 45 Bxd7 Qe7!! 45...Qxd7 46
Rf8+ Kg7 47 Qg8+ Kh6 48 Qh8+
Kh7 49 Qf6! +− **46 Qe6!?** 46 Rd1±
Lein Qxe6 47 Bxe6 Kg7 48 g4! +−
Bd3 49 Rd1 e4 50 Kf2 Kf6 51 Bb3
Nb5 52 Ke3 Nd6 52...Nc3! 53 Rd2!
+− **53 Rc1!** +− Bb5 54 Rc7 Be8
55 Bd5 Bb5 56 Bxe4 Nxe4 57 Kxe4
Bf1 58 Rc6+ **1-0** 58...Ke7 59 Rc1!
Bg2+ 60 Ke5 Bxh3 61 Rg1! +− Δ
Ke4-f3-g3 **Gheorghiu**

21 Suba-Mourier
Buenos Aires 78

**1 c4 Nf6 2 Nc3 c5 3 Nf3 Nc6 4 d4
cxd4 5 Nxd4 e6 6 Ndb5 Bb4** 6...
d5!?; 6...d6 7 Bf4 e5 8 Bg5 a6 9
Bxf6 gxf6 10 Na3∝ **7 Bf4 0-0 8
Bd6!** += 8 Bc7 Qe7 9 Bd6 Bxd6 10
Qxd6 Rd8 11 0-0-0 Ne8= Ungureanu-
Suba, Bucharest 75 **Bxd6 9 Nxd6
Ne8 10 e3 b6 11 Be2 Nxd6 12 Qxd6
Bb7 13 0-0 Qe7 14 Rad1 Rfd8 15
f4! Qxd6 16 Rxd6 Kf8 17 Rfd1 Ke7**
17...Ke8 18 c5! bxc5? 19 Na4±
18 a3 18 c5 bxc5 19 Na4; 18...Nb4!
19 cxb6 Nd5∝ **Rb8 19 b4 Ba8 20
Na4 Re8 21 c5 b5 22 Nc3 a6 23
Kf2 Bb7 24 Bf3 Rbc8 25 h4 Rc7 26
h5 Ra8 27 h6 gxh6 28 Rh1 Kf8 29
Rxh6 Kg7 30 Rh1 Ne7 31 Rhd1**

Bxf3 32 Qxf3 Raa7 33 g4 Ng6 34
R6d3 Rcb7 35 Ne4 f6 36 Rd6 Δ c6
f5 37 gxf5 Nh4+ 38 Kf2 Nxf5 39
R6d3 h6 Zeitnot **40 c6!** +− dxc6
41 Nc5 Re7 42 e4 Nh4 43 Rg3+ Kh7
43...Kf6/f8/h8 44 Rh1; 43...Kf7 44
Rdg1 a5 45 Ke3 axb4 46 Rg7+ Kf8
47 Rg8+ Kf7 48 R1g7+ Kf6 49
e5+ Kf5 50 Rg5+ hxg5 51 Rxg5 mate
**44 Rd6! Ng6 45 Nxe6 Rf7 46 f5
Ne5 47 Rd8 h5** 47...a5 48 Rgg8 Δ
Rh8 mate **48 Ng5+ Kg7 49 Nxf7+
Kxf7 50 Rh8 1-0 Suba**

22 Suba-Bertok Athens 78

1 c4 Nf6 2 Nc3 c5 3 Nf3 Nc6 4 d4
4 g3 d5!? 5 cxd5 Nxd5 6 Bg2 g6
7 d3!? N Bg7 8 Bd2 0-0 9 Qc1 Nc6
10 Bh6 e5 11 h4 += Uhlmann-Alburt,
Bucharest 78 **cxd4 5 Nxd4 e6 6
Ndb5 Bc5** N **7 Bf4 e5 8 Be3!?** 8
Bg3 Qb6 =+ Ungureanu-Rogulj,
Athens 78; 8 Bg5 Bxf2+?! 9 Kxf2
Ng4+ 10 Ke1 Qxg5 11 Nc7+ Kd8
12 Nxa8± 8...Qb6 9 e3 a6 10 Bxf6
axb5 11 Bxg7 Rg8 12 Bf6 bxc4∝
**Bxe3 9 Nd6+ Kf8 10 fxe3 g6 11
g3 Kg7 12 Bg2 Ne8 13 0-0 Nxd6
14 Qxd6 Qe7 15 Rad1!± Bf8 16
Ne4 Qe6?** 17 Nc5 Qxd6 17...Qxc4
18 Bd5 Qxe2 19 Qf6+ Kh6 +− [20
Rae1 Δ Ne4!] **18 Rxd6 f5 19
Nxd7 Rd8 20 Bxc6 bxc6 21 Rfd1
+−** Bxd7 **22 Rxd7+ Rxd7 23 Rxd7+
Kh6 24 Rc7? Rd8 25 Kf2! Rd2 26
b4! Rxa2 27 Rxc6** Δ b5, e4, Ke3 +−
a5 **28 b5 a4?** 28...Rb2 29 e4!± **29
Ra6 a3 30 c5 Rb2 31 b6 a2 32 Rxa2!
1-0 Suba**

23 Rogers-Masculo
Buenos Aires 78

**1 c4 c5 2 Nc3 g6 3 Nf3 Bg7 4 d4
cxd4 5 Nxd4 Nc6 6 Nc2 Nf6 7 g3**

d6 8 Bg2 Be6 9 Ne3 0-0 9...Qd7!
10 0-0 Bh3 +=/= **10 0-0 Qd7 11 Re1!**
Bh3 12 Bh1 Nfc8 13 Bd2 Rab8 14
Rac1 Ne5 14...Nd4 15 a4! Kochiev-
West, Mexico 78; 14...e6! **15 b3 Neg4**
16 Nxg4 Bxg4 17 Be3 b6 18 Qd2
h5?! 19 Bd4 Qe8 Δ Bd7, b5 **20 a4**
Be6?! Δ Nd7-c5; 20...Bd7 **21 e4 Nd7**
22 Bxg7 Kxg7 23 f4 f6

24 Nb5! Nc5 24...a6 25 Nd4 Bf7
26 e5 Δ Nc6 **25 Nd4 a5 26 e5 dxe5**
27 fxe5 f5 27...Rd8 28 Bd5! Rxd5
29 exf6+! **28 Ncd1 Rc7 29 Bd5 Qf7**
30 Qe3 Bxd5?! 30...Rd7 31 Bxe6
Nxe6 32 Nxf5+ **31 cxd5 Kh7?! 32**
Nf3 Ne4 33 Qf4! Δ Rxe4/e6!; 33
Qxe4 Qe8 **34 Rxe4 fxe4 35 Ng5+**
Kg8 36 e6 Rbc8 37 Rf1! Δ Qf7+;
37 Nf7? Qf8 **Kh8? 38 Nf7+ Kg8**
39 Qh6 1-0 Rogers

24 Schmidt-Haik
Buenos Aires 78

1 Nf3 g6 2 c4 Bg7 3 d4 Nf6 4 g3
0-0 5 Bg2 c5 6 Nc3 cxd4 7 Nxd4
Qc7!? N 8 Qd3 8 b3? d5! **Nc6 9**
Ndb5 Qa5 10 Bd2 a6 11 Nd5 Qd8
12 Na3 b5 12...Nxd5 13 cxd5 Bxb2
14 dxc6 15 Qxd8 Rxd8 16 Nc2
Bxa1 17 Nxa1 Be6∞; 14 Rb1!? **13**
Bc3 Rb8? 13...Nxd5 14 cxd5 Bxc3+
15 Qxc3 b4∞ **14 Nxf6+ exf6 15**

cxb5 axb5 16 Nxb5± Ba6?! 16...Ne5
17 Bxe5 fxe5 18 0-0± **17 a4 Ne5**
18 Qc2 Qb6 19 0-0 Rfc8 20 Rfd1
Ng4?! 20...Bxb5 21 e3 **21 Nd4!?**
f5 22 e3 Bb7 23 Qe2 Bxb5 **22 axb5**
f5 **23 h3 Ne5 24 Rd5 Nc4 25 Ra6**
Qd8 26 Ra7 Nb6 27 Rd3 Rc5 28
Qb3 Rbc8? 28...Rxc3 29 Ba5 +−
Qf6 30 Bxb6 Qxb6 31 Rdxd7 Kh8
32 Qxf7 Rg8 33 Ra8 1-0 Schmidt

1 c4 e5

25 Seirwan-Browne
Lone Pine 78
1 c4 e5 2 Nc3 Nc6 3 Nf3 f5 4 d4
e4 5 Ng5 5 d5!? exf3 6 dxc6 fxg2
7 cxd7+ = h6! N 5...Nf6?! **6 Nh3**
g5! 6...Nf6? 7 Nf4 Qf7 8 h4 **7 f3**
7 e3 Nf6 8 Be2 Bg7 9 Nh5+ Nxh5
10 Qxh5+ Kf8= **exf3** 7...Nf6? 8
fxe4 fxe4 9 Nf2 Bg7 10 e3± **8 exf3**
8 gxf3!? Bg7 9 d5 Ne5 10 e4 f4!
=+; 9 e3 **Bg7 9 d5** 9 Be3! Qe7? 10
Nd5 Qe7+! **10 Qd2!?** 10 Be2 Nd4
11 0-0 Nxe2+ 12 Qxe2 Qxe2 =+;
12 Nxe2 Qc5+ 13 Kh1 Ne7∓ **Nd4!**
11 Bd3 Qd8! 11...Nd6!? **12 Ng1!**
12 Re1? Qd6!∓; 12 Ne2? Qb4+!
b5! 13 Nge2 13 Nxb5 Nxb5 14
cxb5 Bb7∓; 13 cxb5! a6! 14 bxa6
Bxa6 15 Nge2 =+ **bxc4 19 Bxc4 Qc5!**
14...Nb4? 15 Qa4 **15 Qd3??** 15
b3! Nxe2 16 Qxe2 Qd4+ 17 Qd3;
15...Ba6!? 16 Bxa6 Nxe2 17 Kxe2!
Qxc3 18 Rb1 Qf6 19 Bc4!; 18...Qa5
=+ **Rb8 16 Be3?** 16 b3! Nxe2 17
Nxe2 Bxa1 18 Be3 Qa5 =+; 16...
Qa6! 17 Bxa6 Nxe2 18 Nxe2 Qxd5+
−+

Diagram

16...Qxc4+! 17 Kxc4 Ba6+ 18 Kb5

18 ♔c5 d6 mate ♞xb5! 0-1 19 ♕a4
♘a3+ 20 ♔c5 d6+ 21 ♔c6 ♘e7 mate;
19 ♘d4 ♘xd4+ 20 ♔c3 ♘e2+ 21
♔d2 ♖xb2+ 22 ♔e1 ♗c3+ 23 ♔f2
♘f4+ 24 ♔g1/g3 ♖xg2 mate **Browne**

✓ 26 Filguth-Byrne
Sao Paulo 79

**1 c4 ♞f6 2 ♘c3 e5 3 ♘f3 ♘c6 4 e3
♗b4 5 ♕c2 0-0 6 ♘d5 a5 N** 6...♖e8
7 ♕f5! += **7 ♗d3 g6 8 ♘xf6+ ♕xf6
9 ♘e4 a4!** =+ **10 0-0 ♖e8 11 d3 ♗f8
12 ♗d2 ♕e7** Δ f5 **13 ♗c3 ♘b4 14
♕d2 f5 15 ♗xe5?!** 15 ♗d5+ ♘xd5
16 cxd5 d6∓ **fxe4 16 ♘g4 ♗g7! 17
f3** 17 dxe4 h5 −+ **h5 18 ♗xb4 c5!
19 ♘f2 cxb4 20 ♘xe4 b6 21 ♖fe1
♗b7 22 ♘g3 d5 23 cxd5 ♗xd5 24 e4**

24...♗f7! −+ 25 d4 ♖ad8 26 d5
a3! 27 ♖ad1 axb2 28 ♖f1 ♕c5+
29 ♔h1 ♖a8 30 e5 ♖xe5 31 ♘e4

♖xd5 0-1 Gheorghiu

✓ 27 Tompa-Hammer Biel 78

**1 c4 e5 2 ♘c3 ♞f6 3 ♘f3 ♘c6 4 e3
d5 4 cxd5 ♘xd5 6 d3?!** 6 ♗b5! ♘xc3
7 bxc3 ♗d6 8 d4± **g6 7 ♗e2 ♗g7 8
♗d2 0-0 9 0-0 ♘de7** 9...h6!? **10 a3
a5 11 ♕c2 h6 12 ♖fd1** += **♔h7 13
♖ab1 ♘d5 14 ♘xd5 ♕xd5 15 b3
♗e6 16 ♗c3 ♘b8?!** 17 **e4!?** 17 d4!±
**♕c5 18 ♘xe5 ♗xe5 19 d4 ♗xd4 20
♖xd4 ♘c6 21 ♖dd1 ♕xa3 22 ♗f6**
+= **a4 23 bxa4 ♕xa4 24 ♕d3 ♘a5!
25 ♕g3! ♕xe4 26 ♗d3 ♕g4 27 ♕xc7
♘d5 28 ♗f1 ♗e6 29 ♗c3! ♕h5 30
♖e1**± **♖fc8 31 ♕f4?** 31 ♕e7! ♖xc3
**32 ♖xe6 ♔g8 33 ♖f6 ♖f8 34 ♖b5
♕d1 35 ♖d6!** ♕a1 36 ♖d8 +−; 33...
♕d5 34 ♖d1 ♕a2 35 ♖xg6+ +−;
32...g5 33 ♕f6 **♖xc3 32 ♖xe6 ♕f5=
33 ♕xf5 gxf5 34 ♖f6 ♗g7 35 ♖xf5
♗b3 36 ♖fb5?!** 36 ♖e1 += Zeitnot
**♗c5 37 ♖5b2 ♖aa3 38 h3 ♖ab3 39
♗e2 ♖xb2 40 ♖xb2 ♖b3 41 ♖c2 ♘e6
42 ♗c4 ♖b1+ 43 ♔h2** ½-½ **Tompa**

✓ 28 Koszorus-Tompa
Hungary ½-Final 78

**1 c4 e5 2 ♘c3 ♞f6 3 ♘f3 ♘c6 4 e3
♗e7 5 d4 exd4 6 ♘xd4 0-0 7 ♗e2
d5 8 ♘xd5!?** 8 cxd5 ♘b4! 9 0-0
♘bxd5=; 9 e4? ♘xe4 10 ♘xe4 ♕xd5∓;
8 ♘xc6 += **♘xd5 9 cxd5 ♕xd5 10
♗f3 ♕c4! 11 ♘xc6 bxc6 12 ♗e2?!**
12 ♗d2 ♗f6 =+; 12 ♕d4 ♗b4+ 13
♗d2 ♕xd4 14 exd4 ♖e8+ 15 ♔d1
♖b8≈ **♕b4+ 13 ♕d2?** 13 ♔f1 ♖d8
=+; 13 ♗d2 ♕xb2∓ **♖d8! 14 ♕c3**
14 ♕xb4 ♗xb4+ 15 ♔f1 ♗a6! −+
♕xc3+ 15 bxc3 ♗f6 16 0-0 16 ♗d2
♖b8 Δ ♖b2∓ **♗xc3 17 ♖b1 ♗e6 18
♗a3 ♖d2!**∓ **19 ♗f3 ♗d5 20 ♖bc1**
20 ♗xd5 cxd5 21 ♖fc1 ♗a5∓ **♗a5
21 e4 ♗e6 22 ♖xc6 ♖xa2 23 ♗c1**

♗d7 −+ 24 ♖c5 ♗b6 25 ♖d5 ♗c6 26 ♖d2 ♖a4! 27 ♖fd1 27 ♖e1 ♗a5; 27 ♖e2 ♗b5 h6 28 ♖e2 ♖e8 29 ♖de1 ♗a5 30 ♗d2 ♗b5 0-1 Tompa

29 Uhlmann-Meduna Halle 78

1 c4 e5 2 ♘c3 ♘f6 3 ♘f3 ♘c6 4 g3 ♗b4 5 ♗g2 5 ♘d5 Korchnoi-Karpov (27) 78 0-0 6 0-0 e4 6...♖e8; 6...d6 7 ♘e1 7 ♘g5 ♗xc3 8 bxc3; 8 dxc3 ♖e8 7...♗xc3 8 dxc3 h6 8 ♘d5 ♗f8 9 d3 ♗xd5 10 cxd5 exd3 11 ♘xd3 ♗b4 12 ♘f4! a5!? 12...c5 13 a3 ♘a6 14 d6!? 13 ♗d2 c5 14 a3 ♘a6 15 d6 ♖b8 15...♗xd6 16 ♗xa5 ♘c7 17 ♗xc7 ♕xc7 18 ♘d5± 16 e4 ♗xd6 16...c4!? △ ♘c5 17 ♗xa5 b6 18 ♗c3 ♗xf4 19 gxf4 ♗b7 20 ♕g4 g6 21 f5 ♘c7 22 ♖ad1 d6

23 a4! b5 24 ♕f4 ♕e7 25 ♖xd6 bxa4 26 ♗f6 ♕f8 27 ♖d7 ♘b5 28 fxg6 +− fxg6 28...hxg6 29 ♕h4 +− 29 ♕h4 h6 30 e5 △ ♕c4+ +− ♘d4 31 ♕g4 ♘e2+ 32 ♕xe2 ♕xf6 33 ♖xb7 1-0 Malich

30 Gheorghiu-Hebert Buenos Aires 78

1 c4 e5 2 ♘c3 ♘f6 3 ♘f3 ♘c6 4 g3 g6 5 d4! += exd4 6 ♘xd4 ♗g7 7 ♘xc6 bxc6 8 ♗g2 0-0 9 0-0 a5 10 ♗e3!± ♖e8 11 ♗d4 ♖b8 12 b3 ♗b7 13 ♖c1

d6 14 c5! d5 15 ♖e1 △ e4± ♘e4 16 ♗xg7 ♕xg7 17 ♘xe4 dxe4 18 ♕c2 ♕d4! += 19 ♖ed1 ♕e5 20 ♕c3 ♗a6 21 ♖d4! ♖b4! 21...♗xe2 22 ♖xe4 ♕xc3 23 ♖xc3±; 21...f5? 22 ♖d7+ +− 22 e3 ♗d3! 23 ♖d7! ♕xc3 24 ♖xc3 a4!!∞ 24...♖b7 25 ♖dxd3! exd3 26 ♗xc6 d2 27 ♖d3; 26...♖d8 27 ♗xb7 d2 28 ♗f3! +− 25 ♗f1 ♗xf1 26 ♔xf1 axb3 27 axb3 ♖b7 28 ♔g2 ♖e5 29 g4 h5 30 h3 hxg4 31 hxg4 ♔f6 32 ♖d4 ♔e6 33 ♔g3 ♖b8 34 b4?! 34 ♖a4! += f5 35 ♖a3 ♖d5 36 ♖xd5!? ♔xd5 37 ♖a7 ♖xb4 38 ♖xc7 fxg4 39 ♖g7 ♔xc5 40 ♖xg6 ♖b1?! 41 ♔f4! ♖f1 42 ♔xe4 ♖xf2 43 ♖xg4 ½-½ Gheorghiu

31 Andersson-Gheorghiu Sao Paulo 79

1 ♘f3 ♘f6 2 g3 g6 3 ♗g2 ♗g7 4 c4 0-0 5 0-0 d6 5...c5 6 ♘c3 ♘c6 7 d4 +=; 6...d5∞ 6 ♘c3 ♘c6 7 d3 7 d4 a6 8 d5 ♘a5 9 ♘d2∞ e5 8 ♖b1 a5! Smyslov 8...♘d4 9 b4 c6 10 b5 ♘xf3+ 11 ♗xf3 d5 12 bxc6 bxc6 13 cxd5 cxd5∞ 9 a3 ♘d4!= 10 b4 axb4 11 axb4 ♘xf3+ 12 ♗xf3 c6! 13 b5 d5 14 bxc6 bxc6 15 cxd5 cxd5 16 ♗g5 ♗e6 16...♖a5!?∞ 17 ♖b5! ♖a5!= 18 ♕b1! ♖xb5 19 ♕xb5 d4 20 ♘e4 ♗f5! 20...h6?? 21 ♘xf6+ △ ♗xh6 21 ♘xf6+ 21 ♖c1 ♗xe4 22 ♗xe4 h6 23 ♗xf6=; 21 ♕xe5! ♗xe4! 22 ♕xg7+! ♔xg7 23 ♗xd8 ♘xg3! 24 hxg3 ♖xd8= ♗xf6 22 ♗xf6 ♕xf6 23 ♖c1= ½-½ Gheorghiu

32 Ghitescu-Calvo Buenos Aires 78

1 c4 e5 2 ♘c3 ♘c6 3 ♘f3 g6!? 4 d4! exd4 5 ♘xd4 ♗g7 6 ♘xc6 bxc6 7 g3 ♘e7 8 ♗g2 0-0 9 0-0 ♖b8 10 ♕c2! 10 ♕a4! △ ♖d1 += Gheorghiu-Radovici, Rumania Final 77 d6 11

♖b1 ♗f5!? N 11...♗e6± **12 e4 ♗e6
13 b3 ♕d7?!** 13...c5 14 ♗b2 ♘c6
15 ♘e2 **14 ♗e3 a5 15 c5!± d5 16
♖bd1 ♗g4 17 f3 ♗e6 18 ♗d4 ♖fd8
19 ♗xg7 ♕xg7 20 ♘e2** Δ ♘d4/♘f4±
♕c8 21 ♕c3+ ♔g8 21...f6? 22 g4 h6
23 h4 g5 24 ♘g3 +− **22 ♕f6 ♖e8
23 h4** Δ 24 h5 gxh5 25 ♘f4! +− ♗h3
**24 ♘f4! ♗xg2 25 ♔xg2 dxe4 26 fxe4
♕g4 27 ♖d4!** h6 27...♘f5 28 exf5
♖e3 29 ♖d8+ ♖xd8 30 ♕xd8+ ♔g7
31 ♕d4+ +−; 27...♖b4 28 ♖xb4 axb4
29 ♘h5! +−; 27...♘d5 28 exd5 ♖e3
29 ♕g5! +− **28 ♘d3! ♕e6 29 ♕xe6!
fxe6 30 ♘e5!± ♖b5 31 ♖f6!** 31
♖d7 ♖xc5 32 ♘g4!±

31...♖xc5 **32 ♖xe6 ♖c2+ 33 ♔h3
g5 34 ♖d7!** +− gxh4 34...♔f8 35
♖exe7 +− **35 ♖exe7 ♖xe7 36 ♖xe7
hxg3 37 ♔xg3 ♖xa2 38 ♘g4 h5 39
♘f6+ ♔f8 40 ♖xc7 ♖a3 41 ♔f4
♖xb3 42 e5 1-0 Gheorghiu/Ghitescu**

33 Tompa-Szurovszky
Hungary ½-Final 78
**1 c4 e5 2 ♘c3 d6 3 g3 g6 4 d4 ♘d7
5 ♘f3 ♗g7 6 ♗g2 ♘e7?! 7 0-0 c6 8
e4?!** 8 e3 Δ b3, ♗b2/♗a3 += **0-0 9
♗e3 ♕c7 10 c5!?** exd4 11 cxd6 ♕xd6
12 ♗xd4 ♗xd4 13 ♕xd4 ♕xd4 14
♘xd4 ♘c5 14...♘e5 15 f4 ♘c4 16
♖f2 ♖d8=; 16 ♖ad1! += **15 ♖ad1**

a5 **16 h3?!** 16 ♖fe1!? **f5 17 exf5
♗xf5 18 ♖fe1 ♖d8 19 ♘b3!± ♖xd1
20 ♖xd1 ♘e6** 20...♘xb3 21 ♖d8+
♔f7 22 axb3± **21 ♘a4 ♘e7 22 ♘b6
♖a6 23 ♘xc8 ♘xc8 24 ♗f1 b5 25
a4! ♖b6 26 ♗xa5 ♔g7** 26...bxa4?
27 ♗c4 ♔f7 28 ♖e1 c5 29 ♘b7! +−
**27 ♖d7+ ♔f6 28 axb5 cxb5 29 ♖xh7
+− ♘e7 30 ♖h4 ♖a6 31 b4 ♘f5 32
♖e4 ♘g5 33 ♖f4 ♔g7 34 ♔g2 ♖d6
35 ♘b3 ♖d5 36 h4 ♘f7 37 ♘c5
♖d2 38 ♗xb5 ♘e5 39 ♖e4 ♕f6 40
♗f1 ♘d6 41 ♖f4+ 1-0 Tompa**

1 c4 ♘f6

34 H.Olafsson-Ermenkov
Buenos Aires 78
**1 c4 ♘f6 2 ♘c3 d5 3 cxd5 ♘xd5 4
♘f3 ♘b6** 4...e6 **5 d4 ♗g4 6 ♘e5
♗e6 7 e4 c6 8 h3 g6 9 ♗e2 ♗g7 10
♘f3 0-0 11 0-0** += **a5** 11...♘a6 **12
♗f4 a4 13 ♕c1 ♘a6 14 ♖d1 ♘c7
15 ♗e5 f6 16 d5!?** 16 ♗h2 += Δ d5
cxd5? 16...fxe5! 17 dxe6 ♕e8∞;
17...♕c8 18 ♕e3 **17 ♘xa4! ♘xa4
18 ♗xc7 ♕d7 19 exd5 ♗f7 20 ♗f4
♖fc8 21 ♕d2 ♖c5 22 d6 exd6** 22...
e5 23 ♗e3 ♖d5 24 ♕b4± **23 ♕b4
d5 24 ♖ac1 ♗f8 25 ♕d4 ♕e6 26 ♗f1
b6 27 ♖e1 ♕c6 28 b4! ♖xc1 29
♖xc1 ♕e6 30 ♖e1 ♕c6 31 ♖c1 ♕e6
32 ♗b5! ♗g7?? 33 ♗c6 +−** f5 33...
♖a7 34 ♗xd5! ♕xd5 35 ♖c8+ ♗f8
36 ♗h6 ♖a8 37 ♖xf8+! ♖xf8 38
♕xf6 +− **34 ♕d2 ♖a7 35 ♘g5 ♕f6
36 ♗xa4 ♖xa4 37 ♖c8+ ♗f8 38 ♖xf8+
1-0 Sigurjonsson**

35 Suba-Roos
Buenos Aires 78
**1 c4 ♘f6 2 ♘c3 d5 3 cxd5 ♘xd5 4
g3 g6** 4...c5 5 ♗g2 ♘c7; 5...e6 **5
♗g2 ♘xc3 6 bxc3** += **♗g7 7 h4!?** 7

目b1! ⒩d7 8 ⒩f3 += Botvinnik ⒱d7
N 7...h6 **8 ⒲b3 c5 9 h5 ⒲c7 10 ⒧a3**
10 a4!? 目b8 11 ⒧a3 b6 12 目c1
⒧b7 13 ⒩f3∝ **目b8 11 ⒩f3 b5?!** 11...
b6 12 d4 ⒧b7 **12 hxg6 hxg6 13
目xh8+ ⒧xh8 14 ⒩g5 e6** 14...c4 15
⒲b4 ⒩e5 16 f4 a5? 17 ⒲c5 ⒲xc5
18 ⒧xc5 ⒩d7 19 ⒧a7 +– **15 ⒩xe6!±
⒲e5** 15...fxe6 16 ⒲xe6+ ⒲f8 17
⒧d5 ⒩f6 18 ⒧xc5+± **16 ⒩f4 b4 17
d4! ⒲d6 18 cxb4 ⒲xd4**

11...e5! 12 ⒩xe5 12 bxc5? ⒧c6! –+
⒧xg2 13 ⒲xg2 ⒩c6! 14 ⒩xc6 14
⒩f3 ⒩xb4∓ **⒲xc6+ 15 ⒲g1 cxb4
16 d3** 16 ⒧xd4 ⒲xc4 17 ⒧xf6 ⒧xf6∓
⒲d7 17 目a1 目fe8 18 a3 目ac8! 18...
bxa3 19 ⒧xa3 ⒧xa3 20 目xa3 ⒲h3
21 f3 目e3? 22 ⒩xb6! **19 f3? b5!
20 cxb5 bxa3 21 ⒧xa3 ⒧xa3 22
目xa3 ⒩d5! –+ 23 b6** 23 目f2 ⒩e3
24 ⒲b1 ⒲xb5! –+ **⒩e3 24 ⒲b1 ⒧xf1
25 ⒲xf1 目c2 26 目a1 axb6 27 ⒩xb6
⒲e6 28 ⒩c4 目xe2 0-1 Letzelter**

19 目c1!!± cxb4 20 e3! ⒲g7? 20...
⒩c5! 21 ⒲xb4 ⒲xb4+ 22 ⒧xb4 目xb4
23 目xc5 ⒧a6± **21 ⒲xb4! ⒲e5** 21...
目xb4 22 目xc8+ ⒲e7 23 ⒧xb4+ ⒲f6
24 ⒧c3+ ⒩e5 25 目e8 +– **22 ⒩d3!**
+– **⒲f6 23 ⒧h3 1-0** 23...⒲d8 24 ⒲c4!
⒲a6 25 ⒲xf7 ⒲xa3 26 目xc8+ Δ
⒲xd7 mate **Suba** 24 Db8! will not
work due to ...Dc3+!

36 Rivas-Pastor-Letzelter
Buenos Aires 78

**1 c4 e6 2 ⒩f3 d5 3 b3 ⒩f6 4 ⒧b2
b6 5 g3 ⒧b7 6 ⒧g2 ⒧e7 7 0-0 0-0 8
⒩c3?!** 8 e3 c5 9 ⒲e2 ⒩c6 10 目fd1
目ac8 11 d3 ⒲c7 12 ⒩c3 目fd8 13
⒩h4?! dxc4 14 bxc4 a6 15 目ab1
⒩a7 =+ Korchnoi-Spassky, 68 **d4!
9 ⒩a4 c5 10 b4 ⒲e8! 11 目b1** 11
bxc5? ⒧c6! 12 cxb6 ⒩a6! –+

Diagram

37 Gipslis-Vitolins USSR 79

**1 c4 ⒩f6 2 ⒩c3 e6 3 e4 c5 4 e5 ⒩g8
5 ⒩f3 ⒩c6 6 d4 cxd4 7 ⒩xd4 ⒩ge7**
N **8 f4** 8 ⒩db5 ⒩f5! ⒩xd4 **9 ⒲xd4
⒩c6 10 ⒲e4 d6 11 ⒧d2** 11 ⒧d3 dxe5
12 fxe5 ⒩xe5∓ **dxe5 12 fxe5 ⒲d4
13 ⒲xd4 ⒩xd4 14 0-0-0 ⒧d7! 15 ⒧f4
⒩f5 16 ⒧d3 目c8! 17 ⒲b1 ⒩h4 18
目d2 ⒧b4 19 ⒧g5 ⒧e7!** 19...⒩g6 20
⒧xg6 hxg6 21 目hd1± **20 ⒧e3** 20
⒧xe7!? **⒩g6! 21 ⒧d4 b6 22 目hd1
⒧c6 23 ⒩e4! 0-0** 22...⒧xe4 23 ⒧xe4
目xc4 24 ⒧d3!∝ **24 ⒩d6 ⒧xd6 25
exd6 目fd8 26 c5 ⒩f4 27 ⒧a6 目b8
28 cxb6 axb6 29 ⒧e5 ⒩g6** 29...⒩xg2
30 d7!± **30 ⒧g3 b5 31 d7 e5 32
目d6 ⒧e4+ 33 ⒲c1 f6 34 ⒧e1!± Δ
⒧a5 ⒩f4 35 ⒧a5 ⒩e2+ 36 ⒲d2 ⒩d4
37 ⒧xd8** 37 ⒧c8!? **目xd8 38 ⒲e3 ⒧xg2
39 目1xd4! exd4+ 40 ⒲xd4 ⒲f7**

40...b4 41 ♔c5 ♕f7 42 ♔b6 Δ ♔c7 +−
**41 ♗xb5 ♔e7 42 ♔c5 ♗h3 43 a4 ♗xd7
44 ♖xd7+ 44 a5!? +− ♖xd7 45 ♗xd7
♔xd7 46 a5!** f5 47 a6 ♔c7 48 b4
f4 49 b5 f3 50 b6+ ♔d7 50...♔b8
51 ♔c6 f2 52 a7+ ♔a8 53 b7+ ♔xa7
54 ♔c7 f1♕ 55 b8♕+ ♔a6 56 ♕b6
mate **51 a7 f2 52 a8♕ f1♕ 53 ♕d5+
+− ♔e7 54 ♕d6+!** ♔e8 54...♔f7 55
b7 ♕c1+ 56 ♔b6 ♕b2+ 57 ♔c7 ♕c1+
58 ♔d8 ♕g5+ 59 ♔c8! +− **55 ♕e6+
♔d8** 55...♔f8 56 b7! ♕c1+ 57 ♔b6
♕b2+ 58 ♔c7 ♕c3+ 59 ♔d7! +−
**56 ♕g8+ ♔d7 57 ♕xg7+ ♔d8 58
♕g8+ ♔d7 59 ♕xh7+ ♔d8 60 ♕h8+!**
♔d7 61 **♕d4+ ♔e7** 61...♔c8 62 ♕c4!
+− **62 b7! +− ♕f5+ 63 ♔b6 ♕b1+
64 ♔c6! ♕g6+ 65 ♔b5! ♕e8+** 65...
♕b1+ 66 ♕b4+ +−; 65...♕f5+ 66
♕c5+ +− **66 ♔b6 ♕g6+ 67 ♔a7!**
1-0 Gipslis

1 c4 g6

38 Ghitescu-Sax Warsaw 79

1 c4 g6 2 e4 e5 3 d4 ♘f6 4 ♘f3 4
dxe5 ♘xe4 5 ♕d5 f5 6 exf6 ♘xf6
7 ♕d1∞; 5 ♕e2 ♗b4+∞ **♗b4+ 5 ♗d2
♗xd2+ 6 ♕xd2 ♘xe4 7 ♕e3 d5!** 8
cxd5 ♕xd5 9 ♗d3 ♕a5+! **10** ♔e2
10 ♘bd2 ♘xd2∓ ♘f6 **11 ♕xe5+**
♕xe5 **12 ♘xe5** 12 dxe5∞ ♗e6 **13
♘c3 ♔e7!** 14 f4 ♖d8! 15 ♖hf1 15
♔e3! +∓ ♘c6!∓ 16 ♘xc6+ bxc6 17
f5 gxf5 18 ♗xf5 ♖xd4 19 ♗xe6 fxe6
20 ♖ac1 ♖g8 21 g3 ♖g5 22 ♖cd1
c5 23 ♖d3 ♘g4! 24 ♖xd4 cxd4 25
♘e4 ♖b5 26 b3 ♘e3 27 ♖c1! ♘d5
28 ♔d3 e5 29 ♖f1 ♖b6 30 ♖f5!
♔e6 31 ♖h5!∞ ♘f6 32 ♘xf6 ♔xf6
33 ♖xh7 c5 34 ♔e4 34 ♖xa7 ♖d6!!
Δ e4+ −+ ♖d6 35 ♖h6+ ♔e7 36
♖h7+ ♔f6 37 ♖h6+ ♔e7 ½-½
Gheorghiu

39 Speelman-Hartston
Hastings 78/9

**1 c4 g6 2 e4 e5 3 d4 ♘f6 4 ♘f3
♗b4+ 5 ♗d2 ♗xd2+ 6 ♕xd2** 6 ♘xd2
♘xe4 7 ♕e3 f5! 7...d5 Speelman-
Sax, Hastings 77/8 **8 dxe5 ♕e7 9 ♘c3
♘xc3 9**...♕b4!? **10 ♕xc3 ♘a6 11
♗e2 ♕b4?** 11...b6 **12 ♕xb4 ♘xb4
13 0-0** Δ c5/a3, b4 **♘c6 14 c5!** 0-0
**15 ♖fe1 ♖e8 16 ♗b5 ♖e7 17 ♖ad1
♔g7 18 h4 a6 19 ♗a4 ♖b8 20 ♘d4**
20 e6 ♔f6 **♘xd4! 20**...♘xe5?; 20...
♖xe5? **21 ♖xd4 b5 22 ♗b3** 22 cxb6?!
♖xb6 **♗b7 23 ♖ed1? ♗c6 24 f4 ♔f8
25 ♖1d3 ♖g7 26 ♖g3 ♖e8 27 ♔f2
♖ee7 28 a4 h6!? 29 ♖h3 ♖e8 30
axb5 axb5 31 ♗d5 g5? 31**...♖a8

32 ♗xc6 dxc6 32...g4!? **33 hxg5 hxg5
34 ♖h8+ ♔e7 35 ♖h6 gxf4 35**...
♖d8 36 ♖xd8 ♔xd8 37 g4! +− **36
♖xc6 ♔f8 37 ♖f6+ ♔f7 38 ♖d7!
♖xf6 39 exf6 ♖e6? 39**...c6 +− **40
♖xc7 b4 40**...♖xf6 41 ♖b7 **41 ♖c8+!
♔f7 42 c6 1-0 Speelman**

Queen's Pawn

40 Botterill-Hartston
Hastings 78-9

**1 d4 c5 2 c3 ♘f6 3 ♘f3 b6 4 dxc5
bxc5 5 e4 e6 6 e5 ♘d5 7 c4 ♘b4**
7...♘e7!? **8 a3 ♘4c6 9 ♘c3 ♗e7 10**

♗d3 ♗b7 10...0-0? 11 h4± **11 h4!?**
11 ♘e4! += ♗d4! **12 ♘xd4 cxd4**
13 ♗b5 a6 14 ♘d6+ ♗xd6 15 exd6
0-0 15...♗xg2? 16 ♕g4 +− **16 ♗g5**
♕a5+ **17 ♔f1 ♘c6 18 f4?!** △ b4,
♗f6, ♗xh7+ ♔c5! **19 b4 ♕xd6 20 c5**
♕d5?! 20...♕c7∓ **21 ♕c2 f5** 21...f6!?
22 ♖d1! h6 23 ♗c4 d3? 24 ♕c3±
½-½ 24...♕e4 25 ♗xd3 ♕d5 26 ♗e2
♘d4 27 ♗f3 +−; 24...♕d4 25 ♕xd4
♘xd4 26 ♖xd3± **Botterill**

✓ **41 Gliksman-Sapi**
Budapest 2 78
1 d4 d5 2 ♘f3 ♘f6 3 ♗f4 e6 3...c5
4 c3 ♕b6 5 ♕b3 c4 6 ♕xb6 axb6
7 ♘e5!? ♘c6 8 a3 ♖a5 9 ♘xc6 bxc6
10 ♗c7 ♖a6 11 ♘c2 c5 =+ **4 e3 c5**
5 ♘bd2 5 c3 ♗d6 5...♕b6 6 ♖b1 ♘c6
7 ♗d3 cxd4 8 exd4 ♗e7 9 0-0 0-0 10
♕e2 += **6 ♗g3 ♗c6 7 c3 ♗xg3 8 hxg3**
♕e7 △ e5 **9 ♗b5 ♗d7 10 ♗xc6! ♗xc6**
11 ♘e5 ♗b5? 11...cxd4 12 exd4 +=
12 ♕b3 ♗c6 13 g4 ♘d7 14 ♘df3
♘f8 **15 ♘xc6 bxc6 16 ♘e5 ♖c8 17**
dxc5 ♘g6 18 ♘xg6 fxg6 19 ♕c2 0-0
20 b4 e5 21 0-0 ♕g5 22 c4!? 22
♕e2 ♕xg4 **23 cxd5 ♕xb4 24 d6±**
♖b8 25 ♖ab1 ♕g4 26 ♖xb8 ♖xb8
27 f3 ♕g5 28 ♕e4 ♖b2 29 f4 ♕g4
30 ♖e1 h5 1-0 time 31 ♕f3 ♕e6
32 fxe5 ♖xa2 33 ♖d1 +− **Balogh**

✓ **42 Magrin-Bohm**
Monte Carlo 78
1 d4 d5 2 ♘f3 ♘f6 3 ♗f4 e6 4 e3
♗e7 4...♗d6!? **5 ♗d3 c5 6 c3 ♘c6 7**
♘bd2 ♘h5?! 7...0-0 8 ♗g3 ♘xg3 9
hxg3 h6 10 ♘e5! ♘xe5 10...♗d7 11
♕h5 ♘xe5 12 dxe5 0-0 △ ♗e8, f5
11 dxe5 ♗d7 12 ♕g4! ♗f8 13 ♕e2
♕b6 **14 b3 ♕a5 15 ♖c1! ♕xa2 16**
0-0∞ ♕a5 17 f4 b5 17...g6 18 g4 △
f5± **18 f5 c4 19 fxe6 ♗xe6 20 bxc4**

---

dxc4 20...bxc4 21 ♗c2 △ ♖a1, ♗a4
21 ♗e4± ♖c8 22 ♘f3 ♗c5 23 ♘d4
♗xd4 24 exd4 ♕b6 25 ♔h2 ♖d8 26
♕f3 0-0 27 d5! f5!? 27...♗c8 28
♗b1 ♕c5 29 ♕e4 g6 30 e6! +−

28 dxe6 fxe4 29 ♕g4 ♕c7 30 ♕h4!
+− **♖xf1 31 ♖xf1 ♖e8 32 ♕f4!** ♕e7
32...♖xe6 33 ♕f8+ ♔h7 33 ♖f7 +−
33 ♕f7+ ♔h8 33...♔h7 34 ♖f6 (△
♕g6) ♕xf7 35 exf7 ♖f8 35 e6 gxf6
36 e7 ♔g7 37 e8♕ +− **34 ♕g6 ♖g8**
34...♕xe6? 35 ♖f8+ +− **35 ♖f7 ♕e8**
35 e7 e3 36 e6 ♕a8 37 ♖xg7 ♖xg7 38
e8♕+ 1-0 Maric

✓**43 Botterill-Andersson**
Hastings 78/9
1 d4 ♘f6 2 ♘f3 e6 3 ♗g5 h6 4 ♗xf6
♕xf6 5 e4 d6 6 ♘bd2 ♘d7 7 ♗d3
g6 8 ♕e2 ♗g7 9 c3 a6 10 a4!? b6
11 0-0 0-0 12 b4 △ a5, c4 **♗b7 13**
a5 b5 14 c4 bxc4 15 ♗xc4 △ b5
♖a7! 16 ♕e3!? 16 ♖ac1!? △ d5 ♕e7
17 ♖a2 17 d5? ♖aa8 18 dxe6 ♗xa1∓
♖fa8! △ c5 **18 ♘b3 ♘f6** △ d5; 18...
d5? 19 exd5 ♕xb4 20 dxe6 ♕xc4 21
exd7 +− **19 ♗d3 ♗c6!** =/=+ **20 ♖c1**
♗e8 21 h3 ♖b7 22 ♕e1 ♕d8 23 ♘a1
♗f8 23...♕b8! △ ♕a7 =+ **24 ♘c2 c5**
25 d5? 25 bxc5 dxc5 26 ♕e2 cxd4
27 ♘cxd4=; 25 e5!? dxe5? 26 dxc5±;
25 e5!? ♘d5! **exd5 26 exd5 ♘xd5**

---

27 bxc5 27 ♗e4? ♖e7 −+ ♖e7 **28
♕d2 dxc5 29 ♗c4 ♘c7 30 ♕xd8 ♖xd8
31 ♘e3 ♔g7 32 ♘d2 ♖b8 33 ♗f1
♖e6 34 ♘dc4 ♘b5** 34...♗b5!∓ **35
♘b6 ♖d8 36 ♘ec4 0-1** time 36...♖e4
37 ♘a4 += △ ♘cb6 **Botterill**

1 d4 d5 2 c4 dxc4

44 Bagirov-Romanishin
USSR Final 78
**1 d4 d5 2 c4 dxc4 3 e4 e5 4 ♘f3
exd4** 4...♗b4+ 5 ♘c3 exd4 6 ♘xd4
♕e7 7 ♗xc4 ♕xe4+ 8 ♔f1∝ Alburt-
Romanishin, Kiev 78 **5 ♗xc4 ♗b4+
6 ♗d2?!** 6 ♘bd2!? **♗xd2+ 7 ♘bxd2
♘c6** 7...♘h6 Miles **8 0-0 ♕f6!** N 8...
♘f6 9 e5 ♘d5 **9 e5 ♕g6 10 ♕b3
♘ge7 11 ♖fe1 0-0 12 ♖ac1 ♖b8 13
♗d3** 13 e6 ♘a5? 14 exf7+ ♔h8 15
♕a3 ♘xc4 16 ♕xe7; 13...fxe6 14
♗xe6+ ♔h8 15 ♗xc8 ♖fxc8 16 ♖xe7
♘xe7 17 ♘e5 △ ♘f7+; 14...♗xe6
15 ♖xe6 ♕f7 16 ♘g5? ♕xf2+ −+
♕h6 14 a3 ♗e6∓ **15 ♕c2 ♘g6 16
b4 ♖bd8 17 b5 ♘ce7 18 ♘e4** 18
♕xc7 ♖c8 19 ♕d6 ♘d5!; 19 ♕xb7
♖xc1 20 ♖xc1 ♗d5 −+ **♘f4 19 ♖cd1
♘xg2! −+ 20 ♘eg5** 20 ♔xg2 ♕h3+
−+ **♗xe1 21 ♗xh7+ ♔h8 22 ♖xe1
g6 23 ♕xc7 ♘f5 0-1 Keene**

45 Miles-Portisch
Buenos Aires 78
**1 d4 d5 2 c4 dxc4 3 e4 ♘f6 4 e5
♘d5 5 ♗xc4 ♘b6! 6 ♗b3 ♘c6 7 ♘e2?!**
7 ♘f3 ♗g4? 8 ♗xf7+! +− **♗f5! 8 ♘bc3
e6= 9 ♗f4 ♘b4** △ ♘4d5 =+ **10 0-0
♗e7 11 ♕d2 ♘4d5 12 ♗e3 0-0 13
♘g3 ♗g6 14 f4 c5! 15 ♗xd5 ♘xd5
16 dxc5 ♘xe3 17 ♕xe3 ♕d3!∓**

Diagram

**18 ♖xd3 ♗xc5+ 19 ♔h1 ♖xd3 20
♖fd1 ♖ad8 21 ♘ge4 ♗e3! 22 g3 f6!
23 ♘d6 ♗g6 24 ♘c4 ♗d4!** 24...fxe5?
25 ♘xe5∝ **25 ♔g2 ♗e8!** △ ♗c6+∓
**26 exf6 gxf6 27 ♖ac1 ♗c6+ 28 ♔f1
♗c5 29 ♔e2 a6 30 ♘d2 ♔f7 31 ♘ce4
♗d4!** 32 **♘c3 ♔e7 33 ♘f3 ♗a7 34
♘e1 ♖xd1 35 ♖xd1 ♗e8** △ ♗h5+
**36 ♔f3 ♖g8 37 ♖c1 ♗h5+ 38 ♔g2
♗e3 39 ♖c2?! ♗xf4 −+ 40 ♘e4 ♗b8
41 ♘c5 ♖c8 0-1 Gheorghiu** ⟨ ♔ 42 S67, Tc
43 Sc2! Lg6 44 Sb4 Le4+ way 67 ⟩

46 Langeweg-Miles Amsterdam 3 78
**1 d4 d5 2 ♘f3 ♘f6 3 c4 dxc4 4 ♘c3
a6 5 e4 b5 6 e5 ♘d5 7 a4 ♘xc3 8
bxc3 ♕d5** 8...♗b7 9 e6 fxe6 10 ♗e2
♕d5 11 ♘g5 ♕xg2 12 ♖f1 ♗d5 13
axb5 ♕xh2∝ **9 g3 ♗f5** N 9...♗b7 11
♗g2 ♕d7 11 ♗a3 Bronstein-Korchnoi,
Moscow 64; 9...♗e6 10 ♗g2 ♕b7 11
0-0 ♗d5 12 e6! ♗xe6 13 ♘g5
Balashov-Miles, Bugojno 78 **10 ♗g2
e6 11 0-0 ♕b7 12 ♘h4 ♗e4 13 ♕g4!
♗xg2 14 ♘xg2∝ h5?!** 14...g6!? 15
♗g5 △ d5! **15 ♕g5 ♘d7 16 ♗a3!
g6 17 ♗xf8 ♘xf8 18 ♖fb1 c6 19 ♘e3!**
△ ♘xc4/♘f1-d2-e4 **♕c8** 19...♕e7? 20
♕xe7+ ♔xe7 21 axb5 cxb5 22 ♖xb5
+− **20 ♘f1 ♘h7 21 ♕h6 ♔e7 22 ♘d2
♕f8 23 ♕e3 ♕d8 24 ♘e4 ♕d5 25 h4
f5 26 ♘c5** 26 exf6+ ♘xf6 27 ♘c5
♘g4 **♔f7 27 axb5 axb5 28 ♕h6!
♘f6 29 ♖xa8!! +− ♖xh6 30 ♖a7+**

♚g8 31 exf6 ♖h7 32 ♖a8+ ♔f7 33
♖a7+ ♔g8 34 ♖ba1 ♖xa7 35 ♖xa7
b4 36 ♖a8+?? 36 f7+ ♔g7 37 ♘d7
♔xf7 38 ♘b6+ +− ♔f7 37 ♖a7+ ♔g8
38 ♖a8+ ♔f7 39 ♖a7+ ½-½ Keene

47 Marovic-Duckstein
Virovitica 78

1 d4 d5 2 c4 dxc4 3 ♘f3 ♘f6 4 ♘c3
a6 5 e4 5 e3!? c5?! 5...b5! 6 e5 ♘d5
7 a4 c6∞ 6 d5 e6 7 a4! exd5 8 e5
d4? 8...♘g8 9 ♕xd5 ♘c6 10 ♗xc4
♗e6 11 ♕e4 += Vladimirov-Hodos,
USSR 58 9 ♗xc4!± ♗e6?? 9...dxc3
10 ♗xf7+!; 9...♘fd7 10 ♘e4± 10
♗xe6 fxe6 11 exf6 +− dxc3 12 f7+
1-0 12...♔e7 13 ♗g5+ Maric

48 Miles-Bellon Amsterdam 3 78

1 d4 ♘f6 2 ♘f3 d5 3 c4 dxc4 4 e3
♘bd7!? 5 ♗xc4 ♘b6 6 ♗e2 ♗f5 7
♘c3 e6 7...h6!? 8 ♘h4 ♗g6 8...♗e4!?
9 ♘xg6 hxg6 10 e4 += ♗b4 11 ♕d3
c5!? 12 a3? 12 ♗e3 +=/± ♗xc3+ 13
bxc3 cxd4 14 cxd4 ♕c7! 15 g3? 15
e5 ♘fd5∞ ♗xe4!∓ 16 ♗f3 16 ♕xe4?
♕c3+ −+ ♘d6 17 ♗f4 ♘d5 18 ♗e5
18 ♗xd5 ♕a5+ −+ ♕a5+ 18...0-0∓
19 ♔f1 ♘f5 20 ♖c1! 20 g4 ♘h4 21
♗xg7 ♘f4 22 ♕e3 ♕b5+ 23 ♗e2
♘xe2 24 ♕xe2 ♕d5 −+; 20 ♔g2 f6
−+ b6? 20...0-0∓; 20...f6!? 21 g4∞
21 g4! ♘h4 22 ♗xg7∞ ♖h7 22...
♘f4? 23 ♗c6+ ♔e7 24 ♕c3 +− 23
♗e5 23 ♗f6? ♘xf3 24 ♕xf3 ♕d2∓
♘xf3 24 ♕xf3 ♖d8 25 ♔g2 f6 25...
g5!? 26 ♗g3 ♖e7 27 h4! f5?! 28 h5
fxg4? 28...g5 29 h6±; 29 gxf5 exf5
30 ♕xf5?? ♘e3+ −+ 29 ♕xg4 gxh5
30 ♕xh5+ ♔d7

Diagram

31 ♕e5! +− ♖g8 31...♕xa3 32 ♖c7+

+− 32 ♕d6+ ♔e8 33 ♖c8+ ♔f7 34
♖xg8 ♔xg8 35 ♕d8+ ♔g7 36 ♗e5+
♔g6 37 ♕g8+ ♔f5 38 ♖h5+ 1-0 38...
♔e4 ♕g6 mate **Miles**

49 Beljavsky-Gulko
USSR Final 78

1 d4 d5 2 c4 dxc4 3 ♘f3 ♘f6 4 e3
e6 5 ♗xc4 c5 6 0-0 ♘c6 7 ♕e2 cxd4
8 ♖d1 ♗e7 9 exd4 0-0 10 ♘c3 ♘a5?!
10...♘b4 11 ♗d3 b6 12 ♗g5 ♗b7
13 ♖ac1 ♘d5?! 13...♖c8 14 ♕e4 g6
14...♘f6 (Δ ♗xe4) 15 ♕h4 h6 16
♗xh6 ♘d5 17 ♗g5! +− 15 ♕h4 h6
16 ♗h6 ♘xc3 17 ♖xc3 ♗xf3 18
gxf3 f5 19 ♕f4? 19 ♕g3! ♖f7??
19...g5! 20 ♕e3 ♖f6 21 ♗xg5 ♖g6
22 f4 h6 23 h4 hxg5 24 fxg5 ♔f7
20 ♖dc1 g5 21 ♕e5 ♖f6 22 ♗a6!±
♔f7 22...♕d6! 23 ♖c7! ♖xh6 24
b4! +− 24 ♖xe7+? ♕xe7 25 ♖c7
♘c6! ♖f6 25 bxa5 ♔g6 26 ♖1c6
bxa5 27 ♗c4! ♖b8 28 ♗xe6 ♖b6
29 ♗xf5+ ♔f7 30 ♕xf6+ 1-0 Keene

50 Hubner-Miles
Wijk aan Zee 79

1 d4 d5 2 c4 dxc4 3 ♘f3 ♘f6 4 e3
♗g4 5 ♗xc4 e6 6 h3 ♗h5 7 ♘c3 ♘bd7
8 0-0 ♗d6 9 ♗e2 0-0 10 e4 e5 11
dxe5 ♘xe5 12 ♘d4 ♗c5 13 ♗xh5 N
13 ♘b3 Portisch-Miles, Lone Pine 79
♗xd4 14 ♘d5! 14 ♗g5? ♗xc3 c5!=

15 ♗g5 ♘ed7 16 ♖e1 h6 17 ♗h4 17
♗e3!? ♖e8 17...g5 18 ♗g3 ♘xd5 19
exd5 ♗xb2 20 ♖b1 ♗c3 21 ♖e2∞
18 ♗f3 18 ♕b3 g5 =+ **♕b8** 18...g5!? **19
♔h1 ♘xd5** 19...♗xb2?! 20 ♖b1 ♗e5
21 ♘xf6+ ♘xf6 22 ♗xf6 gxf6 23
♕d7 b6 24 ♕g4+; 23 ♗e2!? △ ♗c4-d5;
22...♗xf6? 23 e5 △ ♗xb7 **20 exd5
♕d6 21 ♕c2** 21 ♕b3!? **♗f6?!** 21...
♗e5! △ g5 =+ **22 ♗xf6 ♘xf6 23 ♕b3!
♖ab8** 23...b6 24 ♕b5 △ ♕c6 **13
a4!= ♖e7 25 ♖xe7 ♕xe7 26 a5 ♕d6**
26...♘e8 27 ♕c3 △ ♖e1 **27 ♕b5
♘d7 28 g3 a6 29 ♕e2 ♔f8 30 ♕c2
g6 31 ♕d2 ♔g7 32 ♖e1 b5 33 axb6
♖xb6 34 ♖e3 ♕f6 35 b3 ♖b4 36
♔g2 a5 37 d6 a4 38 bxa4 ♖xa4
39 ♗c6 ♖d4 40 ♕c3 ♖xd6 41 ♗xd7
½-½ Miles**

51 Kuligowski-Ghitescu
Warsaw 79

1 d4 d5 2 c4 dxc4 3 ♘f3 3 e4∞
**♘f6 4 e3 ♗g4 5 ♗xc4 e6 6 ♘c3 ♘bd7
7 0-0 ♗d6 8 h3 ♗h5 9 e4 e5 10 ♗e2!**
+= **0-0** 10...exd4 11 ♘xd4± **11 dxe5
♗xe5 12 ♘d4! ♗xe2 13 ♕xe2 ♘g6
14 ♘db5! ♗c5 15 ♘a4!± N ♕e7 16
♘xc5 ♕xc5 17 ♘c3 ♖fe8 18 ♗e3
♕a5 19 f3 c6** 19...b6!∞ **20 ♕f2 b6
21 ♖ad1± ♖e6?** 21...♖ad8! **22 ♗d4**
+= **22 ♖d4 b5 23 b4! ♕a3 24 ♕c2
♖ae8 25 ♗c1! ♕a6 26 f4 ♕b6 27
♗e3! ♘f8 28 e5 ♕b7**

Diagram

**29 ♗f2! ♘d5 30 ♘xd5 cxd5 31
♕d3 ♖a6 32 ♖xd5 ♘e6 33 ♗e3
♖xa2 34 ♕xb5 +− ♕xb5 35 ♖xb5
g6 36 ♖b7 a6 37 f5! ♘g7 38 fxg6
fxg6 39 ♖ff7 ♘f5 40 ♗c5 ♖a1+
41 ♔h2 ♖e1 42 g4! ♖e2+ 43 ♔h1
1-0** 43...♘g3+ 44 ♔g1 **Gheorghiu**

52 Eperjesi-Marszalek
Pazardjik 78

**1 d4 d5 2 ♘f3 ♘f6 3 c4 dxc4 4 e3
♗g4 5 ♗xc4 e6 6 h3 ♗h5 7 0-0 ♘bd7
8 ♘c3 ♗d6 9 e4 e5 10 ♗e2 0-0 11
dxe5 ♘xe5 12 ♘d4 ♗xe2?!** 12...♗c5!
Miles; 12...♗g6!? **13 ♕xe2 ♘g6 14 ♘f5
♗e5 15 f4 ♗xc3 16 bxc3 ♖e8 17 e5
♘d5 18 ♕f3** 18 c4 ♘de7 19 ♘g3
♘c6 20 ♗b2 ♕e7 21 ♔h2 ♖ad8 22
♖f2 ♕d7 △ f6≈ Quinteros-Ghitescu,
Polanica 77 **♘de7** N 18...♘b6 19 ♖d1
♕c8 20 ♕g4 ♕e6!= Lukacs-Marszalek,
Budapest 76; 20 ♘e3!?± Kondratiev
19 ♖d1 19 ♘xe7+ ♕xe7 20 ♕xb7
♕c5+ = **♕c8 20 ♘g3 ♘c6 21 c4!** 21
♖b1! **♖d8 22 ♗b2 ♖xd1+ 23 ♖xd1
♕e8 24 ♘h5± ♖d8 25 ♖d5! ♘ce7
26 ♖xd8 ♕xd8 27 e6! f6 28 f5 +−
♕d2!** Zeitnot 28...♘h4 29 ♘xf6+
gxf6 30 ♕g4+ ♘eg6 31 fxg6; 28...
♘e5 29 ♗xe5 fxe5 30 f6; 28...♘f8
29 ♕g4 +− **29 ♘xf6+?** 29 ♕xb7?
♕d1+ 30 ♔h2 ♕xh5? 31 fxg6±;
30...♕d6!=; 29 ♗xf6 ♕e1+ 30 ♔h2
gxf6 31 ♘xf6+ △ fxg6 +− **gxf6 30
♗xf6 ♗xf5 31 ♕xf5 ♕c1+! 32 ♔h2
♕f4+! 33 ♕xf4 ♘xf4 34 e7 ♔f7=
35 ♔g3?? ♘h5+ 0-1 Marszalek**

1 d4 d5 2 c4 c6

53 Tal-Dorfman
USSR Final 78
**1 c4 c6 2 d4 d5 3 ♘c3 e6 4 e4 dxe4
5 ♘xe4 ♗b4+ 6 ♗d2 ♕xd4 7 ♗xb4
♕xe4+ 8 ♗e2 ♘a6 9 ♗d6 e5?! 10
♘f3 ♗g4?!** N 10...♗f5 11 ♗xe5 ♖d8∞
Euwe **11 0-0 0-0-0 12 ♗d3 ♕f4** 12...
♗xf3? 13 ♗xe4 ♗xd1 14 ♗f5+ +−
**13 ♗xe5 ♕xe5 14 ♘xe5 ♗xd1 15
♗f5+ ♔c7 16 ♘xf7 ♘e7** 16...♘h6!?
**17 ♗xh7 ♗g4 18 ♘xh8 ♖xh8 19
♖fe1 ♘c8 20 ♗c2 ♘b4 21 ♗e4 a5
22 f3 ♗d7 23 ♖ad1 ♘d6 24 c5 ♘xe4
25 ♖xe4 ♘d5 26 g4± ♗f8 27 ♔g2
a4?!** 27...♗e8 Δ ♗g6 **28 a3 ♖a8 29
h4 ♖a5 30 ♖c1 ♖b5 31 ♖c2 ♖b3
32 ♔f2 ♔d8 33 ♖xa4 ♔e7 34 ♖e2+
♔f7 35 h5 ♗e6 36 ♖ae4 ♗d7 37 ♖d2
♔f6 38 ♔g3 ♗c8 39 ♖f2 ♖d3 40 ♖e8
♗d7 41 ♖b8 ♗e3 42 ♔f4 ♘d5+ 43
♔g3 ♘e3 44 ♖e2 ♖b3 45 ♖f8+ ♔e7
46 ♖f4 ♔d8 47 ♖f7 1-0 Keene**

54 Marszalek-Mechkarov
Pazardjik 78
1 d4 d5 2 c4 ♗f5 3 ♘c3 3 cxd5 ♗xb1
4 ♕a4+ c6!? 5 ♖xb1 ♕xd5 6 ♘f3
♘d7 7 ♗d2 ♘b6 8 ♕a5 ♘c4 9 ♕xd5
cxd5 10 e3 ♘d6 11 ♖c1 += Farago-
Kuligowski, Polanica 78; 5 dxc6?!
♘xc6 6 ♖xb1 e5! 7 a3 ♕d5!? 8 ♗d2
exd4 9 ♖c1 ♘f6 =/=+ Marszalek-
Lipski, Lublin 77 **e6 4 ♗f4** 4 ♘f3
♘f6 5 cxd5 exd5 6 ♗g5 c6 7 ♕b3
♘bd7 8 ♕xb7 ♖b8 9 ♕xc6 ♖xb2
10 g4 ♗c2 11 ♗xf6 += Farago-
Bielczyk, Polanica 78 **c6 5 e3 ♘bd7
6 ♕b3 ♕b6 7 c5!? ♕xb3 8 axb3 e5
9 ♗g3∼a6 10 b4 exd4 11 exd4 ♖c8
12 ♘f3 f6?!** 12...g6! Δ ♗g7= **13
♘d2!** Δ ♘b3, ♘a5 **♗e7 14 ♘b3 ♗d8
15 ♘a5 ♗xa5 16 bxa5!± ♘h6 17**

**♖a4 ♘f7 18 ♖b4 ♘d8 19 ♗e2 ♔f7
20 ♗d6 h5 21 h4 g6 22 f3 ♖h7 23
♔d2 ♖h8 24 ♖e1 ♖e8 25 g4 ♗e6**
25...hxg4 26 fxg4 ♗e4 27 ♘xe4 dxe4
28 ♗c4+ Δ ♔e3±; 27...♖xe4 26
♗f3± **26 gxh5 gxh5 27 f4! ♖h8**
27...♗g4 28 ♗xg4 hxg4 29 ♖xe8 ♔xe8
30 f5! Zugzwang **28 ♖g1 ♗f5 29
♘d1! ♗g6** 29...♗e4 30 ♘e3 Δ f5±
**30 ♘e3 f5 31 ♗d3 +− ♗f6 32 ♖xg6
♔xg6 33 ♗xf5+ ♔f7 34 ♗xc8 ♘e4+
35 ♔c2 ♖g8 36 f5 1-0 Marszalek**

55 Gheorghiu-Smyslov
Buenos Aires 2 78
1 ♘f3 d5 2 c4 c6 3 d4 ♘f6 4 ♕b3!?
4 cxd5 cxd5 5 ♗f4; 4 ♘c3 ♕b6 5
♘c3 dxc4 5...♕xb3 6 axb3 e6 7
♗f4 += **6 ♕xc4 ♗f5 7 g3 e6 8 ♗g2
♕b4 9 ♘e5! += ♘bd7 10 ♕xb4 ♗xb4
11 ♘xd7 ♘xd7 12 0-0 0-0 13 ♗f4
♖ad8** 13...♖fe8 Δ e5∞ **14 ♖ac1
♘b6 15 ♖fd1 ♖d7** 15...♘c4 16 b3!±
16 e4!

16...♗g6 16...♗g4! 17 f3 ♗h5= **17 a3
♗e7** 17...♗xc3 18 ♖xc3 += **18 d5!**
+= **cxd5 19 exd5 ♖fd8!** 19...♘xd5
20 ♘xd5 exd5 21 ♖xd5± **20 dxe6
fxe6 21 ♖xd7 ♖xd7 22 ♖d1 ♖xd1+
23 ♘xd1 ♘d5 24 ♗e5∞ ½-½**
Gheorghiu

56 Polugaevsky-Romanishin
USSR Final 78

1 d4 d5 2 ♘f3 ♘f6 3 c4 dxc4 4 ♘c3 c6 5 a4 ♗f5 6 e3 e6 7 ♗xc4 ♗b4 8 0-0 0-0 9 ♕e2 ♘e4 10 ♗d3!? ♗xc3?! 10...♘xc3 11 bxc3 ♗xd3! 12 ♕xd3 ♗e7 13 a5 +=; 11... ♗xc3 12 ♗xf5! ♗xa1 13 ♗a3 ♖e8 14 ♘c2! 11 bxc3 ♘xc3 12 ♕c2 ♗xd3 13 ♕xd3 ♘d5 14 ♖b1 b6 15 ♗a3 ♖e8 16 ♖fc1 f6? N 16...a5? 17 ♘e5± Euwe-Alekine (17) 37; 16...♘f6! 17 e4 e5∞ 17 e4 ♘f4 18 ♕e3 ♘g6 19 h4 h5? 19...♘h8! 20 e5 f5 21 ♗d6 ♘h8 22 ♘g5 ♘f7 23 ♗xf7 ♔xf7 24 ♕f4 ♔g8 25 ♖b3 ♕d7 26 ♖g3± ♘a6 27 ♕h6 c5 28 ♖cc3 ♖ad8 29 ♖xg7+ ♕xg7 30 ♖g3 ♖d7 31 ♖xg7+ ♖xg7 32 ♕xh5 ♖d8 33 ♕h6 ♖e8 34 d5! +− exd5 35 e6 ♘c7 36 e7 ♖exe7 37 ♗xe7 ♖xe7 38 ♕g5+ ♔f8 39 h5 c4 40 h6 c3 41 ♕f6+ 1-0 Keene

57 Hubner-Donoso
Buenos Aires 78

1 c4 ♘f6 2 ♘c3 e6 3 ♘f3 d5 4 d4 c6 5 e3 ♘bd7 6 ♕c2 ♗d6 7 b3 0-0 8 ♗b2 ♕e7 9 ♗e2 9 ♗d3 e5 10 cxd5 cxd5 11 dxe5 ♘xe5 12 ♘xe5 ♗xe5= dxc4 9...♗a3 10 ♗xa3 ♕xa3 11 0-0 ♕d6 12 ♖ad1 Δ e4 += 10 bxc4 e5 11 0-0 ♖e8 12 ♖fe1 b6 12...e4 13 ♘d2 ♘f8 14 f3 exf3 15 ♗xf3 ♘g6 16 g3 Δ e4 += 13 a4 a5 14 ♖ab1 ♗a6 15 ♗a1 ♘c7?! 15...♖ab8? 16 c5 +−; 15...e4!? 16 ♘d2 ♗b4 (1) 17 f3 exf3 18 ♗xf3 ♖ac8 19 e4? ♕d6 20 ♕d3 ♘e5 −+; (2) 17 ♗f1 ♘f8 18 g3 ♗c8 19 ♗g2 ♗f5= 16 g3 Δ 17 dxe5 ♘xe5 18 ♘xe5 ♕xe5 19 ♘d5 ♖ab8 17 ♗f1 ♕f8 18 ♘e2 Δ ♗g2, dxe5 c5? 18...exd4 19 ♘exd4 ♕c5 20 ♘d2 ♘e5 21 h3 Δ f4 += 19 dxe5 19 d5 ♖e7 Δ ♘e8-d6 += ♘xe5 20

♘xe5 ♗xe5 21 ♗xe5 ♖xe5 22 ♘c3± ♕e8 22...♖h5 23 ♕e2 Δ e4-e5; 22...♕d6 23 e4 ♗b7 24 ♗g2 ♖be8 25 ♖ed1 ♕c6 26 f4 ♖5e6 27 e5 ♕xg2+ 28 ♔xg2 ♗xg2 29 ♔xg2 ♘g4 30 ♘d5 Δ h3± 23 e4 ♕c6 24 f4 ♖ee8 25 ♗g2 ♗b7 25...♗xc4 26 e5 ♘d5 27 ♕e4 +− 26 ♖ed1 26 ♘d5!? ♗xd5 27 cxd5 ♕g6 28 ♕c4 h5 29 e5 h4 30 ♖b3 ♘g4 27 ♕e2 f5 28 h3 ♘f6 29 e5 ♘e4 29...♕xg2+ 30 ♕xg2 ♗xg2 31 ♔xg2 ♘e4 32 ♘xe4 fxe4 33 ♔f2 Δ ♔e3xe4 +− 30 ♘xe4 30 ♗xe4 fxe4 31 ♖d6 ♕c7 32 ♖bxb6 ♗a8 33 ♕b2 ♖xb6 34 ♕xb6 ♕xb6 35 ♖xb6 ♖d8 fxe4 31 ♖d6 ♕c7 31...♕xa4 32 ♖dxb6 ♕d7 33 ♕b2 ♖e7 34 ♗xe4 ♕xh3 35 ♕g2 ♕xg2+ 36 ♗xg2 a4 37 ♗b7 +− 32 ♖bxb6 32 ♖dxb6 ♗c6∞ 33 ♖b5 33 ♕xe3? ♗xg2 34 ♖xb8 ♕xb8 35 ♔xg2 ♕xd6 −+; 33 ♗xb7!? ♖xb7 34 ♖b5 ♗xg2 34 ♔xg2 ♖bd8 35 ♖d5 ♕c6 36 ♖bxc5?! 36 ♕d3 +− ♕xa4 37 ♖xa5 ♕b3 38 ♔f3 ♖c8 39 ♖ab5 39 ♕xe3 ♕xc4∞ ♕c3 40 c5 ♖ed8 41 ♖d6 ♕c1 41...♖xd6 42 exd6 ♖xc5 43 d7 +− 42 ♔g4 Δ ♕d3 ♖f8 43 ♖d1 1-0 Hubner

58 Orso-Tompa Hungary Final 78

1 d4 ♘f6 2 c4 c6 3 ♘c3 d5 4 e3 e6 5 ♘f3 ♘bd7 6 ♗d3 dxc4 7 ♗xc4 b5 8 ♗d3 a6 9 0-0?! 9 e4! c5 10 b3 ♗b7 11 ♕e2 ♖c8 11...♗e7 12 ♗b2 0-0 13 ♖fd1 ♕b6 14 ♖ac1 ♖ac8= 12 ♗b2 ♕b6 13 ♖fd1 ♗e7 14 a4!? c4!? 14...b4!? 15 ♘b1 += 15 bxc4 bxc4 16 ♗xc4 16 ♗b1 ♗xf3 17 gxf3 e5∞ ♗xf3 17 gxf3 ♖xc4 18 ♕xc4 ♕xb2 19 d5? 19 ♖db1 ♕c2 20 e4! ♕d2 21 e5; 20...0-0 21 ♖a2 ♘b6!? 22 ♕c6! ♕d3 23 ♖xb6 ♕xf3 24 ♖e2 a5 +=; 22 ♖xb6 ♕c1+ 23 ♔g2 ♘h5 24 ♖b1 ♘f4+ = 0-0! ∓ 20 ♖a2

20 dxe6 ♘e5 21 exf7+ ♔h8 22 ♕c7
♘xf3+ 23 ♔g2 ♘h4+ −+; 21...♖xf7!?
**♕b4 21 ♕xb4 ♗xb4 22 dxe6 fxe6
23 ♘e2 a5! −+ 24 ♘d4 ♘c5 25 ♖c2
♖d8 26 ♖dc1 ♖d5 27 ♔g2 ♘fd7 28
♘c6 ♘d3! 29 ♘xb4** 29 ♖b1 ♖g5+
30 ♔f1 ♘7c5 **♖g5+ 30 ♔f1 ♘xc1
31 ♖xc1 axb4 32 ♖b1 ♖a5 33 ♖xb4
♖a7! 34 ♖c4 ♔f7 35 ♖f4+ ♔e8 36
♖h4 h6 37 ♖g4 ♘c5 38 a5 ♘b3 0-1
Tompa**

---

59 Browne-Stolyarov
Lone Pine 78

1 d4 d5 2 c4 e6 3 ♘c3 c6 4 e3 4 e4?!
dxe4 5 ♘xe4 ♗b4+ 6 ♗d2 ♕xd4 7
♗xb4 ♘f6 5 **♘f3 ♘bd7 6 ♗d3 dxc4
7 ♗xc4 b5 8 ♗d3** 8 ♗b3?! b4 9 ♘e2
♗b7 10 0-0 ♗d6 11 ♘f4 0-0 12 ♖e1
c5 =+ Browne-Polugaevsky, Reykjavik
78 **a6** 8...♗b7 9 e4 b4 10 ♘a4 c5
11 e5 ♘d5 12 0-0 cxd4 13 ♖e1 g6
14 ♗g5; 9 0-0!? **9 e4 c5 10 d5!** 10
e5?! cxd4 11 ♘xb5 axb5 12 exf6
c4 10...e5 11 b3 += **11 dxe6** 11
♗c2? e5 fxe6 **12 ♗c2** 12 e5!? **♕c7
13 0-0 ♗d6 14 ♘d4** 14 ♘g5!?; 14
e5 ♘xe5 15 ♘e4! **♘b6** 14...♘xh2+?
15 ♔h1 ♘c5 16 f4 e5 17 ♘dxb5±
15 ♔h1! 15 f4 ♗c5! 16 ♗e3 ♕d7!
17 e5 ♘fd5 **♗d7** 15...e5?? 16 ♘dxb5
+− **16 f4 e5** 16...♗c5 17 e5 ♘fd5
18 ♘e4± **17 ♘f3!** 17 ♘f5? ♗xf5 18
exf5 0-0 =+ **♗g4 18 a4!?** 18 f5±
**b4 19 a5 ♗xf3! 20 ♖xf3 ♘bd7 21
♘d5 ♘xd5 22 ♕xd5** 22 exd5 0-0
23 ♖h3 ♘f6 **0-0-0!**

Diagram

23 ♗e3! 23 f5 ♔b8! 24 ♗g5 ♘f6∓
♘c5! 23...b3? 24 ♗xb3; 23...exf4
24 ♕a8+ ♘b8 25 ♗b6 ♕c6 26 ♕xc6+
♘xc6 27 ♗xd8 ♖xd8∓; 24 ♗b6!

♘xb6 25 axb6 ♕xb6 26 ♕xc4+ ♔b7
27 ♗d3! a5 28 e5!± **24 fxe5** 24
♕xc4? ♗xe3 25 ♕xa6+ ♔b8 −+;
25 ♕xc7+ ♔xc7 26 ♖xe3 exf4∓
**♗xe3 25 ♖xe3 ♘xe5 26 ♕a8+ ♔d7
27 ♕xa6 ♔e7!** 27...b3 28 ♗xb3!
28 ♖g3! g6 29 ♖g5?! 29 ♕b5 ♖b8!
30 ♕d5?? ♖hd8 −+ **b3 30 ♕b5 ♘f7??**
30...♘g4! −+ 31 ♖xg4 bxc2 32 ♕g5+
♔e6!; 32 ♕b4+ ♔d6 33 ♕e1 ♕d1
34 ♖f4 −+ **31 ♖c5! ♕f4 32 ♗xb3!
cxb3 33 ♖f1 ♕b8?** 33...♕d6 34
♖c6 ♕d7 35 ♕c5+ ♔e8 36 ♖c7 ♕d6
37 ♕b5+ +− **34 ♕xb8 ♖xb8 35 ♖c7+
♔e6 36 ♖fxf7 ♖hd8 37 ♖ce7+ ♔d6
38 h4 ♔c5 39 ♖f2?!** 39 a6! +− **♔b4
40 a6 ♖a8 41 a7 ♖d1+ 42 ♔h2 ♖a1
43 ♖ff7! 1-0 Browne**

---

60 F.Portisch-Ribli Warsaw 79

**1 d4 d5 2 c4 c6 3 ♘f3 ♘f6 4 ♘c3
e6 5 ♗g5** 5 e3 ♘bd7 6 ♗d3 += **dxc4
6 e4 b5 7 e5 h6 8 ♗h4 g5 9 exf6**
9 ♘xg5 hxg5 10 ♗xg5 ♘bd7∞ **gxh4
10 ♘e5 ♕xf6 11 g3! ♘d7!** 11...♗b7?
12 ♗g2± **12 f4 ♗b7 13 ♗g2 ♘xe5
14 fxe5** 14 dxe5 ♕d8 15 ♕h5 ♕d3∓
♕e7 14...♕g5 15 0-0!? hxg3 16 ♕f3∞
**15 0-0 0-0-0 16 ♕h5 ♖xd4 17 ♖xf7
♕g5! 18 ♕xg5 hxg5 19 ♘e4!** 19
♖af1? ♗c5!∓

Diagram

19...h3!!∓ 20 ♗h1 ♖d5! 21 ♖af1 ♗b4 22 a3 ♗a5 23 ♗f3 23 ♘d6+ ♖xd6 24 exd6 ♗b6+∓ ♗c7! **24 ♘xg5 ♖xe5 25 ♘xe6 ♖xe6! 26 ♗g4 ♗b6+ 27 ♔h1 ♖he8 28 ♖e1 c5+! 29 ♖xb7** 29 ♔g1 ♗d5 30 ♖f6 c3!! −+ ♔xb7 **30 ♗xe6 ♔c7 31 ♖e2 a6 32 ♔g1** 32 ♗xc4 ♖xe2 33 ♗xe2 c4! −+ ♔d6 **33 ♗xc4 ♖xe2 34 ♗xe2 c4+ 35 ♔f1 ♗d4 36 a4 ♗xb2 37 axb5 axb5 38 ♔e1 ♔c5 39 ♔d2 b4 0-1 Gheorghiu**

√ **61 Knaak-Georgadse Halle 78**
1 d4 ♘f6 2 c4 e6 3 ♘c3 d5 4 ♗g5 c6 5 ♘f3 dxc4 5...h6!? **6 e4 b5 7 e5** 7 ♕c2; 7 a4 **h6 8 ♗h4 g5 9 ♘xg5** 9 exf6 gxh4 10 ♘e5 ♕xf6≈ **hxg5** 9...♘d5!? **10 ♗xg5 ♘bd7 11 g3** 11 ♕f3; 11 exf6 ♕a5?! 11...♗b7; 11...♖g8!?; 11...b4 12 ♘e4 ♘xe4 13 ♗xd8 ♔xd8 14 ♗xc4 ♘b6 15 ♗d3∝ **12 exf6 b4** 12...♗a6 13 a3!?± **13 ♘e4 ♗a6 14 b3** 14 ♕f3; 14 ♗g2 c3 15 bxc3 bxc3 16 ♕c2 ♖b8∓; 14 a3!? Flohr; 14 ♗d2 0-0-0!; 14 ♗e2!? ♕f5?! 14...♕d5 15 f3 ♘b6 +=; 14...0-0-0 15 ♕c2 ♘b6 16 ♗e3≈; 14...c3 15 ♗xa6 ♕xa6 16 ♕e2± 14...♘b6 += **15 f3 0-0-0?!** 15...♘b6!?∝ **16 ♗xc4 ♗xc4 17 bxc4 ♘c5? 18 g4! ♕g6 19 dxc5!! ♖xd1+ 20 ♖xd1 ♗h6** 20...♗xc5 21 h4! Δ 22 h5± **21 ♗xh6 ♕xh6 22 ♔e2 ♕h3 23 ♖dg1 ♔c7 24 ♖g3 ♕h4 25 g5 ♕f4 26 g6!** 26 h4! fxg6 **27 ♖xg6 ♖f8** 27...♖xh2!? **28 h4! +− ♕e5 29 h5 ♕b2+ 30 ♔e3 ♕a3+** 30...♕xa2 31 h6 b3 32 h7 b2 33 ♖g7+! ♔b8 34 h8♕ +− **31 ♕f4 e5+ 32 ♔g3 ♕e3 53 h6 ♕f4+ 34 ♔g2 1-0 Knaak/Malich**

1 d4 d5 2 c4 e6

62 Knezevic-Santos Algarve 78
1 d4 d5 2 c4 e6 3 ♘c3 ♗b4!? 4 cxd5 exd5 5 ♕a4+ ♘c6 6 a3!? ♗xc3+ 7 bxc3 ♘f6 8 e3 0-0 9 ♗d3 ♗d7 10 ♕c2?! 10 ♕d1 ♘a5! **11 ♘f3 ♖e8 12 ♘e5 c5 13 0-0 c4 14 ♘xd7 ♕xd7 15 ♗f5 ♕c6 16 ♗b2 g6 17 ♗h3 ♘e4 18 g3 ♘b3 19 ♖ad1 f5 =+ 20 ♗g2 ♖e7 21 ♖fe1 ♖ae8 22 ♖e2 b5 22...a5 23 a4!? bxa4 24 ♗a3 ♖e6 25 ♖de1 a6 26 f3 ♘f6! 27 ♔f2 ♖b8 28 h3 ♖b7! 29 g4?! fxg4 30 hxg4 ♖f7 31 ♔g1 ♕c7∓ 32 e4 ♕g3! 33 exd5?** 33 e5∓ ♕xe1+!! 33...♖xe2? 34 ♕xe2 ♘xd5 35 ♕e8+ ♔g7 36 ♕e5+ ♕xe5 37 dxe5± **34 ♖xe1 ♖xe1+ 35 ♔f2 ♖a1 36 ♗b2 ♖xg4+ 37 ♔g3** 37 ♔e2?? ♖e7+ ♘e3 38 **♕e4?!** 38 ♕e2∓ ♗f5+?? 38... ♖e1! −+ **39 ♔h3 ♖e7?!** 39...♖a2? 40 ♕b1; 39...♖d1 =+ **40 ♕f4 ♖a2 41 d6! ♖d7 42 ♕e4!=** ♘xd6! 43 ♕b1 ♖xb2 44 ♕xb2 ♘b5 45 ♕e2 ♖c7 46 ♕e6+ ♔g7 47 ♕xa6 ♘xc3! 48 ♕d6 ♖a7? 48...♘b5!= 49 ♕e5+ ♔f7?? 49...♔h6 50 ♕e3+ ♔g7 51 ♕xc3 a3 52 d5+ ♔g8 53 ♕xc4 a2 54 d6+ ♔g7? 55 ♕c3+ +−; 54...♔f8!∝ **50 ♗f1! +− ♘d2 51 ♕f4+ ♔e7 52 ♕xd2 a3 53 ♕e3+?! ♔d7 54 ♕xc3! a2 55 ♕a1 c3 56 ♗d3 ♔e7 57 ♔g3 ♔f6 58 ♗c2 ♖a3 1-0 Santos**

63 Tseitlin-Volchichin USSR 78
1 d4 ♘f6 2 c4 e6 3 ♘f3 d5 4 ♘c3 ♗b4 5 ♕a4+ ♘c6 6 ♗g5 h6 7 cxd5 exd5 8 ♗xf6 ♕xf6 9 e3 0-0 10 ♗e2 ♗e6 10...♖d8 11 0-0 ♗f8 12 ♖fc1 a6 13 ♕d1 ♗e6 14 ♘a4 ♗d6 15 ♘c5 ♗c8 16 a3 a5 17 b3 ♕e7 Uusi-Nikolaevsky, USSR 66 **11 0-0 a6 12 a3** N **♗d6 13 b4 ♘e7** 13...g5 **14 ♕c2 g5 15 e4! dxe4 16 ♘xe4 ♕g6** 16...♕g7 **17 ♗d3 ♗f5 18 ♘e5± ♕g7 19 ♖ae1 ♘g6 20 ♘xd6 ♗xd3** 20...cxd6 21 ♘xg6 fxg6 22 ♕c4+ ♕f7 23 ♖e7±; 22...♔h8 23 ♗xf5 ♖xf5 24 ♖e6±

21 ♕xd3 ♘f4 22 ♕f5 cxd6 23 ♘d7 ♖fd8 24 ♖e7 ♘e6 25 ♖d1! ♖ac8 25...♘xd4? 26 ♖xd4 **26 g3 ♖c7 27 ♘f6+ ♔f8** 27...♔h8? 28 ♖e8+ ♖xe8 29 ♘xe8 ♘xd4 30 ♘xg7 ♘xf5 31 ♘xf5± **28 ♘h5 ♖xe7** 28...♘xd4 29 ♘xg7 ♘xf5 30 ♖xc7± **29 ♘xg7 ♔xg7 30 ♖d3 ♖c7 31 h4 d5 32 hxg5 hxg5 33 ♖f3 ♔f8 1-0 Tseitlin**

✓64 Szmetan-Browne
Buenos Aires 2 78
1 ♘f3 c5 2 c4 ♘f6 3 ♘c3 e6 4 e3 ♘c6 5 d4 d5 6 a3 a6!? 7 dxc5 7 cxd5 exd5 8 dxc5 ♗xc5= **♗xc5 8 b4 ♗a7! 9 ♗b2 0-0 10 ♕c2?!** 10 ♗d3! **♕c7! 11 cxd5 exd5 12 ♗e2** 12 ♗d3

♗g4! **♖e8!** 12...d4? 13 ♘e4! ♘xe4 14 ♕xe4 dxe3 15 ♘g5 exf2+ 16 ♔f1 f5 17 ♗c4+ ♔h8 18 ♕h4 +- **13 0-0 d4!** 13...♗g4?! 14 ♘xd5! ♘xd5 15 ♘g5 **14 exd4 ♘xd4 15 ♘xd4 ♗xd4 16 ♖ac1 ♗g4! 17 ♗d3 ♕e5! =+ 18 ♘a4 ♖ad8! 19 ♗xd4 ♕xd4 20 ♘b2 ♖c8 21 ♕b1 g6!** Δ ♘d5 **22 h3 ♗e6 23 ♖xc8 ♖xc8 24 ♖c1 ♖c3! −+ 25 ♖xc3 ♕xc3 26 b5 axb5 27 ♗xb5 ♕xa3 28 ♗c4 ♘d5! 28...**♗xc4 29 ♘xc4 ♕c5 30 ♘e3 b5 31 ♕b2! **29 ♕c2 ♕c3! 30 ♕b1 h5 31 ♗f1 ♕d4 32 ♘d3 b6 33 ♘e1 ♘c3 34 ♕b2 ♗d5 35 ♘d3 ♗c4 36 ♕c2** 36 ♘c1 ♘e2+ −+ b5 **37 g3 b4! 38 ♘b2 b3 39 ♕c1 ♗d5 40 ♗d3 ♕xd3! 0-1 Browne**

✓65 Suba-Peters Hastings 78/9
1 c4 ♘f6 2 ♘c3 c5 3 g3 ♘c6 4 ♗g2 e6 5 ♘f3 ♗e7 6 0-0 0-0 7 d4 d5 8 cxd5 ♘xd5 9 ♘xd5 9 e4 ♘db4 10 ♗e3 cxd4 11 ♘xd4 ♘xd4 12 ♗xd4 ♗d7 13 ♖c1 ♗c6 14 a3 e5!? Christiansen-Hartston, Hastings 78/9 **exd5 10 dxc5 ♗xc5 += 11 b3** 11 ♗f4 ♗f5 12 ♕b3 ♗b6 13 ♖ad1 ♗e4 14 ♗e3 ♖e8 15 ♗xb6 ♕xb6 16 ♕xb6 axb6 17 a3∞ Andersson-Peters, Hastings 78/9 **♗f5 12 ♗b2 ♗e4 13 ♖c1 ♕e7?!** 13...♗b6 14 ♘d4 += **14 ♘h4! ♗xg2 15 ♔xg2** Δ ♗xg7 **d4 16 e3 ♗a3!** 16...dxe3? 17 ♕g4 ♘e5! 18 ♕e4 ♖fe8 19 ♘f5 ♕c7 20 b4 ♘g6! 21 ♖xc5!; 17 ♘f5! ♕e4+ 18 ♕f3 ♕xf3+ 19 ♔xf3 ♗b6 20 ♗xg7 exf2 **17 ♗xa3 ♕xa3 18 exd4 ♖ad8 19 d5 ♕a5 20 d6 ♕e5 21 ♖e1 ♕f6?!** 21...♕xd6 22 ♕xd6 ♖xd6 23 ♘f5 += ♖d7 24 ♖cd1 **22 d7 ♘b8 23 ♖c7 ♕b6 24 ♕c1 ♖xd7 25 ♖xd7 ♘xd7 26 ♘f5 ♘f6 27 ♖e7 g6 28 ♘e3 ♘e8 29 ♕c3 ♘d6 30 ♘g4 ♘b5? 31 ♘h6 mate 1-0 Speelman**

QGD 4 cxd5/5 &f4/5 &g5

66 Deze-Kovacs Bajmok 78
**1 d4 ♘f6 2 c4 e6 3 ♘c3 d5 4 cxd5
exd5 5 ♗g5 ♗e7 6 e3 c6 7 ♕c2 ♘bd7
8 ♗d3 ♘f8 9 ♘f3 ♘e6 10 ♗h4 g6
11 h3 ♘g7!?** 11...♘h5 12 ♗xe7 ♕xe7
13 0-0-0 ♘f6 14 g4 ♘g7 15 ♘e5 ♘d7
16 f4 ♘xe5 17 dxe5 += Thorbergsson-
Jimenez, Leipzig 60 **12 g4 h5** N 12...
0-0 13 0-0-0 b6 14 ♘e5 += Suetin-
Espig, Kecskemet 72; 12...♗e6 13
0-0-0 ♕a5 14 ♘e5 ♘g8 15 ♗g3±
Titenko-Krasnov, USSR 64 **13 0-0-0**
13 ♗xg6!? fxg6 14 ♕xg6+ ♔f8 15
♘e5∞ **♗e6 14 ♘e5 ♘d7 15 ♗g3 h4
16 ♗h2 ♗f6 17 f4 ♗xe5! 18 dxe5
♘c5 19 e4**

19...d4 20 ♗e2 ♕a5 21 ♖xd4 ♗xa2
22 ♘xa2 ♘ge6! 23 ♖b4 ♕xa2 =+
24 ♖d1 ♕a1+ 25 ♔d2 0-0-0+ 26 ♔e3
♕a5 27 ♖c4 ♖xd1 28 ♗xd1 ♖d8!
29 b4 ♕a1 30 ♗e2 ♕h1 31 ♗f3 ♕e1+
32 ♗e2 ♖d3+ −+ 33 ♕xd3 ♘xd3
34 ♔xd3 ♕f2 35 f5 ♘g5 36 e6 ♕xh2
37 exf7 ♘xf7 38 ♔d2 ♘e5 39 ♖c5
0-1 Kovacs

67 Forintos-Zaitsev Dubna 79
**1 d4 d5 2 c4 e6 3 ♘c3 ♘f6 4 ♘f3
♗e7 5 ♗f4 0-0 6 e3 c5 7 dxc5 ♗xc5
8 a3 ♘c6 9 ♕c2 ♕a5 10 ♖d1 ♗e7
11 ♘d2 e5 12 ♗g5 d4 13 ♘b3 ♕d8
14 ♗e2 g6** 14...♘g4!?∞ Portisch-

Spassky, Havana 66; 14...h6?! 15
♗xf6 ♗xf6 16 0-0 += Korchnoi-
Karpov (9) 78 **15 exd4!** 15 0-0?
♗f5 16 e4? ♘xe4! 17 ♗xe7 ♘xc3;
15 ♗xf6? ♗xf6 16 0-0 ♗g7 17 ♗f3
♕h4= Keene-O.Jacobsen, Buenos Aires
78 **exd4 16 0-0 ♗f5 17 ♕c1 d3 18
♗xd3! ♗xd3 19 ♖fe1** Δ ♖e3 ♖e8
20 ♗xf6 20 ♖xe7!? ♘xe7 21 ♗xf6
♕b6 22 ♗xe7 ♕xb3 23 ♘d5; 20...
♕xe7 21 ♘d5 **♗xf6 21 ♖xe8+ ♕xe8
22 ♘d5** 22 ♖xd3 ♘e5 ♕e6 23 ♘xf6+
23 ♘c7 ♕xc4; 23 ♖xd3 ♗xb2! **♕xf6
24 ♖xd3 ♖e8∞** Δ ♕xb2! **25 ♖e3
♖xe3 26 fxe3 ♘e5 27 ♕c3 ♕h4!**
½-½ 28 h3 ♕xc4 29 ♕xe5 ♕xb3
Keene

68 Botterill-Csom Hastings 78-9
**1 d4 d5 2 c4 e6 3 ♘c3 ♗e7 4 ♘f3
♘f6 5 ♗g5 0-0 6 cxd5 exd5 7 e3 c6
8 ♗d3 ♘bd7 9 ♕c2 ♖e8 10 0-0-0
♘f8 11 h3 b5** 11...♘e4 12 ♗xe7
♕xe7 13 ♗xe4 dxe4 14 ♘d2 f5 15
g4! **12 ♘e5 ♗b7 13 ♔b1 ♕b6 14
g4 a6 15 ♖hg1 c5 16 ♗f5! ♖ad8**
16...c4!? 17 f4 b4 18 ♗xf6 gxf6?!
19 ♘a4 ♕b5 20 g5! fxe5 21 g6 +−
17 dxc5?! 17 f4! ♗xc5 18 ♘f3 ♗e7
18...g6 19 ♘d4!? gxf5 20 gxf5 ♔h8
21 ♘a4!? bxa4 22 ♕xc5 ♖d6 23
♘e6∞ **19 ♘d4 g6 20 ♗d3 ♘8d7** 20...
♖c8! =+ **21 f4 ♖c8 22 ♕g2! ♗f8**
Zeitnot **23 ♖ge1 ♗g7 24 ♗c2 ♘c5?**
24...♘e4? 25 ♘xe4 dxe4 26 ♘f5!±;
24...b4!? **25 ♗xf6 ♕xf6 26 ♘xd5
♕h4 27 ♘f3!± ♕d8 28 e4 ♗xd5 29
♖xd5 ♕f6 30 ♘e5?** 30 e5! ♕xf4?
31 ♖d4 ♕h6 32 g5 ♕h5 33 ♖h4
+−; 30...♕e7 31 f5± **♕xf4?** 30...
♘e6! =+ **31 ♖f1 ♕e3 32 ♘xf7 ♘e6?**
32...♖f8!? **33 ♖d3 +− ♕c5 34 ♘d6
♕e5 35 ♗b3 ♖f8 36 ♖xf8+??** 36
♗xe6+ ♕xe6 37 ♘xc8 +− ♖xf8 37

78

♘f5± ♔h8 38 ♗xe6 gxf5?! 39 gxf5 b4 40 ♖d2 a5 41 ♖d7 41 ♖d5 +– a4 41...♗f6? 42 ♖xh7+ Zeitnot! 42 ♕xg7+ ♕xg7 43 ♖xg7 ♔xg7 44 e5 ♔h6? Zeitnot 44...♖d8! 45 ♕c2 ♕g5 46 ♗d7 ♖d8 47 e6?? 47 h4+ +– ♕f6 48 ♗xa4 ♖d4 48...♖d5= 49 ♗d7 49 ♔b3= △ ♗b5-c4 ♖h4 50 ♔b3 h5 51 a4 bxa3 52 bxa3 ♖xh3+ 53 ♔b4 ♖h1 54 a4 h4 55 a5?? 55 ♗c6= ♖b1+ 56 ♔a4 56 ♔c5 h3 57 ♗c6 ♖c1+ –+ ♖c1! 57 e7 57 ♗e8 h3 58 ♗h5 ♖c3 **0-1 Botterill**

69 Rocha-Byrne
Sao Paulo 79

1 d4 ♘f6 2 c4 e6 3 ♘f3 d5 4 ♘c3 ♘bd7 5 ♗g5 ♗e7 6 cxd5 exd5 6... ♘xd5± 7 e3 0-0 8 ♕c2 ♖e8 9 ♗d3 ♘f8 10 0-0 c6 11 ♖ab1 a5 12 a3 ♘g6 13 b4 ♗d6 13...axb4 14 axb4 h6 15 ♗xf6 ♕xf6 16 b5∞ 14 ♗f5 ♗xf5 15 ♕xf5 △ ♗xf6± ♖e6 16 ♖b3 h6 17 ♗xf6 ♖xf6 18 ♕g4 ♖e6 19 g3 ♕e7 20 ♖fb1 axb4 21 axb4 △ b5± b5 22 ♘e1! △ ♘d3± ♖f8 23 ♘d3 f5 24 ♕f3 ♘h8 25 ♘e2 g5 26 ♖c3! ♗b8 27 ♖bc1 ♖ff6

28 ♘e5! g4 29 ♕g2 ♗xe5 30 dxe5 ♖xe5 31 ♘d4 ♖e4 32 ♘xc6 ♕d6 33 ♖c5 ♗f7 34 ♖xd5!! +– ♕xc6 34...♕xd5 35 ♘e7+ ♖xe7 36 ♕xd5

+– 35 ♖xc6 ♖xc6 36 ♕f1 ♘e5 37 ♕a1 ♘f3+ 38 ♔g2 ♖ec4 39 ♖d7 ♖c3 40 ♕a8+ ♖c8 41 ♕d5+ ♔h8 42 ♕f7 **1-0 Gheorghiu**

70 Kovacs-Barczay
Hungary Final 78

1 ♘f3 ♘f6 2 c4 e6 3 ♘c3 d5 4 d4 c6 5 cxd5 exd5 6 ♗g5 ♗e7 7 e3 0-0 8 ♗d3 ♘bd7 9 0-0 ♖e8 10 ♕c2 ♘f8 11 ♘e5 ♘g4 12 ♗xe7 ♕xe7 13 ♘xg4 ♗xg4 14 ♖ae1 ♖ad8 N 14...♕f6 15 a4 ♖e7 16 b4 ♖ae8 17 b5 ♕g5 18 f4 += Pillsbury-Showalter, USA 1898; 14...♗h5 15 ♘e2 ♗g6 16 ♘f4 ♗xd3 17 ♘xd3 a5= Ivkov-Gufeld, Jugoslavia-USSR 75 15 a3 h5!? 16 b4 h4 17 f3 ♗c8 18 ♖e2 ♘e6 19 f4 ♕f6 20 ♘b1!? h3 21 g3 ♗c7! 22 ♘d2 ♗g4 23 ♖ee1 ♖e7 24 ♘f3 ♗xf3 25 ♖xf3 ♘e8?! 25...♕b5! 26 ♗xb5 cxb5 =+ 26 g4! ♕h4 27 ♖g3 ♘f6 28 ♕e2 ♖de8 29 ♕f3∞ ½-½ **Kovacs**

71 Gheorghiu-Radulov Balkaniad 78
1 c4 ♘f6 2 ♘c3 e6 3 ♘f3 d5 4 d4 ♘bd7 5 ♗g5 ♗e7 6 ♖c1! 0-0 6...dxc4 7 e4± 7 e3 c6 8 ♗d3 8 ♕c2!? △ ♖d1 += h6 8...dxc4 9 ♗xc4 ♘d5 10 ♗xe7 += 9 ♗h4 ♘e8!? 9...dxc4 10 ♗xc4 b5 11 ♗d3 a6 △ c5 += Alekhine-Euwe 35 10 ♗g3! ♗d6 10...dxc4 11 ♗xc4 ♗d6 12 e4!± Bukic-Radulov, Uljma 76 11 ♘e5!± ♗e7?! 12 0-0 ♗h4 13 ♗xh4 13 ♗f4 ♗g5 14 ♗xg5 ♕xg5 15 f4± ♕xh4 14 ♘f3! ♕e7 15 e4!± dxc4 16 ♗xc4 e5 17 ♘xe5! ♘xe5 18 dxe5 ♕xe5 19 ♔h1! △ f4± ♗e6 20 f4 ♕d6 21 ♕b3! ♘c7 21...♗xc4 22 ♕xc4± 22 ♗xe6 ♘xe6 22...♕xe6 23 ♕xb7 23 e5 ♕e7 24 ♘e4! ♖ad8 25 ♘d6± ♘xf4?! 25...♖d7 26 ♕g3! +– 26 ♗xf4 ♕xe5 27 ♘xf7!! +– 27 ♖xf7? ♖xd6 28 ♖f5+ ♕e6; 28

♖e7+ ♕d5; 28 ♖xb7= ♕xf4 28 ♘xd8+
♔h8 28...♔h7 29 ♕d3+ +−

29 ♕d1!! +− ♕e4 30 ♘xb7 ♖f2 31
♔g1 ♖xb2 32 ♘c5 ♕d5 33 a4 ♖d2
34 ♖e1! ♖c2 35 ♘e6 c5 36 ♕f1 ♔h7
37 ♘f8+ ♔g8 38 ♘g6 ♕f7 39 ♕d3!
♖f2 40 h4! +− Δ ♕d8+, h5 +− h5
41 ♖e7 ♕f5 42 ♕d8+ 1-0 42...♔h7
43 ♕h8+ ♔xg6 44 ♕xg7 mate
Gheorghiu

✔ 72 Gulko-Bleiman
Buenos Aires 78

1 d4 d5 2 c4 e6 3 ♘c3 ♘f6 4 ♗g5 ♗e7
5 e3 h6 6 ♗h4 0-0 7 ♘f3 b6 8 ♖c1
♗b7 9 ♗e2 9 ♗xf6 ♗xf6 10 cxd5
dxc4 10 0-0 ♘bd7 11 ♗xc4 a6 12
a4 c5 13 ♕e2 ♘d5 14 ♗g3 ♘xc3 15
♖xc3 15 bxc3 += ♘f6 16 dxc5 ♗xc5
17 ♖d1 ♕e8 18 ♗e5 ♕xa4! 19 ♗xf6
gxf6 20 ♘d4 ♖fd8 21 ♕g4+ ♔h8
22 ♕h5 ♗f8 23 ♗b3 ♕e8 24 ♖c7 ♗e4!
25 ♖xf7 ♖a7! 26 ♗xe6 ♖xf7 27
♗xf7 27 ♕xf7! ♕e5 28 ♕g4 ♗c5 29
♘e6?! ♖xd1+ 30 ♕xd1 ♗d6! 31
f4?? 31 ♕h5! ♕xh5 32 ♗xh5 ♗e5
33 ♘d4 ♕xb2 32 ♕f1 ♕d2 33 h3
♕xe3+ 34 ♔h2 ♗d5! 35 ♕xa6 ♗xf4+
35...♗xe6? 36 ♕a8+ +− 36 ♘xf4
♕xf4+ 0-1 Keene

73 Gheorghiu-Spassky
Buenos Aires 78

1 d4 ♘f6 2 c4 e6 3 ♘f3 d5 4 ♘c3
♗e7 5 ♗g5 h6 6 ♗h4 0-0 7 e3 b6 8
♗d3 8 cxd5 ♘xd5= ♗b7 9 0-0 ♘bd7
10 ♕e2 c5 11 ♖fd1 ♗e4! 12 ♗xe7
♕xe7 13 ♖ac1 ♖fd8 14 cxd5 ♘xc3!
14...exd5 15 dxc5! ♘xc3 16 bxc3
bxc5 17 c4!± ; 15...bxc5 16 ♗xe4!
dxe4 17 ♘d2 += 15 ♖xc3 ♗xd5 16
e4 ♗b7 17 h3 ♖ac8 18 a3 cxd4 19
♖xc8 ♖xc8 20 ♘xd4 ♘e5 21 ♗b1
♖d8 22 ♘f3!= 22 f4? ♕c5!∓ ♖xd1+
23 ♕xd1 ♘xf3+ 24 ♕xf3 ♕d6 25
♕d3 ♕xd3 26 ♗xd3 e5 27 ♔f1 ♔f8
28 g3 ♔e7 29 ♔e2 ♔d6 30 ♔e3 a5
31 b4 ½-½ **Gheorghiu**

74 Gheorghiu-Radulov
Buenos Aires 78

1 c4 ♘f6 2 ♘c3 e6 3 ♘f3 d5 4 d4
♗e7 5 ♗g5 0-0 6 e3 b6 7 ♗d3 ♗b7
8 ♗xf6! += ♗xf6 9 cxd5 exd5 10
♕b3! a5 10...c6 11 0-0 ♘d7 12 e4
+= 11 0-0 ♘a6 12 ♖fd1 ♘b4 13
♗e2 c5 14 ♗b5!± a4!? 14...c4 15
♕a4± 15 ♗xa4 ♗e7 16 ♖d2 c4 17
♕d1 ♖a5 18 a3 ♘a6 18...♘d3 19
♕b1 Δ ♗c2 +− 19 ♕b1!? 19 b4!
♘xb4! 20 axb4 ♗xb4∞ ♘c7 20 b4
♖a7 21 ♖da2 f5 22 ♗c2 g6 23 a4
♗f6 24 b5 Δ a5± ♖a5 25 ♘e5! ♗xe5
26 dxe5 d4!∞ 27 exd4 ♕xd4 28
♕e1 ♖e8 29 ♖d1! ♖xe5?! 29...
♕xe5 +=

Diagram

30 ♘e4!! +− ♖xe4 31 ♗xe4 ♕xe4
32 ♖d8+ ♔f7 33 ♖d7+ ♔f6 33...
♔e6 34 ♖e2!?± 34 ♕xe4 ♗xe4 35
♖xc7 +− ♗d3 36 f4! c3 37 ♖xc3
♗xb5 38 ♖b2! 1-0 38...♗xa4 39
♖xb6+ Δ ♖c7+ +− **Gheorghiu**

♘b6 16 a3! ♛c5 17 ♗a2 ♗g4 18
♖c1 ♗h5 19 ♗xf6! ♗xf6 20 ♕f5!±
♗g5 21 h4 ♗xe3 21...♗g6?? 22 ♕xg6
22 ♘de4 ♕d4 23 ♖c2! +− g6 24
♘f6+ ♔h8 25 ♕h3 ♗f4 26 ♘xh5
gxh5 27 g3 ♕d3

75 Beljavsky-Tal
USSR Final 78

1 d4 ♘f6 2 c4 e6 3 ♘f3 d5 4 ♗g5
♗e7 5 ♘c3 0-0 6 e3 ♘bd7 7 ♖c1 a6
8 a3 8 cxd5!?; 8 c5!? dxc4 9 ♗xc4
c5 10 0-0 b5 11 ♗a2 ♗b7 12 ♗b1
♖c8 13 ♕d3?! 13 ♕e2 ♗xf3! 14 gxf3
cxd4 15 ♘e4 15 ♕xd4 ♘c5 =+ ♖xc1
16 ♖xc1 dxe3? 16...♘xe4 17 ♕xe4
g6 18 ♗xe7 ♕xe7 19 ♕xd4 += **17
♗xf6 exf2+ 18 ♔f1 ♗xf6 19 ♘c5?**
19 ♖d1! ♗xb2? 20 ♘f6+! +−; 19...
♕c7 20 ♘c5! +− g6 20 ♘xd7 ♗xb2
21 ♖d1 ♖e8 22 ♔xf2 ♕h4+ 23 ♔g2
♖c8∞ 24 ♕e3 ♕e7 25 ♗e4 ♕g7 26
a4 Zeitnot bxa4 27 ♘b6 ♖c3 28
♕d4+ e5 29 ♕d2 29 ♕xa4 ♖b3 30
♘d5 30 ♘xa4 ♗d4 ♕h4 31 ♗c2 ♖b7
32 ♖e1 a3 −+ 33 ♖e4 ♕d8 34 ♖a4
♖b6 35 ♗e4 ♗d6 Δ f5 36 f4 exf4 37
♗f3 ♕g5+ 38 ♔f1 ♕e5 39 ♔g2 ♕f5
40 ♕d1 ♕g5+ 41 ♔f2 0-1 Keene

76 Ribli-Prandstetter
Warsaw 79

1 ♘f3 d5 2 d4 ♘f6 3 c4 e6 4 ♘c3
♗e7 5 ♗g5 0-0 6 e3 ♘bd7 7 ♕c2 7
♖c1 += c5! 8 ♖d1 ♕a5 9 ♘d2 cxd4
10 ♘b3 ♕b6 10...♕c7 =+ 11 ♖xd4
h6 12 ♗h4 e5! 13 ♖d1 dxc4 14
♗xc4 ♕b4?! 14...♕c6!∓ 15 ♘d2

28 ♗b1!! +− ♖g8 29 ♖e2 ♕d4 30
♕f5! ♖g7 31 gxf4 ♘c4 32 ♕d3 ♕xf4
33 ♖e4 ♘xb2 34 ♕c2 ♕f3 35 ♖f1
♖g2 36 ♖xe5 1-0 Gheorghiu

77 Tal-Geller
USSR Final 78

1 c4 e6 2 d4 d5 3 ♘c3 ♘f6 4 ♗g5
♗e7 5 e3 0-0 6 ♘f3 h6 7 ♗xf6 ♗xf6
8 ♖c1 c6 8...♘c6; 8...♖e8; 8...b6
9 ♗d3 ♘d7 10 cxd5 exd5 11 b4
♗e7 11...a6 12 a4 a5 13 b5 ♘b6 14
0-0 += Gligoric-Benko, Palma de
Mallorca 68 **12 b5 ♗a3! 13 ♖c2**
13 ♖b1? ♕a5 ♗d6 **14 0-0 ♘f6 15
bxc6 bxc6 16 ♘a4 ♘e4 17 ♘e5 ♕e8
18 f3** 18 ♘xc6 ♗d7 19 ♕c1 ♖c8
20 ♗b5 a6 21 ♘b6 axb5 22 ♘xc8
♗xc8 **c5 19 fxe4 cxd4** 19...♕xa4
20 exd5 cxd4 21 ♖xc8 ♕xd1 22
♖xf8+ ♖xf8 23 ♖xd1 ♗xe5; 21
♘c4 ♘c5 22 e4 **20 ♘g4** 20 ♘c6!?
dxe4 21 ♗c4 **dxe4 21 ♗c4 ♗xg4
22 ♕xg4 ♕xa4**

Diagram

23 Xxf7! 23 Ab3 a5 24 Ecf2 e5
Xxf7 24 Axf7+ xf7 25 f5+ e7
25...g8 26 d5+ h7 27 xe4+
g6 28 b7+ +− **26 xe4+ d7 27
b7+ e6 28 e4+ d7 ½-½ Keene**

Catalan

78 Vukic-Sydor Stip 78

1 d4 f6 2 c4 e6 3 f3 d5 4 g3
dxc4 5 g2 bd7 6 bd2 b6 7
0-0 d7!? 8 a4 8 e5? a4! 9 b3
xd4 −+ c6 9 a5 bd7 9...bd5?!
10 e5! **10 xc4 a6 11 g5 e7
12 xf6 xf6** 12...xf6?! 13 ce5!
d5 14 a4+ d7 15 Efc1 +=; 13...
b5? 14 g5 0-0 15 xb7± **13 c2
0-0 14 e4 g6 15 Efd1 e7 16 e3**
16 d5!? exd5 17 exd5 b5 18 a3
Eac8 17 h4?! 17 f1 Δ d5 g7 18
f1 f6 19 d3 Efd8= 20 e5 e8
21 f1 c5 22 dxc5 Exc5 23 5c4
Exd1+ 24 Exd1 d7? 24...h6!
=+ **25 d2!± e5 26 d8 f8?!**
26...f6!? 27 xe7 xe7 28 b4
xc4!; 27 a8!? **27 a8 Ec7 28
b6 f3+ 29 g2 d4 30 ec4
c5** 30...f5 31 e5 c6 32 f4 Δ c8
**31 d8 +− Ee7 32 b4 xb4 33
Exd4 xd4 34 xd4 g8 35 d8
f6 36 d6 f8 37 d7+ 1-0 Vukic**

1 d4 f6 2 c4 e6 3 g3 d5 4 g2 e7
5 f3 0-0 6 0-0 dxc4 7 c2 7 e5
c6 a6 8 xc4 8 a4 c5!; 8...c6
9 xc4 d5 10 c3!? **b5 9 c2 b7
10 d2!?** 10 f4 c6 **11 e3!** N 11
c3 xd4 12 xd4 xg2 13 xe6
+= **b4 12 xb4 xb4 13 a3 d6
14 bd2 e7 15 e4 e5 16 h4!** g6
16...exd4 17 e5 +− **17 f4 exd4 18
e5 d3 19 xd3** 19 exd6? e3+ c5+
**20 h1 Efd8 21 c2 xg2+ 22 xg2
d5 23 e4±** d4 24 Ead1 b6
24...c5 25 b4 ac8 26 bxc5 xc5
27 Exd5 +− **25 Ede1 c4 26 f6+
g7 27 b3!** xa3 28 e4 e6 29
h4 c5 29...xb3 30 f5+ gxf5
31 xf5 Eh8 32 h5+ f8 33 e6
+− **30 f3 xb3 31 f5 Ea7 32 h4
Eh8 33 h5+ gxh5 34 f6+ g8
35 d8+ g7 36 f6+ 1-0 Keene**

Dutch

1 c4 f5 2 f3 f6 3 g3 d6 4 d4 e6
5 g2 e7 6 0-0 0-0 7 b3 7 c3
a5 8 Ee1 e4!? 9 c2 c6!? 10
xe4 b4 11 c3?!; 11 b1 Raicevic-
Maric, Bar 77 e4!? 7...e8 8 b2
f6 9 c2 c6 10 Ed1 10 bd2!?
e8 11 c3 xc3 12 xc3 e5=
13 d5?! 13 dxe5!? e7 14 Eac1 f4!
15 gxf4?! exf4 16 d4

Diagram

16...xd4! 17 Exd4 h5!∓ 18 d2
g6 19 h1 h3 20 xh3 20 Eg1!?
xh3 21 Eg1 Eae8 22 f3 Ee7 23
c2 Efe8 24 Ed2 h4! −+ 25 d4
f5 26 f2 g6 27 d3 f7?! 27...

🗒a3 1-0 Vukic

🗒e3! **28 b4?** 28 🗒g2!? 🗒e3! **29** ♗xe3
29 ♕c2 🗒xe2! ♘g3+ **30** 🗒xg3 fxg3
31 ♔g1 31 ♗g1 g2 mate ♕xh2+ **32**
♔f1 g2+ **0-1 Ciocaltea**

✓81 Vukic-Bjelajac
Novi Sad 78

**1 d4 f5 2 c4 ♘f6 3 ♘f3 g6 4 g3 ♗g7
5 ♗g2 0-0 6 0-0 d6 7 ♘c3 ♘c6 8 d5
♘a5 9 ♘d2** 9 ♕d3!? c5 10 b3 a6 11
♗b2 🗒b8 12 ♘d2 += **c5 10 ♕c2
e5!?** 10...a6 11 b3 🗒b8 12 🗒b1 b5
13 ♗b2 e5 14 dxe6 ♗xe6 15 ♘d5
♗xd5 16 cxd5 🗒c8!= Vukic-
Matulovic, Jugoslavia Final 78 **11
dxe6 ♗xe6 12 🗒d1 ♘c6** 12...♘xc4
13 ♘xc4 ♗xc4 14 ♗xb7 🗒b8 15
♗g2 △ ♗f4 **13 e3 ♕e7 14 ♕a4 ♘e5?!**
14...🗒fd8! 15 ♗xc6 bxc6 16 ♕xc6
d5! **15 f4 ♘d3 16 ♘f1 ♘xc1 17
🗒axc1** += ♗d7 18 ♕c2 ♗c6 19 🗒d3
🗒fd8 20 🗒cd1 ♗d7 21 b3 🗒ad8 22
h3 a6 23 a4 🗒b8 24 ♔h2 🗒bd8 25
♘d5 ♗xd5 26 ♗xd5+ ♘xd5 27 🗒xd5
♕e6 28 🗒1d3 ♕f6 29 ♔g2 ♔b2 30
♕xb2 ♗xb2 31 g4!± fxg4 32 hxg4
♘f6 33 ♘d2 b6 34 e4! ♗d4? 34...
♔f7?! 35 e5 ♗e7 36 f5 +- **35 ♘f3
b5??** 35...♗g7 36 e5 ♗f8 37 ♘g5 +-
36 cxb5 +- axb5 37 ♘xd4 cxd4
38 🗒xb5 d5 39 🗒xd5 🗒xd5 40 exd5
🗒xd5 41 g5 🗒d8 42 b4 ♔f7 43 ♔f3
♔e6 44 ♔e4 🗒c8 45 a5 🗒c1 46

82 Miles-Meulders
Amsterdam 3 78

1 d4 f5 2 ♗g5 c5? 3 dxc5 3 d5±; 3
e3±; 3 c3±; 3 ♘c3!? **♘a6** 3...♕a5+
4 ♘c3 ♕xc5 5 e4± **4 e4!** N 4 c4
♘xc5 5 ♘c3 += Cuderman-Vukcevic,
Jugoslavia 57 **fxe4 5 ♘c3 ♗xc5 6
♗e3± ♘e6** 6...b6? 7 ♗xc5 bxc5 8
♕d5 🗒b8 9 ♕h5+ g6 10 ♕e5 +-;
6...d6? 7 ♗xc5 dxc5 8 ♗b5+ ♗d7
9 ♕h5+ +-; 6...e6?? 7 ♗xc5 ♗xc5
8 ♕h5+ +- **7 ♗xe4 ♘f6 8 ♗d3 g6
9 h4** 9 ♘xf6+ exf6 10 ♘f3± ♗g7
10 ♗xf6+ 10 h5 ♘xh5 11 🗒xh5
gxh5 12 ♕xh5+ ♔f8 △ ♕e8∞; 10
♘g5!? ♕a5+! △ d6∞ **exf6 11 ♘f3
b6 12 ♕e2** 12 ♗e4 🗒b8 13 c3± ♗b7
13 0-0-0 ♕c7!? 13...♕e7 **14 h5 0-0-0**
14...f5? 15 hxg6 hxg6 16 🗒xh8+
♗xh8 17 ♗g5 ±/+- **15 🗒h4** 15 hxg6
hxg6 16 ♗xg6 ♘f4 17 ♗xf4 ♕xf4+
18 ♔b1 ♕g4∞; 18...f5∞; 15 h6 ♗f8
16 🗒h4± **f5 += 16 ♗a6 f4 17 ♗d4
♗xd4 18 ♘xd4 🗒he8 19 ♗xb7+
♔xb7 20 ♘f3+ ♔b8 21 🗒hh1 g5
22 h6 ♗e5** 22...♗xd4 23 🗒xd4±
**23 ♘b3!? ♕c6 24 🗒d5 🗒c8 25 c3
🗒c7** 25...♗xc3? 26 bxc3 🗒e3 27
fxe3 ♕xc3+ 28 ♔d1 +- **26 ♕d3
d6?** 26...♕e6 **27 🗒d1?** 27 ♔b1±
🗒e6 28 🗒h1 28 ♕f5 🗒f6! 29 ♕xg5
♗xc3 🗒g6 29 ♔b1 += ♕c4 30 ♕xc4
🗒xc4 31 ♘d2 🗒c7 32 ♘e4 g4 33
♔c2 🗒f7 34 ♔d3 f3 35 g3 ♔c7 36 b4
🗒f5 37 c4 ♔c6 38 a4 🗒f7 39 🗒h5
🗒e7 40 a5 🗒ee6 41 🗒f5 41 b5+!
♔c7 42 🗒f5± ♗e7 **42 🗒h5 🗒e8** 42...
🗒ee6 43 b5+! **43 a6 🗒f8 44 ♔e3!?**
🗒e8?! 44...🗒f7 **45 🗒f5!? ♗e7** 45...
🗒xh6? 🗒f7 +- **46 🗒f8 ♔d7** 46...
🗒xh6? 47 🗒a8 🗒c7 48 🗒d8 🗒d7 49
b5+ △ 🗒a8 +- **47 b5 ♔e6** 47...🗒xh6

48 c5 bxc5 49 b6 +−; 48...♚e6 49
♖d1! ♖g6 50 cxd6 ♖d7 51 ♖e8+
♔f5 52 ♖h1! ♗f6 53 ♖h5+ ♗g5+ 54
♖xg5+ ♖xg5 55 ♖f8+ +−; 49...dxc5
50 ♘g5 mate; 49...♖h5 50 cxb6 axb6
51 ♖b8 +−; 49...bxc5 50 b6 axb6
51 ♘g5+ Δ ♖a8 +− **48 ♔d3 ♖d7** 48...
♖xh6 49 ♘g5+ Δ ♖a8 +− **49 ♖e8+
♖e7 50 ♖d8 ♖d7 51 ♖b8** 51 ♖xd7
♔xd7 52 c5 ♔e6 53 cxb6 axb6 54
♔c4 ♖g8 55 ♖d2 d5+ 56 ♖xd5 ♖c8+
57 ♘c5+ bxc5 58 ♖xe5+ ♔xe5 59
b6 +−; 55...♖c8+ 56 ♔b3 d5 57 ♘g5+
♔d6∝; 53...♔xd5? 54 bxa7 ♖g8
55 b6 ♗d4 56 ♘f6+! ♗xf6 57 b7 +−;
52...bxc5 53 b6 axb6 54 a7 ♖g8
55 ♖xe5+ +−; 53...♔c6 54 b7 ♖g8
55 ♔c4 ±/+−; 52...♔c7 53 ♘xd6
♗xd6 54 ♖xd6 ♖xd6 55 cxd6+ ♔xd6
56 ♔d4 +− **♖c7?** 51...♖xh6! 52 ♖b7
♖h1 ∝/∓; 52 ♖e8+ ♖e7 53 ♖xe7+
♔xe7 54 c5 bxc5 55 b6 ♖g6 56
b7 ♖g8 57 ♔c4∝; 53 ♖d8 ♖d7 **52
♖b7 ♔d7 53 c5!** bxc5 54 ♘xc5+
Zugzwang 54 b6 axb6 55 a7 ♖g8 56
♖b8 +− **♔c8 55 b6! ♖xb7** 55...axb6
56 a7 +−; 55...♖xc5 56 bxa7! ♖xd5+
57 ♔e4 +− **56 axb7+ ♔b8 57 ♘d7+
♔xb7 58 bxa7 ♔xa7** 58...♖xh6 59
♖a5 +− **59 ♘xe5 dxe5 60 ♖d7+
♔b6 61 ♖xh7 +− ♖d6+** 61...♖g5
62 ♖h8 ♖h5 63 h7 ♔a7 64 ♔e3!
Zugzwang ♔b7 65 ♔e4 ♔a7 66 ♖g8
+− **62 ♔e4 ♖d2 63 ♖h8 ♖xf2 64
h7 ♖e2+ 65 ♔d5 ♖d2+ 66 ♔xe5 f2
67 ♖f8 ♖e2+ 68 ♔d4 ♖d2+ 69 ♔e3
f1♘+ 70 ♖xf1 1-0 Miles**

Benko Gambit

83 Radev-Mihalchishin
Pazardjik 78
1 d4 ♘f6 2 c4 c5 3 d5 b5 4 a4 bxc4
5 ♘c3 g6 6 e4 d6 7 f4 ♗g7 8 ♘f3

0-0 9 ♗xc4 ♗a6 10 ♗xa6 ♘xa6 11
e5 ♘d7 12 ♕e2 ♘c7 13 0-0 ♖b8
14 ♗e3 ♖b4 15 a5 ♕b8 16 ♖a2 ♕b7!
17 ♖d1 ♖b8 18 a6 ♕b6 19 ♖d2 ♘b5!
20 g3 ♘d4 21 ♗xd4 cxd4 22 ♘a4
♕a5 23 ♘xd4 ♕xd5 23...♖xa4!?
24 ♘c3 ♕c5 25 ♘a4 ♕d5 26 ♘c3
♕c5 27 ♘a4 ½-½ Mechkarov

84 Gheorghiu-Diez del Corral
Buenos Aires 78
1 d4 ♘f6 2 c4 c5 3 d5 b5!? 4 cxb5
a6 5 bxa6 ♗xa6 6 g3 d6 7 ♗g2 g6
8 b3! += ♗g7 9 ♗b2 0-0 10 ♘h3!
♘bd7 11 0-0 ♕b6! 11...♕a5; 11...
♕b8!? 12 ♘c3! ♕c7 12...c4? 13 b4
Δ a4± 13 ♖e1 ♘b6 14 a4 ♖ab8
15 e4!? 15 ♘f4 ♘bd7 16 ♘a3! ♘h5
17 ♗xg7 ♘xg7 18 ♖ab1 ♕a5 19
f4 c4!∝ 20 ♘xc4 ♗xc4 21 bxc4
♖xb1 22 ♕xb1 ♕xa4 23 ♗f1! +=
♖b8 24 ♕a1! ♕b4 25 ♘f2 ♘c5 26
♖e3 h5 27 ♖a3!± Δ ♖a8 ♕d2 28
♖a8 ♖xa8 29 ♕xa8+ ♔h7 30 ♕a7
♘b3 31 ♘h3! Δ ♘g5+ +− f6 32 ♕f2!
♕c3! 33 ♕e2 ♘c1 34 ♕d1 h4 35
♔g2 hxg3 36 hxg3 ♘h5 37 ♕f3 ♕c2+
38 ♘f2 ♕d2 39 ♗d3! Δ e5 +− ♘xd3
40 ♕xd3 ♕c1 41 ♕b3 41 e5 dxe5
42 fxe5 fxe5 43 ♕f3 ♔g7; 43 ♕e2
♕g5!∝ ♗g7 42 ♕b7 ♔f7 43 ♕c8!
♕e3 44 ♕e6+ ♔f8 45 ♕g4! ♔f7 46
f5 ♕h6 47 ♕xg6+ ♕xg6 48 fxg6+
♔xg6 49 ♔f3 ♘g7 50 ♘d3 ♔f7!
50...♘e8? 51 ♘f4+ Δ ♘e6 +−
Zugzwang 51 ♘f4 f5 52 exf5? 52
g4!± ♘xf5 53 g4 ♘d4+ 54 ♔e4 54
♔e3! += ♘b3! 55 g5 ♘d2+ 56 ♔f5
56 ♔d4 ♘f3+ ♘xc4 57 g6+ ♔g7 58
♘h5+ ♔f8 59 ♔f4 ♘b6 60 ♔e4 ♔g8
61 ♘f4 ♔g7 62 ♔f5 ♘xd5! ½-½ 63
♘xd5 e6+! 64 ♔xe6 ♔xg6 Gheorghiu

85 Nadjorf-Vaganian
Buenos Aires 2 78

1 d4 ♘f6 2 ♘f3 c5 3 d5 3 c4 cxd4
4 ♘xd4 b5 4 ♗g5 d6 5 ♗xf6 exf6
6 e3 a6 7 a4! b4 8 a5 ♗e7 9 ♘bd2
+= f5 10 ♘c4 ♘f6 11 ♗e2 0-0 12
0-0 ♖a7 13 ♖b1 ♖e8 14 ♕d2! △ c3
+= ♖b7! 15 c3 ♖b5 16 cxb4 ♖xb4
17 b3 ♕e7 18 ♗d3 g6 19 ♗e1! △
♘c2, b4± ♗d7 20 ♘c2 ♖b8 21 f4??
21 b4 ♗b7!∞; 21 ♖fe1∞ ♗g7 22 b4
♗b7 23 bxc5 ♘xc5∓

24 ♘b4 ♖bc8! 25 ♖fc1 ♖c7 26 ♖c2
h5 27 h3 ♗f6 28 ♔h2 h4 29 ♕e2
♗g7 30 ♖bc1 ♘f8! 31 ♕d1 ♘xd3
32 ♕xd3 ♖c5! 33 ♔g1 ♕e4! −+ 34
♕xe4 ♖xe4 35 ♔f2 ♗xd5 36 ♘xd5
♖xd5 37 ♘b6 ♖xa5 38 ♖c8 ♔g7 39
♖a8 ♖a2+ 40 ♔f1 ♖xe3 41 ♘d7
♗e7 0-1 Gheorghiu

Benoni

86 Haik-Gheorghiu
Buenos Aires 78

1 d4 ♘f6 2 ♘f3 c5 3 d5 g6 4 ♘c3
♗g7 5 e4 d6 6 ♗b5+ ♗d7 7 a4 0-0
8 ♘d2! e6! 9 ♗xd7 ♕xd7 10 0-0 ♘a6
11 ♘c4 ♘c7!= 12 ♕d3 12 dxe6 ♕xe6
13 ♕xd6 ♕xc4 14 ♕xc7 ♘xe4 =+
b6 13 ♖d1 exd5! 14 exd5 △ ♗f4±
♘h5! 15 ♘e4 ♘e8 16 ♖e1 h6 16...

f5? 17 ♘g5± **17 ♖a3 ♖ad8 18 ♕f3
f5! 19 ♘g3 ♗xg3 20 ♕xg3 g5 =+ 21
h4 f4 22 ♕d3 ♕f5 23 hxg5 hxg5
24 ♖e7! ♕g4!** 24...♕xd3 25 ♖xd3
♖f7 26 ♖xf7 ♔xf7 27 g3! **25 ♖xa7
♘f6!! 26 ♕f3!** 26 ♔g6? ♕d1+ 27
♔h2 ♘g4+ −+ **♖fe8 27 ♘d2** 27 ♕xg4?
♖e1+ 28 ♔h2 ♘xg4+ −+ **♕f5 28 ♖d3
♘e4 29 g4! ♕g6! 30 ♔g2 ♗d4! 31
♘c3! ♖xc3 32 bxc3 ♘f6 33 ♘xb6
♖e1 34 ♖d1 ♖de8 35 ♘d7**

35...♖xd1?? 35...♘xd7! 36 ♖xd7
♕h6 37 ♖xe1 ♖xe1 38 ♕h3 ♖g1+
−+ **36 ♕xd1 ♘e4 37 ♕f3 ♘d2 38
♕d3 f3+! 39 ♔g3!!** 39 ♔h2 ♕h6+
−+ ♘e4+ 39...♕h6! **40 ♕xd2 ♕h4+
41 ♔xf3 ♕h3 mate;** 40 ♘f6+!! ♕xf6
41 ♕xd2 ♖e2∞ **40 ♔h2 ♕h6+ 41
♔g1 ♕h3 42 ♘f6+!! ½-½** 42...♔f8
43 ♘d7+ **Gheorghiu**

87 Gheorghiu-Chen Te
Buenos Aires 78

1 d4 c5 2 d5 ♘f6 3 ♘c3 d6 4 e4 g6
5 ♘f3 ♗g7 6 ♗b5+ ♗d7 6...♘fd7!
7 a4 0-0 8 ♗xd7!? 8 0-0 ♗g4 9 ♗e2
+= ♘bxd7 9 0-0 ♕a5 10 ♖e1! ♘b6
11 ♘b5!± ♖ac8 12 ♗d2 ♕a6 13
b3 ♘fd7 14 ♖b1 14 c4 ♗xa1 15
♕xa1 f6∞ **c4! 15 ♗g5 ♖fe8 16 ♕d2
♘c5 17 ♘fd4 ♘bd7 18 f3!** △ ♗e3±
cxb3 19 cxb3 ♘e5 20 ♖ec1 ♕b6 21

a5 **♕d8 22 ♘xa7! ♖ed3!** 22...♖a8
23 ♘ab5 **23 ♖c4! ♗xd4+! 24 ♖xd4
♖a8 25 ♗e3!!± ♖xa7 26 ♖xd3 ♖xa5**
26...♘xd3 27 ♗xa7 +− **27 b4 ♖b5
28 ♖c3 ♘a6 29 ♖c4 ♕d7 30 ♖bc1**
e5 **31 dxe6! ♕xe6 32 ♖d4 ♕b3 33
♖xd6 ♕xb4 34 ♖d8! +− ♕e7** 34...
♕xd2?? **35 ♖xe8+ +− 35 ♖cc8 ♘c7
36 h3 ♖xd8 37 ♖xd8+ ♘e8 38 ♕d4!**
△ **♗h6 ♖b1+ 39 ♔h2 f6 40 ♕d5+
♔h8** 40...♔g7 41 ♖d7 **41 ♗c5 ♕c7+
42 ♕d6! 1-0** 42...♕xd6+ 43 ♗xd6 △
♖xe8+ +− **Gheorghiu**

88 Segal-Riemsdyk
Sao Paulo 79
**1 d4 c5 2 d5 ♘f6 3 ♘c3 d6 4 e4 g6
5 ♘f3 ♗g7 6 ♗e2** 6 ♗b5+! **♘fd7 7**
a4± **♘a6 7 ♘d2 ♘c7 8 a4 a6 9 ♘c4
b5!? 10 ♘b6** 10 axb5? axb5 11 ♖xa8
♘xa8 12 ♘xb5 ♘xe4∓ **b4! 11 ♘xa8
♗xa8 12 ♘b1 ♗xe4∞ 13 ♘d2 f5?!**
13...♘f6!∞ **14 0-0 0-0 15 ♗f3 ♘g5**
15...♘f6∞ **16 ♗e2 ♘c7** 16...♘e4∞
17 ♘c4 f4 18 h4!± ♘h3+!? 18...
♘e4 19 ♗d3±; 18...♘f7 19 ♗xf4±
**19 gxh3 e6! 20 ♘b6 ♗b7 21 ♗f3
♕xh4 22 ♔h2 ♗d4 23 ♕e2 ♖e8?**
Zeitnot; 23...exd5 **24 ♗g2 h5 25 c3
♗e5 26 ♔g1 exd5 27 ♕d3! ♔g7 28
♗d2 ♘e6 29 ♘xd5 ♘g5 30 ♖fe1 ♖f8**

31 ♘xf4!± ♗xg2 32 ♔xg2 ♗xf4 33

♗xf4 ♖xf4 **34 ♕g3!** bxc3 **35 bxc3
♖c4** 35...♖xf2+ 36 ♔xf2 ♘xh3+ 37
♔g2 ♘f4+ 38 ♔f3 +− **36 ♖e7+ ♔h6
37 ♕xh4 ♖xh4 38 ♖a7 ♖xh3??**
Zeitnot **39 f4 ♖xc3 40 fxg5+ ♔xg5
41 ♖xa6 +− ♖c2+ 42 ♔f3 1-0
Gheorghiu**

89 Vukic-Jansa Novi Sad 78
**1 d4 g6 2 c4 c5 3 d5 e5 4 e4 d6 5
♘c3 ♗g7 6 ♗d3 ♘h6?!** 6...♘f6!? **7
♘ge2 0-0 8 0-0 ♘h5** △ f5 **7 h4! 0-0?**
7...f6!? **8 h5 ♘f7 8 h5 g5 9 ♕d2!** +=
f6 9...g4? **10 ♕c2** △ ♘ge2, ♘g3 **10
♘ge2 ♘a6 11 a3 ♗d7 12 ♘g3 ♖f7
13 ♕c2 ♗f8 14 ♗e3 ♗e7 15 f3 ♔h8
16 ♔f2 ♕f8 17 ♘f5! ♗xf5 18 exf5
♗d8 19 g4± h6 20 ♖ab1 ♗e8 21
♖hc1 ♕e7 22 ♔g2 ♔g7 23 ♕f2 ♗c7
24 b4 b6 25 ♖b2 ♗d8 26 ♖cb1 ♖c8
27 ♕e2 ♕f8 28 ♘e4 ♖fc7 29 bxc5
♘xc5 30 ♗xc5 bxc5** 30...♖xc5? **
31 ♘xc5 ♖xc5 32 a4! ♖a5 33 ♗c2
♗d7 34 ♖b5! ♗xb5 35 cxb5 a6 36
bxa6 ♖xd5 37 ♗e4 ♖a5 38 ♗c6** △
♗b5 +− **31 ♗c2! ♖f7 32 ♕d1 +−
♗b6 33 ♗a4 ♖d8 34 ♗b5 ♖c7 35
♕a4 ♗xb5 36 ♖xb5 ♖cc8 37 ♕a6
1-0 Vukic**

90 Panno-Ljubojevic
Sao Paulo 79
**1 d4 ♘f6 2 c4 c5 3 d5 e6 4 ♘c3 exd5
5 cxd5 d6 6 ♘f3 g6 7 ♘d2 ♘bd7 8
e4 ♗g7 9 ♗e2 0-0 10 0-0 ♖e8 11 a4
a6 12 a5 b5 13 axb6 ♘xb6 14 ♖a3!**
+= **c4 15 ♖e1 ♕c7 16 ♕c2 ♗d7 17
♘f1 ♗b5!? 18 ♗e3 ♘fd7 19 ♖aa1
♘c5 20 ♘d2 ♖ab8 21 ♖ac1 ♖b7 22
g3 ♕d7 23 ♗f1 ♘ba4 24 ♘xc5?!
♘xc5 25 ♗xc4 ♗xc4 26 ♘xc4 ♖b4!∞**
=+ Ljubojevic **27 ♘a2 ♖xc4! 28
♕xc4 ♗xb2 29 ♖e3 ♗xc1 30
♘xc1**

30...♕b5!∓ 31 ♕c2 a5 32 ♘b3 ♖xe4!
33 ♖xe4 ♘xe4 34 ♘xa5 ♕xd5 35
♘c6 ♔g7 36 ♕b2+ ♘f6! 37 ♘d4
♔e5 38 ♔g2 h5 39 ♕c3 ♘d5 40 ♕d3
♘b4 41 ♕c4 ♕c5! −+ 42 ♕xc5 dxc5
43 ♘b5 ♔f6 44 ♔f3 ♔e5 45 ♔e3 ♔d5
46 ♘c3+ ♔c4 47 ♘e4 ♘d5+ 48 ♔d2
f6 0-1 Gheorghiu

91 Smirnov-Kapengut Minsk 79

1 d4 ♘f6 2 c4 c5 3 d5 e6 4 ♘c3 exd5
5 cxd5 d6 6 e4 g6 7 f4 ♗g7 8 e5 ♘fd7
9 ♘b5 dxe5 10 ♘d6+ ♔e7 11 ♘b5!?
11 ♘xc8+ ♕xc8 12 ♘f3 ♖e8 13
fxe5 ♘xe5 14 ♗b5 ♘bd7 15 ♘xe5
♔f8! 16 0-0 ♖xe5 17 ♗f4 c4! 18
♗xd7 ♕c5+! 19 ♔h1 ♖xd5 20 ♕g4
f5 21 ♕h3 ♖xd7 22 ♕xh7 ♔f7 23
♗h6∓ Shofman-Kapengut, Jaraslavl
75; 23 ♖ad1∓ Juferov-Kapengut,
Minsk 76; 18 ♕d4!= Shakarov-
Shumlensson, corr 76/77 ♖e8! 11...
♔f8? 12 ♘f3 e4 13 ♘g5 ♘f6 14 d6
h6 15 ♘xf7 ♔xf7 16 ♗c4+ ♔f8 17
♘c7 ♘c6 Brinck-Claussen-Fedder,
Denmark Final 72; 11...a6? 12 d6+
♔f8 13 ♘c7 ♖a7 14 ♘f3 ♕f6 15
♗c4 b5 16 ♗xf7! +− 12 d6+ ♔f8
13 ♘c7 exf4+ 14 ♘xe8? 14 ♗e2!?
♕h4+ 15 ♔f1∞; 14...♘c6! 15 ♘xe8
♕xe8 16 ♘f3 ♘d4 17 ♘xd4 ♗xd4
18 ♗xf4 ♘e5 ∞/=+ ♕xe8+ N 14...
♕h4+ 15 ♔d2 ♔xe8 16 ♕e1+ ♕xe1+

17 ♔xe1 ♗e5∞ Hartston; 15 g3 fxg3
16 ♘f3 g2+ 17 ♘xh4 gxh1♕∞ 15
♗e2 ♘e5!∓ 16 ♗xf4 ♘bc6 17 ♘h3
17 d7 ♘xd7 18 ♕d6+ ♔g8 19 0-0-0
♘d4∓ ♖xh3 18 gxh3 ♘f3+ 19 ♔f2
♕e4 20 ♗xf3 ♕xf4 21 ♔g2 ♘d4! −+
21...♖d8 22 ♔c1 22 ♖c1 ♘f5! 0-1
Kapengut

92 Szymczak-Rigo
Budapest 2 78

1 d4 ♘f6 2 c4 e6 3 ♘c3 c5 4 d5 exd5
5 cxd5 d6 6 ♘f3 g6 7 ♗f4 a6 7...
♗g7 8 ♕a4+! ♗d7 9 ♕b3 ♕c7 10
e4 0-0 11 ♗e2 ♘h5 (11...a6 12 e5±)
12 ♗e3 f5 13 e5± 8 a4 ♗g7 9 e4 0-0
10 ♗e2 10 ♘d2 ♘h5 11 ♗e3 ♘d7
12 ♗e2 ♘e5! 13 0-0 ♕h4 =+ ♖e8
11 ♘d2 ♘bd7 12 0-0 += ♘e5 13 h3
♖b8 14 ♗e3! b6 15 ♖a3 ♖e7!?±
16 f4 ♘ed7 17 ♖b3 ♕c7 18 ♗f2 c4
19 ♖b4 ♘c5 20 ♖xc4 b5 21 axb5
axb5 22 ♖xc5 dxc5 23 e5 ♘e8 24
d6! ♗xd6 25 ♘d5! ♕d8 26 ♘xe7+
♕xe7 27 exd6 ♕xd6 28 ♘e4 1-0
Balogh

93 Vukic-Planinc Novi Sad 78

1 d4 ♘f6 2 c4 c5 3 d5 e6 4 ♘c3
exd5 5 cxd5 d6 6 ♘f3 g6 7 ♗f4 ♗g7
8 e4 8 ♕a4+ ♗d7 9 ♕b3 ♕c7 10
e4 += 0-0 9 ♗e2 b5! 10 ♘d2 b4?!
10...a6! 11 ♕c2 ♖e8 12 a4 b4 13
♘d1 b3!= 11 ♘b5 ♗a6 12 ♖b1!
12 ♘xd6? ♗xe2 13 ♕xe2 ♘h5 14
♕f3 ♗xb2∓; 12 a4? bxa3 13 ♘xa3
♗xe2 14 ♕xe2 ♘h5 △ ♗xb2∓ ♖e8
13 ♘xd6 ♗xe2 14 ♕xe2 ♘xd5? 14...
♘h5? 15 ♕f3!± 15 ♕c4 +− ♘xf4
16 ♕xf7+ ♔h8 17 ♘xe8 ♘d3+ 18
♔f1 ♘h6 19 ♘f6 ♗g7 20 ♘e8 ♗h6
21 ♘c4 ♘d7 22 ♖d1 ♕xe8 23 ♕xe8+
♖xe8 24 ♖xd3 ♘b6 25 ♘d6! 25
♘xb6?! axb6 26 f3 c4 ♖e7 26 b3

♗f4 27 ♔e2! ♗xd6 28 ♖xd6 ♖xe4+ 29 ♔f3 ♖e7 30 ♖c6 ♘d7 31 ♔g3 ♖e5 32 f4 ♖d5 33 ♖e1 ♔g7 34 ♖e7+ ♔h6 35 ♔f3 ♖d3+ 1-0 36 ♔e2 ♖d4 37 g4! **Vukic**

94 Petran-Nicevski
Budapest 2 78

1 d4 e6 2 c4 c5 3 d5 exd5 4 cxd5 ♘f6 5 ♘c3 d6 6 e4 g6 7 ♘f3 ♗g7 8 ♗g5 a6 N **8...h6 9 ♗h4 g5 10 ♗g3 ♘h5 11 ♗b5+ ♔f8 12 e5± 9 ♘d2 b5 10 a4 b4 11 ♘cb1 ♕e7 12 ♗d3 ♘bd7 13 ♘c4!?** N 13 0-0 ♘e5 14 ♗e2 h6 15 ♗h4 g5 16 ♗g3 ♘g6 17 ♘c4 ♘xe4=; 13 f4 h6 14 ♗h4 g5 15 fxg5 ♘h7 16 0-0 ♘xg5 =+ **♘e5 14 0-0 ♘xc4 15 ♗xc4 0-0 16 ♖e1 h6 17 ♗h4 g5 18 ♗g3 ♘d7 19 ♖a2 ♗b7 20 ♘d2 ♖ae8** 20...♖fe8! 21 ♘f1 ♘f8 22 f3 ♘g6 += **21 f3 ♗d4+ 22 ♔h1 ♗e5 23 ♕e2 ♗xg3? 24 hxg3 ♘f6 25 ♘f1 ♘e5 26 ♖a1 a5 27 ♕f2 ♗c8 28 ♗b5 ♖e7 29 ♘e3 g4 30 ♘c4 ♕h5+ 31 ♔g1 gxf3 32 gxf3 ♘h7 33 g4 ♔g6 34 ♔g3 h5 35 ♕xd6 ♔g5 36 ♕g3 hxg4 37 f4 ♕g6 39 e5! +– ♗b7 40 ♖ad1 ♖d8 40 ♘e3 f5 41 ♘c4 ♔g7 42 ♕h4 1-0 Balogh**

Isn't 30 ♘f5 much stronger?

95 Schmidt-Kuligowski
Warsaw 79

1 d4 ♘f6 2 c4 c5 3 d5 e6 4 ♘c3 exd5 5 cxd5 g6 6 ♘f3 d6 7 ♗g5 ♗g7 8 e4 h6 9 ♗h4 a6 9...g5 10 ♗g3 ♘h5 11 ♗b5+! **10 ♘d2** 10 a4 g5 △ ♘h5∝ **b5 11 a4! b4 12 ♘cb1 ♕e7 13 f3 g5 14 ♗f2!** += **0-0** 14...♘h5 15 ♘c4!± **15 ♗e2 ♘bd7 16 ♘c4! ♘h5!?** 16...♘e5 17 ♘bd2 ♘fd7∝ **17 ♘bd2 ♘f4 18 0-0!± f5** 18...♘xe2+ 19 ♕xe2 f5 20 ♖ae1± **19 ♖e1 ♘xe2+ 20 ♖xe2 f4** 20...fxe4? 21 ♘xe4±

21 e5!± dxe5 21...♘xe5 22 ♘xe5 △ ♘c4± **22 ♘e4! a5 23 ♖c1 ♗a6 24 ♖ec2 ♗xc4 25 ♖xc4 ♖fd8 26 ♗xc5 ♕f7** 26...♘xc5 27 ♖xc5± **27 ♗d6 ♘b6** 27...♘f6 28 ♗xe5 **28 ♖c5 ♖d7 29 ♖b5 ♘c8 30 ♖c6??** 30 ♖b8! +– **♕g6!! 31 ♖xa5** 31 ♗xe5 ♕xc6! –+ **♖xa5 32 ♖xc8+ ♔f7 33 ♗c5 ♕a6!** –+ △ ♖xa4/♕xc8 **34 ♗xb4 ♖axd5 0-1 Gheorghiu**

96 Alburt-Tukmakov
Ashkabad 78

1 d4 ♘f6 2 c4 c5 3 d5 e6 4 ♘c3 exd5 5 cxd5 d6 6 e4 g6 7 ♘f3 ♗g7 8 ♗g5 h6 9 ♗h4 a6 9...g5 10 ♗g3 ♘h5 11 ♗b5+ ♔f8 12 e5!± **10 ♘d2 b5 11 a4!?** 11 ♗e2 **b4 12 ♘cb1 0-0** 12...♕e7 13 ♗d3?! g5 14 ♗g3 ♘xd5?! 15 ♘c4 ♘f4 16 ♗xf4 gxf4 17 ♘b6 ♗b7 18 ♘xa8 ♗xa8 19 0-0 ♗xb2 20 ♖a2 ♗d4 +=/∝ Botterill-Fedorowicz, Hastings 77/8; 13...♘bd7 14 0-0 ♘e5 15 ♗e2 g5 16 ♗g3 ♘fd7 17 ♘b3 a5 18 ♘1d2 0-0 19 ♗b5 ♘b6 20 ♘c1 ♗g4 21 ♘e2 ♗d7 22 ♗xd7 ♘exd7 23 ♖b1 c4∓ Gorhjak-Nevidnichij, Kishinev 78; 16...♘g6 17 ♘c4 ♘xe4 18 ♗d3 ♘xg3 19 ♖e1 ♘e5 20 hxg3 0-0! =+ Ripley-Denman, London 78; 18 ♘b6 0-0!? 19 ♘xa8 ♕b7∝; 13 ♗e2 g5 14 ♗g3 ♘bd7 15 0-0 0-0 16 ♖e1 ♘e5 17 ♕c2 ♘fd7

18 ⌾f1 b3!= Vaganian-Hort, Niksic
78 **13 ♗d3 ♖e8** 13...♖a7 14 0-0 g5
15 ♗g3 ♖e7 16 a5 ♘e8 17 ♘c4±
Diesen-Robatsch, Karlovac 77 **14 0-0
♘bd7!?** N 14...♕c7 15 ♕c2 ♘bd7
16 ♘c4 b3! 17 ♕xb3 ♘xe4 18 ♗xe4
♖xe4 19 ♗g3 ♖b8 =+ Veresov-Suetin,
Minsk 61 **15 ♖e1** 15 f4 ♕c7! 16 ♕c2
♖b8 =+; 16 ♕f3 c4! 17 ♖c1 c3!
18 bxc3 g5! 19 fxg5 ♘e5 20 ♕e2
♘fg4∓ **♘e5 16 ♗f1 g5 17 ♗g3 ♖a7**
=+ **18 ♖a2 ♖ae7 19 b3 ♘h5! 20**
♗xe5 20 ♕xh5?? ♗g4; 20 ♗xa6 ♗xa6
21 ♕xh5 ♘d3 22 ♖d1 f5 −+ **♖xe5
21 g3** 21 ♕xh5?? g4; 21 ♗xa6 ♗xa6
22 ♕xh5 ♖xd5∓ **g4∓ 22 ♗g2 f5 23
f4 ♖5e7 24 ♔h1 ♗d4 25 ♕c2 ♘f6
26 ♕d3 ♔g7 27 ♖c2 ♘xd5 28 ♖c4
♘f6 29 ♖xd4!?** cxd4 30 ♕xd4 ♗b7
31 ♔g1 ♗xe4! 32 ♗xe4 d5 33 ♕xb2
fxe4 −+ 34 ♕d4 e3 35 ♘f1 ♖e4 36
♕a7+ ♕e7 27 ♕xa6 ♘b4 28 ♕e2
♕xb3 29 h3 d4 40 hxg4 d3 41 ♕f3
d2 42 ♖d1 ♕xd1 0-1 Kapengut

97 Smyslov-Portisch Hungary 78
**1 d4 ♘f6 2 c4 e6 3 g3 c5 4 d5 exd5
5 cxd5 d6 6 ♘c3 g6 7 ♗g2 ♗g7 8
♘f3 0-0 9 0-0 ♘bd7 10 ♗f4?!** 10 ♘d2
♕e7 11 ♖e1 a6 12 a4 ♖b8 13 e4 ♘g4!?
14 ♘d2 ♘de5! △ ♘d3 **15 ♘f1 ♘c4
16 ♕e2 b5 17 axb5 axb5 18 h3
♘ge5 =+ 19 ♗c1 b4 20 ♘d1 ♘b6 21
f4?!** 21 ♘de3 c4 22 ♖d1 ♕c7 =+ **♘ec4
22 ♘de3 ♘xe3 23 ♗xe3 ♖e8 24 ♖ad1**
24 ♖ed1 **♕a7! 25 e5?!** 25 ♖a1 ♗a6
26 ♕f2 26 ♖a1 ♖a8 **♘c4!∓ 27 b3
♗xe3 28 ♘xe3 dxe5 29 f5 e4! 30
f6 ♗f8 31 ♕f4 c4! 32 bxc4 ♖xc4
33 ♗xe4 ♗b3 34 ♖d2 ♖b6! 35 ♔h2
♕b8 36 ♕h4** 36 ♕xb8 ♖exb8∓ **♕d8
37 ♘g4 ♗a4 38 ♖f2 b3 39 ♗xg6?!**
hxg6 40 ♖e7 △ ♖xf7! **♕xd5! 40...**
♗xe7?? 41 ♘h6+ ♔f8 42 fxe7+ ♖xe7

43 ♖xf7+ +− **41 ♘e3** 41 ♘h6+ ♗xh6
42 ♕xh6 ♖xf6 43 ♖xe8+ ♗xe8 44
♖xf6 b2 45 ♖b6 ♕b5!! −+ **♕c6
0-1 Maric**

98 Kakageldiev-Tsheshkovsky
Ashkabad 78
**1 d4 ♘f6 2 c4 c5 3 d5 e6 4 ♘c3 exd5
5 cxd5 d6 6 ♘f3 g6 7 g3 ♗g7 8 ♗g2
0-0 9 0-0 ♖e8 10 ♘d2 a6 11 a4 ♘bd7
12 h3 ♖b8 13 ♘c4 ♘e5 14 ♘a3 ♘h5**

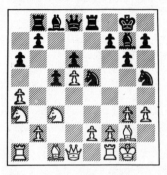

15 g4?! N (1) 15 f4 ♘d7 16 ♔h2
f5 17 ♖e1 ♘hf6 18 ♘c4 ♘b6 19 ♘d2
♘bd7 20 a5 b5 21 axb6 ♘xb6 22
e4 Zakharov-Bangiev, Odessa 71; 15...
♘xg3!? 16 fxe5 ♘xf1 17 ♕xf1 Raksin-
Zhuravlev, Kronstadt 75; 17...b5! 18
axb5 axb5 19 ♘axb5 ♗xe5 20 ♖a7
♖b7 21 ♖xb7 ♗xb7 22 ♗f4 ♗a6 =+;
(2) 15 e3 f5 16 ♖b1 ♗d7 17 b4 cxb4
18 ♖xb4 ♕a5 19 ♘a2 ♖ec8 20 ♗d2
♕c5 21 ♕b1 a5 22 ♖b3 ♗xa4 23 ♖c1
♕a7 24 ♖xc8+ ♖xc8 25 ♖xb7 ♕c5
26 ♖b8! Osnos-Petkevich, Daugavpils
74; 19...b5! 20 ♗d2 ♕c7 21 axb5
axb5 22 ♕b1 ♕a7 23 ♖b3 ♘c4 =+
Osnos-Stein, Tbilisi 66/67; (3) 15
♗d2 f5 16 ♖b1? f4! 17 ♗xf4 ♘xf4
18 gxf4 Liptay-Adamski, Hungary
70; 18...♕h4! −+; 16 e3 ♗d7 17 ♕e2
♘f7 18 ♕d3 g5 19 ♕e2 ♘f6 20 f4 b5!
21 axb5 axb5 22 ♘axb5 ♘e4!? Peev-

Spassov, Cienfuegos 73; (4) 15 ♔h2
f5 16 ♗d2? Butnorius-Nicevski, Vilnius
69; 16 f4 ♘f7 17 ♘c4 b5 18 axb5
axb5 19 ♘a5 ♕c7 20 ♘c6 ♖b6 21
♗f3 b4 =+ Juferov-Kapengut, Minsk
71; 17 e3 ♗d7 18 ♕d3 Veremeichik-
Mochalov, Minsk 77; 18...♘f6 Δ 19...
b5 20 axb5 axb5 21 ♘axb5 ♘e4
(5) 15 e4 f5 16 exf5 ♗xf5 17 g4
♘xg4?! 18 hxg4 ♕h4 19 gxf5 ♗e5
20 ♖e1± Juferov-Vasjukov 68; 17...
♗xg4! 18 hxg4 ♕h4 19 gxh5 ♖f8!
20 h6 ♗h8 21 ♘e4 ♘g4 22 ♕xg4
♕xg4 23 ♘c4 ♖be8?± Marovic-
Kapengut, Erevan 71; 23...b5! =+
Kivlan-Petkevich, Riga 74; 23...♖f3
24 ♘cxd6 ♖d8 Δ ♗e5 Hartston; 24
♗e3!; 23 ♘c2 ♖be8 24 f3 ♕h4 25
♗g5 ♕h5 26 f4 ♕e2 ½-½ Minev-Spassov,
Albena 75; 23...♖f3! 24 ♘g5 ♖f5
25 f4 ♕e2 26 ♖f2 ♕d1+ 27 ♔h2
♖xg5 —+ **♕h4!** 15...♗xg4?! 16 hxg4
♕h4 17 gxh5 ♘g4 18 ♗f4 ♗e5 19
♕d3 ♗xf4 20 ♕h3!± **16 ♘e4!?** 16
gxh5 ♗xh3 17 ♗xh3 ♕xh3 18 ♗f4
♘f3+! 19 exf3 ♖e5! —+ **h6 17 gxh5**
♗xh3 18 ♘g3 18 f3? ♘xf3+ 19 exf3
♗d4+ **♘g4 19 ♗f4 ♗d4 20 e3 ♗xe3!**
21 fxe3 ♗xg2 22 ♔xg2 ♕h2+ 23
♔f3 ♖xe3+! 24 ♗xe3 ♘e5+ 25 ♔e4
f5+ 26 ♖xf5 gxf5+ 27 ♔xf5 27 ♘xf5
♕g2+ 28 ♔f4 ♖f8 20 ♕g1 ♘d3 mate
♕h3+ 28 ♔e4 ♕g2+? Zeitnot 28...
♖e8! —+ **29 ♔f5 ♕h3+ 30 ♔e4 ½-½**
Kapengut

99 Vukic-Minic Pula 78
1 d4 ♘f6 2 c4 c5 3 d5 d6 4 ♘c3 g6
5 ♘f3 ♗g7 6 e4 0-0 7 ♗e2 e6 8 dxe6
♗xe6 9 ♗f4 ♕a5?! 9...♘c6!? 10 ♗xd6
♖e8 11 0-0 ♘d4≈ **10 0-0 ♖d8 11**
♕b3 ♘c6 12 ♖ad1 ♘e8 13 ♕xb7?
13 ♘d5! += **♘d4?** 13...♗xc3! —+
14 bxc3 ♖ab8 15 ♕xc6 ♖dc8! **14**

♘xd4 cxd4 14...♗xd4 15 ♕b3 ♖ab8
16 ♕c2 ♕b4 17 ♘b5! ♕xb2 18 ♕xb2
♗xb2 19 ♘xa7± **15 ♕b5 ♕c7 16**
♘d5 ♗xd5 17 ♕xd5 ♗e5 18 ♗g5 ♘f6
19 ♗xf6 ♗xf6 20 b3 ♖ab8 21 ♖d3
♖e8 22 f4 ♕e7 23 ♗f3 ♖ec8 24 ♕a5
♗c5 25 ♕e1 ♕c7 26 g3 ♗g7 27 ♖f2
a5 28 e5! dxe5 29 ♗d5 ♖f8 30 ♖df3
♗h6 31 fxe5! ♗e3 32 e6!! +— ♗xf2+
33 ♕xf2 ♕e5 33...♔g7? 34 ♖xf7+
♖xf7 35 exf7 ♔f8 36 ♕xd4 +— **34**
♖xf7 ♖e8 35 ♖f8+!! 1-0 35...♖xf8
36 e7+ **Vukic**

100 Kovacs-Matulovic
Bajmok 78
1 d4 g6 2 c4 ♗g7 3 ♘c3 c5 4 d5 d6
5 e4 ♘f6 6 ♗e2 0-0 7 ♘f3 e6 8 0-0
exd5 8...♖e8 9 ♘d2 exd5?! 10 cxd5
♘bd7 11 a4 a6 12 ♖a3! ♖b8 13 a5!
♕c7 14 h3 b5?! 15 axb6 ♖xb6 16
♕c2± Petrosian-Quinteros, Lone Pine
76 **9 exd5** 9 cxd5 ♖e8 10 ♘d2 ♘a6
11 f3 ♘c7 12 a4 b6 13 ♘c4 ♗a6
14 ♗g5! h6! 15 ♗h4 ♗xc4 16 ♗xc4=
Beljavsky-Rogulj, USSR-Jugoslavia 77
♗g4= 10 ♘g5!? ♗xe2 11 ♕xe2 ♖e8
12 ♕c2 ♘bd7 13 ♘f3 ♘g4 14 ♗g5
♕b6 15 ♖ae1 a6 16 b3 ♕c7 17 h3
♘ge5 18 ♘xe5 ♗xe5 19 ♖e2 ♗f6 20
♗xf6 ♖xe2 21 ♕xe2 ♘xf6 22 ♘e4
♕e7 23 ♘xf6+ ♕xf6 24 ♖e1 ♔f8
25 a4 h5 26 g3 ♖b8 27 h4 b6 28
♔g2 ♕d8 29 ♕b2 ♔g8 30 ♖e4 b5 31
axb5 axb5 32 ♕e2 bxc4 33 bxc4
♕f6 34 ♖f4 ♕d8 35 ♕f3 ♖b7 36
♖e4 ♖e7 37 ♕f6 ♖d7 38 ♕b2 38
♕xd8+ ♖xd8 39 ♖e7= **♖e7 39 ♖f4**
♖e5 40 ♖f3 ♖e8= ½-½ Kovacs

101 Padevski-Ghitescu
Balkaniad 78
1 d4 ♘f6 2 c4 c5 3 d5 d6 4 ♘c3 g6
5 e4 ♗g7 6 f4 0-0 7 ♘f3 e6 8 ♗e2

exd5 9 cxd5 ♗g4! 9...♖e8 10 e5!∝
10 0-0 ♗xf3 11 ♗xf3 ♘bd7 12 ♗e3
12 g4!?∝ ♖e8 13 ♗f2 a6 14 ♕c2 ♖c8
15 a4 c4! 16 ♖fe1 ♕a5 17 ♔h1 h6
18 ♗g3 ♘h7!= 19 ♗g4 ♘hf6 20 ♗f3
♘h7 21 ♗g4 ♘hf6 22 ♗h3?! ♖cd8
23 e5 ♘xd5! 23...dxe5 24 fxe5 ♘xd5
25 e6! 24 ♘xd5 ♕xd5 25 ♖ed1 ♕c5
26 ♖xd6 ♘f8 27 ♗f2 ♕b4 28 ♖ad1
♖xd6 29 ♖xd6 c3!!∓ 30 ♗d4??
30 ♕xc3 ♕xf4; 30 bxc3 ♕xf4∓;
30 ♖d4 ♕xb2 ♕xd6! 0-1 31 exd6
♖e1 mate **Gheorghiu**

Nimzo-Indian

✓103 Giffard-Kuligowski
Buenos Aires 78
1 d4 ♘f6 2 c4 e6 3 ♘c3 ♗b4 4 ♗d2!?
d5 5 cxd5 exd5 6 ♘f3 0-0 7 g3 b6
8 ♗g2 ♗b7 9 0-0 ♖e8 10 ♖c1 c6 11
♖e1 ♘bd7 12 a3 ♗f8 12...♗xc3 13
♗xc3 +=; 12...♗d6∝ 13 ♗f4! h6
14 ♕b3 ♖c8 15 ♖cd1 c5 16 ♕a2 c4
17 ♘e5! a6 18 ♗h3 b5 19 ♕b1 ♖a8
20 ♗f5 ♘b6 20...♘xe5?! 21 dxe5±
21 g4!± ♘e4 21...g6? 22 ♗xg6±
22 f3 g5?! 23 ♗c1! ♘f6 23...♘xc3
24 bxc3 24 h4! ♘bd7 24...gxh4 25
g5± 25 hxg5 hxg5 26 ♗xg5 ♗g7?
27 ♘xd7 1-0 **Gheorghiu**

✓102 Korchnoi-Miles
Buenos Aires 78
1 d4 ♘f6 2 c4 g6 3 f3!? c5 4 d5 ♗g7
5 e4 0-0 5...d6! 6 ♘h3! += △ ♘f2
d6 7 ♗f2 e6 8 ♘c3 ♘a6 8...exd5 9
cxd5 b6 △ ♗a6 9 ♗e2 ♘c7 10 0-0
a6 11 ♗g5! h6 12 ♗e3 exd5 13 cxd5
b5 14 ♕d2 ♔h7 15 e5!? 15 ♖ad1
♘d7∝ b4 15...dxe5 16 ♗xc5 ♖e8
17 ♖ad1± 16 exf6 bxc3 17 bxc3
♕xf6 18 ♖ac1 ♕d8?! 18...♘b5!?
19 ♘e4 ♕d8 20 a4! f5!∝ 19 g4!
♖e8 19...f5 20 g5! += 20 ♘d1 ♖b8
21 ♖f2 ♗d7 22 ♗f4! ♕f6 22...♗e5!?
23 ♗xh6 +=; 23 ♗xe5 += 23 c4 ♖b6
24 ♗d3 ♖eb8 25 ♔g2 ♘e8 26 ♖e2
♗a4 27 g5! ♕d8 27...hxg5? 28 ♗xg5
♕d4 29 ♖e4!± 28 gxh6 ♗f6 29 ♗c2!
♗xc2 30 ♖xc2 ♕d7 31 ♗f2 △ ♘g4±
♗d4 32 ♗e3 ♗xe3 33 ♕xe3 ♘f6

Diagram

34 ♘h3! △ ♘g5+ +- ♖e8 35 ♘g5+
♔g8 35...♔xh6? 36 ♘e4+! ♔g7 37
♕c3!? ♕f5; 37 ♘xf6!! ♖xe3 38
♘xd7 +- 36 ♕c3 1-0 **Gheorghiu**

✓104 Vaisman-Kojder Krosno 78
1 d4 ♘f6 2 c4 e6 3 ♘c3 ♗b4 4 e3
0-0 5 ♗d3 c5 6 ♘ge2!? 6 ♘f3 d5 7
cxd5 cxd4 7...exd5 8 a3 ♗xc3+
9 bxc3± 8 exd4 ♘xd5 9 0-0 ♘f6
10 ♗c2! ♘bd7 11 ♕d3 b6 12 ♗g5
♗b7 13 ♖ad1 ♖c8 14 a3 ♗e7 14...
♗xc3 15 ♘xc3! △ 16 ♕h3 15 ♕h3!
♖e8 15...h6 16 ♗xh6! 16 d5! exd5
16...♗xd5 17 ♘f4!≈ 17 ♘d4 a6
17...♘f8 18 ♗a4± 18 ♘f5 ♘f8 19
♖fe1 ♖a8? △ ♗c8 20 ♖xe7!! ♖xe7
21 ♗xf6 gxf6 22 ♕h6 1-0 22...♘e6

23 ♘xe7+ ♕xe7 24 ♕xh7+ ♔f8 25 ♕h8 mate **Ciocaltea**

√**105 Knaak-Malich Halle 78**
1 d4 ♘f6 2 c4 e6 3 ♘c3 ♗b4 4 e3 0-0 5 ♗d3 d5 6 ♘f3 c5 7 0-0 dxc4 8 ♗xc4 ♘bd7 9 ♕e2 a6 10 a4 cxd4 10...♕c7 11 ♘a2 b5 11 ♗d3 ♗a5 13 axb5 axb5 14 ♗xb5 ♗b7 15 ♘c3 cxd4 16 ♘xd4 ♕d6 Knaak-Balashov, Halle 76 **11 exd4 ♘b6 12 ♗d3 ♘bd5 13 ♗d2** 13 ♗g5!? **♗a5?!** 13...♗e7; 13...♗d6 **14 ♖ac1 ♗d7 15 ♘xd5! exd5** 15...♘xd5 16 ♗g5 f6 17 ♕e4 g6 18 ♗h6 **16 ♗g5 h6 17 ♗h4 ♗g4?** 17...♗b6 **18 ♕e3 ♗b6 19 ♘e5 ♗c8 20 ♗b1 ♕d6 21 ♔h1! ♖e8** 21...♘e4 22 ♗xe4 dxe4 23 ♘c4 ♕g6 24 a5 ♗a7 25 ♗e7 ♖e8 26 ♘d6 ♖xe7 27 ♖xc8+; 23...♕e6 24 f3 **22 ♕d3 ♗d8** 22...g5 23 ♘xf7; 22...♗xd4 23 ♗xf6 ♕xf6 24 ♕h7+ ♔f8 25 ♖xc8 **23 ♗xf6 ♗xf6 24 ♕h7+ ♔f8 25 ♘xf7! ♕xf7 26 ♗g6+ ♔e7 27 ♗xe8 ♔xe8 28 ♕g8+ ♕f8 29 ♖fe1+ ♗e7 30 ♖xe7+ ♔xe7 31 ♖e1+ ♗e6 32 ♕xe6+ 1-0 Knaak**

106 Gutman-Vitolins USSR 79
1 d4 ♘f6 2 c4 e6 3 ♘c3 ♗b4 4 e3 0-0 5 ♗e2 b5 N **6 cxb5 a6 7 ♘g3** 7 a3 axb5 8 ♗d2 ♗e7 9 ♘xb5 ♘e4 10 ♘bc3 ♘xd2 11 ♕xd2 d5 12 ♘f4 c5 13 dxc5 ♗xc5 14 ♗e2 d4∞ Shakhovich-Vitolins, USSR 78 **♗b7 8 ♗d2 ♗xc3 9 ♗xc3 axb5 10 ♗xb5 ♗xg2 11 ♖g1 ♗c6 12 ♘h5! ♘xh5 13 ♕xh5 ♗xb5?? 13...d5∞ 14 ♕h6! +– g6 15 d5 e5 16 ♗xe5 f6 17 ♖xg6+! hxg6 18 ♕xg6+ ♔h8**

Diagram

♖g1 +– ♗d3!! 20 ♔xd3 ♕e7 –+ 21 e4 21 ♕h6+ ♔h7+ –+ ♕g7 22 ♕h5+ ♔g8 23 ♗d4 c5! 24 ♗xc5 ♖c8 25 f4 ♘a6! 25...♖xc5 26 ♕e8+ = **26 ♗f2** 26 ♖g1 ♘xc5+ Δ ♕xg1 –+ ♘b4+ **27 ♔e2 ♖xa2 0-1** 28 ♖g1 ♖xb2+ –+ **Gipslis**

107 Hartston-Suba √
Hastings 78/79
1 d4 ♘f6 2 c4 e6 3 ♘c3 ♗b4 4 ♗g5 h6 5 ♗h4 5 ♗xf6 ♗xc3+!= c5 6 d5 **d6** 6...b5!? 7 e4 d6! **7 e3 ♗xc3+! 8 bxc3 e5 9 f3 ♕a5 10 ♕d2** 10 ♕c2 **♘bd7 11 ♗d3 ♘b6!? N 12 ♘h3?!** 12 ♗xf6! gxf6 13 a4! += g5 13 ♗g3 **♗xh3! 14 gxh3 0-0-0 15 a4 h5! 16 h4** 16 0-0 h4 17 ♗f2 e4!∓ **♖dg8 17 hxg5 h4! 18 ♗f2** 18 ♗xe5 dxe5 19 gxf6 h3!∞ **♖xg5 19 ♖g1 ♖xg1+ 20 ♗xg1**

19 ♔d2?? 19 ♕h6+ ♔g8 20 ♔d2 Δ **20...e4! –+ 21 ♗e2 exf3 22 ♗xf3 ♘xc4**

23 ♕c2 ♘e5 24 ♖h1 c4 Δ ♘d3+,
♘xd5 25 ♖d1 ♘fd7 26 ♔f1 ♘c5 27
♖a1 ♘cd3 28 ♗e4 ♕d8 29 ♗f5+ ♔b8
30 e4 ♕g5 31 ♕g2 ♕f4+ 32 ♔e2 ♕h6!
33 ♖f1 33 ♗e3 ♘f4+ 34 ♔f1 ♘xg2
—+ ♘f4+ 34 ♖xf4 ♕xf4 35 ♗e3 h3!
36 ♕f2 ♕xf2+ 37 ♔xf2 a5 Δ b5
38 ♗b6 ♘d3+ 39 ♔g3 ♘c5 40 ♗xa5
♘xa4 41 ♗xh3 b6 42 ♗b4 ♘c5 43
♗f5 ♔c7 Δ ♘d3, ♖a8 44 ♗a3 ♘d3
45 e5 ♖g8+! 46 ♔h4 ♘xe5 47 ♗c1
♘f3+ 48 ♔h3 ♘g1+ 49 ♔h4 ♖h8+ 50
♔g5 ♖xh2 51 ♔f6 ♘e2 52 ♗d2 ♖f2
0-1 Suba

Bogolyubov Indian

108 Vukic-Nogueiras
Novi Sad 78

1 d4 ♘f6 2 c4 e6 3 ♘f3 ♗b4+ 4
♘bd2 b6 5 a3 ♗xd2+ 6 ♕xd2 ♗a6?!
6...♗b7! 7 b3 0-0 8 ♗b2 ♘e4 9 ♕c2
d6 10 e3 ♘bd7 11 ♗d3 f5= 7 e3 d5
8 ♕c2 0-0 9 b3 ♘bd7 10 ♗b2 c5
11 ♗d3 ♖c8 12 ♕e2 12 0-0? cxd4
13 exd4 dxc4 14 bxc4 ♗xc4! 15
♗xc4 b5!∓ cxd4 13 exd4 dxc4 14
bxc4 ♕c7 15 ♖c1 ♖fe8! 16 0-0 ♗b7
17 ♖fe1 ♘f8?! 17...♗xf3! 18 ♕xf3
e5!= 18 ♘e5 ♘g6 19 ♕d2 ♘d7 20
f4 ♘dxe5 21 fxe5 ♕d7 22 ♕f2 ♖c7
23 h4 ♘f8 24 h5 ♖ec8 25 ♖e3! ♘a6
26 ♖g3 g6 26...♗xc4? 27 ♖xg7+
♔xg7 28 ♕f6+ ♔g8 29 h6 +−; 26...
♕d8 27 ♕e2 Δ ♗c2, ♗c1 27 ♖c2 ♕d8
27...♗xc4? 28 ♕f6 Δ h6 +− 28 ♗c1
♗xc4 29 ♗g5 ♕e8 29...♕d5? 30
♗f6! ♗xd3 31 ♕f4 ♘d7 32 ♕h6 ♘xf6
33 exf6 ♕xd4+ 34 ♖f2 +− 30 ♗h6
♘d7 31 ♗e4 ♗d5 32 ♖xc7 ♖xc7
33 ♗d3 ♖c8 34 ♗a6 ♖c7 35 ♗b5 ♕e7
36 ♗xd7 ♖xd7 37 ♖c3 ♗b7 37...
♖d8? 38 ♖c7 +− 38 ♕f4 ♕d8 39
♖c4?! 39 ♗g5! ♖xd4 40 ♗xd8 ♖xf4

41 ♖c7 Δ ♗f6± b5 40 ♖b4 ♗c6 41
♗g5 ♕f8 42 ♖b3 ♖c7 43 ♗h6 ♕d8
44 ♖c3 ♖c8 45 ♗g5 ♕f8 45...♕d5?
46 ♖f3 f5 47 exf6 ♕f5 48 ♕d6 ♗xf3
49 ♕e7 +− 46 ♕f6 +− ♕g7 46...♗b7
47 ♖xc8 ♗xc8 48 h6 a5 49 ♗d2
b4 50 axb4 a4 51 b5 a3 52 ♗b4 a2
53 ♗xf8 a1♕+ 54 ♔h2 ♔xf8 55 ♕d8
mate 47 ♕f3!! h6 48 ♗f6 ♗xf3 49
♖xc8+ ♕f8 50 ♖xf8+ ♔xf8 51 gxf3
a5 52 ♗d8 b4 53 ♗xa5 b3 54 ♗c3 ♔e8
55 hxg6 fxg6 56 a4 ♔d7 57 d5 1-0
57...exd5 58 a5 Vukic

109 Tatai-Ivkov Albufieri 78

1 d4 ♘f6 2 c4 e6 3 g3 ♗b4+ 4 ♗d2
4 ♘c3!? ♕e7 5 ♘f3 ♘c6 6 ♘c3 6
♗g2 e5!?; 6...0-0; 6...♘e4!? ♗xc3
7 ♗xc3 ♘e4 8 ♖c1 0-0 9 ♗g2 a5 10
0-0 d6 11 ♗e1 (1) 11 d5!? ♘b4 12 a3!
♘a2? 13 ♗xg7!; 12...♘xc3 13 ♖xc3
♘a6 14 dxe6 +=; 11...♘d8!?; 11...
♘xc3 12 ♖xc3 ♘d8; (2) 11 d5!? exd5
12 cxd5 ♘b4 13 a3! ♘xc3 14 ♖xc3
♘a6 15 ♘d4 +=; 13...♘a2 14 ♗xg7!
f5 12 d5 ♘d8 13 ♘d2 ♘c5 14 ♘b3
b6 15 ♘xc5 bxc5 16 ♖c3! 16 dxe6∞
♖b8 17 ♕c2 ♘xe6 18 e3 ♗b7 19
♗xa5 ♗xg2 20 ♔xg2 ♖a8 21 ♗c3
♖xa2; 21 ♕d2!? ♘g5; 17 b3!? a4;
16...♖a7; 16...♗b7 e5 17 f4 e4 18
♖a3 ♘b7 19 ♕c2 ♗d7 20 g4! c6!
20...fxg4? 21 ♗xe4± 21 ♖g3 cxd5
22 cxd5 ♖ae8 23 gxf5 ♗xf5 24 ♗c3
♖f7 25 ♔h1!? 25 e3 c4 (Δ ♘c5-d3)
26 ♗d4 ♖c8 e3 26 ♖xg7+! 26 ♔c1
♗e4! ♖xg7 27 ♕xf5 ♖g6 28 ♕h5
28 ♕h3!? ♕f7 29 f5 ♖g5 30 f6 ♘d8
29 f5 ♖g5 30 ♕f3 30 ♕h4!? ♘f7
♕f7

Diagram

31 ♕f4!? (1) 31 ♖g1!? (Δ h4) ♔f8!

32 ♕f4 ♕xf5! 33 ♕xd6+ ♔g8∞;
(2) 31 ♗xa5? ♕h5∞; (3) 31 h4!!
♕h5? 32 ♕h3! ♕g4 33 ♕xg4 ♖xg4
34 ♗h3! ♖xh4 35 ♖g1+ ♔f8 36
♗g7+! ♔e7 37 f6+ +−; 31...♖h5 32
♕g4+ ♔f8 ±/+− **♕h5! 32 ♗f3** 32
♕xd6? ♕xe2; 32 ♖g1!? ♘f7 33 h4!?
♕h6 33 h4 ♘f7 34 ♔h2? 34 ♗f6!
♕xf6 35 hxg5 ♘xg5 36 ♗g2; 36
♖g1?? ♕h6+; 34...♖g6?? 35 fxg6
♕xf4 36 gxf7+ **♔f8! 35 ♔h3 ♖g8
36 ♕xh6+ ♘xh6 37 ♗h5?** 37 ♗g2
**♖e4 38 f6 ♘g4 39 f7 ♘f2+ 40 ♖xf2
♖xh4+!! 0-1 Speelman**

Queen's Indian

110 Segal-Filguth
Sao Paulo 79
**1 d4 ♘f6 2 c4 e6 3 ♘f3 b6 4 a3
♗b7 5 ♘c3 d5 6 cxd5 exd5** 6...♘xd5
7 e3 ♗e7 8 ♗b5+! c6 9 ♗d3 += **7 g3
♘bd7 8 ♗g2 ♗e7 9 0-0 0-0 10 ♗f4 a6
11 ♘e5 c6** 11...♖e8 12 ♕b3!± **12
♖c1 ♖c8 13 ♕b3 ♘xe5 14 ♗xe5 ♔h8**
14...♘d7 15 ♗f4 f5 16 e4!± **15 ♘a4
♘d7 16 ♗f4 b5?** 16...f5! += **17 ♘c5
♘xc5 18 dxc5 ♕e8 19 e4! dxe4 20
♗xe4 ♖d8?!** 20...♗g5!?∞ **21 ♖fe1!
♗c8 22 ♕f3 ♗d7 23 ♗b1!** +− **g6**
23...♗e6 24 ♕e4! g6 25 ♗h6 +−
24 ♕c3+ f6 25 ♗d6 1-0 Gheorghiu

111 Gheorghiu-Stean
Sao Paulo 79
**1 d4 ♘f6 2 c4 e6 3 ♘f3 b6 4 a3
♗b7 5 ♘c3 d5** 5...♗e7 6 d5± **6 cxd5
♘xd5 7 e3 ♗e7 8 ♗b5+ c6 9 ♗d3 c5
10 e4 ♘xc3** 10...cxd4 11 ♘xd5 exd5
12 e5± **11 bxc3 0-0 12 0-0 ♘c6 13
♗e3** 13 d5 exd5 14 exd5 ♘a5 15
c4 b5!∞ **♘a5 14 ♕e2 ♖c8 15 ♖fd1
cxd4 16 cxd4 ♖c3! 17 a4 ♕a8!∞
18 ♘d2!** 18 ♗d2? ♖xd3! 19 ♕xd3
♗xe4∓ **♖fc8 19 f3 ♘c6! 20 ♘b1
♖b3 21 ♘d2 ♖b2** 21...♖c3 22 ♘b1=
22 d5! ♘e5!= 22...exd5 23 exd5 ♘e5
24 ♗d4± ½-½ 23 dxe6 fxe6 24 ♗d4
♗c5!= **Gheorghiu**

112 L.Popov-Kuligowski
Warsaw 79
**1 d4 ♘f6 2 c4 e6 3 ♘f3 b6 4 a3 ♗b7
5 ♘c3 d5 6 cxd5 ♘xd5** 6...exd5 7
♗g5 += **7 e3 ♗e7 8 ♗b5+! c6 9 ♗d3
0-0 10 e4 ♘xc3 11 bxc3 c5 12 0-0!**
12 ♕e2 cxd4 13 cxd4 ♘c6 14 ♗b2
♗f6 15 e5 ♗e7 16 ♕e4 += L.Popov-
Arnaudov 77 **cxd4 13 cxd4 ♘c6 14
♗e3 ♗f6 15 ♗b1! ♘a6** 15...♘a5 16
♕d3 g6 17 ♖c1 ♖c8 18 ♗a2!± **16
e5! ♗xf1** 16...♗e7 17 ♕c2 **17 exf6
♗b5 18 fxg7 ♖e8** 18...♔xg7 19 ♕c1±
19 ♘g5! ♔xg7 20 ♕h5 +− ♕c7

21 ♕xh7+ 21 ♕h6+!! ♔xh6 22 ♘xe6+

[handwritten top margin: ut after ... kg4? 25 kg2 / won't work after ...Te3:]

Kh5 23 Ng7+!! Kh4 24 g3+ Kh3 25 Bf5 mate **Qf8 22 Bg6 Nd8 23 Bxf7 1-0** 23...Nxf7 24 Bh6+ **Gheorghiu**

113 Malich-Bohlig Halle 78

1 Nf3 Nf6 2 c4 e6 3 d4 b6 4 Nc3 Bb7 5...Bb4!? **5 a3 d5** 5...Ne4 6 Nxe4 Bxe4 7 Nd2 Bb7 8 e4± **6 Bg5** 6 cxd5 exd5 7 g3 Be7 8 Bg2 0-0 9 0-0 Ne4!= Malid-Kuzmin, Budapest 78 **Be7 7 Bxf6!? Bxf6 8 cxd5 exd5 9 g3 0-0 10 Bg2 Nbd7?!** N 10...Re8 11 0-0 Nc6 Fernandez-Malich, Budapest 78 **11 0-0 Re8 12 Rc1 c6 13 e3 Nf8?!** 13...a5!? 14 Re1 Δ e4 += **14 b4 Qe7** 14...Qd6!? **15 Qb3 Rad8 16 Rfd1 Ne6 17 Ne1 Nc7?** 17...h5!? += **18 a4 Qe6 19 Nd3 Qf5 20 b5! c5** 20...cxb5 21 Nxb5 Bxb5 22 axb5± **21 dxc5 Bxc3** 21...d4 22 e4! +- **22 c6! d4 23 cxb7 dxe3?** 23...Ne6 24 e4 Qh5 25 e5 Nc5 26 Nxc5 bxc5 27 f4± **24 Qxc3 Nd5** 24...Rxd3 25 Qxd3 exf2+ 26 Kh1 Re1+ 27 Rxe1 fxe1Q+ 28 Rxe1 Qxd3 29 b8Q+ +- **25 Bxd5 Qxd5 26 fxe3 Rxe3 27 Nf2! 1-0** 27...Rxc3 28 Rxc3! **Malich**

114 Vaganian-Browne Buenos Aires 2 78

1 d4 Nf6 2 c4 e6 3 Nf3 b6 4 a3 Bb7 5 Nc3 Ne4 5...d5 6 cxd5 += **6 Nxe4 Bxe4 7 Bf4!?** 7 e3 Be7 8 Bd3 Bxd3 9 Qxd3 d5 10 e4!± Gheorghiu-Panno, Buenos Aires 2 78 **c5 8 d5 exd5 9 cxd5 Be7 10 Qb3! 0-0 11 Nd2 Bg6 12 e3 d6 13 Be2 a6 14 a4 Nd7 15 0-0 Nf6 16 h3 b5?!** 16...Ne4!∞ Browne **17 axb5 axb5 18 Bxb5! Rb8 19 Ra7!± Ne4** 19...Qb6 20 Rxe7 **20 Nxe4 Bxe4 21 Qc4! Bxd5 22 Qxd5 Rxb5 23**

b3! Re8 24 Rfa1 Rb6 25 Bg5!! Rb8 25...Bxg5?? 26 Qxf7+ **26 R1a6** Zugzwang

26...h6 27 Bxe7 Rxe7 28 Rxd6 Qe8 29 Rxe7 Qxe7 30 Qxc5! +- Qe4 30...Rxb3 31 Qc8+ Kh7 32 Qc2+! +- **31 Rb6 Rd8 32 Rb4 Qb1+ 33 Kh2 Qd2 34 e4 Rd8 35 Qc7 Rd1 1-0 Gheorghiu**

[handwritten: y... Kg8, 33 T96: Tb1+ 34 Db1: g4: 35 DA5]

115 Gheorghiu-Skrobek Warsaw 79

1 d4 Nf6 2 c4 e6 3 Nf3 b6 4 a3!? c5 5 e3 5 d5 Ba6 6 Qc2 Qe7!=+ **Bb7 6 Nc3 d5 7 cxd5 Nxd5** 7...exd5± **8 Bb5+ Bc6! 9 Bd3** 9 Qa4 Qd7!! 10 Ne5?! Nxc3∓ **cxd4 10 exd4 Be7** 10...Nd7 += **11 Ne5!± 0-0** 11...Nxc3? 12 bxc3 Bxg2 12 Rg1 Δ Rxg7 +- **12 0-0 Bb7 13 Qc2!** 13 Bc2 Δ Qd3 += **Nf6 14 Rd1 Nc6 15 Qa4! Rc8 16 Ba6! Qc7** 16...Bxa6 17 Nxc6 +- **17 Bb5! Qb8 18 Nxc6 Bxc6!?** 18...Rxc6 19 Bxb7 Qxb7 20 Qxa7± **19 Bxc8 Rxc8 20 Qxa7! +-**

Diagram

20...Bxb5 20...Qxa7? 21 Nxa7 +- **21 Qxe7 Rc2 22 h3 Bc6 23 Rd2! Rc4 24 Rd3 Be4 25 Rg3! Rxd4 26**

&e3! 26 ♕xf6? ♕xg3!!= ♖d7 27
♕b4! +− ♗g6 28 ♕xb6 ♖b7 29 ♕c6
♖xb2 30 ♖c1 ♖b1 31 ♗a7!! +−
1-0 31...♖xc1+ 32 ♕xc1 ♕a8 33
♖b3! +− **Gheorghiu**

116 Gheorghiu-Sunye
Sao Paulo 79

1 d4 ♘f6 2 c4 e6 3 ♘f3 b6 4 a3 d5
5 ♘c3 ♗e7 6 cxd5 exd5 7 g3 0-0 8
♗g2 ♗b7 9 0-0 c5 9...a6 10 ♘e5
♘bd7 11 ♗f4 ♖e8 12 ♕b3! ♘f8 13
e4! +− Gheorghiu-Hartston, Moscow
77 10 ♘e5!? 10 dxc5 bxc5 11 ♘e5
+= ♘c6!∝ 11 ♗e3! ♘xe5 12 dxe5
♘e4! 13 ♕c2! += 13 ♘xe4 dxe4 14
♕c2 ♕d5! =+ ♘xc3 14 bxc3 ♕c7
15 ♖ad1! ♖ad8 15...♕xe5 16 c4 +=
16 ♕a2! ♕d7 17 ♖d2 ♕a4 18 ♖fd1
d4!? 19 cxd4 cxd4 20 ♗xd4! 20
♖xd4 ♕xd1+! 21 ♖xd1 ♖xd1+ 22
♗f1 △ f3∝ ♗xg2 21 ♔xg2 ♗xa3 22
f3! 22 e6 ♕c6+ 23 f3± b5 23 ♖d3
a5! 24 e6! 24 ♖xa3?? ♕xd1; 24
♕xa3 ♖xd4!!∝ ♗b4

Diagram

25 ♕b2!! +− ♖c8 25...♗a3 26 ♖xa3!
♕xd1 27 ♖d3± 26 ♗xg7 ♖c2 27
exf7+! ♔xf7 28 ♕f6+ ♔g8 29 ♗xf8
♗xf8 30 ♖d4! ♖c4 31 ♖d8 1-0
Gheorghiu

117 Vaisman-Suba
Rumania Final 78

1 d4 ♘f6 2 ♘f3 e6 3 e3 b6 4 ♗d3
♗b7 5 ♘bd2 c5 6 0-0 ♗e7 7 b3 ♘c6
8 ♗b2 0-0 9 c4 ♖c8 9...cxd4 10 exd4
d5 11 ♖c1 dxc4= Tisdall-Gheorghiu,
Orense 77 10 ♖c1 cxd4 11 exd4
d5 12 ♕e2 ♖e8! 13 ♖fd1 ♗f8= 14
♘e5 dxc4! 15 ♘dxc4 15 bxc4 ♘xd4
16 ♕e3 ♗c5 17 ♕h3∝ ♘b4 16 ♗b1
♘bd5 17 ♘e3 ♖e7!? 18 ♖xc8 ♕xc8
19 ♘xd5 ♗xd5?! 19...♘xd5! 20
♗c1! ♖c7 21 ♗f4 ♗d6 22 ♗g5 ♗e7
23 ♗d3 g6 24 ♕d2! ♗d8 25 h4 ♗b7
26 ♖e1 ♘d5 27 ♘g4! ♗e7 28 ♗xe7
♖xe7 28...♘xe7 29 ♕h6! △ ♘f6+
29 ♗c4! △ 30 ♗xd5, ♘f6+ ♖c7 30
♕g5 h5 31 ♗xd5 hxg4 32 ♗xb7 ♕xb7
33 ♕xg4± ♕d5 34 ♖e5 ♕c6 35 h5
♕c1+ 36 ♔h2 ♕h6 37 ♔g3! ♖c3+
37...f5 38 ♕xg6+ ♖g7 39 ♖xe6!!
+− 38 f3 ♖c2 39 ♖g5! ♔g7 40 d5!
exd5 41 hxg6 fxg6 42 ♕d7+ 1-0
42...♔g8 43 ♖e5!: 42...♔f6 43 ♕d6+
♔g7 44 ♕e7+ ♔g8 45 ♖xd5!; 43...
♔f7 44 ♖f5+! **Ciocaltea**

118 Petrosian-Browne
Buenos Aires 78

1 d4 ♘f6 2 ♘f3 b6 3 e3 ♗b7 4 ♗d3
e6 5 0-0 ♗e7 6 b3!? 0-0 7 ♗b2 c5

8 c4 cxd4! 9 exd4 9 ♘xd4 ♘c6= **d5**
9...d6?! += **10 ♘bd2 ♘bd7** 10...♘c6!?
11 ♖c1 ♖c8 12 ♕e2 ♖c7! N 12...♘h5
13 g3 g6 **13 ♘g5?** 13 ♘e5 dxc4! 14
bxc4 ♘xe5 15 dxe5 ♘d7 =+; 13 ♖e1
h6! **14 ♘h3 ♖e8** 14...♕a8!? **15 f4
♕a8 16 ♘f3 dxc4! 17 bxc4 ♗e4** =+
18 ♘d2 18 ♘e5 ♗xd3 **19 ♕xd3 ♗b4
20 ♘f3 ♕e4 21 ♕b3 ♗a5!∓ 22 ♗c3!**
22 g3? ♗g4 23 ♘f2 ♕e3! 24 h3 ♕xb3
−+; 23 ♔h1 ♘e3 24 ♖f2 ♘f6 −+
♗xc3 23 ♖xc3 ♖ec8 24 g3 ♘d5?!
24...♕b7! 25 ♘f2! ♘e8! 26 ♕b4
a5! 27 ♕b3 ♘d6∓ **25 ♖cc1** 25 ♘f2??
♕g6 −+ **♕g6?** 25...♘e7! 26 ♘f2 ♕b7
=+ **26 ♖fe1 ♘e7 27 ♘f2 ♘f5 28
♕d3! ♘e7?** 28...♕h7! 29 ♘e5?! ♘xe5
30 fxe5 b5! 31 c5 ♖d8∓ **29 ♘e4 ♘d5
30 ♕f1! ♘b4 31 a3 ♘c6 32 d5 exd5
33 cxd5 ♘a5 34 f5! ♕h5 35 ♖xc7
♖xc7 36 ♘d6 ♘f6 37 h3 ♖c3!?** 37...
♘b7!= **38 ♔g2 ♘xd5?? +−** 38...♖xa3
+= **39 g4 ♘f4+ 40 ♔g3 ♕xh3+ 41
♕xh3 1-0** 41...♖xh3 42 ♖e8+ ♔h7
43 ♘xf7 +− **Browne**

119 Timman-Giardelli
Buenos Aires 78

**1 c4 c5 2 ♘f3 ♘f6 3 ♘c3 b6 4 e3
e6 5 d4 cxd4 6 exd4 (d5?** 6...♗b4!
7 ♘e5!± ♗e7 8 cxd5 exd5 8...♘xd5
9 ♗b5+ ♔f8 10 ♕f3 **9 ♗b5+ ♔f8
10 0-0 ♗e6 11 ♖e1 a6 12 ♗a4 b5 13
♗b3 b4? 14 ♘e2 ♘bd7 15 ♘f4 +−
♘b6 16 ♘xe6+ fxe6 17 ♘d3 ♗d6
18 ♖xe6 ♔f7 19 ♖e1 ♖e8 20 ♘e5+
♔g8 21 ♗g5 ♖e6 22 ♗c2 ♕e8 23 ♗xf6
♖xf6 24 ♘g4 ♖e6 25 ♘f6+! gxf6 26
♕g4+ ♔f7 27 ♕h5+ ♔e7 28 ♖xe6+
♔xe6 29 ♕f5+ 1-0** 29...♔f7 30 ♕xh7+
♔f8 31 ♕h6+ ♔g8 32 ♗h7+ ♔h8
33 ♗g6+ +− **Keene**

120 Balogh-Rigo
Budapest 2 78

**1 d4 ♘f6 2 c4 e6 3 ♘f3 b6 4 e3 ♗b7
5 ♗d3 ♗b4+ 6 ♘bd2 c5** 6...d5 7 0-0
0-0 8 a3 ♗d6 9 b4 += **7 0-0 cxd4
8 exd4 0-0 9 a3 ♗e7 10 ♕e2** 10 ♖e1
d5 11 b3 ♘c6 12 ♗b2 ♖c8 13 ♘e5
dxc4 14 ♘xc6 ♗xc6 15 bxc4 ♖e8 16
♘f3 ♗f8 17 ♘e5 ♗b7 18 ♕d2 += **d5
11 b3 ♘c6 12 ♗b2 ♘fd7!?** N 12...
♖c8; 12...♖e8 **13 ♖ad1!?** 13 cxd5!
exd5 14 ♘e5 += **♗f6 14 ♘e5 g6 15
♖fe1** 15 f4 ♗g7 16 ♘df3 dxc4 17
bxc4 ♘dxe5 18 fxe5 += **♗g7 16
♘df3 ♘cxe5** 16...dxc4 17 ♗xc4=;
17 bxc4 ♘dxe5 18 dxe5 ♕c7 =+
17 dxe5 dxc4 17...♕c7 18 cxd5 ♗xd5
19 ♘g5± **18 ♗xc4 ♕c7 19 ♘d4!**
19 ♘g5 ♕c6= ♕xe5 20 ♘xe6 ♕xb2
20...♕xe2 21 ♖xe2 fxe6 22 ♖xd7
+− **21 ♕xb2 ♗xb2 22 ♖xd7 fxe6
23 ♖xb7 ♗xa3 24 ♖xe6 ♔h8**

25 ♖c6!? 25 h4! ♗c5 26 h5 ♖xf2?
27 ♔h2 ♖f5 28 hxg6 ♖h5+ 29 ♔g3
♖g5+ 30 ♔h4 ♖xg6 31 ♖xg6 hxg6
32 ♔g5 +−; 29...♖g8? 30 ♖e8 ♖xe8
31 g7 mate; 26...♖ae8 27 ♖xe8
♖xe8 28 ♖xa7 += **♖ad8! 26 ♔f1**
26 h4 **♗d2?? 27 ♖cc7 ♖dxf2+ 28
♔g1 1-0** 28...♖f1+ 29 ♗xf1 ♗c5+
30 ♖xc5 +− **Balogh**

121 Miles-Ligterink
Amsterdam 3 78

1 d4 ♞f6 2 ♞f3 e6 3 c4 b6 4 ♗f4 ♗b7 5 e3 ♗b4+ 6 ♞fd2 d5 7 a3 7 ♕a4+ ♞c6∞ **♗e7 8 ♞c3 0-0 9 cxd5 ♞xd5** 9...exd5!? **10 ♞xd5 ♗xd5 11 ♖c1 c5 12 dxc5 ♗xc5 13 ♗c4!** **♗xc4** 13...♗xg2? 14 ♖g1 ♗b7 15 ♗h6±; 13...♗b7!? 14 0-0 += **14 ♞xc4 ♕xd1+ 15 ♔xd1** += 15 ♖xd1 += **♞d7 16 ♔e2 ♞f6 17 ♗d6!? ♗xd6 18 ♞xd6 ♖fd8 19 ♖c6 ♔f8** 19...♞d5 20 ♖hc1! ♞e7 21 ♖c7± **20 ♖hc1 ♖d7 21 ♞b5** 21 ♞c8 ♞d5! Δ ♞e7; 21 ♞c4!? += **♖ad8 21 ♖1c2 ♞e4 23 f4!** 23 f3? ♖d2+ 24 ♖xd2 ♖xd2+ 25 ♔e1 ♖xb2∓; 23 ♞d4 e5 ♕e7 23...♖d2+ 24 ♔f3 += **24 ♖c7 a6 25 ♞d4 ♔f6** 25...♖xc7 26 ♖xc7+ ♖d7 27 ♞c6+ ♔d6 28 ♖xd7+ ♔xd7 29 ♞b8+ +− **26 b4 h6?** 26...g5!?; 26... ♖xc7 27 ♖xc7 ♖d6 28 ♞f3± **27 ♖xd7 ♖xd7 28 ♔f3 ♞d6 29 ♖c6** +− **♞b5 30 ♞xb5 axb5 31 ♖xb6 ♖a7 32 ♖xb5 ♖xa3 33 h4! 1-0** 33...♖b3 34 h5 +− **Miles**

122 Miles-Hubner
England-BRD 79

1 d4 ♞f6 2 ♞f3 e6 3 c4 b6 4 ♗f4 ♗b7 5 e3 ♗b4+ 6 ♞fd2 0-0 7 a3 ♗e7 8 ♞c3 d5 9 cxd5 ♞xd5 10 ♞xd5 ♗xd5 11 ♖c1 c5 12 dxc5 ♗xc5 13 ♗c4 ♗b7! N 13...♗xc4? 14 ♞xc4 ♕xd1+ 15 ♔xd1** += Miles-Ligterink, Amsterdam 3 78 **14 0-0 ♗d6!=** 15 ♗xd6 ♕xd6 16 ♕e2 ♞d7 17 ♖fd1 ♖ac8 18 ♞f3** 18 ♞e4? ♕c6 19 f3 b5∓ 20 ♞d6 bxc4 21 ♖xc4 ♗a6! 22 ♖xc6 ♗xe2 23 ♞xc8 ♗xd1 24 ♞e7+ ♔h8 25 ♖d6 ♗a4 26 ♖d4 ♖e8 −+; 20 ♗d5 ♕xc1 21 ♗xb7 ♖c2! −+; 20 ♖d6 ♕c7 21 ♖cd1 ♕xc4 22 ♕xc4 ♖xc4 23 ♖xd7 ♗xe4 ∓/−+

123 Miles-Andersson
Buenos Aires 78

1 d4 ♞f6 2 ♞f3 e6 3 c4 b6 4 ♗f4 ♗b7 5 e3 ♗b4+ 6 ♞fd2?! 6 ♞bd2 ♞e4 7 a3 += **0-0 7 ♗d3 d5! 8 0-0 c5!** =+ 9 a3 ♗xd2 10 ♞xd2 cxd4 11 exd4 ♞c6 12 ♞f3 dxc4 13 ♗xc4 ♖c8 14 ♖c1 ♞a5 15 ♗e2** 15 ♗d3? ♖xc1 16 ♕xc1 ♗xf3!∓; 16 ♗xc1 ♗xf3 17 ♕xf3 ♕xd4∓ **♖xc1 16 ♕xc1 ♕d5! 17 ♕d3 ♖c8∓ 18 ♗f4 ♕b3! 19 ♕xb3 ♞xb3 20 ♗d1 ♞d5 21 ♗g5** 21 ♗xb3 ♞xf4∓ **♞c1** Δ ♞d3 −+ **22 ♗xc1 ♖xc1 23 ♗b3 ♖c7 24 ♞e5 ♞f4 25 ♖d1** 25 f3 ♞e2+ Δ ♞xd4 **♗xg2 26 f3 f6! −+**

27 ♞d3 ♗xf3! 28 ♞xf4 28 ♞f1 ♞xd3 −+ **♗xd1 29 ♗xe6+** 29 ♗xd1 ♖c1 **♔f8 30 ♗f5 ♖c1 31 ♔f2 0-1 Gheorghiu**

124 Miles-Rivas
Amsterdam 3 78

1 c4 ♞f6 2 d4 e6 3 ♞f3 b6 4 ♗f4 ♗b7 5 e3 ♗e7 6 h3 0-0 7 ♞c3 d5 8 cxd5 ♞xd5 9 ♞xd5 ♗xd5 10 ♗d3 ♗b4+ 11 ♔e2 ♗d6 12 ♗xd6 ♗xf3+! N 12...cxd6 Miles-Browne, Amsterdam 1 78 **13 ♔xf3!? 13 gxf3 += ♕xd6 14 ♕c2! f5** 14...h6 15 ♖ac1± **15 ♖ac1! f4** 15...c6±; 15...c5 16 dxc5 ♕d5+

17 ♔e2± **16 ♕xc7! ♕d5+** 16...fxe3+?
17 ♔xe3 ♕d5 18 ♗e4 ♕g5+ 19 ♔e2
+− **17 ♔e2 ♘d7** 17...f3+ 18 gxf3
♕xf3+ 19 ♔d2 ♕xf2+ 20 ♗e2 +−
♘a6 21 ♕c4; 17...fxe3 18 ♕e5! ♕xg2
19 ♕xe3 ♘d7 20 ♗e4 ♖xf2+ 21 ♔e1!
+−; 18...♖xf2+ 19 ♔xe3 +−; 18...
♕xa2 19 ♖c7/♕e4 +−; 17...♕xg2?
18 ♖cg1 f3+ 19 ♔e1 +− **18 ♕c6±
♕h5+ 19 f3** 19 ♕f3 ♖ad8 **20 ♕xe6+?!**
20 e4 ±/+− **♕h8 21 e4 ♘f6 22 ♕e5
♕g6 23 ♖hg1 ♕g3 24 ♖c7 ♖fe8 25
♖e7 ♕h2! 26 ♔f1!** 26 ♔f2 ♘g4+! 27
hxg4 ♕h4+∞; 27 fxg4 ♕g3+; 26...
♕g3+ 27 ♔f1 ♖xe7 25 ♕xe7 ♖xd4
♖xe7 27 ♕xe7 ♖c8 27...♖xd4 28
♕f8+ ♘g8 29 ♗c2! ♖c4 30 ♗b3 ♖c1+
31 ♔e2 ♖c2+ 32 ♔d3 +− **28 ♔f2!
♕g3+ 29 ♔e2 ♕h2 30 ♕b7!** +− 30
♕e6?? ♖e8 −+ **♖e8** 30...♕xg1 31
♕xc8+ ♘g8 32 ♗c4 +−; 30...♖d8 31
♔f1 ♖xd4 32 ♗c2! +− **31 ♔f1 ♘h5
32 e5! g6** 32...♘g3+ 33 ♔f2 ♘h1+ 34
♖xh1 ♕xh1 35 ♕f7! ♖g8 36 ♗xh7!
+−; 35...♖c8/♖d8 36 ♕f5 +− **33 e6
♕g3 34 ♗b5 ♖g8 36 e7 ♘g7 36 ♕d5**
△ ♕e5 **a6 37 ♗d7 1-0 Miles**

**125 Browne-Andersson
Buenos Aires 2 78**

**1 d4 ♘f6 2 c4 e6 3 ♘f3 b6 4 g3 ♗a6!?
5 ♕a4 ♗b7** 5...c6 6 ♘c3 b5!? 7 cxb5
cxb5 8 ♘xb5 ♕b6∞ **6 ♗g2 c5 7 0-0
cxd4 8 ♘xd4 ♗xg2 9 ♔xg2 ♗e7**
9...♕c8!= **10 ♘c3 0-0 11 ♖d1 ♕c7
12 ♗f4 ♕b7+ 13 f3 a6 14 e4 d6 15
♘de2 ♖d8 16 ♖d2 ♘c6 17 ♖ad1 ♗e8
18 a3** △ b4; 18 ♕c2 b5 =+ ♖dc8!
**19 h4 h6 20 h5 ♘a5! 21 b3 ♕c7
22 e5! ♖d8!** 22...dxe5!? 23 ♖d7!
♕c6 24 ♗xe5± **23 exd6 ♗xd6 24
♘e4** 24 ♗xd6 ♘xd6 =+ **♗xf4 25 ♘xf4
♖xd2+ 26 ♖xd2 ♘c6 27 b4 ♘e5!
28 c5 ♘f6!∓**

29 cxb6 ♕xb6 30 ♘xf6+ gxf6 31
**♕b3 ♖c8 32 ♖e2 ♖c1 33 ♔e3 ♕c7
34 ♕d4 ♖c3 35 ♖e3 ♖c4! 36 ♕d1
♖c2+ 37 ♔h3 ♖c1 38 ♕d2 ♔g7 39
a4 ♕c4! 40 ♘d3 ♖c2 41 ♕d1 ♕a2**
△ ♖h2+ **42 ♕g1 ♗xd3 43 ♖xd3
♕xa4 44 ♕b1 ♖c4 45 ♖b3 ♕b5!**
−+ **46 g4 ♖d4 47 ♖b2 ♕d5 48 ♕g3
♖d3! 49 ♖f2 ♖b3 50 ♕c1 ♕d6+
51 ♔g2 ♖xb4 52 g5 hxg5 53 h6+
♔g6! 54 h7 ♖h4 0-1 Gheorghiu**

126 O'Kelly-Miles England 78

**1 c4 b6 2 d4 e6 3 ♘f3 ♘f6 4 g3
♗a6 5 b3 ♗b4+ 6 ♗d2 ♗e7 7 ♗g2
c6!? 8 0-0 d5 9 ♘c3 0-0 10 cxd5?!**
10 ♘e5 ♘fd7= **cxd5 =+ 11 ♕b1**
11 ♗c1 △ ♗b2 **♘c6 12 a3** 12 ♖c1?
♗a3 **♖c8 13 ♖c1 ♖e8 14 e3 h6 15
♕b2?** ♗d6! =+/∓ △ ♕e7, e5 **16 b4
♗d3!** 16...♗c4 17 e4! dxe4 18 ♘xe4
♘xe4 19 ♖xc4∞ **17 ♘e1 ♗c4∓ 18
♗f1** 18 e4? ♘xd4 −+ **♗xf1 19 ♔xf1
e5 ∓/−+ 20 ♘b5** 20 dxe5 ♘xe5 △
♘c4; 20 b5 ♘a5 21 dxe5 ♗xe5 −+
exd4 21 ♘xd4 21 ♘xd6 ♕xd6 22
exd4 ♕d7 −+ **♘xd4 22 exd4** 22
♕xd4 ♗e5 −+ **♕d7 −+ 23 ♖xc8
♕xc8! 24 ♔g2 ♖e2 25 ♘f3 ♘g4
0-1** 26 ♖f1 ♘e3+ 27 ♔g1 ♕h3 **Miles**

**127 Barczay-Tompa
Hungary Final 78**

1 d4 ♘f6 2 c4 e6 3 ♘f3 b6 4 g3 ♗a6

5 b3 ♗b4+ 6 ♗d2 ♗e7 7 ♗g2 c6 8 0-0 d5 9 ♘c3!? 9 ♘e5 0-0 10 ♘c3 ♘fd7 11 ♘xd7 ♘xd7 12 ♘d2 ♖c8 13 e4 dxc4 14 bxc4 b5 15 ♕c2 bxc4 16 ♖fd1 ♘f6 17 ♖ab1 ♖b8= Bukic-Tal, Bugojno 78 **♘e4?!** 9...0-0 10 ♘e5 ♘fd7 **10 ♗b2 ♘d7 11 ♘fd2 ♘xd2 12 ♘xd2 b5!? 13 c5!?** 13 ♕c2! += **b4 14 ♖e1 f5 15 e4?! dxe4!** 15...fxe4? 16 ♕g4± **16 f3 0-0 17 fxe4 e5! 18 exf5 exd4 19 ♗xc6?** 19 ♕g4 ♗xc5 20 ♖ac1 ♗b6 21 ♖xc6 ♘f6∞ ♖c8 19...♗xc5? 20 ♕f3 ♖c8 21 ♕d5+ ♖f7 22 ♘e4± **20 ♗d5+ ♔h8 21 ♘e4** 21 ♗xd4? ♘xc5 −+ **♘e5!∓ 22 ♗e6 ♖c6! 23 ♘g5** 23 ♔g2 ♘d3 24 ♖e2 ♖xe6 25 fxe6 ♕d5 26 ♖b1 ♖f4 27 gxf4 ♘xf4+ −+ **♗xg5 24 ♖xe5 ♗e3+ 25 ♔g2?!** 25 ♖xe3!? fxe3 26 ♕xd8 ♖xd8 27 ♖e1 e2 28 ♔f2 ♖f8 29 ♔e3 ♖xc5∓; 26 ♕g4 ♕e7 Δ e2 −+ **♗b7 −+ 26 ♔h3** 26 ♗d5 ♖xc5; 26 ♖d5 ♖xe6 **♕f6 27 ♗xd4** 27 ♖xe3 ♖xe6 28 ♖xe6 ♕xf5+ 29 g4 ♕xe6 −+ Δ ♖f3+; 29 ♕g4 ♗g2+ 30 ♔h4 g5+ −+; 28 fxe6 ♕h6+ 29 ♔g4 ♗g2 30 h4 ♕g6 mate **♕h6+ 28 ♔g4**

28...♖xe6!! 29 ♖xe6 29 ♗xe3 ♖g6+! 30 fxg6 ♗c8+; 29 fxe6 ♗g2! 30 h4 ♕g6+ 31 ♖g5 h5 mate **♕g5+ 30 ♔h3 ♕xf5+ 31 ♕g4 ♗g2+ 32 ♔h4 ♗g5+ 0-1 Tompa**

1 c4 b6 2 d4 e6 3 ♘f3 ♘f6 4 g3 ♗a6 5 b3 ♗b4+ 6 ♗d2 ♗e7 7 ♗g2 7 ♘c3 c6 8 0-0 0-0 9 ♗c3 d5 10 ♘e5 ♘fd7 11 ♘xd7 ♘xd7 12 ♘d2 ♖c8 13 a4!? ♗f6!? 13...f5!?; 13...♖e8 14 e4 += **14 e4 c5** 14...dxc4 15 e5! ♗e7 16 bxc4± **15 exd5 cxd4 16 ♗b4?** 16 dxe6? dxc3 17 exd7 cxd2 18 dxc8♕ ♗xc8 19 ♖a2 ♗c3∓; 16 ♗b2! +=/± **♗e7! 17 ♗xe7 ♕xe7 18 dxe6 fxe6!** =+ **19 ♕c2 ♖ce8 20 ♖ae1 e5 21 ♗c6 ♗c8 22 h4?!** 22 f4!? ♔h8! (Δ d3) 23 ♗xd7 ♕xd7 24 fxe5 ♖xf1+ 25 ♔xf1 ♗b7∓; 25 ♖xf1 d3 26 ♕b2 ♗b7∓; 25 ♘xf1 ♗b7∓; 24 ♖xe5 d3 25 ♕c3 ♖xe5∞ **♔h8 23 ♘e4 ♖d8 24 ♘g5 ♘f6 25 ♗g2 h6 26 ♘e4 ♗f5 27 ♕d3 ♖fe8 28 ♖e2 ♗g4 29 ♖d2** ♗f3? ♘xe4 30 ♕xe4 ♗xf3 31 ♕xf3∓ 32 ♖fe1? d3 −+; 30 ♗xg4 ♘c3 Δ e4∓ **♘d7 30 ♕b1 a5 31 ♖e1 ♖f8 32 ♔h2 ♗f5 33 ♕b2 ♕b4∓ 34 ♗h3? ♗xh3 35 ♔xh3 ♖f3 36 ♖b1 ♘c5 37 ♘xc5 bxc5 −+ 38 ♖e2 ♖df8?!** 38...♖e8 Δ e4 −+ **39 ♕d2** 39 ♖xe5! ♖xf2 40 ♖e8!∓ **♕b6!** 39...♕xd2? 40 ♖xd2 ♖xf2 41 ♖xf2 ♖xf2 42 ♖e1 =; 39...♖xb3 40 ♕xb4 ♖xb4 ♖xb4∞ **40 ♕g2** 40 ♖xe5 ♖xf2 41 ♕d3 ♖2f3 42 ♕e4 ♖e3 43 ♕d5 ♖xg3+ −+ **♕f6 41 ♕xa5 0-1** 41 ♖b2 ♕c6 42 ♔g1 e4 43 ♕xa5 e3 (Δ ♖xg3+, ♖f1+) 44 ♕e1 ♕e4 −+ **Miles**

1 d4 ♘f6 2 c4 e6 3 ♘f3 b6 4 g3 ♗b7 5 ♗g2 ♗b4+ 6 ♗d2 ♗e7 7 ♘c3 0-0 8 0-0 ♘a6!? 9 ♘e5 ♗xg2 10 ♔xg2 ♕b8 11 e4 ♕b7 12 ♕f3 c6 13 ♖fe1 ♘b4 14 ♖ac1 d6 15 ♘d3 ♘xd3 16 ♕xd3 a6 17 d5 += cxd5 18 cxd5

b5 19 a3 ♖ac8 20 ♗f4 ♖c4 △ e5,
♖fc8= **21 dxe6 fxe6 22 f3 ♖d8 23
♖ed1 ♘d7 24 b3** 24 ♗xd6?? ♘c5
♖cc8 25 ♘e2 ♘c5 26 ♕b1 b4∞ **27
♗e3?** bxa3 **28 b4 ♘d7 29 ♘f4 ♘f8
30 ♕b3 d5!∓ 31 exd5 ♕xb4 32
♕xb4 ♖xb4 33 dxe6 ♖xd1 34 ♖xd1
a2 35 ♘d5** 35 ♖a1 ♖c2+ 36 ♔h3
♘xe6 37 ♘xe6 ♗c3 −+; 35 ♗d4 ♖d8
36 ♘e2 ♘xe6 −+ **♖d8! 36 e7 ♖xd5
37 ♖xd5** 37 e8♕? ♖xd1 −+ **a1♕
38 e8♕ ♕a2+ 39 ♗d2! ♖xd2 40 ♖e5
♗b4+ 41 ♔e2 ♕d5 42 h4 a5 −+
43 ♖e4 ♗d6 44 ♖e2 h6 45 g4 ♕d4
46 h5 ♗c5 47 ♔g3 ♕g1+ 48 ♔f4 ♗d6+
49 ♔e4 ♗c5 50 ♕a8 ♕c4+ 51 ♔e3
♗c5+ 52 ♔d2 ♕a2+ 53 ♔d1 ♕b1+
54 ♔d2 ♕b2+ 55 ♔d1 ♕b3+ 56 ♔d2
♗b4+ 57 ♔c1 ♕d3 △ ♗a3+ 0-1 Miles**

130 Sosonko-Miles
Amsterdam 3 78

1 d4 e6 2 g3 c5 3 ♘f3 b6 3...♕a5+!?
4 ♗g2 ♗b7 5 c4 5 0-0 cxd4 6 ♕xd4
♘c6 7 ♕a4 += Sosonko-Timman,
Netherlands Final 78 **cxd4 6 ♕xd4
♘c6 7 ♕f4 ♘f6** 7...♕b8!? **8 0-0 d5!?
9 ♘c3 ♗d6 10 ♕h4 ♘e7 11 ♗g5 ♘e4!**
11...♘g6? 12 ♗xf6± **12 cxd5** 12
♘xe4 dxe4 13 ♘d4 ♗e5; 13 ♘d2
f6!?/f5 **♕xc3** 12...exd5!? **13 bxc3
♗xd5 14 ♖fd1 ♕c7 15 ♘d4 a6 16
♗xd5 exd5** 16...♘xd5? 17 ♕e4! △
c4/♘xe6 +− **17 e4! ♘g6 18 ♕g4 0-0
19 exd5 ♘e5 20 ♕e4 ♕xc3 21 ♖ac1
♕a3 += 22 ♔g2 g6 23 ♗h6?! ♖fe8
24 ♖e1 ♕a4=** 24...♕xa2!? **25 ♖ce2∞
♕a4 26 ♖ce2∞ 25 ♘c6 ♕xe4+ 26 ♖xe4
f5 27 ♖e2?** 27 ♖ee1= **♘g4 28 ♖xe8+
♖xe8 29 ♗f4 ♗xf4 30 gxf4 ♖e2∓**

Diagram

31 d6! ♖xf2+ 32 ♔g3 ♖d2 33 ♘e5!

33 ♘e7+ ♔f7 34 ♖c7!? **♖xd6 34 ♖c8+
♔g7 35 ♖c7+ ♔f6 36 ♘xg4+ fxg4
37 ♖xh7 b5!** 37...♖d3+ 38 ♔xg4
♖a3 39 ♖b7 **38 ♔xg4** 38 ♖b7 ♖d2
39 a3? 39 a4 =+ ♖g2+ 40 ♔f3 ♖a2∓
41 ♖b7 ♔f5 41...♖xa3+ 42 ♔g4
♖e3 43 h4 ♖e6 44 ♖b8 ♖c6 45 ♖b7
♔e6 46 ♔g5 ♔d5 47 h5! gxh5 48
f5!= **42 ♖f7+ ♔e6 43 ♖g7 ♖xa3+
44 ♔g4 b4 45 ♖xg6+ ♔d5 46 ♖b6
♔c5 47 ♖b8 ♖a1** 47...♖a2!? **48 f5
a5 49 ♖c8+ ♔b5 50 ♖b8+ ♔c4 51
f6 ♖f1 52 ♖c8+ ♔b5 53 ♖b8+ ♔c5
54 ♖c8+ ♔d6 55 ♖b8 ♔c5** 55...♖xf6?
56 ♖b5? **♔f2!** 57 ♖xa5 ♖xh2 58
♔f4 ♔c6 59 ♔e3 b3! 60 ♖a3 ♔c5!
−+; 59 ♔e4 b3 60 ♖a3 ♖h3! −+;
56 ♖b6+!= **56 ♖c8+ ♔d4 57 ♖d8+
♔c4 58 ♖c8+ ♔b3 59 ♖c5!=** a4 60
♖f5 ♖g1+ 61 ♔h5 ♖g8 62 f7 ♖f8
63 ♔g6 a3 64 ♔g7 ♖xf7+ 65 ♖xf7
65 ♔xf7?? ♔a4! −+ a2 66 ♖a7 ♔b2
67 ♖xa2+ ♔xa2 68 h4 b3 69 h5 b2
70 h6 b1♕ 71 h7 ♕a1 72 h8♕ ♕b2+
73 ♕g8 ♕xh8+ 74 ♔xh8+ ½-½ **Miles**

131 Korchnoi-Gheorghiu
Sao Paulo 79

**1 c4 c5 2 ♘f3 ♘f6 3 ♘c3 e6 4 g3
b6 5 ♗g2 ♗b7 6 0-0 ♗e7 7 d4 cxd4
8 ♕xd4 d6 9 ♖d1 a6!** 9...0-0?! 10
b3 a6?! 11 ♗a3!± Andersson-Segal,
Sao Paulo 79 **10 ♗g5!** N 10 b3 △ ♗b2;

10 e4 ♘bd7 11 ♗xf6 ♘xf6 12 ♘a4!
♖b8 12...b5 13 cxb5 axb5 14 ♘c3∞
13 c5! ♗xf3 13...bxc5 14 ♘xc5 dxc5??
15 ♕a4+! +–; 14...♘c8! 15 ♘e5!
♕b6 16 ♕a4+ ♔f8 17 ♘ed7+ ♘xd7
18 ♘xd7+ ♗xd7 19 ♕xd7 += 14 ♗xf3
dxc5! 15 ♕e5! 15 ♘c6+? ♔f8∓ ♕c8 16
♖d6!∞ 0-0 16...♖xd6 17 ♕xd6 ♘d5!
18 ♗xd5 exd5 19 ♘xb6 ♖xb6 20
♕xb6 0-0 ∞/± Korchnoi 17 ♖xb6
♖xb6? 17...♘d7! 18 ♖xb8 ♘xe5 19
♖xc8 ♘xf3+! 20 exf3 ♖xc8= 18 ♘xb6
♕d8 19 ♘c4! += ♘d7 20 ♕e3 ♘b6
21 ♘e5! ♕c7 22 ♘c6 ♗d6 23 ♕d3!
23 ♕a3? ♘d5!∞ c4 24 ♕d2!± ♖c8
25 ♖c1 ♗f8 26 b3! cxb3 27 axb3
♔h8! 28 ♖c2?! ♕d7!= 29 ♕xd7 ♘xd7
30 ♖a2 ♘b8! 31 ♘xb8 ½-½ Gheorghiu

Some tricky tactics on both sides.

1 c4 c5 2 ♘f3 e6 3 g3 b6 4 ♗g2
♗b7 5 0-0 ♘f6 6 ♘c3 ♗e7 7 d4 cxd4
8 ♕xd4 0-0 9 e4 9 ♖d1 d6 10 ♘g5!;
9 b3 d6 10 ♗b2 ♘bd7 11 ♖fd1 a6
12 ♕e3 △ ♘d4± d6 10 b3 a6 11
♗b2 ♕c7 12 ♖fd1 ♘bd7 13 ♖ac1
♖fd8 14 ♕e3 ♖ac8 15 ♘d4 ♗f8 16
h3 g6 17 f4? 17 ♔h1! e5 18 ♘de2
d5! 19 fxe5 ♘g5 20 ♘d4 ♕xe5 21
♘xd5 ♗xd5 22 cxd5 ♘xd5 =+ 23 ♕h6
♘5f6 24 b4?! 24 ♖xc5 ♕xc5! 25
♔h2! ♗f8 25 ♕d2 ♕xg3 26 ♘c6?!
♘e5! 27 ♗xe5 ♖xd2 28 ♗xg3 ♖xc6
29 ♖xc6 ♖xd1+ 30 ♔h2 ♘d7 –+
31 ♖c8 ♔g7 32 a3 ♗d6! 33 ♗xd6
♖xd6 34 a4? 34 ♖a8! ♖d4 35 ♖c7
♘e5 36 ♖a7 ♖xb4 37 ♖xa6 ♘d3!
△ ♘c5 38 a4 bxa5 39 ♖xa5 ♘f4!
40 ♗f3 ♖b3 41 ♗g4 h5 42 ♗d7 ♖e3
43 e5 ♘d3 44 e6 fxe6 45 ♖a3 e5
0-1 Ciocaltea

1 ♘f3 ♘f6 2 g3 d5 3 ♗g2 e6 4 0-0
♘bd7?! 4...♗e7 5 d3 0-0 6 ♘bd2 c5
7 e4 ♘c6≈ 5 d4 b6 5...♗e7 6 c4 0-0=
6 c4 ♗b7 7 cxd5 ♘xd5?! 7...exd5!?
8 ♖e1 ♗b4? 8...♗e7 9 ♗g5! ♗e7 10
e4!

10...♗xg5? 10...♘5f6!? 11 exd5! ♗xd5
12 ♘xg5 ♗xg2 12...♕xg5 13 h4
♕f5 14 g4 +– 13 ♘xe6 fxe6 14 ♕xg2
♕f6 15 ♕g4 +– 0-0-0 16 ♖xe6 ♕f7
17 ♘c3 ♖hf8 18 ♕e2 ♔b8 19 ♖e1
h5? 20 ♘d5 ♘f6 21 ♘b4 ♖de8 22
♘c6+ ♔b7 23 ♕f3 ♔c8 24 ♘e5 1-0
Samarian

1 d4 ♘f6 2 c4 e6 3 ♘f3 b6 4 g3 ♗b7
5 ♗g2 ♗e7 6 ♘c3 d5 7 cxd5 exd5 8
♕a4+!? c6?! 8...♕d7! 9 ♕b3 0-0 10
♘e5 ♕d8 9 0-0 0-0 10 ♘e5 ♘fd7?!
10...♕c8! △ ♘bd7 11 ♘d3! ♘f6 12
♖d1 ♗d6 13 ♗g5 ♘bd7 14 e4!± dxe4
15 ♘xe4 ♗e7 16 ♘xf6+ ♗xf6 17 ♗xf6
♕xf6 17...♗xf6? 18 ♘e5+ △ ♗xc6
18 ♖ac1 ♘b8? 18...♖fc8 19 ♘e5
♖c8 20 ♖c3 △ ♖f3 +– ♕d6

Diagram

21 ♘xf7! ♔xf7 22 ♕c4+ ♔e7 22...

♕e6? 23 ♖f3+ ♔e7 24 ♖e3; 22...
♔f8 23 ♖f3+ +− **23 ♖e3+ ♔d8 24
♖e6!** +− ♕f8 **25 d5 cxd5 26 ♕h4+
♔c7 27 ♖e7+ ♘d7 28 ♗xd5 ♖d8 29
♗xb7 ♔xb7 30 ♕e4+ 1-0** 30...♔c7
31 ♖c1+ ♔b8 32 ♕c6 +− **Maric**

135 Pfleger-Browne
Buenos Aires 78
**1 ♘f3 ♘f6 2 d4 e6 3 c4 b6 4 g3 ♗b7
5 ♗g2 ♗e7** 5...♗b4 6 ♗d2 ♗xd2+ 7
♕xd2 0-0 **6 ♘c3 ♘e4** 6...0-0 7 ♕c2!
7 ♕c2 7 ♗d2 f5!?; 7...0-0 8 0-0 ♗f6
9 ♕c2 ♘xd2= **♘xc3 8 ♕xc3 0-0 9
0-0 c5 10 b3?!** 10 ♖d1 d6 11 b3 ♗f6
12 ♗b2 ♕e7 13 ♕c2 ♘c6 14 e4 e5
15 d5 ♘d4 16 ♗xd4 += **♗f6 11 ♗b2
cxd4** 11...♗xf3!? 12 ♕xf3 ♘c6 13 e3
cxd4 14 exd4 d5!= **12 ♘xd4 ♗xg2
13 ♕xg2 ♘c6 14 ♕d2?!** 14 ♕d3!
♗xd4 15 ♗xd4 d5 16 ♗b2 += **♗xd4
15 ♗xd4 d5 16 ♗b2! dxc4 17 ♕c3
♕d5+ 18 f3 e5 19 ♖ac1 ♖fd8** 19...
b5!? 20 bxc4 ♕c5 21 cxb5 ♕xb5
22 ♗a3 ♖fc8 23 ♕c4! += **20 ♕xc4
♕xc4 21 ♖xc4 ♖d2 22 ♗c3! ♖xe2+
23 ♖f2 ♖xf2+ 24 ♔xf2 ♖c8!** 24...
♘d4? 25 ♗xd4 exd4 26 ♔e2 ♔f8 27
♔d3 ♔e7 28 ♖c7+! ♔e6 29 a4!± **25
♗xe5 f6 26 ♗c3 ♔f7 27 ♔e3?!**
27 g4!? ♔e6 28 g5! += **♔e6 28 h4
♔d5** 28...h5? 29 g4! **29 a4=** ½-½
Browne

Grunfeld

136 Polugaevsky-Miles
Wijk aan Zee 79
**1 d4 ♘f6 2 c4 g6 3 ♘c3 d5 4 cxd5
♘xd5 5 e4 ♘xc3 6 bxc3 ♗g7 7 ♗c4
c5 8 ♘e2 0-0 9 0-0 ♘c6 10 ♗e3 b6 11
♖c1 ♗b7 12 d5 ♘e5** N 12...♘a5 13
♗d3 c4 14 ♗c2 e6 15 dxe6 +=/∞
**13 ♗b3 c4 14 ♗c2 e6! 15 dxe6 ♘d3!
16 ♗xd3 ♕xd3** 16...cxd3 17 exf7+
♖xf7 18 ♘g3∞ **17 exf7+ ♖xf7 18
♘g3!** 18 ♕xd3 cxd3 =+ **♗xe4 19
♕a4 ♕d5 20 ♘xe4 ♕xe4 21 ♖fe1 ♕d5**
21...♕h4? 22 ♗xb6± **22 ♖cd1 ♕b7
23 ♕xc4 ♖c8 24 ♕e6** 24 ♕b3!?
♗xc3 25 ♖e2 ♕c6!= **26 ♕xc6 ♖xc6
27 ♖c2 ♖cc7!** 27...♖fc7 28 ♗f4 +=;
27...b5? 28 ♖d8+± **28 ♖d8+** ½-½
Miles

137 Knaak-Ftacnik
CSSR DDR 78
**1 d4 ♘f6 2 c4 g6 3 ♘c3 d5 4 cxd5
♘xd5 5 e4 ♘xc3 6 bxc3 ♗g7 7 ♗c4
0-0 8 ♗e3 c5 9 ♘e2 ♘c6 10 0-0 ♕c7
11 ♖c1 ♖d8 12 ♕a4 ♗d7 13 ♕a3
♗f8 14 f4** 14 ♕b2 b5 15 ♗d3 ♖ab8
16 ♗f4 e5 17 ♗g5 ♖e8 18 d5 ♘a5 19
♕d2 c4 20 ♗b1 ♗b7 21 ♘g3 ♘c5=
Gligoric-Smejkal, Ljubljana 73 **e6
15 ♕b2?!** 15 dxc5 ♘a5 16 ♗b3 ♗b5
17 c4 ♗c6 Andersson-Honfi,
Copenhagen 65 **♘a5 16 ♗d3 b5! 17
f5 exf5 18 ♘g3?!** 18 exf5 ∆ fxg6∞
♘c4! 19 ♗xc4 19 ♕e2? ♘xe3 20
♕xe3 f4! 21 ♕xf4 ♕xf4 22 ♖xf4
♗h6 −+ **bxc4 20 exf5 cxd4 21 ♗xd4=
♗c5! 22 ♕d2?!** 22 ♖cd1 ∆ ♕f2= ♗c6!
=+ **23 ♕h6?? 23 ♖f4 ∆ ♖h4, ♕f2
♖xd4!∓ 24 cxd4 ♗xd4+ 25 ♔h1**

103

♗g7 26 ♕h4 ♕b7! 27 ♖f2 ♗d5 28 ♘f1 28 f6 ♗f8∓ ♖e8 29 h3 ♕b6 30 ♘h2 ♗f6! 31 ♕f4 31 ♔g3!∓ ♗g5 —+ 32 ♔xg5 ♕xf2 33 ♖f1 h6 34 ♖xf2 34 ♔g4 ♖e1! —+ ♖e1+ 35 ♘f1 hxg5 36 ♔g1 ♗e4 △ c3, c2 —+ 0-1 Maric

138 Radnoti-Hardicsay
Hungary 78

1 ♘f3 g6 2 c4 ♗g7 3 d4 ♘f6 4 ♘c3 d5 5 cxd5 ♘xd5 6 e4 ♘xc3 7 bxc3 0-0 8 ♗e3 c5 9 ♕d2 ♕a5 10 ♖ab1!? a6 11 ♖b3 b5 12 d5 c4 13 ♖b4 ♘d7 13...e5!? 14 ♘d4! ♘f6 15 f3 ♗d7 16 ♗e2 ♖fd8 17 0-0 e5 18 dxe6 fxe6 19 ♔b2?! e5 20 ♘c2 ♗f8∓ 21 ♔h1 ♗xb4 22 cxb4 ♕c7 23 ♗d2! ♖e8 24 ♗c3 ♗c6 25 ♘e3 ♖ad8 26 g4 ♕b6! 27 ♘xc4! bxc4 28 ♗xc4+ ♔f8 29 ♗xe5 ♗b5 29...♖xe5?! 30 ♕xe5 ♗b5 31 ♗e6!± 30 ♗xf6 ♗xc4 31 ♗xd8 ♖xd8 32 ♕h8+ ♗g8 33 ♖c1 ♕d4! 34 ♕xd4 34 e5 ♕f4! —+ ♖xd4 35 ♖c6 ♖xb4 Zeitnot 35...♗c4! 36 ♔g2! ♗e2 —+ 36 ♖xa6 ♖b2 37 a4 ♖f2 37...♗c4!? 38 ♖f6+ ♔e7 39 ♔g1 ♖a2? 39...♔xf6! 40 ♔xf2 ♔e5 41 ♔e3 g5 42 h4 h6 43 hxg5 hxg5 44 ♔d3 ♗e6 45 a5 ♗c8 46 ♔c4 ♗a6+ 47 ♔c5 ♗e2! —+ 40 ♖a6 g5 41 a5 ♗c4 41...♗e6!? 42 ♖h6 ♖xa5 42... ♗e2 43 ♔f2 ♗d1+ 44 ♔g3 ♖a3 45 ♖xh7+ ♔f6 46 h4= 43 ♖xh7+ ♔f6 44 ♔f2 ♖a2+ 45 ♔e3 ♔e5 46 ♖e7+ ♗e6 47 h3 ♖b2 48 ♖e8 ♖h2 49 ♖h8 ♗c4 50 ♖e8+ ½-½ Hardicsay

139 Timman-L.Roos
Amsterdam 78

1 d4 ♘f6 2 c4 g6 3 ♘c3 d5 4 ♘f3 ♗g7 5 cxd5 ♘xd5 6 e4 ♘xc3 7 bxc3 0-0 8 ♗e2 c5 9 0-0 ♕c7? 9...♘c6 10 ♗e3 ♗g4 11 d5!; 10...cxd4 11 cxd4 ♗g4 12 d5 ♗xa1 13 ♕xa1 ♗xf3 14 ♗xf3 ♘a5 15 ♗h6 f6 16 ♗xf8 ♔xf8 += 10 ♗e3 ♖d8 11 d5! ♘d7 11... ♗xc3 12 ♖c1 12 ♕c2 b6 13 ♖ac1 ♘f6 14 c4 ♗g4 15 h3 ♗xf3 16 ♗xf3 ♖ac8 17 g3 e5 18 ♗g2 ♘e8 19 f4!± ♘d6 20 f5 ♘e8 21 h4! ♖d6 22 ♗h3 ♖cd8 23 ♖f3 ♕e7 24 ♖cf1 ♘c7 25 ♕f2 f6 26 fxg6 hxg6 27 h5! gxh5 28 ♖f5 ♕f7 29 ♖xh5 ♖h8 30 ♖xh8 ♗xh8 31 ♗f5 ♕f8 32 ♔g2 ♗g7 33 ♖h1 ♔e7 34 ♖h7 ♔d8 35 ♗g4 1-0 Keene

140 Ghitescu-Smejkal
Warsaw 79

1 d4 ♘f6 2 c4 g6 3 ♘c3 d5 4 f3!? c6! N 4...c5 5 dxc5! d4 6 ♘b5 ♘c6 7 e3! e5 8 exd4 exd4 9 ♗f4!±; 4... ♗g7 5 e4 dxe4 6 fxe4 e5 7 d5± 5 e4 5 ♗g5! += dxe4 6 fxe4 e5 7 ♗g5?! 7 d5 ♗c5 8 ♗g5 h6 9 ♗h4 ♘bd7 10 ♕f3! += h6! 8 ♗h4 8 dxe5 ♕xd1+ 9 ♖xd1 hxg5 10 exf6 ♘d7∓ exd4 9 e5 g5∓ 10 exf6 ♕xf6! 11 ♕e2 ♕e6 12 0-0-0 dxc3 13 ♕c2? 13 ♗g3 ♕xe2 △ cxb2+∓

13...♕e3+! 14 ♔b1 gxh4 —+ 15 ♘f3 ♗e6 16 ♗d3 ♗g7 17 ♖he1 ♕b6 18 b3 ♘a6 19 ♖xe6+ fxe6 20 ♗g6+ ♔e7 21 ♖e1 ♖af8 22 ♗f5 ♘c7 23 ♕e4 ♖xf5 24 ♕xf5 ♕f2! 0-1 Gheorghiu

141 Ivkov-Skalkotas
Albufieri 78

1 ♘f3 ♘f6 2 c4 g6 3 ♘c3 d5 4 d4 ♗g7 5 ♕a4+ ♗d7 6 ♕b3 dxc4 7 ♕xc4 0-0 8 e4 ♗g4 9 ♗e3 ♘fd7 10 ♕b3 ♘b6 11 ♖d1 ♘c6 12 d5 ♘e5 13 ♗e2 ♘xf3+ 14 gxf3 ♗h5 15 ♖g1! ♕d7 15...♕b8? 16 f4! ♗xe2 17 ♘xe2 c6 18 dxc6 bxc6 18 h4!± Ivkov-Timman, Bugojno 78; 15...♕c8!? **16 ♖g3 e6?** N 16...c6!; 16...♗e5!? 17 f4 ♗xe2 18 ♘xe2 ♗g7 19 f5 +=; 16...f5!? Ljubojevic **17 a4! exd5 18 a5 ♘c4 19 ♖xd5 ♘d6**

20 ♘b5! △ 21 ♘xd6 cxd6 22 ♖xh5! gxh5 23 ♗h6; 20 ♖xh5?! gxh5 21 ♗h6 ♘e8; 20 e5? ♕e6 21 exd6 c6 **c6 21 ♖xd6 ♕e7 22 ♗c5 cxb5 23 ♖dxg6!** +− ♕xc5 24 ♖xg7+ ♔h8 25 ♖7g5 ♕c1+ 26 ♕d1 ♕xd1+ 27 ♗xd1 ♗g6 28 ♖xb5 f5 29 ♖xb7 ♖ab8 30 ♖xb8 ♖xb8 31 b3 ♖b5 32 f4! fxe4 33 ♖g5 ♖b4 34 ♖c5 ♗f7 35 ♖c7 ♗xb3 36 ♗xb3 ♖xb3 37 ♖xa7 ♖b2 38 a6 ♖a2 39 f5 1-0 **Speelman**

142 Keene-Smyslov
Buenos Aires 2 78

1 d4 ♘f6 2 c4 g6 3 ♘c3 d5 4 ♘f3 ♗g7 5 ♕b3 dxc4 6 ♕xc4 0-0 7 e4 ♗g4 8 ♗e3 ♘fd7 9 ♕b3 ♘b6 10 ♖d1 c6

10...♘c6 11 d5 ♘e5 12 ♗e2! ♘xf3+ 13 gxf3 ♗h5 14 ♖g1± **11 ♗e2 ♘a6 12 0-0 ♕d6 13 a3 ♘c7 14 h3 ♗e6 15 ♕c2 ♖ad8 16 ♘g5!± ♗c4 17 e5 ♕d7 18 ♗g4!** e6 19 ♖fe1 ♘cd5 20 ♘ge4 20 ♘ce4 h6 **♗xe3 21 fxe3 ♕e7 22 b3 ♗d5** 22...♗a6 23 ♘c5!± **23 ♘f6+!?** 23 ♘c5 ♗xe5 24 ♘xd5 ♖xd5 25 ♗f3 ♗g3∞; 23 ♘d6 f3∞ **♗xf6 24 exf6 ♕xa3! 25 ♖b1** 25 e4 ♗xb3 26 ♕d2 ♕h8!∓ **e5! 26 dxe5 ♖fe8 27 ♘xd5 ♘xd5 28 ♖bd1 ♖xe5! 29** e4 **♕b4! 30 ♕f2** 30 ♕c1 ♕b6+ 31 ♔h1 ♘xf6; 30 ♕d2 ♕xd2 31 ♖xd2 ♖de8∓ **♖xe4 31 ♖xe4 ♕xe4 32 ♕xa7 ♖e8 33 ♕xb7 ♘xf6 34 ♗f3 ♕e3+ 35 ♔h1 c5! 36 ♗d5 ♖e7 37 ♕b8+ ♔g7 38 ♗f3 h5 39 ♖f1 ♕d3 40 ♖d1 ♕c3∓ 41 ♖d8!?** 0-1 41...♖e1+ 42 ♔h2 ♕c1 43 ♖h8 ♖h1+ 44 ♔g3 h4+!! 45 ♖xh4 ♕e1+ −+; 45 ♔xh4 g5+ 46 ♔g3 ♕e1 mate **Gheorghiu**

143 Kuligowski-Smejkal
Warsaw 79

1 d4 ♘f6 2 c4 g6 3 ♘c3 d5 4 ♘f3 ♗g7 5 ♕b3 dxc4 6 ♕xc4 0-0 7 e4 ♗g4 7...a6!?; 7...♘a6 △ c5 **8 ♗e3 ♘fd7 9 ♕b3 ♘b6 10 ♖d1 e6!?** 10...♘c6 11 d5 ♘e5 12 ♗e2 ♘xf3+ 13 gxf3 ♗h5± **11 ♗e2 ♘c6 12 ♘g1!** += ♗xe2 13 ♘gxe2 ♕e7 14 0-0 ♘a5 **15 ♕c2 ♘ac4 16 ♗c1 e5 17 d5!?** 17 dxe5 ♘xe5 18 f4 ♕c5+ 19 ♔h1 ♘g4 20 ♘g3 += **♘d6 18 b3 f5 19** exf5 gxf5 20 f4 e4 21 ♗e3 ♖f7 22 ♖f2 ♖c8 23 ♘d4 a6 24 ♕e2 △ ♕h5+± ♖f6 25 ♕e1 ♖g6 26 ♖c2 ♕f7 27 ♘de2 ♔h8 28 ♘g3 ♖h6!∓ 29 ♘f1 ♘d7 30 ♗d4 ♗xd4+ 31 ♖xd4 ♘c5! 32 ♖dd2 ♘d3 33 ♕e3 ♖g8 34 ♘e2?

Diagram

34...♘e1! −+ 35 ♘eg3 ♞xc2 36 ♖xc2 ♖g7 37 ♕c1 ♕xd5 38 ♖xc7 ♕d4+! 39 ♔h1 ♖xc7 40 ♕xc7 ♖g6 41 h3 e3! 42 ♕e7 ♖g8! △ ♖e8 −+ 0-1 Gheorghiu

144 Kaunas-Levchenkov USSR 78
1 d4 ♘f6 2 c4 g6 3 ♘c3 d5 4 ♗f4 ♗g7 5 e3 0-0 6 cxd5 ♘xd5 7 ♘xd5 ♕xd5 8 ♗xc7 ♗f5 9 ♘e2 ♖c8 10 ♘c3 ♕c6 11 ♗g3 ♘a6 12 ♗e2!? N 12 a3 e5! 13 d5 ♕b6 14 e4 ♖xc3 15 bxc3 ♗xe4 16 f3 ♕xe3+ 17 ♗e2 ♕xc3+ 18 ♔f2 ♗c2 19 ♕c1 e4∓ Tamme-Gulko, USSR 77 ♕xg2 12... e5 13 0-0± **13 ♗f3 ♕h3 14 ♗xb7 ♘b4 15 ♗xa8 ♖xa8 16 ♕f3 ♖d8?** 16...♖c8!? 17 ♔d2 e5!∞; '17 0-0-0 ♘xa2+ 18 ♔d2 ♘b4∞ **17 0-0-0 ♘d3+ 18 ♖xd3 +− ♗xd3 19 ♖d1 ♗c4 20 ♕b7 ♕d7 21 ♕xd7 ♖xd7 22 b3 ♗a6 23 ♘a4 ♖d8 24 ♘c5 1-0 Gipslis**

145 Kovacs-Pribyl Decin 78
1 d4 ♘f6 2 c4 g6 3 ♘c3 d5 4 ♗f4 ♗g7 5 ♘f3 c6 6 e3 ♗e6 6...♗g4 7 ♕b3 ♕b6=; 6...♕a5 7 cxd5 cxd5 8 ♕b3 ♘c6 9 ♗e2 0-0 10 0-0 ♘h5 11 ♗e5 f6 12 ♗g3 ♖d8!= Uhlmann 7 ♕b3 ♕b6 8 c5 ♕xb3 9 axb3 0-0 10 h3 ♘bd7 11 ♗e2 h6 12 g4!? ♘h7 13 ♗g3 f5 14 gxf5 ♗xf5 15 b4 a6 16 h4 ♗g4 17 ♘e5 ♘xe5 18 ♗xe5

♗xe2 19 ♘xe2 ♗f6 19...♗xe5 20 dxe5 △ ♘d4 += **20 f4 ♕f7 21 ♔d2 ♖g8=** △ ♘f8-e6-g7-f5∞ ½-½ Kovacs

146 Pinter-Honfi Budapest 78
1 d4 ♘f6 2 c4 g6 3 ♘c3 d5 4 ♘f3 ♗g7 5 ♗f4 0-0 6 e3 c6 7 ♗e2 dxc4 8 ♗xc4 ♘bd7 9 h3 b5 10 ♗e2 ♗b7 N 10...a6 **11 0-0** 11 a3 a6 12 b4 ♘d5= b4 12 ♘a4 c5 13 dxc5 ♕a5 14 ♘d4 ♘xc5 14...e5? 15 c6± **15 ♘xc5 ♕xc5 16 ♖c1?!** 16 ♕a4; 16 ♗f3 ♕d5 17 ♗f3 ♘e4 18 ♗h2 ♕xa2!∓ 19 ♖c7 ♗d5 20 ♖xe7 ♖fe8 21 ♖d7 ♗c4! 22 ♕a1 a5 23 ♕xa2 ♗xa2 24 ♖d1 a4 25 ♘c6 ♗xb2! 26 ♘e7+ 26 ♗xe4 ♖xe4 27 ♖1d2 ♗e6 −+; 27 ♖7d2 ♗b3 −+ ♖xe7 27 ♖xe7 f5 28 ♗xe4 fxe4 29 ♖xe4 b3 30 ♗d6 a3 31 ♖b4 ♗f6! 32 ♖b6 b2 33 ♗xa3 ♖xa3 34 ♖xf6 ♗b3 35 ♖b6 ♖a1! 0-1 Honfi

147 Browne-Strauss
Lone Pine 78
1 d4 ♘f6 2 c4 g6 3 ♘c3 d5 4 ♘f3 ♗g7 5 ♗g5 dxc4 5...♘e4 6 ♗h4 ♘xc3 7 bxc3; 5...c6 **6 e4 c5 7 ♗xc4!** d5 b5! 8 e5 b4 9 exf6 exf6 10 ♕e2+ ♔f8∞; 10...♕e7?? 11 ♘e4 fxg5 12 d6 ♕e6 13 ♘fxg5 ♕f5 14 ♘f6+ ♔d8 15 ♘xf7 mate ♕a5?! 7...cxd4 8 ♕xd4! ♕xd4 9 ♘xd4 ♘xe4 10 ♘xe4 ♗xd4 11 0-0-0±; 9...♘c6?! 10 ♘xc6 bxc6 11 0-0 ♘g4 12 ♖ac1 h6 13 ♗d2 0-0 14 ♖fd1 ♖d8 15 ♗e1 ♗d7 16 ♘a4± Dorfman-Smyslov, Lvov 78 **8 e5!** 8 0-0 cxd4 9 ♘d5 ♘c6 10 ♘xd4 ♘xe4! ♘g4 8...♘e4 9 0-0 ♘xg5 10 ♘xg5 0-0 11 ♕b3 e6 12 d5!∞ **9 0-0** 9 ♕b3? cxd4! 10 ♗xf7+ ♔f8 11 ♘xd4 ♕xe5+ −+ cxd4 9...♘c6 10 e6! ♗xe6 11 d5 ♖d8 12 ♕b3 +−; 10...fxe6 11 d5! exd5 12 ♕xd5± **10 ♘d5 ♘c6**

11 b4! Qd8 12 b5 Be6 12...Ncxe5 13 Bxe7 Qd7 14 Re1 +− **13 bxc6 Bxd5 14 c7!** 14 cxb7 Bxb7! 15 Qb3 Bxf3 16 Bxf7+ Kf8 17 gxf3 += **Qd7 15 Bxd5** 15 Qxd4!? Bxc4 16 Qxc4 Nxe5 17 Nxe5 Bxe5 18 Rae1 f6!; 18 Rfe1! f6! 19 Rad1 Qc6 **Qxd5 16 Rc1 Rc8 17 Qa4+ Qd7** 17...b5 18 Qb4! 0-0 19 Bxe7 Rfe8 20 Rc5! Qxa2 21 Bd6 f6!± **18 Qxd7+! Kxd7 19 Rfd1 Bxe5** 19...Ke8 20 Nxd4 Bxe5 21 f3! Nf6 22 Nb5 a6 23 Re1! axb5 24 Rxe5 +− **20 Nxd4! Ke8** 20...f6 21 Nf5+? Ke6 22 Nxg7+ Kf7; 21 Nc6+! Ke6 22 Nd8+ Kf5 23 Be3± **21 f4! h6** 21...Ng4 22 Nb5 Ne3 23 Nxa7? Rxc7 24 Rxc7 Nxd1 25 Rxe7+ Kf8 26 Rd7 +−; 23 Rd3! +− **22 Bh4 g5! 23 Nf5 Rg8??** 23...Rh7? 24 fxe5 gxh4 25 Rd5 f6 26 e6 +−; 23...gxh4? 24 Nxg7+ Kf8 25 Nf5 +−; 23...Bf8! 24 fxe5 gxh4 25 e6 fxe6 26 Nd4 Bg7! 27 Nxe6 Be5; 27 Nb5 Be5 28 Rc5 a6! 29 Na7 Rxc7 30 Rxe5 b5=; 25 Rc3 e6 26 Rcd3 Bc5+ 27 Kf1 exf5 28 Rd8+ Ke7 29 R1d7+ Ke6 30 Rxh8 Bxd7 −+; 25 Nd4! Bg7 26 Re1! Kd7 27 e6+ fxe6 28 Nxe6 +−; 25...a6 26 Nf5 Rg8 27 e6!± **24 fxe5 gxh4 25 Rd8+! Rxd8 26 c8Q 1-0 Browne**

√148 Vukic-Popovic
Novi Sad 78

1 d4 Nf6 2 c4 g6 3 Nf3 Bg7 4 g3 0-0 5 Bg2 d5 6 cxd5 Nxd5 7 0-0 Nc6 8 Nc3 Nxc3 9 bxc3 e5!? 9...Be6 10 e4 Bc4 11 Re1 += **10 d5 Na5 11 Ba3 Re8 12 Qa4 b6** 12...c6?! 13 Bb4 Nc4 14 dxc6 Nb6 15 cxb7 Bxb7 16 Qa5 += **13 Nd2 Bd7?!** 13...Ba6! 14 Rfe1 c5!= **14 Qd1 Rc8** 14...c5!= **15 Bb4 Nb7 16 c4 += a5 17 Ba3 c6 18 Rb1 cxd5 19 Bxd5 Nc6 20 Qb3 Bxd5 21 cxd5 e4 22 Rfc1 Rxc1+ 23 Rxc1 Re5?** 23...e3!? 24 fxe3 Bh6 **24 Nc4! +− Re8** 24...Rxd5?? 25 Nxb6 Δ Rc8 +− **25 Nxb6 Bg5 26 e3 Rd8 27 Nc8 Rd7 28 d6 h5 29 Rc7 Qg4 30 Ne7+** 30 h3!! Qxh3 31 Qxb7 +− **Kh7 31 Rxd7 Bxd7 32 Qxf7 Qg4 33 h3 Qd1+** 33...Qxh3?? 34 Qxg6+ Kh8 35 Bb2! +− **34 Kh2 Qf3 35 Qxg6+ Kh8 36 Qf5 Qxf5 37 Nxf5 Bf6 38 d7 Kg8 39 Nd6 Nd8 40 Bxe4 1-0 Vukic**

149 Kochiev-Botterill
Hastings 78-9

1 Nf3 g6 2 c4 Bg7 3 d4 Nf6 4 g3 0-0 5 Bg2 d5 6 cxd5 Nxd5 7 0-0 Nc6 8 e4 Nb6 9 d5 Na5 10 Nc3 c6 11 Re1?! 11 Bg5 h6 12 Bf4 cxd5 13 exd5 Nac4 14 Qe2 g5 15 Bc1 Bg4=; 11 Bf4!? **Re8 12 Bg5 h6 13 Bf4 Nac4 14 Qb3 e5!** 14...cxd5 15 exd5 e5= **15 dxe6 Bxe6 16 Qc2** 16 Rad1 Qe7 17 Nd4 Bxd4! 18 Rxd4 g5! 19 Bc1 Ne3 20 Nd5 Nexd5 21 exd5 Bxd5!∓ **Qe7 17 Rad1 Qb4 18 Bc1 Rad8 19 h3?** 19 Rxd8 Rxd8 20 Rd1 =/=+ **Na3! 20 bxa3** 20 Qe2? Bc4 **Qxc3 21 Qb1 ½-½** 21...Rxh3?! 22 Bd2∞; 21...Qc4 22 Be3 Qxa2 23 Bxb6 Qxb1 24 Rxb1 axb6 25 Rxb6 Bc8 =+ **Botterill**

150 Cornelius-Browne
Lone Pine 78
**1 c4 ♘f6 2 ♘c3 d5 3 d4 g6 4 ♗g5
♘e4** 4...dxc4?! 5 e4! **5 ♗h4 ♘xc3**
5...c6 **6 bxc3 ♗g7 7 e3** 7 ♘f3 c5 8
cxd5 ♕xd5 9 e3 ♘c6 10 ♗e2 cxd4
11 cxd4 0-0 12 0-0 b6= Beljavsky-
Grigorian, USSR Final 77 **c6!?** 7...c5
8 ♗d3! 0-0 9 ♘e2! dxc4 9...♗f5? 10
♗xf5 gxf5 11 ♘g3±; 9...♘d7 10
0-0 ♘f6 += **10 ♗xc4 c5 11 0-0 ♘c6
12 ♕a4 ♕c7** 12...♘a5?? 13 ♗xe7 +−;
12...♗d7 13 ♕a3 += **13 ♖ac1** 13
♗g3 e5; 13 ♘f4 e6 14 d5! exd5 15
♘xd5± **e6** 13...♕a5 14 ♗b5! **14
♖fd1 ♗d7** 14...b6? 15 ♗g3!±; 14...
♕a5 15 ♕xa5 ♘xa5 16 ♗d3 += **15
♕a3 ♘a5 16 ♗d3 b6** 16...♖fc8 17
♗g3! **17 dxc5! bxc5** 17...♕xc5 18
♕xc5 bxc5 19 ♗xg6 hxg6 20 ♖xd7
♖fb8!?∝ **18 ♗e4**

18...♘b7? 18...♘c4? 19 ♕a6 ♖ab8
20 ♖xd7 +−; 18...♗c6 19 ♕xc5 ♖fc8
20 ♗xc6 ♘xc6 21 ♘d4 ♕b7! += **19
♕a6 ♖ab8 20 ♕xa7** 20 ♖ab1 ♘a5!
♗e5 20...♗c6? 21 ♗xc6 ♕xc6 22
♖b1± **21 ♗g3 ♗xg3 22 hxg3 ♗c6
23 ♗xc6 ♕xc6 24 ♖b1 ♖bd8 25
♖xd8 ♘xd8 26 a4±** ♕d6! **27 ♕b6?**
27 a5 ♘c6 28 ♕a6 ♕d5 29 ♖b6 ♘e5!?
**♘c6 28 ♕b3 ♖a8 29 ♖d1 ♕c7 30
c4?** 30 ♘f4! += **♖b8!= 31 ♕c3**

151 Segal-Lein
Sao Paulo 79
1 d4 ♘f6 2 c4 g6 3 ♘c3 d5 4 ♗g5
4 ♘f3 ♗g7 5 ♗g5 **♘e4 5 ♗h4 ♘xc3
6 bxc3 ♗g7?!** 6...c5 7 cxd5 ♕xd5
8 e3 cxd4 9 ♕xd4 ♕xd4 10 cxd4
e6!= **7 e3 0-0? 8 cxd5 ♕xd5 9 ♗xe7
♖e8 10 ♗a3!± c5** 10...♕a5 11 ♗b4
+− **11 ♕f3! ♕e6 12 ♗xc5 ♘d7 13
♗a3! ♘e5?!** 14 dxe5 ♗xe5

**15 ♗b2 +− ♕b6 16 ♕e2 ♗g4 17 ♘f3
♖ac8 18 ♕b5! ♕c7 19 ♘xe5 ♖xe5
20 ♕b4 ♕d7 21 c4 ♖d8 22 ♗e2 ♗xe2
23 ♗xe5 +− ♗d3 24 ♖d1 ♕g4 25
♖xd3 ♖xd3 26 0-0! ♖d7 27 ♗b2
♖d1 28 f3 ♕d7 29 ♕c3 ♖xf1+ 30
♔xf1 ♕d1+ 31 ♔f2 ♔f8 32 ♕h8+
♔e7 33 ♕e5+ ♔d7 34 ♕d4+ ♕xd4
35 exd4 b6 1-0 Gheorghiu**

152 Gheorghiu-Jansa Warsaw 79
**1 d4 ♘f6 2 c4 g6 3 f3!? d5 4 cxd5
♘xd5 5 e4 ♘b6 6 ♘c3 ♗g7 7 ♗e3
0-0 8 f4! +=** ♘c6 8...c6; 8...a5!?
9 d5 ♘a5 9...♘b8 10 a4!± **10 ♗d4
♗g4** 10...c6?! 11 ♗xg7 ♔xg7 12
♕d4+ Δ b4 +− **11 ♕d3!** N 11 ♗e2
+= e5!? **12 fxe5 ♘ac4 13 ♕g3! ♗g5
14 ♘f3!± ♕h5 15 0-0-0** 15 ♗xc4;
15 b3 += c5!!∝ **c5 16 ♗xc5 ♖fc8**

17 ♗d4 ♘xe5 18 ♗e2 ♘bc4 19 ♕b1!
b5 20 h3±

20...♘xf3 20...♗xf3 21 gxf3 Δ f4 +−
21 gxf3 ♗xd4 22 ♖xd4 ♗d7 23 ♗xc4!
bxc4 24 h4 ♖ab8 25 ♖f1 25 ♖xc4
♖xb2+ 26 ♔xb2 ♖xc4±; Δ ♕g5
♕h6 26 f4 ♕f8 27 d6 ♗c6 28 f5 ♕d8
29 ♕f2! ♕d7 29...♕f6 30 fxg6 ♕xf2
31 gxh7+ +− 30 h5 ♖e8 31 ♕g2 ♔g7
32 ♕d2! h6 33 hxg6 fxg6 34 fxg6
♖f8 35 ♖h1! +− h5 36 ♖xh5 ♖f1+
37 ♘d1 ♖h8 38 ♖xh8 ♔xh8 39 ♕h6+!
1-0 time 39...♔g8 40 ♕h7+! ♔xh7
41 gxh7+ ♔xh7 42 d7 +− Gheorghiu

King's Indian

Simple & v. subtle!
Gt accuracy

153 Andersson-Byrne
Sao Paulo 79

1 ♘f3 ♘f6 2 c4 g6 3 ♘c3 ♗g7 4 e4
d6 5 d4 0-0 6 ♗e2 e5 7 dxe5!? dxe5
8 ♕xd8 ♖xd8 9 ♗g5 ♖e8 9...c6 10
♘xe5 10 ♘d5! ♘xd5 11 cxd5 c6 12
♗c4 += cxd5 13 ♗xd5 ♘d7 14 ♘d2
♘b6 15 ♗b3 ♗e6 16 ♔e2!± Δ ♖c1
♗f8 17 ♖hc1 ♗d6 18 ♗xe6 ♖xe6 19
♗e3! ♔f8 19...♖c8 20 ♖c3! ♖c8
21 ♖ac1 ♖xc3 22 ♖xc3 ♔e8 23
g4! f6 24 ♖b3 ♗c7

Diagram

25 a4!± ♖e7 25...♘xa4 26 ♖xb7±
26 a5 ♘c8 27 ♘c4 ♗d8 28 ♖b5 ♖c7
29 b3 a6 30 ♖d5 ♖d7 31 g5! ♖xd5
32 exd5 fxg5 33 ♔d3! g4 34 ♔e4
♗e7 35 ♘xe5 ♗b4 36 ♘xg4 ♗xa5
37 ♔e5 ♔e7 38 ♗c5+ ♔f7 39 d6
♘b6 40 ♗xb6 40 ♘h6+! ♔g7 41
♗e3 +− Andersson ♗xb6 41 ♔d5
♗d8 42 ♘e5+ 1-0 42...♔f6 43 ♘d7+
Δ ♘c5 +− Gheorghiu

154 Malich-Hort Halle 78
1 d4 ♘f6 2 c4 g6 3 ♘c3 ♗g7 4 e4 d6
5 ♗e2 0-0 6 ♘f3 ♘bd7 6...e5 7 0-0
c6!? 7...e5 8 ♖e1 c6 9 ♗f1 a5 10 ♖b1;
10 ♗e3; 10 dxe5 dxe5 11 ♘a4 ♕e7
12 ♕c2 Malich-Vogt, Halle 78 8 ♖e1
a6 9 h3 9 a4 a5; 9 d5 cxd5 10 cxd5
♘c5 11 ♗f1 ♗g4= b5 10 e5!? ♘e8 11
♗f4 ♗b7 12 ♖c1 12 exd6 ♘xd6 13
c5 ♘f5 14 g4? ♘xd4 15 ♗xd4 e5∓;
12 ♕c2!? Δ ♖ad1 += dxe5 13 dxe5
♘c7 14 ♕c2 ♘e6 15 ♗g3 b4! 16
♘e4 ♘dc5!= 16...♘ec5 17 ♖cd1!
♕b6 18 e6! fxe6 19 ♘c5 ♘xc5 20
♘e5 ♗xe5 21 ♗xe5 ♖xf2 22 ♗d4∞
19 ♘fg5!± 17 ♘xc5 ♘xc5 18 ♖cd1
♕b6 19 ♘d4 19 b3 a5∓ ♖ad8 20
♗f3 a5 21 ♕e2!? Δ 22 ♕e3+ ♗h6!
22 h4!? 22 ♗h4 ♘a4 23 ♘b3 ♗c8!
24 h5 ♗g5 25 ♗e4 Δ 26 hxg6 hxg6
27 e6 ♗xe6 28 ♗xg6± ♔g7 26 ♕h1!
Δ f4≈ Zeitnot ½-½ Malich

Diagram

155 Speelman-Biyiasas Hastings 78/9

**1 c4 g6 2 e4 ♗g7 3 d4 d6 4 ♘c3 ♘f6
5 ♘f3 0-0 6 ♗e2 e5 7 0-0 ♘c6 8 d5
♘e7 9 b4!? ♘h5 10 c5** 10 g3 ♘f4
11 ♗xf4 exf4 12 ♖c1 ♗g4!? N 12...
h6 Δ g5; 12...a5 **13 ♘d2 ♗xe2** 13...
♕d7 14 c6! **14 ♕xe2 g5 15 ♕h5!?**
15 ♕g4!? ♘g6 16 ♘f3 ♘e5! 17 ♘xe5
♗xe5 18 h4!? ♘h8 19 ♕xg5 ♘g6
16 ♘f3 h6 17 ♘b5 a5 18 ♘bd4 18
a3! axb4 19 axb4 ♖a4 (19...♕d7)
20 cxd6 cxd6 (20...♕d7? 21 dxc7)
21 ♘bd4 ♖xb4 22 ♘f5 ♖f6 **axb4
19 cxd6 cxd6 20 ♘f5 ♕f6 21 ♖c7!**
21 ♘xh6+?! ♗xh6 22 ♕xh6 g4 23
♘g5 ♕g7 24 ♕xg7+ ♔xg7 25 ♖c7
♔g8; 23...♕h8 24 ♘xf7 **♖fc8** 21...
♖xa2 22 ♘xh6+ ♗xh6 23 ♕xh6 ♖a1
(23...♕g7 24 ♕xg7+ ♔xg7 25 ♘xg5±;
23...♕h8) 24 ♘xg5 (24 e5!) ♖xf1+
25 ♔xf1 ♕a1+ =; 21...b3 22 axb3
♖a1 23 ♖cc1 += **22 ♖d7** 22 ♖xb7
♖xa2 23 ♖xb4 **b3** 22...♖xa2 23 ♖xd6
♕c3 24 ♖xg6 fxg6 25 ♕xg6 ♕f6 26
♘xh6+! ♔f8? 27 ♕h7!! ♗xh6 28
e5! +−; 26...♔h8 27 ♘f7+ ♔g8 28
♘h6+ =; 22...♖d8 23 ♖xb7 **23 ♖xd6**
23 axb3 ♖a1∓

23...♕xd6 23...b2 (23...bxa2?! 24
♖xf6 a1♕ 25 ♖xg6 fxg6 26 ♕xg6
♕f6 27 ♘xh6+ ♔f8 28 ♕xf6 ♗xf6
29 e5; 24...♗xf6 25 g3 a1♕ 26 ♖xa1±)

24 ♖xf6 ♗xf6 (Δ ♖c1) 25 ♘xh6+
♔f8 26 e5! (26 ♘g4? ♖c1 27 ♘d2
♗c3 28 ♘b1 ♖xa2! 29 ♘xc3 ♖aa1!
−+; 26 ♕h3! ♖c1 27 ♘d2 ♖xa2 28
♕d7! [28 ♕b3? ♖aa1 29 d6 ♘h8!∓]
28...♘e7 [28...♘e5 29 ♕d6+ ♔g7
30 ♘f5+ ♔g6 31 ♕f8! +−] 29 d6
♖aa1 30 dxe7+ ♗xe7 31 ♕d3 ♖xf1+
32 ♕xf1!) 26...♖c1 27 ♘d2 (1) 27...
♖xa2? 28 exf6 ♖aa1 29 ♕e2! ♖xf1+
30 ♕xf1!; (2) 27...♘xe5 28 ♘f5
(Δ ♕h6+) ♘g6 29 h4 gxh4 (29...
♖xa2 30 ♕h6+ ♔e8 31 ♘d6+ Δ
♘6c4, ♗xb2; 30...♔g8? 31 h5!) 30
♕h6+ ♔g8 (30...♔e8 31 ♘d6+ Δ ♘6c4,
♗xb2) 31 d6 (Δ ♘e7+) ♖e8 32 ♘e7+
♗xe7 33 dxe7 ♖xe7 (Δ ♖e2) 34
♕h5! (Δ ♕b5) ♖d7 35 ♘b1±; (3)
27...♗xe5 28 ♕h3 (28 ♕xg5±) ♖xa2
29 ♕b3 (29 ♕d7) ♖ca1 30 d6!±;
(4) 27...♖e8? 28 e6!± **24 ♘xd6 bxa2
25 ♘xc8 a1♕ 26 ♘d6** 26 d6 **♕b2**
26...♕f6 27 e5! ♕xe5 28 ♘xe5 ♕xe5
29 ♕xf7+ ♔h7 30 ♕xb7! ♖a1 31
♘c4 ♖xf1+ 32 ♔xf1±; 31...♕d4
♘d2!± **27 h4! ♖a1 28 ♖xa1 ♕xa1+
29 ♔h2 ♕f6 30 ♘e8** 30 e5 **♕e7 31
♘xg7 ♕xg7 32 hxg5 hxg5 33 ♘xg5
b5 34 ♘f3 ♕xe4** 34...b4!? 35 e5 b3
36 ♕f5± **35 d6 ♕b7** 35...♕d3 **36
♕f5 ♔f8 37 ♕f6?** 37 ♘g5?? ♕xg2+;
37 ♘d4 b4 38 ♘e6+ ♔e8 (38...♔g8
39 ♘c5 Δ d7 +−) 39 ♘c7+ ♔d8
(39...♔f8 40 ♕c5!) 40 ♕xf7 ♕c6
41 ♘e6+ ♔c8 42 d7+! ♕xd7
♕g8+ ♔b7 44 ♘c5+ +−; 37...♔e8
38 f3! b4 39 ♘b5 b3 40 ♘c7+ ♔f8
41 ♗c5 ♔g8 42 d7 ♕b8 43 ♘e6!
+−; 41...♔g7 42 d7 ♕b8 43 ♕d4+
38 ♘xb5 ♕xg2+!; 38 ♕xb5 **♕e8 38
♘e5** 38 ♘d4!? **♕xe5 39 ♕xe5+ ♔d7
40 ♕e7+ ♔c6 41 ♕e4+ ½-½** 41...♔b6
42 ♕e8 ♕d5! 43 ♕d8+ ♔c5 44
♕c7+ ♔c6 Δ f5, ♕d5; 43 d7 ♕h5+

=; 42 ♕xf4?! ♕d5 =+ △ ♔c6, ♕e6, f6, ♕xd6 **Speelman**

156 Eslon-Ochoa Manresa 78

1 d4 ♘f6 2 c4 g6 3 ♘c3 ♗g7 4 e4 0-0 5 ♘f3 d6 6 ♗e2 e5 7 0-0 ♘c6 8 d5 ♘e7 9 ♘e1 ♘d7 10 ♘d3 f5 11 ♗d2 c5 12 f4 fxe4!? 13 ♘xe4 ♘f5 14 g4?! ♘d4 15 ♘xd6 exf4 16 ♘xc8 ♖xc8 17 ♗xf4 ♕e7 18 ♖f2 g5! 19 d6! ♕e4 20 ♗xg5 ♖xf2 21 ♘xf2! ♘xe2+ 22 ♔f1 ♖f8 23 ♕d5+ ♕xd5 24 cxd5 ♗d4 25 ♔xe2 ♖xf2+ 26 ♔d3 ♘e5+ 27 ♔e4 ♔f7 28 ♖e1 ♘f3 29 d7 ♘xg5+ 30 ♔d3 ♗f6 31 h4! ♖d2+! 32 ♔c4 ♘e4?? 32...♖d4+ △ ♘e4 −+ 33 ♖xe4 ♖d4+ 34 ♖xd4 cxd4 35 g5 ♗d8 36 ♔xd4 ♔e7 37 ♔e5 ♔xd7 38 ♔f5 ♔e7 39 h5 ♔f7 40 d6 ♗b6 41 g6+ hxg6 42 hxg6+ ♔g7 43 ♔e6 ♔xg6 44 b4 ♗d4 45 a4 ♗f6 46 ♔d7 ♔f7 47 ♔c8 b6 48 d7 ♔e6 ½-½ **Ochoa**

157 Kovacs-Balogh Hungary 78

1 d4 ♘f6 2 c4 g6 3 ♘c3 ♗g7 4 e4 d6 5 ♘f3 0-0 6 ♗e2 e5 7 0-0 ♘bd7 8 ♗e3 8 ♕c2 c6 9 ♖d1 ♕e7 10 d5 c5 11 ♖b1 +=; 8 ♖e1 c6 9 ♗f1 a5 10 ♖b1 exd4 11 ♘xd4 ♖e8 12 b3 ♘g4! 13 ♕xg4 ♗xd4 14 ♕g3 ♕f6 =+ ♘g4 9 ♗g5 f6 10 ♗h4!? 10 ♗d2! c6 11 b4 f5 12 d5 f4= **c6 11 d5 c5 12 ♘e1 ♘h6 13 ♘d3 g5 14 ♗g3 f5 15 exf5 ♘f6= 16 ♕d2 ♘f7 17 h4 h6 18 ♖ae1 ♗xf5 19 hxg5 hxg5! 20 ♗f3 ♗h6 21 ♗e4 g4 ∓ 22 ♕e2 ♘xe4 23 ♘xe4 ♘g5 24 ♘xg5** 24 ♗h4 ♘f3+! ♕xg5 25 b4 ♕g6 26 ♖d1 b6 27 b5 ♖f7 28 ♖fe1 ♖h7 △ ♕h5, ♗f4 29 ♘xe5!? dxe5 30 ♕xe5 ♗g7 31 ♕d6 ♕h5 32 ♗h2 ♖f8 33 ♕g3 ♗c2 34 ♖c1 ♗d3 35 ♖e7 ♕g5 36 ♕e3 ♕xe3 36 fxe3 ♗h6 0-1 **Balogh**

158 Uhlmann-Knaak Halle 78

1 c4 g6 2 ♘c3 ♗g7 3 d4 d6 4 e4 ♘d7 5 ♗e2 e5 6 ♘f3 ♘gf6 7 0-0 0-0 8 ♗e3 8 ♖e1 c6 9 ♗f1 a5; 8 ♕c2 c6 9 ♖d1 ♕e7 10 d5 c5 11 ♖b1 ♘h5 12 g3 ♘b6?± Dorfman-Grigorian, USSR Final 77 a5!? N 8...♕e7!? 9 dxe5 dxe5 10 ♘d5 Miles-Hort, Rejkjavik 78; 8...♘g4 9 ♗g5 f6 10 ♗d2!± Uhlmann-Knaak, Leipzig 77 9 d5 ♘g4 10 ♗g5 f6 11 ♗d2 ♘c5 11...♘h6!? 12 ♘e1 f5 13 ♗xg4 13 f3?! ♘f6 =+; 13 exf5 gxf5 14 ♗xg4 fxg4 15 ♗e3 △ ♗xc5, ♕c2≈ fxg4 14 ♕e2 ♗d7 15 ♗d3 ♘xd3 16 ♕xd3 b6 17 b3 h5 18 a3 h4 19 ♗e3 ♔h7 20 ♕d2 h3 21 g3 ♕f6 22 ♕e2 ♗h6!= 23 ♗xh6 ♔xh6 24 ♖ac1

24...♕f3? 25 ♕xf3 ♖xf3 26 ♖fd1 △ ♖d2, ♘d1-e3 += ♖af8 27 ♖d2 ♗c8 28 ♔f1 ♗a6 29 a4! += ♖8f7 30 ♕e1 ♔g7 31 ♖b2 ♖d3 32 ♘b1! ♖df3 32...♖ff3 33 ♘d2 ♖c3 34 ♖bc2 ♖xc2 35 ♖xc2 ♖f8 36 ♖c3± 34...♖xb3!≈; 34 ♖1c2! ♖fd3 35 ♖xc3 ♖xc3 36 ♔d1 △ ♘f1, ♘e3± **33 ♖c3 ♖3f6 34 ♖e2 ♗b7 35 ♘a3 c5?! 36 dxc6 ♗xc6 37 ♖ce3 ♔f8 38 ♖d2 ♔e7 39 c5!! dxc5 40 ♘c4 ♖f3! 41 ♖xf3!** 41 ♘xe5 ♖xe3+ 42 fxe3 ♖f6 43 ♘xg4 ♖e6≈ **gxf3** 41...♖xf3 42 ♘xe5 ♖f6 43 ♘xg4 ♖e6 44 f3 ♗xe4 45

fxe4 Rxe4+ 46 Re2 +− **42 Nxe5 Rf6
43 Nxc6+ Rxc6 44 Rd3! c4 45 Rxf3**
45 Rc3? Kd6 cxb3 45...c3 46 Kd1
+−; 45...Re6 46 bxc4 Rxe4+? 47 Re3
+− **46 Rxb3 Rc4 47 Ke2 Rxa4** 47...
Rxe4+ 48 Re3 +− **48 Kf3 Ra2** 48...
Rb4 49 Rxb4 axb4 50 Ke3 +− **49
Rxb6 Kf7 50 e5 a4 51 Rf6+ Kg7
52 Kg4 Re2 53 f4! Rxh2 54 Ra6 Rh1
55 Rxa4 Kf7** 55...h2 56 Ra2 +− **56
Ra7+ Kg8 57 Rb7 Kh8 58 Rd7 Kg8
59 Rc7 Kh8 60 Kg5 Rg1 61 Kh6!
Kg8 62 e6** △ Rc8 mate **Kf8 63 Kxg6!
h2 64 Kf6 Kg8 65 e7 Re1 66 Rc1!
1-0 Malich**

✓ **159 Sapi-Ozsvath Budapest 2 78**
**1 d4 g6 2 Nf3 Bg7 3 e4 d6 4 Nc3
Nf6 5 Be2 0-0 6 0-0 Bg4 7 Be3 e5!?**
N 7...Nc6 8 Qd2 e5 9 d5 Ne7 10
Rad1 Bd7 11 Ne1 Ng4= **8 dxe5!
dxe5 9 Nxe5 Qxd1** 9...Bxe2 10 Qxe2
Nxe4 11 Nxe4 Bxe5 12 Qb5± **10
Bxd1 Bxd1 11 Raxd1 Nxe4 12 Nxg6
Nxc3 13 Ne7+ Kh8 14 bxc3** +−
**Nxc3 15 Nd5 Be5 16 f4 Bd6 17 Bd4+
f6 18 Bxf6 Nc6 19 Bb2 Bc5+ 20
Kh1 Bd4 21 Bxd4 Nxd4 22 Nd7
Nxc2 23 Nxf8 Rxf8 24 Rd7 Ne3
25 Re1 Rxf4 26 Kg1 1-0 Balogh**

✓ **160 Kuligowski-Liberson
Buenos Aires 78**
**1 d4 Nf6 2 c4 g6 3 Nc3 Bg7 4 e4 d6
5 f3 0-0 6 Be3 a6 7 Qd2! b6 8 Rd1**
N 8 0-0-0 c5 9 dxc5 bxc5 10 e5 Ne8
11 Bh6± Gheorghiu-Sax, Teesside 75
**c5!? 9 dxc5 bxc5 10 Bxc5! Nc6
11 Be3± Ne5 12 b3 a5 13 Bd3 Nxd3+
14 Qxd3 Bd7 15 Nge2 Qb8** △ a4
16 Rb1 Qb4 17 0-0 a4 18 a3! Qb7
18...Qxa3 19 b4! △ Bc1 +− **19 b4
Rfc8 20 Rbc1 e6 21 Rfd1 Be8 22
Bf4!** 22 Qxd6 Rxc4± Qa6 22...e5

23 Bg5! +− **23 Bxd6 Qxc4 24 Qxc4
Rxc4 25 Be5! Rac8 26 Nb1! Rxc1
27 Rxc1 Rxc1+ 28 Nxc1 Bh6! 29 Ne2
Nd7 30 Bd4 Nb8 31 Kf2 Nc6 32
Bf6! Bf8 33 Nd4 Nxd4 34 Bxd4 f5
35 exf5 exf5** 35...gxf5 36 f4!± **36
Nc3 Kf7 37 f4 Ke6 38 Ke3 h6 39 Kd3
g5 40 g3! gxf4 41 gxf4 Bd6 42 Be3
Kf6 43 Kd4 Bc6 44 Bc1!** △ b5 +−
Kg6 45 b5 Bf3 45...Bd7 46 Kc4±
**46 Nxa4 Kh5 47 Nb6 Kh4 48 Nc4
Bb8 49 b6 Kh3 50 Ne3 Be4 51 a4
Kxh2 52 a5 Bb7 53 Nxf5 h5 54
Kc5 Bc8 59 Nd6 1-0 Gheorghiu**

161 Knaak-J.Fernandez Halle 78
**1 d4 Nf6 2 c4 g6 3 Nc3 Bg7 4 e4
d6 5 f3 0-0 6 Be3 a6!? 7 Qd2 b6 8
0-0-0 c5 9 dxc5 bxc5 10 e5 Ne8 11
exd6** 11 Bh6 **Nxd6! 12 Nd5** 12
Bxc5 Qa5 13 Nd5 Qxc5! 14 Nxe7+
Kh8 15 Qxd6 Qe3+ 16 Kb1 Nd7 △
Rb8 **Nd7 13 Bg5** 13 g4 Rb8; 13
Bf4 Rb8! 14 Nxe7 Qxe7 15 Bxd6
Bxb2+ 16 Kc2 Qf6 17 Bxb8 Nxb8∓
f6 14 Be3 14 Bf4! **Nf5** 14...Rb8!
**15 Ne2 e5 16 h4!± Bb7 17 h5 Nb6
18 Nec3 Ng3 19 h6 Bh8**

20 Bxc5!! +− Nxd5 21 cxd5 Nxh1
22 Bc4 Rc8 22...Ng3 23 d6+ Rf7
24 d7! Nf5 25 Bxf7+ Kxf7 26 Qc2
Nd4 27 Rxd4 **23 d6+ Rf7 24 b4! Ng3**

25 d7 Xxc5 26 bxc5 ♘f5 27 ♕b2 ♗e3 28 ♕b6 1-0 Knaak

162 Gheorghiu-F.Portisch
Warsaw 79

1 d4 ♘f6 2 c4 g6 3 ♘c3 ♗g7 4 e4 d6 5 f3 0-0 6 ♗e3 ♘c6 7 ♘ge2 Xb8 8 ♕d2 Xe8 9 h4! a6 9...h5 10 0-0-0 a6 11 ♗h6 ♗h8 12 g4± **10 h5 b5 11 hxg6 fxg6 12 ♘f4?!** 12 ♗h6! ♗h8 13 ♗g5± e5! **13 dxe5 dxe5 14 ♘fd5** 14 ♕xd8! ♘xd8 15 ♘fd5∞; 15 ♘d3!? **♘d4! 15 ♗h6 ♗h8 16 0-0-0 c6 17 ♘e3 ♕a5 18 ♔b1 ♗e6∓ 19 ♗g5 ♘d7 20 ♘e2 ♕b6 21 ♘c2!?** 21 ♘xd4 exd4 −+ **bxc4! 22 ♘e3 ♕b5?!** 22...♘c5! 23 ♘c3 ♘d3! −+ **23 ♘c3 ♕b4 24 ♘e2 ♕a3 25 ♘xd4 c3!!** 25... exd4 26 ♘xc4∞

26 ♘b3!!∞ ♕xa2+! 27 ♔xa2 ♗xb3+ 28 ♔a3 cxd2 29 ♗c4+ ♗xc4 30 ♘xc4 ♘c5 31 Xxd2 31 ♗xd2 △ ♗c3 **♘e6!= 32 ♗e3 ♘d4 33 Xhd1 Xb3+ 34 ♔a2 Xeb8 35 Xd3 X3b4 36 Xc1 ♗g7 37 Xa3! ♘e2! 38 Xc2 ♘d4 39 Xc1** ½-½ Gheorghiu

163 Gheorghiu-Sznapik
Warsaw 79

1 d4 ♘f6 2 c4 g6 3 ♘c3 ♗g7 4 e4 d6 5 f3 0-0 6 ♗e3 e5 7 d5 c6 8 ♗d3 cxd5 9 cxd5 ♘e8 9...♘bd7; 9...♘h5

10 ♕d2! 10 ♘ge2 ♗h6!∞ **f5 11 exf5** 11 ♘ge2 f4 12 ♗f2 ♗f6 13 0-0-0 ♗h4 14 ♗g1! += **gxf5 12 ♘ge2 ♘d7 13 0-0 ♘df6 14 Xac1 ♕e7 15 ♗g5 ♕f7 16 ♘g3! f4!** N 16...♘g6 17 ♘b5 △ Xxc8 +− **17 ♘ge4!** 17 ♗xf6? ♗xf6 18 ♘ge4 ♗d8! △ ♗b6± ♗e3∞ **♔h8 18 ♗b5! ♗d7 19 ♗xd7 ♕xd7 20 ♕d3!± ♘xe4 21 ♘xe4 ♗f6 22 Xf2!** △ Xfc2+ **♗d8 23 ♗xd8 ♕xd8 24 Xfc2 Xg8 25 ♕b5! ♕e7 26 Xc8** 26 a4!± **♕g7! 27 ♕e2 Xxc8 28 Xxc8 ♕d7!∞ 29 Xc2** 29 ♕c2 ♕b5! **♕e7 30 Xc8 ♕d7 31 Xc2 ♕d8 32 ♕b5 ♕h4 33 Xe2 ♕e7∞** ½-½ Gheorghiu

164 Marszalek-Zoltek
Poland 78

1 d4 ♘f6 2 c4 c5 3 d5 g6 4 ♘c3 ♗g7 5 e4 d6 6 f4 0-0 7 ♘f3 e6 8 ♗e2 exd5 9 cxd5 Xe8 10 e5 dxe5 11 fxe5 ♘g4 12 ♗g5 ♕b6 12...f6!? **13 0-0 c4+?!** 13...♘xe5 **14 ♔h1 ♘xe5** N 14...♘f2+ 15 Xxf2 ♕xf2 16 ♘e4 ♕b6 17 ♘d6+ **15 ♘xe5 ♗xe5 16 ♗xc4 ♕xb2 17 ♕f3 ♗f5 18 Xac1** 18 Xae1 ♘d7 19 ♘e4∞ Xec8!? 18... ♘d7 19 ♗b5! **19 ♘d1!** 19 ♘b5?! Xxc4 20 Xxc4 ♕xb5 21 Xc8+ ♗g7∓; 19 ♘e4!? ♕d4 20 ♗d3∞ **♕d4** 19... ♕xc1 20 ♗xc1 Xxc4 21 ♘e3 **20 ♘e3± ♘d7!?** 20...♕e4 21 ♕xe4 ♗xe4 22 d6± **21 Xcd1!** 21 ♘xf5!? gxf5 22 ♕xf5 Xxc4 23 ♕xf7+ ♔h8 24 ♕xd7 Xg8 += **♕c3** 21...♕e4 22 ♕xe4 ♗xe4 23 d6 ♗f5 24 ♗d5± **22 ♘xf5 ♕xf3?** 22...gxf5 23 ♗d3!± **23 ♘h6+ ♔g7** 23...♔h8!? 24 Xxf3 Xxc4 25 ♘xf7+ ♔g8 26 ♘h6+ ♔h8 27 Xf7±; 25... ♔g7 26 ♘xe5 △ ♗f6+ +− **24 Xxf3 f6 25 ♗b5 ♘b6 26 ♘g4 Xc5 27 ♘xe5 fxg5 28 a4 a6 29 ♗f1 Xae8 30 Xf7+ ♔g8 31 Xxb7 1-0 Marszalek**

165 Segal-Panno
Sao Paulo 79
**1 d4 ♘f6 2 c4 g6 3 ♘c3 ♗g7 4 e4
d6 5 f4 0-0 6 ♘f3 c5 7 d5** 7 ♗e2
cxd4 8 ♘xd4 ♘c6 **e6 8 dxe6** 8 ♗e2
exd5 9 cxd5 ♗g4!= Tal **fxe6** 8...♗xe6
9 ♗d3 ♘c6 10 f5! Δ 0-0± **9 ♗d3 ♘c6
10 0-0 a6 11 ♕e1 ♗d7 12 ♗d2 ♘d4
13 ♘g5!± h6 14 ♘h3 ♗e8 15 ♖d1
b5 16 e5!** ♘h7 **17 exd6 ♕xd6 18
♘e4 ♕c6 19 ♘hf2 ♖a7 20 b3 ♖af7
21 cxb5 axb5 22 ♖c1!** ♕a6

**23 ♘xc5± ♕xa2 24 ♗xg6 ♖e7 25
♗b1 ♕a8 26 ♗e3 ♘c6 27 ♗e4! ♖d8
28 ♗xc6 ♕xc6 29 ♘fd3 ♕d5 30 b4
♘f5 31 ♗f2 ♖a8 32 ♖d1 ♕c6 33 ♘e5!
♗xe5 34 ♕xe5 ♖a2 35 ♖a1 ♘h4 36
♘e4 ♖xa1 37 ♖xa1 ♘g6 38 ♕d4** 38
♘f6+ **♗xf4! 39 ♖e1 e5!! 40 ♕d8+
♖e8 41 ♕d2 ♘g5!=** ½-½ Gheorghiu

166 Bonon-Soltis
New York 78
**1 ♘f3 g6 2 d4 ♗g7 3 c4 d6 4 ♘c3
♘f6 5 g3 0-0 6 ♗g2 c6 7 0-0 ♕a5 8
d5 ♕b4 9 ♘d2 ♗d7 10 a3 ♕b6 11
♖b1** 11 e4! a5 **12 b4? axb4 =+ 13
♖xb4** 13 axb4 cxd5 14 cxd5 ♖c8
15 ♗b2 ♕xb4; 15 ♕b3 ♕d4; 14 ♘xd5
♘xd5 15 cxd5 ♗a4 **♕c7 14 ♕b3?!**
♖a7 **15 ♘de4 ♗xe4** 15...c5 16 ♘xf6+
♗xf6 17 ♘b5 **16 ♘xe4 c5 17 ♕e3!**

17 ♖b6 ♗a4 18 ♕b1 ♗c2 19 ♕b5
♘d7 −+ ♕a5 17...♗d4 18 ♕h6 cxb4??
19 ♘g5; 17...♖xa3 18 ♕xa3 cxb4
19 ♕xb4 ♘a6 =+ **18 ♖b1 ♕a4! 19
♕b3?!** 19 ♕d3 ♗f5 20 ♗d2 ♗e5
**♕xb3∓ 20 ♖xb3 ♗a4 21 ♖b1 ♗c2!
22 ♖b5 ♘d7 23 f4 ♖b8!** Δ 24...♗a4
25 ♖b1 b5 **24 ♗h3 f5! −+ 25 ♘g5
♗d4+ 26 e3 ♗f6! 27 ♖f2** 27 ♘e6
♗d3 **♗d3 28 ♗f1 ♗xf1 29 ♔xf1 ♖a4
30 ♖c2 ♗xg5! 31 fxg5 ♘e5 0-1 Soltis**

167 Brown-Soltis USA 78
**1 c4 g6 2 ♘c3 ♗g7 3 g3 ♘f6 4 ♗g2
0-0 5 ♘f3 d6 6 0-0 c6 7 d4 ♕a5 8
e4 ♗g4! 9 h3 ♗xf3 10 ♗xf3 ♘fd7
11 ♖b1** N 11 ♗e3 a6 12 a3 c5 13
b4?! ♕d8! 14 ♖c1 cxd4 15 ♘xd4
♗h6! 16 ♖c2 ♘c6 =+ Rohde-Soltis,
New York 77 **a6 12 b4 ♕d8 13 ♖b3**
13 ♗e3 c5 14 bxc5 dxc5 15 ♖xb7?
♘c6 **a5 14 bxa5 ♖xa5** 14...♕xa5??
15 ♖a3 **15 ♗e3 ♘b6 16 ♕e2?!** 16
♕d3 **♘8d7 17 ♖fb1 c5 18 dxc5**
18 d5 ♖a6 Δ ♘e5/♕a8 **dxc5!? 19 ♘d5
♘c8!** =+ **20 ♗f4** 20 ♖xb7 ♘d6 21
♖7b3 ♘e5 22 ♖b8 ♕xb8 23 ♘xe7+
♔h8 24 ♖xb8 ♖xb8 25 ♔g2 ♘dxc4
♘e5 21 ♖xb7 e6 22 ♗xe5 22 ♘e3
♘xf3+ 23 ♕xf3 e5 **♗xe5 23 ♘e3 ♘d6
24 ♖d1?** 24 ♖7b3 ♕a8 25 ♘g4 ♖xa2
26 ♕f1 **♕a8 25 ♖b2?!** 25 ♖bb1 ♖xa2∓
**♗xb2 26 ♕xb2 ♘e8 27 ♘g4 h5 −+
28 ♘f6+ ♗xf6 29 ♕xf6 ♖xa2 30 e5
♕a5 31 ♗xh5 ♖a1 32 ♗xg6 ♖xd1
33 ♔h2 ♕d8! 0-1 Soltis**

168 Botterill-Biyiasas
Hastings 78/9
**1 d4 ♘f6 2 c4 g6 3 ♘f3 ♗g7 4 g3 0-0
5 ♗g2 d6 6 ♘c3 ♘bd7 7 0-0 e5 8 e4
c6 9 h3 ♕b6 10 ♖e1 ♖e8** 10...♘e8!?
Suetin; 10...exd4 **11 ♘xd4 ♘g4?!**
12 ♘ce2! ♘ge5 13 b3 ♘c5 14 ♗e3

a5 15 ♖b1 ♖e8 16 ♘c3!± Portisch-Gligoric, Budapest 64; 11...♖e8 12 ♘c2! ♘c5 13 b4 ♘e6 14 ♗e3 ♕c7 += Portisch-Stein, Sousse 67 **11 d5 c5 12 ♖b1** 12 ♖e2!? △ ♘e1-d3 **a6 13 a3 ♕c7 14 ♗e3 ♖f8** 14...b6 15 ♗f1 ♘f8 16 b4 ♗d7 Sherwin-Fischer, USA Final 66/7 **15 ♘d2 ♘e8 16 ♕c2 b6 17 b4 ♔h8 18 bxc5 bxc5 19 ♘b3 ♘df6 20 ♘a4 ♘h5?!** 20... ♗d7 21 ♘d2 += **21 ♗d2± ♖b8 22 ♘a5 ♖xb1 23 ♖xb1 f5 24 ♘c6** △ ♖b8, ♗a5, ♘b6 **♘ef6 25 ♖b8! ♗f7** 25...♘xe4 26 ♗a5 +– **26 ♘b6 ♘d7** 26...♗d7 27 ♖b7 +– **27 ♖xc8 ♗xb6 28 ♖xf8+ ♔xf8 29 exf5 gxf5 30 ♕b3** +– **♘d7 31 ♕b7 ♘df6 32 ♕xa6 ♘e4 33 ♗xe4 fxe4 34 ♕b7 ♕f3 35 ♕c8+ ♗f8 36 ♗h6??** Zeitnot 36 ♔g4 +–; 36 ♗f4 +–

36...e3! 37 ♗xe3 ♘xg3 38 fxg3 ♕xe3+ 39 ♔g2 ♕e2+ 40 ♔g1 ♕e1+ 41 ♔g2 ♕e2+ ½-½ **Botterill**

169 Botterill-Taulbut
Hastings 78/9

1 d4 g6 2 c4 ♗g7 3 ♘f3 d6 4 g3 ♘f6 5 ♗g2 0-0 6 0-0 ♘c6 7 ♘c3 a6 8 d5 ♘a5 9 ♘d2 c5 10 ♕c2 ♖b8 11 ♖b1!? e6 11...b5 12 cxb5 axb5 13 b4 **12 a3 exd5 13 ♘xd5** 13 cxd5? c4∓ **♘c6** 13...♘xd5? 14 cxd5 b5

15 b4± **14 ♘xf6+ ♗xf6 15 ♘e4 ♗f5** 15...♗g7 16 ♗g5± **16 ♗h6 ♖e8 17 ♘xf6+** 17 ♖bd1? ♗h8∓ **♕xf6 18 e4 ♗g4?!** 18...♗e6 19 ♗d2 +=; 18...g5!? **19 ♕d2 ♘e5 20 f3 ♗d7** 20...♘xc4 21 fxg4 ♘xd2 22 ♖xf6 ♘xb1 23 ♖xd6! ♖bd8 24 e5± **21 b3 ♘c6 22 ♗f4** 22 ♗e3 += **♘d4 23 b4 b6 24 ♗e3 b5** 24...♘a4!? **25 cxb5** 25 ♗xd4?! cxd4 26 ♖fd1 bxc4 27 ♕xd4 ♕xd4 28 ♖xd4 ♗e6=; 28...♖ec8!? **♗xb5 26 ♖f2 ♖bc8 27 ♕b2 ♗a4 28 ♖c1** 28 ♖bf1!? △ ♖d2 ♕g7 29 bxc5 dxc5 30 ♖xc5 ♖xc5 31 ♗xd4 ♕f8 32 ♗xc5 ♕xc5 33 ♗f1 a5 34 ♔g2 ♖d8 35 ♖d2?! 35 h4, 35 ♕f6 += ♖xd2 36 ♕xd2 ♕xa3 37 ♕d8+ ♔g7 38 ♕xa5 ♕b2+ 39 ♔g1 ♕d4+ 40 ♔g2 ♕b2+ 41 ♔g1 ½-½ **Botterill**

170 Suba-Skalkotas
Balkaniad 78

Remarkable vision & conviction!

1 c4 ♘f6 2 ♘c3 g6 3 e4 d6 4 d4 ♗g7 5 h3?! 0-0 **6 ♗d3?!** 6 ♗e3 △ ♕d2, 0-0-0 **e5 7 d5 ♘h5! 8 g3 a5 9 ♗e2?** 9 ♗e3 **♘a6! 10 ♗xh5 gxh5 11 ♕xh5 f5 12 ♗g5 ♕d7 13 f3 ♘c5 14 0-0-0 ♖a6!! 15 ♘ge2 ♖b6 16 g4?** 16 ♗e3 △ ♗xc5∞ **f4 =+ 17 ♔c2 ♖b4 18 b3 b5! 19 cxb5 ♖xb5 20 ♘xb5 ♕xb5**

21 ♘c3 ♕b4 22 ♗e7? 22 ♗h6!= a4!∓ **23 ♖b1 ♗a6 24 ♖hd1 axb3+ 25**

axb3 ♖b8 —+ 26 ♘a2 26 g5 ♘xb3!
Δ ♘a1+ —+ ♕a3 27 ♘c1 ♗c4!! 28
bxc4 ♕a4+ 29 ♔d2 ♖xb1 30 g5 ♘d3!
31 ♕g4 31 ♔xd3 ♕xd1+ —+ ♖b2+
0-1 Maric

171 Suba-Botterill Hastings 78/9
1 c4 ♘f6 2 ♘c3 g6 3 e4 d6 4 d4 ♗g7
5 h3 0-0 6 ♗g5!? h6 6...c5 7 d5 b5 8
cxb5 ♕a5 9 ♗d2 a6 10 a4 axb5 11
♗xb5 ♗a6 12 ♖a3 += Suba-Plachetka,
Moscow 77; 7 dxc5! +=; 6...♘bd7
7 ♘f3 e5 8 d5 h6 9 ♗e3 ♘c5 10
♘d2 a5≈ Gheorghiu-Stein, Hastings
67/8 **7 ♗e3 e5 8 d5 ♘bd7** 8...c6!?
9 ♗d3 ♘c5 10 ♗c2 a5 11 ♕d2 11 g4
h5 12 g5 ♘h7 13 ♕d2 f6 14 gxf6
♖xf6 15 0-0-0 ♗d7 16 ♘ge2 ♖f3 17
♖dg1 ♕e8 18 ♘g3 ♔h8 19 ♗d1 ♖f4!
=+ Mititelu-Botterill, Bath 1973 **♔h7
12 g4 ♘g8** Δ ♗f6-g5 **13 ♘ge2 ♗d7
14 ♘g3 b6** 14...♗f6!? **15 f3 ♗f6 16
h4! ♗xh4 17 ♔f2 ♔g7 18 ♖xh4
♕xh4 19 ♖h1 ♕d8 20 ♗xh6+ ♘xh6
21 ♕xh6+ ♔f6 22 ♘h5+** 22 ♕h4+
♔g7 23 ♕g5+ f6 23...♔e8?? 24
♘g7! mate **24 ♘xf6! ♖xf6! 25 ♖h7+
♔e8**

26 ♕h6 26 ♖h8+ ♔f7 27 ♖h7+ =;
27 ♖xd8 ♖xd8∞; 26 ♔g2!! ♕e7
27 ♖xe7+ ♔xe7 28 f4! exf4 29 e5
dxe5 30 d6+! ♔f7 31 ♘d5± ♖e6 32

♘xc7 ♗c6+ 33 ♔f1 ♖xd6 34 ♘xa8
♗xa8 35 ♕xe5 +— **♕e7 27 g5 ♖f7
28 ♕xg6** 28 ♖h8+ ♖f8 29 ♖h7=
♕f8 29 f4 ♔e7 30 f5? 30 ♕f6+!
♔e8 31 ♕g6 ♔e7= **♖xh7∓ 31 ♕xh7+
♔f7 32 f6+ ♔e8?** 32...♔f8! 33 ♕h8+
♕g8 34 ♕h6+ ♔f7 35 ♗d1 ♘d3+ Δ
♘f4 —+ **33 ♕h8+ ♕f8 34 ♕h4 ♔g8
35 ♔e3 ♕g6** 35...♔f7 36 ♗d1 ♗e8??
37 g6+! +— Suba **36 ♗d1 ♔d8 37
♖h5 ♕h7! 38 ♘e2 ♔c8 39 ♘g1 ♔b7
40 ♘f3 ♖h8 41 g6 ♕h6+ 42 ♔e2**
42 ♕g5 ♕xg5+ 43 ♘xg5 ♖xh5 44 f7
♖xg5 45 f8♕ ♖xg6 —+; 42 ♔f2 ♘d3+
43 ♔f1 ♕c1+ —+ **♗e8!** 42...♕c1!
43 f7 ♕xc4+ 44 ♔f2 ♘d3+ —+ Suba
42...♕c1!? ∞/∓; 42...♘xe4!? 43 ♕xe4
♕xh5 44 g7 ♖g8 45 ♕h4! ♗g4 46
♕xh5 ♗xh5 47 ♔e3 ♔c8 48 ♘h4 ♔d8
49 ♘f5 ♔e8 50 ♘h6 ♗f7 51 a4!=
43 f7 ♗xf7 44 gxf7 ♘d7 45 c5!
♗g4 ♕xh4 46 ♘xh4 ♖xh4 47 ♗xd7
♖xe4+ Δ ♖f4 —+ **dxc5! 46 ♕e7 ♕xh5
47 ♕xd7 ♖f8 48 ♕c6+ ♔a6!** 48...
♔b8 49 d6∓ **49 a4 ♕xf7 50 ♘d2
♕h5+ 51 ♔e1** 51 ♘d3 ♕d1 —+ **♕h1+
52 ♔e2 ♕h5+ 53 ♔e1 ♕g4!** Δ ♖h8
**54 ♕b5+ ♔a7 55 ♕c6 ♖f7 56 d6
♕e6 0-1 Botterill**

172 Kovacs-Nagy Budapest 78
1 e4 g6 2 d4 ♗g7 3 c4 d6 4 ♘c3 c6
5 f4 a6 5...♘b6! 6 ♘f3 N 6 a4 ♘d7 7
♘f3 e5 8 fxe5 dxe5 9 d5 ♘gf6 10
♗e2 0-0 11 ♗g5 ♕b6 12 ♕c2 ♘g4
13 ♘d1 f6 14 ♗d2 cxd5 15 cxd5
f5 16 a5 ♕d6 17 ♖a4 += A.Zaitsev-
Szily, Busum 69 **b5 7 ♗e3 ♗g4 8
h3 ♗xf3 9 ♕xf3 e6 10 e5! bxc4 11
♘e4 d5 12 ♘d6+ ♔f8∞ 13 g4 f5 14
gxf5 exf5 15 h4 ♘h6 16 0-0-0 ♘f7
17 ♘xc4! dxc4 18 ♗xc4 ♘d7 19
d5 c5 20 d6 ♘b6 21 ♗xf7 ♔xf7
22 ♕b7+ ♘d7 23 e6+! ♔g8** 23...♔xe6?

24 ♕d5+ ♔f6 25 ♗d2 △ ♗c3 mate **24 exd7 ♖b8 25 ♕d5+ ♔f8 26 ♖h2 ♕xd7 27 ♗xc5 +− ♗f6 28 ♔b1 ♕b5 29 h5 ♕d7** 29...♕xb2? 30 d7+ ♔g7 31 h6+ ♔f6 32 ♕d6 mate **30 h6 ♔e8 31 ♖e2+ ♔d8 32 ♖de1 ♕b5 33 ♕f7** △ ♕c7 mate/♕xf6+ **1-0 Kovacs**

173 Djindjihashvili-Torre
Buenos Aires 2 78

1 ♘f3 c5 2 c4 g6 3 d4 ♗g7 4 e4 ♘c6 4...♕a5+ 5 ♗d2 ♕b6! 6 ♗c3 cxd4=; 5 ♘c3 ♘c6 6 d5 ♘d4 7 ♗d2 ♘xf3+ 8 ♕xf3 d6 += **5 d5 ♘d4 6 ♗xd4 cxd4 7 ♘a3 ♕b6 8 ♗d3 d6 9 c5!?** 9 0-0± ♕xc5 **10 ♗b5+ ♔f8 11 0-0 ♘f6 12 ♗d3 ♗g4 13 ♘c4 ♘e5** 13...b5 14 ♘d2; 14 ♘a5, 14 b4!? **14 ♘xe5 ♗xe5 15 ♗h6 + ♗g7 16 ♕d2 ♕b6 17 a4!** △ a5, ♖fc1± **a5 18 ♗b5 e5**

19 ♕g5!! +− △ ♕f6 +− ♔g8 **20 ♕e7! ♗d7** 20...♗xh6 21 ♗e8! +− **21 ♗xg7 1-0** 21...♗xb5 22 ♗h6 +− **Gheorghiu**

174 Ghitescu-Sikora Warsaw 79

1 c4 g6 2 e4 ♗g7 3 d4 d6 4 ♘c3 ♘c6!? 5 ♗e3 e5 6 d5 ♘ce7 6...♘d4 7 ♘ge2± **7 g4! f5 8 f3 ♘f6?!** 8...♗h6 9 g5 ♗g7 10 h4± **9 h3 0-0 10 ♗d3 c5 11 ♘ge2 ♗d7 12 a3!±** △ b4 fxe4?! **13 ♘xe4! ♘xe4 14 ♗xe4 b5 15 cxb5 ♗xb5 16 ♘c3 ♖b8** 16...♗c4? 17 ♕a4! +− **17**

h4 ♗e8 **18 ♕c2 ♔h8?** 18...h6!± **19 h5! gxh5 20 gxh5 h6 21 0-0-0 ♖b7 22 ♖dg1 ♘g8 23 ♖h3! ♗f6 24 ♗g6! e4 25 fxe4 ♘d7 26 ♕d2 ♗e5?**

27 ♗d4!! +− 1-0 27...cxd4 28 ♕xh6+ **Gheorghiu**

175 Gheorghiu-Djindjihashvili
Buenos Aires 2 78

1 d4 g6 2 c4 ♗g7 3 ♘c3 d6 4 e4 e5 5 dxe5! 5 ♘f3!? ♘c6! 6 dxe5 dxe5= Ghitescu-Kagan, Buenos Aires 78 **dxe5 6 ♕xd8+ ♔xd8 7 f4! f6!?** N **8 fxe5! fxe5 9 ♗g5+ ♗f6** 9...♔e8? 10 ♘d5± **10 ♘f3 ♘d7 11 ♘d5! h6!** 11...c6?? 12 ♘xf6 ♘gxf6 13 ♘xe5 +−; 11...♗xg5 12 ♘xg5 △ ♘e6+ +− **12 ♗xf6+ ♘gxf6 13 ♘xf6 ♗xf6 14 ♘xe5 ♖g8 15 0-0-0+ ♔e7 16 ♗d3 ♗g4!** △ ♘f2 **17 ♘xg4 ♗xg4 18 ♖de1 ♖ad8 19 ♔c2 ♖hf8 20 ♖hf1 c5! 21 ♔c3 g5** △ ♔e6-e5∞ **22 e5!± b6 23 h3 ♗e6 24 g4** △ ♗f5± **♖xf1 25 ♖xf1 h5** 25...♖f8± **26 gxh5! ♖h8 27 ♗g6! ♖xh3 28 ♖g1 g4 29 ♔d3 ♖d8+ 30 ♔e4 ♖d4+ 31 ♔e3 ♔e6 32 h6 ♔xe5 33 h7 ♖d8 34 ♗e4 ♔f6 35 ♖d1! +− ♖e8 36 ♔f4! ♗g7 37 ♖d7+ ♔h8 38 ♗g6 ♖f8+ 39 ♔g3 ♗f1 40 b3 ♗e2 41 ♖xa7** △ ♖b7 **♖b8 42 ♖d7 ♗f3 43 ♖d6 ♔g7 44 ♗f5 ♔h8 45 ♔h4! ♔g7 46 ♖g6+ ♔h8** 46...♔xh7?? 47

♖xb6+ 47 ♔g5! +– 1-0 47...g3 48 ♔h6 g2 49 ♗e6 △ ♖g8+ **Gheorghiu**

176 Nemet-Smejkal
Virovitica 78

1 d4 ♘f6 2 c4 g6 3 d5?! c6 4 ♘c3 cxd5 5 cxd5 d6 6 ♘f3 ♗g7 7 g3?! ♕a5! △ ♘xd5∓ 8 ♕d2 b5! 9 b4!? ♕xb4 10 ♖b1

10...♘xd5!! 11 ♘xd5 11 ♖xb4 ♗xc3; 11 ♕xd5? ♗c3+ △ ♕xb1 –+ ♕xb1∓ 12 ♗g2 ♘c6 13 ♘c7+ ♔d7 14 ♘xa8 ♗b7 15 0-0 ♗xa8 16 ♘g5 ♘d4! 17 ♗h3+ 17 ♗xa8 ♖xa8 28 ♘xf7 ♔e4∓ f5 18 ♗b2 18 ♗a3 ♕c2∓ ♕xb2 19 ♕xb2 ♘f3+ 20 ♘xf3 ♗xb2 21 ♖b1 ♗c3 22 ♖xb5 ♖c8∓ 23 g4 e6 24 gxf5 gxf5 25 ♔f1 ♗c6 26 ♖b3 ♗d5 27 ♖a3 a5 –+ 28 ♔g1 ♗b4 29 ♖d3 ♗xa2 30 ♘d4 ♖c1+ 31 ♔g2 ♗d5+ 32 f3 ♗c4 33 ♖e3 ♗c5 34 ♘xf5 ♗xe3 35 ♘xe3 a4 0-1 Maric

177 Terebesi-Hardicsay
Hungary 78

1 d4 g6 2 ♘f3 ♗g7 3 ♗f4 d6 4 e3 ♘d7 5 c4 5 c3 e5 6 dxe5 6 ♗g3 ♘h6 △ f5 =+ dxe5 7 ♗g5 f6 8 ♗h4 ♘h6! 9 ♘c3 9 e4 ♕e7 △ ♘c5∓ ♘f5 10 ♗g3

c6 11 e4 ♘xg3 12 hxg3 ♕e7 13 ♗e2 ♘c5 14 ♕d2 a5 15 b3 ♗e6 16 ♖d1 0-0 17 ♕d6 ♕xd6 18 ♖xd6 ♖fe8 19 0-0 ♗f8 20 ♖d2 ♘a6! 21 ♘a4 ♗b4 22 ♖d3 ♘c5 23 ♘xc5 ♗xc5 24 a4 ♔f8 25 ♖fd1 ♗e7 26 ♔f1 ♖ab8 27 ♘e1 f5 28 ♗f3 ♖f8 29 ♖1d2 g5! 30 exf5 30 ♔g1 g4 –+ ♗xf5 31 ♖e2 ♗xd3 32 ♘xd3 ♗d4 35 ♘xe5 ♔d6 36 ♘d3 ♖be8 37 ♗e4 h5 36 f4 h4 36... gxf4 37 gxf4 h4∓ 37 gxh4 gxf4 38 ♗f3 ♗e3 39 ♖c2 b6 40 h5 ♖f5 41 ♗g4 ♖g5 42 ♗f3 ♖h8 43 ♘e1 ♔c5 44 ♘d3+ ♔d4 45 ♔e2 c5 46 ♘b2 ♖h6 47 ♘d1 ♖hxh5! 48 ♗xh5 ♖xg2+ 49 ♘f2! ♗xf2+ 50 ♔d1 ♖f1+ 51 ♔e2 ♖b1 52 ♗e8 ♖xb3 53 ♗b5 ♖a3 54 ♔f3 ♗d2+ 55 ♔e2 ♗b4 56 ♖c1 f3+ 57 ♔f2 ♔e4 58 ♖h1 ♖a2+ –+ 59 ♔g3 ♖g2+ 60 ♔h3 ♖g6 61 ♖d1 f2 62 ♗e8 ♖g1 63 ♗c6+ 0-1 Hardicsay

Sicilian

2 b3

178 Spassky-Herbert
Buenos Aires 78

1 e4 c5 2 b3!? d6 3 ♗b2 a6 3...♘c6 △ e6 4 f4 ♘c6 5 ♘f3 e6 6 g3 ♘f6 7 e5 dxe5 8 fxe5 += ♘g4 9 ♕e2 h5 10 ♗g2 ♘b4 11 ♘a3! ♗d7 △ ♗c6 12 h3 ♘h6 13 c3 ♘d5 14 0-0 ♗c6 15 ♘c2 ♕b6 16 c4! ♘b4 17 ♘xb4 ♕xb4 18 ♘g5!± ♗xg2 19 ♔xg2 ♗e7 20 ♘e4 0-0-0 20...♘f5∞ 21 ♗c3 ♕b6 22 ♕xh5! ♕c6 23 ♖ae1 ♗f5 24 ♕f3 ♔b8 25 a4 ♖h6 26 ♘f2! ♖g6 27 ♘g4!± 27 ♕xc6? ♖xg3+∞ ♔c8 28 ♕e4 ♖h8 29 ♖f3 ♖h5 30 ♖d3 ♕e8 31 ♖b1 ♔c8 32 b4! ♕c6 33 ♕xc6 bxc6 34 bxc5 ♗xc5 35 ♗a5 △ ♖d8 mate ♖h8 36 ♖db3! ♗a7 37 ♖b7 1-0 **Gheorghiu**

2 c3

179 Jamieson-F.Olafsson
Buenos Aires 78
**1 e4 c5 2 c3 d5 3 exd5 ♕xd5 4 d4
♘f6 5 ♘f3 ♗g4** 5...e6 **6 ♗e2 e6 7 0-0
♘c6 8 h3** 8 ♘a3 cxd4 9 ♘b5 ♗c8=
**♗h5 9 c4 ♕d7 10 dxc5 ♗xc5 11
♘c3?!** 11 ♕xd7= **♕c7! 12 a3 a6 13
b4 ♗a7 14 ♗g5 ♖d8 15 ♕a4 0-0 =+
16 ♖ac1 ♗xf3! 17 ♗xf3 ♘d4 18 ♕d1
♘f5 19 ♕c2 ♘d4 20 ♕d1 ♕xc4 21
♗xf6 gxf6 22 ♘e4** 22 ♗xb7 ♘b3 **♕b5
23 ♘xf6+ ♔h8 24 ♖e1 ♕f5 25 ♘e4
♖g8∓ 26 ♗g4 ♕f4 27 g3 ♕h6 28 ♘c5
f5 29 ♗f3 e5** △ e4, ♘f3+ **30 ♖c4
♕g7** △ e4 **31 ♗g2 b5 32 ♖c3 e4 −+
33 ♕c1 ♖d6 34 ♔f1 ♗b8! 35 ♕e3
♕g6 36 ♖d1 ♗e5 37 ♖cc1 h5 38
h4 ♖f8 39 ♗h3 f4 40 ♕xe4 fxg3
0-1 Sigurjonsson**

180 Timoshenko-Kasparov
USSR Final 78
**1 e4 c5 2 ♘f3 e6 3 c3 d5 4 exd5 exd5
5 d4 a6 6 ♗e2 c4?!** 6...♘f6 **7 0-0 ♘c6
8 ♗e3 cxd4 9 cxd4 0-0 10 ♘c3 ♕d6
+= 7 ♗f4 ♗d6 8 ♗xd6 ♕xd6 9 b3
cxb3 10 axb3 ♘e7 11 0-0 0-0 12
c4 ♘bc6 13 c5 ♕f6 14 ♘c3 ♗f5 15
♕d2 ♗e4 16 ♖fd1 +=♘f5 17 ♖a4
♖ad8 18 ♘e1 ♘fe7 19 b4 ♖fe8 20 b5
axb5 21 ♘xb5 ♘g6 22 ♖a3 +=♘f4
23 ♗f1 h5 24 ♘d6 ♖e7 25 ♖b3 h4 26
f3 ♗g6 27 ♖xb7 ♖xb7 28 ♘xb7
♖b8 29 ♘a5 ♗xa5 30 ♕xa5 ♖b2 31
♕a1 ♘e2+ 32 ♔h1**

Diagram

**32...♘g3+? 33 hxg3 hxg3 34 ♕a8+
± ♔h7 35 ♕c8 ♖f2** 35...♗f5 36 ♕xf5+
△ ♗d3 +− **36 ♕h3+ ♔g8 37 ♕c8+
♔h7 38 ♕h3+ ♔g8 39 ♔g1 ♕f4 40**

♕c8+ ♕h7 41 ♕h3+ 1-0 Suetin

181 Holmov-Malich Halle 78
**1 e4 c5 2 ♘f3 e6 3 c3 ♘f6 4 e5 ♘d5
5 d4 cxd4 6 cxd4 d6 7 ♘c3!? dxe5**
7...♘c6 **8 ♘xe5 ♗b4 9 ♗d2 0-0 10
♗e2!?** N 10 ♗d3 ♘d7 11 0-0?! ♘xe5
12 dxe5 ♘xc3=; 11 ♘xd5 ♗xd2+
12 ♕xd2 ♘xe5!= **♗xc3?** 10...♘d7
11 ♘xd5 ♗xd2+ 12 ♕xd2 ♘xe5 13
dxe5 exd5 +=; 10...♘c6 11 ♘xc6
bxc6 12 0-0 ♗xc3! 13 bxc3 ♗d6 14
♗f3 ♕c7 15 g3 ♖b8 △ c5=; 12 ♘e4!?
+=; 10...♘e7 11 ♗e3 ♘d5=; 11 a3
♗a5 12 ♘c4 ♘bc6 13 ♖xa5 ♘xa5≈
**11 bxc3 ♘d7 12 0-0 ♘xe5 13 dxe5
♗d7** 13...♘e7 14 ♗g5!±; 13...b6 14
c4 ♘e7 15 ♗f3 ♖b8 16 ♗b4± **14
c4 ♘b6 15 ♗b4 ♖e8 16 ♕b3 ♗c6**
16...♗a4 17 ♕e3 ♖c8 += **17 ♕e3!
♘d7?!** 17...♕h4!? **18 ♗d6 ♕a5** 18...
♕h4 19 f4 f5± **19 ♖fd1 ♘f8** 19...b6
20 ♖d4 ♘c5 21 ♖g4± **20 ♖d4 ♘g6
21 ♗d3 ♖ad8 22 c5!** 22 h4 ♖xd6 23
exd6 e5 **b6 23 cxb6 axb6 24 h4
♗b5** 24...h6 25 ♖g4± **25 ♗e4 ♖c8 26
h5 ♘f8 27 ♗b4! ♕a7 28 h6 f5 29
exf6 gxf6 30 ♕g3+ ♔h8 31 ♖ad1**
△ ♖d7 +− **♕f7 32 a4 ♗c6** 32...♗xa4
33 ♗xf8 +− **33 ♗xc6 ♖xc6 34 ♖d8
♖c8 35 ♖xe8 ♖xe8 36 ♖d6 ♘g6**
36...e5 37 ♖xb6 ♘e6 △ ♖g8, ♘f4;
37 ♕g7+ ♕xg7 38 hxg7+ ♔xg7 39

罩xb6 ♘e6 40 a5 +− **37 罩xb6 ♛d7?**
38 ♛f3! 38 a5? ♛d1+ 39 ♔h2 ♛h5+
40 ♔h3 ♛e5+ 41 g3 ♛e2 △ ♘e5≈
f5 39 ♗c3+ e5 40 a5 +− ♗c8 41 g3
♔g8 42 ♗b2 e4 43 ♛b3+ ♔f7 44
罩xg6+! 1-0 Malich

182 Sanz-Miles
Amsterdam 3 78
1 e4 c5 2 c3 ♘f6 3 e5 ♘d5 4 d4 cxd4
5 cxd4 b6!? 6 ♘f3 e6 6 a3 ♗e7 8
♗d3 ♗b7 8...♗a6!? 9 ♗e4!? **9 0-0**
♘a6 10 罩e1 ♘ac7 11 ♘bd2 0-0 11...
♘f4!? △ ♘cd5∞ **12 ♘e4 f5!?** 12...
罩c8; 12...♘e8!? **13 exf6 gxf6?!** 13...
♘xf6≈ **14 ♛d2! 罩f7 15 ♛h6 罩g7 16**
♛h3! △ ♗h6 **f5 17 ♗h6!** 17 ♘g3 ♘f6
18 ♗h6 ♗xf3! 19 ♗xg7 ♗g4 20 ♛h6
♘fe8! △ ♘xg7/♗g5∓ **fxe4 18 罩xe4!**
18 ♗xg7 ♘f4 19 ♛g4 exd3 ∞/=+;
19 ♛h6? ♘xd3∓; 19 ♛g3 ♘h5 **♘f6**
18...罩g6 19 罩g4! ♛e8 20 ♘e5! +−

19 罩h4?! 19 ♗xg7 ♘xe4 20 ♛g4 h5
21 ♛g6 ♛e8 22 ♛h6 d6 23 ♘e5!
dxe5 24 ♗xe5 ♘f6 25 ♗h7+ ♔f7 26
♗g6+ ♔g8 27 ♗xf6 ♗xf6 28 ♛h7+
♔f8 29 ♗xe8 +−; 20...♘g5 21 ♘xg5
♗xg5 22 ♗h6 +−; 19...♗xe4 20 ♗xf6
♗xd3 21 ♛g3+! ♗g6 22 ♗xe7 ♛xe7
23 ♛xc7±; 19...♛xg7 20 罩g4+!
♔h8 21 ♘e5! +− **♗f8 20 ♗xg7 ♗xg7**
21 罩e1? 21 ♘e5! △ 罩xh7 **♗xf3!∓**

22 gxf3!? 22 ♛xf3 ♘cd5 **♛e7 23 ♔h1**
♛f7 24 f4 24 罩g1 罩g8 25 ♗xh7
♘xh7 26 罩xh7 ♘e8∓ **♛g8 25 f5 ♛d6**
26 fxe6+ dxe6 27 ♛f3 ♛e7 27...♛d5
28 ♗e4∞ **28 ♗c4** 28 ♗xh7? 罩h8 −+
♘cd5 29 罩e5? 29 ♗xd5 ♛xd5 30
♛xd5 罩xd5 31 罩xh7 ♘f6∓ **♛c6!**
−+ 30 ♗f1 30 ♗xd5 ♛c1+ 31 ♔g2
♗f8+ 32 ♔h3 ♛f1+ −+; 30 b3 b5
−+ **♗h8! 31 罩h3** 31 ♗h3? ♛c1+ −+;
31 罩h6 ♛c1 −+ **h5 32 罩g3 罩f8**
33 ♗h3 ♘g4 0-1 time **Miles**

183 Castro-Ochoa Manresa 78
1 e4 c5 2 c3 ♘f6 3 e5 ♘d5 4 d4 cxd4
5 cxd4 d6 6 ♘f3 ♘c6 7 ♗c4 dxe5
7...♘b6!? **8 dxe5 e6 9 0-0 ♘b6 10**
♛xd8+ ♘xd8 11 ♗b3 ♗d7 12 ♘c3
♗c6 13 ♘d4 ♗e7 14 ♗e3 0-0 15 罩fd1
罩fe8!? 16 ♘db5 ♗f8 17 ♘xa7 罩xa7
18 ♗xb6 罩a6 19 ♗e3?! 19 ♗d4!?
罩a5! 20 ♗d4 b5! 21 a3 ♘b7 22
罩ac1 罩a6! △ ♘a5-c4= **23 ♘xb5**
♗xb5 24 ♗c7 ♘a5! 25 ♗c2 罩c6
26 ♗xh7+? ♔xh7 27 罩xe7 罩d8
0-1 Ochoa

184 Tompa-Szekely Hungary 78
1 e4 c5 2 c3 ♘f6 3 e5 ♘d5 4 d4 cxd4
5 ♛xd4 e6 6 ♘f3 ♘c6 7 ♛e4 d6 8
♘bd2 dxe5 9 ♘xe5 ♘f6 9...♘xe5
10 ♛xe5 ♛d6 11 ♗b5+ ♗d7 12 ♗xd7+
♛xd7 13 ♘f3 ♛c7= Bronstein-Hort,
Monte Carlo 69; 13...♘e4! **10 ♛a4**
10 ♘xc6 ♛xd2+! **♛c7 11 ♘df3** 11
♘dc4?! a6 12 ♘xc6 b5 13 ♛a5 ♛xc6
14 ♘b6 罩b8 15 ♘xc8 罩xc8=
Polugaevsky **♗d6 12 ♘xc6 ♗d7 13**
♗g5! ♗d5? 13...♗xc6 14 ♗b5 ♗xb5
15 ♛xb5+ ♛d7 16 ♛e2 +=; 13...♛c6=
14 ♛d4 +− f6 15 ♘xa7 ♗c5 15...fxg5
16 ♘b5 **16 ♛d2 ♗xa7 17 ♗h4 罩d8**
18 ♗g3 ♛c5 19 ♗d3 e5?! 20 0-0
20 ♛c2 ♗b5 21 ♗xh7? ♘e3! −+ **0-0**

21 ♕c2 g6 21...h6 22 ♘h4 **22 ♗xg6!**
hxg6 23 ♕xg6+ ♚h8 24 ♕h6+ ♚g8
25 ♕g6+ ♚h8 26 ♘xe5 ♕e7 27 ♕h5+
♚g7 28 ♕g6+ ♚h8 29 ♕h6+ ♚g8
30 ♘g6 ♕g7 31 ♕xg7+ ♚xg7 32
♘xf8 ♖xf8 33 ♖ad1 +− **♗c6 34 c4**
34 ♖fe1 **♘b6 35 b3!?** 35 ♗d6! ♖c8
36 b3; 35...♖e8 36 ♗c5 **♘d7 36**
♖fe1 **♘e5 37 h3 ♚g6 38 ♚f1 ♗c5 39**
f3 ♚f5 40 ♗f2 ♗b4 41 ♖e3 b5 42
cxb5 ♗xb5+ 43 ♚g1 ♖a8? 44 f4!
♗c5 45 fxe5 ♗xe3 46 ♗xe3 ♖xa2 47
exf6 ♚xf6 48 ♖d2 ♖a1+ 49 ♚h2 ♖b1
50 ♖b2 ♖d1 51 b4 ♖d3 52 ♖f2+
♚g6 53 ♗c5 ♖b3 54 ♗e7 1-0 Tompa

2 ♘c3/2 d3

185 Ermenkov-Minic Plovdiv 78
1 e4 c5 2 ♘c3 ♘c6 3 ♘ge2 ♘f6 4 d4
cxd4 5 ♘xd4 e6 6 ♗e2 ♗b4 7 0-0!?
7 ♘xc6? bxc6 8 0-0 d5! =+ Taimanov
♗xc3 8 bxc3 ♘xe4 9 ♗d3! 9 ♗f3
d5 10 ♘xc6 bxc6 11 ♗xe4 dxe4 12
♕xd8+ ♚xd8 13 ♖e1 f5 14 ♗g5+
♚e8 15 ♖ad1∝ Taimanov **♘xc3?**
9...d5!? 10 ♗a3 ♘xd4 11 cxd4 ♕a5
12 ♕c1 ♗d7 13 ♖b1 ♗c6 14 ♗b4
♕c7 Geller-Hasin, USSR 78 **10 ♕g4!±**
0-0 10...♕f6? 11 ♘xc6 dxc6 12 ♗g5
♕e5 13 ♖fe1 ♗c5 14 ♗e3 Δ ♕xg7 +−
11 ♗b2 f5 11...♘d5? 12 ♘f5! +−
12 ♘xf5! exf5 13 ♕c4+ d5 14 ♕xc3
d4 15 ♕b3+ ♚h8 16 ♖fe1!± ♕c7
16...♕b6!? 17 ♕f7 ♗e6∝ **17 ♗a3 ♖d8**
18 ♖e2! ♗d7 19 ♖ae1 ♕a5 19...♖e8?
20 ♕f7! ♖xe2 21 ♖xe2 ♕a5 22 ♗f8!
+− **20 ♗d6 ♕b6 21 ♕f7** +−**h6**

Diagram
22 g4 22 ♖e7! ♘xe7 23 ♖xe7 ♕b1+
24 ♗f1 ♖g8 25 ♗e5 +− **♕a5 23 gxf5**
♖ac8 24 h4 24 ♗e5 ♘xe5 25 ♖xe5

♕b6 26 ♖e7 +− **♘b4 25 ♖e7 ♖g8 26**
♗e5 1-0 Maric

186 Roos-Miles
Amsterdam 3 78
1 e4 c5 2 ♘c3 ♘c6 3 g3 ♖b8!? 4
f4 g6 5 ♘f3 ♗g7 6 ♗g2 b5 7 0-0 d6
8 d3 b4 9 ♘d5!? 9 ♘e2 e6 10 ♘e3
♘ge7 11 a3 a5 11...bxa3 12 ♖xa3
♗xb2?? 13 ♗xb2 ♖xb2 14 ♕a1 ♕b6
15 ♖b3! +− **12 axb4 axb4 13 f5?!**
exf5 14 exf5 ♘xf5!? 14...♗xf5 15
♘xf5 ♘xf5 16 ♘g5 ♘e5 17 ♗d5
0-0? 18 ♖a7± Kopilov-Bevlov, USSR
63; 17...♕d7 **15 ♘xf5 ♗xf5 16 ♘g5**
♘e5 17 ♗d5 17 ♖a7 ♕b6 **♕d7!∓**
17...0-0 18 ♖a7∝ **18 c3 bxc3 19**
bxc3 0-0 20 d4 cxd4 21 cxd4 ♘d3
22 ♗e3 ♘b4?! 22...♕e7 23 ♕f3 ♖be8
−+ **23 ♗xf7+! ♖xf7** 23...♚h8!? 24
♗b3 h6 25 ♘f3 ♗g4∓ **24 ♕b3 ♗h6!**
25 ♘xf7 ♗xe3+ 26 ♕xe3 ♕xf7 27
♖ab1! ♕d5! 27...♕d7 28 ♖b2∝;
27...♕c4? 28 ♖xf5=; 27...♕e6 28
♕xe6+ ♗xe6 29 ♖b2 ♗f5 30 g4 ♗e4
31 d5= **28 ♖b2 ♗h3! 29 ♖fb1** 29
♖ff2 ♖a8 −+; 29 ♗f3 ♖a8 30 ♖xb4
♖a1+ 31 ♚f2 ♕a2+ 32 ♕e2 ♖f1+
33 ♚e3 ♕a3+ −+ **♖f8 30 g4! ♖f3 31**
♕e8+ ♚g7 32 ♕e7+ ♖f7 33 ♕e3 h5!
33...h6 Zugzwang **34 gxh5** 34 ♖xb4
♕g2 mate; 34 ♕xh3 ♕xd4+ 35 ♚h1
♘d3 36 ♕g2 ♘f2+ 37 ♖xf2 ♖xf2

38 ♖b7+ ♔f6 39 g5+ ♔e6 −+; 36 gxh5 ♘xb2 37 ♔g2 ♖f6 38 ♕xb2 ♕e4+ 39 ♔g1 gxh5∓ **♕f5! −+ 35 ♕e2** 35 ♕f2 ♕g4+ −+ **♕g5+ 36 ♔h1 ♕d5+ 37 ♔g1 ♕g5+ 38 ♔h1 ♕d5+** Zeitnot **0-1** 39 ♔g1 ♕xd4+ 40 ♔h1 ♕d5+ 41 ♔g1 ♕g5+ 42 ♔h1 ♗g4 −+ Miles

187 Skrobek-Knaak Halle 78

1 e4 c5 2 ♘c3 e6 3 ♘f3 d6 4 d4 cxd4 5 ♘xd4 ♗e7 6 f4 ♘f6 7 ♕f3 0-0 8 ♗e3 e5 9 ♘f5 ♗xf5 10 exf5 ♕a5 10...e4?! **11 0-0-0** 11 ♕xb7 ♘bd7∞ **e4 12 ♕h3** 12 ♘xe4 ♕xa2 13 ♘c3 ♕a1+ 14 ♔d2 ♕xb2 15 ♖b1 ♕a3 16 ♖xb7 d5!∓ Filipowicz-Vogt, Polanica Zdroj 77 **♖c8 13 ♗d4** 13 g4 ♖xc3∞ **♘c6 14 g4?!** 14 ♗c4 ♕b4 15 ♗xf6 ♗xf6 16 ♗b3 ♘d4 17 ♘d5 Sigurjonsson-Malich, Telex 78; 17... ♖xc2+!? 18 ♔b1 ♘xb3! 19 ♘xf6+! gxf6 20 ♔xc2 ♖c8+ 21 ♔b1 ♘d2+ 22 ♔a1 ♖c2 23 ♕a3! += **♘xd4∓ 15 ♖xd4 ♕b6 16 ♖d2** 16 ♖d1 ♕f2∓ **d5 17 ♘xd5** 17 g5 e3 18 ♖d3 d4 19 ♘a4 ♕c6 −+ **♘xd5 18 ♖xd5 ♕f2 19 ♕b3** 19 ♖d2 ♕xf4 △ ♗g5 −+ **e3 20 ♕d3 ♖d8 21 c4 ♖xd5 22 ♕xd5** 22 cxd5 ♕e1+ 23 ♕d1 ♖c8+ −+; 23 ♔c2 ♖c8+ 24 ♔b3 ♕b4 mate **♖d8 0-1 Knaak/Malich**

188 Gaprindashvili-Miles
Wijk aan Zee 79

1 e4 c5 2 ♘f3 e6 3 ♘c3 a6 4 g3 b5 5 ♗g2 ♗b7 6 d3 ♘c6 7 0-0 d6 8 ♖e1 ♘f6 9 e5 dxe5 10 ♘xe5 ♕c7 11 ♘xc6 11 ♗f4 ♗d6=; 11 ♕f3 ♘d8= **♗xc6 12 a4 ♖c8?** 12...♖d8 13 axb5 axb5 14 ♖a7!?∞; 12...b4= **13 axb5 axb5 14 ♗f4± ♕b7** 14...♗d6 15 ♗xc6+ ♕xc6 16 ♗xd6 ♕xd6 17 ♘xb5 ♕b6± **15 ♗xc6+ ♖xc6** 15...♕xc6 16

♖a5! b4 17 ♘b5 ±/+− **16 ♕f3! b4 17 ♖a7 ♕xa7 18 ♕xc6+ ♕d7 19 ♕a8+ ♕d8 20 ♕a4+ ♕d7 21 ♘b5 ♗e7** 21... ♘d5 22 ♕a8+ ♕d8 23 ♖a1 +− **22 ♘c7+ ♔f8**

23 ♕xd7? 23 ♕a8+ ♕d8 24 ♖a1 ±/+−; 23...♗d8 24 ♖a1 ♘h5 25 ♗e5 f6 26 ♖a7! fxe5 27 ♘xe6+ ♔xe6 28 ♕xd8+ ♔e8 29 ♕d6+ ♔g8 30 ♕d5+ +− **♘xd7 24 ♖a1 g5! += 25 ♗e3 ♔g7 26 ♖a7 ♖d8 27 ♘a6 ♔g6 28 ♖b7 ♗d6! 29 d4 cxd4 30 ♗xd4 ♘b8!= 31 ♗xb8** 31 ♘xb4? ♗xb4 32 ♖xb4 ♘c6 −+ **♖xb8 32 ♖xb8 ♗xb8 ½-½ Miles**

189 Botterill-Speelman
Hastings 78/9

1 e4 c5 2 ♘f3 e6 3 d3 d5 4 ♕e2 ♗e7 5 g3 ♘f6 6 ♗g2 ♘c6 7 0-0 b6 8 e5 ♘d7 9 c4! ♘f8!? 10 h4 h6 11 ♘c3 ♗b7 12 ♖e1 12 ♖d1! (△ d4) d4 13 ♘b5 a6 14 ♘a3 f5 15 exf6 gxf6 += **♕d7 13 ♗f4?!** 13 b3 **d4 14 ♘b5?** 14 ♘e4 ♘g6 =+; 14 ♖b1! a6 15 ♘a3 △ 16 ♗d2 g5 17 h5, ♘h2-g4 **g5! 16 hxg5 ♘g6 17 ♗d2 hxg5 18 ♗xg5 0-0-0! 19 ♗f6 ♖h6 20 ♘d2?** 20 ♕d2 ♖h5 21 g4 ♖h7 22 ♘g5 ♖h4∓; 21... ♗xf6 22 gxh5 ♘gxe5 23 ♕f4 ♖g8 −+; 20 ♘b1!? △ ♘d2-e4 **♖g8! 21 ♕g4** 21 f4 ♘xf4 −+; 21 ♘e4 ♘gxe5 22 ♗xe5 ♘xe5 23 ♘xc5 bxc5 24

122

♕xe5 f5! −+ ♘cxe5! −+ 22 ♗xe5 ♗xg2
23 f3 23 ♔xg2 ♘h4+ **f5 0-1 Botterill**

190 Biyiasas-Suba
Hastings 78/79
**1 ♘f3 c5 2 g3 b6 3 ♗g2 ♗b7 4 0-0
♘f6 5 d3 d5?** 5...g6 **6 ♘bd2 g6 7 e4
dxe4? 8 dxe4!±** 8 ♘g5 ♗g7 9 ♘gxe4
Lein-Suba, Hastings 78/79 ♕c8 **9 e5
♘h5 10 ♖e1 ♘g7 11 ♘e4 h6 12
b4! +−** cxb4 **13 ♗b2 ♗e6 14 ♘d4
♘a6 15 ♘xe6** 15 ♕d3 ♘ac7 **fxe6 16
♕g4 ♕f7 17 ♖e3** 17 ♘d6+! exd6 18
♗xb7 ♕xb7 19 exd6 ♘c5 20 ♗xh8
♗xd6 21 ♗d4 +− **♖h7!±** **18 ♖ae1**
18 ♖f3+ ♔g8 19 ♕xg6+ ♖g7 Δ ♗xe4
−+ **♘c5 19 ♘xc5 bxc5 20 ♗xb7
♕xb7 += 21 ♖f3+ ♔g7 22 ♖d3** 22
♖f6? exf6 23 exf6+ ♔h8 24 f7+ e5!!
Csom −+; 24...♗g7 25 ♕xe6 ♖f8 26
♕e8 +− **♕c6 23 ♕c4 ♔g8 24 ♕g4**
♖g7 **25 ♖ed1 c4 26 ♖d4 ♖c8= 27
♗c1 ♔h7 28 h4 ♖f7 29 ♕e4 a5 30
♗e3 ♗g7 31 f4 ♕xe4= 32 ♖xe4 g5
33 hxg5 hxg5 34 ♖d7 gxf4 35 gxf4
♔g6 36 ♖a7 ♔f5 37 ♖d4 ♗h6 38
♖xa5 ♖g7+ 39 ♔f2 b3 40 axb3 cxb3
41 cxb3 ♔g4 42 ♖aa4 ♖c3 43 ♖ac4!?
=+** 43 ♖ab4 ♖h4 44 ♖b7 ♖h2+ 45
♔g1 ♖e2 46 ♗d2 ♖c2 47 ♖bd7 ♖b2
48 ♔f1 ♖h2 49 ♔g1 ½-½ **Suba**

191 Makropoulos-Gheorghiu
Balkaniad 78
**1 e4 c5 2 g3 g6 3 ♗g2 ♗g7 4 d3 ♘c6
5 f4 d6 6 ♘h3!?** 6 ♘f3; 6 ♘c3∞ **e5!
7 c3!?** 7 0-0∞ **exf4! 8 ♘xf4** 8 gxf4??
♗xh3 9 ♗xh3 ♕h4+ −+ **♘ge7 9 ♗e3
♖b8 10 0-0 0-0 11 a4** 11 d4 cxd4 12
cxd4 ♕b6!∓ **a6 12 ♘a3 b5 13 axb5
axb5 14 d4 =+ b4 15 ♘c4!?** 15 ♘c2!
bxc3 16 bxc3 cxd4 17 cxd4 ♘b4!∓
Δ d5 **18 ♘a5!? ♗a6 19 ♖f2 ♕c7
20 ♖b2 ♖fc8** Δ ♘c2, ♕c3∓ **21 ♗h3**

21...♘c2!! −+ 22 ♖xc2 22 ♗xc8
♖xb2! 23 ♗xa6 ♘xe3∓; 22 ♖xb8
♖xb8∓ **♕xc2 23 ♗xc8 ♕xc8! 24
♖c1 ♕e8!** Δ ♘f5 −+ **25 ♖c7 ♘f5! 26
♗f2** 26 exf5 ♕xe3+ −+ **♕xe4 27
♖a7 ♖b1! 0-1 Gheorghiu**

192 Rickford-Browne
Lone Pine 78
**1 g3 c5 2 ♗g2 g6 3 e4 ♗g7 4 f4 ♘c6
5 ♘e2** 5 ♘f3 d5 **e6** 5...♘f6? **6 e5
6 d3 ♘ge7 7 0-0 0-0 8 g4 f5!** 8...d5
9 f5! exf5 10 gxf5 gxf5 11 exd5
♘xd5 **9 ♘g3 d5 10 gxf5** 10 h3!?
**exf5! 10...gxf5? 11 ♘h5 += 11 e5
d4!** 11...♗e6?! 12 c3! d4 13 c4 +=
12 ♘a3 ♗e6 13 ♘c4 ♘d5 13...♗xc4?
14 dxc4 +=; 13...b5 14 ♘d6 ♖b8
15 a4 a6 16 axb5 axb5 17 ♖a6 ♖b6
18 ♖xb6 ♕xb6 19 ♗d2 ♘c8 =+ **14
a4 ♕h4 15 ♗d2** 15 ♕e1 ♖ae8? 16
♘d6 ♖e7?? 17 ♘gxf5! +−; 15...♘cb4
16 ♕f2 ♗h6∓ **♗h6 16 ♘e2 ♖ad8!**
16...♖ae8? 17 ♘d6 ♖e7 18 ♖f3!
17 ♖f3 ♕e7 18 ♖h3 ♗g7 19 ♗e1?
19 ♖g3! **g5! 20 ♕d2** 20 fxg5 f4 −+
♔h8 21 ♖h5 ♗xf4! 21...g4? 22 ♗h4?
♕f7 23 ♗xd8 ♕xh5 24 ♗g5 h6 −+;
22 ♘d6! **22 ♘xf4 gxf4 23 ♗h4** 23
♕xf4 ♗xc4 24 ♗h4? ♕f7 −+; 24 dxc4
♗xe5 25 ♕h4 ♗f6∓ **♕f7 24 ♕e2 ♖d7
25 ♘d6 ♕g8 26 ♗h3?** 26 ♖g5 ♘xe5
−+ **♗xe5+ 27 ♖g5 ♖g7 −+ 28 ♕h5**

♗xd6 29 ♕f2 ♗e7 30 ♖xg7 ♕xg7
31 ♖g1 ♕f7 32 ♕h6 ♗xh4+ 33 ♕xh4
♘e5 34 ♕xf4 ♘g4+ 0-1 Browne

3 ♗b5

√193 Kapengut-Mochalov Minsk 79
**1 e4 c5 2 ♘f3 ♘c6 3 ♗b5 ♘f6 4 ♘c3
♘d4 5 e5 ♘xb5 6 ♘xb5 ♘d5 7 0-0
a6 8 c4! ♘b6?** 8...♘b4!? 9 ♘c3 d6
10 exd6 ♕xd6 11 ♘e4 ♕c7 12 d4
cxd4 13 ♖e1 ♗g4 14 ♕a4+ ♘c6 15
♘xd4 0-0-0 16 ♘xc6 ♕xc6 17 ♕xc6+
bxc6 18 ♗e3 e6 19 ♗b6 ♖d7 20
f3 ♗f5 21 ♖ad1 ♗xe4 22 ♖xd7 ½-½
Tukmakov-Sveshnikov, Ashkabad 78
9 ♘c3 d6?! N 9...d5 10 d4! e6 11
♗g5 ♕d7 12 cxd5 ♘xd5 13 ♘xd5
♕xd5 14 dxc5 ♗xc5 15 ♕c2± Sax-
Sveshnikov, Hastings 77/8 **10 d4!
♗g4 11 exd6 exd6 12 ♖e1+ ♗e7
13 ♗g5 f6 14 ♗f4± ♔f7** 14...0-0
15 dxc5 dxc5 16 ♕xd8 ♗xd8 17
♗d6 ♘xc4 18 ♗xc5 +- **15 dxc5 dxc5
16 ♕b3 g5** 16...♗d7? 17 ♖xe7+
♔xe7 18 ♕xb6 +-; 16...♖e8 17
♖ad1 ♗d7 18 a4 a5 19 ♘b5 +- **17
♖ad1 ♘d7 18 ♘d5 ♖e8 19 ♕d3!
+- ♘f8** 19...♔g7 20 ♘c7 ♕c8 21
h3 ♗xf3 22 ♕xf3 ♗f8 23 ♗g3 +-
**20 ♗xg5! ♘g6 21 ♖xe7+! ♖xe7
22 ♗xf6 1-0 Kapengut**

√194 Kindermann-Fleck BRD 78
**1 e4 c5 2 ♘f3 ♘c6 3 ♗b5 g6 4 0-0
♗g7 5 c3 ♘f6 6 ♖e1 0-0 7 d4 cxd4
8 cxd4 d5 9 e5 ♘e4 10 ♘c3 ♘xc3
11 bxc3 a6?!** 11...♘a5 12 ♕a4 a6
13 ♗f1 ♗g4 += Sax-Janosevic, Italy
74 **12 ♗d3 ♘a5 13 ♘g5!** △ e6 **h6**
13...f6? 14 ♘xh7 ♔xh7 15 ♕h5+
14 ♘f3 △ e6, ♗xg6 **♗e6** 14...♔h7
15 e6! ♗xe6 16 ♗xg6+! ♔xg6 17
♕d3+; 14...♗g4 15 h3 **15 ♘h4! ♖c8**

16 f4! ♖xc3 17 f5 gxf5 17...♕b6 18
♗e3 **18 ♗xf5 ♖c6! 19 ♗e3** 19 ♕h5
♕b6 20 ♗e3 ♘c4≈ ♕c8! **20 ♗xe6
♕xe6 21 ♖g3** 21 ♕h5 f5 22 exf6?
♖xc1+! -+ **♖fc8** 21...♔h7 22 ♕d3+
♔h8 23 ♗d2! ♘c4 24 ♖xg7! ♔xg7
25 ♗xh6+!! ♔xh6 26 ♘f5+ ♔g6 27
♕g3+ ♔xf5 28 ♖f1+ ♔e4 29 ♖f4
mate; 21...♔h8 22 ♕h5 ♖g8 23 ♘f3
♖f8 24 ♗f4 △ ♖f1± **22 ♗d2** 22 ♗xh6
♕xh6 23 ♘f5 ♕c1 24 ♖xg7+ ♔f8 +=
b6! 22...♘c4 23 ♗xh6! +- **23 ♕h5
♘c4 24 ♗f4!** 24 ♘f5 ♗xd2! 25 ♖xg7+
♔f8≈; 25 ♘xg7? ♖c1+ 26 ♖xc1
♖xc1+ 27 ♔f2 ♘e4+ △ ♘xg3 -+
♕h8 25 ♖f1 b5 25...♖g8 26 ♘f5 ♗f8
27 ♖xg8+ ♔xg8 28 ♗xh6! ♗xh6 29
♘xh6+ ♔xh6 30 ♕xf7+ ♔h8 31
♕e8+ ♔h7 32 ♖f7+ ♔g6 33 ♖f6+ +-

26 ♖xg7! ♔xg7 27 ♗xh6+ 1-0 27...
♔h8 28 ♘f5 (△ ♗g7+, ♕h8 mate)
28...f6 29 ♕g6 ♖g8 30 ♗g7+ ♖xg7
31 ♕xg7 mate **Kindermann**

4...♕b6

195 Kavalek-Hubner
Buenos Aires 78
**1 e4 c5 2 ♘f3 ♘c6 3 d4 cxd4 4 ♘xd4
♕b6!? 5 ♘b3 ♘f6 6 ♘c3 e6 7 ♗d3 ♗e7
8 ♗e3 ♕c7 9 f4 d6 10 ♕f3 a6 11 g4**
11 0-0 b5 12 ♖ae1 ♗b7 += **b6** △

♘d7-c5 **12 g5 ♘d7 13 0-0-0 ♘c5 14 ♔b1 ♗d7** 14...♘xd3 15 cxd3 Δ ♖c1± **15 h4 ♕b7!? 16 ♗e2 ♘a7 17 f5! ♘b5 18 ♗d4! ♗c6** 18...♘xd4 19 ♘xd4 e5 20 ♘b3 += **19 fxe6 ♘xc3+** 19... ♘xe6 20 ♘xb5 axb5 21 ♗c3± **20 ♗xc3 ♘xe6 21 ♖hf1 0-0 22 ♗d3 b5 23 a3 ♘c5 24 ♘xc5 dxc5 25 ♕f5! ♖ae8** 25...g6?? 26 ♕e5 +−

26 ♗xg7!! +− ♗d7 26...♔xg7 27 e5 +− **27 ♕e5 ♗d8 28 ♕d6!!** 28 ♕c3 b4∞ **♔xg7 29 ♕h6+ ♔g8 30 e5! f5 31** exf6 **♗e6 32 ♖de1 c4 33 ♗g6! ♖f7 34 ♗xf7+ ♕xf7 35 · g6! ♕xg6 36 f7+! 1-0** 36...♗xf7 37 ♖xe8+ ♗xe8 28 ♖f8 mate; 36...♕xf7 37 ♖g1+
Gheorghiu

5...e5

196 Alexandria-Akhmilovskaya
Piatgorsk 78
1 e4 c5 2 ♘f3 ♘c6 3 d4 cxd4 4 ♘xd4 ♘f6 5 ♘c3 e5 6 ♘db5 d6 7 ♘d5 ♘xd5 8 exd5 ♘b8 8...♘e7 9 c4 ♘f5 10 ♗d3 a6 11 ♕a4! Mestel-Fedorowicz, Hastings 77/8; 10...♗e7 11 0-0 a6 12 ♘c3 0-0 13 a4 Westerinen-Kirpichnikov, Jurmala 78 **9 c4 ♗e7 10 ♗d3 0-0 11 0-0 ♘d7** 11...f5!? **12 ♖b1** 12 ♕c2 g6 13 ♗h6 ♖e8 14 ♗e3 a6 15 ♘c3 f5 16 f3 += **f5= 13**

f3 Δ 14 ♗e3 ♗g5 15 ♗f2; 13 f4 a6 14 ♘c3 g6 15 b4?! b5∓ 16 cxb5 axb5 17 ♗xb5 exf4 18 ♗xf4 ♗f6 Δ ♗xc3, ♕b6+ **a6 14 ♘c3 ♗g5 15 f4** exf4 **16 ♘e2** 16 ♗xf4 ♘e5 17 b4? ♗xf4 18 ♖xf4 ♕b6+ 19 c5 dxc5 20 ♘a4 ♕h6 −+; 19 ♔h1 ♕e3 −+ **f3∓ 17 gxf3** 17 ♖xf3 ♘e5 18 ♖f1 ♗xc1 19 ♘xc1 ♕b6+ 20 ♔h1 ♘g4 **♗xc1 18 ♘xc1** 18 ♕xc1 ♘e5 **f4 19 ♕c2 ♕h4 20 b4?!** 20 ♗e4 Δ ♘d3 **♘e5** Δ 21...♗h3 22 ♖f2 ♘xf3+ 23 ♖xf3 ♕g4+ **21 ♗e4 ♗h3 22 ♖f2 ♖f5? 22...** ♖ae8! 23 ♘d3 ♘g4 **23 ♘d3** 23 ♗xf5? ♘xf3+ 24 ♖xf3 ♕e1+; 24 ♔h1 ♗xf5 −+ **♘xd3 24 ♗xd3 ♖g5+ 25 ♔h1 ♖e8 26 ♗e4 ♗f5** Δ ♖xe4, ♕xf2! −+ **27 ♖bf1 +=♕h5 28 c5 ♕g6 29 ♗xf5 ♖xf5 30 c6 ♖xd5 31 ♕c4** 31 cxb7!? ♕xc2? 32 ♖xc2 ♖b5 33 ♖c7 ♔f8 34 ♖fc1 ♖xb4 35 ♖d7 Δ ♖c8 +−; 33 ♖c8 ♔f7=; 31...♖b5 32 ♔c8 ♕f7 33 ♖e2! ♖f8!=; 33...♔f8? 34 ♖fe1 +−; 32...♕e6 33 ♖c2 ♔f7 34 ♖c7+ ♔f6∞ **♕f7 32 cxb7 ♖b5 33 ♕c6 ♖xb7 34 ♕xd6 ♕c4 35 a3 ♖be8 36 ♖g1 ♖f7** Zeitnot **37 ♖fg2 ♔h8 38 ♖d2 ♕c3 39 ♖d3 ♕c4 40 ♖d4 ♕c3 41 ♖d3 ½-½ Alexandria**

197 Veingold-Levchenkov
USSR 78
1 e4 c5 2 ♘f3 ♘c6 3 d4 cxd4 4 ♘xd4 ♘f6 5 ♘c3 e5 6 ♘db5 d6 7 ♘d5 ♘xd5 8 exd5 ♘e7 9 c3 9 c4 ♘f5 10 ♗d3 ♗e7 11 0-0 0-0 12 ♔h1 a6 13 ♘c3 ♘d4 14 ♗e3± Voronova-Fatalibekova, Moscow 77 **♘g6** 9...♘f5!? **10 ♕a4 ♕e7** 10...♗d7 11 ♕b4 ♗f5 12 ♕c4! ♕e7± Dolmatov-Chekhov, Moscow 77 **11 h4! a6 12 h5 ♘f4 13 ♗xf4 exf4 14 0-0-0 f6 15 ♘d4 ♗d7**

Diagram

**16 ♘c6+! bxc6 17 dxc6 ♗e6 18 ♗c4!
+− ♗xc4 19 ♖he1+! ♗e6** 19...♔f7
20 ♕xc4+ 20 ♕b3 ♔e8 20...♕c8 21
♖xe6+ ♕xe6 22 ♕b7+ ♔e8 23 ♕xa8+
♔f7 24 c7 +−; 22...♔d8 23 c7+ +−
21 ♕xe6+ ♗e7 22 ♖xd6 1-0 Gipslis

**198 Kapengut-Timoshenko
Ashkhabad 78**

**1 e4 c5 2 ♘f3 e6 3 d4 cxd4 4 ♘xd4
♘f6 5 ♘c3 ♘c6 6 ♘db5 d6 7 ♗f4 e5
8 ♗g5 a6 9 ♘a3 b5 10 ♘d5 ♕a5+ 11
♗d2 ♕d8 12 ♗g5** 12 ♘xf6+?! ♕xf6
13 c4 bxc4?; 13...b4 14 ♘c2 ♕g6 15
♕f3 ♖b8 Sorokin-Korchnoi, Leningrad
50; 15 f3 ♖b8 16 ♘e3 ♗e7 17 g3
0-0 18 ♗g2 ♗d8 19 0-0 ♗b6 20 ♔h1
♗c5 21 f4 += Petrushin-Semenuk
76; 13...♕g6 14 f3 ♗e7 15 cxb5?
♗h4+∓ Radulov-Cobo, Havana 69;
15 ♔f2 0-0 16 cxb5 ♘d4 17 ♗e3
f5∓ Kurajica-Radojevic, Sombor 68;
15 g3 0-0 16 cxb5 ♘d4 17 ♗e4 Minic-
Radojevic, Sombor 68, 17...f5!∞; 12
c4!? ♘xe4 13 cxb5 ♘e7 14 ♗e3 ♖b8
15 ♗c4 ♕a5+? 16 b4 +− Mihalchishin-
Timoshenko 73; 15...♗e6 16 0-0
Petrushin-Timoshenko, Tbilisi 73; 16
b6! ♘xd5 17 ♗xd5 ♗xd5 18 ♕xd5
♘f6 19 ♕a5 d5 20 0-0 ♗d6 21 f4±
**♗e7 13 ♗xf6 ♗xf6 14 c3 0-0 15 ♘c2
♖b8** 15...a5 **16 ♗e2 ♗g5 17 0-0 a5**
17...♗e6 **18 b4 ♘e7** 18...axb4 19

♘cxb4 ♘xb4 ½-½ Jansa-Sveshnikov,
Sochi 76; 20 cxb4 ♗e6 21 a4! +=;
18...♗e6 19 a4 bxa4 20 b5 ♘e7 21
c4 ♘xd5 22 cxd5 ♗d7 23 ♘a3 ♕c7
24 ♕xa4 ♕c3 25 ♖ab1 ♕c5 26 ♗d3
♖fc8 27 ♖fd1 g6 28 h3 f5 29 exf5
gxf5 30 ♖b3 ♔h8 31 ♗f1 ♗f6 32
♘c4 ♗d8 Belov-Filipenko 77; 20
♖xa4 axb4 21 cxb4 ♘e7 22 ♗c4 ♘xd5
23 ♗xd5 ♕c7 24 ♖a2 ♔h8 25 ♕d3
f5 26 exf5 ♖xf5 Tseshkovsky-Jusupov,
Ashkhabad 78 **19 ♘xe7+ ♗xe7 20 ♘e3**
+= 20 a4 bxa4 21 b5 ♗e6 22 c4
♕d7 23 ♕d2 ♗d8 24 ♖fd1 ♗b6 25
♖xa4 ♖fd8 26 ♘a1 ♖bc8 Sznapik-
Sveshnikov, Sochi 74 **♗g5 21 ♘d5
♗e6 22 a4 bxa4 23 ♖xa4 axb4 24
cxb4 ♕d7 25 b5 ♗d8! 26 ♖a6?!**
26 ♘b4! += **♗xd5 27 ♕xd5 ♗b6 28
♖d1** 28 ♕c6! += **♖fd8 29 ♗c4 ♗c5
30 g3 g6 31 ♖d3 ♔g7 32 ♖c6 ♔e7
33 ♖f3 ♖f8 ½-½ Kapengut**

199 Klovan-Gaidarov USSR 79

**1 e4 c5 2 ♘f3 ♘c6 3 d4 cxd4 4 ♘xd4
♘f6 5 ♘c3 e5 6 ♘db5 d6 7 ♗g5 a6
8 ♘a3 b5 9 ♗xf6 gxf6 10 ♘d5 f5
11 c3 ♗g7 12 exf5 ♗xf5 13 ♘c2 0-0
14 ♘ce3 ♗e6** 14...♗d7 15 g4 e4 16
♗g2 ♖e8 17 h3?! ♖c8 18 ♕b1 ♘e7!∓
Ostojic-Simic, Jugoslavia Final 77;
17 ♕c2! ♖e8 18 ♗xe4 ♗xg4 19 ♖g1
f5 20 ♖xg4∞ Barle-Ljubojevic,
Jugoslavia 75; 16...f5?! 17 gxf5
♗xf5 18 ♘xf5 ♖xf5 19 ♘e3 ♖e5
20 ♗xe4 ♕h4 21 ♗d5+ ♔h8 22 ♕f3∓
Rodriguez-Bueno, Havana 78 **15 g3!?**
15 g4∞ **f5 16 f4** 16 ♗h3 b4?! 17 0-0
bxc3 18 bxc3 ♕a5 19 ♖b1! ♔h8
20 ♖b7± Sigurjonsson-Rohde, New
York 77; 16...♖b8 17 0-0 ♘e7 +=
**♖a7 17 ♗g2 ♔h8 18 0-0 ♘e7 19 ♕d2
♘g6 20 ♔h1± exf4 21 ♘xf4 ♘xf4
22 ♖xf4 ♗e5 23 ♖f2 ♕g5 24 ♗d5!**

♘xd5 25 ♘xd5 ♕g4 25...♕xd2 26
♖xd2± 26 ♕d3 ♖af7 27 ♖af1 ♕h5
28 ♖f3 ♖g8 29 ♘f4 ♕h6 30 ♘e2 ♕e6
31 a3 ♖gf8 32 ♖1f2 ♔c4 33 ♘f4
♕xd3 34 ♖xd3 ♗xf4 35 ♖xf4± ♖f6
36 ♔g2 ♖e8 37 ♔f2 ♔g7 37...♖fe6
38 ♖d2 38 ♖fd4 ♖ee6 39 a4! ♖e4
40 axb5 ♖xd4 41 ♖xd4 axb5 42
♖b4 ♖h6 43 h4 ♔f6 44 ♔f3 f4 45
♖xf4+ +− ♔e6 46 ♔g4 ♖g6+ 47 ♔h3
♔d5 48 g4 ♖e6 49 g5 ♖e2 50 ♖b4
♔c5 51 ♔g4 d5 52 h5 ♖g2+ 53 ♔f4
♔c6 54 ♔f5 ♖h2 55 h6 ♖f2+ 56 ♔f4!
♖xb2 57 g6 hxg6+ 58 ♔xg6 ♔d6 59
h7 ♖h2 60 ♖f5 1-0 Gipslis

200 Marcovici-Kertesz Jasi 78

1 e4 c5 2 ♘f3 ♘c6 3 d4 cxd4 4 ♘xd4
♘f6 5 ♘c3 e5 6 ♘db5 d6 7 ♗g5 a6
8 ♘a3 b5 9 ♗xf6 9 ♘d5 ♗e7 10
♗xf6 ♗xf6 11 c3 0-0 12 ♘c2 ♖b8;
12...♗g5 gxf6 10 ♘d5 f5 11 c4?!
♕a5+ 12 ♕d2 ♕xd2+ 13 ♔xd2 ♗h6+
14 ♔d1 0-0 15 cxb5 axb5 16 ♗xb5
16 ♘xb5!? ♘d4 17 ♗d3 ♗a6! 18
♗xa6 ♖xa6 19 ♘e7+ ♔h8 20 ♖e1
♖b8! 21 ♘xf5 21 ♘c4 ♖b4!∓ ♘xf5
22 exf5 ♖xb2 23 ♘c2 23 ♘c4 ♖xf2
−+ ♖a5 24 ♖e2 ♖axa2! 25 f6 ♖xa1+
26 ♘xa1 ♖b1+ 0-1 Ciocaltea

201 Stanciu-Urzica
Rumania Final 78
1 e4 c5 2 ♘f3 ♘c6 3 d4 cxd4 4 ♘xd4
♘f6 5 ♘c3 e5 6 ♘db5 d6 7 ♗g5 a6
8 ♘a3 b5 9 ♗xf6 9 ♘d5 ♗e7 10
♘xe7 gxf6 10 ♘d5 f5 11 ♗d3 11 g3
fxe4 12 ♗g2 ♗e6 13 ♗xe4 ♗g7 14 ♕h5
♖c8 15 0-0 ♘e7 16 ♖ad1 ♖c5 Lanka-
Minasian, USSR 78; 11 ♘xb5 axb5
12 ♗xb5 ♗d7 13 exf5 ♖b8 14 a4
♕g5 15 ♘e3 ♘d4 16 ♗xd7+ ♕xd7≈
Bronstein-Kim, USSR 78 ♗e6 12 ♕h5
12 c4 ♕a5+ 13 ♔f1; 12 0-0 ♗g7 13

c4 ♗xd5?; 12 c3 ♗g7 13 0-0 f4 14 c4
bxc4 14...b4 15 ♘c2 a5 16 b3 += 15
♗xc4! 0-0 16 ♖ac1 ♖a7 N 16...♖b8?!
17 b3 ♗xd5 18 ♗xd5 ♘b4? 19 ♖fd1±
♘xa2 20 ♖c6 Stean-Sax, Las Palmas
78 **17 ♖fd1 ♔h8**

18 ♘xf4! exf4 18...♗xc4!? += 19
♗xe6 ♘e7 20 ♗xf7 ♗xb2 21 ♘c4!
♘c8 21...♗xc1 22 ♖xd6! Δ ♕e5
22 ♘xb2 ♖axf7 23 ♘c4 ♕e7 24
♕d5 f3 25 g3 ♕d7 26 ♘e5 ♕h3 27
♘xf7+ 1-0 27...♖xf7 28 ♖xc8+; 27...
♔g7 28 ♕g5+ ♔xf7 29 ♕f5+ **Ciocaltea**

202 Matanovic-Sax
Buenos Aires 78
1 e4 c5 2 ♘f3 e6 3 d4 cxd4 4 ♘xd4
♘f6 5 ♘c3 ♘c6 6 ♘db5 d6 7 ♗f4
e5 8 ♗g5 a6 9 ♘a3 b5 10 ♗xf6 gxf6
11 ♘d5 f5 12 ♗d3 ♗e6! 13 ♕h5!
♗g7 14 0-0 f4! 15 c4 bxc4 15...b4?!
16 ♘c2 += 16 ♗xc4 0-0 17 ♖ac1 ♘e7
18 ♖fd1 ♖c8 19 ♘xe7+ 19 ♖c2!±
Ciocaltea ♕xe7 20 ♕e2 ♔h8!!∞ 21
♗xa6 ♖xc1 22 ♖xc1 f5∓ Ciocaltea
23 exf5 23 ♗d3 fxe4 24 ♗xe4 d5∞
♗xf5 24 ♘b5 e4! 25 ♘c3 ♕g5 26 f3
26 ♘xe4 ♗xe4 27 ♕xe4 f3 −+ **exf3**
27 ♕xf3 ♗g4 28 ♕d5 ♗e5 29 ♘e4
♕g7 30 ♗f1 f3! 31 ♖c2 fxg2 32
♗xg2 ♗f3 −+ 0-1 time 33 ♖f2 ♗d4
Gheorghiu

203 Bondoc Nicolaide Iasi 78

1 e4 c5 2 ♘f3 ♘c6 3 d4 cxd4 4 ♘xd4 ♘f6 5 ♘c3 e5 6 ♘db5 d6 7 ♗g5 a6 9 ♗xf6 gxf6 9 ♘a3 b5 9...d5!? **10 ♘d5 f5 11 ♗d3 ♗e6 12 ♕h5 ♗g7 13 0-0 f4 14 ♖fd1** 14 c4!? **0-0 15 c3 ♗e7!** 15...♖a7 16 ♘c2± **16 ♘c2?!** 16 ♘xe7+ ♕xe7 17 ♘c2 += **♗xd5 17 exd5 f5∓ 18 ♘b4** 18 a4 ♖f6 **19 ♘c6 ♘xc6 20 dxc6 e4 21 ♗c2 ♖c8 22 ♗b3+ ♔h8 23 ♗d5 ♕f8** 24...♖h6 **24 g4?! ♖g6 25 ♔h1 ♗e5!** 25...♖xg4 26 ♗e6!; 25...fxg4 26 ♗xe4± **26 f3 exf3 27 gxf5** 27 ♕xf5!? **♖h6 28 ♕g4** 28 ♕xf3 ♕xf5∓ **f2! 29 ♖d2?** 29 ♗f3!? **♖xh2+!! 30 ♔xh2 f3+ 31 ♔h3 ♕h6+ 32 ♕h4 ♕xd2 -+ 33 ♗xf3 ♕d3** 33...♕e3! **34 ♕xf2 ♖g8** 34...♕xf5+ **35 ♕e2 ♖g3+ 36 ♔h4 ♕xf5 37 ♗g4 ♕f6+ 38 ♔h5 ♕g6+ 0-1 Ciocaltea**

204 Browne-Adorjan IBM 78

1 e4 c5 2 ♘f3 ♘c6 3 d4 cxd4 4 ♘xd4 ♘f6 5 ♘c3 e5 6 ♘db5 d6 7 ♗g5 a6 8 ♗xf6 gxf6 9 ♘a3 b5 10 ♘d5 f5 11 exf5 ♗xf5 12 ♗d3 e4!? 13 ♕e2 ♘d4 14 ♕e3 ♗g7 15 f3 15 ♗xe4 0-0 16 0-0-0 ♗xe4 17 ♕xe4 ♖e8 18 ♕g4 h5! 19 ♕h3 ♕g5+ 20 ♘e3 ♕f6∓ Matulovic-Rajkovic 75; 16 0-0 ♖e8 17 f3 b4 18 ♘xb4? (18 ♘c4!? ♘xc2 19 ♕f4∝ Radev-Georgadze 77) d5! 19 ♘xd5 ♗xe4 20 fxe4 ♕xd5∓ **♕h4+!** 16 g3 ♘xf3+! **17 ♕xf3** 17 ♔f2 ♕d8 18 c3 ♘e5! -+ **exf3 18 gxh4 ♗xd3 19 cxd3 ♗xb2 20 ♔f2** N 20 ♘c2 ♗xa1 21 ♘xa1 ♖c8 22 0-0 ♖g8+ 23 ♔h1 ♖g2∓; 20 ♖b1? ♗xa3 21 ♘c7+ ♔d7 22 ♘xa8 ♗c5! 23 ♖f1 f2+∓; 20 ♖d1 ♗xa3 21 ♘c7+ ♔d7 22 ♘xa8 ♖xa8 =+ **♗xa1** 20...♗xa3!? 21 ♘c7+ ♔d7 22 ♘xa8 ♖xa8 =+ **21 ♖xa1 ♖c8 22 ♖e1+?** 22 ♔xf3 ♖c5 23 ♔e4!∝

22...♕f8? 22...♔d8 23 ♖e7 ♖c5 24 ♖a7 ♖xd5 25 ♖a8+ ♔e7 26 ♖xh8 ♖xd3 27 ♘b1 b4 (27...♖d1!?) 28 ♖g8! a5 ∓/-+ **23 ♕xf3 ♖c5 24 ♘f4 ♖c3 25 ♘b1 ♖c2 26 a3** 26 a4!? **♖g8! 27 h3 ♔g7 28 ♘d5** Zeitnot 28 ♘h5+!? **♖gc8 -+ 29 ♘e7 ♖8c5?!** 29...♖c1 30 ♖e2 ♖e8! **30 d4 ♖c1! 31 ♖e2 ♖f1+ 32 ♔e4** 32 ♔g2 ♖cc1 33 ♘d2 ♖ce1! -+ **♖cc1 33 ♘d2 ♖ce1?** 33...♖fe1! -+ **0-1** time 34 ♘f5+ ♔f6 35 ♘xf1 ♖xe2+ 36 ♘1e3 ∓/∝

Adorjan

4...g6

205 A.Smith-Petersen Corr. 78

1 e4 c5 2 ♘f3 ♘c6 3 d4 cxd4 4 ♘xd4 g6 5 ♘c3 ♗g7 6 ♗e3 ♘f6 7 ♗c4 ♕a5 8 0-0 0-0 9 ♘b3 ♕c7 10 f4 d6 11 ♗e2 a5 11...b6; 11...♖d8 **12 a4 ♘b4 13 ♖f2! +=** ♗e6 14 ♘d4 ♗c4 15 ♗f3 **♖fd8 16 ♖d2 ♕c8 17 ♘db5 ♘d7 18 ♗g4 f5!?** 18...♗xb5? Westerinen-Jansson, Suomi, 69 **19 exf5 ♘f6 20 ♗b6!** N 20 ♗f3 gxf5 21 ♗b6 ♗d7 =+; 20 ♗h3 gxf5 21 ♗b6 ♖f8 22 ♘c7 ♖b8 (∆ ♘a6 =+) 23 ♗xa5? ♘a6 24 ♘xa6 bxa6 25 b4 ♘e4∓; 20 ♗e2 gxf5 21 ♕f1 ♗f7= **gxf5! 20...♘xg4 21 ♕xg4 gxf5** (21...♖f8 22 ♘c7 ♖b8 23 ♖e1±) 22 ♕g5±; 20...♖f8 21 ♘c7 ♖b8 22 ♗e2± **21 ♗xd8 ♕c5+ 22 ♔h1 ♘xg4 23 ♗xe7 ♘f2+ 24 ♖xf2 ♕xf2 25 ♘xd6**

♘xc2?! 25...♕xf4 26 ♘xc4 += **26 ♘xc4 ♘xa1 27 ♘d6!± △ ♕d5+;** 27 ♕xa1? ♗xc3 28 bxc3 ♖e8 −+ **♗xc3 28 bxc3 ♕a2 29 c4 ♕b2 30 h3** 30 ♕d5+ ♔h8 31 ♕e5+ ♔xe5 32 fxe5 ♔g8 ♖a6 += **♘c2?** 30...♔h8 31 ♘xf5 ♖g8 32 ♘h4± △ ♕d6 **31 ♕d5+ ♔h8 32 ♕xf5 1-0** A.Smith/Ciamarra

206 Browne-Whitehead
Lone Pine 78

1 e4 c5 2 ♘f3 ♘c6 3 d4 cxd4 4 ♘xd4 g6 5 c4 ♘f6 6 ♘c3 d6 7 ♗e2 ♘xd4 8 ♕xd4 ♗g7 9 ♗g5 0-0 10 ♕d2 ♕a5 11 ♖c1 ♗e6 12 f3 ♖fc8 13 b3 13 ♘d5!? ♕xd2+ 14 ♔xd2 ♘xd5 15 cxd5 ♗d7 16 ♖xc8+ ♖xc8 17 ♗xe7 ♗h6+ 18 ♔e1 ♖c1+ 19 ♗d1 ♖b1 **a6 14 ♘a4 ♕xd2+ 15 ♔xd2 ♘d7!** N 15...♖c6 **16 ♖c2!?** 16 ♘c3 b5! 17 ♘d5 ♗xd5 18 cxd5 b4! 19 ♖xc8+ ♖xc8 20 ♗xe7?? ♗h6+ 21 ♔d3 ♖c3+ 22 ♔d4 ♗e3 mate **♔f8 17 ♖hc1 ♗d4!** 17...♖c6 18 ♘c3 ♖ac8 19 ♘d5 += **18 ♘c3 f6 19 ♗e3!** 19 ♗h6+ ♔f7 20 h4 ♘e5 21 ♘d5 ♘c6! **♗xe3+ 20 ♔xe3 a5** 20...f5 21 f4 fxe4 22 ♘xe4 ♗f5 23 ♗f3 +=; 20...♘e5 21 f4 ♘c6?! 22 ♘d5± **21 f4 += ♖c5 22 a3** 22 ♘a4 ♖c7 23 c5? ♗xc5 24 ♘xc5 ♖xc5 25 ♖xc5 dxc5 26 ♖xc5 a4 27 ♖b5 ♗xb3!∓ **♘b6 23 ♘d5** 23 ♘b5 ♖ac8 24 ♘d4 ♗f7= **♘xd5+!** 23...♖a6? 24 b4!±; 23...♗xd5? 24 exd5± **24 exd5** 24 cxd5 ♖xc2 25 ♖xc2 ♖c8!= **♗f5 25 ♖c3! b6 26 ♔d4 ♖a7 27 g4 e5+!?** 27...♗d7 28 ♖h3 h5? 29 ♖h4 hxg4 30 ♗xg4 g5 31 fxg5 fxg5 32 ♖f1+ ♔g7 33 ♖h5± 28...♔g7 29 ♖e3 ♔f7 30 ♖ce1 += **28 fxe5 fxe5+** 28...dxe5+? 29 ♔e3 ♗d7 30 b4± **29 ♔e3 ♗c8?!** 30 b4 axb4 31 axb4 ♖cc7 32 c5!± bxc5 33 bxc5 ♖xc5 34 ♖xc5 dxc5 **35 ♖xc5 ♗d7 36 d6!** ♖a3+ 37 ♔e4 ♖a2 38 ♗f3 ♖a3! 39 ♗e2 39

♗d1 ♖a1 40 ♗b3 ♖e1+ 41 ♔d5 ♗xg4 42 ♖b5!? ♖a2 40 ♗c4 ♖xh2= 41 g5 ♖g2? 41...♖h4+! 42 ♔xe5 ♖g4 43 ♔f6 ♖f4+ = **42 ♖c7 ♔e8 43 ♖a7 ♗c6+ 44 ♔xe5 ♖xg5+ 45 ♔e6 ♖g4! 46 ♗b3 ♖e4+ 47 ♔f6 ♖d4 48 ♔e5 ♖e4+ 49 ♔f6 ♖d4 50 ♔e5 ½-½ Browne**

3 ♗b5+

207 Taulbut-Csom Hastings 78/9

1 e4 c5 2 ♘f3 d6 3 ♗b5+ ♘c6 4 0-0 ♗d7 5 ♖e1 a6 6 ♗f1 ♗g4 7 h3 ♗h5?! 8 c3 e6 9 g4! ♗g6 10 d4 h5 11 g5 ♗e7 12 ♗g2 h4 13 d5! ♘e5 14 dxe6 ♘xf3+ 15 ♕xf3?! 15 ♗xf3! fxe6 16 ♕b3+; 15...♗xg5 16 e5± **fxe6 16 c4?!** 16 e5! d5 17 c4 ♗e4 18 ♖xe4 dxe4 19 ♕g4± **e5 17 ♘c3 ♗f7 18 ♘d5! ♗xd5 19 exd5 ♗xg5 20 ♕g4 ♗f6 21 f4 ♕d7 22 fxe5 ♗xe5 23 ♕g6+ ♔d8 23**...♕f7 **24 ♕xd6! +− 24 ♖xe5! dxe5 25 ♕b6+** Zeitnot **♕c7 26 ♗g5+ ♔c8 27 ♕e6+ ♔b8 28 d6 ♕b6 29 ♕f7 ♔a7 30 ♖f1** 30 ♕xg7 ♕xb2 31 ♖f1 ♗h6! **♗h6 31 ♕d5** 31 ♕xg7 ♖ag8 32 ♕xe5± **♖ad8?** 31...♖hd8 32 b4! cxb4+ 33 c5 ♕c6 34 ♕xe5 +−; 32...♖ac8 33 d7 ♖c6 34 b5 +−; 32...♕xb4 33 ♗e4 △ ♖b1 +−

32 d7?? −+ 32 ♗e3 ♖xd6 33 ♕xc5 ♕xc5 34 ♗xc5+ ♖b6 35 a4 a5 36 b4

♔a6 37 b5+ ♔a7 38 ♗d5 ♖d8 39
♔h2 +− ♕c7 33 ♗e3 ♖xd7 34 ♕xc5+
♕xc5 35 ♗xc5+ ♔b8 36 ♗d5 ♖e8
37 ♗e3 ♘g8 38 ♗f7 ♖f8 39 ♗e6 ♖xf1+
40 ♔xf1 ♖d8 41 ♗g5 ♘f6 0-1 Taulbut

208 Gaprindashvili-Djindjihashvili
Wijk aan Zee 79

1 e4 c5 2 ♘f3 d6 3 ♗b5+ ♘c6 4 0-0
♗d7 5 ♖e1 ♘f6 6 c3 a6 7 ♗xc6 N 7
♗a4; 7 ♗f1 ♗xc6 8 d4!? ♘xe4 8...
cxd4 9 cxd4 d5!? 10 e5 ♘e4 11 e6∞;
8...e6 9 d5 ♗d7; 8...g6 9 ♗g5 d5 10
♘bd2 ♗g6?! 10...♗xf3 △ e6= 11
dxc5 e6 12 ♕a4+! ♕d7 13 ♕d4 ♖c8
14 b4 ♗e7 15 a4 0-0 16 ♘c4!? 16
♘e5!? △ ♖e3 dxc4 17 ♕xd7 ♘xd7
18 ♗xe7 ♖fe8 += 19 ♗d6 b6?! 19...
f6 △ e5 20 ♘e5 ♘xe5 21 ♖xe5 bxc5
22 bxc5± ♗c2 23 ♖e2 ♗b3 24 f4!
f6 25 ♕f2 ♔f7 26 ♕e3 e5?! 27 f5!
g6 28 ♕e4 gxf5+ 29 ♔d5! +− f4 30
c6 ♖g8 31 c7 h5 32 ♔c6 ♔e6 33
♗c5 h4 33...♔g7 34 ♗b6 △ ♔b7
34 ♔b7 h3 35 gxh3 f3 36 ♖d2 e4
37 ♖e1 f5 38 ♖d6+ ♔e5 39 ♖xa6
♗c2 40 ♗d4+ ♔d5 41 ♖f6 1-0 41...
♗xa4 42 ♖a1 Miles

209 Adorjan-Radio Listeners
Hungary 78

1 e4 c5 2 ♘f3 d6 3 ♗b5+ ♗d7 4
♗xd7+ ♘xd7 5 0-0 ♘gf6 6 ♕e2 e6 7
c3 ♗e7 8 d4 0-0 9 e5 ♘e8 10 ♖d1!
d5 11 c4! ♘b6 12 cxd5 ♘xd5 13
dxc5 ♗xc5 14 ♘bd2 ♘ec7 14...♘f4?
15 ♕c4 15 ♘e4 ♗e7 16 ♘fg5! h6 17
♘h3 ♕e8! 18 ♕g4 18 ♕h5? f5! f5
18...♔h8 19 ♖d3 △ 20 ♗xh6! gxh6
21 ♕h5 ♔h7 22 ♘hg5+ ♔g7 23 ♖g3
+− 19 exf6 ♘xf6 20 ♘xf6+ ♖xf6
21 ♘f4± ♕a4? 22 h3! △ ♘h5! ♕c2?
23 ♗e3 ♘d5 24 ♘xd5 exd5 25 ♕d7 +−
♕e4 26 ♖d4 ♕e6 27 ♖xd5 ♖d8 28

♕xe6+ ♖xe6 29 ♖xd8+?! 29 ♖ad1
♗xd8 30 ♗xa7?? ♗f6! 31 ♗e3 ♖a6!
32 ♗c1 ♖c6? 32...♖d6! 33 ♔f1 ♖d1+
34 ♔e2 ♖g1 35 g3 ♗g5! 36 f4 ♗f6 △
♗xb2!= 33 ♔f1 ♖c2 34 ♖b1 ♗d4
35 ♗e3 ♗xb2 35...♗xe3 36 fxe3 b5
37 a3 ♔f7 38 b3 ♖a2 39 ♖c1! ♖xa3
40 ♖c3 ±/+− 36 a4 ♔f7 37 a5! ♗c3
38 ♖b5 ♖a2 39 ♗b6 ♕g6 40 ♖d5
△ 41 ♖d7 ♗xa5 42 ♗d4 +− ♕f6 41
♖d7 g6 42 ♗d8+! ♕e6 43 ♖e7+ ♕d6
44 ♖xb7 ♗d4 45 ♗b6! 1-0 Adorjan

210 Botterill-Lein
Hastings 78-9

1 e4 c5 2 ♘f3 d6 3 ♗b5+ ♗d7 4 ♗xd7+
♕xd7 5 c4 ♘c6 5...e5 6 d4 cxd4 7
♘xd4 g6 8 ♘c3 ♗g7 9 ♗e3 ♘f6 9...
♘h6 10 f3 f5 11 ♕d2 ♘f7 12 exf5
gxf5 13 f4 ♗xd4 14 ♗xd4 ♕e6+ 15
♔d1!± Hort-Jansson, Skopje 72; 15
♔f2? ♖g8 16 b3 ♕g6 17 g3 ♘h6∓
Minic-Stein, Zagreb 72 10 f3 0-0 11
0-0 ♖fc8 11...♖ac8 12 b3 e6 13 ♖c1
♖fd8 14 ♕d2 d5!? 15 exd5 exd5
16 c5 += Blau-Fischer, Zurich 59
12 ♘de2 12 b3 ♕c7 13 ♕d2 ♕a5
14 ♖ac1 a6 15 ♘xc6! ♖xc6 16 ♖fd1
Hecht-Sosonko, Amsterdam 2 73;
16...♖ac8!= Hecht b6?! 12...♖ab8
13 ♕d2 ♕d8 Botterill-Hodgson,
England 76 △ a6, ♘d7 13 ♕d2 ♕b7
14 ♖ac1 ♖ab8 15 ♘d5! += ♘e8
15...♘xd5? 16 cxd5 ♘e5 17 b3 △
♘d4± 16 b3 ♖d8 17 ♘d4 ♖d7 18
♘xc6 ♕xc6 19 b4!? ♕a4 19...a6?
20 a4! +−; 19...b5?! 20 a4! bxc4
21 b5± 20 b5 ♘c7 21 ♘b4!?
♕b4 ♕xa2 22 ♖f2 ♘xd5 23 cxd5
♕a5 24 ♕b3 a6!∞; 24 ♕xa5 bxa5
25 ♖a2 += a6 22 ♘c6 ♖b7 22...♖a8?!
23 ♗xb6 axb5 24 c5! ♕xa2 25 ♘xe7+!
♖xe7 26 ♕xa2 ♖xa2 27 cxd6 +−
23 ♖b1! 23 e5 ♘e6! axb5 24 cxb5?

24 ♖b4 ♛a6 25 ♖fb1!± bxc4? 26 ♖xb6 +− ♞xb5 25 ♖fc1 25 ♖b4 ♛a6 26 ♖fb1? ♗c3 −+ h5 26 ♖b4 ♛a6 27 ♛d3 ♞c7= 28 ♛xa6 ♞xa6 29 ♖xb6

29...♗h6! 30 ♞xe7+! ♖xe7 30...♔h7 31 ♗xh6 ♖xb6 32 ♘d5 ♖bb7 33 ♗g5± 31 ♖c8+ ♔h7 32 ♗d4! ♗g7 33 ♗xg7 ♛xg7 33...♖xb6? 34 ♗f6 +− 34 ♖xa6 d5!= 35 ♖c2 dxe4 36 fxe4 ♖xe4 37 g3 h4 38 ♔g2 ♖d7 39 ♖a3 ♖de7 40 ♖ac3 ♖a4 41 a3 ♖ea7 42 ♖a2 f5 43 ♖f3 hxg3 44 hxg3 ♔h6 45 ♖e3 ♔g5 46 ♔f3 ♖7a6 47 ♖b3 ♖c4 48 ♖e3 ♖ca4 49 ♖b3 ♖c6 50 ♖e3 ♖b6 51 ♖c3 ♖b1 52 ♖d3 ♖b6 53 ♖c3 ♖ba6 54 ♖b3 ♔f6 55 ♖e3 g5 56 ♖b3 g4+ 57 ♔g2 ♔g5 58 ♖b5 ♖xa3 59 ♖f2 ♖f6 60 ♖c5 ♖f8 61 ♖b5 ♖a6 62 ♖c5 ♖h6 63 ♖a5 ½-½ Botterill

Najdorf

211 Stanciu-Vaisman
Rumania Final 78

1 e4 c5 2 ♘f3 d6 3 d4 cxd4 4 ♞xd4 ♞f6 5 ♞c3 a6 6 a4 ♞c6 6...e6; 6... g6 7 ♗e2 e5 8 ♞xc6 8...♘b3 bxc6 9 f4 ♛a5! 10 0-0 ♗e7 11 ♗e3 ♖b8 12 ♖b1 ♔b4 12...0-0 13 ♛e1 △ ♘d5 13 ♗f3 ♗e6 14 ♔h1 ♗c4 15 ♖e1 a5 16 ♗d2 ♔b6 17 b3 ♗a6 18 ♞e2! △ 19

fxe5 dxe5 20 ♗c3 ♛c7 21 ♛d2 ♛c7 19 ♞g3 g6 20 ♗e2 ♗c8!? 21 ♖f1 h5! 22 fxe5 dxe5 23 ♗g5 ♞h7 23...♘g4 24 ♗xe7 ♛xe7 25 ♗xg4 ♗xg4; 25... hxg4 24 ♗xe7 ♛xe7 25 ♗c4 ♞g5 26 ♛e1 26 h4? ♘e6 h4 27 ♞e2 h3 27...♖a8!? 28 g3 ♖a8 29 ♛f2

29...0-0 30 ♛e3 ♔g7 31 ♞g1 ♗g4 32 ♗e2 ♗e6 33 ♞f3 ♞xf3 34 ♖xf3 ♖fd8 35 ♖af1 ♖d4 36 ♔g1! ♖ad8 37 g4 ♖h8 38 ♗c4 ♗xc4 39 bxc4 ♖d7 40 ♖xf7+ 40 ♖xh3 ♖xh3 41 ♔xh3 ♛c5+ 42 ♔h1 ♛xc4; 40...♛e6! ♛xf7 41 ♖xf7+ ♖xf7 −+ 42 ♛c3 42 ♛d3 ♖f4! ♖d8! 43 ♛xh3 43 ♛xe5+ ♔h7 44 ♛a1 ♖d2 ♖d1+ 44 ♔g2 ♖d2+ 45 ♔g1 45 ♔g3 ♖df2! ♖b7! 46 ♛f1 ♖b2 47 h4 ♖bxc2 48 h5 48 g5 ♔g8! 49 c5 ♖e2 50 ♔h1 ♖f2 51 ♛g1 ♔g7 Zugzwang gxh5 49 gxh5 ♔h6!! 49... ♖g2+ 50 ♛xg2 ♖xg2+ 51 ♔xg2 ♔h6 52 ♔h3 ♔xh5 53 ♔g3 ♔g5 54 c5= 50 c5 ♖b2! 50...♔xh5? 51 ♛h3+! ♔g5 52 ♛g3+ ♔f6 53 ♛h4+ 51 ♔h1 51 ♛e1 ♖g2+ 52 ♔f1 ♖h2! ♛f2 52 ♛d3 52 ♛g1 ♔xh5 53 ♛d1+ ♔h4 54 ♛e1 ♖be2 ♖bd2 53 ♛e3+ ♔h7! 54 ♔g1 ♖fe2 0-1 Ciocaltea

212 Bielczyk-Pokojowczyk
Slupsk 78

1 e4 c5 2 ♘f3 d6 3 d4 ♞f6 4 ♞c3 cxd4

5 ♘xd4 a6 6 a4 e5 7 ♘f3 7 ♘b3! +=
h6 8 ♗c4 ♕c7 9 ♗a2 ♗e7 10 0-0 0-0
11 ♕e2 ♗e6 12 ♖d1 ♘bd7 13 ♘d2
♖fc8 14 ♘f1 ♕c6 15 f3 ♖ab8 15...b5
16 axb5 axb5 17 ♗d5 += **16 ♘e3
♗d8 17 ♕d3 ♗b6 18 ♕xd6 ♕xd6 19
♖xd6 ♗d4! 20 ♔f1 ♘f8!** 20...♗f8 21
♗xe6 += **21 ♘e2 ♗xe3 22 ♗xe3 ♖xc2
23 ♖d2 ♖bc8 24 ♔e1 ♗xa2 25 ♖xa2
♘e6 26 ♖a3 ♖xd2 27 ♔xd2 ♖c4 ½-½**
Zeitnot 28 ♖b3 += ♖c7! Bielczyk

213 Sequeira-Silva
Portugal Final 78

**1 e4 c5 2 ♘f3 d6 3 d4 cxd4 4 ♘xd4
♘f6 5 ♘c3 a6 6 ♗c4 e6 7 ♗b3 b5 8
0-0 ♗e7 9 ♕f3 ♕c7** 9...♕b6!? **10 ♕g3
♘c6 11 ♘f5!?** N exf5 **12 ♕xg7 ♖f8
13 ♗g5 ♕d8 14 exf5 ♘e5 15 ♘d5
♘xd5 16 ♗xd5 ♗xg5 17 ♗xa8 ♗xf5
18 ♖ae1 ♗f6 19 ♗c6+ ♔e7 20 ♕g3
♖g8 21 ♕e3 ♗e6 22 ♘e4 ♘c4 23 ♕e2
♘xb2 24 ♗d5 ♗e5 25 ♗xe6 fxe6 26
f4 ♗d4+ 27 ♔h1 ♕c8 28 ♕e4 ♕c4?!
29 f5 e5 30 f6+ ♔d8 31 ♕xh7 ♗e6
32 f7 ♖f8 33 ♕g7 ♕e7 34 ♕e4 ♘a4 35
♖h4 ♘c5 36 ♖h6 ♘d7 37 ♕g6 ♗c5**
Zeitnot **38 ♕f5 ♕c7 39 ♖e6 ♕d8 40
♕g6 ♖h8 41 ♖e8? ♖xh2+ 0-1 Ochoa**

214 Fuller-Browne
Buenos Aires 78

**1 e4 c5 2 ♘f3 d6 3 d4 cxd4 4 ♘xd4
♘f6 5 ♘c3 a6 6 ♗c4 b5 7 ♗b3** 7
♗d5!? ♘xd5 8 exd5 g6 **e6 8 0-0 ♗e7
9 ♕f3 ♕c7** 9...♕b6!? **10 ♗e3 ♕b7
10 ♕g3 0-0** 10...♘c6 **11 ♗h6 ♘e8
12 a3 ♗d7!** 12...♘f6!? **13 ♖fe1 ♘c6
14 ♘xc6** 14 ♖ad1 ♗xc6 **15 ♖ad1 a5**
15...♖b8!? **16 ♗g5! ♗xg5** 16...b4?! **
17 axb4 axb4 18 ♘d5! 17 ♕xg5 b4
18 b4 18 axb4 axb4 19 ♘a2! 19**
♘b5?? ♕a5 −+

19...♗a4! =+ 19...♘f6?! 20 f3? ♖xa2∓
21 ♗xa2 ♕a7+; 20 e5! += **20 ♘xb4
♗xb3 21 cxb3 ♕b6 22 ♘d3 ♕xb3 23
e5?! h6?!** 23...d5! 24 ♕e7 ♖c8! 24
♘c5 ♕b5 25 ♕e7 ♕b4!∓ **24 ♕e3!
♖b8!** 24...d5?! 25 ♘c5 ♕b5 26 ♖d3!
♘c7 27 ♖b3 += **25 exd6 ♘xd6 26
♘e5 ♘f5 27 ♕xb3 ♖xb3 28 ♖d2 ♖c8
29 g3? f6!** 30 ♘g4 30 ♘g6 ♔f7 31
♘f4 e5 32 ♖d7+ ♔e8 33 ♖d2 ♖d8∓
**e5 31 ♘e3 ♗xe3 32 ♖xe3 ♖xe3 33
fxe3 ♖b8 34 g4 ♔f7 35 ♔g2 ♔g6 36
♔g3 ♖b3 37 ♔f3 ♔g5 38 ♖d7 g6
39 ♖g7** 39 ♖f7 ♖xb2 40 h4+ ♔xh4
41 ♖xf6 e4+! 42 ♔xe4 ♖b4+ 43 ♔d5
♖xg4∓ **h5 40 gxh5** 40 h4+ ♔h6!
−+ **♔xh5 −+ 41 ♖h7+** 41 h4 ♔h6
42 ♖f7 f5 −+ **♔g5 42 h3! f5?!** 42...
♔f5 −+ **43 h4+ ♔f6 44 ♖c7! ♖xb2
45 ♖c6+ ♔f7 46 ♖c5 ♔f6 47 ♖c6+
♔g7 48 h5! gxh5 49 ♖e6 ♖b5 50 ♔g3
♔f7 51 ♖h6 ♖b3 52 ♔f2 ♖b2+ 53 ♔g3
♖e2 54 ♔f3 ♖h2 55 ♔g3??** 55 e4!!
f4? 56 ♖f6+!=; 55...♖h4 56 exf5 ♖
♖f4+ 57 ♔e3 ♖xf5 58 ♔e4 ♖g5 59
♖a6 ♔g7 60 ♖a7+ ♔h6 61 ♖a8!=
♖h1 56 ♖a6 56 ♔g2 ♖h4 57 ♔g3 ♖g4+
−+ h4+ **57 ♔g2 ♖e1 58 ♔f2 ♖b1
59 ♖h6 ♖b4 −+ 60 ♔f3 ♖g4 61 ♖h5
♔f6 62 ♔f2 ♔e6 63 ♔f3 ♖g3+ 64
♔f2 ♖h3 65 ♖h6+ ♔d5 66 ♖a6 ♖h2+!
67 ♔f3 e4+ 68 ♔f4 ♖f2+ 69 ♔g5 h3
70 ♖h6 h2 71 ♖h3 ♔c4 72 ♔f6**

♕d3 73 ♔e5 ♔e2 0-1 Browne

215 Skrobek-Schurade DDR 78

**1 e4 c5 2 ♘f3 d6 3 d4 cxd4 4 ♘xd4
♘f6 5 ♘c3 a6 6 ♗c4 e6 7 ♗b3 b5 8
0-0 ♗e7** 8...♗b7 9 ♖e1 ♘c6!? 10 a4
b4 11 ♘xc6 ♗xc6 12 ♘d5 ♗e7 13
♘xe7 ♕xe7 14 ♗g5 0-0= Skrobek-
Szilagy 78, 9...♘bd7 **9 f4 0-0** 9...♗b7
10 e5 dxe5 11 fxe5 ♗c5 12 ♗e3 ♘c6
13 exf6 ♗xd4 14 ♕e1 ♗xe3+ 15
♕xe3 ♕d4 16 ♖ae1 +=; 12...♘d5 13
♗xd5 ♗xd5 14 ♘f5 +=; 12...♘fd7
13 ♖xf7 ♔xf7 14 ♕g4! +=; 11...♘fd7
12 ♖xf7 ♔xf7 13 ♘xe6 ♔b6+ 14 ♔h1
♔e8 15 ♘xg7+ ♔d8 16 e6 += **10 a3**
10 f5 b4!; 10 e5!? dxe5 11 fxe5
♘fd7 12 ♔h5!? **♗b7 11 f5! e5 12 ♘de2
♘xe4** 12...♘bd7 13 ♘g3 ♖c8 14
♗g5 a5 15 ♗xf6 ♘xf6 16 ♘h5 ♘xh5
17 ♕xh5 b4 18 axb4 axb4 19 ♘d5
♗xd5=; 13...♘c5 14 ♗d5 ♗xd5 15
exd5 ♖c8 16 ♗g5 ♘cd7 17 ♗xf6 ♘xf6
18 ♘ce4 ♖c4 19 ♕d3! += **13 ♘xe4
♗xe4 14 ♘g3 ♗b7** 14...d5!? 15 ♘xe4
dxe4 16 ♗d5 += **15 ♘h5** 15 f6!? ♗xf6
16 ♘h5 ♔h8!∞; 16...♘d7 17 ♕g4 g6
18 ♕xd7 +– **♗f6 16 ♕g4 ♔h8 17
♗xf6 gxf6** 17...♕xf6? 18 ♗g5 +–
**18 ♖f2! ♘d7 19 ♔h5 ♔b6 20 ♗xf7
♖xf7 21 ♔xf7 ♖g8 22 ♔f1 ♔c6 23
♗e3 ♖xg2 24 ♖xg2 ♕xg2+ 25 ♔e1
♔h1+** 25...♗f3 26 ♔e8+ ♔g7 27
♕xd7+ ♔g8 28 ♕c8+ ♔f7 29 ♕c7+
♔e8 30 ♕b8+ ♔d7 31 ♔a7+ ♔e8 32
♗f2 ♔h1+ 33 ♗g1 +– **26 ♔d2 ♕g2+
27 ♔c3 ♕c6+ 28 ♔b3 ♕d5+ 29 ♕xd5
♗xd5+ 30 ♔c3 ♗e4 31 a4 ♗xf5 32
axb5 axb5 33 ♖d1 ♘c5 34 ♗xc5 dxc5
35 ♖f1 1-0 Bielczyk**

216 Sigurjonsson-Portisch
Buenos Aires 78

1 e4 c5 2 ♘f3 d6 3 d4 cxd4 4 ♘xd4

**♘f6 5 ♘c3 a6 6 ♗e2 e5 7 ♘b3 ♗e7 8
0-0 ♗e6 9 f4 ♕c7 10 a4 ♘bd7 11 ♗e3**
11 f5 ♗c4 12 a5∞ **0-0 12 f5 ♗c4 13
a5 ♖fc8 14 ♔h1** 14 ♖a4!? **♗xe2 15
♕xe2 d5!∞ 16 exd5** 16 ♘xd5? ♘xd5
17 exd5 ♖xc2∓ **♗b4 17 ♗d2 ♗xc3
18 ♗xc3 ♘xd5 19 ♖f3 ♖e8!** △ e4∓
**20 ♖a4 ♘7f6! 21 ♘d2 ♕d7 22 ♖h4
♘xc3 23 bxc3** 23 ♖xc3 ♕xf5∓ **e4!
24 ♖f1 ♕c6 25 h3 e3! 26 ♘c4 ♗e7
27 ♖f3** 27 ♘xe3 ♖ae8 **♖ae8 28 ♖d4**
28 ♖xe3 ♖xe3 29 ♘xe3 ♕xc3 –+
♘d5 29 f6 ♖e4! –+

30 ♖g3 30 fxg7? ♘xc3 –+ **g6 31 ♖g4
♖xg4 32 hxg4 ♘xc3 0-1 Gheorghiu**

217 Hartston-Csom
Hastings 78/9

**1 e4 c5 2 ♘f3 d6 3 d4 cxd4 4 ♘xd4
♘f6 5 ♘c3 a6 6 ♗e3 e5 7 ♘b3 ♗e7
8 ♕d2 ♗e6 9 f3** △ ♘d5 **♘bd7 10 g4**
10 0-0-0? b5 11 g4 ♘b6 =+ **h6** 10...
♖c8 11 g5 ♘h5 12 ♖g1 (12 0-0-0
♘f4!?) 0-0 13 0-0-0 b5 14 ♘d5 ♗xd5
15 exd5 ♘b6 16 ♘a5!? ♘xd5 17 ♕xd5
♕xa5 18 ♗d3∞ Eales-de Fotis, Graz
72; 10...♘b6 11 g5 ♘fd7 12 0-0-0
♕c7 13 h4 0-0-0 14 ♘d5 ♗xd5 15
exd5 += Hartston-Browne, Hastings
72/3; 10...b5 11 a4 b4 12 ♘d5 ♗xd5
13 exd5 ♘b6? 14 a5! ♘bxd5? 15 g5
♘xe3 16 gxf6 ♘xf1 17 fxe7 +– **11**

♘d5 11 0-0-0 b5 12 ♘d5 ♗xd5 13 exd5 ♘b6 =+ **♗xd5 12 exd5 ♘h7** 12... ♘b6 13 c4 ♘fd7!? **13 0-0-0 ♗g5** △ ♗xe3, ♕g5 **14 ♔b1 ♗xe3 15 ♕xe3 ♕b6 16 ♘d2 ♘hf6 17 ♗e2** 17 h4 **♖c8 18 h4 ♘c5 19 ♘xc5 ♕xc5 20 c4 ♖c7 21 ♖c1 ♘d7 22 g5 ♘f8 23 f4 ♘g6 24 fxe5** 24 f5? **♘xe5 25 ♖hf1 hxg5 26 ♕xg5 f6 27 ♕f4 ♖e7 28 h5 ♘f7 29 ♕g4 ♘e5 30 ♕f4 ♘f7 31 ♕g4 ♘e5** ½-½

218 Kapengut-Savon Ashkabad 78
1 e4 c5 2 ♘f3 d6 3 d4 cxd4 4 ♘xd4 ♘f6 5 ♘c3 a6 6 f4 ♕c7 7 ♗d3 e5 8 ♘f3 ♗e7 9 0-0 ♘bd7 10 ♕e1 b5 11 ♔h1 0-0 12 fxe5 dxe5 13 ♗g5 13 a3 ♗b7 14 ♘h4 g6 15 ♗g5 ♔g7 16 ♕d2 ♘g8 17 ♘f5+ gxf5 18 ♗xe7 ♘xe7 19 ♕g5+ ♘g6 Troianescu-Sajtar 59 **b4** 13...♗b7 14 ♘h4 g6 15 ♘f5 gxf5 16 ♖xf5 b4 17 ♘e2 ♖fe8 18 ♕h4 ♗d8 19 ♖af1 ♖e6 20 ♖1f3 ♕c6 21 ♖g3 ♘xe4 Ghizdavu-Munteanu 71 **14 ♘d5!± N** 14 ♘d1 ♘c5 15 ♘e3 ♗e6 16 ♗xf6 ♗xf6 17 ♗c4 ♗xc4 18 ♘xc4 ♕b7 19 ♕e3 ♘a4= Bronstein-Boleslavsky, Grozny 60; 14...h6 15 ♗h4 ♘c5 16 ♗xf6 ♗xf6 17 ♕xb4 ♗e6 18 b3 ♖fd8 19 ♘f2 ♖ac8 20 ♕d2 a5∞ Miles-Marjanovic, Teesside 73 **♘xd5 15 exd5 f6** 15...♗xg5 16 ♘xg5 g6 17 ♕h4 h5 18 ♘xf7! +– **16 ♕e4 g6** 16...f5 17 ♕c4! ♗d6 18 ♗e7!± **17 ♗h6 ♗b7!±** 17...♖d8 18 d6 ♗xd6 19 ♕d5+ ♔h8 20 ♕f7 ♖g8 21 ♘h4 +– **18 ♗xf8 ♖xf8 19 ♕e2 a5 20 ♖ad1 ♗d6 21 h3 ♘c5 22 ♗b5 ♕e7 23 ♘d2! f5 24 ♘c4 ♘e4 25 ♖f3 ♕c7 26 ♘xd6 ♕xd6 27 c4?** 27 c3± **♘c5 +=/∞ 28 a3 e4 29 ♖e3 ♗c8 30 axb4 axb4 31 ♕e1** 31 g3 g5∞ **f4 32 ♖xe4 ♗xe4 33 ♕xe4 f3! 34 ♖f1 fxg2+ 35 ♕xg2?=** 35 ♔xg2! ♗xh3+! 36 ♔xh3

♖xf1 37 c5! ♕f6 38 ♗xf1 ♕xf1+ 39 ♔h4 ♕f2+ 40 ♔g5 ♕xc5 41 ♕e6+ ♔g7 42 ♕d7+ ♔g8 43 ♕f6 ♕f2+ 44 ♔e7± ♖xf1+ 36 ♕xf1 ♕g3 37 ♕g2 ♕e1+ 38 ♔h2 ♕e5+ 39 ♔g1 ♕e1+ 40 ♕f1 ♕g3+ 41 ♕g2 ♕e1+ ½-½ Kapengut

219 Kapengut-Zilberstein Minsk 79
1 e4 c5 2 ♘f3 d6 3 d4 cxd4 4 ♘xd4 ♘f6 5 ♘c3 a6 6 f4 ♕c7 7 ♗d3 g6 8 0-0 ♗g7 9 ♔h1 0-0 10 a4 b6 10... ♘bd7 11 a5 ♘c5 12 f5 e5 13 fxe6 ♘xe6! 14 ♗e3 ♗d7 15 ♕d2 ♖ae8 16 ♘xe6 ½-½ Kapengut-Juferov, Minsk 79; 11 f5!? ♘e5 12 ♗g5 e6 13 ♕d2 ♗d7 14 ♖ad1 ♖ac8 15 ♕f4!? ♕b6 16 ♘b3 ♘h5 17 ♕h4 ♘xd3 18 ♖xd3± Kapengut-Gofstein, Frunze 77 **11 ♕e2 ♗b7 12 f5 ♘bd7 13 ♗g5 ♘e5 14 ♖ad1 ♕d7 15 ♘f3! ♘fg4 16 ♘xe5 ♘xe5 17 ♕f2 ♗c6! 18 ♗e2 b5 19 axb5 axb5 20 b4!? ♖fc8 21 f6! exf6 22 ♗xf6 ♗xf6 23 ♕xf6 ♖d8 24 ♘d5 ♗xd5 25 ♖xd5 ♕e6 26 h3 ♕xf6 27 ♖xf6 ♖a2 28 ♗d3!?** 28 ♖fxd6 ♖xd6 29 ♖xd6 ♖xc2 30 ♗xb5 ♖b2 31 ♖d5 f6 32 ♖d8+ ♔g7 33 ♖d4 += **♘xd3 29 cxd3 ♖c8 30 ♖xb5 ♖c1+ 31 ♔h2 ♖cc2** 31...h6! 32 ♖f3 += **32 ♖g5 ♖ab2 33 b5 h6 34 ♖g3 ♖xb5 35 ♖xd6 ♖bb2?** 35...♖e2! += **36 e5 ♖e2 37 e6!± fxe6 38 ♖xg6+ ♔f7 39 ♖g4 h5 40 ♖g5 ♔f6 41 h4 ♖bd2 42 ♖d8 ♔e7 43 ♖dg8! ♖xd3 44 ♖xh5 ♔f7 45 ♖gg5 ♔e7 46 ♖h7+ ♔f6 47 ♖h6+ ♔f7 48 h5 ♖d5 49 ♖h7+ ♔f8 50 ♖xd5 exd5 51 ♖d7 +– ♖e5 52 g4 ♔e8 53 ♖a7 ♖e6! 54 g5! ♖e5 55 ♖g7 d4 56 h6 ♔f8 57 ♔g3 d3 58 ♔f4 ♖d5 58...d2 59 ♖d7 59 ♖a7 ♔g8 59...d2 60 h7 ♖d4+ 61 ♔e3 ♖d3+ 62 ♔f2 60 g6 ♖d4+ 60... ♖d8 61 h7+ ♔h8 62 ♔g5 d2 63 ♔h6 d1♕ 64 g7 mate 61 ♔e3 ♖d8 62 ♔d2 ♔h8 63 ♖f7 1-0 Kapengut**

220 Vitolins-Arakas USSR 78
**1 e4 c5 2 ♘f3 d6 3 d4 cxd4 4 ♘xd4
♘f6 5 ♘c3 a6 6 ♗g5 ♘bd7 7 f4!?**
7 ♗c4 ♕a5 8 ♕d2 e6 9 0-0-0 b5 10
♗b3 ♗b7 11 ♖he1 0-0-0 12 a3 ♔b8
13 f4 ♖c8 14 ♖e3± Matulovic-Baretic,
Jugoslavia 77 **♕b6 8 ♕d2!** 8 ♘b3
h6 9 ♗h4 ♕e3+ 10 ♗e2 ♕xf4 11
♗g3 ♕e3 12 ♘d5 ♘xd5 13 exd5 ♘f6
14 ♗f2 ♕e5 15 c4 g6∞ **♕xb2 9 ♖b1
♕a3 10 ♗xf6! gxf6** 10...♘xf6 11
e5!± **11 ♘d5 ♖b8 12 ♖b3 ♕a4** 12...
♕xa2!? ±/∞

13 ♗xa6! N 13 ♖b4 ♕a5 14 f5 ♘e5?
15 ♗xa6 h5 16 ♗b5+ ♗d7 17 ♗xd7+
♘xd7 18 ♘c6! +– Rogulj-Nemet,
Jugoslavia 77; 14...h5!? **bxa6 14 ♕c3!**
+– Δ ♖xb8 **♕xb3** 14...♖xb3?? 15
♕xc8 mate **15 cxb3 ♗b7 16 ♘c7+ ♔d8
17 ♕a5 ♔c8 18 0-0?!** 18 ♘e8! +–
**♗xe4 19 ♖c1 ♘c5 20 b4 e5 21 ♘xa6
♖b7 22 bxc5 1-0 Gipslis**

221 Rogobete-Buzbuchi
Poiana Brasov 78
**1 e4 c5 2 ♘f3 d6 3 d4 cxd4 4 ♘xd4
♘f6 5 ♘c3 a6 6 ♗g5 e6 7 f4 b5 8 e5
dxe5 9 fxe5 ♕c7 10 ♕e2!? ♘fd7 11
0-0-0 ♗b7 12 ♕g4 ♕b6** 12...♕xe5
13 ♗e2 ♗c5!? 14 ♖hf1! Δ ♗f4!± **
13 ♗e2** 13 ♗d3 **♘xe5?!** 13...h6!? 14
♕h3 ♘xe5 15 ♖he1 ♘bd7 16 ♗h4 g5

17 ♗xg5 ♖g8!≈ Kavalek-Polugaevsky,
Manila 75 **14 ♕h3!?** 14 ♕g3 ♘bd7 15
♗f4 f6 16 ♗g4!± **♘bd7 15 ♖he1 ♗c5?**
15...g6 16 ♗g4 h5 17 ♗xe6! fxe6
18 ♘xe6 ♖h7 19 ♘c7+! ♕xc7 20
♕e6+; 15...♗e7!? **16 ♘xe6! fxe6** 16...
♕xe6 17 ♗g4! +– **17 ♗h5+ ♔f8 18
♖f1+ ♘f6** 18...♔g8 19 ♖xd7! **19
♗xf6 gxf6 20 ♖xf6+ ♔g7** 20...♔e7 21
♕h4! **21 ♖xe6 ♗e3+ 22 ♔b1 +– ♖hd8**
22...♕c5 23 ♕g3+ **23 ♖xb6 ♗xb6
24 ♕e6 1-0**

222 Geszosz-Tringov
Bulgaria-Greece 78
**1 e4 c5 2 ♘f3 d6 3 d4 cxd4 4 ♘xd4
♘f6 5 ♘c3 a6 6 ♗g5 e6 7 f4 ♕b6 8
♕d2 ♕xb2 9 ♖b1 ♕a3 10 f5 ♘c6 11
fxe6 fxe6 12 ♘xc6 bxc6 13 e5 dxe5
14 ♗xf6 gxf6 15 ♘e4 ♗e7 16 ♗e2
h5 17 ♖b3 ♕a4 18 ♘xf6+! ♗xf6 19
c4 ♗h4+ 20 g3 ♗e7 21 0-0**

21...♗d7 21...♖a7 22 ♖b8 ♖c7 23 ♕d3
♗c5+ 24 ♔h1 ♕e7 25 ♕g6 ♔d6 26
♕f6 ♖e8 27 ♗xh5 ♖ce7 28 ♖d1+
♗d4 29 ♖xd4+ exd4 30 ♕xd4+ =
Vitolins-Gavrikov; 23 ♗d3 ♖g8 24
♗h7 ♖g7 25 ♕h6∞ Korfman **22
♕c2?!** Δ ♖b8+ +–; 22 ♖b7! ♖d8?!
23 ♗d3! ♗c5+ 24 ♔h1 ♖g8 25 ♗e2!!±
Timman-Ribli, Niksic 78 **♕a5! 23
♖fb1** 23 ♕g6+ ♔d8 24 ♖d1 ♕c5+ Δ

135

♔c7∓ **e4!! 24 ♕xe4 ♕f5 —+ 25 ♖b8+ ♖xb8 26 ♖xb8+ ♗d8 27 ♕h4 0-0!** 0-1 Maric

223 Auzins-Ausmanis Corr. 77/78
1 e4 c5 2 ♘f3 d6 3 d4 cxd4 4 ♘xd4 ♘f6 5 ♘c3 a6 6 ♗g5 e6 7 f4 ♘bd7 8 ♕f3 ♕c7 9 0-0-0 b5 10 ♗xb5 axb5 11 e5 ♗b7 11...♕b7 12 ♘dxb5 dxe5 13 fxe5 ♖xa2 14 ♔b1! ♖a5 15 exf6 ♕xf3 16 ♘c7+ +— Polescuk-Foigel, Corr. 77; 11...♖a5 12 exf6 gxf6 13 ♖he1 b4 14 ♘c6 ♖g8! 15 ♘e4 ♖xa2∓ Semkov-Georgiev, Varna 77; 11...♕b8 12 gxf6 gxf6 13 ♖he1! h5 14 ♕h3! e5 15 ♘d5!± Sibarevic-Bukic, Banja Luka 76 **12 ♘dxb5 ♕b8** 12...♕c8!? 13 ♕e2 dxe5 14 fxe5 ♘d5 15 ♘xd5 ♗xd5 16 ♖xd5 exd5 17 e6!?∞; 12...♕b6!? **13 ♕e2 d5 14 exf6 gxf6 15 f5!** N 15 ♗h4 ♕xf4+ 16 ♔b1 ♖c8 17 ♗g3 ♕c4 18 ♕h5 ♗e7 19 ♗d6 Nejolov-Stengrigt, Corr 75; 16...♕xh4! 17 ♘c7+ ♔d8 18 ♘xa8 ♕b4!∓ **fxg5 16 fxe6 ♘f6 17 ♖hf1 ♗e7** 17...♗g7 18 exf7+ ♔f8 19 ♖de1 ♕d8 20 ♘c7! ♕xc7 21 ♕e8+ +— **18 exf7+ ♔f8** 18...♔xf7 19 ♖de1 ♕d8 20 ♕e6+ ♔f8 21 ♘d6! +— **19 ♖de1!** 19 ♘d4 ♖a6 ♘e4 19...♕d8 20 ♘d4 ♖a6 21 ♘e6+±; 21 ♘f5!? **20 ♖f5!** 20 ♘xe4 dxe4 21 ♕c4 ♕e5! ♗b4

21 ♘xe4! dxe4 21...♗xe1 22 ♘ed6! +— **22 ♕c4 ♖a4** 22...♗xe1 23 ♕c5+ ♔g7 24 ♕d4+ +— **23 ♕d4 ♗d2+ 24 ♕xd2 h6 25 ♕c3** 1-0 Gipslis

224 Hubner-Hort
Wijk aan Zee 79
1 e4 c5 2 ♘f3 d6 3 d4 cxd4 4 ♘xd4 ♘f6 5 ♘c3 a6 6 ♗g5 e6 7 f4 ♘bd7 8 ♕f3 ♕c7 9 0-0-0 ♗e7 10 g4 b5 11 ♗xf6 gxf6!? 11...♘xf6 12 f5 ♘c5! 12...♘e5 13 ♕h3 0-0 14 ♘ce2 (14 ♕h6!) ♔h8 15 ♘f4 ♖g8 Gligoric-Fischer, Candidates 59 **13 fxe6 fxe6 14 b4!** 14 a3 0-0 15 ♗d3 += Capelan-Donner, Solingen 68 **♘a4 15 ♘xa4 bxa4 16 ♖d3!± 0-0** 16...♗d7 17 g5! fxg5 18 ♕h5+ ♔d8 19 ♗h3 ♕c4 20 ♕f7 ♖f8 21 ♘xe6+ ♗xe6 22 ♕xe6 ♕xe6 23 ♗xe6± **17 ♖c3! ♕b6** 17...♕b7 18 ♘c6±; 18 ♗c4±; 18 a3± **18 ♘c6 ♖f7 19 ♘xe7+ ♖xe7 20 ♗c4** 20 a3 ♖f7 21 ♗c4 ♖f7 20...♕xb4 21 ♖f1 ♖f7 22 g5 +—; 21 g5! fxg5 22 ♕f6! +— **21 a3 ♖aa7** 21...♗d7 **22 ♖d1 ♖ac7 23 ♕g3** +— Δ ♖xd6/g5 **♖c6 24 g5 fxg5 25 ♕xg5+ ♔f8 26 ♖dd3! ♕c7 27 ♖f3! ♖xc4 28 ♖xc4** 1-0 28...♕xc4 29 ♕d8+ ♔g7 30 ♖g3+ ♔h6 31 ♕g5 mate Miles

Sozin

✓ **225 Skrobek-Radulov Warsaw 79**
1 e4 c5 2 ♘f3 ♘c6 3 d4 cxd4 4 ♘xd4 ♘f6 5 ♘c3 d6 6 ♗c4 6 ♗g5 ♕b6!? 6...e6 **7 ♘b3 e6 8 0-0 a6 9 a4 ♗e3 ♕c7 10 f4 b5 11 ♗d3∞ ♕c7 10 a5 ♘b4?!** 10...♘xa5 11 ♘xa5 b6 **11 ♗d3 d5** 11...♗e7 12 ♗e3 += **12 ♗e3 ♗d6 13 f4 e5?!** 13...dxe4 14 ♘xe4 ♘xe4 15 ♗xe4 0-0 += **14 ♗b6! ♕e7 15 exd5 0-0** 15...♘bxd5 16 ♘xd5 ♘xd5 17 ♗b5+± **16 ♖e1± ♘bxd5 17 fxe5**

♗xe5 17...♘xc3 18 exd6 +− **18 ♘xd5 ♘xd5**

19 ♕h5! +− 19 ♗xh7+ ♚xh7 20 ♕h5+ ♚g8 21 ♖xe5 ♘f6+ **f5 20 ♗c4 ♕d6** 20...♕e6 21 ♖ad1 +− **21 ♗c5! ♕e6 22 ♖ad1 ♖d8 23 ♖xd5! 1-0** 23... ♖xd5 24 ♗xd5 ♕xd5 25 ♕e8 mate **Gheorghiu**

226 Velimirovic-Santos
Albufieri 78
1 e4 c5 2 ♘f3 ♘c6 3 d4 cxd4 4 ♘xd4 ♘f6 5 ♘c3 d6 6 ♗c4 e6 7 ♗e3 a6 8 ♕e2 ♕c7 9 ♗b3!? 9 0-0-0 ♘a5 **10 g4 b5 11 g5 ♘d7 12 f4!?** 12 0-0-0 b4 13 ♘a4 ♘xb3+ 14 axb3 ♘c5 15 ♘xc5 dxc5=; 12 ♗xe6? fxe6 13 ♘xe6 ♕c4! ∓/−+ 14 ♕xc4 ♘xc4 15 ♘c7+ ♚d8 16 ♘xa8 ♘xe3 17 fxe3 ♗b7; 12 ♘xe6?! fxe6 13 ♗xe6 ♘b6!? **b4** 12...♘c5!? **13 ♘a4 ♘c5** 13...♘xb3 14 axb3 ♗b7; 14...♘c5 15 ♘xc5? dxc5 16 ♘b5? ♕b6 −+; 15 f5! **14 ♘xc5! dxc5 15 ♗a4+! ♗d7 16 ♗xd7+ ♕xd7 17 ♘b3 ♗b7** 17...♖xb3?± **18 ♘d2 ♗e7 19 h4 ♕c6 20 h5 ♘d6 21 0-0-0! c4!?** 21...♘xe4? 22 ♕f3 **22 e5 ♘f5 23 ♕xc4** 23 ♘xc4!? **♕b7!?** 23...♕xc4 24 ♘xc4 ♖c8 25 ♘d6+ ♗xd6 26 exd6 ♚d7!∝; 26...♖xc2+? 27 ♚xc2 ♘xe3+ 28 ♚b3 ♘xd1 29 ♖xd1 ±/+−; 25 ♘b6!? ♖xc2+! 26 ♚xc2 ♘xe3+ 27 ♚b3 ♘xd1 28 ♖xd1

h6!? **24 ♗f2± 0-0 25 g6 ♖fc8 26 gxf7+ ♚xf7 27 ♕e4 ♕b5 28 ♘b3 ♖ab8 29 ♘d4! ♘xd4 30 ♗xd4 b3 31 axb3 ♕xb3 32 ♕xh7! +−** ♕a2 **33 ♖hg1 ♕a1+ 34 ♚d2 ♕a5+ 35 ♚e3 ♗f8 36 h6 1-0 Speelman**

✓227 Gurevich-Elvest USSR 78
1 e4 c5 2 ♘f3 d6 3 d4 cxd4 4 ♘xd4 ♘f6 5 ♘c3 a6 6 ♗c4 e6 7 ♗b3 ♘c6 8 ♗e3 ♗e7 9 ♕e2 ♕c7 10 0-0-0 ♘a5 11 g4 b5 12 g5 ♘xb3+ 13 axb3 ♘d7 14 h4 14 ♘f5?! exf5 15 ♘d5 ♕d8 16 exf5 ♗b7 17 f6 gxf6 18 ♖he1 ♗xd5 19 ♖xd5 ♖g8∓ Guseinov-Korsunsky, USSR 78 **♗b7 15 h5! b4** 15...♘f8 16 ♕g4 0-0-0?; 16...b4!? 17 ♘d5! ♗xd5 18 exd5± Stanciu-I.Szabo, Rumania Final 76 **16 ♘a4 ♗xe4** 16...0-0-0!? **17 f3 ♗b7 18 g6 hxg6 19 hxg6 ♖xh1 20 ♖xh1 ♗f6** N 20...♘c5 21 ♘xc5 dxc5 22 gxf7+ ♚xf7 23 ♘xe6! +− Podgaets-Butnoris, USSR 75

21 ♘xe6! fxe6 22 ♗b6 0-0-0 22... ♘xb6 23 ♕xe6+ △ ♖h8 mate **23 ♗xc7 ♚xc7 24 ♕xe6 ♗xf3 25 ♕c4+ ♚c6 26 ♖d1 a5 27 ♚b1 ♖b8 28 c3 ♘e5 29 ♕a6 bxc3 30 ♕xa5+ ♚d7 31 ♘c5+ ♚e8 32 ♕c7 ♖b5 33 ♕c8+ ♚e7 34 ♕e6+ ♚f8 35 ♕xd6+ ♗e7 36 ♘e6+ 1-0 Gipslis**

228 Bielczyk-Cylwik
Bialystok 78

1 e4 c5 2 ♘f3 ♘c6 3 d4 cxd4 4 ♘xd4
e6 5 ♘c3 d6 6 ♗e3 ♘f6 7 ♗c4 ♗e7 8
♗b3 0-0 9 f4 ♗d7 9...♘xd4 10 ♗xd4
b5!= 10 ♕d3! ♘xd4 11 ♗xd4 ♗c6
12 0-0-0 a6 13 ♖he1 ♕a5 14 ♕g3 ♘h5
15 ♕g4 g6 15...♘f6! += 16 f5! +−
exf5 17 exf5 ♖ae8 18 ♖xe7! ♖xe7 19
fxg6 h6 20 gxf7+ ♔h7 21 ♕g8+ 1-0
Bielczyk

Richter-Rauzer

229 Radulov-Sigurjonsson
Buenos Aires 78

1 e4 c5 2 ♘f3 e6 3 d4 cxd4 4 ♘xd4
♘f6 5 ♘c3 d6 6 ♗g5 ♗e7 7 ♕d2 a6
8 0-0-0 b5 9 ♗d3 ♗d7 9...♗b7 10
♖he1 ♘bd7 11 f4 ♕b6 12 ♘xe6!?
10 f4 ♘c6 11 ♘f3 11 ♘xc6 ♗xc6 12
e5 b4 12 ♘e2 ♕b6?! 12...♕a5; 12...
0-0 13 h3?! 13 e5 dxe5 14 fxe5 ♘d5
15 ♗e4 += a5 14 g4 a4 15 ♔b1 0-0
16 f5?! △ ♗e3, g5; 16 ♘g3! ♘e5!
17 ♘ed4 17 ♘xe5 dxe5 =+ b3!∓
18 cxb3 axb3 19 a3 ♘xd3 20 ♕xd3 e5
21 ♗xf6 gxf6 22 ♕xb3 22 ♘xb3 ♗b5!;
22 ♘e2 ♗b5 23 ♕xb3 ♖fb8∓; 23...
♕a6∓; 23 ♕d2 d5! 24 exd5 e4 ♕a7
23 ♘c2 ♖fb8 24 ♘b4 24 ♕d3 ♗b5 △
♕b7, d5 d5 25 ♖xd5 ♗xb4 26 axb4
♗c6 27 ♖hd1 ♖c8 △ ♗xd5, ♕a1 mate
28 ♕a3 ♗xd5 29 ♖xd5 ♕xa3 30
bxa3 ♖xa3 −+ 31 ♘d2 ♖b8 32 g5
♖xb4+ 33 ♔c2 fxg5 34 f6 h6 35
♖xe5 ♖xh3 36 ♖d5 ♔h7 37 e5 ♔g6 38
♖d8 ♔f5 39 ♖d5 ♔e6 40 ♖c5 ♖d4
41 ♘c4 g4 0-1 **Sigurjonsson**

230 Gheorghiu-Horitver
Torremolinos 78

1 e4 c5 2 ♘f3 d6 3 d4 cxd4 4 ♘xd4
♘f6 5 ♘c3 a6 6 ♗g5 ♘c6 7 ♕d2 ♗d7

8 0-0-0 e6 9 f4 b5 10 ♗xf6 10 ♘xc6
♗xc6 11 ♕e1 ♗e7 12 e5 ♘d5 13 ♗xe7
♕xe7 14 ♘xd5 ♗xd5 15 ♔b1= Jovicic-
Smejkal, Belgrade 77 gxf6 10...♕xf6?
11 e5 dxe5 12 ♘dxb5± 11 ♕b1
11 f5!? ♘xd4 12 ♕xd4 ♗h6+ 13 ♔b1
♗f4∞ Speelman-Dorfman, Mexico 77;
11 ♘xc6 ♗xc6 12 ♕e3 ♕e7 13 ♗d3
♕a7! 14 ♕e1! 0-0-0 15 ♔b1 ♕c5!
16 ♖f1 += Zaid-Lanka, USSR 77;
14 ♕h3 ♕c5 15 f5 b4 Torre-Kinlay,
London 77 b4 11...♕b6! 12 ♘ce2
♕b6 13 f5 e5 14 ♘f3 h5 15 ♘c1 ♖c8
16 ♗d3 ♗h6 17 ♕e2 a5 18 ♗b5 ♕e7!
19 ♖d5 ♗xc1 20 ♖xc1 ♘a7 21 ♗xd7
♔xd7 22 ♖cd1 ♖c6∞ △ ♘b5 ½-½
Ciocaltea

231 Sax-Ribli Warsaw 79

1 e4 c5 2 ♘f3 d6 3 d4 cxd4 4 ♘xd4
♘f6 5 ♘c3 a6 6 ♗g5 ♘c6!? 6...e6 7
f4 ♕b6!?; 7...♗e7 8 ♕f3 ♕c7 9 ♗d3 +=
7 ♕d2 e6 8 0-0-0 ♗d7 9 f4 b5 9...h6
10 ♗h4 ♘xe4 11 ♕e1± 9...♗e7 10
♗xf6 gxf6 11 g3 11 ♘xc6 ♗xc6 12
♕e3 ♕e7!∞ ♕b6 12 ♘ce2 0-0-0 13
♔b1 ♔b8 14 ♗g2 ♗g7?! N 14...h5;
14...♘a5!? 15 ♖hf1 ♖he8 16 ♕d3!
♔a7

17 e5!± dxe5 18 ♕xh7 dxe4 19 ♕xg7
e5 20 fxe5 fxe5 21 ♖xf7 ♘b8 22
♕h7 ♖e6 23 c3! ♕d6 24 cxd4 e4 25

♘f4 ♖ee8 26 ♗xe4 ♘c6 27 ♕g6! +–
♕xg6 28 ♗xg6 ♘e7 29 ♖e1! 1-0 29...
♘xg6 30 ♖xe8 ♖xe8 31 ♖xd7+ +–
Gheorghiu

232 M.Tseitlin-Makarichev
USSR Final 78
**1 e4 c5 2 ♘f3 ♘c6 3 d4 cxd4 4 ♘xd4
♘f6 5 ♘c3 d6 6 ♗g5 e6** 6...♕b6;
6...♗d7 7 ♕d2 ♘xd4 8 ♕xd4 ♕a5 9
f4 **7 ♕d2 ♗e7 8 0-0-0 0-0 9 f4 ♘xd4
10 ♕xd4 ♕a5 11 ♗c4 ♗d7 12 ♖hf1!?**
12 e5 dxe5 13 fxe5 ♗c6 14 ♗d2 ♘d7
15 ♘d5 ♕d8 16 ♘xe7+ ♕xe7 17
♖he1 ♖fd8 N Khait-Lysenko, USSR
76; 14 ♕f4 ♘h5 15 ♕e3 ♗b4!?
Osachuk-Lysenko, USSR 76 **b5 13
♗b3 b4 14 e5!!** dxe5 14...bxc3 15
exf6± **15 fxe5 bxc3 16 ♗xf6! ♗xf6
17 exf6 cxb2+ 18 ♔b1 ♖fd8 19
♕g4 g6** 19...g5 20 ♕h5 ♕c5 21 ♖d5
**20 ♕f4 g5 21 ♕g4 ♗e8 22 ♖xd8 ♖xd8
23 ♕h5 ♕c5 24 ♗xe6! h6** 24...fxe6
25 f7+ ♗xf7 26 ♕xf7+ ♔h8 27 ♕f6+
+– **25 ♕g6+ 1-0 Tseitlin**

Scheveningen

233 A.Smith-L.D.Evans USA 78
**1 e4 c5 2 ♘f3 d6 3 d4 cxd4 4 ♘xd4
♘f6 5 ♘c3 a6 6 a4 e6 7 ♗e2 ♗e7 8
0-0 0-0 9 f4 ♘c6 10 ♗e3 ♕c7 11 ♘b3**
11 ♔h1 b6 12 ♗f3 ♖b8 13 ♕e2 ♘a5
14 ♘d2 ♖d8 14...♖e8!? A.Smith-
Fiedler, Canada 77; 15 ♔h1= **15 ♕f2?!**
N 15 ♔h1 ♗b7 16 ♕f2 ♘d7 17 ♖ae1
♘c4 18 ♘xc4 ♕xc4= Witt-Larsen,
Canada 74 **d5! 16 e5 d4 17 ♗xd4
♖xd4 18 exf6 ♗c5 19 ♔h1 ♕xf4 20
♖ad1 ♕xf6?!** 20...gxf6! =+; 20...♖b4?
21 ♘e4± **21 ♘de4 ♕d8?** 21...♕e5 22
♕h4 ∝/+= **22 ♕g3! +– ♖b7** 22...♗b7
23 b4! +–

**23 b4! ♗xb4 24 ♖xd4 ♕xd4 25
♖d1 ♗xc3** 25...♕c4 26 ♖d8+ ♗f8 27
♘f6+ ♔h8 28 ♖xf8 mate **26 ♖xd4
♗xd4 27 c3** 27 ♘f6+ ♗xf6 28 ♗xb7
♘xb7 29 ♕b8 **f5 28 ♘g5 f4 29 ♕xf4**
1-0 A.Smith/Ciamarra

234 Klovan-Petkevic USSR 79
**1 e4 c5 2 ♘f3 d6 3 d4 cxd4 4 ♘xd4
♘f6 5 ♘c3 a6 6 ♗e2 e6 7 0-0 ♗e7 8
f4 0-0 9 a4 ♕c7 10 ♔h1** 10 ♗e3 ♘c6
11 ♘b3 b6 12 ♗f3 ♗b7 13 ♕e1 ♘b4
14 ♕f2 ♘d7 15 g4∝ Ivanka-Feustel,
Tbilisi 76; 12...♖b8 13 ♕e2 ♘a5 14
♖ae1?! ♘c4 15 ♗c1 b5! 16 axb5 axb5
17 ♔h1 b4 18 ♘d1 ♗a6∓ Grotke-
Vogt, DDR Final 77; 12 ♕d2 ♖b8!?
13 g4 d5 14 e5 ♘e4 15 ♘xe4 dxe4
16 c3 += Kosansky-Gligoric, Osijek
78 **♘c6 11 ♗e3 ♗d7** 11...♖e8!? 12
♘b3 b6 13 ♗f3 ♗b7 14 ♕e2 ♘d7=
Smyslov-Radulov, Leningrad 77; 11...
♖d8 12 ♕e1 ♘xd4 13 ♗xd4 e5 14
♗g1 exf4 15 a5! += Geller-Tal, Sochi
77 **12 ♘b3 Δ a5 b6 13 ♕e1** 13 ♗f3
♖ab8 Δ ♘a5 **♘b4 14 ♘d4 ♖fc8** 14...
e5 15 fxe5 dxe5 16 ♕g3 **15 ♕g3 ♔h8
16 e5!± ♘fd5 17 ♗d2 ♘xc3 18 ♗xc3**
dxe5 18...♘d5 19 exd6 Δ ♘f5 +–

Diagram

19 ♘xe6!! ♗xe6 20 ♗xe5 ♕xe5 21

fxe5 +− ♖xc2 22 ♗g4 ♗c4 23 ♖f4 ♖d8 24 ♗f5! ♖cd2 25 h3 ♗d5 26 ♗e4 ♘d3 27 ♗xd3! ♖xg2 28 ♕xg2 ♗xg2+ 29 ♔xg2 ♖xd3 30 ♖xf7 ♗c5 31 e6 ♕g8 32 ♖d7! ♖xd7 33 exd7 ♗e7 34 ♖d1 ♗d8 35 ♖e1 1-0 Gipslis

√ 235 Jakobsen-Browne
Buenos Aires 78

1 e4 c5 2 ♘f3 d6 3 d4 cxd4 4 ♘xd4 ♘f6 5 ♘c3 a6 6 a4!? e6 6...g6?!; 6...♘c6 7 ♗e2 ♗e7 8 0-0 ♘c6 9 ♔h1!? 9 f4; 9 ♗e3 ♕c7 9...♗d7 10 ♘b3! 10 f4 0-0 11 ♗f3 ♖e8 12 ♗e3 ♖b8! 12...♘xd4? 13 ♕xd4 e5 14 ♕d2 exf4 15 ♗xf4 ♗e6 16 ♖ad1 += 13 ♕e2 ♘xd4! 13...♘a5 14 ♗xd4 e5 15 ♗a7 ♖a8 16 ♗e3 ♗e6! 17 ♖fd1 17 ♕f2 exf4 18 ♗xf4 ♘d7= ♖ac8 18 f5 18 fxe5 dxe5 =+ ♗c4 19 ♕f2 b5! 20 axb5 axb5 21 ♖a7 21 b3! ♗xb3!∓; 21 ♗g5 b4∓ ♕c6! 22 ♖d2 b4 23 ♘d5 ♗xd5 24 exd5 ♕c4 25 ♗e2! 25 b3? ♕c3∓ ♕e4 26 ♗d3 ♕xd5! 26...♕g4 27 ♗e2= 27 ♗a6 ♕c6 27...♖xc2? 28 ♖xc2 ♕d1+ 29 ♗f1 ♘g4 30 ♕e2 ♘xe3 31 ♖xe7 +− 28 ♗xc8 ♕xc8 =+ 29 ♕f3! h6 30 h3 d5 31 ♗g1? 31 ♖xd5! ♘xd5 32 ♕xd5 ♕xf5 33 ♕b5 ♕c8 34 ♕xe5 =+; 33...♔f8?? 34 ♖xe7! ♖xe7 35 ♕b8+ ♖e8 36 ♗c5+ +− d4 32 ♖e2 ♗c5 33 ♖a5 e4 34 ♕f4 34 ♕b3 e3! 35 ♕c4 ♘e4 −+

e3 −+ 35 ♗h2 b3! 36 ♕c7 ♗b6 37 ♕xb6 bxc2 0-1 Browne

√ 236 De Boer-Tompa
Biel 78

1 e4 c5 2 ♘f3 e6 3 d4 cxd4 4 ♘xd4 ♘f6 5 ♘c3 d6 6 ♗e2 ♗e7 7 0-0 0-0 8 f4 a6 9 ♔h1 ♘c6 10 ♗e3 ♗d7 11 ♕e1 b5 12 a3 ♕b8 13 ♗f3 13 ♕g3 b4 14 axb4 ♕xb4 15 ♘xc6 ♗xc6 16 e5 dxe5 17 fxe5 ♘e4 18 ♘xe4 ♗xe4 19 ♖xa6 ♖xa6 20 ♗xa6 ♗xc2?! 21 ♕f2 ♗f5 22 ♗d4 ♖d8 23 ♗c3= Tompa-Sax, Hungary 77; 20...♕xb2! =+ ♘xd4 14 ♗xd4 e5 15 ♗e3 15 ♘d5 ♘xd5 16 exd5 exd4! 17 ♕xe7 ♗f5 18 ♖ac1 ♖e8 19 ♕g5 ♕c8 20 c3 h6 21 ♕h5 d3!∓ Szabo-Larsen, Costa Brava 76 ♗c6 16 ♖d1 ♖e8! 17 ♘d5 ♗xd5 18 exd5 exf4 19 ♗xf4 ♕c7 20 c3 ♗f8 20...♘d7 21 ♕g3 21 ♕f2 21 ♕g3 ♘e4! ♖ab8 21...♘e4 22 ♕c2 22 ♖d4 g6 23 ♕g3 ♘d7 24 h4?! ♘e5 25 h5 ♗g7 =+ 26 ♖e4 ♘c4 27 ♖xe8+ ♖xe8 28 ♕f2 ♕d8 28...♕d7! 29 ♗d1 ♕d7 30 ♗c1 ♖e5 31 ♗f3 ♕e7 32 hxg6 hxg6 33 ♗f4 ♖f5 34 ♖e1 ♕e5∓ 35 ♗xe5 ♘xe5 36 ♔g1 36 ♕e3 ♘xf3! −+ ♘xf3+! 36...♖xf3? 37 ♖xe5!= 37 gxf3 ♕g5+ 38 ♔f1 38 ♕g2 ♕h5∓ ♖xd5 39 f4 ♕g4 40 ♖e8+ ♔g7 0-1 41 ♖e3 ♖d1+ 42 ♖e1 ♕h3+ 43 ♔g1 ♖d3 44 ♕h2 ♕g4+ Tompa

237 Jansa-Radulov
Warsaw 79

1 e4 c5 2 ♘f3 d6 3 d4 cxd4 4 ♘xd4 ♘f6 5 ♘c3 a6 6 ♗e2 e6 7 0-0 ♗e7 8 f4 0-0 9 ♔h1 ♕c7 10 ♕e1 b5 11 ♗f3 ♗b7 12 e5 ♘e8! 12...dxe5 13 fxe5 ♘fd7 14 ♗xb7 ♕xb7 15 ♕g3± 13 f5!? 13 ♕g3∞ ♗xf3 14 ♘xf3 b4! 15 f6 15 ♘e4?! exf5∓ gxf6 16 exd6 ♗xd6 17 ♘e4

17...♔h8!!∓ 18 ♘xd6 18 ♗h6 ♖g8; 18
♕h4 ♗e7 ♕xd6 19 ♕e4 ♘c6 20 ♗h6
♖g8 21 ♖ad1 ♕c7 22 ♖d2 ♖d8! 23
♖xd8 ♘xd8 24 ♕xb4 ♕xc2! 25 ♗d2
25 ♕d2 ♘c4 −+ ♘c6 26 ♘c3 ♕g6! 27
♘h4 ♕e4! 28 ♖e1 28 ♖xf6 ♘xf6
29 ♕xf6+ ♖g7 −+ ♕d5 29 ♘f3 ♘e5
30 ♕d4 ♘b7 31 ♖f1 ♘c7 32 ♕h4 ♘d5
33 ♘xe5 fxe5 34 ♕e4 ♕c7! 35 h3 f5
−+ 36 ♕e2 e4 37 ♖c1 ♕g7 38 ♗c3 e5
39 ♗d2 e3 40 ♗e1 0-1 40...♘f4
Gheorghiu

238 Sznapik-Jansa Warsaw 79

1 e4 c5 2 ♘f3 d6 3 d4 cxd4 4 ♘xd4
♘f6 5 ♘c3 e6 6 ♗e2 a6 7 f4 ♗e7 8
0-0 0-0 9 ♔h1 ♕c7 10 ♕e1 b5 11
♗f3 ♗b7 12 e5 ♘e8! 13 ♕g3 ♘d7 14
a3 ♖c8!? 14...♘b6! 15 ♗e3! ♘b6 16
♖ae1 ♘c4 17 ♗xb7 ♕xb7 18 ♗c1!±
g6 19 ♘e4 ♕d5!∝ 20 ♘f3 ♘g7?
20...dxe5 21 fxe5 f5!∝ **21 b3! ♘f5 22
♕f2! ♘a5 23 g4 dxe5** 23...♘g7? 24
exd6 +− **24 gxf5?!** 24 fxe5! ♘g7 25
♗h6; 25 ♘f6+ ♗xf6 26 exf6 ♘e8
29 ♗h6+ **exf5∝ 25 ♘g3 e4 26 ♕d4
♖fd8! 27 ♗b2 f6! 28 ♕xd5 ♖xd5 29
♖f2??** 29 ♘d4 ♗xa3 30 ♘dxf5!∝

Diagram

29...exf3!! −+ 30 c4 30 ♖xe7 ♖xc2!!
31 ♖xc2 ♖d1+ **♖d7! 31 cxb5 axb5**

32 ♖xf3 ♖c2 33 ♗a1 ♔f7 34 a4 bxa4
35 bxa4 ♖a2 36 h4 h5 37 ♘f1 ♘c4 38
♘g3 ♖xa4 0-1 Gheorghiu

239 Bellon-Suba Bucharest 79

1 e4 c5 2 ♘f3 d6 3 d4 ♘f6 4 ♘c3 cxd4
5 ♘xd4 e6 6 ♗e3 a6 7 ♗d3 N b5 8 ♕e2
♘bd7 9 g4 9 a4!? ♗b7! 9...h6 10 g5
b4 11 gxf6 bxc3 12 fxg7 ♗xg7 13
b4!∝ ♘e5 14 ♖g1 ♗f6 15 a4?! 15 f4
♘xd3+ 16 cxd3 +=; 15...♘c6 16 ♘xc6
♗xc6 17 ♗xa6 ♗xe4∝ **d5! =+ 16 exd5
♕xd5 17 ♖d1 ♖d8 18 b5 ♘xd3+ 19
♖xd3 ♕e4?** 19...♕a2!∓ **20 f3± ♕h4+
21 ♗f2 ♕h6** 21...♕xh2 22 ♘xe6 ♖xd3
23 ♘c7+ ♔d7 24 ♕xd3+ ♔c8 25
♕f5+ ♔b8 26 ♕xf6 +− **22 ♖g4 axb5
23 f4?!** ♕xh2! **24 ♘xe6 ♖xd3! 25
♘c5+ ♗e7 26 ♕xd3 ♗xc5 27 ♕xb5+
♔d8 28 ♗h4+ ♔c7 29 ♕xc5+ ♗c6 30
♕a7+** 30 ♕e5+? ♗b7 31 ♕xh8 ♕d2+
32 ♔f1 ♕d1+ 33 ♔f2 ♕xg4 −+ **♗c8
31 ♕a6+ ♗b7 32 ♕e2 ♕h1+ 33 ♔f2 h5
34 ♕e5! ♕h2+** Zeitnot **35 ♔e1 ♕d2+
36 ♔f1 ♕d1+ 37 ♔f2 ♕xc2+ 38 ♔g1
♕d1+ 39 ♔f2 ♕d2+ 40 ♔g1 ♖f8?**
40...hxg4∓ **41 ♕c5+ ♔d7 42 ♕e7+!
½-½** 42...♔c6 43 ♕f6+ ♕d6 44 ♖g3!=;
43 ♖g2? ♕d6 44 ♕xd6+ ♔xd6 45
♖e2 ♖g8+ 46 ♔f1 ♖g4!∓ **Suba**

240 Ostojic-Bukic Virovitica 78

1 e4 c5 2 ♘f3 e6 3 d4 cxd4 4 ♘xd4

♘f6 5 ♘c3 d6 6 ♗e3 a6 7 f4 b5 8 a3 ♗b7 9 ♗d3 ♘bd7 10 0-0 ♗e7 11 ♕f3 ♘c5 12 ♖ae1 0-0 13 ♔h1 13 ♗f2 ♖c8 14 ♕h3 ♕d7 15 ♗h4 ♖fe8 16 ♗g5 ♗a8 17 ♔h1 ♕a7∝ Ligterink-Kavalek, Wijk aan Zee 77 ♕h8?! 13...♖c8 **14 b4! ♖c8!? 15 ♗d2** 15 bxc5? dxc5 △ c4 =+ **♘xd3 16 cxd3 ♕d7** 16...♕b6 **17 ♕h3 g6?!** 17...♗d8 △ ♗b6 **18 ♘f3 ♘h5 19 f5± exf5 20 exf5 ♗f6** 20...♕g7?? 21 f6! ♕xh3 22 fxg7+ +— **21 ♘e4 ♗xe4 22 dxe4 ♕g8** 22...♖c2 23 g4 ♘g7 24 ♘g5! ♗xg5 25 ♗xg5 **23 g4 ♘g7 24 ♕h6 ♖c4 25 ♘g5 ♗xg5 26 ♗xg5 ♕b7 27 ♖f4! f6** 27...gxf5 28 ♗f6 +—

28 fxg6 hxg6 29 ♗h4! +— 29 ♗xf6 ♖xf6! 30 ♖xf6 ♖xe4∝ **f5** 29...g5? 30 ♗xg5! fxg5 31 ♖xf8+ ♔xf8 32 ♕h8+ ♔f7 33 ♖f1+ ♔e6 34 ♕h6+ +— **30 gxf5 ♖xf5 31 ♖g4 ♖fe5 32 ♕xg6 ♕f7 33 ♖eg1 ♕f3+ 34 ♖4g2 1-0** 34...♖c7 35 ♗f6 +— **Maric**

241 Prandstetter-Gheorghiu
Warsaw 79
1 e4 c5 2 ♘f3 d6 3 d4 cxd4 4 ♘xd4 ♘f6 5 ♘c3 a6 6 ♗e3 e6 7 f4 b5 8 a3!? 8 ♗d3 △ ♕f3 **♗b7 9 ♗d3 ♘bd7 10 0-0 g6!** N 10...♖c8; 10...♗e7; 10...♕c7 **11 ♕f3 ♗g7 12 ♖ad1 0-0** 12...e5!? 13 ♘b3 exf4 14 ♕xf4 ♘e5 15 ♗xb5+∝

13 ♘de2! ♖c8 14 g4 ♘c5 15 ♗d4! h6! 16 ♘g3 ♘cd7 17 ♗e2?! 17 ♗e3!∝ e5!∓ 18 ♗e3 18 fxe5 dxe5∓ exf4 19 ♗xf4 ♗e8! 20 ♕e3 ♕b6! 21 ♕xb6 ♘xb6 22 ♗xd6 ♘xd6 23 ♖xd6 ♗e5! —+ 24 ♖dd1 24 ♖xb6? ♗d4+ ♗xc3 25 bxc3 ♖xc3 26 ♗f6 ♘c4 27 a4?! ♘b2! 28 ♖df1 28 ♖d7 ♗c8! —+ ♘xa4 29 ♗d3 ♖c6! 29...♘c5? 30 ♘e2! △ ♘f4∝ 30 e5 ♘c5 31 ♖xc6 ♗xc6 32 ♖f6 ♖c8! △ ♘d7 —+ 33 e6 ♘xe6 34 ♗xg6 fxg6 35 ♖xe6 ♕f7 36 ♖d6 a5! —+ 37 ♘e2 a4 38 ♘d4 ♗e8 39 ♖b6 a3 40 ♔f2 a2 41 ♖a6 ♖c4 42 c3 ♖a4! 0-1 43 ♖xa4 bxa4 44 ♘c2 ♔f6 —+ **Gheorghiu**

242 Litvinov-Kapengut Minsk 79
1 e4 c5 2 ♘f3 ♘c6 3 d4 cxd4 4 ♘xd4 e6 5 ♘c3 d6 6 ♗e3 ♘f6 7 ♗e2 ♗e7 8 0-0 0-0 9 f4 ♗d7 10 ♘db5?! ♕b8 10...♗e8!? 11 a4 a6 12 ♘a3 d5!; 12 ♘d4 ♘xd4 13 ♗xd4 ♗c6 14 ♗d3 ♘d7 11 a4 ♖d8 11...♖c8 Torre-Larsen, Manila 74 12 ♗f3 12 ♕e1 ♘b4 13 ♗d1 Tseshkovsky-Gufeld, Tbilisi 73; 13 ♖e1 Ljubojevic-Calvo, Madrid 73 ♘b4! 12...♗e8 Podgaets-Polugaevsky, Moscow 71; 12...a6 13 ♘a3 d5 Litvinov-Kjarner, USSR 75; 14 exd5 ♗e8 15 ♘c4!± 13 ♕e2 e5! N 13...♗c6 14 ♕f2 b6 15 ♘d4 ♗e8 16 ♖ad1 a6 17 ♕g3 ♖a7 18 ♖d2 ♖c8 19 e5± Saharov-Zilberstein 74 14 ♘a3?! 14 ♖ad1!? ♗c6 15 fxe5 dxe5 16 ♖xd8 ♕xd8 17 ♘xa7 ♖xa7!? 18 ♗xa7 b6∝ ♕c8 15 ♕f2 exf4 16 ♗xf4 ♗e6 17 ♘ab5 d5! 18 ♘c7 dxe4 19 ♘xe6 ♘fd5 20 ♘xe6 ♕xe6 21 ♗g5 f6 22 ♗c1 ♖ac8∓ 23 c3 ♘d3 24 ♕e2 ♘5f4 24...♘xc1 25 ♖axc1 ♘f4 26 ♕c2 f5 27 ♘g3 ♘d3 28 ♖cd1 ♕e3+ 29 ♔h1 g6∓ 25 ♗xf4 ♘xf4 26 ♕b5? 26 ♕e3?? ♗c5; 26 ♕c2 ♘d3 27 ♖ad1 a6! 28

♛xb7 f5 −+ 29 ♘g3 ♖b8 30 ♛c7 ♗d6!
30...♗c5+ 31 ♔h1 ♗b6 32 ♛xb8!∞
**31 ♛a5 ♗c5+ 32 ♔h1 ♘f2+ 33 ♔g1
33** ♖xf2 ♖xd1+ 34 ♗xd1 ♗xf2 −+
0-1 33...♘e4+ 34 ♔h1 ♘xg3+ 35 hxg3
♛h6+ −+ **Kapengut**

243 Orgovan-Tompa
Hungary ½-Final 78

**1 e4 c5 2 ♘f3 e6 3 d4 cxd4 4 ♘xd4
♘f6 5 ♘c3 d6 6 ♗e3 ♗e7 7 ♗c4 0-0
8 ♛e2?!** 8 ♗b3 ♘a6≈; 8 f4 d5 9 ♗d3
dxe4 10 ♘xe4 ♘d5 11 ♛f3 ♘xe3
12 ♛xe3 ♛b6 =+ Hubner-Petrosian,
Malaga 71 **d5! 9 exd5 exd5 10 ♗d3**
10 ♗b3 ♖e8 11 0-0 ♘c6 12 ♛d2 ♗b4∓
Huguet-Hartston 69 **♘c6 11 ♛f3**
11 0-0 ♘g4; 11 0-0-0 ♗b4 **♘e5 12 ♛g3
♘fg4∓ 13 ♗f5** 13 h3? ♗h4 14 ♛f4 g5

**13...♗h4! 14 ♛h3 ♘xe3 15 ♛xe3
♘c4 16 ♛h3 ♖e8+ 17 ♘ce2 ♛f6!** −+
18 0-0-0 18 0-0 ♖xe2; 18 c3 ♘e3! −+
**♖xe2! 19 ♗xc8 ♗g5+ 20 ♔b1 ♘d2+
21 ♖xd2 ♖xd2 22 ♖e1 ♛e7 0-1
Tompa**

Dragon

244 Barczay-Adorjan Budapest 78
**1 e4 c5 2 ♘f3 ♘c6 3 ♘c3 g6 4 d4 cxd4
5 ♘xd4 ♗g7 6 ♗e3 ♘f6 7 ♗e2 0-0 8
♛d2?! d5! 9 exd5 ♘xd5 10 ♘xc6 bxc6**

---

11 ♖d1 ♗e6!∓ 12 ♗d4 12 ♘xd5 ♛xd5!
13 ♛xd5 ♗xd5 14 ♗f3 ♗xf3 15 gxf3
♗xb2 16 ♖d7 ♗a3! 17 ♗xa7 ♖fd8 18
♖xd8+ ♖xd8 19 ♔e2 ♖a8 20 ♗d4
♗d6 21 ♖a1 ♗xh2∓ **♗xd4 13 ♛xd4
♛a5! 14 ♛a4** 14 ♛e5 ♛b4 **♛b6 15
♛a3 ♖fb8! 16 ♘a4 ♛a5+ 17 ♖d2**
17 c3 ♘b6∓; 17...♘f4! 18 ♗f3 ♛e5+
19 ♔d2 ♘xg2! 20 ♗xc6 ♛f4+ 21 ♔c2
♗f5+ −+ **♖b4 18 ♘c3** 18 b3 ♖ab8
19 ♛c1 ♖xa4! 20 bxa4 ♘c3 21 0-0
♖b1 22 ♛a3 ♖xf1+ 23 ♗xf1 ♖b1!? −+
**♛xa3 19 bxa3 ♖b2 20 ♘e4 ♖xa2 21
c4 ♖a1+ 22 ♖d1 ♖xd1+ 23 ♗xd1
♘f4 24 g3 ♘d3+ 25 ♔d2 ♖d8 0-1
Adorjan**

245 Byrne-Braga
Sao Paulo 79

**1 e4 c5 2 ♘f3 d6 3 d4 cxd4 4 ♘xd4
♘f6 5 ♘c3 g6 6 ♗e3 ♗g7 7 f3 ♘c6 8
♛d2 0-0 9 0-0-0 9** ♗c4 ♗e6!? 9...
♘xd4 10 ♗xd4 ♗e6 **10 ♘xe6 fxe6 11
♗c4 +=** ♛c8 12 ♗b3 ♘a5 13 ♗d4!
♘xb3+ 14 axb3 ♘h5 15 ♛g5!± ♛e8
15...♖f7 **16 ♖he1! ♛f7 17 e5 d5**
17...♛f4+ 18 ♛xf4 ♘xf4 19 g3 ♘h5
20 exd6 **18 ♛b1 b6 19 ♖f1 h6 20
♛d2 ♛f4 21 g3!± ♛xd2 22 ♖xd2**
△ f4± **g5 23 ♖d3 ♗h8** △ ♘g7-e8!?
**24 ♖e1 ♘g7 25 ♗f2 ♘e8 26 ♘b5!
♖f5 27 ♖de3 ♘g7 28 g4! ♖ff8** 28...
♖f4 29 ♗g3 **29 ♖c3 ♘e8 30 ♗g3 ♖f7
31 ♖c6 1-0** 31...♖xf3 32 ♖xe6; 32
♘d4 △ ♘xe6 +− **Gheorghiu**

246 Suba-Taimanov Bucharest 79
**1 c4 g6 2 e4 ♗g7 3 d4 c5 4 ♘f3 cxd4
5 ♘xd4 ♘c6 6 ♗e3 ♘f6 7 ♘c3 ♘g5
8 ♛xg4 ♘xd4 9 ♛d1 ♘e6 10 ♖c1 b6
11 b4! += ♗b7 12 ♗d3 0-0 13 0-0
♘d4 14 ♗b1 ♘c6 15 a3 ♖c8 16 f4 d6
17 ♛d3 ♛d7 18 ♖fd1** 18 h3 += ♛g4 **19
♛f1 ♛h8 20 h3 ♛h4 21 ♔h2 f5 22**

exf5 gxf5 23 **♕f2! ♕h5! 24 ♖d5** Δ
g4 +−; 24 ♗d3! Δ ♗e2-f3 e5!∝ **25
♖xd6 exf4 26 ♗xf4 ♘e5 27 ♕e2 ♕xe2
28 ♘xe2 ♗e4!≈ 29 c5 ♗xb1 30 ♖xb1
bxc5 31 bxc5 ♘g6!** 31...♖xc5 32
♘d4± **32 ♖d2**

32...♖xc5! 32...♘xf4 33 ♘xf4 ♗e5
34 g3 ♗xf4 35 gxf4 ♖xc5 36 ♖b7
Δ ♖xa7/♖dd7±; 33...♗h6 34 ♖f2!
♗xf4+ 35 ♖xf4 ♖xc5 36 ♖b7 Δ ♖h4
+− **33 ♗d6 ♖d8!=** 33...♗e5+ 34 ♗xe5+
+= **34 ♖b8 ♖xb8 35 ♗xb8 ♗e5+! 36
♗xe5+ ♖xe5 37 ♖d8+ ♔g7 38 ♘d4
♖a5 39 ♖d7+ ♔h6 40 ♘c6** ½-½ Suba

**247 Vaisman-Pavlov
Rumania Final 78**
**1 ♘f3 ♘f6 2 c4 c5 3 ♘c3 g6 4 e4
♗g7 5 d4 cxd4 6 ♘xd4 ♘c6 7 ♗e3
7** ♘c2!? **0-0** 7...♘g4 8 ♕xg4 ♘xd4
9 ♕d1! += **8 ♗e2 d6 9 0-0 ♗d7** 9...
♘xd4 10 ♗xd4 ♗e6 11 f4 ♕c8 12 b3
♖d8 13 ♕d3 ♗g4 14 ♖ad1 +=; 9...♘d7
10 ♕d2 ♘c5 11 ♖ad1! ♗d7 12 f4 +=
10 ♖c1 ♘xd4?! 10...a6 11 ♘b3 ♖b8?!
12 f3 b6 13 ♕d2± Smejkal-Andersson,
Sochi 73; 11...♘e5!= Gufeld **11 ♗xd4
♗c6 12 ♗f3!?** N 12 f3 ♘d7?; 12...a5;
12 a3 a5 Δ ♘d7 **a5 13 ♖e1 ♘d7!?
14 ♘d5 ♗xd5 15 exd5 +=/± ♖e8 16
♖e4 ♘c5 17 ♖e2 ♖b8 18 ♗xg7 ♔xg7
19 ♕d4+ ♔g8 20 h4! e5?! 21 dxe6**

♖xe6 **22 g3!± ♖xe2 23 ♗xe2 ♕e7
24 ♗f3 ♕e5 25 ♕d2 a4?** 25...♖e8!?
26 ♖d1= **26 ♖e1 ♕f6 27 ♘d5 ♕g7 28
♖e3± ♖f8 29 ♔g2 h5!?** 29...h6 30
**b4! axb3 31 axb3 b6 32 ♕b4 ♕d8 33
♖f3 f5?! 34 ♕c3+ ♕f6 35 b4?!** 35
♕e3! Δ b4 **♘d7?** 35...♕xc3!? 36 ♖xc3
♘d7 37 ♖a3 +−; 36...♘a6 += **36
♕e3 ♖b8 37 ♕f4 ♖c8 38 ♖a3 ♖c7
39 ♖a6 ♔h7? 40 c5! +− bxc5 41
♖xd6 ♕g7 42 ♖xg6!** 1-0 42...♔xg6
43 ♕xc7 cxb4 44 ♗e6 ♘f8 45 ♗xf5+
♔f6 46 ♕f4!; 46 ♕c8 +− **Ciocaltea/
Speelman**

248 Ribli-Gheorghiu Warsaw 79
1 c4 g6 2 e4 c5 2...e5 3 ♘f3 ♘f6∝
3 ♘f3 ♗g7 4 d4 cxd4 4...♕a5+!?
5 ♘c3 ♘f6∝; 5...♘c6 6 d5 ♘d4 7
♗d2 +=; 5 ♗d2 ♕b6!∝ **5 ♘xd4 ♘c6
6 ♗e3 ♘f6 7 ♘c3 d6 8 ♗e2 0-0 9
0-0 ♗d7 10 ♕d2 ♘xd4 11 ♗xd4 ♗c6
12 f3 ♘d7** 12...a5! **13 ♗e3** 13 b4!
+= a5!= **14 ♖fd1 ♘c5 15 ♖ac1 ♕b6
16 ♗f1 ♖fc8 17 ♖c2!=** ½-½ Gheorghiu

249 Mestel-Christiansen Hastings 78/9
**1 e4 c5 2 ♘f3 d6 3 d4 cxd4 4 ♘xd4
♘f6 5 ♘c3 ♘c6 6 g3 ♗g4!? 7 f3
♗d7 8 ♗e3 g6 9 ♕d2 ♗g7 10 0-0-0
♖c8** 10...0-0?! **11 g4 ♗e5 12 h4 b5!?**
12...h5!? **13 ♘cxb5 0-0 14 h5 ♗xf3!?
15 ♘xf3 ♗xg4 16 ♕g2** 16 ♗e2 ♘xe4
17 ♕e1 **♕a5 17 a3** 17 ♔b1 **♖xc2+
18 ♔xc2** 18 ♕xc2 ♖c8 19 ♗c4 ♗xf3
20 hxg6 hxg6 21 ♗xf7+ ♔xf7 22
♕xc8 ♕xb5 **♕a4+ 19 ♔d2 ♕b3 20
♘c3 ♕xb2+ 21 ♔d3 ♕xa3**

Diagram

22 ♗c1 22 ♖c1!? ♖c8 23 ♘d4! ♘d7
24 ♖c2 ♘e5+ 25 ♔d2 (1) 25...♖xc3
26 ♖xc3 ♕b2+ 27 ♖c2 ♕b4+ 28 ♔c1

♕a3+ 29 ♔b1 ♕xe3 30 ♕f2 +−; (2)
25...♘f3+ 26 ♘xf3 ♗xc3+ (26...♖xc3
27 ♕xg4!) 27 ♔e2 ♕b3 28 ♕xg4
♕xc2+ 29 ♘d2; 24...♘c5+ 25 ♔d2
♘b3+? 26 ♘xb3 ♕xb3 27 ♕xg4 ♗xc3+
28 ♔d1 +−; 23 hxg6; 22...♖b8?! 23
♘d4 ♘d7 24 ♕a2?? ♖b2! −+ ♕b4 23
♗d2 ♖c8 △ 24...♖xc3+ 25 ♗xc3
♕xe4+ 26 ♔d2 ♗h6+ 24 hxg6 24 h6
hxg6 24...h5 25 ♖h4 ♖xc3+ 26 ♗xc3
♕xe4+ 27 ♔d2 ♘d5? 27...♗xf3 28
♖xe4 ♘xe4+ 29 ♔e3 ♗xg2 30 ♗xg7
♔xg7! 31 ♗xg2 ♘c5 ∞/±; 30...♗xf1
31 ♗a1 ♗g2 32 ♖g1 +− 28 ♗xg7
♕e3+ 29 ♔c2 ♗xf3 30 ♗b2! e5 31
♕d2 ♕c5+ 32 ♔b1 ♘e3 33 ♖c1 ♕b6
34 ♕h2 ♘f5 35 ♖c8+ ♔g7 36 ♖b4!
1-0

250 Paoli-Bielczyk Albena 78
1 e4 c5 2 ♘f3 ♘c6 3 d4 cxd4 4 ♘xd4
♘f6 5 ♘c3 d6 6 g3 ♗g4 6...♘xd4 7
♕xd4 g6= 7 f3 ♗d7 8 ♗e3 g6 9 ♕d2
♗g7 10 0-0-0 0-0 11 h4 ♕a5 12 ♘b3
12 g4 ♖fc8 ♕c7 13 h5 ♘e5 13...♘xh5
14 ♖xh5 (14 g4 ♘f6 15 ♗e2 +=)
gxh5 15 ♗h6 ♗xh6 16 ♕xh6 ♗e6 17
f4 ♔h8∞ 14 ♗e2 ♖fc8 15 hxg6 fxg6
16 ♗h6 ♖h8 17 ♖h2 b5 18 ♖dh1
♘c4 19 ♗xc4 bxc4 20 ♘d4 ♕b6 21
♘d1 21 ♗e3? ♖ab8 22 ♘d1 c3! −+
♖c5 22 c3 ♕a5 23 b4 23 ♔b1 ♖b8
24 ♗e3 ♕a6 25 ♘c2 ♖a5∞ cxb3

24 ♘xb3 ♕a3+ 25 ♔b2 ♕xb2+ 26
♔xb2 ♖ab8 27 ♗e3 ♖c7 28 ♗d4 ♖b5
29 ♗xf6 ♗xf6 30 ♖xh7 a5 31 ♔c2
a4 32 ♘c1 32 ♘d2 ♗e6 −+ ♗e6 33
♖7h2 ♔f7 34 ♖d2 ♖bc5 35 ♖d3 d5
36 ♖he1 dxe4 36...d4? 37 f4! +=
32 fxe4 ♗g4 38 ♘e2 ♗e6 39 ♘c1
♖h5 40 ♖de3 ♖h2+ 41 ♖1e2 ♖xe2+
42 ♖xe2 ♗g4 43 ♖e3 ♗xd1+ 44 ♔xd1
♗xc3 45 ♖f3+ ♔g7 45...♔e6? 46 ♘c2=
46 ♘d3 e5 47 ♖f2 ♖d7 48 ♔e2 ♖d8
49 ♖h2 ♗d4 50 ♖h1 ♖c8 51 ♖c1
51 ♔d2 ♔f6 =+ ♖h8 52 ♖c7+ ♔f6 53
♘b4 ♔g5 54 ♘c2 ♖h2+ 55 ♔d3 ♗b2
56 ♖a7 ♖g2 57 ♖xa4 ♖xg3+ 58
♔e2 ♖g2+ 59 ♔d3 ♔f4 60 ♖c4 ♗a3!
60...g5 61 a4!= 61 ♖c6 ♖g3+ 62 ♔e2
g5 63 ♖c4 ♖h3 64 ♘e1 ♖h2+ 65
♔f1 ♗b2 66 ♘d3+ ♔f3 67 ♘e1+ ♔e3
68 ♘g2+ ♔d3 69 ♖c7 ♗d4 70 ♘e1+
♔xe4 71 ♘c2 ♗b6 72 ♖c6 ♗a5 73
♖c5 ♗d2 0-1 Bielczyk

251 Mestel-Speelman Hastings 78/9
1 e4 c5 2 ♘f3 ♘c6 3 d4 cxd4 4 ♘xd4
♘f6 5 ♘c3 d6 6 g3 g6 7 ♘de2 ♗g7
8 ♗g2 ♗d7 9 h3 ♕c8!? 10 g4 ♖b8
11 g5?! 11 a4 ♘h5 12 ♘d5? 12 ♗f3
f5 f5! 13 ♗f3? 13 gxf6 fxe4 14 ♗xh5
gxh5 15 ♘g3 ♘d4! −+ 16 ♘f6+ 16
♕xh5+ ♔d8 17 ♕f7 ♗f8; 16...♔f8!
♗xf6! 17 ♕xh5+ ♔d8 18 gxf6 ♕c4!
−+ 19 fxe7+ ♔c8 20 ♖b1 ♘xc2+
21 ♔d1 ♘d4 22 ♔d2 22 ♕a5 ♗a4+!
23 b3 ♕c2+ 24 ♔e1 ♗b5 −+; 22
♖a1 ♕d3+ 23 ♔e1 ♘c2 mate 0-1
Speelman

4 ♕xd4

252 Schneider-Ribli
Buenos Aires 78
1 e4 c5 2 ♘f3 d6 3 d4 cxd4 4 ♕xd4
♘c6 4...a6 5 ♗g5∞ 5 ♗b5 ♕d7!?

5...♗d7 **6 ♕d3 a6 7 ♗xc6 ♕xc6 8 c4 b5 9 ♘a3 ♘f6 10 e5!** 10 cxb5 axb5 11 ♘xb5? ♘xe4 =+ **b4! 11 exf6 bxa3 12 b3 gxf6 13 0-0 ♖g8 14 ♔h1 ♗b7 15 ♗xa3 e6 16 ♖fd1 e5 17 ♕f5 ♖g6 18 ♖d2 ♖d8 19 ♖ad1 ♗e7 20 ♖d5!?** ♕d7! =+ **21 ♕xd7+ ♔xd7 22 ♖5d2** ♔c7 23 ♘e1 f5 24 f3 e4!∓ 25 fxe4 fxe4 26 ♘c2 f5 27 c5 f4! 28 cxd6+ ♗xd6 29 ♗xd6+ ♖gxd6 30 ♖xd6 ♖xd6 31 ♖xd6 ♔xd6 32 ♔g1 e3! △ ♗e4 −+ **33 ♔f1 ♗e4 34 ♘e1 h5 35 ♔e2** 35 g3?? f3 −+ **h4! 36 ♘d3** 36 g3? fxg3 37 hxg3 h3 −+ **♗xd3+! 37 ♔xd3 a5 38 a3 ♔d5 39 h3 ♔e5 40 ♔e2 ♔e4 0-1 Gheorghiu**

2...e6, 4...a6

253 Skrobek-Jansa Warsaw 79
1 e4 c5 2 ♘f3 ♘c6 3 d4 cxd4 4 ♘xd4 e6 5 ♘c3 5 ♘b5 a6 6 g3 ♘ge7 6...d6! **7 ♗g2 ♗d7**= **7 ♘b3! += d6 8 ♗g2 ♗d7 9 a4 ♘c8 10 a5 ♗e7 11 0-0 0-0 12 ♔e2** ♕c7 **13 ♖d1 ♘e5 14 ♗f1** 14 ♗e3 ♘c4 **♗f6 15 ♗e3 ♗c6 16 ♘d4 ♖e8 17 f4 ♘d7 18 ♕c4! d5!?∝ 19 exd5 ♘d6 20 ♕b4 += exd5 21 ♘xc6 bxc6 22 ♗b6 ♕b8** 22...♘xb6 23 axb6± **23 ♖e1 ♖xe1 24 ♖xe1 ♘xb6 25 axb6 ♘b5 26 ♘a4! ♗d4+ 27 ♔g2 ♗xb6**

28 c4!± dxc4 29 ♖xc4 h6 30 ♖e7

♔h7 **31 ♗xf7 ♗d4 32 ♖e6 ♔c7 33 ♕c4 c5 34 ♕d3+ ♔h8 35 ♕e4 ♖f8 36 ♗g6 ♕d7 37 ♘b6 ♕d8 38 ♘c4 ♗f6 39 ♖xa6± 1-0** time **Gheorghiu**

√254 Riemsdyk-Andersson
Sao Paulo 79
1 e4 c5 2 ♘f3 e6 3 d4 cxd4 4 ♘xd4 a6 5 ♘c3 ♘c6 5...♕c7 **6 g3** 6 ♘xc6 +=; 6 ♗e3 ♘ge7 **7 ♗e3 ♘xd4 8 ♗xd4 ♘c6 9 ♗g2?!** 9 ♗e3 ♕c7 **10 0-0 ♘xd4 11 ♕xd4 ♕c5 12 ♕xc5 ♗xc5 13 e5!∝ ♗d4 14 ♖fe1 ♔e7 15 a4! ♖b8 16 ♖e4!** ♗xc3 **17 bxc3 ♖d8 18 ♖d4 b5?!** 18...d5! **19** exd6+ ♖xd6 =+ **19 ♖b4! d5 20 exd6+ ♖xd6 21 c4!** ♖d2 21...♖db6 22 axb5 axb5 23 c5 ♖a6∝; 22 cxb5 axb5 23 ♖ab1 ♗d7 24 c4! +− **22 cxb5 a5 23 ♖c4 e5 24 ♖c7+ ♔f6 25 b6 ♗f5 26 b7 ♖xc2 27 ♖xc2 ♗xc2 28 ♖c1 ♗f5 29 ♖c6+ ♔e7 30 ♖c5! 1-0 Gheorghiu**

√255 Bouaziz-Gheorghiu
Buenos Aires 78
1 e4 c5 2 ♘f3 e6 3 d4 cxd4 4 ♘xd4 a6 5 ♘c3 ♕c7 6 ♗d3 ♘f6 7 0-0 ♘c6 8 ♘b3 b5 9 f4 d6 10 ♕e2 10 ♕f3 **♗e7 11 ♗d2 0-0 12 ♖ae1 ♗b7 13 a4!? b4 14 ♘d1 d5! 15 e5** 15 exd5!? ♘xd5 **16 f5∝;** 15...exd5!∓ **♘e4!∓ 16 ♘f2** 16 ♗xe4 dxe4 17 ♕xe4 ♖ad8∓; 17...♘a5! **♘xd2 17 ♘xd2** 17 ♕xd2 =+ **♘d4! 18 ♔h5 g6 19 ♕h6 f5 20 exf6 ♗xf6 21 ♘g4 ♗g7 22 ♕g5 ♖ae8 23 ♔h1 ♕e7! 24 h4 ♘f5! 25 ♗xf5 ♖xf5 26 ♕xe7 ♖xe7 27 ♘e5 ♖c7! 28 ♘b3! ♗xe5 29 ♖xe5 ♖xe5 30 fxe5 ♖c4!** 30...♖xc2 31 ♘d4! △ ♘xe6 **31 g3 d4+!**

Diagram

32 ♔g1 ♖xc2 33 ♖f2 d3 34 ♖d2

146

♗d5! −+ 35 ♖xd3 ♖g2+! 36 ♔f1
♖xb2 37 ♘d2 ♖a2 38 ♔f2 ♖xa4 39
♔e3 ♖a3 40 ♔d4 ♖xd3+ 41 ♔xd3
a5 0-1 Gheorghiu

✓ 256 J.Meyer-E.Meyer USA 78
1 e4 c5 2 ♘f3 e6 3 d4 cxd4 4 ♘xd4
a6 5 ♘c3 ♕c7 6 ♗d3 ♘f6 7 0-0 ♗e7
7...b5 8 a4 b4 9 ♘a2 ♗b7 10 ♕e2±;
7...♘c5 8 ♘b3 ♗a7 9 ♕e2±; 7...♘c6
8 ♕e2 d6 9 ♔h1 ♘bd7 10 f4 b5 11
a4 b4 12 ♘a2 ♗b7!? 12...a5 13 ♗d2
△ c3± 13 ♘xb4 ♘c5 14 e5 dxe5
14...♘d5 15 ♘xd5 ♗xd5 16 exd6
♕xd6 17 ♗c4± 15 fxe5 ♘fe4 16
♘xa6?! 16 ♗f4?! g5; 16 ♘xe4! ♘xe4
17 ♘d3±; 16...♗xe4 17 ♘d3 +=/±
♗xa6 16...♖xa6? 17 ♗b5+ +− 17
♗xa6 ♖xa6 18 b4 ♕xe5 19 bxc5 ♖a5
20 ♗e3 20 ♘c6?? ♘g3+ −+ ♖xc5
20...♗xc5? 21 ♘c6 +−; 20...♘xc5?
21 ♕f3 +− 21 ♖ad1!? 21 ♘f3 ♕h5
△ ♘g3+ ♘c3 21...0-0 22 ♕f3 ♘xd1
23 ♕xf7+ ♔d7 24 ♖xd1 ♖d5∞ 25
♗g5! ♖e8 25...♕xg5 26 ♕xe6+ ♔c7?
27 ♕c6+ +−; 26...♔d8 27 ♖b1! ♔e8
(27...♖xd4 28 ♖b8+ ♔c7 29 ♕b6+
♔d7 30 ♕xd4+ +−) 28 ♕c6+ ♔f7 29
♕e6+ ♔f8 30 ♖f1+ ♔e8=; 26...♔e8 27
♕c6+ ♔f7 28 ♕e6+ ♔f8 (28...♔e8=)
29 ♖f1+ ♗f6 30 ♕c8+ 26 c3 h6 26...
♕f5 27 ♕xf5 exf5 28 c4 ♖d6 31
♗f4±; 26...♕xg5? 27 ♕xe6+ ♔d8 28

♖b1 +− 27 ♖b1 hxg5 28 ♖b7+ ♔d6
28...♔d8 29 ♘c6+ ♔c8 31 ♖b8+ +−;
28...♔c8 29 ♕xe8+ ♔xb7 30 ♕xe7+∞
29 ♖b6+ ♔c7 30 ♖xe6 ♖xd4 31 cxd4
♕xd4 32 ♖xe7+ ♖xe7 33 ♕xe7+ ♔b6
½-½ A.Smith/Ciamarra

257 Kasparov-Polugaevsky
USSR Final 78
1 e4 c5 2 ♘f3 e6 3 d4 cxd4 4 ♘xd4
a6 5 ♘c3 ♕c7 6 ♗e2 b5 7 ♗f3 ♗b7 8
0-0 ♘c6 9 ♘xc6 9 ♖e1 ♗d6 10 g3
♘xd4 11 ♕xd4 ♗e5= dxc6 10 e5?!
N 10 g3!? △ ♗g2 ♕xe5 11 ♖e1 ♕c7
12 ♗h5 ♗e7! 13 ♖xe6 g6! 13...♘f6?
14 ♘e4! 0-0 15 ♗xf6+ ♗xf6 16 ♖xf6
gxf6 17 ♗h6± 14...♘xh5 15 ♕xh5
0-0 16 ♗f4 += 14 ♖e1 14 ♕d4? fxe6
15 ♕xh8 0-0-0 16 ♗g4 ♗f6∓ ♖d8?
14...gxh5 15 ♕d4 f6 16 ♕d1! ∞/∓
15 ♕f3 c5 16 ♗f4

16...♕b6 16...♗xf3? 17 ♗xc7 ♗xh5
18 ♗xd8 ♔xd8 19 f3±; 16...♕c8?
17 ♗g4 f5 18 ♕g3 fxg4 19 ♗e5 +−
17 ♕g3 gxh5 18 ♗c7 18 ♕g7? ♕g6
19 ♖xe7+ ♘xe7! 20 ♕xh8+ ♔d7 21
♖d1+ ♗d5 −+ ♕g6 19 ♗xd8 ♕xg3
20 hxg3 ♔xd8 21 ♖ad1+ ♔c7 22
♘d5+ ♗xd5 23 ♖xd5 h6! 24 ♖xh5
♖h7≈ 25 ♖he5 ♔d7 26 ♖5e3 ♖g7
27 ♖d3+ ♔c7 28 ♖a3 ♖g6 29 ♖f3
♗f6?! 29...♖g7 30 ♖a3 ♖g6= 30 c3!

♛d7 31 ♖d3+ ♚c7 32 ♖e8 ♘e7?!
32...♗e7 += 33 ♖ed8 ♘c6 34 ♖8d7+
♛b6 35 ♖xf7 ♗e7 36 ♖e3 ♗d6 37 f4
c4 38 ♚h2 ♗c5 39 ♖e2 b4 40 ♖e4
bxc3 41 bxc3 ♗f2 42 ♖xc4 ♗xg3+
43 ♚h3 ♗e1 44 a4! +− ♘a5 45 ♖b4+
♛c5? 46 ♖f5+ 1-0 Kasparov

258 van der Lely-Tompa
Biel 78

1 e4 c5 2 ♘f3 e6 3 d4 cxd4 4 ♘xd4
a6 5 ♘c3 ♛c7 6 ♗e2 ♘f6 7 0-0 d6 8
f4 ♗e7 9 ♚h1 0-0 10 ♕e1 ♘c6 11
♘f3? 11 ♗e3 b5 12 a3 ♗b7 13 ♕g3
b4 14 axb4 ♘xb4 15 ♗d3 d5 16 e5
♘e4 17 ♗xe4 17 ♕e1 ♖ac8 dxe4
18 ♘d4 ♗c5 19 ♘ce2 ♖xd4 20 ♘xd4
♗xc2 21 ♘xc2 ♕xc2 =+ 22 f5 ♕d3
23 ♗e3 23 ♕xd3 exd3 24 ♗d2 exf5
=+ exf5 24 ♖xf5 ♖ac8 25 ♖af1?!
25 ♖g5!? g6 24 ♕f4 Δ ♖f1, h4, h5∞
♖c6! 26 e6? ♖xe6 27 ♖xf7 ♕xf1+!
28 ♖xf1 ♖xf1+ 29 ♗g1 ♗d5 30 h3 e3
0-1 Tompa

259 Vogt-Hesse DDR Final 79

1 e4 c5 2 ♘f3 e6 3 d4 cxd4 4 ♘xd4
a6 5 ♘c3 ♛c7 6 g3 ♘c6 7 ♗g2 ♘ge7
8 ♘b3 d6 9 a4 ♗d7 10 0-0 ♘c8 11
♗g5!? h6?! 11...♗e7 12 ♗xe7 ♘8xe7
13 ♕d2 += 12 ♗e3 ♗e7 13 f4 b6 14
♕h5 ♖b8 15 ♖f2 ♗f6 16 e5 16 ♖af1!±
♗e7 16...dxe5 17 ♘e4± 17 ♖d1 ♘b4
18 ♘d4 g6 19 exd6 ♘xd6 20 ♕f3
20 ♕e5 f6 21 ♘xe6 ♕c4 22 ♘g7+
♚f7∓ h5 21 f5!? gxf5 22 ♗f4 ♖d8
23 ♘xf5 exf5 24 ♕e3 ♕c5! 24...♗e6
25 ♕d4 0-0 26 ♕xb4 ♘c4 27 ♗xc7
♖xd1+ 28 ♘xd1 ♗xb4 29 b3 ♖c8 30
♗f4 += 25 ♕xc5 bxc5 26 ♗xd6 ♗e6
27 ♗e5 0-0 28 ♗f3 ♗g5 29 ♖e1 ♖d7
30 ♗xh5 ♖fd8≈ 31 ♗f4 ♗f6 32 ♗e3
♗d4 33 ♘d1 ♚g7 34 ♗xd4+ cxd4
35 ♖d2 f4! 36 gxf4 ♗f5 37 c3 ♘d3

38 ♖f1 ♛f6 39 cxd4 ♖xd4 40 ♘e3
♘h3 41 ♖fd1 ♗e6? 41...♖g8+ 42 ♚h1
♖gd8∞ 42 ♘g4+ ♛f5 42...♗xg4 43
♗xg4 ♖xf4 44 h3 ♖fd4 45 ♚h2! Δ
♗e2 +− 43 ♘f2 ♗c4 44 ♗g4+ 44
♗e2 ♘xf4! ♛xf4 45 ♗e2 +− ♛e3
45...♖g8+ 46 ♚f1 +− 46 ♗xd3 ♗b3
46...♗xd3 47 ♖xd3+ ♖xd3 48 ♖xd3+
♖xd3 49 ♘xd3 ♚xd3 50 ♚f2 a5 51
♚f3 +− 47 ♖e2+ ♛f3 48 ♖dd2 ♗xa4
49 ♖e4 ♖g8+ 50 ♚f1 ♖xe4 51 ♗xe4+
♛e3 52 ♖d3+ ♛f4 53 ♗h7 1-0 Vogt

260 Szmetan-Gheorghiu
Buenos Aires 2 78

1 e4 c5 2 ♘f3 e6 3 d4 cxd4 4 ♘xd4
a6 5 ♘c3 5 ♗d3 ♛c7 6 g3 ♘f6 7 ♗g2
♗e7 8 0-0 0-0 9 f4 d6 10 g4! 10 ♗e3=
♘c6 11 ♘b3! 11 g5? ♘xd4!∓; 11
♘xc6 bxc6 12 g5 ♘e8! 13 f5 exf5
14 exf5 d5∞ Dueball-Gheorghiu,
Vratsa 75 d5! 12 exd5 ♖d8 13 a3!
13 g5? ♘xd5 14 ♘xd5 exd5 =+ ♘xd5
14 ♗xd5 ♗f6! 15 ♕f3 exd5 15...♘d4??
16 ♕f2! +− 16 ♘xd5 ♖xd5! 17 ♕xd5
♕b6+! 18 ♚h1 18 ♕c5?? ♗d4+! −+
♗xg4 19 ♕g2 ♗f5! 20 ♗d2 ♗xb2
20...♗xc2 21 ♘c3! ♗xc3 22 ♕xc2 +=
21 ♖ab1 ♗f6 22 ♘a5 ♕d4! 23 ♘xc6
bxc6 24 ♖b4 ♕d6 25 ♖c4!?

25...♗h3!! −+ 25...♖e8∓ 26 ♕xh3
♕d5+ 27 ♛f3 ♕xc4 28 ♕d3 ♕a4!

29 ♖e1 h6 30 ♖e4 ♛b5 31 ♛xb5 axb5 32 ♗b4 ♗b2 33 ♖e3 ♗d4 34 ♖d3 ♖d8 35 ♔g2 35 ♗c5 ♗f6; 35 ♗a5 ♖d5 −+ **d5! 36 ♘f3 f5 37 ♗c3 ♗c5!** −+ **38 ♖xd5 cxd5 39 ♗b2 ♛f7 40 h3 g5 41 ♗c1 ♔g6 42 ♗b2 ♗d6! 43 fxg5 hxg5 44 ♗c1 ♔h5 46 ♗b2 ♔h4 46 ♗c1 f4!! 47 ♔g2 ♗e7 48 ♗b2 f3+ 49 ♔xf3 ♔xh3** Δ g4+ **0-1 Gheorghiu**

√ 261 Ljubojevic-Gheorghiu ✗
Balkaniad 78

1 e4 c5 2 ♘f3 e6 3 d4 cxd4 4 ♘xd4 a6 5 c4!? ♘f6 6 ♘c3 d6 6...♗b4!?
7 ♗d3 7 f4 ♛c7 8 ♗d3 g6!∞ 9 0-0 ♗g7 10 ♔h1 0-0 11 ♛e2 ♘bd7! 11...
♘c6 12 ♘xc6!? bxc6 13 e5∞; 12 ♘f3!± **12 ♘f3 b6 13 ♗d2 ♗b7 14 ♖ac1 ♖ac8 15 b4 ♛b8! 16 ♖fe1** 16 e5 dxe5 17 fxe5 ♘g4∓ **♖fe8 17 ♛f2! ♛a8!**
18 h3 Δ e5± **d5! 19 cxd5 exd5 20 e5 ♘e4 21 ♛d4** 21 ♗xe4 dxe4 22 ♘g5 f5 23 ♛h4 ♘f8∓ **♗xd2 22 ♘xd2 f6!∓ 23 ♘f3** 23 e6 f5! Δ ♘f6∓ **fxe5 24 fxe5 b5 25 ♖cd1!?** 25 ♘e2!∞
Ljubojevic **♛b8!∓ 26 ♘xd5 ♘xe5 27 ♘xe5 ♗xe5 28 ♛e4 ♛d6** 28...♔g7∓
29 ♗b1 ♔g7 30 ♛f3 ♗g3 30...♖cd8
31 ♗e4∓ **31 ♖xe8 ♖xe8 32 ♗e4! ♖f8 33 ♛b3 ♖f2** 33...♛e5!? **34 a3 ♖e2**
34...♛e5 **35 ♛c3+! ♛e5 36 ♛xe5+ ♗xe5 37 ♘c3!!= ♗xc3** 37...♖xe4?
38 ♘xe4 ♗xe4 39 ♖e1!± **38 ♗xb7 a5 ½-½ Gheorghiu**

262 Adorjan-Miles IBM 78

1 e4 c5 2 ♘f3 e6 3 d4 cxd4 4 ♘xd4 a6 5 ♗d3 ♘c6 6 ♘xc6 dxc6 7 ♘d2 e5 8 ♘c4 ♘f6 8...♘e7 9 ♗e3 ♘g6 10 ♘b6 ♖b8 11 ♘xc8 ♖xc8 12 g3 += **9 0-0 ♗g4 10 ♛e1! ♘d7 11 f4 ♗c5+ 12 ♔h1 exf4 13 ♗xf4 0-0 14 e5! ♗h5** 14...♖e8 15 ♛g3 ♗h5 16 ♗xh7+!
♔xh7 17 ♛h3 g6 18 ♖ad1! Δ g4 ±/+−

15 e6! ♘f6 15...fxe6 16 ♛xe6+ ♗f7
(16...♗f7 17 ♛h3 ♘f6 18 ♗d6! ♗xd6
19 ♖xf6 +−) 17 ♘d6 ♗xd6 18 ♗xd6
♘f6 19 ♗c4 ±/+−; 15...♖e8 16 exd7!
♖xe1 17 ♖axe1 f6 (17...♛xd7 18
♖e5 ♗g6 [18...b5 19 ♖xh5 bxc4 20
♗xh7+] 19 ♖xc5 ♗xd3 20 ♘e5! Δ
♘xd3 +−) 18 ♗f5 ♗f7 19 ♘d6 ♗xd6
20 ♗xd6 g6 21 ♗e7 ♛c7 22 ♗h3 f5
23 ♖d1 ♖d8 24 ♗xd8 ♛xd8 25 ♖fe1
+−; 23...♗d5 24 d8♛+! ♖xd8 25 ♗xd8
♛xd8 26 c4 +− **16 ♗g5 ♗e7** 16...♗g6
17 exf7+ ♗xf7 18 ♛h4 ♗g6 19 ♗xg6
hxg6 20 ♘e5 ♛e8 21 ♗xf6 gxf6 22
♘g4 +−; 17...♖xf7 18 ♘e5 +−; 16...
fxe6 17 ♛xe6+ ♖f7 (17...♔h8 18
♛f5) 18 ♘e5 +− **17 ♛h4 b5** 17...g6
18 exf7+ ♖xf7 19 ♗xg6! hxg6 20
♘e5 Δ ♗xg6 +− **18 ♘e5 ♛d5 19 ♗xf6 ♗xf6 20 ♛xh5 g6 21 ♘d7!**
1-0 Adorjan

263 Nuktu-Jaurdran Corr. 78

1 e4 c5 2 ♘f3 e6 3 d4 cxd4 4 ♘xd4 a6 5 ♗d3 ♛c7 6 0-0 b5!? 7 a4 b4 8 c3 ♘f6 8...♗b7 9 cxb4 ♗xb4 10 ♛g4
9 cxb4 ♗xb4 10 ♗d2 ♗d6!? 11 ♘a3! Δ 12 ♘db5! axb5 13 ♘xb5
♛b6 14 ♗e3 ♗c5 15 ♗xc5 ♛xc5
16 ♖c1 **0-0** 11...♗xh2+? 12 ♔h1 ♛d6
13 ♘c4! ♛c7 14 ♗a5; 13...♛xd4?
14 ♗e3 **12 ♖c1 ♘c6 13 ♘xc6 dxc6 14 ♘c4!? ♗xh2+ 15 ♔h1 ♗f4 16 ♗a5**

[handwritten top margin: 24 Sd2 Lb2·. / if. 23.Db1, La4 ~24 Sc1 De1]

♕e7! **17 ♖c2** 17 ♘b6 ♘xe4 △ ♕h4+
−+ **♗b7 18 g3 ♗c7 19 ♗xc7 ♕xc7
20 e5 c5+ 21 f3 ♘g4 22 ♕e2 ♖ad8
23 ♔g1 ♖d4!?** 23...♕d7?! 24 ♖d2!
♕d4+ 25 ♔h1 f5 26 ♗b1!±; 25...f6?
26 ♗xh7+ **24 fxg4 ♕c6 25 ♗xh7+!?**
25 ♖d2 ♕h1+ 26 ♔f2 ♕g2+ 27 ♔e1
♕xg3+ 27 ♔d1 ♗d5 **♕xh7 26 ♕h2+
♔g8 27 ♕h3!? f5!** 27...♕e4? 28 ♖h2
f5 29 exf6! **28 ♘d6** 28 exf6? ♖xf6
29 ♖xf6 gxf6 30 ♖h2 ♖d1+; 28
♖h2 ♕e4 29 ♕h7+ ♔f7 30 gxf5 ♖xc4
31 fxe6+ ♔xe6 32 ♕xe4 ♖xf1+!;
32 ♕h3+ ♔e7 **♖xd6 29 exd6 ♕xd6 30
g5** 30 gxf5 ♖f6 **♔f7 31 ♔h2** 31 ♕h4
♖h8 32 ♕f4 ♖h1+ 32 ♔f2 ♖xf1+
33 ♔xf1 ♕d1+ **♔e7** 31...♕d8? 32
♖xf5+ exf5 33 ♕xf5+ ♔g8 34 ♕e6+
♔h8 35 ♕h3+ △ g6 **32 ♖e2** 32 ♕h4!?
♔d7!? **♕d8 33 ♔g1!** 33 ♖xe6+ ♔xe6
34 ♖e1+ ♔d6 35 ♖d1+ ♗d5; 33 ♖fe1
♗d5 34 ♖d2 ♖h8 35 ♖xd5 ♖xh3+;
33 ♖f4 ♖h8 34 ♖h4 ♕d1 35 ♖g2
♖d8! 36 ♖f4 ♖d2; 36 ♖h7 ♗xg2
**♕d4+ 34 ♖ef2 ♕d7 35 ♕h4 ♗e4 36
g6 ♖b8! 37 ♕h5! ♕e3** 37...♖xb2 38
♕d1 ♖xf2 39 ♕xd4+; 37...♗d3 38
♖d1 c4 39 ♕e2 **38 ♖d1+ ♔c6** 38...
♔c7 39 ♕h4; 38...♗d5 39 ♖xd5+
**39 ♕e2 ♕xg3+ 40 ♔f1 ♖b6 41 ♖h2
♗d5 42 ♖h8** 41 b4 c4 **c4 43 ♖d4**
43 ♖d8 ♔c5; 43 ♖xd5 ♕xd5; 43
♖c8+ ♔b7 44 ♖g8 ♖b3 45 ♖xg7+
♔c6 **♕c5 44 ♖xc4+ ♗xc4 45 ♖c8+
♔d6 46 ♖xc4 ♖b3 47 ♖c3 ♖xc3 48
bxc3 ♕f4+ 0-1 Jaudran**

✓264 Moraza-Gheorghiu
Buenos Aires 78
**1 e4 c5 2 ♘f3 e6 3 d4 cxd4 4 ♘xd4
a6 5 ♗d3 ♘f6 6 0-0 d6 7 c4 g6 7...**
♗e7∝ **8 ♘c3 ♗g7 9 ♗e3 0-0 10 ♕e2
♘bd7 11 f4 e5!** =+ **12 ♘b3** 12 fxe5
♘xe5∓ **exf4 13 ♗xf4 ♘e5 14 ♘d5!?**

14 ♗xe5! dxe5 15 ♘d5= **♘xd5 15
cxd5 ♗d7!∓** △ ♘xd3, ♗b5/♗xb2;
15...♘xd3 **16 ♖f2 ♖c8 17 h3 ♖e8 18
♖c1 ♗b6! 19 ♖xc8 ♕xc8 20 ♗e3
♕b4! 21 ♕h2** 21 ♗d2 ♕a4!∓ **♘xd3
22 ♕xd3 ♗b5! 23 ♕d2 ♕xe4 24
♗f4 ♗c4 25 ♗xd6 ♗xd5 26 ♖e2
♕f5! 27 ♕e3 h5 28 ♖f2 ♕d7 29 ♗f4
♖c4! 30 ♗g5 ♖e4 31 ♕d2 ♕c7+ 32
♗f4 ♖xf4! −+ 33 ♖xf4** 33 ♕xf4?
♗e5 **♗xb3 34 axb3 g5! 0-1 Gheorghiu**

265 Stean-Gheorghiu
Buenos Aires 78
**1 e4 c5 2 ♘f3 e6 3 d4 cxd4 4 ♘xd4
a6 5 ♗d3 ♘f6 6 0-0 d6 7 f4 ♘bd7 8
♕f3** 8 c4 ♘c5! =+ **♘c5 9 ♗e3 ♗e7 10
♘c3 ♘xd3 11 cxd3 0-0 12 ♖ad1
♗d7!=** 13 ♕g3 ♗h4 14 ♕h3 ♗f6 15
♘f3! △ e5 += b5 16 ♖d2 ♖b8 17
♕g3! b4 18 ♘d1 ♖e8 19 ♘f2 g6 20
♘g4 ♗g7 21 f5 △ f6 += exf5 22 exf5
♗f6! 23 ♘h6+! ♗xh6 24 ♗xh6 ♕b6+!
25 ♔h1 ♗xf5 26 h3! ♘h5! 27 ♕h4
♕d8∝ ½-½ 28 ♕d4 ♕f6; 28 ♗g5 f6∝
Gheorghiu

✓266 Westerinen-Andersson
Buenos Aires 78
**1 e4 c5 2 ♘f3 e6 3 d4 cxd4 4 ♘xd4
a6 5 ♗d3 g6 6 0-0 ♗g7 7 c3 d6 8
♘d2 ♘f6 9 ♕e2 0-0 10 ♘c4 e5∝ 11
♘b3 b5 12 ♘ca5 ♗d7!** △ ♘c6 **13
♗d2 ♘c6 14 c4 ♘d4! 15 ♗xd4 exd4
16 h3** △ ♘g4∓ **♖e8! 17 ♕f3 ♕b6!
18 b4 ♗e6∓ 19 cxb5 axb5 20 ♕e2
♗f5!**

Diagram

**21 ♗xb5 ♖xe4 22 ♕c4 ♖c8 23 ♗c6
d3!! 24 ♕c1 ♖e2 −+** △ ♘e4 **25 b5
♘e4 26 ♘c4 ♕d4! 27 ♗e3 ♕xa1 28
♕xa1 ♗xa1 29 ♖xa1 d5! 30 ♗xd5**

d2 31 **♕f1 ♞c3 32 ♞b2 ♖xe3 0-1**
33 fxe3 ♘xd5 −+ **Gheorghiu**

2...e6, 4...♞f6

✓267 Bruggemann-Vogt DDR 78
1 e4 c5 2 ♞f3 e6 3 d4 cxd4 4 ♞xd4
♞f6 5 ♞c3 d6 6 g4 a6 7 g5 ♞fd7
8 ♝e3 b5 9 a3 ♞b6 9...♝b7 10 ♖g1
♘b6 11 ♕g4! ♘8d7 12 0-0-0 g6 13
f4 ♖c8 14 f5 exf5 15 exf5 ♘e5 16
♕g3 ♖xc3 17 bxc3 ♕c7 18 ♝f4 ♕c5
19 ♖e1!± Matulovic-Malich, Siegen
70 **10 h4 ♞8d7 11 ♕e2?! ♝b7 12
♖h3 ♞c4 13 ♝c1?!** 13 0-0-0∝ **♕b6
14 ♞f3 ♖c8 15 ♞d2** 15 b3? ♘xa3∓
**♞a5 16 h5 ♝e7 17 g6 ♝f6 18 gxf7+
♔xf7 19 h6 g6 20 e5?! ♝xe5 21
♞de4 ♖he8 22 ♕g4 ♞f6∓ 23 ♖f3
♖xc3! 24 bxc3** 24 ♘xc3 ♝xf3 25
♕xf3 ♕c6∓; 24 ♖xf6+ ♝xf6 25
♘xf6 ♖f3! −+ **♝xe4 25 ♕xe4 ♝xc3+
26 ♝d2 ♝xa1 27 c3 ♕c5 −+ 28 ♕h4
♕e5+ 29 ♔d1 ♖c8 30 ♝g5 ♝xc3 31
♖xf6+ ♔g8 32 f3 ♕d5+ 33 ♔e2 ♕a2+
34 ♔d3 ♕b1+ 35 ♔e3 ♕c1+ 36 ♔d3
♕xf1+ 0-1 Vogt**

268 Kovacs-Tompa
Hungary Final 78
1 e4 c5 2 ♞f3 d6 3 d4 cxd4 4 ♞xd4
♞f6 5 ♞c3 e6 6 g4 a6 7 g5 ♞fd7 8
♝e3 ♞c6 8...b5 9 a3 ♝b7 10 ♕g4!?

♞c6! 11 0-0-0 ♞ce5 12 ♕h3 g6 13 f4
♞c6 14 ♖g1± Fedorowicz-Petrosian,
Hastings 77/78 **9 ♝g2!?** 9 ♕d2 ♕c7
10 0-0-0 b5 11 ♘xc6 ♕xc6 12 ♝g2
+= Gufeld-Tukmakov, USSR 71 **♞de5!
10 ♞xc6** 10 f4 ♘c4 11 ♝c1 h6 =+
Malich **bxc6 11 b3 ♝e7 12 f4 ♞d7
13 h4 h6 14 ♕d2 hxg5 15 hxg5 ♖xh1+
16 ♝xh1 += ♕a5 17 ♞a4 ♕xd2+ 18
♔xd2 ♝b7 19 ♝f3 c5 20 c4 f6 21
gxf6** 21 ♝g4!? fxg5 22 ♝xe6∝ ♝xf6
22 ♖h1 ½-½ Kovacs

269 Skrobek-Bonsch Halle 78
1 e4 c5 2 ♞f3 d6 3 d4 cxd4 4 ♞xd4
♞f6 5 ♞c3 e6 6 g4 a6 7 g5 ♞fd7 8
♝g2 ♞c6 9 ♝e3 ♞de5= **10 b3!?** N
♕a5 11 ♞de2 h6! 12 gxh6?! 12 h4
hxg5 13 hxg5 ♖xh1+ 14 ♝xh1 ♝d7=
gxh6 13 f4 ♞g4 14 ♝g1 14 ♝d2 ♕b6∓
♖g8 15 ♕d2 ♝d7 16 ♞a4 ♞f6

17 ♝f3 17 ♕xa5 ♞xa5 18 ♞b6 ♖xg2
19 ♞xa8 ♞xe4 20 ♞c7+ ♔d8 21
♝b6 +−; 19...♝c6 20 ♝b6! +−; 18...
♖d8 19 ♞xd7 ♖xd7 20 ♝f3 d5 21 e5
♞e4∓ **♖c8 18 ♝e3 d5! 19 e5 ♞b4!
20 ♞ac3 ♞g4 21 ♝xg4 ♖xg4 22
♔f2 ♝c5 23 ♖hg1 ♝xe3+ 23 ♕xe3
♞xc2! 25 ♕d3 ♕c5+ 26 ♔f3 ♖xg1
27 ♖xg1 ♕xg1! −+ 28 ♕xc2** 28
♘xg1 ♞e1+ −+ **♕f1+ 29 ♔g3 ♔e7 30
♕h7 ♕e1+ 31 ♔g4 ♖xc3 32 ♞xc3**

♕xc3 33 ♕xh6 ♗e8 34 h4 f5+! 35
exf6+ ♚xf6 36 ♕g5 d4 37 ♕c5+ ♚f7
38 ♕c7+ ♚g8 39 ♕c8 ♚g6+ 40 ♚f3
d3 41 ♚e3 ♚g3+ 42 ♚d2 ♕xf4+ 0-1
Malich

270 Sax-Ghinda Warsaw 79

1 e4 c5 2 ♘f3 d6 3 d4 cxd4 4 ♘xd4
♘f6 5 ♘c3 a6 6 ♗e3 e6 7 g4 7 f4
b5 8 ♕f3 ♗b7 9 ♗d3 ♘bd7∝ h6 8
♕e2 b5 9 a3 ♗b7 10 f3 ♘bd7 11 h4
d5!? 11...g6∝ 12 exd5 ♘xd5 13 ♘xd5
♗xd5 14 0-0-0 ♖c8 15 ♔b1 ♘c5 16
♘f5!± △ ♗d4 ♖c7 17 ♗d4 ♖d7 18
♘xg7+ ♗xg7 19 ♗xg7 ♖g8 20 ♗c3
♘a4 20...♗a2+ 21 ♔xa2 ♖xd1 22
♕xd1 ♕xd1 23 ♗xb5+! 21 ♗e5 ♖xg4

22 ♖xd5! +− ♖xd5 23 fxg4 ♖d1+
24 ♔a2 ♕d5+ 25 c4! bxc4 26 ♗g2
1-0 **Gheorghiu**

271 Chi Chin-hsuan—Andersson Buenos Aires 2 78

1 e4 c5 2 ♘f3 d6 3 d4 cxd4 4 ♘xd4
♘f6 5 ♘c3 e6 6 g4 h6 7 g5 hxg5 8
♗xg5 ♘c6 9 ♕d2 ♕b6! 10 ♘b3 a6
11 0-0-0 ♗d7 12 h4 ♗e7 13 ♗e2
♕c7 14 f4 0-0-0 14...♖c8!? 15 ♔b1
♔b8= 16 ♗f3 ♖c8 17 ♕e2 △ e5 ♘g8!
18 ♗xe7 ♘gxe7 19 h5 g6! 20 a3
20 hxg6 ♘xg6= gxh5 21 ♖xh5 ♖xh5

22 ♗xh5 f5! =+ 23 ♕d2 23 exf5
♘xf5 =+ fxe4 24 ♘xe4 e5 25 ♘g5
♘f5 26 ♗g4 a5! 27 ♘e4 a4 28 ♘c1
d5∓ 29 ♘f6 exf4! 30 ♗xf5 30 ♘xd5
♖xd5! 31 ♕xd5 ♘e3! ♗xf5 31 ♖f1
♘d4!! −+ 32 ♘d3 32 ♕xd4 ♕xc2+
△ ♕b1 mate f3 33 ♕c3 ♕b6! 34
♘b4?? ♕xf6 0-1 **Gheorghiu**

2...♘f6

272 A.Smith-Regan USA 78

1 e4 c5 2 ♘f3 ♘f6 3 e5 ♘d5 4 ♘c3
e6 5 ♘xd5 exd5 6 d4 ♘c6 7 dxc5
♗xc5 8 ♕xd5 d6 9 exd6 ♕b6 10
♗c4 ♗xf2+ 11 ♔e2 0-0 12 ♖d1 ♗e6
13 ♕b5!? 13 ♕e4 ♘d4+ 14 ♘xd4
♗xd4 15 ♔f3 ♗xc4 16 ♕xc4 ♗g1!∝
N 16...♗e5 17 ♕d5 += Prokos-Rozkov,
corr. 64 **17 ♚g3! ♖ac8 18 ♕d3** 18
♕e2 ♖ce8 19 ♕f3 ♖e6∓ **♖fd8!?**
18...♕f2+ 19 ♚h3 ♖xc2 20 ♖d2?
♕f4! 21 ♖xc2 ♕xh2+ 22 ♚g4 f5+ 23
♚f3 ♕h5+ 24 ♚f4 ♕h4+ (24...♚g4+
25 ♚e5 ♖e8+ 26 ♚d5 ♖e4 27 ♖c4
+−) 25 ♚e5 ♕f6+ 26 ♚f4 (26 ♚d5
♕f7+ 27 ♚e5 ♖e8+ 28 ♚f4 ♖e4+ −+)
♕h4+ =; 26...g5+ 27 ♚f3 +−; 20 ♖xg1!
♖c5 21 ♕d1 g6 22 g4 +−; 18...♖c6
19 ♗g5 ♕xb2 20 ♗xd8 20 ♖xg1 ♖c3
21 ♗xd8 ♖xd3+ 22 cxd3 ♕e5+ 23
♚h3 ♕xd6∝ **♕e5+ 21 ♚f3 ♖c3 22
♖xg1 ♖xd3+ 23 cxd3 ♕xd6 24 ♗g5
♕d5+ 25 ♚g4 h5+ 26 ♚xh5** 26 ♚h4
♕d4+ 27 ♚xh5? g6+ 28 ♚h6 ♕h8
mate; 27 g4 ♕f2+ ∝/=+ **f6 27 h4 ♕d7**
27...f5!?; 27...fxg5∝ **28 ♖gf1** 28 ♗e3?
♕f5+ 29 ♗g5 ♚h7 △ g6 mate **f5!?
29 ♗e3 ♕e7 30 ♖ae1?** 30 ♖xf5 ♕xe3=
♚h7! △ g6 mate **31 ♖xf5 g6+ 32
♚g4 gxf5+ 33 ♚xf5 ♕f8+ 34 ♚g4??**
Zeitnot 34 ♚e6 =+ **♕b4+ 0-1 A.Smith/
Ciamarra**

273 Jekabson-Shabalov
USSR 78

1 e4 c5 2 ♘f3 ♘f6 3 e5 ♘d5 4 ♘c3
e6 5 ♘e4 ♘c6 6 c4 ♘b6 7 b4!? ♘xb4
8 ♗b2 ♕c7 8...♗e7 9 h4! h6 10 a4 a5
11 ♖a3 ♕c7 12 ♖h3 ♕c6 13 ♕b1±
Gurgenidze-Matsakanian, Tbilisi 77;
8...d5!? ∝/+= 9 a4 a5 10 ♖a3 ♕c6
11 ♕b1 h6 11...♘xa4 12 ♗a1∝ 12
♗e2 ♗e7 13 0-0 0-0?

14 ♘f6+! ♗xf6 14...gxf6 15 exf6 ♗d8
16 ♘g5 △ ♖h3 +− 15 exf6 d6 15...
g6 16 ♘e5 △ ♘xg6 +− 16 fxg7 ♖e8
17 ♘g5! f5 17...hxg5 18 ♖h3 +− 18
♖h3 e5 19 ♖xh6 +− ♔xg7 20 ♖h7+
♔g6 21 f4! ♗d7 22 ♗h5+ 1-0 22...
♔f6 23 ♖f7 mate **Gipslis**

2 f4

274 Sikora-Ermenkov Warsaw 79
1 e4 c5 2 f4 ♘c6 3 ♘f3 g6 4 ♗b5
♗g7 4...♕b6 5 ♗xc6 dxc6 6 d3 ♘f6 7
♘c3 0-0 8 0-0 b6 9 ♕e1 ♗e8!? 10
♕h4 ♘d6 11 f5!∝ gxf5 12 ♗h6 ♗xh6
13 ♕xh6 △ ♘g5 +− f6 14 ♘h4! ♘f7
15 ♕h5 fxe4 16 ♖ae1 ♘e5 17 ♖xe4
♖f7 18 ♘f3 ♘g6 19 ♖e3 ♖g7 20 ♘e4
♗e6 21 ♘g3 21 ♘eg5∝ ♕d7 22 ♕h6
♘f8 23 ♘h4 ♖e8 24 ♘gf5 ♗xf5 25
♘xf5 ♖g6 26 ♕h3 26 ♕f4! e6 27 ♘h4
♕h8 27 ♘h4 ♖g5 28 ♘f5 ♘g6 29 ♖g3

♖xg3 30 hxg3 ♖g8 31 ♕h6 e6 32 ♘h4
♕f7 33 ♕f4?? ♘xf4 0-1 **Gheorghiu**

1 e4 c6

275 Soltis-Shamkovich Phoenix 78
1 e4 c6 2 d3 g6 3 ♘d2 ♗g7 4 g3 d5
5 ♗g2 ♘f6!? 6 ♘gf3 6 e5 ♘g4 7 d4
h5 dxe4 6...0-0 7 0-0 ♘a6 8 e5 ♘g4
9 d4 += 7 dxe4 0-0 8 0-0 ♘a6 9 ♕e2
♘c5 10 ♖d1 10 e5 ♘d5 11 a3 ♗f5
12 ♘d4 ♘f4!; 11 c4 ♘b4 ♕c7 11
♘c4! N ♘g4 11...♘fxe4 12 ♗f4 12 h3
♗xf3 13 ♗xf3± ♘fd7 14 ♗g2 ♖ad8
15 ♗f4 ♘e5 15...e5? 16 ♗g5± 16 c3
♘e6 17 ♘xe5 ♗xe5 18 ♗e3! ♕a5 19
a3 19 ♕c4 ♕a4! 20 f4

20...♘c7! 21 e5 ♗b6 22 ♗xb6 axb6
23 ♗e4 △ ♘c2, ♔g2, f5 ♖xd1+ 24
♖xd1 ♖d8 25 ♖xd8+ ♘xd8 26 ♗c2
♕a5 27 ♕d3 ♘e6 28 h4 ♘g7 29 h5
♕a6! 29...♘c7 30 ♕d8 ♕c5+ 31 ♔f1
♕b5+? 32 ♔e1 ♕xb2 33 h6+!; 31...
♘e6 30 c4 30 ♕xa6 bxa6 31 hxg6
hxg6 32 ♗e4 c5 33 ♗b7 ♘c7 34 ♔f2
f6 b5 31 cxb5 ♕b6+ 32 ♔g2 cxb5=
33 hxg6 hxg6 34 ♗d1 ½-½ **Soltis**

276 Mariotti-Santos Albufieri 78
1 e4 c6 2 ♘c3 d5 3 ♘f3 ♗g4 4 h4
♗h5 5 exd5 cxd5 6 ♗b5+ ♘c6 7 g4
♗g6 8 ♘e5 ♖c8 9 h4!? f6 10 ♘xg6

hxg6 11 d4 e6 12 ♕d3 ♗f7 13 a3!?
N 13 ♗e3 ♕a5 14 h5 gxh5 15 gxh5
♘ge7 16 ♔f1? ♘b4! △ ♘xc2, ♕xb5
Usacij-Usov, USSR 59; 13 h5 gxh5 14
gxh5 ♘ge7 15 ♗e3 ♘f5 Fischer-
Smyslov, Jugoslavia 59 **♗d6 13...**
♕a5!? △ ♘b4 14 ♗e2 ♘ge7 15 c3 a6!?
16 ♗a4 b5 17 ♗c2 e5 18 f3 exd4?!
18...♔c7 19 ♗e3 exd4!? 20 ♘xd4
♘e5; 19...f5∞ **19 cxd4 ♕c7 20 ♕d1!**
♘a5? 20...g5; 20...a5 **21 b3 ♘ac6**
22 ♗d2 ♘d8 23 a4 b4 24 ♖c1 ♕b6?
24...g5! **25 f4! f5? 25...♘e6 26 h5**
♘e6 27 hxg6+ ♔f6 28 ♖h5 ♖xh5 29
gxh5 ♖h8 30 ♕h3! ♘xd4 31 a5 ♕a7
32 ♗e3 ♘c5 33 ♗b1 △ ♖xc5 ♘xb3
33...♘ec6 34 ♘xd4 ♘xd4 35 ♗xd4+
♗xd4 36 ♕xf5+ **34 ♖xc5! d4?** 34...
♘xc5 35 ♘d4! (△ ♕h4 mate) ♘xg6
36 ♕xf5+ ♔e7 37 ♘c6+ **35 ♖xf5+**
1-0 Speelman

277 Spassky-Pfleger Munich 79
1 e4 c6 2 d4 d5 3 ♘c3 dxe4 4 ♘xe4
♘d7 5 ♗c4 ♘gf6 6 ♘xf6+ 6 ♘g5 exf6!?
7 ♘e2 ♘b6 8 ♗b3 ♗d6 9 c4 ♗c7 10
♗f4 += 0-0 11 ♗xc7 ♕xc7 12 c5?!
♘d7 13 0-0 b6? 13...♖d8! (△ ♘xc5)
14 ♖c1 ♘f8 △ ♗e6= **14 ♖e1 ♗b7**
14...bxc5 15 ♖c1! **15 cxb6 axb6 16**
♘g3± ♖fe8?

17 ♗xf7+! +− ♔xf7 18 ♕h5+ g6

18...♔f8 19 ♕xh7 (△ ♘f5) ♕f4 20 ♘f5
♕g5 21 ♕h8+ ♔f7 22 ♘d6+ **19 ♕xh7+**
♔f8 20 h4! △ 21 h5 gxh5 22 ♘f5
1-0 Stean

✓278 Zaharov-Shakarov Corr 78
1 e4 c6 2 d4 d5 3 ♘c3 dxe4 4 ♘xe4
♗f5 5 ♘g3 ♗g6 6 h4 h6 7 ♘f3 ♘d7 8
h5 ♗h7 9 ♗d3 ♗xd3 10 ♕xd3 ♕c7
11 ♗d2 11 ♖h4 e6 12 ♗f4 ♕a5+!
♘gf6 12 0-0-0 e6 13 ♕e2 0-0-0 13...
c5!? 14 ♖h4 ♖c8 15 ♗f4 ♕a5 16 d5
♕xa2 17 c4 ♗e7! 18 ♗d6! (18 dxe6
fxe6 19 ♗d6 ♖c6! 20 ♘f5 ♖b6!∓)
18...♗xd6 19 dxe6 ♕a1+ 20 ♔c2
♕a4+ 21 ♔b1 0-0 22 ♖xd6 fxe6 23
♕xe6+ ♔h8 24 ♘f5 ♖ce8 25 ♘e7
♖xe7! 26 ♕xe7 ♖e8 27 ♖xd7! ♖xe7
28 ♖xe7 ♕d1+ 29 ♔a2 ♕a4+ ½-½
Shakarov-Asrian, Corr 73; 15 ♘f5
cxd4 (15...c4 16 ♘e3! △ d5±) 16
♘3xd4 ♕c4! 17 ♕xc4 ♖xc4=
Mihalchishin-Kasparov, USSR 78 **14**
♘e5 ♘b6 15 ♗a5 ♖d5 16 ♗xb6 axb6
17 c4 ♖a5 17...♖d8 18 ♘e4 ♘xe4
19 ♕xe4 ♗d6 20 f4 f5 21 ♕e2 ♗xe5
22 ♕xe5 ♕xe5 23 dxe5 g5! 24 hxg6
♖dg8=; 20 ♘f3 ♗e7 △ ♗f6= **18 ♔b1**
♗d6 19 f4 ♖d8 20 ♖d2 b5 21 c5 ♗xe5
22 fxe5 ♖a4! 23 ♖h3?! 23 ♖h4?!
♘d5 24 ♘e4 ♕a5 25 b3 ♖a3 26
♖g4 f5 27 exf6 gxf6∓; 23 ♕f2 ♘g4
24 ♕f4 ♘xe5 25 b3∞ **♘d5 24 ♘e4**
♘f4 25 ♕f2 ♘xh3 26 gxh3 ♔b8 27
♘d6 ♖f8 28 b3 ♖a6? 28...♖a8!
29 ♕g2! 29 ♕g3? f6 30 ♖g2 fxe5 31
♕xe5 ♖f1+ 32 ♔b2 ♖xa2+! −+; 30
♖f2 f5∓ **f6 30 exf6 gxf6 31 ♕g6 e5**
32 ♖g2! += 32 ♕xh6? ♖g8∓ **exd4**
33 ♕xh6 ♖d8 34 ♕xf6 ♕a7! 34...
♕a5? 35 ♕e7 ♖a7 36 h6± **35 h6 ♕h7+**
36 ♕g6 36 ♔b2 ♕d3!= **♕e7 37 ♕e4**
♕xe4 38 ♘xe4 ♖h8 39 ♖g6 b4 40
♘f2 ♖a5 41 ♘d3 ♖h7 42 h4 ♔a8 43

🖺d6 ♕b8 44 🖺xd4 🖺xh6 45 🖺xb4
🖺a8 ½-½ 46 ♘e5 ♔c7 47 🖺f4 🖺e8
48 🖺f7+ ♔b8 49 ♘d7+ ♔c8 50 ♘b6+
♔b8 51 🖺f4 🖺eh8=; 49 ♘c4 🖺xh4
50 🖺xb7 =; 46 🖺f4 ♔a7= **Shakarov/
Kasparov**

vicious sacrificial attack

279 Gaprindashvili-Nikolac
Wijk aan Zee 79
**1 e4 c6 2 d4 d5 3 ♘d2 dxe4 4 ♘xe4
♗f5 5 ♘g3 ♗g6 6 h4 h6 7 h5 ♗h7
8 ♘f3 ♘d7 9 ♗d3 ♗xd3 10 ♕xd3 e6
11 ♗f4 ♕a5+ 12 c3** N 12 ♗d2 ♕c7
♘gf6 13 a4 △ b4, a5 **c5 14 0-0 🖺c8?!**
△ c4?!; 14...♗e7; 14...cxd4 15 b4
15 🖺fe1 c4 16 ♕c2 ♗e7 17 ♘e5 0-0?
17...♘xe5 *B. looks quite safe on
the K-side...!*

18 ♘f5!± 🖺fe8 18...exf5 19 ♘xd7
♘xd7 20 🖺xe7± **19 ♘xg7!** +− 19
♘xh6+? gxh6 20 ♘xf7 ♕xh5∓ **♕xg7
20 ♗xh6+!** ♔xh6 20...♔g8 21 🖺e3 +−
(21 ♘xf7? ♕xh5∓) ♘xe5 22 dxe5
♘xh5 23 ♕e2 ♘g7 24 ♗xg7 ♔xg7 25
♕h5 ♗d8 (25...♗c5 26 ♕g5+ △ 🖺h3)
26 🖺g3+ ♔f8 27 🖺d1 **21 ♘xf7+ ♔xh5**
21...♔g7 22 ♕g6+ ♔f8 23 ♘g5 +−
22 g4+! ♔h4 22...♘xg4 23 ♕h7+ +−;
22...♔xg4 23 ♕g6+ ♔h4 (23...♔f4
24 ♕g3+ ♔f5 25 ♘h6 mate) 24 ♕g2
♕d5+ 25 f3 △ 🖺h1 mate **23 f3** △
♕h2 mate **♘xg4** 23...♗d6 24 ♕f2+
(24 ♔g2) ♗g3 25 ♔g2! ♗xg2 26 🖺h1

mate **24 🖺e4! 1-0** 24...♕h5 25 🖺xg4
△ ♕h7 mate **Miles**

280 Kapengut-Roizman Minsk 79
**1 e4 c6 2 d4 d5 3 ♘d2 dxe4 4 ♘xe4
♗f5 5 ♘g3 ♗g6 6 ♘f3 ♘d7 7 h4 h6
8 h5 ♗h7 9 ♗d3 ♗xd3 10 ♕xd3
e6 11 ♗f4 ♕a5+ 12 ♗d2 ♕c7 13
♕e2 ♘gf6 14 c4 ♗d6 15 ♘f5 0-0 16
♘xd6 ♕xd6 17 a3!** N 17 0-0-0 b5!
18 cxb5 cxb5 19 ♔b1 b4 20 ♘e5
♘d5 21 🖺h3 f6∓ Lukin-Gozshkov,
USSR 75; 17 🖺h4? b5 18 ♔f1 bxc4
19 ♕xc4 ♕d5∓ Lanka-Kasparov, Riga
77; 17 ♗c3? b5 18 cxb5 cxb5 19
♕xb5 ♘d5 20 ♘e5 ♘xe5 21 dxe5
♘xc3 22 bxc3 ♕c7 23 🖺h3 🖺fd8 24
♕e2 🖺d5 25 🖺e3? 🖺xe5 −+ Beljavsky-
Bagirov, Baku 77; 24 f4 =+ Kapengut-
Kasparov, Daugavpils 78 **c5** 17...a5
18 🖺h4 b5 19 ♗f4 ♕e7 20 c5± **18
🖺h4 🖺fc8** 18...🖺fe8 **19 🖺d1± cxd4
20 🖺xd4 ♕c7 21 ♗f4 ♕c6 22 ♘e5?!**
22 g4!± **♘xe5 23 ♗xe5 ♘e8 24 🖺g4
f6 25 ♗f4 ♕xc4 26 ♗xh6 ♕xe2+ 27
♔xe2 🖺c7! 28 ♗e3 f5!= 29 🖺g6 ♔f7
30 f3 ♘f6 31 g4 🖺c2+ 32 ♔e1!? 🖺ac8**
32...🖺xb2? 33 ♗d4 🖺h2 34 ♗xf6
🖺h1+ 35 ♔e2 🖺xd1 36 g5! +− **33
♗d4 e5 34 ♗c3 🖺h2 35 🖺g5 fxg4
36 fxg4 🖺c4 37 🖺d6 🖺e4+ 38 ♔d1
🖺f4= 39 🖺xe5 🖺xg4 40 🖺e2 🖺xh5
41 ♗xf6 gxf6 42 🖺d7+ ♔g6 43 🖺xb7
🖺d5+ ½-½ Kapengut**

281 Peters-Andersson USA 78
1 e4 c6 2 d4 d5 3 ♘c3 3 ♘d2 g6 4
h3 ♗g7 5 ♘f3 ♘h6!? 6 ♗d3 0-0 7 0-0
f6 8 c4 dxe4 9 ♘xe4 ♘f5 10 ♗c2 +=
Kavalek-Andersson (9) 78; 5...♘f6 6
e5 ♘e4 7 ♘xe4 dxe4 8 ♘g5 c5!=
**dxe4 4 ♘xe4 ♘f6 5 ♘xf6+ exf6 6
♗c4** 6 ♘f3 ♗d6 7 ♗d3 0-0=; 6 g3
♗e6 7 ♗g2 ♗e7 8 ♘e2 ♗d5 9 ♗xd5

155

cxd5 10 ♘f4 ♘c6 11 c3 ♕d7 12 ♕f3!
0-0-0 13 h4 +=; 6...♕d5!; 6 c3 ♗d6 7
♗d3 0-0 8 ♘e2 ♖e8 (8...♕c7? 9 ♕c2
g6 10 h4 ♘d7 11 h5 f5 12 hxg6
hxg6 13 ♗g5 c5 14 ♗xf5 f6 15 ♗e6+
1-0 Bronstein-Rotov, Tallinn 78; 8...
♘d7!?) 9 ♕c2 g6 10 h4 ♘d7 11 h5
♘f8 12 ♗h6! (12 hxg6 fxg6 13 ♕b3+
♗e6 14 ♕xb7 ♗d5 15 ♔f1 a6 16 c4
♖b8 17 ♕xa6 ♖a8= Szabo-Flohr,
Groningen 46) 12...♕c7?! (12...♗e6!?
13 0-0-0 ♕a5! ∞/+=; 12...♕e7 13 0-0-0
♗f5!? 14 ♗xf8 ♗xd3 15 ♗xe7 ♗xc2
16 ♗xd6 ♖xe2 17 ♖d2 +=) 13 0-0-0
♗e6 (13...b5!?) 14 c4± Kavalek-
Andersson (7) 78 ♕e7+ 7 ♕e2 7 ♘e2?
♕b4+ ♗e6! 8 ♗xe6 8 ♗b3 ♘d7! 9 ♗f4
♘b6 10 0-0-0 ♘d5=; 8 ♗d3 ♕c7=
♕xe6 9 ♗f4 9 ♘h3!? g5 10 ♗d2!?
♘a6 10 0-0-0 10 c3 0-0-0 11 ♕xe6+
fxe6 12 ♘e2 c5 13 ♗e3 ♗d6=
Gaprindashvili-Andersson, Dortmund
78 0-0-0 11 ♕xe6+ fxe6 12 h4!?
N 12 ♘e2 ♘b4 13 c3 ♘d5 14 ♗g3
♗d6!?= c5!= 13 ♗e3 13 dxc5 ♖xd1+!?
14 ♔xd1 ♗xc5 15 ♘h3 ♖d8+ 16 ♔c1
♘b4 ∞/=+ cxd4 14 ♗xd4 ♗c5 15 ♘e2
15 ♗xc5 ♖xd1+ 16 ♔xd1 ♖d8+ 17
♔c1 ♘xc5 18 ♖h3!? e5; 18 ♘e2 e5 △
♘e6 =+ e5 16 ♗xc5 ♘xc5 17 h5
17 ♖xd8+ ♖xd8 18 ♖d1 ♘e6 =+
♖d7! =+ 18 ♘g3 ♖hd8 19 ♘f5 ♘e6
20 g3 ♔c7 21 ♖xd7+ ♖xd7 22 ♖e1
22 ♖d1 ♘d4!? g6 23 hxg6 hxg6 24
♘e3 ♘d4∓ 25 ♘g4 ♖d6 26 c3 ♘c6 27
f3 27 ♖h1 ♔d7 28 ♖h1 ♔e6 29 ♘f2
f5 30 ♖h6 30 ♖e1!? ♔f6 31 ♖h7
♘d8! 32 ♔c2 ♔f7 33 f4? e4 34 ♖h1
34 ♘d1 ♖d3 35 ♖h3 g5 ♖d8 35 b3
g5 36 fxg5+ ♘xg5 37 ♖h6+ ♔g7 38
♖h1 ♘f3 39 ♘d1 ♖d2+ 40 ♔b1
♔f6 41 c4 ♘e5 42 ♘e3 ♖d3 43 ♘d5+
♔g5 44 g4 fxg4 45 ♖h8 ♔f5 46
♘e7+ ♔f6 47 ♘d5+ ♖xd5! 48 cxd5

g3 0-1 Diesen/Ciamarra

282 Timman-Bellon
Amsterdam 3 78

**1 e4 c6 2 d4 d5 3 ♘d2 dxe4 4 ♘xe4
♘f6!? 5 ♘xf6+ gxf6** 5...exf6 6 c3!?
+= **6 ♗e2 ♖g8!?** 6...♗f5 7 ♗f3 ♕a5+
8 c3 h5?! 9 ♗xh5 ♘d7 10 ♗g4 ♗xg4
11 ♕xg4 0-0-0 12 ♘e2 e6 13 ♗f4
♕b5! 14 0-0-0 ♘b6 15 ♘g3 ♕d5 =
Lasker-Nimzovich, St. Petersburg 14
7 ♗f3 e5?! 8 ♘e2 ♗g4 9 ♗xg4 ♖xg4
10 0-0 ♕d5 10...exd4? 11 ♖e1 ♗e7
12 ♘g3 +− **11 f3 ♖g6 12 b3?!** 12
♗e3!± **♘d7 13 c4 ♕e6 14 ♖e1 ♖g8
15 d5?** 15 ♘g3 0-0-0 16 d5 cxd5 17
cxd5 ♕b6+ 18 ♗e3 ♗c5 19 ♗xc5
♕xc5+ 20 ♔h1 ♕b8 21 ♖e2!? ∞/+=
♗c5+ 16 ♔h1 ♕f5∓ 17 ♘g3??

17...♖xg3! −+ **18 b4** 18 hxg3 ♕h5
mate **♗f2 19 ♖e2** 19 ♖f1 ♗d4 **♖xf3!
20 ♗d2 0-0-0 21 ♖c1 ♖h3!** △ ♖xh2+,
♕h5 mate **22 ♖xf2 ♕xf2 23 gxh3
♖g8 0-1 Bellin**

283 Donaldson-Maddigan USA 78
**1 e4 c6 2 d4 d5 3 exd5 cxd5 4 c4 ♘f6
5 ♘c3 ♘c6 6 ♘f3 ♗g4 7 cxd5 ♘xd5
8 ♕b3 ♗xf3 9 gxf3 ♘b6** 9...e6 10
♕xb7 ♘xd4 11 ♗b5+ ♘xb5 12 ♕c6+
♔e7 13 ♕xb5 ♘xc3 14 bxc3 ♕d7 15
♖b1!± Fischer-Euwe, Leipzig 60;

13...♕d7 14 ♘xd5 ♕xd5 15 ♕xd5 exd5 16 ♗e3 += **10 ♗e3!** 10 d5 ♘d4 11 ♕d1 e5 12 dxe6 fxe6 13 ♗e3 ♗c5 14 b4 ♕f6! 15 bxc5 ♘xf3+ 16 ♔e2 0-0 17 cxb6 ♖ad8! 18 ♕c1 ♕f5 19 ♕b1 ♕h5 20 ♕b2 ♕g4∓ Hermlin-Piskin, Corr 76 **e6 11 0-0-0** 11 ♖g1!? ♖c8 12 ♖d1 g6 13 d5 ♘xd5 14 ♕xb7 ♗b4 15 ♗b5 ♕c7 16 ♕xc7 ♖xc7 17 ♖g4! += Velimirovic-Nikolac, Jugoslavia 78 **♗b4** N 11...♖c8 12 ♕b1 ♕c7 13 ♘b5 ♕b8 14 ♘xa7± Sisniega-Groszpeter, Innsbruck 77 **12 d5 ♘xd5 13 ♘xd5 exd5 14 ♖xd5** 14 ♗b5!? ♕e7 15 ♖g1; 14 ♖g1 **♕c7 15 ♔b1 0-0 16 ♖g1 ♖fd8 17 ♖dg5 ♗f8 18 ♗d3** Δ 19 ♖h5 g6 20 ♗xg6 hxg6 21 ♖xg6+ ♗g7 22 ♖hg5± **♘d4 19 ♖xd4 ♖xd4 20 ♗e4** 20 ♖h5 g6 21 ♗xg6 hxg6 22 ♖xg6+ ♗g7 23 ♖hg5 ♖d1+! 24 ♕xd1 fxg6∓ **♖ad8 21 a3** Δ ♖h5 **♕d6?** 21...g6 22 ♕xb7 ♕xb7 22 ♗xb7 ♖d2∓; 22 h4 ♖d2 23 h5 ♗g7 24 hxg6 hxg6 25 ♖xg6 ♖xb2+ 26 ♕xb2 fxg6 27 ♕b3+ ♕f7 28 ♕xf7+ ♔xf7= **22 ♗xh7+± ♔xh7 23 ♕xf7 ♖d1+ 24 ♖xd1 ♕xd1+ 25 ♔a2 ♖d6 26 ♕xf8 ♕d4 27 ♖h5+ ♖h6** 27...♔g6 28 ♕f5 mate **28 ♕f5+ ♔h8 29 ♖xh6+ gxh6 30 ♕c8+ ♔h7 31 ♕xb7+ ♔h8 32 ♕c8+ ♔h7 33 ♕c2+ ♔g8 34 ♕g6+ 1-0 Donaldson**

284 Sveshnikov-Kasparov
USSR Final 78
1 e4 c6 2 d4 d5 3 exd5 cxd5 4 c4 ♘f6 5 ♘c3 e6 6 ♘f3 ♗e7 7 cxd5 ♘xd5 8 ♗d3 0-0 9 h4?! 9 0-0 ♘c6; 9...b6 **♘c6 10 ♕c2 f5** 10...♘f6!? 11 ♘e4 ♘b4 12 ♘xf6+ ♔h8! 13 ♕d2 ♘xd3+ 14 ♕xd3 ♗xf6 15 ♗g5 ♕d5 16 ♗xf6 gxf6 =+ **11 a3 b6?!** 11...♘f6 12 ♗g5∝ **12 0-0 ♔h8 13 ♖e1 ♘f6**

14 ♕a4 ♗d7 15 ♘g5?! 15 ♗b5 a6 16 ♗xc6 b5 17 ♕d1! ♗xc6 18 ♘g5 +=; 15...♕c8 16 ♘g5 ♗d6! 17 ♘xe6 ♖e8 18 d5? ♘xd5! 19 ♘xd5 ♗xe6 20 ♗xc6 ♗d7!∓; 18 ♗g5 a6 19 ♗xc6 ♗xc6 20 ♕b3 ♘e4 21 ♘xe4 ♗xe4 22 d5 ♕b7 23 ♖ad1 ♖ac8 ∝/≈ **♘g4! 16 f3** 16 ♗f4 ♘xd4! 17 ♕xd4 ♗c5∓; 16 ♗b5 ♕c7∓ **♘ce5?!** 16...♘xd4! 17 ♕xd4 ♗c5 18 ♕xc5 bxc5 19 fxg4 h6 20 ♘f3 fxg4 21 ♘e5 ♗e8 22 ♗e3 ♕xh4 23 ♗xc5 g3! 24 ♗xf8 ♗h5 ♖c5 ♕h2+ 26 ♔f1 ♖f8+ −+ **17 ♕d1** 17 ♗b5 ♗xb5 18 ♘xb5 a6 19 ♘xe6 axb5 20 ♘xd8 bxa4 21 dxe5 ♖axd8 22 fxg4 ♗xh4∓; 19 ♘c3 ♗d3∓ **h6 18 fxg4** 18 dxe5 ♗c5+ 19 ♔f1 ♘f2 20 ♕c2 ♘h1 21 ♕e2 ♘g3+ 22 ♔d1 hxg5 23 ♗xg5 ♕e8∝; 20 ♕e2? ♘h1! −+ **♘xd3 19 ♖xe6 ♗xe6 20 ♕xd3 ♗g8 ½-½** 21 g5 f4 22 ♕e4 ♗d6 23 gxh6 gxh6 24 ♘b5 f3! 25 gxf3 ♗d5∓; 21 gxf5 ♗xh4 22 ♖f1 ♗h7 =+ **Kasparov**

285 Szell-Orso
Hungary Final 78
1 e4 c6 2 d4 d5 3 exd5 cxd5 4 ♗d3 ♘c6 5 c3 ♕c7!? 6 ♘a3?! 6 ♘e2 e6 7 ♗f4 ♗d6 8 ♗xd6 ♕xd6 9 ♘d2 e5 10 dxe5 ♘xe5 11 ♗b5+ ♗d7 12 ♗xd7+ ♕xd7 13 0-0 += **a6 7 ♘c2 ♘f6 8 ♗e3 e5! 9 dxe5 ♘xe5 10 ♕e2 ♗e6 11 ♘f3 ♗d6! 12 ♘f5** 12 0-0? ♘xf3+ ♗xf5 **13 ♗xf5 0-0 14 h3 ♗xf3+ 15 ♕xf3 ♖fe8+ 16 ♗e3**

Diagram

16...d4! 17 cxd4 ♕c4! 18 ♕e2 ♕d5 19 ♗g4 19 ♕f3 ♕b5!∓ **♕xg2 20 ♕f3? ♖xe3+! 0-1** 20 fxe3 ♗b4+ 21 ♔d1 ♕d2 mate **Tompa**

1 e4 e5 2 ♘c3

286 Soltis-Westerinen
New York 78

1 e4 e5 2 ♘c3 ♘c6 3 g3 ♗c5 4 ♗g2 d6
5 ♘a4 N ♗e6 6 d3 ♕d7 7 ♗f3?! 7
♘xc5!? dxc5 8 ♗e3; 7 ♘e2 f6 8 0-0
♘ge7 9 c3 ♗g4! 10 b4 ♗b6 11 b5
♘d8 12 ♘xb6 axb6 13 a4 0-0= 14 d4
♘f7 14...♗e6? 15 dxe5 fxe5 16 ♘xe5
15 ♕d3 ♘g6 16 ♘e1 ♗h3 17 f3 ♖fe8
=+ 18 ♗d2? ♖ad8? 18...exd4 19 cxd4
♖ad8 Δ d5∓ 19 d5 ♖a8 20 c4 ♘f8?
20...♖a7 21 ♘c2= ♖a7 22 ♖a3 ♖ea8
23 ♖fa1 ♘g5?! 24 ♗xg5 fxg5 25 ♘e3
+= ♗xg2 26 ♔xg2 ♕d8 Δ ♘d7 27
♕c3 ♖a5? 27...♘d7 28 a5 bxa5 29
♖xa5 ♖xa5 30 ♖xa5 b6 31 ♖a3 ♘c5
28 c5!! bxc5 28...dxc5 29 ♘c4 29
♘c4± ♖5a7 30 b6 cxb6 30...♖a6!
31 ♕b3 ♖a6 32 ♖b1 ♖8a7 33 ♘xb6
g4 34 ♘c4 34 fxg4 ♕g5 gxf3+ 35
♕xf3 ♘d7 35...♖xa4 36 ♖xa4 ♖xa4
37 ♖f1! ♕e7 38 ♘xd6 36 a5 ♘f6
37 ♕f5! +− h6 37...♕d7 38 ♕xd7
♘xd7 39 ♖ab3 ♘f6 40 ♔f3 38 ♖ab3
♕c7 39 g4?? 39 ♖b5! Δ g4, h4, g5
♖xa5! 40 ♘xa5 ♕xa5 41 ♖xb7 ♕d2+
42 ♕f2?! ♕xf2+ 43 ♔xf2 ♘xe4+ 44
♔f3 ♘d2+ 45 ♔e2 ♘xb1 45...♖a2
46 ♖1b2 46 ♖xa7 ♘c3+ 47 ♔d3 ♘xd5

48 ♕e4 ♘c3+? Zeitnot 49 ♔f5 ♔h7 50
♖a6 ♘b5 51 ♖b6 ♘d4+ 52 ♔e4 ♔g6?
52...c4 53 h4! ♔f6 54 ♖xd6+ ♔e7 55
♖d5 +− ♔e6 56 ♖xc5 ♔f6 57 ♖xe5
♘c6 58 ♖f5+ ♔e6 59 ♖b5 ♘e7 60
♖b6+ ♔f7 61 ♖a6 61 h5! h5 62 gxh5
♔g8 63 ♖a7 ♔f8 64 ♖c7 ♘g8 65 ♔e5
65 ♔f5! ♘h6 66 ♖c8+ 66 ♔f4? ♔g8 Δ
♔h7, ♘g8-h6-g8 ♔e7 67 ♔f4 ♔f6
68 ♖c6+ ♔e7 69 ♖a6 1-0 69...♔f7
70 ♔g5; 69...♘f7 70 ♔f5 **Soltis**

287 Babrikowski-Vogt
DDR Final 79

1 e4 e5 2 ♘c3 ♘f6 3 g3 ♗c5 4 ♗g2
0-0 5 ♘f3 d6 6 d3 a6 7 0-0 ♘c6 8 ♘d5
♘xd5 9 exd5 ♘e7 9...♘d4?! 10 ♘g5
Δ c3 10 d4 exd4 11 ♘xd4 ♘f5 =+
12 ♘f3 ♕f6 13 c3 ♗d7 14 ♗f4 h6
14...♖ae8 15 ♘d2 ♗b6 16 ♕f3 16
♕h5 g5 17 ♘e4 ♕g6 =+ ♖ae8 17
♖fe1 ♕g6 18 h3 18 ♘c4 ♗a7 19 ♘e3
♘xe3 20 ♗xe3 ♗xe3 21 ♖xe3 ♕c2∓
h5 19 ♔h2 h4 20 ♗f1? 20 ♘e4 hxg3+
21 fxg3 ♖e7 =+ hxg3+ 21 fxg3

21...♘h4!∓ 22 ♕d3 ♗f5 23 ♕c4 ♗c5
24 a4 b5 25 axb5 axb5 26 ♕xb5
♖b8 27 ♕c4 ♖xb2 28 ♗e2 ♕h7! 29
g4 29 gxh4 ♕xh4 30 ♗f1 ♗xh3! 31
♗xh3 ♖xd2+ −+ ♗d7 −+ 30 ♕a6
♘g6 31 ♗g5 f6 32 ♘c4 fxg5 0-1
Vogt

Far if 32 ♗d2; Dc4;!

288 Tartakovsky-B.Smith USA 79
**1 e4 e5 2 ♘c3 ♘f6 3 f4 d5 4 fxe5
4 d3?!** exf4 5 e5? d4! 6 ♘ce2 ♘d5 7
♘xf4 ♗b4+ 8 ♔f2 ♘c6∓ Lombardy-
Smyslov, Teesside 75; 4...♘c6 5
fxe5 ♘xe5 6 d4 ♘g6 7 exd5 ♘xd5
8 ♘xd5 ♕xd5 ∝/=∓ Steinitz-Lasker,
London 1899 **♘xe4 5 ♕f3!?** 5 ♘f3
♗e7! (Δ 0-0, f5) 6 d4 0-0 7 ♗d3 f5
8 exf6 ♗xf6! 9 0-0 ♘c6 10 ♘xe4
dxe4 11 ♗xe4 ♘xd4 12 ♘g5! ♗f5!;
8...♘xf6!? 9 0-0 ♘c6=; 6 d3 ♘xc3
7 bxc3 0-0; 6 ♕e2 ♘xc3 (6...f5!?)
7 dxc3 0-0 8 ♗f4 c5 9 0-0-0 ♕a5!
10 ♔b1 ♘c6 11 ♕b5 ♗e6 12 ♕xa5
♘xa5 13 ♘g5 ♗xg5 14 ♗xg5 ♘c6=
f5 5...♘c6! 6 ♘xe4? ♘d4 7 ♕d3
dxe4; 6 ♗b5 ♘xc3 7 bxc3 ♗e7 8 d4
0-0 9 ♗d3! f6 10 ♕h5 g6 11 ♗xg6=
Hromadka-Lasker 23; 7...♕h4+ 8 g3
♕e4+ 9 ♕xe4 dxe4 10 ♗xc6 bxc6
11 ♘e2 ♗e7= **6 ♘h3!?** 6 d3 ♘xc3 7
bxc3 d4 8 ♕g3! ♘c6 9 ♗e2 ♗e6 10
♗f3 (10 ♖b1!?) ♕d7 (10...♗d5 11
♘e2 ♗xf3 12 ♕xf3 dxc3 13 ♖b1!
Keres) 11 ♘e2 0-0-0!? (11...♗c5 12
c4 0-0∝) 12 0-0 ♗c5 13 c4 ♗xc4!
14 ♘f4 ♘xe5! 15 dxc4 d3+ 16 ♔h1
dxc2∓ Vorotnikov-Kapengut, USSR
75 **♗c5** 6...♘c6 7 ♗b5 ♕h4+ 8 ♔f1
+=; 6...c6 7 ♘e2?! ♗e7 8 d3 ♘c5
9 a3? 0-0 10 ♗e3 ♘bd7 11 ♗xc5
♘xc5∓ Blackburne-Lasker, London
1892; 7 d3 **7 d3 ♘xc3! 8 bxc3 d4
=∓ 9 ♕g3 0-0 10 ♗g5 ♕e8 11 ♗e2
♕h8?** 11...dxc3 12 ♗e3 +=; 11...♘c6!
=∓ **12 0-0 ♘c6 13 ♖ae1± dxc3+ 14
♔h1 ♗d4** 14...♘xe5? 15 ♗f3 ♗d4
16 ♗f4 +−; 14...♕xe5 15 ♕h4! Δ ♗f3,
♘f4± **15 ♕h4 ♗e6** 15...♕xe5 16 ♗f3
♕c5 17 ♗xc6 bxc6 18 ♗e7 +−; 15...
♗xe5 16 ♗f3 +− **16 ♗h5 ♗f7** 16...
♕d7 17 ♘f4; 17 ♗g6 **17 ♗f3 ♗c5 18
e6 +− ♗g6 19 e7 ♖g8 20 ♗d5 ♗f7**

21 ♖xf5 ♗xd5 22 ♖xd5 ♗d6 23 ♖f6!
♕g6 23...gxf6 24 ♕xf6+ ♖g7 25
♖g5 ♕f7 26 e8♕ +−; 23...♕f7 24
♘g5 ♕g6 25 ♕xh7+! ♕xh7 26 ♘f7
mate **24 ♖xc3 ♗e7** 24...h6 25 ♖h5
♔h7 26 ♘g5+ +−; 24...♖ae8 25 ♖g5
♕f7 26 ♖h5 ♕g6 27 ♘g5 +− **25
♖xe7 ♗xe7 26 ♕xe7 ♖ge8 27 ♕h4
♕f7 28 ♖h5 1-0 Ciamarra**

289 Snyder-Shmeteff Corr 79
**1 e4 e5 2 ♘c3 ♘f6 3 g3 d5 4 exd5
♘xd5 5 ♗g2 ♗e6?!** 5...♘xc3 **6 ♘f3
♘c6 7 0-0 ♗e7 8 ♖e1 ♗f6 9 ♘xd5!±**
N 9 ♘e4 0-0 10 d3 += Smyslov-
Polugaevsky, USSR 61 **♗xd5 10 d4**

10...e4 10...♗xf3 11 ♗xf3 ♘xd4 12
♗xb7 ♖b8 13 ♗g2 0-0 14 c3 ♘b5
15 ♗e3 ♕e7 16 a4 ♘d6 17 ♗xa7
♖xb2 18 ♕c1! +− Snyder-Oppenrieder,
Corr 78; 14...♘e6 15 ♕a4! **11 ♘d2
♗xd4 12 ♘xe4 0-0 13 c3 ♗b6 14
♕xd5! ♕xd5 15 ♘f6+ gxf6 16 ♗xd5**
Δ ♗xc6 +− **♘e5 17 ♗xb7 ♖ad8 18
♔g2! ♘d3 19 ♖e2 ♖fe8 20 ♗e3 ♖b8**
20...♗xe3 21 fxe3 ♖b8 22 ♖d1! +−
**21 ♗a6 ♗xe3 22 ♗xd3 ♗c5 23 ♖xe8+
♖xe8 24 ♖d1 +− a5 25 ♗c4 ♖e4
26 ♗b5 ♖e6** Δ ♖b6 **27 ♖d5 ♖e5
28 ♖d7 ♖e7** 28...♗xf2? 29 ♗c4!
**29 ♖xe7 ♗xe7 30 f4 ♗c5 31 ♔f3
♔f8 32 ♔e4 ♔e7 33 f5 ♗g1 34 h3**

♗f2 35 g4 ♗e1 36 ♕d5 ♗d2 37 a4!
♗c1 38 b4 axb4 39 cxb4 ♗e3 40 ♔c6
♕d8 41 ♔b7 ♗d2 42 a5 1-0 Snyder

Spanish

290 Radulov-Westerinen
Buenos Aires 78
1 e4 e5 2 ♘f3 ♘c6 3 ♗b5 a6 4 ♗a4
d6 5 0-0 ♗d7 6 c4!? ♗g4?! 6...♘f6
7 ♘c3 ♗e7 8 d4 ♘xd4 9 ♘xd4 exd4
10 ♗xd7+ ♘xd7 11 ♕xd4 ♗f6 12
♕d5!? ∞/+=; 6...g6!? 7 h3 ♗xf3 8
♕xf3 ♘f6 9 ♘c3 ♗e7 10 d4!? b5?!
10...exd4 11 e5?! dxe5 (11...dxc3?!
12 exf6 ♗xf6 13 ♗xc6+ bxc6 14
♕xc6+ ♔f8 15 bxc3 ♗xc3 16 ♖b1∞)
12 ♗xc6+ bxc6 13 ♕xc6+ ♘d7 14
♘d5 0-0 =+; 11 ♘e2 b5!? (11...0-0
12 ♗xc6 bxc6 13 ♘xd4 +=) 12 cxb5
♘e5 13 bxa6+ ♔f8∞ 11 ♘xb5 0-0
12 ♘c3 ♘xd4 13 ♕d3 ♗e6 14 b4 +=
♘h5 15 g3 ♗g5 16 ♗b2 ♖b8 17 ♕e2
g6 17...♖xb4?? 18 ♗a3 +− 18 ♘d5
f5 19 exf5 ♖xf5 20 c5! ♗h6 20...
dxc5? 21 ♗b3; 20...c6 21 ♗xc6 dxc5
22 ♗xe5 ♘d4 23 ♗xd4 cxd4 24
♕c4+ +− 21 ♗b3 ♘h8 22 ♖ad1 Δ
♘xc7 ♕d7 22...♗g7 23 ♘e3 +− 23
♘xc7! ♘ef4 23...♘xc7 24 ♖xd6
♕e7 25 ♖fd1! ♘f6 26 g4 ♖g5 27 f4
+− 24 gxf4 ♕xc7? 24...♘xf4 25 ♗xe5+
dxe5 26 ♕xe5+ ♖xe5 27 ♖xd7 ♘xh3+
∞/± 25 cxd6 ♕b7 26 ♗xe5+ ♗g7 27
d7 ♖d8 28 ♗xg7+ ♘xg7 29 ♕e7 +−
♖ff8 29...♕b6 30 ♖d6 ♕c7 31 ♖c6!
♕xd7 32 ♕xd7 ♖xd7 33 ♖c8+ +−
30 ♕xf8+! ♖xf8 31 d8♕ ♖xd8 32
♖xd8+ ♘e8 33 ♖xe8+ ♔g7 34 ♖fe1
♕xb4 35 ♖1e7+ ♔h6 36 ♗g8 ♕xf4
37 ♖xh7+ ♔g5 38 h4+ 1-0 38...♔g4
39 ♗e6+ ♔f3 40 ♖f7 Bellin

291 Kozlov-Vorotnikov USSR 79
1 e4 e5 2 ♘f3 ♘c6 3 ♗b5 a6 4 ♗a4
d6 5 0-0 ♗g4 6 h3 h5 7 ♗xc6+ bxc6
8 d4 ♕f6 9 ♘bd2 ♗e6 10 ♘b3 10
dxe5 dxe5 11 ♘b3 ♗d6 12 ♕e2 ♘e7
13 ♘a5 ♕g6 14 ♘h4 ½-½ Hait-
Vorotnikov, Vilnius 77 ♕g6 11 ♘g5!?
N 11 ♘h4 ♕xe4 12 ♘f3 f6 13 ♖e1
♕d5 14 ♗d2 ♘e7 15 ♖c1 ♗f5 16 c4∞
Bangiev-Vorotnikov, Vilnius 77; 11
dxe5 ♗xh3 12 ♘h4 ♕xe4 13 gxh3
♕xh4 14 ♕f3 d5 15 ♘a5± Ivanov-
Vorotnikov, Yalta 76; 11 ♕d3 ♗e7
12 dxe5 ♗xh3 13 ♘h4 ♗xh4 14
♕xh3 ♗e7 15 ♗f4± Faibisovich-
Vorotnikov, Daugavpils 78; 11...f6!?
12 ♘h4 ♕f7 13 ♕c3 ♘e7 14 f4 ♗c4
15 ♖f2 exd4 16 ♘xd4 c5∞ Kim-
Vorotnikov, Daugavpils 78 ♗c8 12
dxe5 12 f4!? exf4 13 ♗xf4 f6 14
♘f3 ♗xh3 15 ♕d2 ♘e7 16 ♖ae1 Δ
e5 ±/∞ f6!? 13 exf6 gxf6 14 ♕d4
♘e7 15 f4 ♕g8 15...c5?! 16 ♕c3 ♗g7
17 ♘f3 ♗b7 18 f5 ♕g3 19 ♕c4 ♗c6
20 a4 ♖b8 21 ♗d2 ♖g8 22 ♖f2
Peshina-Vorotnikov, USSR 79; 17 f5
fxg5! 16 f5 fxg5 17 f6 ♗e6 17...
♖h7!∞ 18 ♕a4 ♗xb3 19 cxb3 ♕d7
20 fxe7 ♗xe7 21 ♗e3 ♕b8 22 ♖f5
♕b7 23 ♖af1 ♖ae8 24 ♕c4 ♕c8 25
♕a4? 25 ♖a5± g4 26 hxg4 hxg4 27
♖a5 ♖h4 28 ♖xa6 g3 29 ♖f4 ♖xf4
30 ♗xf4 ♕d7 31 ♗xg3 ♗f6 32 ♖a5
♖xe4! 33 ♕xe4 ♕b6+ 34 ♔h1 ♕xa5
35 ♕g4+ ♕e7 36 ♗h4 ♗xh4 37 ♕xh4+
♔d7 38 a4 ♕d2 39 ♕h3+ ♔d8 40
♕h8+ ♔d7 41 ♕g7+ ♔c8 42 ♕c3
♕d1+ ½-½ Kapengut

292 Arseniev-Vorotnikov USSR 79
1 e4 e5 2 ♘f3 ♘c6 3 ♗b5 a6 4 ♗a4
d6 5 0-0 ♗g4 6 h3 h5 7 d4 b5 8
♗b3 ♘xd4 9 hxg4 hxg4 10 ♘g5 ♘h6
11 ♗d5!? c6 11...♗e7 12 f4?! c6 13

♘xf7 ♘xf7 14 ♗xf7+ ♔xf7 15 fxe5+
♘f3+! 16 gxf3 g3!∓ Scharther-Marjan,
corr 70; 12 c3 ♖xg5 13 cxd4 ♗f4
14 g3!± Haag-Vucenovic, Hungary 75;
13...♖c8 14 f4?! Sigurjonsson-Marjan,
Novi Sad 76; 14 ♗c6+ ♔f8 15 g3±
**12 c3 cxd5 13 cxd4 ♗e7 14 dxe5
♗xg5 15 ♕xd5 ♖c8 16 ♘c3 ♗xc1!?**
N 16...♗e7 17 ♗e3 dxe5 18 ♕xe5
♕d6 19 ♕xd6 ♗xd6 20 ♖fd1 ♖c6 +=
Haag-Ciocaltea, Zinnowitz 66 **17 ♖fx
c1 g3**

**18 ♘d1!± ♗g4 19 ♖xc8 ♕xc8 20
exd6 ♕d8 21 ♕c6+ ♕d7 22 ♕a8+**
22 ♕xa6 0-0 23 ♖c1± ♕d8 **23 ♕xd8+
♔xd8 24 f3 ♗e5 25 ♘e3 ♔d7 26 ♖c1
g6 27 ♘f1 ♖c8! += 28 ♖xc8 ♔xc8
29 ♗xg3 ♘d3 30 b3 ♘c1 31 e5 ♗xa2
32 ♘e4 a5 33 ♘c5 ♘c3 34 ♔f2 a4
35 bxa4 bxa4 36 ♔e3 a3 37 ♔d2
a2 38 ♘b3 ♘b5 39 ♔c1 ♘d4 40
♘a1 ♘c6 41 f4 g5 42 g3 ½-½ Kapengut**

293 Donaldson-Opl Graz 78

1 e4 e5 2 ♘f3 ♘c6 3 ♗b5 a6 4 ♗a4
♘f6 5 d4 exd4 6 0-0 ♗e7 7 ♖e1 0-0
7...b5 8 e5 ♘xe5 9 ♖xe5 d6 10 ♖e1
bxa4 11 ♘xd4 ♗d7 12 ♕f3 0-0 13
♘c6 ♗xc6 14 ♕xc6 ♖e8 15 ♘c3 ♕d7
16 ♕xd7 ♘xd7 17 ♘xa4 += Ribli-
Karpov, Hungary-R.S.F.S.R. 69; 11...
♕d7 12 ♕f3 d5 13 ♗g5 0-0 14 ♘c3

+= Weinstein-Chellstorp, USA 73, 9...
bxa4 10 ♘xd4 0-0 11 ♘f5 ♖e8 12
♗g5 d6 13 ♘xe7+ ♖xe7 14 ♗xf6
gxf6 15 ♖h5! (15 ♖xe7? ♕xe7 16
♘c3 ♗b7 17 ♕e1 ♕e5 =+ Donaldson-
Bisguier, Lone Pine 78) 15...♖e5 16
♘c3 ♗b7 17 ♖h4 ♕e8? 18 f4! ♖e3
19 ♔f2!± Ghizdavu-Andersson,
Groningen 68/69; 8...♘d5 9 ♗b3
♘b6 10 ♘xd4! ♘xd4 11 ♕xd4 c5
12 ♕g4 c4 13 ♕xg7 ♖f8 14 ♗h6±
Timman-Balshan, Lone Pine 78 **8
e5 ♘e8** 8...♘d5 9 ♗b3 ♘b6 10 ♘xd4
♘xd4 11 ♕xd4 d5 12 exd6 ♕xd6
13 ♕e4 ♗f6 14 ♘c3 += Suetin-
Petrosian, USSR 50 **9 ♗f4 b5** (1) 9...
f6 10 ♗xc6 dxc6 11 ♕xd4 ♕xd4 12
♘xd4 f5 13 ♘f3 h6 14 h4 ♗e6 15
♘c3 c5 16 ♖ad1 c6 17 ♘a4 b5 18
♘b6 ♖d8 19 ♖xd8 ♗xd8 20 ♘d7!
♗xd7 21 e6 += Gaprindashvili-
Tarjan, Lone Pine 77; (2) 9...d5 10
♗xc6 bxc6 11 ♘xd4 ♗d7 12 c4! +=;
(3) 9...d6 10 ♗xc6 bxc6 11 ♘xd4
♗d7 12 c4 d5 13 ♘c3 c5 14 ♘b3
dxc4 15 ♘a5 += Torre-Shaw, Hong
Kong 79 **10 ♗b3 d5 11 c3 ♗g4** 11...
♘a5 12 cxd4 ♘xb3 13 ♕xb3 c6 14
♕e3 h6 15 ♘bd2 ♘c7 16 ♗g3 ♘e6
17 ♖ac1 += Tarjan-Taylor, Lone
Pine 78 **12 h3 ♗h5 13 g4 ♗g6 14
cxd4** 14 ♘xd4 ♘xd4 15 cxd4 c6 16
♗e3 f5 Grunberg-Vogt, DDR 78 **♘b4
15 ♗g3 a5 16 a3 a4!?** 16...♘d3 17
♖e2 c5 18 dxc5 ♘c7 19 c6!? ♖a6 20
♘d4 += Ghizdavu **17 axb4 axb3 18
♖xa8 ♕xa8 19 ♕xb3 c6 20 ♘bd2
♘c7 21 ♗h4 ♖xh4 22 ♘xh4 ♘e6
23 ♕e3!±** 23 ♕c3 ♕d8 24 ♘g2 f5=
Shmit-Tseitlin, USSR 76 **♕a7 24
f4 ♗c2 25 ♘hf3± ♕a4 26 f5 ♘c7
27 ♕c3 △ b3 ♗e4 28 ♘b3 △ ♖a1
♘a6 29 ♖a1 ♕xb4 30 ♖xa6 ♕xc3
31 bxc3 ♗xf3 32 ♖xc6 h6 33 ♔f2**

♗d1 34 ♘c5 h5 35 g5 ♗c2 36 f6 gxf6 37 ♘d7 1-0 Donaldson

294 Rosario-Joynt USA 78

1 e4 e5 2 ♘f3 ♘c6 3 ♗b5 a6 4 ♗a4 ♘f6 5 0-0 ♘xe4 6 d4 b5 7 ♗b3 d5 7...exd4? 8 ♘xd4 ♘e7 9 ♖e1! (9 ♗xf7+ ♔xf7 10 ♕f3+ ♔g8 11 ♕xe4 d5∝) d5 (9...♘f6 10 ♗g5!) 10 ♘c6 ♘xc6 11 ♗xd5 ♗b7 12 ♕h5! N g6 13 ♗xe4 (13 ♗xc6+? ♗xc6 14 ♕e5+ ♕e7 15 ♕xh8 0-0-0 16 ♕xh7 ♘g5 −+) ♗e7 (13...gxh5? 14 ♗xc6 mate) 14 ♕h6! +− Petrosian-Grinberg, simul. USA 78 8 dxe5 ♗e6 9 c3 ♗c5 10 ♘bd2 0-0 11 ♗c2 ♘xf2!? 12 ♖xf2 f6 13 exf6 ♗xf2+ 13...♕xf6 14 ♕f1 ♗g4 15 h3 ♗xf3 16 ♕xf3 ♘e5 17 ♗d1 Korchnoi 14 ♔xf2 ♕xf6

15 ♘b3?! 15 ♔f1 ♘e5 16 ♗e3 ♖ae8 17 ♗d4 (17 ♗c5) ♗g4 18 ♘1d2 ♕f4 19 ♔g1 ♘xf3+ 20 ♘xf3 c6≈ Balashov-Tukmakov, USSR Final 77; 15 ♔g1 ♖ae8 16 ♘f1 ♘e5 17 ♗e3 ♗xf3+ 18 ♕xf3 ♕xf3 19 gxf3 ♖xf3 20 ♗f2 ♗h3 21 ♘g3 g6 ≈/∝ ♘e5 16 ♘bd4 ♗g4 17 b4 ♖ae8∓ 18 ♗d2 ♕b6! 19 ♔f1!? ♗xf3 20 gxf3 20 ♘xf3? ♖xf3+! −+ ♖xf3+ 21 ♔g1? 21 ♕xf3?! ♗xf3 22 ♘xf3 ♕f6 23 ♗d1 (23 ♔f2 ♖f8 24 ♗d1 g5 =+) 23...♖f8 24 ♔g2 ♕g6+ 25 ♔f2 ♕d3 26 ♗e3 (26 ♗e1 d5 −+)

26...♕xc3 27 ♖c1 ♕e5 =+; 21 ♔g2! Δ ♕xf3 h5! 22 ♔g2 ♖fe3 23 ♕c1 ♖e2+ 24 ♔g1 ♗f3 25 ♗f4 ♖g2+ 26 ♔f1 ♖ee2 −+ 27 ♗d3 ♖ef2+ 28 ♔e1 ♗e4 29 ♗f1? ♖xf1+ 30 ♔xf1 ♕f6! 0-1 A.Smith/Ciamarra

295 Prainfalk-Kuuskmaa Corr 77

1 e4 e5 2 ♘f3 ♘c6 3 ♗b5 a6 4 ♗a4 ♘f6 5 0-0 ♘xe4 6 d4 b5 7 ♗b3 d5 8 dxe5 ♗e6 9 ♕e2 ♗e7 10 ♖d1 0-0 11 c4 bxc4 12 ♗xc4 ♗c5!? 12...♕d7 ∝/+= 13 ♗e3 ♗xe3 14 ♕xe3 ♕b8 15 ♗b3 ♘a5 15...♘b6; 15...♘a7? N 16 ♕xa7! (16 ♕e2 ♖fd8 17 ♘bd2 ♘c5 18 ♖ac1 h6 19 ♗c2 ♗g4 20 ♘b3 ♘xb3 21 ♗xb3 ♗xf3 22 ♕xf3 ♘d4≈ Nunn-Bellin, England 77) 16...♘xa7 17 ♘bd2 ♖fe8 18 ♖ac1± Nicevski-Bellin, Bilisi 77 16 ♘e1 16 ♘bd2 ♕a7!= ♘xb3 17 axb3 f5! 17...♕b6 18 ♕xb6 cxb6 19 b4!± 18 exf6 ♖xf6 19 ♘f3? 19 f3 ♘d6 20 ♘d2 ♖h6 21 ♘f1≈ ♗g4! 20 ♖xd5 ♗xf3 21 gxf3 c6! 22 ♖h5? 22 ♖d1 ♖g6+ 23 ♔h1 23 ♔f1 ♕b5+ 24 ♕e2 ♖g1+ −+ ♕f4!! 0-1 24 ♕xf4 ♘xf2 mate; 24 fxe4 ♕g4! Bellin an 2343, De3; & 24...Sg wins R,

296 Kupreichik-Kakageldiev Ashkabad 78

1 e4 e5 2 ♘f3 ♘c6 3 ♗b5 a6 4 ♗a4 ♘f6 5 0-0 ♗e7 6 ♖e1 b5 7 ♗b3 d6 8 a4!? ♗b7 8...b4!? 9 c3 0-0 10 d4 h6 10...♘a5 11 ♗c2 c5!?∝ 11 ♘bd2 ♖e8 12 ♕e2 ♕b8 13 ♗c2 ♗f8 14 d5 ♘a7? 14...♘e7 15 c4 c6 16 b3 cxd5 17 cxd5 ♘d7 18 b4± f5? 19 ♘h4! ♕c7 20 ♗b1 fxe4? 20...f4± 21 ♘xe4! ♗xd5

Diagram

22 ♗xh6!! gxh6 22...♗xe4 23 ♕xe4

♘f6 24 ♗a2+ d5 25 ♗xd5+ ♘xd5
26 ♕xd5+ ♔f7 27 ♕xf7+ ♔xf7 28
♗d2 +=; 23 ♖xe4! gxh6 24 ♕g4+
♗g7 25 ♗d5+ ♔h8 26 ♘g6+ ♔h7 27
♕e4 ♘f6 28 ♘f8+ ♔h8 29 ♕h7+ ♘xh7
30 ♘g6 mate **23 ♕g4+ ♔f7** 23...♗g7
24 ♘f5 ♘f8 25 ♗a2+! ♔h8 26 ♖ac1
♘c6 (26...♕d7 27 ♘f6! +−) 27 ♘exd6
+− **24 ♕g6+ ♔e7 25 ♘xd6** Δ ♘hf5+,
♕xe8 mate **♗e6 26 ♘hf5+ ♗xf5 27
♕f7+! ♔xd6 28 ♖d1+ ♔c6 29 ♕d5+
1-0** 29...♔b6 30 a5 mate **Bellin**

297 Hardicsay-Windischman
Hungary 78
**1 e4 e5 2 ♘f3 ♘c6 3 ♗b5 a6 4 ♗a4
♘f6 5 0-0 b5 6 ♗b3 ♗e7 7 ♖e1** 7 d4
d6 8 c3± **d6** 7...0-0! **8 c3 ♘a5 9 ♗c2
c5 10 d4 ♕c7 11 ♘bd2 0-0 12 b3
♗g4 13 d5 c4?** 13...b4 += **14 b4 ♘b7
15 a4 ♖fc8 16 ♘f1 ♗h5 17 ♘g3 ♗g6
18 ♘h4 +−** ♕d7 **19 ♘hf5 ♗d8 20 ♗e3**
a5 21 h3 axb4 22 cxb4 ♖a6 23 a5
h6 24 ♔h2 ♔h7 25 ♖a3! ♗c7 26 f4
♖e8 27 ♖f1 exf4 28 ♖xf4 ♗d8 29
♗d4 ♖g8 30 ♕f3 ♘e8 31 h4! ♗f6 32
♗xf6 ♘xf6 33 ♘xg7 ♔xg7 34 ♖xf6
♕e7 35 ♖f4 ♕e5 35...♘d8 36 ♖g4 +−
**36 h5 ♗h7 37 ♖xf7+ ♔h8 38 ♖xb7
♖aa8 39 ♕f7 1-0 Hardicsay**

298 Diesen-Kovacs Bajmok 78
1 e4 e5 2 ♘f3 ♘c6 3 ♗b5 a6 4 ♗a4

♘f6 5 0-0 ♗e7 6 ♖e1 b5 7 ♗b3 0-0 8
d4 d6 9 c3 ♗g4 10 d5 ♘a5 11 ♗c2
c6 12 h3 ♗c8!?** 12...♗xf3 13 ♕xf3
cxd5 14 exd5 ♘c4 15 ♘d2 ♘b6 16
♘f1 ♘e8! 17 a4! ♘xa4?! Romanishin-
Karpov, USSR Final 76; 17...g6 Tal-
Gligoric, Bugojno 78 **13 dxc6 ♕c7
14 a4 ♕xc6** 14...♗e6 15 axb5 axb5 16
♘g5 ♕xc6 17 ♘xe6 fxe6 18 ♘d2
♖fc8 19 ♗d3 ♕b7! Schrancz-Hardicsay,
Hungary 78 **15 ♘bd2 ♗b7 16 ♘f1
♘c4 17 ♘g3 g6 18 ♗h6 ♖fd8 19 ♕c1
♗f8 20 ♘f5!** ♕d7 **21 ♗xf8 ♖xf8 22
a5?** 22 b3! ♘a5 23 ♕g5 Δ ♖ad1 +−
**♘xb2! 23 ♘h6+ ♔g7 24 ♘f5+∝
½-½ Kovacs**

299 Ivanov-Borisenko USSR 79
**1 e4 e5 2 ♘f3 ♘c6 3 ♗b5 a6 4 ♗a4
♘f6 5 0-0 ♗e7 6 ♖e1 b5 7 ♗b3 0-0 8
d4 d6 9 c3 ♗g4 10 d5 ♘a5 11 ♗c2
c6 12 h3 ♗c8 13 dxc6 ♕c7** 13...♘xc6
14 ♘bd2 ♗b7 15 ♘f1 ♘b8 16 ♘g3
♖e8 17 a4 ♗f8 18 ♕e2 += Nunn-
Goday, Haifa 76 **14 ♘bd2** 14 a4 ♕xc6
15 ♘bd2 ♗e6 16 ♘g5 ♗d7 17 ♘f1
♘c4 18 b3 ♘b6 19 a5 ♘c8 20 ♕d3±
Stein-Gershberg 66; 14...♗e6 15 axb5
axb5 16 ♘g5 ♕xc6 17 ♘xe6 Schrancz-
Hardicsay, Hungary 78 **♕xc6 15 ♘f1**
15 ♖e3!? g6 16 b4 ♘c4 Soltis-
Reshevsky, USA Final 77 **♘c4** 15...
♗e6 16 ♘g3 g6 17 ♗h6 ♖fc8 18 ♘g5
♗f8 19 ♗xf8 ♖xf8 20 ♕c1 ♗d7 21
♘f3 ♔g7 22 ♘f5+ Ligterink-Timman,
Amsterdam 3 78; 16...♖fe8 17 ♕e2
♗f8 18 ♘g5 ♗d7 19 ♘h5 += Tseshkovsky-Savon, Ashkabad 78 **16 ♘g3**
16 ♕e2 h6 17 ♘g3 ♖e8 18 ♘h4 ♗f8
19 ♕f3 += Stein-Kavalek, Caracas
70 **g6** 16...♖e8 17 a4 ♗f8 18 b3?♘b6
19 a5 ♘bd7 18 ♗d2 Nunn-P.Little-
wood, London 78; 18 ♘h4! += Nunn
17 b3 17 ♕e2 ♗b7 18 a4 ♖fc8 19 axb5

axb5 20 ♖xa8 ♖xa8 21 ♗d3 ♖a2
22 ♗b1 ♖a1 23 ♗d3 ♖a2 ½-½ Ciocaltea-
Gligoric, Moscow 77 **♗b6 18 ♗h6
♖e8 19 ♕d2** △ ♘f5 **♔h8 20 ♘g5 ♗e6
21 ♘xe6 fxe6** += **22 ♖ac1 ♖ac8 23
♗d3 ♘fd7 24 ♗e2 ♘c5 25 ♗g4 ♗h4
26 ♖cd1** 26 ♕e3 △ ♘f1-h2-f3 +=
**♖cd8 27 ♗g5 ♗xg5 28 ♕xg5 ♕c7
29 ♖d2 ♕e7 30 h4 ♕xg5 31 hxg5
♔g7 32 ♖ed1 ♗b7 33 ♖b2?!** △ a4;
33 ♘e2 d5? 34 ♗f3±; 33...h6 34 gx
h6+ ♔xh6 35 g3 △ f4 += **♖e7 34
♗e2 h6 35 f4?!** exf4 36 **♗xf4 ♖de8
37** gxh6+ **♔xh6 38 g3 ♘d7** =+ **39
♘d3 ♘f6 40 ♗f3 ♖c8 41 e5!?** 41
♖c2 e5! 42 ♘b4 a5 43 ♘d5 ♘xd5 44
♖xd5 ♖c5 =+ **dxe5 42 ♘xe5 ♖xc3
43 ♖e2 ♘c5 44 ♔g2 ♘cd7?!** 45 **♗xd7
♘xd7 46 ♖d6=** ♘c5 **47 b4 ♘d3 48
♖xa6 ♗xb4 49 ♖axe6 ♖xe6 50 ♖xe6
♖a3 51 ♖b6 ♖xa2+** ½-½ **Kapengut**

**300 Tseshkovsky-Romanishin
USSR 79**

**1 e4 e5 2 ♘f3 ♘c6 3 ♗b5 a6 4 ♗a4
♘f6 5 0-0 ♗e7 6 ♖e1 b5 7 ♗b3 d6 8
c3 0-0 9 d4 ♗g4** 9...exd4?! 10 cxd4
♗g4 11 ♘c3!±; 9...♘a5?! 10 ♗c2!
♗g4 11 h3± **10 d5** 10 ♗e3 d5!? 11
exd5 exd4 12 ♗g5? ♘xd5!∓ J.Toth-
Perenyi, Hungary 77; 12 ♗xd4 ♘xd4
13 cxd4 ♗b4 14 ♘c3 a5?! (14...♗xc3
15 bxc3 ♘xd5 16 ♕d3 ∝/+=) 15 a3
♗xc3 16 bxc3 a4 17 ♗a2 ♕d6 18 h3±
Gulko-Geller, Lvov 78; 10...exd4!
♘a5 11 ♗c2 ♕c8!? N 11...c6 12 h3
♗xf3 13 gxf3 cxd5 14 exd5 ♘c4 15
♘d2 ♘b6 16 ♘f1 +=; 11...♘c4!?; 11...
c5?! **12 a4** 12 h3 ♗d7 13 ♘bd2 c6
14 dxc6!?≈ **c6 13 ♗g5! h6** 13...
♘xd5?! 14 exd5 (14 ♗xe7? ♘xe7 15
♕xd6 ♗xf3) 14...♗xf3 15 ♕xf3 ♗xg5
16 dxc6±; 13...cxd5∝ 14 exd5 ♘xd5?
15 ♕xd5 ♗xf3 16 ♕xf3 ♗xg5 17 axb5

axb5 18 ♗e4 ♖a7 19 b4 ♘c6 20 ♘a3
+– **14 ♗xf6 ♗xf6 15 dxc6 ♖d8?!**
15...♕xc6 **16 axb5 axb5 17 ♕d5**
♕xc6 **18 ♗d3 ♕xd5?** 18...♗d7!?
19 exd5 ♘b3 20 ♖a3! 20 ♖xa8 ♖xa8
21 ♗xb5 ♖a2; 21 ♘a3 b4! 22 cxb4
e4!∝ **♘c5 21 ♖xa8** 21 ♗xb5 ♖ab8!
22 c4 e4∓ **♖xa8 22 ♗xb5** += e4 23
**♘fd2 ♖a1 24 ♔f1 ♗f5 25 ♘a3 ♖a2
26 ♘dc4 ♗g6 27 h3 h5 28 ♔g1 ♘d3
29 ♖b1 ♗g5 30 ♘c2** Zeitnot 30
♗a4? (△ ♗b3) e3 31 fxe3 (31 ♗b3
e2 32 ♗xa2 ♘c1 –+) ♘e5 –+ **♘xf2!**
30...e3 31 fxe3 ♘xb2 32 ♖xb2 ♖xb2
33 ♘xb2 ♗xc2 34 ♔f2 += **31 ♔xf2
e3+ 32 ♘4xe3 ♗xe3+ 33 ♔xe3 ♗xc2
34 ♖c1 ♖xb2= 35 ♘f1** 35 ♗e2 ♗e4
♔f8 36 c4 ♔e7 37 ♔d4 37 ♗e2 **f5??**
+– 37...♗f5 **38 ♔c3 ♖a2 39 ♖xc2
♖a1 40 ♗e2 ♖a3+ 41 ♔d4** 1-0 **Bellin**

Pity !

**301 Lodz-Ivanovo
Telex 78**

**1 e4 e5 2 ♘f3 ♘c6 3 ♗b5 a6 4 ♗a4
♘f6 5 0-0 ♗e7 6 ♖e1 b5 7 ♗b3 0-0
8 c3 d6 9 h3 ♘a5 10 ♗c2 c5 11 d4
♕c7 12 ♘bd2 cxd4 13 cxd4 ♗b7 14
♘f1 ♖ac8 15 ♖e2** 15 ♗d3; 15 ♗b1
♘h5!? 16 d5 ♘c4 17 b3 ♘b6 18 g4?!
**♕c3! 19 ♗e3 ♘f4! =+ 20 ♖d2 ♘d7
21 ♔h2 ♖c7 22 ♘g3 ♖fc8 23 ♘e2
♘xe2 24 ♖xe2 h6?** 24...a5 △ b4,
♗a6 **25 ♗d3 ♘c5 26 ♗c2 ♘d7 27** a3
a5 **28 ♔g2 b4 29** axb4 ♗a6 **30 ♖d2
♕xb4**

Diagram

31 ♖a4! += ♕c3 **32 ♗d3 ♗xd3! 33
♖xd3 ♕b2 34 ♖xa5 ♘c5 35 ♗xc5
♖xc5 36 ♖xc5 ♖xc5 37 ♖d2 ♕a3
38 ♕b1 +=** ♖c3 **39 ♖b2 ♕b4 40
♘g1 ♗h4! 41 ♘e2 ♖c8 42 ♔f1 ♕c5
43 ♘g1 g6 44 b4 ♕c4+ 45 ♔g2**

♗d8!≈ 46 b5 ♗b6 47 ♘f3 ♔g7 ½-½
Suetin

302 Kapengut-Agzamov
Minsk 79
1 e4 e5 2 ♘f3 ♘c6 3 ♗b5 a6 4 ♗a4
♘f6 5 0-0 ♗e7 6 ♖e1 b5 7 ♗b3 d6 8
c3 0-0 9 h3 ♘a5 10 ♗c2 c5 11 d4
♕c7 12 ♘bd2 cxd4 13 cxd4 ♘c6 14
♘b3 a5 15 ♗e3 a4 16 ♘bd2 ♗d7!?
16...♘b4 17 ♗b1 ♗d7 18 a3 ♘c6 19
♗d3 ♕b8? 20 b4! axb3 21 ♕xb3 exd4
22 ♘xd4 ♘xd4 23 ♗xd4 ♘e8 24 e5!±
Boleslavsky-Goldenov, Leningrad 47;
19...♘a5 Tal-Kuzmin, Leningrad 77
17 a3 17 ♖c1 ♖fc8 18 ♗b1 ♕b8 19
♘f1 ♘a5 20 ♖xc8+ ♗xc8 21 ♗g5
h6 22 ♗h4± Smyslov-Reshevsky,
Hague 48, 21 ♗d2 ♘c4 22 ♗b4 ♖a7
23 b3± Keres-Skold, Moscow 56
♖fc8 18 ♗d3 18 ♖c1 ♕b7 19 ♗b1
♗e8 20 ♕e2 ♖c7 21 ♘f1 ♖ac8 22
♖cd1 += Keres-Borisenko, USSR 67;
19...b4?! 20 ♘c4 bxa3 21 bxa3 exd4
22 ♘xd4! Petrosian-Pfleger, Bamberg
68 **♕b8 19 b4!? axb3 20 ♕xb3 ♘a5
21 ♕b4 ♘c4**

Diagram

22 ♘xe5!? 22 dxe5 ♖a4 **dxe5 23
♕xe7 ♖e8! 24 ♕c5** 24 ♕b4 ♘xe3
25 fxe3 exd4 26 exd4 ♕g3 27 ♗f1

♗xh3 α/∓; 25 ♖xe3 ♖a4 **♖c8 25
♕e7** 25 ♕b4 ♘xe3 26 ♖xe3 ♖a4 27
♕b2 exd4 28 ♖f3 ♖c3 =+ **½-½**
Kapengut

303 Kapengut-Didishko Minsk 79
1 e4 e5 2 ♘f3 ♘c6 3 ♗b5 a6 4 ♗a4
♘f6 5 0-0 ♗e7 6 ♖e1 b5 7 ♗b3 d6 8
c3 0-0 9 h3 ♘a5 10 ♗c2 c5 11 d4
♕c7 12 ♘bd2 ♗d7 13 ♘f1 cxd4 14
cxd4 ♖ac8 14...♖fc8 15 ♖e2 ♘h5
16 dxe5 dxe5 17 ♘xe5! ♗xh3 18
♘xf7!± Lasker-Ed.Lasker, New York
29; 15 ♗d3 ♘c6 16 ♗e3 ♕b7 Maroczy-
Reti, New York 29 **15 ♘e3** 15 ♗b1
♖fe8 16 ♘g3 ♘c6 17 ♗e3 g6 Gufeld-
Bisguier, Moscow 61; 15 ♖e2 ♖fe8
16 ♘g3 g6 17 ♕d2 exd4 18 ♕xd4
♘c6 19 ♕d1 ♘e5 20 ♔h2 ♗e6=
Vasyukov-Judovich, Moscow 62; 15
♗d3 ♘c6 16 ♗e3 ♘b4 17 ♖c1 ♕b8
18 ♗b1 += Rabor-Pirc, Jugoslavia 49
♘c6 15...♖fe8 16 d5 g6 17 b3 ♘b7
18 b4 ♘h5 Robatsch-Bisguier, Hastings
61/62; 16 ♗d2 ♘c6 17 d5 ♘d4=
Darga-Bisguier, Bled 61; 16 b3! exd4
17 ♘xd4 ♗f8 18 ♗b2! ♕d8 19 ♘df5±
Spassky-Keres, Riga 65 **16 a3?!** 16
d5 **♘xd4! 17 ♘xd4 exd4 18 ♕xd4
d5!** N 18...♗e6 19 ♗d2 ♘d7 20 ♖ac1
♗f6 21 e5 dxe5 22 ♗xh7+ ♔h8 23
♕b4 ♘c5 Shamkovich-Judovich,
Moscow 62; 24 ♗f5!± **19 exd5** 19 e5

165

♗c5 20 ♕f4 ♖fe8 21 b4 ♗b6!∓; 19
♘f5? ♗xf5 20 exf5 ♗c5 21 ♕d3 ♗xf2+
∓ **♗c5 20 d6!= ♗xd4** 20...♕c6 21
♕c3 ♕xd6 22 ♕d3= **21 dxc7 ♖xc7
22 ♗d3 ♖e8 23 ♖d1 ½-½ Kapengut**

304 Kasparov-Kuzmin
USSR Final 78
**1 e4 e5 2 ♘f3 ♘c6 3 ♗b5 a6 4 ♗a4
♘f6 5 0-0 ♗e7 6 ♖e1 b5 7 ♗b3 d6 8
c3 0-0 9 h3 ♘a5 10 ♗c2 c5 11 d4
♕c7 12 d5 ♘c4** 12...c4 Δ ♘b7-c5;
12...♗d7 **13 a4 ♗d7** 13...♘b6!? 14 b3
c4 **14 b3 ♘a5 15 axb5 axb5 16 ♘bd2
♘b7 17 ♗b2 g6 18 c4 ♘h5?!** 18...b4
19 ♘h2 += **19 cxb5 ♗xb5 20 ♘c4 f6**
20...♘g7 21 ♘fxe5! dxe5 22 ♗xe5±
**21 ♕d2 ♖fb8 22 ♗c3 ♗f8 23 ♘h2
♘f4 24 ♘g4 ♘g7 25 h4 ♕c8 26 ♘ge3±
♗xc4 27 bxc4 ♘h6 28 ♖xa8 ♖xa8 29
♗d1! ♖a3** 29...f5 30 exf5 gxf5 31
♕c2 e4 32 ♗g4!! fxg4 33 ♕xe4 ♕f8
34 ♘f5 +− **30 g3 ♘h5 31 ♔b2 ♕a8
32 ♗xh5 ♗xe3 33 ♖xe3 gxh5 34 ♔g2
♘d8 35 ♕e2 ♘f7 36 ♕xh5 ♕a6 37
♖f3 ♕b7** 37...♕xc4 38 ♕g4+ ♔f8 39
♕c8+ ♔g7 40 ♕f5 +− **38 ♕g4+ ♔f8
39 ♕f5 ♕e7 40 ♕xh7 ♖a4 41 ♗d2!
1-0** 41...♖xc4 42 ♗g5 +− **Kasparov**

305 Kasparov-Dorfman
USSR Final 78
**1 e4 e5 2 ♘f3 ♘c6 3 ♗b5 a6 4 ♗a4
♘f6 5 0-0 ♗e7 6 ♖e1 b5 7 ♗b3 d6
8 c3 0-0 9 h3 ♗b7 10 d4 ♖e8 11 ♘bd2
♗f8 12 a4?!** 12 ♗c2 ♘b8 13 b3 g6 14
a4 ♘bd7 15 d5 += **h6!** 12...♘b8? 13
axb5 axb5 14 ♖xa8 ♗xa8 15 dxe5
dxe5 16 ♗xf7+! ♔xf7 17 ♕b3+ ♔e7
18 ♕a3+ +−; 12...exd4 13 cxd4 ♘b4
14 ♘g5 ♖e7 15 ♗xf7+!? ♖xf7 16
♕b3 d5 17 ♘xf7 ♔xf7 18 e5 ♘e8 19
♘f3 += **13 d5 ♘b8 14 c4 c6 15 axb5
axb5 16 ♖xa8 ♗xa8 17 dxc6 b4** 17...

---

bxc4 18 ♘xc4 ♗xc6 (18...♘xc6 19
♗a4≈) 19 ♘cxe5? dxe5 20 ♘xe5
♕xd1 21 ♗xf7+ ♔h7 22 ♗g6+ ♔h8
23 ♖xd1 ♖xe5 24 ♗f4 ♘bd7∓; 19
♗a4≈ **18 ♗a4 ♘xc6 19 ♘f1 ♕b8 20
g4!?** 20 ♘g3 g6 Δ ♖c8 =+ **♖c8 21
♘g3 ♗d8 22 g5 hxg5 23 ♘xg5 ♖xc4?**
23...♘e6 24 ♘xe6 fxe6 25 ♘h5 ♖c7!
26 ♘xf6+ gxf6 27 ♕f3 ♕d8 28 ♔h2
♔h8 29 ♖g1 ♖h7 =+ **24 ♗b3 ♖d4?**
24...♖c7 25 ♘h5 ♘h7!∞ **25 ♕c2**
25 ♕f3!?

25...♘d7! 25...d5 26 ♗e3 dxe4 27
♗xd4 exd4 28 ♘3xe4 ♘xe4 29 ♖xe4
♗xe4 30 ♕xe4 +−; 26...♖xe4 27 ♘3x
e4 ♘xe4 28 ♘xe4 dxe4 29 ♖d1±
**26 ♗e3 ♘c5 27 ♗xd4 exd4 28 ♗d5
♗e7 29 h4 ♘de6** 29...♗xg5 30 hxg5
♘de6 31 g6 fxg6 32 ♗xe6+ ♘xe6 33
♕c4 ♕e8 34 ♕xb4± **30 ♗xe6 fxe6
31 ♕c4 d3?!** 31...d5 32 ♕xd4 dxe4
33 ♘3xe4 ♘xe4 34 ♘xe4 ♗xh4 35
♘c5 ♗f6 36 ♕g4±; 34...♕f4 35 ♕d7!
+− **32 ♘xe6 d2 33 ♖d1 d5 34 exd5
♘xe6 35 ♕e4!** +− **♗c5 36 ♕xe6+
♔h8 37 ♔g2 ♕f4 38 ♕c8+ ♔h7 39
♕xc5 1-0 Kasparov**

**1 e4 e5 2 ♘f3 ♘c6 3 ♗b5 a6 4 ♗a4
♘f6 5 0-0 ♗e7 6 ♖e1 b5 7 ♗b3 d6 8
c3 0-0 9 h3 ♗b7 10 d4 ♖e8 11 ♗g5!?**

h6 **12 ♗h4 ♘d7** 12...♘h7 13 ♗g3
♗f6 14 ♗d5 ♖b8 15 ♘a3 ♘g5 16 ♘xg5
hxg5 17 ♘c2 exd4?! Kapengut-
Podgaets, Belcy 77; 18 cxd4! ♘xd4
19 ♗xf7+!± **13 ♗g3** 13 ♗xe7 ♘xe7
14 ♘h4 c5 15 d5 c4 16 ♗c2 ♖f8 17
♘d2 ♘xd5 18 ♘df3 ♘5f6 19 ♕xd6
♕b8= Tal-Razuvaev, Tbilisi 78 **♗f6**
14 ♕d3 ♘a5 15 ♗c2 ♘c4!? 15...c5
16 ♘bd2?! cxd4 17 cxd4 ♘c6 18
a3? ♘xd4 19 ♘xd4 ♘c5 −+ Kapengut-
Beljavsky, Ashkabad 78; 16 d5! ♘c4
17 b3 ♘b6 18 c4 +=; 16...c4 17 ♕e2
Δ b4 += **16 b3 ♘cb6 17 a4 bxa4 18**
bxa4 a5 19 ♘a3 ♗a6 20 ♕d1 c6 20...
♘c4 21 ♘xc4 ♗xc4 22 ♗d3 ♗xd3
23 ♕xd3 ♕b8 24 ♖ab1 ♖a7 25 ♕c4
+= **21 ♗b3 ♖a7 22 ♕c2 c5 23 ♕a2**
♗f8 24 ♖ad1 ♕c7 25 dxe5 dxe5 26
♘c4! ♘xc4 27 ♗xc4 ♗g6 28 ♗xa6
♖xa6 29 ♕c4 ♖d6 30 ♖b1± ♖d7 31
♖b5 ♖c8 32 ♖eb1 ♔h7 33 ♖b6 ♖cd8
34 ♔h2 ♖c8 35 ♖1b5?! 35 h4 h5 36
♕e2 Δ ♘d2± **h5! 36 h4 ♕d8 37 ♔h3**
♖d1 38 ♕xf7 ♖h1+ 39 ♘h2 ♕d1 40
f3 ♖f8 41 ♕e6 ♕d2 42 ♕f5 ♕h6
42...♔h6? 43 ♗xe5 +− **43 ♖xc5!?**
♗e7 44 ♖xg6 ♕xg6 45 ♕xg6+ ♔xg6
46 ♖xe5!? 46 ♖xa5 ♗d6? 47 ♖d5
♖f6 48 a5±; 46...♗f6! 47 ♗xe5 ♗xe5
48 ♖xe5 ♖c8 49 ♖g5+ ♔h6 50 g4
hxg4+ 51 ♔g2 ♖xh2+ 52 ♔xh2 gxf3=
♗d8 47 f4 ♖a1 48 ♘f3 ♖h1+ 49 ♘h2
♖a1 50 f5+ ♔h7 51 ♘f3 ♖h1+ 51...
♖xa4?! 52 ♘g5+ ♔g8 53 ♖e6 Δ ♗d6±
52 ♔h2 ♗c7 52...g6 53 g4 **53 ♖c5**
♗xh2 54 ♘xh2 ♖e8?! 55 e5 ♖a8 56
♔g3 ♖a1

Diagram

57 ♖c7!± ♔g8 58 ♘f3 ♖xa4 59 ♘d4
♖a1 60 ♘e6 ♖f1 61 ♖xg7+ ♔h8
62 f6 ♖g8 63 ♖g5! a4? 63...♖f5 64

♔h3 ♖gxg5 65 hxg5 ♔h7! 66 g4!
♖f3+ 67 ♔h4 hxg4 68 ♔xg4 ♖f1 69
♘f4 a4 70 g6 +− **64 ♘f4 ♖c1 65 e6**
♖xc3+ 66 ♔h2 ♖xg5 67 hxg5 1-0
Kapengut

307 Poleschuk-Umansky Corr 78

1 e4 e5 2 ♘f3 ♘c6 3 ♗b5 a6 4 ♗a4
♘f6 5 0-0 ♗e7 6 ♖e1 b5 7 ♗b3 d6 8
c3 0-0 9 h3 ♘b8 10 d4 ♘bd7 11 c4
c6 12 ♘bd2?! c5! 13 d5 ♘b6 14 ♕e2?!
♘h5! 15 ♗c2 15 cxb5? ♘f4 16 ♕f1
axb5 17 ♕xb5 ♗a6 18 ♕a5 ♘e2+ −+
19 ♔h1 ♗d3 **♘f4 16 ♕e3 ♗d7!** 16...
bxc4 17 ♕c3 **17 b3 ♕e8 18 ♗b2?!**
♕c8 Δ ♗xh3 −+ **19 ♗d3 ♘xd3!? 20**
♕xd3 f5 21 exf5 ♗xf5 22 ♘e4 ♕e8
23 ♗c3 bxc4 24 bxc4 ♕a4 25 ♘fd2
♘g5∓ 26 ♕f1 ♖xd2 27 ♘xd2 ♖a7 28
♖e3 ♗c2! 29 ♕e2 ♖af7 30 ♖f1 ♗g6
Δ ♕xa2 **31 f3 ♖f4 32 g3 ♖xc4!! 33**
♘a5 33 ♘xc4 ♗xc4 −+ ♗c2 34 ♗xb6
♖b8 35 ♗c7 35 ♖b3 ♕xa2 −+ **♖bb2**
36 ♖d1 ♕xa2 −+ 37 ♗xd6 ♖xd2
38 ♖xd2 ♖xd2 39 ♕f1 ♕xd5 40
♗xe5 ♕a2 41 g4 h6 42 ♕c1 ♗f7 43
♗f4 ♖b2 43...♖g2+! 44 ♔h1 ♖b2 45
♖e1 ♗d5 46 ♕d1 ♖b1! −+ **44 ♖e1**
♗d5 45 ♕d1 ♖g2+ 46 ♔h1 ♖f2 47
♖e8+ ♔f7 48 ♖e3 ♖b2 49 ♖a3! ♖b1
50 ♗c1 ♕c4 51 ♖c3 ♕d4 52 ♕c2
♖a1 53 ♔g2 ♖a2 54 ♗b2 a5 55 ♕c1
a4 56 ♖c2 ♕d3 57 ♕f4+ ♔g8 58

**♖d2 ♛b3 59 ♛e5 ♛xf3+ 60 ♔h2
♖xb2 61 ♖xb2 a3 —+ 62 ♖d2 ♗e4
63 ♖a2 ♛h1+ 64 ♔g3 ♛e1+ 65 ♔h2
♛b1 66 ♛e6+** 66 ♖xa3 ♛h1+ 67 ♔g3
♛e1+ 68 ♔h2 (68 ♔f4 g5+) ♛f2 mate
♔h7 67 h4 67 ♖xa3 ♛b2+ 68 ♔g3
♛xa3+ **♛h1+ 68 ♔g3 ♛f3+ 69 ♔h2
♛f4+ 70 ♔h3** 70 ♔g1 ♛g3+ 71 ♔f1
♗d3+ **h5 0-1 Bellin**

308 Kapengut-Malevinsky USSR 79

**1 e4 e5 2 ♘f3 ♘c6 3 ♗b5 a6 4 ♗a4
♘f6 5 0-0 ♗e7 6 ♖e1 b5 7 ♗b3 d6 8
c3 0-0 9 h3 ♛d7 10 d4 ♖e8 11 ♗g5
h6 12 ♗h4 ♗b7 13 ♘a3!?** N 13 ♘bd2
♗d8 14 a3 ♘h5 15 ♘f1 ♘f4 16 ♘g3
♘g6 17 h4 ♗f6 18 h5 ♘f8 19 d5 ♘e7
+= Balashov-I.Zaitsev, USSR 69; 13...
g5!? 14 ♗g3 ♗f8 15 dxe5 dxe5 16
♛e2 ♗c5 17 ♖ad1 ♛e7 18 ♗h2 ♖ad8
19 ♘f1 ♖xd1 20 ♖xd1 ♘a5= Shmit-
I.Zaitsev, USSR 69; 13...♘h7 14 ♗g3
♗f6 15 ♗d5 ♖ab8 16 dxe5 ♘xe5 17
♗xb7 ♖xb7 18 ♘xe5 ♗xe5 19 f4
♗f6 20 ♘b3 ♛c6 21 ♛d5 += Sakharov-
Malevinsky, Rostov 76 **♘h7 14 ♗g3
♗f6 15 d5 ♗e7 16 c4 += ♘g6 17 cxb5
axb5 18 ♘c2 ♗g5 19 ♗b4 ♘xf3+
20 ♛xf3 ♗g5 21 ♖e2 ♖f8 22 ♖c2 f5
23 exf5 ♖xf5 24 ♛g4** 24 ♖xc7!
♖xf3 25 ♖xd7 ♖xb3 —+ ♗af8 **25
a4 ♘f4** 25...bxa4 26 ♖xa4± **26 a5?!**
26 ♗xf4 ♗xf4 27 a5± **h5 27 ♛d1 h4?!**
27...♘xh3+! 28 gxh3 h4 29 ♗h2 ♖f3
30 ♖a3 ♛xh3 △ ♛g4+∓ **28 ♗xf4 ♗xf4
29 ♛g4 ♛e7?** 30 ♘c6 ♛d7 31 a6 ♗a8
32 ♖e2 ♛e8 33 ♘d4?! 33 ♗c2±
♖5f6 34 ♘c6 34 ♘e6? ♖g6 35 ♘xc7
♛f7 **♛h8 35 a7 ♖h6 36 ♗c2! ♗b7**
36...♗xc6 37 dxc6 ♛xc6 38 ♗e4 d5
39 ♖c2 ♛b7 40 ♖xc7! ♛xc7 41
a8♛ +— **37 ♗e4 ♛f7 38 ♖c2 ♖f6 39
♛xh4+ ♗h6 40 f3 g5 41 ♛g4 ♖a8
42 ♘b8 1-0 Kapengut**

309 Dubinin-Brglez Corr 78

**1 e4 e5 2 ♘f3 ♘c6 3 ♗b5 a6 4 ♗a4
♘f6 5 0-0 ♗e7 6 ♖e1 b5 7 ♗b3 d6 8
c3 0-0 9 h3 ♗e6!? 10 d4 ♗xb3 11
axb3** 11 ♛xb3!? d5! 12 exd5 ♘a5
13 ♛c2 +=; 11...♛b8!? **♛c8** 11...exd4
12 ♘xd4!? +=; 12 cxd4 d5 13 e5
♘d7!?∞ **12 d5** 12 ♗g5!? **♘d8** 12...
♘b8 13 ♗g5 ♘bd7 += **13 c4 c6 14
♘c3 b4 15 ♘a4 ♛c7 16 dxc6 ♘xc6**
16...♛xc6 17 ♗g5 ♘e6 18 ♗xf6 ♗xf6
19 ♛d5 += **17 ♗g5 ♘d7 18 ♗xe7 ♘xe7
19 ♛d2 a5 20 ♖ed1?** 20 ♖e3! △ ♖d3,
♖d1± **♖a6 21 ♛e3 ♘g6 22 g3 ♖c8
23 ♖d5 ♘gf8 24 ♖ad1 ♗e6 25 ♛d2
♘dc5 26 ♘xc5 ♘xc5 27 ♘xe5 ♘xb3
28 ♛e3**

28...♘c5?! 28...dxe5 29 ♛xb3 (29
♖d7 ♛b8 30 ♛xb3 a4!∞) g6 30 c5!
+=/± **29 ♘f3** △ 30 e5 dxe5 31 ♖xc5
♛xc5 32 ♖d8+ **♛e7 30 ♘d4± ♗b7**
30...♛xe4?? 31 ♖xc5 +— **31 ♘f5
♛f6 32 g4!** h6 32...♖xc4 33 e5 +—
**33 e5 +— dxe5 34 ♖d7 ♖b8 35 ♘e7+
♔h8** 35...♔f8 36 ♖xb7! ♖xb7 37
♛c5 **36 ♖xb7! 1-0** 36...♖xb7 37 ♖d8+
♔h7 38 ♛e4+ **Bellin**

310 Kapengut-Nei Tallinn 79

**1 e4 e5 2 ♘f3 ♘c6 3 ♗b5 a6 4 ♗a4
♘f6 5 0-0 ♗e7 6 ♖e1 b5 7 ♗b3 d6**

8 c3 0-0 9 h3 ♗e6!? 10 d4 ♗xb3 11 axbg3 exd4 12 cxd4 ♘b4 13 d5 c5 13...♘d7 14 ♘c3 ♗f6 15 ♘a2 ♘xa2= Kotkov-Holmov, USSR 62; 14 ♘a3! c5 15 dxc6 ♘xc6 16 ♘c2 ♘c5 17 ♘fd4 ♘xd4 18 ♘xd4 ♗f6 19 ♘c6 ♕d7 20 ♘b4 ♖fe8 21 ♘d5± Vasjukov-Judovich, Moscow 64; 14...♗f6 15 ♘c2 c5 16 ♘xb4 cxb4 17 ♘d4 ♗xd4 18 ♕xd4± Fischer-Szabo, Havana 65 **14 dxc6 d5!** 14...♘xc6 15 ♘c3 ♘e5 16 ♘d4 ♖e8 17 ♗f4 ♗f8 18 f3 += Tukmakov-Romanovsky, Kiev 63 **15 e5 ♘e4 16 ♘c3 ♘xc3** 16...♘c5?! 17 ♗e3 ♘e6 18 ♖e2 ♖c8 19 ♖d2 ♘xc6 20 ♘xd5± Zuckerman-Ostojic, Wijk aan Zee 68 **17 bxc3 ♘xc6 18 ♕d3 ♖e8!** 18...♕d7 19 ♗g5 ♖fe8 20 ♗xe7 ♘xe7 += Suetin-Holmov, Leningrad 62; 19...♖fd8 20 ♖ad1 ♕e6 21 ♗xe7 ♕xe7 22 b4 h6 23 ♕e3 ♕e6 24 ♘d4 ♘xd4 25 ♖xd4 ♖ac8 ½-½ Zakharov-Nei, Moscow 63; 20 ♗xe7 ♕xe7 21 ♘d4 += Polugaevsky; 21 ♕e3 ♕a7 22 ♕g5 d4 Karklins-Chellstorp, Chicago 73 **19 ♗f4 ♕d7 20 ♖a2! += ♕e6 21 ♖ea1 ♖ed8!** 21...h6? 22 ♖xa6 ♖xa6 23 ♖xa6 ♘b4 24 ♕xb5 +− **22 ♕e3 ♕c8!= 23 ♘d4 23** ♕b6?! b4 24 ♖c1 ♕f5 **♘xd4 24 cxd4 ♕e6 25 ♗g5 ♗xg5 26 ♕xg5 ♖dc8 27 ♖ac1 h6 28 ♕d2 ½-½ Kapengut**

311 Ghinda-Ciocaltea
Rumania Final 78

1 e4 e5 2 ♘f3 ♘c6 3 ♗b5 a6 4 ♗a4 ♘f6 5 0-0 ♗e7 6 ♖e1 b5 7 ♗b3 d6 8 c3 0-0 9 h3 h6 10 d4 ♖e8 11 ♗e3 11 ♘bd2 ♗f8 12 ♘f1 ♗d7 13 ♘g3 ♘a5 14 ♗c2 ♘c4 15 ♘h2 c5 16 b3 ♘b6 17 f4 cxd4 18 cxd4 ♕c8≈ Tal-Geller, USSR 77; 12 ♗c2 ♗d7 13 ♗d3 ♕b8 14 b3 g6 15 ♗b2 ♗g7 16 d5 ♘d8

17 c4 += Savon-Geller, Lvov 78 ♗f8 12 ♘bd2 ♘a5 12...♗b7; 12...♗d7 **13 ♗c2 c5** 13...♗b7 **14 d5** 14 a3 c4 15 a4 ♗d7 16 ♕e2 ♕c7 17 ♖a2±; 14 ♖c1 ♗d7 15 ♗b1 ♘c6 16 d5 += **♗d7 15 b4! ♘b7 16 a4 g6** 16...cxb4 17 cxb4 a5 18 bxa5 ♘xa5 19 axb5 ♗xb5 20 ♕b1± **17 ♕b1 ♕c7 18 ♖c1 ♖eb8 19 axb5 axb5 20 ♗d3 c4 21 ♗f1 ♘e8 22 ♗a7 ♖c8 23 ♖c2! △** ♖ca2, ♗b6 **♕d8! 24 ♖ca2 ♕e7 25 ♗e2 f5 26 ♗d1 f4 27 ♘b6 ♖ab8! 28 ♘h2 h5 29 ♗a7 ♖a8 30 ♗b6 ♖ab8= ½-½ Ciocaltea**

312 Guttierez-L.Bronstein
Buenos Aires 78

1 e4 e5 2 ♘f3 ♘c6 3 ♗b5 ♗c5 4 c3 f5 5 ♗xc6 dxc6 6 ♘xe5 ♗d6 7 d4 7 ♕h5+ g6 8 ♘xg6 ♘f6 9 ♕h4 ♖g8 10 e5 ♖xg6 11 exf6 ♗e6 12 0-0 ♕d7 13 d4 0-0-0∓ fxe4 8 ♕h5+ g6 9 ♘x g6?! 9 ♕e2 **♘f6 10 ♕h4** 10 ♕h6 ♖g8 **11 ♘h4 ♗f8 12 ♕e3 ♕e7∓ ♖g8 11 ♘e5**

11...♗xe5! 12 dxe5 ♕d3 13 h3 13 ♕xf6 ♗g4! 14 f3 exf3 15 gxf3 ♖f8 16 ♕g5 ♗xf3 −+; 13 exf6 ♗g4 −+ **♗e6! 14 ♘d2** 14 exf6 ♗c4 −+ **0-0-0! 15 ♕h6** 15 ♕xf6 ♗c4 16 ♘xc4 ♕d1 mate **♘d5!! 16 ♕xe6+ ♔b8 17 ♕f5 ♘e3! 18 fxe3 ♕xe3+ 19 ♔d1 ♖xg2 −+ 20 ♔c2 ♖dxd2+ 21 ♗xd2 ♕xd2+**

22 ♔b3 ♕xb2+ 23 ♔c4 ♕b5+ 24 ♔d4 ♕d5+ 0-1 Samarian

313 Russowsky-Snyder Corr 78

1 e4 e5 2 ♘f3 ♘c6 3 ♗b5 ♗c5 4 c3 f5?! 5 d4 fxe4 6 ♗xc6 dxc6 7 ♘xe5 7 ♘fd2! ♗d6 8 dxe5 e3 9 exd6!± **♗d6 8 ♕h5+ g6 9 ♕e2 ♕h4 10 h3 ♗e6 11 ♘d2 ♗xe5 12 dxe5 ♕g5 13 0-0 ♗xh3 14 ♕xe4 ♗f5 15 ♕f3** 15 ♕a4!? ♗h3! 16 ♕e4 ♗f5= **0-0-0 16 ♘e4** N 16 ♘b3 ♕h4 17 ♘g3 ♘e7 18 ♕f4 ♕xf4 19 ♗xf4 ♗d3 20 ♗g5?! 20 ♖fe1 ♗xf1 21 ♗xe7 ♗d3 22 ♗xd8 **♖xd8 23 ♖d1?!** 23 ♖e1 ♖d5! =+ **24 f4 ♗c4 25 ♖xd5 cxd5 26 b3 ♗b5 27 ♔f2 c5 28 ♔e3 ♗d7 29 ♘h1 ♗c6 30 ♘f2 d4+!∓ 31 cxd4 cxd4+ 32 ♔xd4 ♗xg2 33 ♘g4 ♔e6 34 f5+ gxf5 35 ♘f6 h6 36 ♘h5 ♗e4 0-1 Snyder**

1 e4 e5 2 ♘f3 ♘c6 3 ♘c3

314 Bernard-Pytel
Poland Final 79

1 e4 e5 2 ♘f3 ♘c6 3 ♘c3 ♗c5?! 4 ♘xe5! ♘xe5 5 d4 ♗d6 6 dxe5 ♗xe5 7 f4 ♕h4+!? N 7...♗xc3+ 8 bxc3± **8 g3 ♗xc3+ 9 bxc3 ♕e7 10 ♗g2 d5! 11 ♕xd5 ♘f6 12 ♕d4 0-0 13 0-0 ♖d8 14 ♕e3** 14 ♗a3 ♕e8! △ ♕a4 **♗e6 15 h3 ♗c4 16 ♖e1 c5 17 ♕f3 ♕c7 18 f5?! += ♘d7 19 e5 ♘xe5**

Diagram

20 ♕xb7 20 ♕f4 ♖e8 21 ♖xe5 ♕xe5 22 ♕xc4 ♕e1+∓ **♕d6 21 ♗f4 f6 22 ♗xe5** 22 ♖ed1!? fxe5 23 ♕e4 ♗d5 24 ♕xe5 ♗xg2 25 ♕xd6 ♖xd6 26 ♔xg2 ♖d2+ 27 ♔f3 ♖xc2 28 ♖e3 ♔f8 29 a4 ♖e8 30 ♖ae1 ♖xe3+ 31 ♖xe3 ♖a2 31...c4 32 ♔e4 ♖a2 33 ♔d4

♖xa4 34 ♔c5 a6 36 g4± **32 ♖e4 ♖a3 33 ♖c4 ♔e7 34 ♖xc5?** 34 ♔e3!± ♖xa4 35 ♖c6 ♖a1 36 ♖c7+ ♔f6 37 g4 a5 38 ♔e4 h6 39 ♖c6+ ♔f7 40 ♖a6 a4 41 ♔d5 a3 42 c4 42 ♔c4 += a2!= **23 ♔c5 ♔e7 44 ♖e6+ ♔f7 45 ♖a6 ½-½ Pytel**

1 e4 e5 2 ♘f3 ♘c6 3 ♗c4

315 Miles-Keogh
Amsterdam 3 78

1 e4 e5 2 ♘f3 ♘c6 3 ♗c4 ♗c5 4 c3 ♘f6 5 d3 d6 6 b4 ♗b6 7 a4 a6 8 0-0 0-0 9 ♗g5 ♗g4 10 ♘bd2 h6 11 ♗h4 11 ♗xf6 += g5 12 ♗g3 ♘h5 13 ♗a2 **♕f6** 13...♘f4!? **14 ♘c4 ♗a7 15 ♘e3 ♗xe3?** 15...♗xf3 16 ♕xf3 ♕xf3 17 gxf3 ♘e7∝ **16 fxe3 ♘xg3 17 hxg3± ♕e7 18 ♖f2 ♗e6** 18...♔g7 19 ♘h4/ ♕f1± **19 ♘h2 +− ♗xa2 20 ♖axa2 ♕e6 21 ♘g4 ♔g7** 21...f5? 22 exf5 ♖xf5 23 ♘xh6+ +− **22 ♘f6 ♘e7 23 ♖a1 ♘g8 24 ♘h5+ ♔g6 25 ♖f5 f6 26 ♕g4 ♔f7 27 ♖af1 ♔e7 28 d4** △ d5 +− **c6** 28...♕c4 29 d5 ♕xc3 30 ♖5f3 △ ♕e6+ +− **29 ♖d1 ♔c4 30 dxe5 1-0** 30...fxe5 31 ♖xe5+ dxe5 32 ♕d7 mate **Miles**

316 Kovacs-Hess
Reggio Emilia 78/79

1 e4 e5 2 ♘f3 ♘c6 3 ♗c4 ♘f6 4 d3

♗e7 5 ♘c3 d6 6 a3 0-0 7 ♗e3 N 7
0-0 ♘d7 8 ♘d5 ♘b6 9 ♘xe7+ ♕xe7=
S.Nikolic-Matanovic, Jugoslavia Final
69 ♗e6! 8 ♘d5 ♕h8!? 9 h3 ♘g8 10
g4 ♕d7 11 ♕d2 ♘d8!? 12 d4 f6 13
♘h4 c6 14 ♘xe7 ♘xe7 15 ♗xe6
15 d5!? cxd5 16 exd5∞ ♘xe6 16 dxe5
16 0-0-0 d5 17 f3 exd4 18 ♗xd4 c5
19 ♗f2 d4 =+ fxe5 17 0-0-0 d5 18
♘f5 d4 19 ♗g5 ♘g6 20 h4 ♘gf4 21
♗e7 ♖xf5! =+ ½-½ 22 gxf5 ♕xe7 23
fxe6 ♕xe6 Δ c5/♕a2 =+ **Kovacs**

Scotch

317 Prandstetter-Kovacs Decin 78
1 e4 e5 2 ♘f3 ♘c6 3 d4 exd4 4 ♘xd4
♘f6 5 ♘xc6 bxc6 6 e5 ♕e7 7 ♕e2
♘d5 8 c4 ♗a6 9 ♕e4 ♘f6!?= 10 ♕e2
♘d5 11 ♘d2 0-0-0!? 11...♘b4 12 ♘f3
c5 13 a3 ♘c6 14 ♗d2 ♕e6 15 ♗c3
♗e7 16 0-0-0 f6 17 exf6 ♕xe2 18
f7+ ♔xf7= Barczay-Forintos, Hungary
Final 64 **12 b3 ♖e8 13 ♗b2 f6 14 ♕e4
♘b6 15 f4 fxe5 16 fxe5 ♗b7 17 0-0-0
g6 18 ♗d3** 18 e6 d5 Δ ♗g7= **♗g7 19
♖he1 d5 20 ♕g4+** 20 exd6 ♗xb2+
21 ♔xb2 ♕g7+ Δ ♖xe4 −+ **♕b8 21
♔b1 ♖hf8 22 ♕g3 ♗h6 23 cxd5 cxd5
24 ♖e2 ♘d7 25 ♘f3 ♗f4 26 ♕e1** +=
♘c5 27 ♗b5? 27 ♗a3! ♘xd3 28 ♕a5
+− **c6 28 ♗a3 cxb5 29 ♕g1 ♖c8 30
♖c2**

**30...d4! 31 ♖xc5 ♗e4+! 32 ♕a1 ♖xc5
33 ♕xd4 ♗xf3 34 ♗xc5 ♕xe5 35
gxf3 ♖d8!! 0-1 Kovacs**

1 e4 e5 2 ♘f3 d6

318 Shakarov-Riabchonok
USSR 79
1 e4 e5 2 ♘f3 d6 3 d4 exd4 4 ♘xd4
♘f6 5 ♘c3 ♗e7 6 ♗f4 6 ♗e2 0-0 7
0-0 ♖e8 8 f4 ♗f8 9 ♗f3 += **0-0 7 ♕d2
a6** 7...d5!? 8 ♘db5 ♗b4 **8 0-0-0 d5**
8...b5 9 f3 b4 10 ♘d5± **9 exd5 ♘xd5
10 ♘f5 ♘xf4** 10...♗xf5? 11 ♘xd5
♗d6 12 ♗xd6 ♕xd6 13 ♕g5 +− **11
♘xe7+** 11 ♕e3!? **♕xe7 12 ♕xf4 ♗e6
13 ♗d3** += **♘d7 14 ♖he1 ♕f6** 14...
♘f6 15 g4 c6 16 g5 ♘d5 17 ♕h4 h6
18 ♘xd5 cxd5 19 f4!± Marjanovic-
Kalashan, Kirovakan 78 **15 ♕e3** Δ
♘e4-g5; 15 ♕g3 ♘c5 **♖fe8 16 f4**
16 ♘e4 ♕e5 17 f4 ♕a5∞ **♘f8 17
f5! ♗d7** 17...♗xa2? 18 ♕d2 +−; 17...
♗xf5 18 ♘d5± **18 ♘d5 ♕d6** 18...
♕h4!? 19 ♕g3 ♕xg3 20 hxg3 c6? 21
♘e7+ ♔h8 22 ♗c4 f6 23 ♖xd7! ♘xd7
24 ♘g6+ +−; 20...♖xe1 21 ♖xe1 c6
+= **19 ♘e7+ ♔h8 20 ♗c4 ♕f6** 20...
♖xe7? 21 ♕xe7 ♕f4+ 22 ♔b1 ♕xc4
23 ♖xd7 ♘xd7 24 ♕e8+! +− **21 g4
♗e6!** 21...h6? 22 g5! ♕xg5 23 ♕xg5
hxg5 24 ♗xf7 +−; 22...hxg5 23 ♖xd7!
♘xd7 24 ♘g6+ +− **22 ♘d5! ♗xd5
23 ♕xe8 ♖xe8 24 ♖xe8 g6!** 24...
♕d6? 25 ♖xd5 ♕f4+ 26 ♔b1 +−
25 ♖xd5 ♕g7 25...♕c6? 26 ♖xf8+
♔g7 27 ♖xf7+! +− **26 ♖dd8 ♕g5+**
26...♕c6? 27 g5! **27 ♔b1 ♕xg4 28 b3
b5 29 ♗d3** 29 ♗e2 ♕xf5 30 ♖xf8 ♕e5
31 ♖fe8 ♕xh2∞; 29 ♗xf7 ♕xf5! 30
♖xf8 ♕f1+ 31 ♔b2 ♕f6+∞ **c5! 30 c3
♘d7! 31 ♖xd7 ♕d1+ 32 ♔b2 ♕d2+
33 ♔b1** 33 ♔a1? ♕xc3+? 34 ♔b1 +−;
33...♕c1+ −+ **1-0 Shakarov/Kasparov**

319 Karolyi-Tompa
Hungary ½-Final 78

**1 e4 e5 2 ♘f3 d6 3 d4 exd4 4 ♘xd4
4 ♕xd4!? g6 5 ♗c4** 5 ♘c3 ♗g7 6 ♗e3!
♗g7 6 ♘c3 ♘c6 7 ♗e3?! 7 ♘xc6 bxc6
8 0-0 ♘e7 9 f4 ♗e6 10 ♗d3 ♕d7 11
♕f3 f5= Browne-Larsen, San Juan 69
♘f6 8 f3 0-0 9 a3? 9 ♕d2 ♖e8 10
0-0-0 ♘e5 11 ♗b3 a6 =+ **♖e8 10 ♕d2
d5! 11 ♘xc6** 11 ♗xd5 ♘xd5 12 ♘xd5
♘xd4 13 ♗xd4 ♗xd4 14 ♕xd4 c6 −+;
11 ♘xd5? ♘xd5 12 ♘xc6 bxc6 13
exd5 ♕h4+ −+ **bxc6 12 exd5?!** 12 ♗e2
♕e7∓ **♗h6! −+ 13 ♘d1 cxd5 14 ♗b5
♖xe3+!** 14...♗d7?! 15 ♗xd7 ♕xd7 16
0-0! ♖xe3? 17 ♘xe3 d4 18 ♘d5!! +−
15 ♘xe3 d4 16 ♖d1 ♕e7 16...♗d7!
17 ♕xd4 ♕e7! 18 ♗xd7 ♗xe3 19
♕d3 ♘xd7 20 ♕xd7 ♗d2+!! −+; 20
♕e4 ♖e8 △ ♘f6∓ **17 ♕xd4 ♗xe3?!**
17...♗d7! **18 ♕d8+ ♕xd8 19 ♖xd8+
♔g7 20 ♗a6 ♗b7! 21 ♖xa8 ♗xa8 22
♔e2 ♘f4?!** 22...♗d4! 23 c3 ♗e5∓ **23
c4! =+ ♘d7 24 ♖d1?!** 24 b4!? ♔f6
25 ♖d1 ♔e7 =+ **♘c5 25 ♖d8 ♗c6 26
♗b5 ♘e6! 27 ♖b8 ♗xb5 28 cxb5
♗xh2 29 a4 ♘c5** 29...c6!? **30 ♖b7
cxb5 31 ♖xa7 ♗g1 =+ 30 b3 ♘xb3
0-1 Tompa**

1 e4 e6

320 Browne-Paolozzi
Lone Pine 79

**1 e4 e6 2 d3 c5 3 ♘d2 ♘c6 4 g3 g6
5 ♗g2 ♗g7 6 f4** 6 ♘gf3 ♘ge7 7 ♘gf3
7 e5!? **d6 8 g4!** 8 0-0 f5! **f5?!** 8...0-0
9 gxf5 gxf5 10 ♘f1! 10 ♘h4? ♘g6 =+
♘g6 11 exf5! 11 ♘g3 ♗h6 12 ♘h5
0-0 13 ♘g5? ♘xf4! −+ **exf5 12 ♘g3
0-0** 12...♕e7+ 13 ♕e2 ♕xe2+ 14 ♔xe2
0-0 15 ♘h5 ♗h8 16 ♘g5! **13 0-0 h6
14 ♘h5 ♗h8 15 ♕e1! ♘ce7 16 ♗d2!
♕e8** 16...♗xb2 17 ♖b1 ♗h8 18 ♗c3

♘d5?! 19 ♗xh8 ♔xh8 20 ♕g3 ♖g8
21 ♕h3 +=; 17 ♗c3!? **17 ♕g3 ♕f7
18 ♖ae1 ♖fe8 19 ♖e2** 19 ♘c3 ♗xc3
20 bxc3 ♗d7 21 ♘h4!± **♗d7 20 ♖fe1
♔f8!** 20...♔h7? 21 ♕h3 ♘d5 22
♘g5+! hxg5 23 ♘f6+ ♔g7 24 ♕h7+
♔xf6 25 fxg5 mate **21 ♗c3! ♗xc3
22 bxc3 ♘g8** 22...♘c6?? 23 ♖e6 +−;
22...♘d5? 23 ♘h4! ♗xh4 24 ♗xd5
♕g6 25 ♘f6! +− **23 ♘d2! ♘f6 24
♘xf6 ♕xf6 25 ♗xb7 ♖ab8 26 ♗f3**
26 ♗d5 ♖xe2 27 ♖xe2 ♘e7! 28 ♗b3
♕xc3 **♖xe2 27 ♖xe2 ♖b2 28 ♘c4!
♖xa2 29 ♘e3 += ♖a1+ 30 ♔g2!**
30 ♔f2? ♕h4 31 ♘c4 a5 32 ♘xd6 a4
−+ **♘h4+ 31 ♔h3 ♗xf3 32 ♕xf3 ♖g1**
32...♗e6! 33 ♕a8+ ♔f7? 34 ♘d5 ♕g6
35 ♕b7+ +−; 33...♔g7! 34 ♖g2+
♔h7 35 ♘d5? ♕f7!; 33 ♕c6!± **33
♕a8+ +− ♗e8** 33...♔g7 34 ♘d5 +−
34 ♘d5 ♕f7 35 ♘f6! +− ♕g7 35...
♕xf6 36 ♕xe8+ ♔g7 37 ♖e7+ +−
**36 ♖xe8! ♖g4 37 ♘xg4 ♕h5+ 38
♔g3 ♕xg4+ 39 ♔f2 ♕xf4+ 40 ♔f3
1-0 Browne**

√321 Chen Te-Ornstein
Buenos Aires 78

**1 e4 e6 2 d4 d5 3 ♘c3 ♗b4 4 e5 c5
5 a3 ♗xc3+ 6 bxc3 ♘e7 7 ♘f3 ♕a5
8 ♗d2 ♗d7 9 a4** 9 c4!? **♘bc6 10 ♗e2
f6! 11 exf6** 11 c4 ♕c7 12 exf6 gxf6
13 cxd5 ♘xd5 14 c3 0-0-0 15 0-0=
Spassky-Korchnoi (4) 77; 14 c4!?
gxf6 12 0-0 0-0-0 12...c4!? **13 c4
♕c7 14 cxd5 ♘xd5 15 c3** 15 c4!?
♖hg8 16 ♖e1 e5 17 dxe5? 17 c4 ♗h3
18 ♗f1 ♗b6 (18...♘f4!?) 19 d5 ♘xc4!
20 dxc6! ♕xc6 Spassky-Korchnoi (4)
77; 21 g3 (21 ♗xc4!?) ♗xf1 22 ♖xf1
e4 23 ♕b3 ♕d5 24 ♖ac1 ♘xd2! 25
♘xd2 ♕xd2= **fxe5? 17...♘xc3! 18
♗xc3 ♗h3 △ ♗xg2; 17...♘xe5 18 ♗g5!
♖xg5 19 ♘xg5 ♗xc3 20 ♕c2 ♘xe2+**

21 ♕xe2 ♘d4?! 21...♖g8

22 ♔c4? 22 ♕xe5 ♘c2 23 ♖ac1 ♘xe1 24 ♖xc5 ♗c6 25 ♕xc7+ ♔xc7 26 ♘e6+ ♔d6 27 ♖xc6+!; 26...♕b6?? 27 a5+ **♗c6 23 ♖xc5 h6! 24 ♕xe5!?** 24 ♘e4 ♘b3 **hxg5 25 ♕xg5 ♕f7!** 25... ♘c2?? 26 ♕f5+ **26 ♕g4+ ♔b8 27 ♖ad1?** 27 ♖e5! **♕d5! 28 f3 ♗xa4! 29 ♖b1 ♖g8 30 ♕f4+ ♔a8 31 ♖e4? ♕a2! 0-1 Speelman**

322 Hecht-Botterill BRD-Wales 79

1 e4 e6 2 d4 d5 3 ♘c3 ♗b4 4 e5 c5 5 ♕g4 ♘e7 6 dxc5 d4!? N 6...♘bc6 7 ♗d2 0-0 8 ♘f3 f5 9 exf6 ♖xf6 10 0-0-0 e5 11 ♕h5 ♖f5 12 ♕h4 ♗xc3! 13 bxc3 ♕a5∓ Pietzsch-Uhlmann, DDR 63; 9 ♕h4 d4 10 ♘e2 ♗xd2+ 11 ♘xd2 ♕d5 =∓ Estrin-Rittner, Corr. 66 **7 a3 ♕a5 8 ♖b1!** 8 ♕xd4 ♘bc6 9 ♕d3 ♗xc3+ 10 ♕xc3 ♕xc3+ 11 bxc3 ♘xe5 =∓ **♗xc3+ 9 bxc3 ♕xc3+ 10 ♔d1 ♘bc6?** 10...♗d7!? △ ♗a4 **11 ♘f3 a6** 11...♘g6 12 ♖b5 △ ♗b2 **12 ♗d3 ♕xc5 13 ♖e1! ♘g6** 13...♕d5!?; 13...h5!?; 13...b5 14 ♕x g7± **14 h4 0-0 15 ♕g3!± ♘ce7?!** 15...♔h8!? **16 h5 ♘d5 17 ♖b3 ♘c3+ 18 ♖xc3 dxc3 19 hxg6 fxg6 20 ♖h1 ♖f5** 20...♗d7 21 ♖xh7 +− **21 ♗xf5 exf5 22 ♕h4 ♕d5+ 23 ♕d4 ♗e6 24 ♕xd5 ♗xd5 25 ♔e2 ♖e8 26**

♗e3 +− ♗xf3+ 27 ♔xf3 ♖xe5 28 ♖b1 b5 29 ♖b3 h6 30 ♖xc3 ♖e4 31 ♖c6 ♖a4 32 ♖xg6 ♖xa3 33 ♕f4 ♔h7 34 ♔xf5 b4 35 ♖b6 ♖c3 35...a5 36 ♗d4 +− 36 ♖xb4 ♖xc2 37 ♖b6 ♖a2 38 ♗d4 ♖a4 39 ♗e5 ♖a2 40 ♗d4 ♖a5+ 41 ♔e4 ♖g5 42 g3 ♖g4+ 1-0 Botterill

323 Ghinda-Ungureanu
Rumania Final 78

1 e4 e6 2 d4 d5 3 ♘c3 ♘f6 4 e5 ♘fd7 5 f4 c5 6 ♘f3 ♘c6 7 ♗e3 a6 7...cxd4 8 ♘xd4 ♘xd4 9 ♗xd4 ♕b8=; 7...♕b6∝ 8 ♘a4 ♕a5+ 9 c3 cxd4 10 b4 ♘xb4 11 cxb4 ♗xb4+ 12 ♗d2 **8 ♕d2 ♕a5?!** 8...b5 **9 a3 b5 10 dxc5 ♘xc5 11 ♗d4 ♕c7** 11...♘xd4?! 12 ♗xd4 b4?! 13 ♘a2 ♘e4 14 axb4 ♕a4 15 b3!± ♕a3?! (15...♕c6) 16 ♕d1 ♗xb4+? (16...a5!) 17 c3 +− ♗e7 (17...♗a5 18 b4) 18 ♘b4 ♕b2 19 ♘d3!; 12 ♕xd4 b4!? 13 ♕xb4?? (13 ♘a2) ♘d3+ **12 ♗d3 ♗b7 13 0-0 ♗e7 14 ♕f2** △ ♘dxb5 **♘xd4 15 ♗xd4 g6 16 b4 ♗xd3?!/? 16...♘e4!? 17 ♗xe4 dxe4 18 ♕e3 17 cxd3± 0-0 18 ♖fc1 ♕d7 19 ♘e2 ♖fc8** 19...a5 20 ♗c5 **20 ♗b6! ♖xc1+** 20...d4!? **21 ♖xc1 ♖c8 22 ♕d4 ♖xc1+ 23 ♘xc1 ♕c6 24 ♗c5 ♗xc5 25 ♕xc5 f6 26 ♘b3! fxe5 27 ♕xc6 ♗xc6 28 fxe5 ♔f7 29 ♔f2 g5 30 ♘c5 1-0 Speelman**

324 Spassky-Dankert Munich 79

1 e4 e6 2 d4 d5 3 ♘c3 ♘f6 4 ♗g5 dxe4 5 ♘xe4 ♗e7 6 ♗xf6 gxf6 7 ♘f3 b6?! 7...f5! 8 ♘g3 c5∝ **8 ♗c4 ♗b7 9 ♕e2 c6 10 0-0-0 ♘d7 11 ♗a6± ♗xa6 12 ♕xa6 ♕c7 13 ♕e2!? f5 14 ♘g3 ♕f4+** 14...0-0-0? **15 ♘xf5 ♕f4+ 16 ♘e3 15 ♔b1 0-0-0 16 d5!! cxd5 17 ♘xf5! ♗c5** 17...♕xf5 18 ♕a6+ ♔b8 19 ♘d4 ♕f6 20 ♘b5! **18 ♘5d4**

**♕b7 19 ♖he1 a6 20 g3 ♕f6 21 c4!
♗xd4** 21...dxc4? 22 ♕e4+ **22 ♖xd4
♘c5 23 cxd5 +− ♕f5+ 24 ♔a1 e5**
24...♖xd5 25 ♖f4 ♕h5 26 g4 ♕g6 27
♘e5 +− **25 ♗xe5 f6 26 ♘f7 1-0
Stean**

✓325 Hess-Nikolac
Reggio Emilia 78/9

**1 e4 e6 2 d4 d5 3 ♘c3 ♘f6 4 ♗g5
♗e7 5 e5 ♘fd7 6 ♗xe7 ♕xe7 7 f4
a6 8 ♘f3 c5 9 dxc5 ♘xc5!?** 9...♘c6
10 ♕d2 ♕xc5 11 a3 b5 12 ♕f2 ♗b7
13 ♕xc5 ♘xc5 14 0-0-0 +=; 10...
♘xc5!?; 9...♕xc5 10 ♕d4! ♘c6 11
♕xc5 ♘xc5 += **10 ♕d2 ♘c6 11 0-0-0!?**
11 ♗d3 △ 0-0 **b5 12 ♘d4 ♗xd4 13
♕xd4 ♗b7** 13...b4 14 ♘e2 ♗b7!?
15 ♔b1 a5!? 16 f5!? exf5 17 ♘g3
g6 18 ♗b5+ ♔f8 19 e6∝; 15...♘e4;
14...♗d7?/?! 15 f5; 14...0-0!? 15
f5 exf5!?; 15...♘e4; 14 ♕xb4??
♘xd3+ **14 ♔b1** 14 g3?! b4 **♖c8 15 g3
0-0 16 ♗g2 ♖c7** 16...♘d7! 17 ♘e4?!
♖c4 18 ♕d2 ♘xe5! 19 fxe5 dxe4;
18 ♕a7!? ♘xe5 19 ♘d2 ♘c6 20 ♕b6
♖a4 21 ♘b3 ♖b8!; 17...♘xe5; 17 ♘e2
17 ♖hf1 ♘d7! 18 ♘e2 18 ♕e3?? d4!
**♖fc8 19 ♖d2 a5 20 ♕e3 a4 21 ♘d4
♘b6** 21...a3? 22 ♘xb5 △ ♕xa3; 21...
b4 22 f5!

22 ♘f5! ♕b4! 22...exf5? 23 ♕xb6 b4

24 ♗xd5!? ♗xd5! 25 ♖xd5 ♖xc2 ∝/±
26 ♖hd1 h5 27 ♖d8+ ♔h7 28 ♖xc8
♖xc8 29 ♖d4 a3!?; 24...♖d8? 25 ♖hd1
♖cd7 26 ♗xf7+!! +−; 24 ♖hd1; 24
♖c1; 24 ♕d6!; 23...a3?!; 23...♕b4
24 ♖d4! **23 a3!** 23 ♘d6? a3! **♕a5
24 ♘d6 b4!?** 24...♘c4! 25 ♘xc4 ♖xc4
26 f5 d4 27 ♕f2 ♗xg2 28 ♕xg2 exf5
29 ♖xf5∝ b4 30 ♕b7!; 29...♕c7!?;
26...b4 27 f6 ♕c5!; 27 fxe6 fxe6
Hess/Nikolac; 25...bxc4 26 c3! **25
f5! ♘c4** 25...bxa3? 26 f6! (△ ♕g5)
♕b4 27 c3! ♖xc3 28 ♕g5 a2+ 29
♔xa2 +− **26 ♘xc4 ♖xc4 27 fxe6!
fxe6 28 ♗h3! ♖4c6 29 ♕f4 ♕c7 30
♕xb4 ♗a6 31 ♖f3 ♕xe5 32 ♕d4
♕e1+** 32...♕xd4 33 ♖xd4± **33 ♖d1
♕a5 34 ♕e5 ♖e8 35 ♖d4 ♘c4??**
35...♕c5 36 ♖c3 ♗c4 37 ♗f1!? ♘ec8
38 ♗xc4 dxc4 39 ♕xc5 (39 ♕e4!?)
♖xc5 40 ♖d7± (△ ♖a7xa4) ♖5c7
41 ♖xc7 ♖xc7 42 b3 axb3 43 cxb3
♖b7 44 b4!; 42...♖b7 43 ♖xc4 axb3
44 c3; 40...♖d5; 40...e5; 40...♖e8
36 ♖xc4! ♕a6 36...♖xc4 37 ♕xe6+
+− **37 ♖xc6 ♕xc6 38 ♖c3 1-0
Speelman**

✓326 Bisguier-Rubinsky USA 78
**1 e4 e6 2 d4 d5 3 ♘c3 ♘f6 4 ♗g5
♗e7 5 e5 ♘fd7** 5...♘g8?! **6 ♗xe7
♕xe7 7 f4** 7 ♕d2 0-0! a6!?
7...0-0 **8 ♘f3** 8 ♕g4 f5!? 9 exf6 ♘xf6
10 ♕g5 0-0 11 0-0-0 += **c5 9 dxc5
♘c6 10 ♗d3 ♕xc5 11 ♕d2** +=/∝ **b5
12 ♘e2** N **♘b6** 12...♗b7; 12...0-0 △
f6 **13 b3 ♗d7** 13...♘c4?! 14 bxc4
bxc4 15 ♕c3; 13...♗b7 **14 c3 b4
15 ♖c1±** bxc3 15...a5 **16 ♖xc3 ♕e7
17 0-0 f6 18 ♕e3?!** 18 ♖fc1! **d4!
19 ♘exd4 ♘d5 20 ♘xc6 ♘xe3 20...
♗xc6? 21 ♕c5 21 ♘xe7 ♘xf1 22 exf6**
22 ♘g6?! hxg6 23 ♗xg6+ ♔e7 24
♔xf1 f5∓ **gxf6 23 ♘g6** 23 ♗e4 ♖b8

24 ♘c6 ♖c8 25 ♔xf1 f5 =+/∞ **hxg6**
23...♖g8!? 24 ♘gh4 ♘e3 25 ♗xh7
♘d5∞ **24 ♗xg6+ ♔e7 25 ♔xf1 ♖ac8**
26 ♖e3! 26 ♖xc8 ♖xc8∓ **♖c5?** 26...
♖c1+ △ ♖a1 **27 h4 ♗c6 28 ♘d4 ♗b5+**
29 ♔f2 ♖xh4 30 ♖xe6+ 30 ♘f5+?
♖xf5 31 ♗xf5 ♖xf4+ —+ **♔f8 31 ♔g3**
+— ♖h1 32 ♖xf6+ ♔g7 33 ♖d6 ♖c3+
34 ♔g4 1-0 Ciamarra

327 Miles-Nikolac
Wijk aan Zee 79
1 e4 e6 2 d4 d5 3 ♘d2 b6!? 4 exd5!?
4 ♘gf3; 4 ♗d3 **exd5** 4...♕xd5! **5 ♘df3**
5 ♗d3 ♗a6; 5...♗d6 6 ♘gf3 ♕e7+
♗d6 6 ♗d3 ♗g4!? 7 c3 7 ♘e2 ♗xf3
8 gxf3∞ **♘d7 8 ♕c2 ♘gf6 9 ♗g5 h6**
9...♕e7+ 10 ♔f1; 20 ♘d2?!?∞ **10**
♗e3 10 ♗h4? ♕e7+ △ 0-0 **c5! 11 h3**
♗e6 12 ♘e2 c4 13 ♗f5 ♗xf5 14 ♕xf5
g6? 14...♕c7= **15 ♕c2 += ♕c7** 15...
♔f8 △ ♔g7 += **16 ♕c1! g5 17 ♘d2**
0-0-0 18 ♕c2 ♖de8 19 ♕f5 ♕c6 20
h4 g4 21 ♘f1 ♗c7!= 22 ♘fg3 ♕e6
23 0-0 ♘e4 24 ♖ae1?! 24 ♕xe6 ♖xe6
25 ♘f5 ♔d8= **♘df6 25 ♕xe6+ fxe6**
26 ♘xe4 ♘xe4 27 f3 gxf3 27...♘g3?!
28 ♘xg3 ♗xg3 29 ♗f2 ♗xf2+ 30
♔xf2 += **28 ♖xf3 ♖eg8! 29 ♗f4**
♖g4!∓ 30 ♘xe6 30 h5? ♘g5 △ ♗xf4,
♘h3+ —+ **♗g3** 30...♖8g8!? △ ♘g3
31 ♖ef1 ♖xh4 32 ♗f4 ♖g8 33 ♖e3
33 ♗xg3? ♘xg3 34 ♖f8+ ♖xf8 35
♖xf8+ ♔d7 36 ♘f4 ♖xf4 —+; 33
♗e5? ♗xe5 34 dxe5 ♘g3 △ ♖h1+ —+
♔d7 34 ♗xg3 ♖xg3? 34...♘xg3! 35
♖f7+? ♔d6 —+; 35 ♘f8+ ♔c6; 35
♖fe1 ♘e4! **35 ♘f8+ ♔e8** 35...♔e7??
36 ♖xg3 ♘xg3 37 ♘g7+ +— **36 ♖ff3**
♖xf3 37 ♖xf3 ♖g4 38 ♘e6 ♔d7 39
♘f4 ♔d6 39...♘d2 40 ♖f2 ♘e4 41
♖f1 += ♘d2 42 ♘xd5 **40 ♘e2 ♖g7=**
41 ♖f5 △ ♖h5/♘f4 **♖g5 42 ♖f7 a5**
43 ♘f4 += ♖g4? 43...h5? 44 ♖h7 ♘f6

45 ♖b7 ♔c6 46 ♖f7 ♘e4 47 ♖h7±;
43...b5! 44 ♖h7 b4 45 ♖xh6+ ♔d7
46 ♘e2 ♖f5 47 ♖h4 ♘f2=; 44 a3
♔c6! 45 ♖h7 b4! 46 axb4 axb4 47
♖xh6+ ♔b5 48 cxb4 ♔xb4 49 ♖b6+
♔a4= **44 ♖f5 ♖g5 45 ♖f8 ♖g4 46**
♖f5 ♖g5 47 ♖f7 ♖g4? 47...b5! **48**
a4!± ♔c6 48...♖h4 49 ♘g6 ♖h5 50
♘e5 △ ♖b7 +— **49 ♖f5! ♗d6** 49...
♖g5 50 ♘xd5! +— **50 ♖f6 ♖h4 51**
g3 ♖g4 52 ♔g2 +— h5 53 ♘xh5 ♔d7
54 ♔f3 ♖g8 55 ♘f4! ♖xg3+ 55...
♖g5 56 g4; 55...♘e4 56 ♘xd5; 55...
♔c6 56 g4; 56 ♘g6 +— **56 ♔xg3 ♘e4+**
57 ♔g4 ♘xf6+ 58 ♔f5 ♘e4 58...
♔e7 59 ♔e5 +— **59 ♘xd5 ♘d6+ 60**
♔e5 ♘f7+ 60...♔c6 61 ♘xb6 ♘f7+
62 ♔f6 ♘d6 63 ♔e6 +— **61 ♔f6**
1-0 Miles

√328 Karpov-Unzicker
Munich 79
1 e4 e6 2 d4 d5 3 ♘d2 c5 4 exd5
exd5 5 ♗b5+ ♘c6 6 ♘e2!? 6 ♕e2+!?
♗d6 7 dxc5 ♗xc5 8 0-0 ♘e7 9 ♘b3
♗b6 9...♗d6 10 ♗f4 += **10 ♗f4 0-0**
11 ♕d2 ♗g4 12 h3! += **♗xe2** 12...
♖h5 13 ♘g3 ♗g6 14 ♖ad1± **13 ♗xe2**
♘g6 14 ♗h2 ♕f6! 15 ♗f3 15 ♕xd5
♕xb2= **♖ad8 16 ♗xd5** 16 c3?! ♘ce5
=+ **♕xb2 17 ♖fd1 ♘ge7 18 c4 ♕f6**
18...♕xd2 19 ♖xd2 △ ♖ad1, c5
19 ♕f4 ♕xf4 20 ♗xf4 ♘xd5 21 cxd5
♘a5 22 ♖ac1 += ♘xb3 23 axb3 ♖d7
24 ♔f1 ♖fd8 25 d6 f6 26 g4 a6 27
♖e1 ♔f7 28 ♗g3 ♗d4! △ ♗e5!= **29**
♖c7 ♗e5!= 30 ♗xe5 fxe5 31 ♖xe5
♖xc7 32 dxc7 ♖c8 33 ♖c5 ♔e6 34
♔e2 ♔d6 35 ♖g5 ♖xc7 36 f4 g6 37
♔d3 ♔e6 38 h4 ♖c1 39 h5 ♔f7 40
♖d5 ♔e6 41 ♖e5+ ♔f7 42 h6 ♖h1
43 g5 ♖h3+ 44 ♔c4 ♖f3 45 ♖e4 a5
46 ♔b5 ♖xb3+ 47 ♔xa5 ♖b1 48
♖c4 ♔e6 49 ♖c7 ½-½ Stean

329 Vasyukov-Botterill
Hastings 78/9
**1 e4 e6 2 d4 d5 3 ♘d2 c5 4 exd5
exd5 5 ♗b5+ ♘c6 6 ♕e2+ ♗e7 7 dxc5
♘f6 8 ♘b3 0-0 9 ♗e3 ♖e8** 9...a6 10
♗d3 d4 11 ♗g5 a5 12 a4 ♗e6 13 ♘f3
♗xb3 14 cxb3 ♗xc5 =+ Hubner-
Uhlmann, Palma 70; 10 ♗a4 ♖e8
11 0-0-0 ♘g4!?∝ Kupreichik-Gulko,
USSR 73 **10 0-0-0** 10 ♘f3 ♘e4∝ **a5
11 a4 ♗d7** △ ♘a7xb5, a4 **12 ♘f3 ♘a7
13 c4** N 13 ♘fd4 ♗g4?! 14 ♔b1 ♘xe3
15 fxe3 ♗g5 16 ♕f3! ♖e5 17 ♖hf1 f6
18 ♗xd7 ♕xd7 19 h4! ♗xh4 20 ♘f5±
△ ♖xd5, ♘e7+; 13...♘e4! =+ **♘xb5
14 cxb5 ♗xc5! 15 ♘xc5 ♖c8 16
♕b1** 16 ♕c2? b6 17 ♕b1 bxc5 18
♗xc5 ♗g4 −+ **♖xc5 =+ 17 ♕d3** 17
♖c1 ♖xc1+ 18 ♖xc1 ♗f5+ −+; 17
♘d4 ♖c4 △ ♖xa4/♘e4

17...♖c4! 18 ♘d4 18 b3? ♕c8 19
♘d4 ♖c3∓ **♖xa4** 18...♘e4!? 19 ♖c1
♘c5 20 ♕a3 ♖xd4 21 ♗xd4 ♗f5+
22 ♔a1 ♘d3∝ **19 f3!** 19 b3 ♖b4 20
♗d2 ♘e4 21 ♗xb4 axb4 −+ **♖c4 20
b3 ♖c8 21 ♖c1 ♕e7∓ 22 ♖xc8 ♖xc8
23 ♖c1 ♖xc1+ 24 ♗xc1 ♕e5 25 h3
♘e8?** △ ♘c7xb5/e6; 25...h6! 26
♗d2 ♕h2∓ **26 ♗d2 ♘c7 27 ♔a2
♘e6 28 ♘xe6 ♗xe6 29 ♗xa5 ♗f5
30 ♕d2 d4 31 ♗c3!= h6** ½-½
Botterill

✓ **330 Balshan-Botterill**
Hastings 78/9
**1 e4 e6 2 d4 d5 3 ♘d2 c5 4 exd5
exd5 5 ♕e2+? ♗e7 6 dxc5 ♘f6 7 ♘b3
0-0 8 ♗e3 ♖e8 9 0-0-0 a5∓ 10 ♕b5**
10 a4 ♗d7 **♗d7! 11 ♕xb7 ♘c6 12
♘d4 ♘b4! 13 ♔b1?** 13 c6 ♗xa2+
14 ♔b1 ♘c3+! 15 ♔c1 ♖b8 16 c7
♖xb7 17 cxd8♕ ♖xd8 18 bxc3 ♘e6
19 ♖d3 ♗a3+ 20 ♔d1 ♖b1+ 21 ♔e2
♗b2! −+ △ a4-a3-a2 **♗xc5 −+ 14
♘b3** 14 ♘e6 ♖xe6 15 ♗xc5 ♖b8 16
♕a7 ♘c6 17 ♕a6 ♘e4 −+ **♗xe3 15
fxe3 ♖b8** 15...♘c6 −+ **16 ♕a7 ♘e4 17
♗d3 ♘c6 18 ♕a6 ♖b6 19 ♕xb6 ♕xb6
20 ♗xe4 ♖xe4 21 ♖xd5 ♗e6 22
♖d1 a4 23 ♘c1 h6 24 ♘f3 ♖xe3
25 ♖d2 ♘a5 26 ♖hd1 ♘c4 27 ♖d8+
♔h7 28 b3 ♗f5 29 ♖8d5 axb3!** △
♖xb3+ **0-1 Botterill**

✓ **331 Delaune-Seirawan**
USA 78
**1 e4 e6 2 d4 d5 3 ♘d2 ♘c6 4 ♘gf3
♘f6 5 e5 ♘d7 6 ♘b3 a5 7 a4 ♗e7
♗b5** 8 h4 ♘cb8 9 h4 h6?! 9...b5
**10 c3 b6 11 h5 +=/± c6 12 ♗d3 ♗a6
13 ♗xa6 ♘xa6 14 ♗e3 ♘c7!? 14...c5
15 ♘h2!± △ ♕g4, f4 b5 16 ♕g4 ♔f8
17 f4 ♕b8? 17...bxa4 18 ♖xa4 ♕b6
19 ♕d1 ♕b5! 20 ♖a2± 18 0-0! f5
18...bxa4 19 f5 axb3 20 fxe6 +−
19 exf6 ♘xf6 20 ♕d1 bxa4 21 ♖xa4
♕b5 22 ♖a2 ♖g8 23 f5 exf5 24
♖xf5 ♘e8 25 ♖f3! g5** △ ♔g7; 25...
♘d6 26 ♘c5 **26 ♘g4 ♔g7** 26...♘e4
27 ♘c5 ♘xc5 28 dxc5 ♗xc5 29 ♗d4+
+−; 28...♘f6 29 ♕c2 +− **27 ♘e5 ♖f8
28 ♘c5 +− ♗xc5 29 dxc5 ♘e4** 29...
♖a7 30 ♗d4 △ ♘g4+, ♕c2 **30 ♗d4
♔g8** 30...♘8f6 31 ♘d7 ♖f7 32 ♘xf6
♘xf6 33 ♕c2 **31 ♖xf8+ ♔xf8 32
♕f3+ ♘8f6 33 ♘g4 1-0** A.Smith/
Ciamarra

332 Hort-Seirawan
Lone Pine 79
**1 e4 e6 2 d4 d5 3 ♘d2 ♘c6?! 4 ♘gf3
♘f6 5 e5 ♘d7 6 ♗e2** 6 ♘b3; 6 ♗b5
**♘cb8 7 h4! b6 8 h5 c5 9 c3 cxd4 10
cxd4 ♗a6 11 h6 g6 12 ♘f1 ♗e7 13
♗d2 ♗xe2 14 ♕xe2 ♘c6 15 ♖c1 ♖c8
16 ♘1h2!** △ ♘g4± **♕c7 17 0-0 0-0
18 ♘g4 ♕b7 19 ♖c3 ♘cb8 20 ♗g5!
♗xg5 21 ♘xg5 ♖xc3 22 bxc3 ♕c8
23 ♖c1 ♘c6 24 ♕b5 ♔h8 25 ♕a4
♘a5 26 ♕a3! ♕d8 27 f4 ♔g8** 27...
♘c4 28 ♕xa7 **28 ♕d6! ♔h8** 28...
♘c4? 29 ♕xd7! △ ♘f6+ **29 ♘f6!
♗xf6**

**30 ♘xf7+!! +– ♖xf7 31 ♕xd8+ ♔g8
32 ♕e8 ♖e7 33 ♕f8 ♘c4 34 ♔f2 ♘d2
35 ♔e3 ♘c4+ 36 ♔e2 b5 37 ♖b1
a6 38 a4! +– ♖d7 39 axb5 axb5
40 ♖xb5 ♖a7 41 ♖b8 ♖a2+ 42 ♔e1
1-0 Gheorghiu**

333 Dolmatov-Sisniega Graz 78
**1 e4 e6 2 d4 d5 3 ♘d2 ♘c6 4 ♘gf3
♘f6 5 e5 ♘d7 6 ♗e2** 6 ♘b3 f6 7 ♗b5
a6 8 ♗xc6 bxc6 9 0-0 c5 10 ♖e1
c4 (10...fxe5 11 ♗g5!) 11 ♘a5 ♘b8
12 exf6 gxf6 13 ♘e5!; 6...a5 7 a4
♗e7 8 ♗b5 ♘cb8 9 0-0 0-0 10 ♗f4 b6
11 ♖c1 c6 12 ♗d3 ♗a6 13 ♗xa6 ♘xa6
14 c4 dxc4 15 ♖xc4 ♘b4 16 ♖e1 b5!

△ ♘d5 +=; 6 ♗d3!? ♘b4! (6...f6?!
7 ♘g5! fxg5 8 ♕h5+ g6 9 ♗xg6+ hxg6
10 ♕xg6+ ♔e7 11 ♘e4!) 7 ♗e2 c5 8
c3 ♘c6 9 0-0 ♕b6 (9...cxd4 10 cxd4
f6 11 exf6 ♘xf6 12 ♘e5!? ∝/+=) 10
♘b3 a5? 11 dxc5!; 10...cxd4 11 cxd4
♗e7 **f6** 6...♗e7 7 ♘f1 0-0 8 ♘e3 +=
7 exf6 ♕xf6 7...♘xf6 8 0-0 ♗d6 9
c4 0-0 9 ♖e1 ♗d7 10 ♘f1 += **8 ♘f1**
8 ♘b3?! ♗d6 9 0-0 0-0 10 c4 dxc4
11 ♗xc4 ♘b6 12 ♗b5 a6 13 ♗xc6
bxc6 14 ♕c2 ♗d7 =+ Gligoric-
Bondarevsky, Moscow 47 **e5!?** 8...
♗d6 9 ♘e3 0-0 10 0-0 ♘b6 (10...
♕g6 11 c4 ♘f6 12 g3 +=) 11 ♘g4
♕g6 12 h3! (△ ♗d3, ♖e1) e5 13 ♘gxe5
♗xe5 14 dxe5 ♘xh3 15 ♘h4 ♕e4 16
f4± Dolmatov-Yurtaev, Moscow 78
9 ♘e3 9 dxe5?! ♘dxe5 10 ♕xd5 ♘b4!
(10...♗e6 11 ♕b5 a6! 12 ♕a4 0-0-0≈)
11 ♕xe5+ ♕xe5 12 ♘xe5 ♘xc2+ 13
♔d1 ♘xa1 14 ♘e3 ♗c5 15 b3 ♗xe3
16 ♗xe3 ♗f5 17 ♗d3 0-0-0 18 ♔d2
♖he8 19 ♗f4 ♖d4 20 ♗g3 ♗xd3 21
♘xd3 ♖ed8 –+ Schwarz **e4 10 ♘xd5
♕d6 11 ♗c4!** 11 c4!? exf3 12 ♗f4
♕xf4? 13 ♘xf4 ♗b4+ 14 ♔f1 0-0
15 ♗f4 ♖xf4 16 ♗xc6 bxc6 17 c5!
+– Makarichev-Hubner, IBM 75; 12...
fxg2! 13 ♖g1 ♕xf4 14 ♗h5+! (14
♘xf4? ♗b4+) g6 (14...♕f7 15 ♗xf7+
♔xh7 16 ♕f3+ ♘f6 17 ♘xf6 gxf6 18
♕h5+ +–) 15 ♕e2+ ♔f7 16 ♘xf4
♗b4+ 17 ♔d1 ♘f6! ≈/=+; 15 ♘xf4
♗b4+ 16 ♔e2 0-0 d5 ♖xf4 18 dxc6
♘f6 19 ♖xg2 ♘xh5 20 ♕d5+ +–
exf3 12 ♗f4 12 0-0!? ♕g6 13 ♘xc7+
♔d8 14 ♘e6+ ♔e7 15 ♗g5+ ♘f6 16
♖e1 ♗xe6 17 ♗xf6+ gxf6 18 ♖xe6+
♔d7 19 ♕xf3± **♕g6** 12...♕e6+ 13
♔d2! **13 ♘xc7+ ♔d8 14 ♕xf3** ∝/=+
♘b6 14...♘xd4 15 ♕d5 ♘xc2+ 16
♔d1 ♘xa1 17 ♘e6+ ♔e8 18 ♗d3!
♕g4+ 19 f3 ♕xg2 20 ♖e1± **15 ♗d3**

♗g4 15...♘xd4 16 0-0-0! **16 ♕g3 ♗f5**
17 ♕xg6 hxg6 18 ♘xa8 ♘xa8 19
0-0-0± ♘b6 20 ♗g5+ ♔c7 21 ♗xf5
gxf5 22 h4 22 ♗f4+!? ♗d6 **23 ♖he1**
♔d7 **24 c3 a6 25 ♔c2 ♘d5 26 ♔d3**
b5! 27 ♖a1 ♖b8 28 ♖e2 ♘a5 29 g3
♖c8 30 ♖c2 ♘c4= 31 ♖h1 b4 32
♗c1! bxc3 33 bxc3 ♘f6 34 h5 ½-½
Ciamarra

334 Kovacs-Joksic
Bajmok 78

1 e4 c5 2 ♘f3 a6 3 c3 e6 4 d4 d5 5
e5 ♘c6 6 ♗e2 N 6 ♗d3! cxd4 7 cxd4
♘ge7 8 ♘c3 ♘f5 9 ♗c2± Ivkov-
R.Byrne, Sarajevo 67 **f5!? 7 0-0**
♘h6?! 8 ♗xh6 gxh6 9 ♘bd2 ♖g8
10 ♖e1 ♕b6 11 ♕b3 ♕d8 11...♕xb3
12 ♘xb3 += **12 ♘f1 c4 13 ♕c2 b5**
14 ♘g3 ♖a7 15 ♘h5 ♗e7 16 b3 ♖c7
17 ♖ed1 ♔f8 18 g3 ♕e8 19 ♘f4 ♘d8
20 a4 ♘f7 21 axb5 axb5 22 ♖a8
♘g5 23 bxc4 bxc4 24 ♖b1 ♔g7 25
♖bb8 ♕f7 26 ♕b2 ♘xf3+ 27 ♗xf3
♗g5 28 ♗h5 ♕e7 29 ♘g2 +=♖b7 30
♖xb7 ♕xb7 31 ♕a1 ♔h8 32 ♖a7
♕b6 33 ♖a2 ♖g7 34 h4 ♗d8 35
♔h1 ♖b7 36 ♘f4 ♖b8 36...♕b1+
37 ♕xb1 ♖xb1+ 38 ♔g2 △ ♖a8/
♗f7 +− **37 ♔g2 ♗e7 38 ♗f7 ♕c6**
39 ♖a7 ♗f8 40 ♕a5 △ ♕d8 +− **♖b6**
41 ♖a8 ♔g7 42 ♗e8 ♗d7 42...♕c7
43 ♖a7 ♗b7 44 ♘xe6+ +− **43 ♘h5+**
1-0 Kovacs

335 Sax-Kuligowski Warsaw 79

1 e4 e6 2 d4 d5 3 e5 c5 4 c3 ♘c6 5
♘f3 ♕b6 6 a3 6 ♗d3; 6 ♗e2 c4 7
g3 ♗d7 8 ♘bd2 ♘a5 9 h4 h5 10 ♗h3
f6 11 exf6 gxf6 12 0-0 0-0-0 13
♖e1 ♘h6 △ ♘g4∞ 14 ♘h2! += ♘f7
15 ♗g2 ♗d6 16 ♖b1 ♖e8 17 ♘df1 ♗g7
18 ♗f3!± △ ♗xh5 ♖ef8 19 ♗xh5 e5
20 ♘e3 ♗c6? 21 ♕g4+ f5 22 ♕xg7 +−

22...exd4 23 cxd4 ♕d8 24 ♗f3 f4
25 ♘xd5 ♖f7 26 ♘e7+! ♔c7 27
♕g5! +− fxg3 27...b6 28 ♗xf4 +−
28 ♕xa5+ b6 29 ♕xa7+ ♘b7 30
fxg3 ♗xf3 31 ♖e6 ♕xd4+ 32 ♗e3
1-0 Gheorghiu

1 e4 ♘f6

336 Gofstein-Kengis USSR 78
1 e4 ♘f6 2 ♘c3 d5 3 e5 ♘fd7 4 f4
e6 5 ♘f3 c5 6 d4 ♘c6 7 ♗e3 cxd4
7...a6 8 ♕d2 b5 9 dxc5! ♘xc5 10
♗d3 ♗b7 11 ♕f2 ♘xd3+ 12 cxd3
♗e7 13 0-0 0-0 14 ♘d4± Gheorghiu-
Belkadi, Skopje 72 **8 ♘xd4 ♗e7**
8...a6 9 ♕g4 g6 10 0-0-0 ♘xd4 11
♗xd4 b5 12 ♗d3 ♗b7 13 h4!±
Barle-Padevsky, Pula 75; 8...♗c5 9
♕d2! ♘xd4 10 ♗xd4 ♗xd4 11 ♕xd4
♕b6 12 ♘b5± Tal-Stahlberg, Stockholm 61; 8...♕b8!? **9 ♕f3 ♘xd4 10**
♗xd4 f5 11 0-0-0 0-0 12 g4!± ♘c5
13 gxf5 ♖xf5 14 ♗e3! ♕f8 15 ♖g1
♖f7 15...♖xe5 16 ♗d4 ♖g5 17 ♗xc5
+− **16 ♗h3 b5 17 f5! b4 18 ♘b5**
♗d7 19 ♘d4 ♕c8 20 ♘h6 ♗f8 20...
♔h8 21 ♗xg7+ ♖xg7 22 ♖xg7 ♔xg7
23 f6+ +− **21 f6 g6 22 ♗xf8 ♕xf8**
23 ♕h5 +− ♖c8 24 ♖g2 ♖c7 25
♔b1 a6 26 ♖dg1 △ ♖xg6+ ♗c8 27
♘e2! ♘e4 28 ♖xg6+ hxg6 29 ♖xg6+
♖g7 30 fxg7 ♖xg7 31 ♖h6! 1-0 Gipslis

337 Dobsa-Bullocks Corr. 76/78
1 e4 ♞f6 2 e5 ♞d5 3 d4 d6 4 ♞f3
♝g4 5 ♝e2 c6 6 ♞g5!? 6 0-0 ♝xf3 7
♝xf3 dxe5 8 dxe5 e6 9 ♖e1 += ♞f5
6...♝xe2 7 ♛xe2 dxe5 8 dxe5 e6 9
0-0 ♛c7 10 ♖d1 ♞d7 11 ♞f3 +=
7 ♝d3 7 e6 ♝xe6! 8 ♞xe6 fxe6 9 ♝g4
♞c7 10 0-0 ♞d7 11 ♖e1 e5 12 ♝xd7+
♛xd7 13 dxe5 d5!=; 7 ♝g4!? ♝xd3
8 ♛xd3 dxe5 9 ♛f5 9 dxe5≈ f6 9...
♞f6 10 dxe5 g6 11 ♛f4 h6 12 ♞xf7
♔xf7 13 ♞c3± 10 ♞xh7 exd4 11
0-0 11 ♛g6+ ♞d7∞ ♛d6! N 11...e5
12 c4 ♞c7 13 f4 ♞d7 14 ♞g5!±
Vasyukov-Bagirov, Baku 72 12 c4
dxc3 13 bxc3 13 ♞xc3!? ♞d7 14
♛g6+ ♞d8 15 ♖d1 ♞e5 16 ♛c2 16
♛e4? f5 17 ♛xf5 g6 —+

16...g6? 16...♔c7∞ 17 ♞xf8 ♖xf8
17...♞f3+ 18 gxf3 ♛xh2+ 19 ♔f1
+— 18 ♝a3 ♛c7 19 c4 +— ♞f3+ 20
gxf3 ♖h8 21 cxd5 ♛xh2+ 22 ♔f1
♛e5 23 dxc6+ ♔e8 24 ♛xg6+ ♔f8
25 ♝xe7+! 1-0 25...♔xe7 26 ♛g7+;
25...♔xe7 26 ♖d7 Bellin

338 Beljavsky-Alburt Kiev 78
1 e4 ♞f6 2 e5 ♞d5 3 d4 d6 4 ♞f3
♝g4 5 ♝e2 e6 6 h3 ♝h5 7 0-0 ♝e7
8 c4 ♞b6 9 ♞c3 0-0 10 ♝e3 d5 11 c5
♝xf3 12 ♝xf3 12 gxf3! += ♞c4 13
♝f4 ♞c6 13...b6 14 b3 ♞a5 15 b4

Lukhin-Bagirov, USSR 75 14 b3 ♞a5
15 ♖c1! 15 ♛d2 b6 16 ♞a4 f6! ♛d7!?
15...b6 Geller-Timman, Teesside 75
16 ♖e1 16 ♛d2; 16 ♝g4!? f6 16...b6!?
Δ f6 17 exf6 ♝xf6 18 ♞e2 Δ ♛d2
♞e7! 19 ♛d2 ♞ac6 20 ♝g4 ♞f5= 21
♝xf5 exf5 22 b4 a6 23 a4 ♖fe8
24 b5 axb5 25 axb5 ♞a5 26 ♛d3
c6! =+ 27 bxc6 bxc6 28 ♞g3 g6
29 ♝e5!? ♝xe5 30 dxe5 ♞b7 31 ♛e3
♞d8 32 ♞e2 ♞e6 33 ♞d4 f4?! 33...
♖a4 =+ 34 ♛c3 ♖a4 35 ♞xe6 ♛xe6
36 ♛b3 ♖e4 37 ♛b7! ♛xe5 38 ♖xe4
dxe4 38...♛xe4 39 ♛xc6 f3 =+ 39
♛xc6 e3 40 fxe3 ♛xe3+ 41 ♔h2 f3!?
42 ♖f1! ♛f4+ 43 ♔h1 ♖e3 44 ♛c8+
♔g7 45 ♛d7+ ♔h6 46 ♛g4! =+ ♛xg4
47 hxg4 fxg2+ 48 ♔xg2 ♖c3 49
♖f7!= ♖xc5 50 ♖a7 ½-½ Gufeld

1 e4 g6

339 Bellon-Ciocaltea
Montilla 78
1 e4 ♞f6 2 ♞c3 d6 3 d4 g6 4 ♝c4
♝g7 5 ♛e2 ♞c6 5...c6!? 6 ♞f3 ♝g4 7
♝e3 7 e5?! ♝xf3 8 ♛xf3 ♞xd4 9 ♛xb7
dxe5 10 ♝b5+ ♔f8∓ Tuzovsky-Tal,
USSR 75 0-0 7...e5!= 8 0-0-0 ♞d7
8...e5!? 9 h3 ♝xf3 10 gxf3! ♞b6
11 f4 e6 12 f5 exf5 13 exf5 d5 14
♝b3 ♞a5 15 h4 gxf5? 15...♞xb3+
16 axb3 ♛f6± 16 ♖dg1! ♔h8 17
♖xg7!! ♛xg7 18 ♖g1+ ♔h8 19 ♝h6
♞xb3+ 20 axb3 ♖g8 21 ♛e5+ f6 22
♖xg8+ ♔xg8 23 ♛e6+ 1-0 23...♔h8
24 ♛f7 +— Ciocaltea

340 Sveshnikov-Romanishin
Tbilisi 78
1 e4 g6 2 d4 ♝g7 3 ♞c3 d6 4 ♝e3 c6
5 g3!? N ♞f6 6 h3 0-0 7 ♝g2 ♞bd7
8 a4 ♞b6 8...e5 9 b3 d5? 9...a5!?;
9...c5 10 dxc5 ♞fd7 Δ ♞xc5; 10 a5

cxd4 11 ♗xd4 ♘bd7 **10 a5 ♘bd7 11
e5!±** 11 exd5 cxd5 12 ♘xd5 ♘xd5
13 ♗xd5 ♘f6 14 ♗g2 ♘d5∞ **♘e8 12
f4 ♘c7 13 ♘f3 b6 14 axb6 axb6 15
♖xa8 ♘xa8 16 0-0 ♘c7 17 g4! ♗a6
18 ♖f2 f5?!** 18...e6 Δ c5 **19 gxf5
♖xf5 20 h4 ♘f8 21 ♗h3 ♗c8 22
♘e2!?** 22 ♗xf5 ♗xf5± **♖h5 23 ♕f1
e6** 23...♗xh3 24 ♕xh3 e6 25 ♘g3 +−
**24 ♖h2 ♗a6 25 ♕f2 ♕e7 26 ♘g3 ♖h6
27 f5! +−** exf5 28 ♗xf5 gxf5 29
**♗xh6 ♗xh6 30 ♘xf5 ♕e6 31 ♖g2+
♕f7** 31...♔h8 32 ♘xh6 ♕xh6 33 ♘g5
+− **32 ♘g5+! ♗xg5 33 ♖xg5 ♘g6 34
h5 ♘e8 35 hxg6+ hxg6 36 ♕h4! ♘f6
37 ♕h6 ♘e4 38 ♕h7+ 1-0 Keene**

341 Tseshkovsky-Kuzmin
USSR 79

**1 e4 d6 2 d4 ♘f6 3 ♘c3 g6 4 ♘f3
♗g7 5 ♗e2 0-0 6 0-0 ♗g4 7 ♗e3 ♘c6
8 ♕d2 ♖e8 9 ♖ad1** 9 d5 ♗xf3 10
♗xf3 ♘e5 11 ♗e2 c6 12 ♗d4 ♕a5
Andersson-Keene, Hastings 71/72 **e5
10 dxe5** 10 d5 ♗xf3 11 ♗xf3 ♘d4
♗xf3 **11 ♗xf3 dxe5 12 ♕xd8 ♖axd8**
12...♖exd8 13 ♘b5 ♘e8 **13 ♘b5
♖c8 14 c3 a6 15 ♘a3 h5 16 h3 ♗f8
17 ♘c2 ♘d8 18 a3 ♘e6** 18...a5!?
19 ♘b4! ♘c5 20 ♘d5 ♘xd5 20...
♘cxe4 21 ♗xe4 ♘xe4 22 f3 ♘g3 23
♘f6+ ♔h8 24 ♘xe8 ♗xf1 25 ♔xf1
♖xe8 26 ♖d7 Δ ♖xc7/♖xf7± **21
♖xd5 ♘a4 22 ♖b1 ♖cd8 23 ♗d1
♖xd5 24 ♗xa4** 24 exd5 b5 24...♖dd8
25 ♗xe8 ♖xe8 26 ♖d1 ♗d6 27 c4
♖d8 28 ♗g5! **25 exd5 bxa4 26 b4
f5 27 c4 ♕f7 28 ♕f1** 28 ♗c5 ♖b8
29 ♗xf8 ♕xf8 30 c5 ♖d8 31 ♖d1
♔e7 32 ♕f1 c6 33 d6+ ♔d7 **♖b8
29 ♕e2 a5 30 b5** 30 ♗d2 axb4 31
axb4 a3! **♗xa3 31 ♖a1** 31 c5 f4 32
d6 cxd6 33 c6!; 31...♔e7 32 d6+
♔d7! **♗b4!= 32 ♖xa4 ♕e7 33 ♗d2**

♕d6 34 ♗xb4+ axb4 35 ♖xb4 ♕c5
36 ♖a4 ♕d4 37 h4 ♕c3 38 g3 ♕b3 39
♖a7 ♔xc4 40 ♖xc7+ ♕xd5 41 ♖c6
♖xb5 42 ♖xg6 ♖b2+ 43 ♕f1 ♕e4
½-½ **Keene**

342 Skrobek-Ftacnik
Poland 78

**1 e4 d6 2 d4 ♘f6 3 ♘c3 g6 4 f4 ♗g7
5 ♘f3 0-0 6 ♗d3 ♘c6 7 e5 dxe5**
7...♘e8!? **8 fxe5 ♘d7** 8...♘d5! **9 0-0
♘b6 10 ♗e3 f6 11 exf6 exf6 12
d5! ♘e7** 12...♘xd5? 13 ♗c4 **13 ♗c5
♖e8 14 ♖e1 ♗f8** 14...♘exd5 15 ♖xe8+
♕xe8 16 ♘xd5 ♘xd5 17 ♗c4 c6
18 ♗xd5+ cxd5 19 ♕xd5+ ♗e6 20
♕xb7 +=; 19...♕f7 20 ♕d8+; 19...
♔h8 20 ♖e1 +=; 14...♘bxd5 15
♗c4 += **15 ♘e4 ♗g7** 15...♘exd5 16
♗xb6 axb6 17 ♗c4! ♗e6 18 ♗xd5+
♗xd5 19 ♕xd5+ +−; 17...c6 18 ♗xd5+
cxd5 19 ♘xf6+ +−; 15...♘bxd5
16 c4 += **16 d6 ♘ed5 17 ♕d2 f5 18
♘eg5 ♖xe1+ 19 ♖xe1 cxd6 20 ♗a3
♘c7 21 ♕f4 h6 22 ♕xd6 ♗f6**

23 ♕xc7!! ♗d4+ 23...♕xc7 24 ♖e8+
♔g7 25 ♗f8+ ♔g8 26 ♗xh6 mate
**24 ♘xd4 ♕xc7 25 ♖e8+ ♔g7 26
♘ge6+ ♗xe6 27 ♘xe6+ ♕f7 28 ♘xc7
♖xe8 29 ♘xe8 1-0 Pytel/Bielczyk**

180

343 Sax-Donner
Buenos Aires 78

**1 e4 d6 2 d4 ♞f6 3 ♞c3 g6 4 f4 ♝g7
5 ♞f3 0-0 6 ♝d3 ♞c6 7 0-0 e5** 7...
♝g4 8 e5 dxe5 9 dxe5 ♞d5 10 h3!
+= **8 dxe5** 8 fxe5 dxe5 9 d5 ♞e7
10 ♞xe5 c6! 11 ♝g5 cxd5!= 12 ♝xf6
♛b6+; 10...♞fxd5? 11 ♝xf7! ♞xc3
12 bxc3 ♜xf7 13 ♜xf7 ♚xf7 14
♝c4+± 9...♞d4!? 10 ♞xe5 ♞xe4
11 ♝xe4 ♝xe5= **dxe5 9 f5 ♞b4?**
9...gxf5! 10 exf5 e4 11 ♞xe4 ♝xf5
12 ♞xf6+ ♛xf6 13 ♝g5 ♛e6 14
c3 ♝g6= Sax-Hazai, Hungary 77
10 fxg6 hxg6 10...fxg6? 11 ♝c4+
♚h8 12 ♛xd8 ♜xd8 13 ♝g5± **11
♝g5 c6 12 ♚h1 ♝xd3 13 cxd3 ♛d6?!**
13...♛c7 14 ♜c1 ♝e6 **14 d4 ♞h7 15
d5 ♝xg5 16 ♞xg5 ♛e7?!** 16...♝d7
17 ♛e1 ♝h6; 17 ♛b3 c5! **17 ♞f3 ♝d7
18 ♛b3 b6 19 ♜ad1 ♜ad8** 19...c5
20 d6 ♛e6 21 ♞d5 ♛xd6 22 ♞g5
♜ad8! 23 ♞f6+ ♚xf6 24 ♜xf6 ♝xf6∞;
23 ♛g3! ∆ ♛h4 **20 ♜d2 c5 21 d6
♛e6 22 ♞d5 ♛xd6 25 ♞g5 ♝e6 24
♛g3 ∆ ♛h4 1-0 Keene**

17 ♜e4! f6 17...♞c5 18 ♜xe5 ♝xe5
19 fxe5± **18 ♜c4 ♛b8** 18...♛d8 19
♝g2 ♝b7 20 d6!± **19 ♜c6 ♝b7 20**
♝g2 b5 21 ♜e6 ♜f7 22 fxe5 ♞xe5
23 g5 23 ♜f1!?; 23 ♜b6!? ♛d8 24
♜d1 ♞c4! ∆ ♜c8/f5 **25 d6?!** 25 b3
♛a5 exd6 26 ♜e1 fxg5∓ 27 ♝xb7
♜xb7 28 ♛f3 d5! 29 b3 g4! —+ 30
hxg4 ♝h6+? 30...♜f7 31 ♛d3 ♛g5+
32 ♚b1 ♞d2+ 33 ♚b2 ♞e4/b4 —+
**31 ♚d1 ♜f7 32 ♛xd5 ♝b2+ 33 ♚e2
♛f8??** 33...b4 34 ♜d6 ♛e7+ 35 ♜e6
♛d8=; 33...♜c8!?; 33...♛xd5 34 ♞xd5
♜d8 35 ♝d6 ♜fd7! 36 ♞f6+ ♚f7+
34 ♜f1!! ♜c8 35 ♝e5 ♛c5?? 35...
♝g5 ∆ ♜d8 **36 ♜e8+ 1-0 Botterill**

344 Peters-Botterill
Hastings 78-9

**1 e4 d6 2 d4 g6 3 ♞c3 ♝g7 4 f4 ♞f6
5 ♞f3 0-0 6 ♝e3 b6!? 7 e5!? ♞g4
8 ♝g1 c5 9 h3** 9 dxc5? bxc5!∓ 10
♛d5 ♛b6 **♞h6 10 d5 ♞d7!?** N 10...
♞f5 11 ♝f2 dxe5 12 fxe5 ♞d7 13
♛e2 ♝b7 (13...♛c7!? Kovacevic) 14
0-0-0 ♛b8 15 g4 ♞d4 16 ♞xd4 cxd4
17 ♝xd4 ♝xe5 18 ♝g2± Balashov-
Timman, Tilburg 77 **11 ♛e2 ♛c7
12 ♝h2** 12 e6? fxe6 13 dxe6 ♞f6
14 g4 ♝b7!∓ **♞f5 13 0-0-0 a6** 13...
♞d4? 14 ♞xd4 cxd4 15 ♞b5 ♛c5
16 ♞xd4 ♛xd5 17 ♞b3± **14 g4 ♞d4
15 ♞xd4 cxd4 16 ♜xd4 dxe5**

345 Romanishin-Kuzmin
USSR 79

**1 e4 d6 2 d4 ♞f6 3 ♞c3 g6 4 ♝g5
♝g7 5 ♛d2 h6 6 ♝f4 g5 7 ♝e3?!
♞g4 8 ♞ge2 ♞c6 9 ♞g3 ♞xe3 10
fxe3 h5 11 ♝e2 g4 12 0-0-0?** 12 h3!
h4 13 ♞f5 ♝f6 14 hxg4 e6 15 g5
♝xg5 16 ♞g7+ ♚f8 17 ♞h5 ∆ 0-0-0
**♞xd4! 13 ♝c4 ♞c6 14 ♞f5 ♝f6 15
♞d5 e6 16 ♞xf6+** 16 ♞xc7+ ♛xc7
17 ♞xd6+ ♚f8 18 ♜hf1 ♜h6∓ **♛xf6
17 ♞d4 ♞xd4 18 ♜hf1 ♞f5 19 exf5
exf5 20 e4 ♛h6 21 ♜f4 ♝d7 22
exf5 ♝c6 23 g3** 23 ♛d4!? **♛f6 24
♜e1+ ♚d8 25 ♛a5 a6 26 ♝d5 ♜b8
27 ♚b1?** 27 ♝xc6 bxc6 28 c3 ♜e8

28 ♖xe8+ ♗xe8 29 b3 ♗b5 30 a4 b6
31 ♕d2 ♗d7 32 ♕d3 b5 33 a5 ♔e7
34 ♔e3+ ♔f8 35 ♕a7 ♖e8 −+ 36
♖f1 ♕c3 37 ♕f2 ♖e5 38 ♕g2 ♗xf5
39 ♖c1 c6 0-1 time **Keene**

√346 Romanishin-Donner
Buenos Aires 78

1 e4 d6 2 d4 ♞f6 3 ♞c3 g6 4 ♗g5
♗g7 5 f3 c6 6 ♕d2 h6? 6...b5! 7
♗e3 b5 8 ♗d3 ♞bd7 9 ♞ge2 ♞b6?!
9...a6!? △ c5 10 b3 a5? 10...h5!?
△ 0-0 11 a4! b4 12 ♞d1 ♞fd7 13
c3 e5 14 cxb4 axb4 15 ♖c1± ♗b7
16 0-0 exd4 17 ♞xd4 c5 18 ♞b5
♞c8 19 ♗e2 ♖a6 20 ♞b2! h5 21
♞c4 ♞e5 22 ♖fd1 ♞xc4 23 ♗xc4
△ ♗xc5 +− ♕e7 24 ♗g5 ♕d7 24...
♗f6 25 ♗xf6 ♕xf6 26 ♞c7+ +−

25 e5!! +− ♗xe5 26 ♖e1 △ f4 **1-0**
26...♔f8 27 ♖xe5 +− **Keene**

347 Sveshnikov-Tseshkovsky
Lvov 78

1 e4 g6 2 d4 ♗g7 3 ♞c3 c6 4 g3?!
4 ♞f3 d5 5 h3 +=; 4 e5 ♗g7 5 h3
♞h6 6 ♞f3 0-0 7 ♗f4 f6= **d5 5 e5**
5 exd5 **f6! 6 exf6** 6 f4 fxe5 7 fxe5
♞h6 △ ♕b6, ♗e6, ♞f5 =+ ♞xf6 7
♗g2 0-0 8 ♞f3 8 ♞ge2 e5 9 dxe5
♞g4 10 f4 ♕b6 =+; 8 f4 ♗g4 9 ♞f3
♕b6 ♗g4 =+ 9 h3?! ♗xf3 10 ♗xf3

♞bd7 11 0-0 e5 12 ♞e2 ♕e7 13 ♗g2
♖ae8 14 ♗g5 exd4! 15 ♞xd4 ♕f7∓
16 ♗xf6 ♞xf6 17 ♕f3 ♞e4 18 ♕xf7+
♖xf7 19 ♖ad1 ♞d6! −+ 20 b3 ♗xd4!
21 ♖xd4 ♖e2 22 c4 ♞f5 23 ♖f4 dxc4
23...d4? 24 g4 **24 ♖d1?** c3! 25 ♖c1
♖xa2 26 ♖xc3 ♖d2 27 ♗f1 ♞d4 28
♖e4 28 ♖xd4 ♖xd4 29 ♞c4 ♔g7 −+
♔f8 29 ♗c4 ♞f3+ 29...♖fxf2? 30
♖xd4 30 ♔g2 ♞g5 31 ♖f4 ♖xf4 32
gxf4 ♖xf2+! 33 ♔xf2 ♞e4+ 34 ♔f3
♞xc3 35 f5 gxf5 36 ♔f4 ♞e4 37
♔e5 ♔e7 38 ♗g8 ♞g5 39 ♔xf5 ♞xh3
40 ♗xh7 ♔d6 0-1 **Gufeld**

1 ♞f3

348 Ribli-Ljubojevic √
Buenos Aires 78

1 ♞f3 d5 2 g3 c5 3 ♗g2 ♞c6 4 d4
e6 5 0-0 ♞f6 6 c4 dxc4 7 ♕a4 ♗d7
8 ♕xc4 ♖c8 10 ♞c3 ♞xd4 11 ♞xd4
cxd4 12 ♕xd4 ♗c5 13 ♕h4 ♗c6 14
♖d1 ♕b6 15 ♗xc6+ ♖xc6 16 ♗h6!!±
♗f8 17 ♖d2! e5 18 ♗e3 ♕a6 19
♖ad1 ♗e7 20 ♕g5! 0-0 21 ♕xe5
♗b4 22 ♖d8! ♖c8 23 ♖xc8 ♖xc8
24 ♕d4!± ♕a5 24...♗xc3 25 ♕d8+
25 ♕xa7 ♗xc3 26 bxc3 ♕b5 27
♕b6 ♕a4 28 ♖d8+ ♖xd8 29 ♕xd8+
♞e8 30 f3 h6 31 ♔f2 ♕c6 32 c4!
♕a4 33 ♕c8 ♔h7 34 c5 ♕b5 35 a4!
+− ♕xa4 36 ♕xb7 ♕c4 37 ♕e4+!
♕xe4 38 fxe4 g5 39 c6 f6 40 ♗b6
♔g6 41 ♔e3 ♔f7 42 ♔d4 ♔e6 43
♗d8! g4 44 c7 ♞d6 45 ♔c5 ♞d7 46
♔d5 ♞b5 47 e5! fxe5 47...f5 48
e6+ 48 ♔xe5 ♞c3 49 e4 ♞d1 50
♔f6 1-0 **Gheorghiu**

349 Portisch-Radulov
Buenos Aires 78

1 ♞f3 d5 2 g3 c5 3 ♗g2 ♞c6 4 d4
♞f6 5 0-0 e6 6 c4 dxc4 6...cxd4

7 ♕a4! ♗d7 8 ♕xc4 cxd4 9 ♘xd4
♖c8 9...♘xd4 10 ♕xd4± 10 ♘c3
♘xd4 11 ♕xd4 ♗c5 12 ♕h4 ♘c6
13 ♖d1 ♕b6 14 ♗xc6+ ♖xc6

15 ♗h6!!± gxh6 16 ♕xf6 0-0 17
♘e4 ♕b4! 18 ♕e5 ♗e7 19 a3 ♕b6
20 ♖d7 ♗g5 21 b3! 21 ♘xg5 ♖c5∝
♕xb3 22 ♘xg5 hxg5 23 ♕xg5+ ♔h8
24 ♖ad1 ♕c2 25 ♕f6+ ♔g8 26 ♖1d4!
♕g6! 27 ♕f3 h5 28 ♖xb7 e5 29
♖h4! ♖d8 30 ♕xh5 +− ♕xh5 31
♖xh5 f6 32 ♖xa7 ♖d2 33 e3 ♖c1+
34 ♔g2 ♖dd1 35 ♖f5! 1-0 Gheorghiu

350 Taimanov-Bellon
Bucharest 79

1 ♘f3 d5 2 g3 c6 3 ♗g2 ♗f5 4 b3
♘d7 5 ♗b2 ♘gf6 6 0-0 e6 7 d3 ♕b6
8 ♘bd2 a5 9 a3 ♗e7 10 e4 ♗g6 11
♕e2 11 e5 += 0-0 12 h3 ♘e8 13 ♔h1
♘c7 14 ♘h4!? ♗xh4 15 gxh4 f6 16
f4 ♕c5 17 c4 dxe4 18 ♘xe4 ♕e7 19
h5 ♗xe4 20 ♗xe4 ♘c5 21 d4 ♘xe4
21...♘xb3 22 ♗xh7+ ♔h8 23 ♖ab1!±
22 ♕xe4 ♕f7 23 ♕f3 ♘e8 24 f5
exf5 25 ♕xf5 ♘d6 26 ♕f3 a4 27
h6! g6 28 d5 axb3 29 ♕xb3 ♘e4
30 ♕d3 cxd5 31 cxd5 ♖fe8 32 ♖f4
♖a4 33 ♖af1 ♘c5 34 ♕d2 ♕d7 35
♔g2 ♕b5?! 35...♖xf4 36 ♖xf4 ♕b5∓

Diagram

36 ♖xf6! ♘e4?? Zeitnot 36...♘d3!=;
36...♖e2+?? 37 ♔g1! +− 37 ♖xg6+!!
hxg6 38 h7+ ♔xh7 39 ♖f7+ ♔g8
40 ♖g7+ 1-0 40...♔h8 41 ♕h6 mate;
40...♔f8 41 ♕f4+ +− Suba

351 Martinovic-Ciric
Trstenik 79

1 g3 d5 2 ♗g2 c6 3 ♘f3 ♗g4 4 b3
♘d7 5 ♗b2 ♗xf3?! 5...♘gf6; 5...♕c7
6 ♗xf3 e5 7 ♗g2 ♘gf6 8 0-0 ♗d6
8...♗c5 9 d3 0-0 10 c4 dxc4 10...♕e7!
11 bxc4 ♕e7 12 e3± ♖fd8 13 ♕c2
♘f8 14 a3 14 ♘d2 ♗a3 ♖ab8 15
♘d2 ♘g6 16 ♖fd1 a6 17 a4 ♘f8
18 ♖ab1 ♘g6 19 ♗c3 ♖dc8 20 a5
♘f8 21 ♖e1! ♘e6 22 h3 ♘d8 23 ♕b2
c5 24 f4! ♘c6 25 ♕a1 △ ♗xc6 exf4
26 exf4 ♕d8 27 ♘b3 ♗e7 28 ♖bd1
♕d7 29 ♔h2 ♖e8 30 ♕a3 ♘d4 31
♕b2 ♘f5 32 ♕f2 ♖bc8 33 ♖e5 ♘h6
△ ♘g4 34 ♔h1 ♗d6 35 ♘xc5 ♗xc5
36 ♖xc5 ♘hg4? 37 hxg4 ♘xg4 38
♕d4 +− ♕e6 39 ♕xg7 mate 1-0
Pytel

352 Kochiev-Tseshkovsky
Lvov 78

1 ♘f3 ♘f6 2 g3 d5 3 ♗g2 ♗f5 4 0-0
e6 5 c4 5 d3 c6 6 b3 ♗e7 6...h6 7
♗b2 ♘bd7 8 d3 7 ♗b2 0-0 8 d3 h6
9 ♘bd2 ♘bd7 10 a3 a5 11 ♖a2?!
11 ♖c1 ♗h7 12 ♖c2 ♗d6 13 ♕a1

183

♕e7 14 ♗h3! += ♗h7 12 ♕a1 ♔b6!
**13 ♘e5 ♘xe5 14 ♗xe5 ♖fd8= 15 ♘f3
♘e8** Δ ♗f6 16 ♗c3 ♗f6 16...♔b3?!
**17 ♖b1 ♗xc3 18 ♕xc3 dxc4! 19
♕xc4 ♘d6 20 ♕c1 f6!? 21 ♘d2** Δ
♘c4 += ♕d4 22 ♖c2 ♕a7 23 b4 axb4
24 axb4 e5 25 ♘e4! ♘b5 25...♘xe4
**26 dxe4! 26 ♖cb2 ♔h8 27 ♘c3 ♘d4
28 b5 ♕a3!= 29 bxc6 bxc6 30 ♘e4
f5 31 ♘c5 f4 32 ♔h1?!** 32 e3!=
♗f5 33 ♖d2?

**33...♖db8! 34 ♖xb8+ ♖xb8 35 ♖d1
♕xc1 36 ♖xc1 ♘xe2 −+ 37 ♖e1 ♘d4**
37...♖b5 **38 gxf4 exf4 39 ♗e4 ♗h3
40 ♗g6 f3! 0-1 Gufeld**

353 Rosenberg-Fagerstrom corr. 78

1 ♘f3 ♘f6 2 g3 d5 3 ♗g2 ♗f5 3...c6
4 b3 ♗f5 5 ♗b2 e6 6 0-0 h6 7 d3
♗e7 8 ♘bd2 0-0 9 ♕e1 ♗h7 Vukic-
Miles, Novi Sad **4 0-0** 4 c4 e6! 5 ♕b3
♕c8 6 ♘c3 c6≈ Barcza-Portisch,
Hungary Final 58; 4...c6 5 cxd5 cxd5
6 ♕b3 ♕c8 7 ♘c3 e6 8 d3 ♘c6 9
♗f4 += Barcza-Smyslov, Moscow 56
e6 5 d3 ♘bd7 5...h6 6 ♘bd2 ♗c5 7
♕e1 0-0 8 e4 dxe4 9 ♘xe4 +=
Petrosian-Euwe, Zurich 53; 5...c6 6
♘bd2 ♗e7 **6 ♘bd2 ♗c5?!** 6...♗e7
**7 a3 a5 8 b3 0-0 9 ♗b2 h6 10 ♕e1
♕e7** 10...c6 **11 e4 dxe4 12 dxe4**
12 ♘xe4 **♗h7** 12...♘g6!? **13 ♘d4! +=**

♗xd4 14 ♗xd4 e5 15 ♗b2 ♖ad8
15...♖fd8 **16 ♘c4 b6** 16...♕c5! Δ a4
**17 ♕e2 ♕e6 18 ♖fd1 ♕c6 19 f3!±
♖fe8 20 ♖d2 b5 21 ♘e3 ♕b6 22
♗h3!** 22 ♖ad1? ♖e6! Δ ♖d6 +=/∝
c6 **23 ♖ad1 ♕a7 24 ♖2d6** Δ ♕d2
1-0 Rosenberg

354 Smejkal-Prandstetter
Warsaw 79

**1 ♘f3 d5 2 g3 g6 3 c4 d4 4 b4! ♗g7
5 ♗b2 e5 6 d3 ♘e7 7 ♗g2 0-0 8 0-0
a5!?** 8...c6 Δ a5∝ **9 b5 c6** 9...c5 10
bxc6 ♘xc6 11 ♘a3 Δ ♘b5± **10 ♗a3!
f5 11 ♘bd2 ♖e8 12 ♖b1 ♗f6 13 ♕c2
♔g7 14 e3!± dxe3 15 fxe3 g5 16
h3 ♘g6 17 c5!** Δ ♘c4, ♘d6 **h5 18
♘c4 g4 19 hxg4 hxg4 20 ♘fd2 f4
21 bxc6 ♘xc6 22 ♗xc6! bxc6 23
♘e4 ♗a6 24 ♘cd6 ♖h8 25 exf4 ♗xf4
26 gxf4 ♖h3 27 ♕g2 ♔h8 28 ♘f7+
1-0 Gheorghiu**

355 Nikolac-Timman
Wijk aan Zee 79

**1 ♘f3 ♘f6 2 b3 g6 3 ♗b2 ♗g7 4
g3 d6 5 d4 b5 6 ♗g2 ♗b7 7 ♘bd2
♘bd7 8 0-0 c5 9 c4 bxc4 10 ♘xc4
0-0 11 dxc5 d5** 11...♘xc5 12 ♘ce5
12 c6!? ♗xc6 13 ♘ce5 ♘xe5 14
♗xe5 **♘xc5 13 ♖c1 ♘fe4! =+ 14
b4 ♘e6 15 ♘d4 ♕d6 16 ♘xe6 ♕xe6
17 ♘d3 ♗xb2 18 ♘xb2 ♖fc8 18
♕d4 ♕a6!** Δ ♕xa2, ♘c3 **20 ♘d3**
20 ♖xc8+ ♖xc8 21 ♗xe4 dxe4 22
a4 ♕c6∓ **♕xa2 21 ♗xe4 dxe4 22
♘c5 ♗c6 23 e3 =+ ♕d5** 23...♕b2!?
**24 ♕xd5 ♗xd5 25 ♖fd1 e6 26 ♘d7
♔g7 27 b5 ♗b3 28 ♖xc8 ♖xc8 29
♖a1 ♖c7 30 b6 axb6 31 ♘xb6 ♖c6
32 ♘d7**

Diagram

32...g5!∓ 33 g4? 33 h3 ☖c7 34 ♘b6
h5 35 h3 h4 36 ☖b1 ☖c3 37 ♘d7
♗d5 38 ♘b6 ♗c6 39 ♔g2 f5 40 ☖b4
♔f6 41 ☖c4 ☖xc4 −+ 42 ♘xc4 f4
43 ♘d2 f3+??= 43...♔e5 −+ 44 ♔f1
♔e5 45 ♔e1 ♔d5 46 ♔d1 ♗b5 47
♔c2 ♗d3+ 48 ♔c3 e5 49 ♔b4 49
♘xf3 ♗f1 50 ♘xg5 ♗g2 Δ ♔d6-e7-f6
−+; 50 ♘g1∓ ♔c6 50 ♔c3 ♔c5 51
♘b3+ ♔d5 52 ♘d2 ♗a6 53 ♔b4
♗b7 54 ♔b5 ♗c8 55 ♔b4 ♗a6! 56
♔a5??? ♗f1! 0-1 Miles   ᶜᵒ S-g1 perch =

√356 Vadasz-Honfi Subotica 78

**1 ♘f3 ♘f6 2 g3 g6 3 b3 ♗g7 4 ♗b2
0-0 5 ♗g2 d6 6 d4 a5 7 0-0 ♘bd7
8 ♘bd2 c5! 9 c4 cxd4 10 ♘xd4 ♘c5
11 a3 ♗d7 12 ☖b1! ♕b6 13 ♗a1
☖fc8** 13...e5!? **14 b4 axb4 15 axb4
♘e6 16 c5! ♕a7! 17 ♘xe6 ♗xe6 18
cxd6 exd6 19 ♘b3 ♗f5! 20 ♗d4 ♕a3!**
20...♕a4? 21 ♘a5± **21 ♗xb7 ♗xb1
22 ♕xb1 ♕xb4 23 ♗xc8 ☖xc8 24
♕a1 ½-½ Honfi**

357 Stean-Ljubojevic
Sao Paolo 79

**1 ♘f3 ♘f6 2 g3 b5!? 3 ♗g2 ♗b7 4
0-0 c5 5 d3 ♘c6 6 e4 d6 7 ♘c3!?
b4 8 ♘d5 ♘d7!** 8...e6 9 ♘xf6+ ♕xf6
10 c3!?± **9 c3 e6 10 ♘f4 10 ♘e3!**
+= bxc3 **11 bxc3 ♘ce5! 12 d4 ♘xf3+
13 ♗xf3 ♗e7 14 ☖b1 ☖b8 15 d5!?**

**e5 16 ♘g2 ♗a6 17 ☖xb8 ♕xb8 18
♗e2 ♗xe2** 18...c4?! ∝/+= **19 ♕xe2
0-0 20 ♘e3 g6 21 ♕a6 Δ ♘c4± f5!=**
21...♕b6 22 ♕a4 ♕c7 23 ♕c6 +=/±
22 ♕d3 22 exf5 gxf5 23 ♕a4 (Δ
♕xd7/♘xf5) ♕e8! **fxe4 23 ♕xe4
♘f6 24 ♕a4∝ ½-½ Stean**

√358 Tringov-Popovic
Trstenik 79

**1 ♘f3 ♘f6 2 g3 g6 3 ♗g2 ♗g7 4 0-0
0-0 5 d3 c5 6 ♘bd2 ♘c6 7 e4 ☖b8
8 a4 d6 9 ☖e1 ♘e8 10 c3 ♘c7 11
♘f1 e5 12 ♘h4 d5! 13 exd5 ♘xd5
=∓ 14 ♘e3 ♗e6 15 ♘f3 f6 16 ♕e2
☖e8! 17 ♘d2 b6 18 ♘ec4** 18 ♘dc4
♕e7 **19 h4 ♗f7 20 ♘e4 ☖bd8 21 h5?
21** ♗d2 gxh5 22 ♗f3 h4! **23 ♕g2?!
hxg3 24 fxg3 f5!∓ 25 ♘g5 ♗g6 26
♘h5 ♗xh5 27 ♕xh5 ♘f6 28 ♕f3 ♕d7
29 ☖f1 e4! 30 ♕xf5 ♕xf5 31 ☖xf5
exd3 32 ♗f4 h6 33 ♘f3 ☖e2+ 34
♔h3 ♘e4! 35 ♘fd2 ♘e7 36 ☖h5 ☖d5!
−+ 37 ☖xd5 ♘xd5 38 ♘xe4 ☖xe4
39 ♘d6 ♘xf4+ 40 gxf4 ☖xf4 41
♘b5 a6 42 ♘c7 ☖f2 43 ☖b1 ♗e5
44 ♘xa6 h5! 45 ♔h4 ☖f4+ 46 ♔xh5
☖xa4 47 ☖d1 ☖xa6 48 ☖xd3 ♔f7
0-1 Pytel**

1 g3

359 Gufeld-Dolmatov
USSR 78

**1 g3 d5 2 ♗g2 ♘f6 3 d3 e5 4 ♘f3
♗d6 5 0-0 c6 6 ♘bd2 0-0 7 e4 ♗g4
8 h3 ♗h5 9 c3 ♘bd7 10 ♕c2 ☖e8
11 b3 a5 12 a3 b5 13 ♗b2 ♕b6=
14 ♘h4 ☖ad8 15 b4 dxe4?! 16 dxe4
+= c5?! 17 bxa5 ♕xa5 18 c4 ♘b6
19 g4** 19 cxb5 ♗e2 20 a4 ♗xf1 21
♗xf1 c4!? **♗g6 20 cxb5 ♗c7! 20...**
♕xb5 21 a4 +−; 20...♕a4 21 ☖fc1±
21 ♗c3 ♕xb5 22 a4 ♕d3 23 ♕xd3

23 ♖fc1 ♖xd3 24 ♖fc1± ♖dd8 25 ♘xg6 25 f3!? hxg6 26 ♗f1 ♖b8 27 f3 ♖ed8 28 a5 ♘c8 29 ♘c4 ♘d7 30 ♖ab1 ♘a7 31 ♖xb8 ♖xb8 32 ♖d1 ♖d8 33 ♖b1 Zeitnot ♖b8 34 ♖d1 ♖d8 35 ♘e3 ♘f8 36 ♘d5 ♘e6 37 a6 ♔f8 38 ♖b1 ♖b8 39 ♖d1 ♗d6 40 ♗c4 ♘d4 41 ♔f2 ♘ac6 42 h4?! 42 ♖a1± ♘b5 43 ♗b2 ♘bd4 44 ♗a3 ♘b5 45 ♗xb5?! 45 ♗c1± ♖xb5 46 ♘c3 ♖b3 47 ♖xd6 ♖xc3 48 ♖xc6 ♖xa3 49 ♖c8+ ♔e7 50 ♖c7+ ♔e6 50...♔f6? 51 g5+ +− **51 a7 ♖a2+ 52 ♔e1** 52 ♔e3? c4 53 g5 f5! **g5!! 53 hxg5** 53 h5 ♔f6= **g6 54 ♔d1 c4 55 ♔c1 ♔d6! 56 ♖xf7 ♔c5 57 ♔b1 ♖a4! 58 ♖d7!** 58 ♖g7 ♔d4 59 ♖xg6 ♖xa7 60 ♖f6 ♔d3!= **♔b4! 59 ♔b2 ♖a5! 60 ♖e7 c3+! 61 ♔c2 ♖a2+ 62 ♔b1** 62 ♔d3 ♖d2+! **♖a6 63 ♖xe5 ♖xa7 64 ♖e6** 64 f4 ♔b3 65 ♖b5+

♔c4 66 ♖b6 ♔d3= **♔c4 65 ♖xg6**

65...♔d3 +=66 ♖d6+ ♔e3 67 ♔c2 67 e5 ♔xf3 68 e6 ♖e7! += **♔xf3 68 ♖e6 ♖c7 69 g6 ♔f4!!** 69...♔xg4 70 ♖f6! +− **70 ♖e8?** 70 g7! ♖xg7 71 ♔xc3 += **♔g5! 71 g7 ♖xg7 72 ♔xc3 ♔f6 73 ♔d4 ♖xg4 74 ♔d5 ♔f7 ½-½ Gufeld**

Games Index

189

RICKFORD: Browne **192**
RIEMSDYK: Andersson **254**; Ljubojevic **15**; Segal 88
RIGO: Balogh 120; Szymczak 92
RIVAS: Miles 124
RIVAS-PASTOR: Letzelter **36**
ROCHA: Byrne **69**
ROGERS: Masculo **23**
ROGOBETE: Buzbuchi **221**
ROIZMAN: Kapengut 280
ROMANISHIN: Bagirov 44; Donner **346**; Kuzmin **345**; Polugaevsky 56; Sveshnikov 340; Tseshkovsky 300
ROOS: Miles **186**; Suba 35; Timman 139
ROSARIO: Joynt **294**
ROSENBERG: Fagerstrom **353**
RUBINSKY: Bisguier 326
RUKAVINA: Saladen **11**
RUSSOWSKY: Snyder **313**
SALADEN: Rukavina 11
SANTOS: Knezevic 62; Mariotti 276
SANZ: Miles **182**
SAPI: Gliksman 41; Ozsvath **159**
SAVON: Kapengut 218
SAX: Donner **343**; Ghinda **270**; Ghitescu 38; Kuligowski **335**; Matanovic 202; Ribli **231**
SCHMIDT: Haik **24**; Kuligowski **95**; Miles 14; Portisch **18**
SCHNEIDER: Ribli **252**
SCHURADE: Skrobek 215
SEGAL: Andersson 10; Filguth **110**; Lein **151**; Panno **165**; Riemsdyk **88**
SEIRAWAN: Browne **25**; Delaune 331; Hort 332
SEQUEIRA: Silva **213**
SHABALOV: Jekabson 273
SHAKAROV: Riabchonok **318**; Zaharov 278
SHAMKOVICH: Soltis 275
SHMETEFF: Snyder 289
SIGURJONSSON: Portisch **216**;

Radulov 229
SIKORA: Ermenkov **274**; Ghitescu 174
SILVA: Sequeira 213
SISNIEGA: Dolmatov 333
SKALKOTAS: Ivkov 141; Suba 170
SKROBEK: Bonsch **269**; Ftacnik **342**; Gheorghiu 115; Jansa **253**; Knaak **187**; Radulov **225**; Schurade **215**
SLIWA: Balogh 4
SMEJKAL: Ghitescu 140; Kuligowski 143; Nemet 176; Prandstetter **354**
SMIRNOV: Kapengut **91**
A.SMITH: L.D.Evans **233**; Petersen **205**; Regan **272**
B.SMITH: Tartakovsky 288
SMYSLOV: Gheorghiu 55; Keene 142; Portisch **97**
SNYDER: Russowsky 313; Shmeteff **289**
SOLTIS: Bonon 166; Brown 167; Hoffman 1; Shamkovich **275**; Westerinen **286**
SOSONKO: Miles **130**; Morrison **79**
SPASSKY: Dankert **324**; Gheorghiu 73; Hebert **178**; Pfleger 277
SPEELMAN: Biyiasas **155**; Botterill 189; Hartston **39**; Mestel 251
STANCIU: Stefanov 80; Urzica **201**; Vaisman **211**
STANOJEVIC: Vukic 3
STEAN: Gheorghiu 111, **265**; Ljubojevic **357**
STEFANOV: Stanciu **80**
STOLYAROV: Browne 59
STRAUSS: Browne 147
SUBA: Bertok **22**; Bellon 239; Biyiasas 190; Botterill **171**; Hartston 107; Mourier **21**; Peters **65**; Roos **35**; Skalkotas **170**; Taimanov **246**; Vaisman 117
SUNYE: Gheorghiu 116
SVESHNIKOV: Kasparov **284**;

191